Early Printed Narrative Literature in Western Europe

Early Printed Narrative Literature in Western Europe

———

Edited by
Bart Besamusca, Elisabeth de Bruijn and
Frank Willaert

DE GRUYTER

ISBN 978-3-11-056300-9
e-ISBN (PDF) 978-3-11-056301-6
e-ISBN (EPUB) 978-3-11-056310-8

Library of Congress Control Number: 2019938240

Bibliographic information published by the Deutsche Nationalbibliothek
The Deutsche Nationalbibliothek lists this publication in the Deutsche Nationalbibliografie;
detailed bibliographic data are available from the Internet at http://dnb.dnb.de.

Cover image: Western Europe in the sixteenth century. Source: Abraham Ortelius, *Theatre, oft:
Toonneel des aerdtbodems waer in te siene sijn die landt-tafelen der geheelder weerelt, met
een corte verclaringe der selver*. Printed by Gielis van Diest (Antwerp, 1571), copy: Museum
Plantin-Moretus: Preciosa, R 39.7. Design: Typografie Frederik Hulstaert
Typesetting: Integra Software Services Pvt. Ltd.
Printing and binding: CPI books GmbH, Leck

www.degruyter.com

Acknowledgements

This volume results from the research project 'The Changing Face of Medieval Dutch Narrative Literature in the Early Period of Print (1477–c.1540)' (www.changingface.eu), which was supported financially by the Research Foundation Flanders (FWO) and the Netherlands Organisation for Scientific Research (NWO). We wish to thank all the authors, as well as the participants in the two symposia at the University of Antwerp and the final conference at Utrecht University, for contributing to our project. This book constitutes its most substantial and significant outcome. We express our gratitude to our research assistant Annika van Bodegraven for her invaluable assistance in the preparation of the volume. We would like to thank Imke de Gier (Academic Language Services) for correcting the English contributions written by non-native English authors, Frederik Hulstaert for his cover design, and Hubert Meeus for his advice and administrative support. We are also grateful to Elisabeth Kempf at De Gruyter for both her enthusiasm and patience.

B.B., E.d.B, F.W.

Contents

I The History of Early Printing of Narrative Texts

II Publication Strategies

List of Abbreviations

ABäG	*Amsterdamer Beiträge zur älteren Germanistik*
BNTL	Bibliografie van de Nederlandse taal- en literatuurwetenschap (www.bntl.nl)
DTM	Deutsche Texte des Mittelalters
GW	Gesamtkatalog der Wiegendrucke (http://www.gesamtkatalog derwiegendrucke.de/)
Hod.	Edward Hodnett, *English Woodcuts, 1480–1535*. Oxford 1973
ISTC	Incunabula Short Title Catalogue (http://www.bl.uk/catalogues/istc/)
JEBS	*Journal of the Early Book Society*
Killy²	*Killy Literaturlexikon. Autoren und Werke des deutschsprachigen Kulturraumes*. 2., vollständig überarbeitete Auflage, hg. von Wilhelm Kühlmann, 13 Bde. Berlin 2008-2012
LexMA	*Lexikon des Mittelalters*. Hg. v. Norbert Angermann et al. 9 Bde. München, Zürich, 1980–1998
LCI	*Lexikon der christlichen Ikonographie*. Hg. von Engelbert Kirschbaum und Wolfgang Braunfels. 8 vols. Freiburg im Breisgau 1968-1976
MRFH	Marburger Repertorium zur Übersetzungsliteratur im deutschen Frühhumanismus (http://www.mrfh.de/)
MTU	Münchener Texte und Untersuchungen zur deutschen Literatur des Mittelalters
NK	W. Nijhoff and M.E. Kronenberg, *Nederlandsche bibliographie van 1500 tot 1540*. 3 vols. 's-Gravenhage 1923–1940
ODNB	Oxford Dictionary of National Biography. Ed. by H. C. G. Matthew and Brian Harrison. 61 vols. Oxford 2004. (http://www.oxforddnb.com/)
PBSA	*The Papers of the Bibliographical Society of America*
PMLA	*Publications of the Modern Language Association of America*
SpdL	*Spiegel der Letteren*
STC	*A Short-Title Catalogue of Books Printed in England, Scotland, & Ireland, And of English Books Printed Abroad, 1475–1640*. Ed. by A. W. Pollard and G. R. Redgrave. 2nd ed. rev. by W. A. Jackson, F. S. Ferguson and Katherine F. Pantzer. 3 vols. London 1976–1991.
TMA	Texte des späten Mittelalters und der frühen Neuzeit
TNTL	*Tijdschrift voor Nederlandse Taal- en Letterkunde*
USTC	The Universal Short Title Catalogue, http://ustc.ac.uk/
VD 16	Verzeichnis der im deutschen Sprachbereich erschienenen Drucke des 16. Jahrhunderts (https://www.bsb-muenchen.de/sammlungen/historische-drucke/recherche/vd-16/)
²VL	*Die deutsche Literatur des Mittelalters. Verfasserlexikon*. 2., völlig neu bearbeitete Auflage, hg. von Burghart Wachinger et al. 14 Bde. Berlin, New York 1978–2008.

VL Deutscher Humanismus	*Deutscher Humanismus 1480–1520. Verfasserlexikon.* Hg. von Franz Josef Worstbrock. 3 Bde. Berlin, New York 2008-2015.
ZfdA	*Zeitschrift für deutsches Altertum und deutsche Literatur*
ZfdPh	*Zeitschrift für deutsche Philologie*

Bart Besamusca, Elisabeth de Bruijn, Frank Willaert
Introduction

The essays in this volume are concerned with early printed narrative texts in Western Europe. The aim of this book is to consider to what extent the shift from hand-written to printed books left its mark on narrative literature in a number of vernacular languages. Did the advent of printing bring about changes in the corpus of narrative texts when compared with the corpus extant in manuscript copies? Did narrative texts that already existed in manuscript form undergo significant modifications when they began to be printed? How did this crucial media development affect the nature of these narratives? Where and by whom were they published? Which strategies did early printers develop to make their texts commercially attractive? Which social classes were the target audiences for their editions?

Even though narrative texts represent just a small portion of early book production, these questions have received ample scholarly attention in the various research traditions, resulting in recent and important book-length publications, such as *Eulenspiegel trifft Melusine* (2010) in German studies or *Le Roman français dans les premiers imprimés* (2016) in French studies.[1] However, research that transcends the boundaries of linguistic disciplines tends to be limited to case-studies devoted to adaptations of source texts in another language. The essays in this volume shed light on the development of early printed narratives in various Western European areas. We hope that this book will provide an impetus for cross-linguistic research of early printed narratives in a number of regions.

In 2013, a research project, co-funded by the Research Foundation-Flanders (FWO) and the Netherlands Organisation for Scientific Research (NWO), was launched under the title 'The Changing Face of Medieval Dutch Narrative

---

1 Catherine Drittenbass and André Schnyder (eds), *Eulenspiegel trifft Melusine. Der frühneuhochdeutsche Prosaroman im Licht neuer Forschungen und Methoden*. Akten der Lausanner Tagung von 2. bis 4. Oktober 2008. Amsterdam 2010 (Chloe 42); Anne Schoysman and Maria Colombo Timelli (eds), *Le Roman français dans les premiers imprimés*. Paris 2016 (Rencontres 147).

Note: We would like to thank Christa Bertelsmeier-Kierst, Frank Brandsma, Olivier Delsaux, Anna Katharina Richter and Jordi Sánchez-Martí for their comments on earlier versions of this introduction and Annika van Bodegraven for her assistance.

Bart Besamusca, Utrecht University
Elisabeth de Bruijn, Frank Willaert, University of Antwerp

Literature in the Early Period of Print (1477–c. 1540)'.[2] This collaboration between the universities of Antwerp (Frank Willaert and Elisabeth de Bruijn) and Utrecht (Bart Besamusca and Rita Schlusemann) aimed at taking two important steps forward: the researchers intended (1) to study the corpus of early printed Dutch narratives as a whole and (2) to include the wider European context in their investigations.[3] The first objective was motivated by the fact that our understanding of the whole corpus of these texts was fundamentally flawed, in spite of Luc. Debaene's overview of the Dutch printed prose romances, published in 1951.[4] Although his study provided a solid basis for future investigations into the corpus of early printed Dutch narratives, scholars have generally restricted themselves to a limited number of individual printed narratives, such as the *Borchgravinne van Vergi*, the *Hystorie van Reynaert die vos* and *Margariete van Limborch*, or to a single publisher's list, such as Jan van Doesborch's.[5]

Our second objective has prompted this volume of essays. The early printing of narrative literature truly was an international phenomenon. It involved parallel developments in various language areas, similar interests in subject matter and comparable publishers' strategies to attract audiences. At the same time, the development of narrative literature differed from one language and cultural context to another. In order to better understand the relationships between the early printed Dutch narratives and printed narratives in other Western European languages, the research team organized two expert meetings (September 16–17, 2014; June 9–10, 2016), which brought together around twenty specialists in early printed literature. Departing from Dutch

---

2 www.changingface.eu.

3 For overviews of the corpus, see 'Dutch Corpus' on the website (see note 2) and Rita Schlusemann, '"Mit poetrien". Bucheingänge, Fiktion und Wahrheit gedruckter niederländischer Historien im europäischen Kontext'. In: *ZfdA* 147 (2018), p. 70–99, here p. 97–99.

4 Cf. W. van Anrooij, 'Ridderromans uit de late Middeleeuwen en Vroegmoderne Tijd. Een internationaal onderzoeksthema in opkomst'. In: *Queeste* 11 (2004), p. 163–83; Luc. Debaene, *De Nederlandse volksboeken. Ontstaan en geschiedenis van de Nederlandse prozaromans, gedrukt tussen 1475 en 1540.* Hulst 1977 [1951].

5 See R.J. Resoort, *Een schoone historie vander borchgravinne van Vergi. Onderzoek naar de intentie en gebruikssfeer van een zestiende-eeuwse prozaroman.* Hilversum 1988; Rita Schlusemann, *Die hystorie van reynaert die vos und The history of reynard the fox. Die spätmittelalterlichen Prosabearbeitungen des Reynaert-Stoffes.* Frankfurt a. M. 1991; Rita Schlusemann, *Schöne Historien. Niederländische Romane im deutschen Spätmittelalter und in der frühen Neuzeit.* Berlin, Boston 2016 (Frühe Neuzeit, 203); P.J.A. Franssen, *Tussen tekst en publiek. Jan van Doesborch, drukker-uitgever en literator te Antwerpen en Utrecht in de eerste helft van de zestiende eeuw.* Amsterdam 1990.

studies only, we strove to cover at least the neighbouring – and historically interconnected – language areas of English, French and German, but we also welcomed excursions into Scandinavian and Spanish studies. Many of these experts also participated in the project's final conference (November 24–25, 2016), entitled 'European Narrative Literature in the Early Period of Print'. The present volume consists of the selected proceedings of that conference.[6] Around half of the contributions focus on developments in the history of early printed narrative texts, others discuss publication strategies. We have adopted these two categories in the ordering of the essays in this volume.

1 Initiating a Dialogue

The discussions at the two expert meetings showed that research into fifteenth- and sixteenth-century narrative literature is still mainly carried out within the confines of the different language areas. Differences that are rooted in the various national research traditions make it hard to transcend these boundaries. As a working group we were able to identify three of these obstacles. They are indicated here, as they have left their mark on the design and contents of this volume.

A major source of misunderstanding concerns the different ways in which the corpora of early printed narrative texts in the various linguistic areas are indicated and defined. The French research tradition may distinguish between 'épopées' (epic poetry) and 'romans de chevalerie / chevaleresques' (chivalric romances), but – probably due to Georges Doutrepont's highly influential 1939 study *Les mises en prose des épopées et des romans chevaleresques du XIVe au XVIe siècle*[7] – these texts are often grouped together under the heading 'mises en prose' and are studied as such. This tradition continues up to the present day, as is demonstrated by the *Nouveau Répertoire de mises en prose (XIVe-XVIe siècle)*, published in 2014.[8] This makes sense in the French research tradition because many narrative French texts actually are 'mises en prose': prosifications of medieval subject matter that already existed in verse form.

---

6 With the exception of the essay by Christa Bertelsmeier-Kierst, which we commissioned in order to complement the discussions of the Dutch, English and French corpora with an overview of the German tradition.

7 Georges Doutrepont, *Les Mises en prose des épopées et des romans chevaleresques du XIVe au XVIe siècle*. Bruxelles 1939 (Académie royale de Belgique. Classe des lettres et des sciences morales et politiques. Mémoires, 40).

8 Maria Colombo Timelli et al. (eds.), *Nouveau Répertoire de mises en prose (XIVe-XVIe siècle)*. Paris 2014 (Textes littéraires du moyen âge 30).

Whereas the term 'Volksbuch' is commonly found in German research literature before 1970 to denote narrative literature in print, German scholars have generally adopted the term 'Prosaroman' in the last decades.[9] It is a denotation that refers to the somewhat longer (non-anecdotic) narrative texts and points to the transition from verse to prose that started around 1400 to become the dominant form after the advent of printing.[10] A typical feature of the German prose romances is that many of these texts have a long manuscript tradition and were also copied in codices after the introduction of printing.[11]

In the English research literature, both verse and prose narratives are unproblematically referred to as romances. The term 'prose romance' is mainly used to distinguish the group of prose narratives from the much larger corpus of verse texts.[12] Lastly, Dutch scholars use the term narrative text as a synonym for romance, even though narrative literature may also include anecdotes, fables, short stories and hagiographical texts.

In view of these diverging scholarly opinions on the text corpora involved, we have decided not to impose a unified terminology on the essays in this volume. Authors apply a range of terms, all of them indicating medieval prose and verse texts which feature an extradiegetic narrator who recounts a series of adventures of a predominantly secular nature.

The second issue that may hinder the exchange of ideas between experts in early printed narrative texts concerns the chronological demarcation of the various corpora within the respective research traditions. Scholars are united in their distinction between incunabula, produced in the period before 1501, and books which were printed later. But how much later? In various research areas,

---

9 Jan-Dirk Müller, 'Volksbuch/Prosaroman im 15./16. Jahrhundert – Perspektiven der Forschung'. In: *Internationales Archiv für Sozialgeschichte der Literatur* 1 (1985), p. 1–128.

10 See Christa Bertelsmeier-Kierst, 'Erzählen in Prosa. Zur Entwicklung des deutschen Prosaromans bis 1500'. In: 143 (2014), p. 141–165. For the distinction between 'Schwankroman', often in verse, and 'Prosaroman', see Johannes Klaus Kipf, 'Schwankroman – Prosaroman – Versroman. Über den Beitrag einer nicht nur prosaischen Gattung zur Entstehung des frühneuzeitlichen Prosaromans'. In: *Eulenspiegel trifft Melusine* (see note 1), p. 145–162.

11 See Bertelsmeier-Kierst in this volume.

12 See for instance: Jordi Sánchez-Martí, 'The Printed History of the Middle English Verse Romances'. In: *Modern Philology* 107 (2009), p. 1–31, and Helen Cooper, 'Prose Romances'. In: *A Companion to Middle English Prose*. Ed. by A. S. G. Edwards. Cambridge 2004, p. 215–230. Cf. also J. Burke Severs (ed.), *A Manual of the Writings in Middle English, 1050–1500, fascicule 1: Romances*. New Haven, Connecticut, 1967.

the whole sixteenth century is regarded as a period of early printing, as shown by recent publications on narrative literature in French, German and English.[13] Within that time-frame, research often focuses on specific topics, such as certain centres of printing (i.e. German publishers[14]) or the early and later years of a printer's career (early and later years of Wynkyn de Worde[15]). For scholars of Scandinavian literature, however, using the sixteenth century as a cut-off point does not make sense, as the first editions of medieval romances were published as late as the sixteenth (in Denmark) and seventeenth century (in Sweden). Many of these romances were reprinted up to the first decades of the nineteenth century, often without major changes to lay-out and contents.[16] Dutch scholars, on the other hand, frequently restrict their research to the period up to 1540, due to the fact that their most important bibliographical resources end around that year.[17] This date is quite arbitrary, however. It results from the decision in around 1840 of J.W. Holtrop, then librarian of the Royal Library at The Hague, to group together the so-called post-incunabula, i.e. books printed between 1500 and 1540.[18] In this volume, no strict demarcation in time was imposed on the contributions.

The third issue that hinders the dialogue between specialists in early printed narratives is related to the fact that research communication is firmly rooted in national traditions. It is no exaggeration to state that our research is still compartmentalized. As Karla Mallette has stated recently, literary

---

13 Colombo Timelli et al., *Nouveau Répertoire* (see note 8); André Schnyder, 'Der deutsche Prosaroman des 15. und 16. Jahrhunderts. Ein Problemfeld, eine Tagung und der Versuch einer Bilanz'. In: *Eulenspiegel trifft Melusine* (see note 1), p. 11–39; Jennifer Fellows, 'Printed Romance in the Sixteenth Century'. In: *A Companion to Medieval Popular Romance*. Ed. by Raluca L. Radulescu and Cory James Rushton. Cambridge 2009 (Studies in Medieval Romance 10), p. 67–78.

14 Ursula Rautenberg, 'Typographie und Leseweisen. Überlegungen zu den Melusine-Ausgaben der Frankfurter Offizinen Gülfferich und Weigand Han / Han Erben'. In: *Eulenspiegel trifft Melusine* (see note 1), p. 341–363.

15 N. F. Blake, 'Wynkyn de Worde: the Early Years'. In: *Gutenberg Jahrbuch* (1971), p. 62–69; N. F. Blake, 'Wynkyn de Worde: the Later Years'. In: *Gutenberg Jahrbuch* (1972), p. 128–138.

16 See Jürg Glauser (ed.), *Skandinavische Literaturgeschichte*. 2nd ed. Stuttgart, Weimar 2016, p. 59–60; Henrik Horstbøll, *Menigmands medie. Det folkelige bogtryk i Danmark 1500–1840*. Copenhagen 1999 (Danish Humanist Texts and Studies 19); Anna Katharina Richter, *Transmissionsgeschichten. Untersuchungen zur dänischen und schwedischen Erzählprosa in der frühen Neuzeit*. Tübingen, Basel 2009 (Beiträge zur Nordischen Philologie 41).

17 NK. See also Debaene, *De Nederlandse volksboeken* (see note 4).

18 See J.A. Gruys, 'Post-Incunabula: a Dutch Contribution to Bibliographical Vocabulary'. In: *Across the Narrow Seas. Studies in the History and Bibliography of Britain and the Low Countries Presented to Anna E.C. Simoni*. Ed. by Susan Roach. London 1991, p. 17–22.

historians 'are generally trained to think within the boundaries of disciplines defined by the national languages of modern Europe', in spite of the highly cross-linguistic character of their material.[19] In order to facilitate the exchange of ideas, we have accepted contributions in three major European languages reflecting the literatures that take centre stage in this volume. By publishing these contributions side-by-side, we wish to promote a more outward-looking attitude among experts in early printed narratives. We have, additionally, indicated discussions of related interest by cross-references in footnotes.

Due to the three issues indicated here, the ambitions this volume has are modest. This collection of essays is essentially meant to stimulate the cross-linguistic exchange of knowledge and ideas between specialists in early printed narrative literature in Western Europe. The dialogue between these experts will eventually result, so we believe, in a deeper understanding of similarities and differences in the development of narrative texts in the respective language areas after the advent of printing.

2 The Organization of the Volume: Convergences and Divergences

As mentioned above, the contributions in this volume fall into two categories. Roughly half of the essays, grouped under the heading 'The History of Early Printing of Narrative Texts', discuss larger text corpora. These articles focus on the selection of texts that made it into print or on the various stages in their printed history. The selection of these corpora is based on language (Bertelsmeier-Kierst for German, Besamusca and Willaert for Dutch), on publisher (Delsaux and Van Hemelryck for French, Boffey for English), on source texts (de Bruijn for Dutch, based on French texts), on period (Sánchez-Martí for English) and on genre (Montorsi for French Arthurian romances). The second category of contributions, assembled under the heading 'Publication strategies', focuses on a single text or a small group of texts, examining the motives behind textual transformations and the various ways in which the accessibility and attractiveness of the editions of narrative texts were enhanced. The essays discuss the influence of woodcuts on text transmission (Frick) and on the reception of a text (Potysch), textual adaptations (Richter) and changing title pages of a group of texts (Syrovy) or a single text (Schaeps). Together, the articles in

---

19 Karla Mallette, *The Kingdom of Sicily, 1100–1250. A Literary History*. Philadelphia 2005, p. 6.

this volume bring out convergences and divergences in the production of early printed, vernacular narrative texts in Western Europe. The most important convergences and divergences will be identified below.

Even though printing took the whole of Western Europe by storm in the second half of the fifteenth century, the impact of the new technology on narrative literature varied significantly in the different language areas. These divergent effects were caused by the different social and cultural contexts in which narrative texts functioned. The patrons and readers of French literature, for instance, belonged predominantly to aristocratic circles who favoured narratives in prose over verse texts as early as the thirteenth century.[20] In the second half of the fifteenth century, manuscript copies of these texts were mainly produced for the Burgundian elite, which may have hampered early printers like Colard Mansion in Bruges.[21] Elsewhere in the francophone world, the first printed narratives emerged on the periphery, in cities such as Geneva and Lyon. Printers originating from Germany, like Adam Steinschaber (Geneva) and Nicolas Philippi and Marcus Reinhart (Lyon), tried to reach new audiences with their printed narratives, initially focusing on Trojan material, Charlemagne epics (*Fierabras, Renaut de Montauban*) and hagiographical / historical texts (*Destruction de Jérusalem*). They had a keen eye for printed texts that had met with success in Germany such as *Melusine*. It was only near the end of the 1480s that Paris emerged as the centre for printed narrative texts. Antoine Vérard was the market leader, producing high-quality editions, meant for people of standing (Montorsi). A few decades later, he was succeeded by Galliot du Pré, who tried to sell his narrative texts to the same types of buyers, including aristocrats and lawyers (Delsaux and Van Hemelryck).

As in France, the production of Dutch early printed narratives in the Low Countries started on the periphery (northern Netherlands), failed to attract the attention of the Burgundian elite and focused on historically and/or religiously oriented narratives (Besamusca and Willaert). Printers relied on Dutch and Latin texts that were popular in the manuscript tradition, such as the oeuvre of the immensely influential thirteenth-century author Jacob van Maerlant. Noteworthy is the initial absence of the southern Netherlands in the production of printed narrative texts, probably due to the nobility's preference for French

---

20 See Francis Gingras, *Le Bâtard conquérant. Essor et expansion du genre romanesque au Moyen Âge*. Paris 2011 (Nouvelle bibliothèque du moyen âge, 106), p. 353–377.
21 For these manuscripts, see Tania Van Hemelryck, 'Le livre mis en prose à la cour de Bourgogne. Réflexions pour une approche codicologique d'un phénomène littéraire'. In: *Mettre en prose aux XIVᵉ-XVIᵉ siècles*. Ed. by Maria Colombo Timelli et al. Turnhout 2010 (Texte, Codex et Contexte, 11), p. 245–254.

literature and maybe also because of the chambers of rhetoric, whose members favoured lyrical texts and plays in Dutch. When Antwerp had become the centre of book production around 1490, printers reproduced indigenous narrative texts that had already proven their attractiveness, such as *Karel ende Elegast* and *Margariete van Limborch*, and selected French, English and German sources for their Dutch editions in order to attract larger groups of readers. In this context, it is interesting that the adapters of these non-Dutch sources tried to get rid of passages aimed at aristocratic readers, shortening their texts on the one hand and adding rhetorical verse passages on the other (De Bruijn).

From about 1400 onwards, the German tradition of narrative literature was dominated by the prose form. Up to around 1500, manuscripts and printed books existed side by side, albeit hand-written copies far outnumbered printed editions (Bertelsmeier-Kierst). The printers did not opt for a radical departure from the existing corpus of narratives, but produced editions of texts that were circulating in codices as well, such as Johannes Hartlieb's *Alexander* and *Melusine* by Thüring von Ringoltingen. While printed books with narrative texts made in Ulm, Basel and Strasbourg were often luxury products targeted at upper-class readers, the quarto-sized editions of, in particular, Augsburg tended to be cheaper and show efforts to trivialize both text and presentation.

Initially, English readership, in particular the nobility, was interested in translations of French texts which were the favourites of Burgundian circles, starting with William Caxton's *Recuyell of the histories of Troy* (1473–1474) and a number of his other printed narratives (Sánchez-Martí). However, from 1495 onwards, Caxton's successor Wynkyn de Worde and his contemporaries preferred to attract larger audiences and chose to print editions of indigenous verse romances, whose manuscript copies were still accessible. Notwithstanding, early English printers continued to select and adapt prose narrative texts with proven print circulation on the Continent.

The printing of narrative literature reached the Scandinavian area somewhat later than elsewhere in Western Europe (Richter). Although the first printing press in Denmark dates from 1482 and the first one in Sweden from 1483, the earliest Danish printed narrative text that has come down to us, *Flores oc Blantzeflor*, was published in 1504 and the earliest Swedish narrative, *Josephs historie*, in 1601.[22] Many of the narrative texts in Danish and Swedish

---

[22] For the earliest printed editions in Denmark and Sweden, which were printed first in Latin and subsequently in the vernacular languages (mostly liturgical books and chronicles), see for example Glauser, *Skandinavische Literaturgeschichte* (note 16), p. 55–62. We may assume that narrative texts were well-known in sixteenth-century Sweden. They were read both in Danish and in German, as is evident from Swedish aristocratic book collections such as Hogenskild Bielke's

manuscripts can be traced back, through medieval Norwegian and Icelandic intermediary stages, to French sources. The production of narrative texts in print was essentially a continuation of this manuscript tradition. Other narratives which became very popular in Scandinavia in the sixteenth and seventeenth centuries were mostly translated and adapted from High and Low German printed sources, such as *Griseldis, Eulenspiegel* and *Melusine*.

Convergences and divergences in the production of early printed, vernacular narrative texts in Western Europe also come to the fore in the subject matter. In all parts of Western Europe, the first printers tested the market by publishing texts that dealt with Antiquity. In various language areas, vernacular renditions of Guido de Columnis' *Historia destructionis Troiae* were the first to roll off the press. German printers, for example, published an adaptation of the *Elsässische Trojabuch* and Hans Mair's *Buch von Troja* in a well-known South German edition (Bertelsmeier-Kierst). In France, England and the Low Countries, translations of Raoul Lefèvre's *Histoire de Jason* and the *Recueil des histoires de Troyes* were printed. Whereas Lefèvre's version of the story remained popular in England, printers in the Low Countries, such as Jan van Doesborch, published modernized adaptations of this narrative (De Bruijn).

The story of Alexander the Great was likewise appreciated by early printers. As far as we know, the first printed narrative published in the Low Countries was Gheraert Leeu's *Historie van Alexander*, printed in Gouda in 1477. The text was reprinted three times before 1500 (Besamusca and Willaert). In Germany, Johannes Hartlieb's *Alexander* was not only copied by scribes at least twenty times before 1500, his text has also come down to us in nine incunabular editions (Bertelsmeier-Kierst).

In many language areas of Western Europe, early printers selected texts that had proven their popularity in the manuscript transmission. They must have thought that these domestic texts ensured good sales figures. In France, for example, the Charlemagne epics *Fierabras* (1478) and *Renaut de Montauban*

---

private library in Uppsala or from literary examples such as Per Brahe's *Oeconomia* (1585), a manual for young noblemen. See for example Richter, *Transmissionsgeschichten* (see note 19), p. 7–22; Stina Hansson, *"Afsatt på Swensko". 1600-talets tryckta översättningslitteratur*. Göteborg 1982 (Skrifter utgivna av Litteraturvetenskapliga institutionen vid Göteborgs universitet 11); *Hogenskild Bielke's Library. A Catalogue of the Famous 16th Century Swedish Private Collection*. Reconstructed and compiled by Wolfgang Undorf. Uppsala 1995. For the Medieval transmission of narrative texts, see for example Karl G. Johansson and Else Mundal (eds), *Riddarasǫgur. The Translation of European Court Culture in Medieval Scandinavia*. Oslo 2014.

(1482) were among the first printed narrative texts.[23] In German literature, local traditions encouraged early printed prose versions of Johann von Würzburg's *Wilhelm von Österreich* (1481) and Eilhart von Oberg's *Tristrant* (1484) (Bertelsmeier-Kierst). By publishing indigenous verse narratives, like *Karel ende Elegast* (1484–88) and *Seghelijn van Jherusalem* (1483–86) (Schaeps), the first printers of the Low Countries capitalized on the literary preference of their customers. In striking contrast to this publishing strategy for German and Dutch texts, William Caxton neglected the English narrative tradition, with the notable exception of Thomas Malory's *Morte Darthur* (1485). He seems to have found the traditional verse romances old-fashioned.[24]

Later English printers thought more favourably of the commercial appeal of domestic narrative texts (Boffey, Sánchez-Martí). It is noteworthy, however, that Arthurian romances such as *Arthur and Merlin* (1499?) and the *Jeste of Sir Gawaine* (1528?) were only rarely printed.[25] The same lack of interest in Arthuriana is shown by printers of German texts. Initiated by Bishop Rupprecht von Simmern, the Strasbourg printer Johann Mentelin tried in vain to introduce *Parzival* and the *Jüngerer Titurel* to readers of printed texts in 1477.[26] The only texts they appreciated were *Tristrant und Isalde* and *Herr Wigoleis vom Rade* (Bertelsmeier-Kierst).[27] In the Low Countries, just a single Arthurian narrative, the *Historie van Merlijn* (c. 1540), made it into print.[28] In contrast, French readers were more interested in printed Arthurian romances. This is demonstrated by the eleven printed editions of these texts, all in prose, and their many reprints (Montorsi).

---

23 Giovanni Matteo Roccati, 'Le roman dans les incunables. L'impact des stratégies éditoriales dans le choix des titres imprimés'. In: *Le Roman français dans les premiers imprimés* (see note 1), p. 95–126, here p. 108.

24 See Jordi Sánchez-Martí, 'The Printed Transmission of Medieval Romance from William Caxton to Wynkyn de Worde, 1473–1535'. In: *The Transmission of Medieval Romance: Metres, Manuscripts and Early Prints*. Ed. by Ad Putter, Judith A. Jefferson. Cambridge 2018, p. 170–190.

25 See Sánchez-Martí, 'The Printed History' (note 12), p. 6–7. The *Morte Darthur*, however, was reprinted twice, in 1498 and 1529, by Wynkyn de Worde, see Sánchez-Martí, 'The Printed Transmission' (note 24), p. 186–187.

26 See Volker Mertens, *Der deutsche Artusroman*. Stuttgart 1998, p. 341.

27 For the 1484 and 1498 editions of *Tristrant*, see Dorothee Ader, 'Die Abkehr von der Tradition. Zur Rezeption des Tristrant in den Drucken des 15. Jahrhunderts'. In: *Eulenspiegel trifft Melusine* (see note 1), p. 437–458.

28 See Elisabeth de Bruijn, 'To Content the Continent. The Dutch Narratives *Merlijn* and *Jacke* Compared to Their English Counterparts'. In: *TNTL* 133 (2017), p. 83–108.

A last aspect of the subject matter that should be mentioned here is concerned with the dominant position of French narrative literature in Western Europe. Printers in England, Germany and the Low Countries were united in their efforts to search out French texts that they could translate and adapt for their own markets (Bertelsmeier-Kierst, Besamusca and Willaert).[29] Examples of this phenomenon are *Ponthus et la belle Sidoine*, the *Livre du chevalier de la Tour Landry*, *Paris et Vienne*, *Pierre et Maguelonne* and *Robert le Diable*.

Another characteristic of the production of early printed, vernacular narrative texts in Western Europe is its dependence on a relatively limited number of major printers and centres of printing. For France, we may single out the Parisian printers Antoine Vérard, Michel Le Noir, Denis Janot and Galliot du Pré. The printing of English narrative texts took place in London and, after Caxton's demise, was monopolized, first, by Wynkyn de Worde and, later in the sixteenth century, by William Copland (Boffey, Sánchez-Martí). The German production of narrative texts was divided between Augsburg and Nuremberg on the one hand and Strasbourg, Ulm and Basel on the other (Bertelsmeier-Kierst), focusing on different audiences. The editions which were published in Strasbourg, Ulm and Basel were oriented towards the French-Burgundian manuscript culture (printers such as Heinrich Knoblochtzer, Johann Zainer and Bernhard Richel). In the Low Countries, narrative texts were published especially by Gheraert Leeu in Gouda and, later on, by Jan van Doesborch and Willem Vorsterman in Antwerp.

It should be noted that these printers often had a prolific business, as shown by their extensive publisher's lists, including grammar books, school-books and Latin (spiritual) works, of which narratives made up only a small part. Wynkyn de Worde, for example, printed forty to fifty narrative texts out of a total of around 850 books (including multiple editions) (Boffey). In the period between 1477 and 1540, just around 11 percent of the total production of Dutch texts in the Low Countries consisted of texts which were meant for entertainment, including narrative texts.[30]

Finally, convergences and divergences in the production of early printed, vernacular narrative texts in Western Europe also stand out in the interference of printers, adaptors and translators in existing editions and texts. Some of them tried to arouse the customers' interest in their products by publishing folio-

---

29 For English literature, see Sánchez-Martí, 'The Printed Transmission' (note 24) and Sánchez-Martí, 'The Printed History' (note 12).

30 See Peter M.H. Cuijpers, *Teksten als koopwaar: vroege drukkers verkennen de markt. Een kwantitatieve analyse van de productie van Nederlandstalige boeken (tot circa 1550) en de 'lezers-hulp' in de seculiere prozateksten*. Nieuwkoop 1998, p. 99.

sized editions, such as the books that Wynkyn de Worde printed early in his career (Boffey). Others intended to attract buyers by printing in quarto format, in particular after 1500. The paratextual material that was used to catch the eye of readers included curiosity-arousing title pages (Syrovy), which could be designed rather archaically to meet the audience's expectations (Schaeps). Illustration programmes were used to guide the readers through the stories (Potysch, Frick). Texts were geared towards the presumed taste of the customers by compiling texts from different sources (De Bruijn), by shortening source texts (Richter), by adding moralizing passages (Besamusca and Willaert, Richter), by opting for verse or prose texts (De Bruijn, Sánchez-Martí, Boffey) and by modernizing the language of the texts (Van Hemelryck and Delsaux, Boffey).

It is our hope that the essays in this volume will provide food for thought for scholars working in adjacent research areas. Jordi Sánchez-Martí, for example, makes us realize that political circumstances were by no means a negligible factor in the production of narrative literature. In his essay on English narratives in the period between the deaths of Wynkyn de Worde, in 1535, and William Copland, in 1569, he argues that the printing of English romances flourished under the influence of Catholicism during the reign of Queen Mary I (1553–1558). In her contribution on Thomas Murner's German translation of the *Aeneid* (1515), Julia Frick reveals how translations in the age of print may be related to 'new' features such as woodcuts. She argues that Murner's understanding of the *Aeneid* was influenced by the *Aeneid* woodcuts in Sebastian Brant's Latin edition of Virgil's works. Studying the output of the French printer Galliot du Pré (1512–1560), Tania Van Hemelryck and Olivier Delsaux remind us of the importance of archival sources, such as inventories, in shedding light on the publication strategies of early printers. A cross-linguistic approach may reveal to what extent these tendencies are only found on a local level or testify to international trends. We therefore hope that this book will invite scholars from various disciplines to get involved in this conversation.

Bibliography

Ader, Dorothee, 'Die Abkehr von der Tradition. Zur Rezeption des Tristrant in den Drucken des 15. Jahrhunderts'. In: *Eulenspiegel trifft Melusine. Der frühneuhochdeutsche Prosaroman im Licht neuer Forschungen und Methoden*. Akten der Lausanner Tagung von 2. bis 4. Oktober 2008. Ed. by Catherine Drittenbass and André Schnyder. Amsterdam 2010 (Chloe 42), p. 437–458.

Anrooij, W. van, 'Ridderromans uit de late Middeleeuwen en Vroegmoderne Tijd. Een internationaal onderzoeksthema in opkomst'. In: *Queeste* 11 (2004), p. 163–83.

Bertelsmeier-Kierst, Christa, 'Erzählen in Prosa. Zur Entwicklung des deutschen Prosaromans bis 1500'. In: *ZfdA* 143 (2014), p. 141–165.

Blake, N. F., 'Wynkyn de Worde: the Early Years'. In: *Gutenberg Jahrbuch* (1971), p. 62–69.

Blake, N. F., 'Wynkyn de Worde: the Later Years'. In: *Gutenberg Jahrbuch* (1972), p. 128–138.

Bruijn, Elisabeth de, 'To Content the Continent. The Dutch Narratives *Merlijn* and *Jacke* Compared to Their English Counterparts'. In: *TNTL* 133 (2017), p. 83–108.

Burke Severs, J., (ed.), *A Manual of the Writings in Middle English, 1050–1500, fascicule 1: Romances*. New Haven, Connecticut 1967.

Colombo Timelli, Maria et al. (eds), *Nouveau Répertoire de mises en prose (XIVe-XVIe siècle)*. Paris 2014 (Textes littéraires du moyen âge 30).

Cooper, Helen, 'Prose Romances'. In: *A Companion to Middle English Prose*. Ed. by A. S. G. Edwards. Cambridge 2004, p. 215–230.

Cuijpers, Peter M.H., *Teksten als koopwaar: vroege drukkers verkennen de markt. Een kwantitatieve analyse van de productie van Nederlandstalige boeken (tot circa 1550) en de 'lezershulp' in de seculiere prozateksten*. Nieuwkoop 1998.

Debaene, Luc., *De Nederlandse volksboeken. Ontstaan en geschiedenis van de Nederlandse prozaromans, gedrukt tussen 1475 en 1540*. Hulst 1977 [1951].

Doutrepont, Georges, *Les Mises en prose des épopées et des romans chevaleresques du XIVe au XVIe siècle*. Bruxelles 1939 (Académie royale de Belgique. Classe des lettres et des sciences morales et politiques. Mémoires, 40).

Drittenbass, Catherine and André Schnyder (eds), *Eulenspiegel trifft Melusine. Der frühneuhochdeutsche Prosaroman im Licht neuer Forschungen und Methoden*. Akten der Lausanner Tagung von 2. bis 4. Oktober 2008. Amsterdam 2010 (Chloe 42).

Fellows, Jennifer, 'Printed Romance in the Sixteenth Century'. In: *A Companion to Medieval Popular Romance*. Ed. by Raluca L. Radulescu and Cory James Rushton. Cambridge 2009 (Studies in Medieval Romance 10), p. 67–78.

Franssen, P.J.A., *Tussen tekst en publiek. Jan van Doesborch, drukker-uitgever en literator te Antwerpen en Utrecht in de eerste helft van de zestiende eeuw*. Amsterdam 1990.

Glauser, Jürg (ed.), *Skandinavische Literaturgeschichte*. 2nd ed. Stuttgart, Weimar 2016.

Gingras, Francis, *Le Bâtard conquérant. Essor et expansion du genre romanesque au Moyen Âge*. Paris 2011 (Nouvelle bibliothèque du moyen âge, 106), p. 353–377.

Gruys, J.A., 'Post-Incunabula: a Dutch Contribution to Bibliographical Vocabulary'. In: *Across the Narrow Seas. Studies in the History and Bibliography of Britain and the Low Countries Presented to Anna E.C. Simoni*. Ed. by Susan Roach. London 1991, p. 17–22.

Hansson, Stina, *"Afsatt på Swensko". 1600-talets tryckta översättningslitteratur*. Göteborg 1982 (Skrifter utgivna av Litteraturvetenskapliga institutionen vid Göteborgs universitet 11).

Hemelryck, Tania Van, 'Le livre mis en prose à la cour de Bourgogne. Réflexions pour une approche codicologique d'un phénomène littéraire'. In: *Mettre en prose aux XIVe-XVIe siècles*. Ed. by Maria Colombo Timelli et al. Turnhout 2010 (Texte, Codex et Contexte, 11), p. 245–254.

Hogenskild Bielke's Library. A Catalogue of the Famous 16th Century Swedish Private Collection. Reconstructed and compiled by Wolfgang Undorf. Uppsala 1995.

Horstbøll, Henrik, *Menigmands medie. Det folkelige bogtryk i Danmark 1500–1840*. Copenhagen 1999 (Danish Humanist Texts and Studies 19).

Johansson, Karl G. and Else Mundal (eds), *Riddarasǫgur. The Translation of European Court Culture in Medieval Scandinavia*. Oslo 2014.

Klaus Kipf, Johannes, 'Schwankroman – Prosaroman – Versroman. Über den Beitrag einer nicht nur prosaischen Gattung zur Entstehung des frühneuzeitlichen Prosaromans'. In: *Eulenspiegel trifft Melusine. Der frühneuhochdeutsche Prosaroman im Licht neuer Forschungen und Methoden*. Akten der Lausanner Tagung von 2. bis 4. Oktober 2008. Ed. by Catherine Drittenbass and André Schnyder. Amsterdam 2010 (Chloe 42), p. 145–162.

Mallette, Karla, *The Kingdom of Sicily, 1100–1250. A Literary History*. Philadelphia 2005.

Mertens, Volker, *Der deutsche Artusroman*. Stuttgart 1998.

Müller, Jan-Dirk, 'Volksbuch/Prosaroman im 15./16. Jahrhundert – Perspektiven der Forschung'. In: *Internationales Archiv für Sozialgeschichte der Literatur: Sonderheft Forschungsreferate* 1 (1985), p. 1–128.

Rautenberg, Ursula, 'Typographie und Leseweisen. Überlegungen zu den Melusine-Ausgaben der Frankfurter Offizinen Gülfferich und Weigand Han / Han Erben'. In: *Eulenspiegel trifft Melusine. Der frühneuhochdeutsche Prosaroman im Licht neuer Forschungen und Methoden*. Akten der Lausanner Tagung von 2. bis 4. Oktober 2008. Ed. by Catherine Drittenbass and André Schnyder. Amsterdam 2010 (Chloe 42), p. 341–363.

Resoort, R.J., *Een schoone historie vander borchgravinne van Vergi. Onderzoek naar de intentie en gebruikssfeer van een zestiende-eeuwse prozaroman*. Hilversum 1988.

Richter, Anna Katharina, *Transmissionsgeschichten. Untersuchungen zur dänischen und schwedischen Erzählprosa in der frühen Neuzeit*. Tübingen, Basel 2009 (Beiträge zur Nordischen Philologie 41).

Roccati, Giovanni Matteo, 'Le roman dans les incunables. L'impact des stratégies éditoriales dans le choix des titres imprimés'. In: *Le Roman français dans les premiers imprimés*. Ed. by Anne Schoysman and Maria Colombo Timelli. Paris 2016 (Rencontres 147), p. 95–126.

Sánchez-Martí, Jordi, 'The Printed History of the Middle English Verse Romances'. In: *Modern Philology* 107 (2009), p. 1–31.

Sánchez-Martí, Jordi, 'The Printed Transmission of Medieval Romance from William Caxton to Wynkyn de Worde, 1473–1535'. In: *The Transmission of Medieval Romance: Metres, Manuscripts and Early Prints*. Ed. by Ad Putter, Judith A. Jefferson. Cambridge 2018, p. 170–190.

Schlusemann, Rita, *Die hystorie van reynaert die vos und The history of reynard the fox. Die spätmittelalterlichen Prosabearbeitungen des Reynaert-Stoffes*. Frankfurt a. M. 1991.

Schlusemann, Rita, *Schöne Historien. Niederländische Romane im deutschen Spätmittelalter und in der frühen Neuzeit*. Berlin, Boston 2016 (Frühe Neuzeit, 203).

Schlusemann, Rita, "Mit poetrien". Bucheingänge, Fiktion und Wahrheit gedruckter niederländischer Historien im europäischen Kontext'. In: *ZfdA* 147 (2018), p. 70–99.

Schnyder, André, 'Der deutsche Prosaroman des 15. und 16. Jahrhunderts. Ein Problemfeld, eine Tagung und der Versuch einer Bilanz'. In: *Eulenspiegel trifft Melusine. Der frühneuhochdeutsche Prosaroman im Licht neuer Forschungen und Methoden*. Akten der Lausanner Tagung von 2. bis 4. Oktober 2008. Ed. by Catherine Drittenbass and André Schnyder. Amsterdam 2010 (Chloe 42), p. 11–39.

Schoysman, Anne and Maria Colombo Timelli (eds), *Le Roman français dans les premiers imprimés*. Paris 2016 (Rencontres 147).

I The History of Early Printing of Narrative Texts

Christa Bertelsmeier-Kierst

Durchbruch zur Prosa und der Einfluss des Buchdrucks auf die deutschsprachige Erzählliteratur des 15. Jahrhunderts

Abstracts: The stagnation of German verse romance during the fourteenth century was broken around 1400 when new narratives in prose, combining quite disparate narrative and thematic traditions by transferring material from various cultural spheres and epochs, first appeared. Most of the texts translated into German in the fifteenth century were from the Franco-Burgundian narrative tradition. However, in addition historical subjects from Latin literature, Hellenistic romances, humanistic novels and hagiographical material, as well as Middle High German verse romances, all found their way into Early New High German prose. During this literary development a major event in media history took place, the transition from the hand-written to the printed book. This article analyses which works proved to be successful in the new market for books and which remained in the world of manuscripts. In addition, it asks how far the printed book influenced the development of prose romance and compares the manuscript tradition with the printed editions in North and South Germany during the period of incunabula. Whereas the manuscript tradition consisted of a great many regionally varied versions, only one version was extant in printed editions, or, at most, both an Upper and Lower German version existed in print till 1500, whereas Lower German incunabula mostly follow Upper German editions. There is a clear distinction between Upper German incunabula, especially those printed in Augsburg (the main printing place for vernacular literature in the fifteenth century) and books printed in the South West, where the manuscript tradition, strongly influenced by the French-Burgundian style, still played an important role, also as admired models, for the printed books in this region.

Nachdem der deutsche Versroman im 14. Jahrhundert stagnierte, setzte erst gegen 1400 eine neue Erzählliteratur in Prosa wieder ein, die aus unterschiedlichen Kulturräumen und Epochen teils sehr heterogene Themen und narrative Traditionen verarbeitete. Die meisten Texte, die im 15. Jh. ins Deutsche übertragen wurden, sind der französisch-burgundischen Kultur entlehnt, hinzu kommen Geschichtsepen aus dem Lateinischen, hellenistische Romane, humanistische Novellen und hagiographische Stoffe sowie Bearbeitungen älterer mittelhochdeutscher Versromane, die ebenfalls in frühneuhochdeutsche Prosa gegossen wurden. Im Laufe dieser literarischen Entwicklung fand ein wichtiges mediengeschichtliches Ereignis statt: der Übergang vom handgeschriebenen zum gedruckten Buch. Dieser Beitrag untersucht, welche Werke Aufnahme auf dem neuen Buchmarkt fanden und welche hingegen in der Manuskriptkultur verblieben. Zum zweiten fragt er danach, welchen Einfluss der Buchdruck auf den Prosaroman nimmt und vergleicht hierzu die handschriftliche Überlieferung mit den gedruckten Ausgaben in Nord- und Süddeutschland während der Inkunabelzeit. Während in der Manuskriptkultur eine große Vielfalt an regional unterschiedlichen

Christa Bertelsmeier-Kierst, Universität Marburg

Fassungen existiert, setzt sich im Buchdruck in der Regel nur eine Fassung durch oder es werden je eine oberdeutsche und eine niederdeutsche Fassung bis 1500 gedruckt, wobei die niederdeutschen Ausgaben meistens von den oberdeutschen Drucken abhängig sind. Bei den oberdeutschen Inkunabeln lässt sich eine deutliche Differenzierung zwischen den vor allem in Augsburg (Hauptort der deutschsprachigen Druckproduktion im 15. Jh.) hergestellten Büchern und den Drucken aus dem deutschsprachigen Südwesten nachweisen, wo die Manuskriptkultur, stark von der französisch-burgundischen Tradition beeinflusst, nach wie vor eine bedeutende Rolle spielte und auch noch Vorbildfunktion für das gedruckte Buch in dieser Region hatte.

1 Einleitung

Obwohl mittlerweile eine breite Diskussion über Fragen der narrativen Kommunikation, über Fiktionalität und Poetik im Mittelalter und in der Frühen Neuzeit stattfindet, existiert bislang keine systematische Erforschung der deutschsprachigen Erzählliteratur. Dies gilt vor allem für den Übergang vom Vers zur Prosa, der sich in Deutschland, von Einzelfällen abgesehen, erst am Ausgang des Mittelalters vollzieht. Während im französisch-angiovinischen Kulturraum bereits im 13. Jahrhundert die älteren Versepen durch Prosafassungen abgelöst werden, setzt der Durchbruch zur Prosa in der erzählenden Literatur in Deutschland erst mit der Wende zum 15. Jahrhundert ein.[1] Begleitet wird dieser Wandel ab der Mitte des 15. Jahrhunderts von einem wichtigen mediengeschichtlichen Ereignis, der Einführung des Buchdrucks, der schon bald einen bedeutenden Einfluss auf die Entwicklung der volkssprachlichen Literatur nimmt. Während für die Kleinepik, insbesondere für die neue Form der Prosanovellistik, mittlerweile eine Reihe von Gattungsuntersuchungen und Einzelstudien vorliegen,[2] fehlen

---

1 Vgl. u.a. Johannes Janota, *Orientierung durch volkssprachliche Schriftlichkeit (1280/ 90–1380/90). Geschichte der deutschen Literatur von den Anfängen bis zum Beginn der Neuzeit.* Hg. v. Joachim Heinzle. Band III.1 Tübingen 2004, S. 208; Thomas Cramer, 'Aspekte des höfischen Romans im 14. Jahrhundert'. In: *Zur deutschen Literatur und Sprache des 14. Jahrhunderts. Dubliner Colloquium 1981.* Hg. v. Walter Haug, Timothy R. Jackson und Johannes Janota. Heidelberg 1983, S. 208 ff. [Vgl. für den Übergang zur Prosa im niederländischsprachigen Raum den Beitrag von Besamusca und Willaert (Seite 55) und für die Koëxistenz von Vers und Prosa in England den Beitrag von Sánchez-Martí in diesem Band (Seite 143–166.]
2 Vgl. zum Forschungsstand Wolfgang Achnitz, 'Das Feld der literarischen Kleinformen im Mittelalter'. In: *Deutsches Literatur-Lexikon: Das Mittelalter, Bd. 5: Epik.* Hg v. Wolfgang Achnitz. Berlin, Boston 2013, S. XXVII–XXXVIII. Zur Rezeption italienischer Novellistik vgl. u.a. Ursula Kocher, *Boccaccio und die deutsche Novellistik. Formen der Transposition italienischer "novelle" im 15. u. 16. Jahrhundert.* Amsterdam 2005; Luisa Rubini Messerli, *Boccaccio deutsch. Die Dekameron-Rezeption in der deutschen Literatur (15.–17. Jahrhundert).* Amsterdam 2012

vergleichbare Untersuchungen zum Prosaroman und zur Geschichtsepik, mit denen – nach dem Stagnieren des höfischen Romans – die narrative Großform um 1400 in Deutschland wieder einsetzt. Über ihre Entwicklung sind wir immer noch schlecht unterrichtet,[3] weil sich bei Untersuchung der Gattung die Aufmerksamkeit in der Vergangenheit fast ausschließlich auf die Druckprosa richtete, während die große Anzahl der in der Manuskriptkultur verbleibenden Werke in der Forschung weitgehend unbeachtet blieb. Somit wirkt bis in die jüngste Gegenwart wissenschaftsgeschichtlich immer noch die ältere ‚Volksbuch'-Tradition nach.[4]

Ausgehend von der Materialbasis, die wir als Marburger Forschergruppe in den letzten Jahren zum frühneuhochdeutschen Prosaroman zusammengetragen haben,[5] möchte ich nachfolgend beispielhaft untersuchen, welchen

---

(Chloe 45); Christa Bertelsmeier-Kierst, 'Zur Rezeption des lateinischen und volkssprachlichen Boccaccio im deutschen Frühhumanismus'. In: *Giovanni Boccaccio in Europa. Studien zu seiner Rezeption in Spätmittelalter und Früher Neuzeit*. Hg. v. Achim Aurnhammer, Rainer Stillers. Wiesbaden 2014 (Wolfenbütteler Abh. zur Renaissanceforschung 31), S. 131–154; Christa Bertelsmeier-Kierst, 'Übersetzen im deutschen Frühhumanismus. Ergebnisse des MRFH zur Einbürgerung humanistischer und antiker Autoren bis 1500'. In: *Humanistische Antikenübersetzung und frühneuzeitliche Poetik in Deutschland (1450–1620)*. Hg. v. Regina Töpfer, Johannes Klaus Kipf und Jörg Robert. Berlin, Boston 2017 (Frühe Neuzeit 211), S. 125–150. Sowie die Ergebnisse des MRFH (http://www.mrfh.de).

3 Richtungweisend immer noch Jan-Dirk Müller, 'Volksbuch/Prosaroman im 15./16. Jahrhundert – Perspektiven der Forschung.' In: *Internationales Archiv für Sozialgeschichte der Literatur: Sonderheft Forschungsreferate* 1 (1985), S. 1–128; ergänzend Jan-Dirk Müller, 'Prosaroman'. In: *Reallexikon der deutschen Literaturwissenschaft* 3 (2003), S. 174–177; André Schnyder, 'Der deutsche Prosaroman des 15. und 16. Jahrhunderts'. In: *Eulenspiegel trifft Melusine. Der frühneuhochdeutsche Prosaroman im Licht neuer Forschungen und Methoden*. Hg. v. Catherine Drittenbass und André Schnyder. Amsterdam, New York 2010 (Chloe 42), S. 11–39; André Schnyder, 'Das Corpus der frühneuhochdeutschen Prosaromane: Eine tabellarische Übersicht als Problemaufriss'. In: *Eulenspiegel trifft Melusine*, S. 545–556; Christa Bertelsmeier-Kierst, 'Erzählen in Prosa. Zur Entwicklung des deutschen Prosaromans bis 1500'. In: *ZfdA* 143 (2014), S. 141–165.

4 Vgl. Bertelsmeier-Kierst, 'Erzählen in Prosa' (Anm. 3), S. 161.

5 Das Marburger Prosaroman-Corpus umfasst für den älteren Zeitraum bis 1500 68 Texte, wobei die Grenze zwischen Roman, Geschichtsepik und Legende oftmals unscharf bleibt, so dass die Hybridität sicher zu den auffälligsten Gattungsmerkmalen in der Frühzeit zählt. Hinzu treten noch Grenzfälle zwischen Klein- und Großepik, so vor allem bei Novellen- und Erzählsammlungen, die durch ihre Rahmenhandlung eine Makrostruktur aufweisen und sich somit der Gattung ‚Roman' zumindest annähern. Liste des Textcorpus bei Bertelsmeier-Kierst, 'Erzählen in Prosa' (Anm. 3), S. 163–165.

Einfluss der mediengeschichtliche Wandel auf die Entwicklung des Prosaromans nimmt, welche Texte sich am erfolgreichsten auf dem neuen Buchmarkt durchsetzen bzw. welche noch überwiegend in der Manuskriptkultur verbleiben. Wie erste Fallstudien inzwischen belegen,[6] ist es keineswegs so, dass im neuen Medium, dem gedruckten Buch, die formal oder inhaltlich innovativsten Werke tradiert werden, sondern gerade die Texte, die Kontinuität verbürgen und oftmals in einer langen mittelalterlichen Tradition stehen, finden eine frühe und langanhaltende Aufnahme im Repertoire der Buchdrucker.

2 Antike Stoffe

Nachdem der Versroman im 14. Jahrhundert in Deutschland stagnierte, setzt „an der Wende zum 15. Jahrhundert in auffälliger Parallele zum Versroman des 12. Jahrhunderts"[7] der Neubeginn in Prosa wiederum mit antiken Stoffen ein.[8] Am Beginn steht das *Elsässische Trojabuch* eines südwestdeutschen Anonymus (vor 1386), das den *Trojanerkrieg* Konrads von Würzburg mit der *Historia destructionis Troiae* Guidos de Columnis kompiliert,[9] und die süddeutsche Bearbeitung des *Buch von Troja* durch Hans Mair (um 1391), die sich ausschließlich auf den mittellateinischen Text stützt.[10] Ebenfalls noch vor 1400 dürfte Meister Wichwolt seine *Cronica Alexander* verfasst haben,[11] der dann um 1450 der

---

6 Vgl. hierzu Bertelsmeier-Kierst, 'Übersetzen' (Anm. 2), mit dem Nachweis speziell für Übersetzungen aus der antiken Literatur im deutschen Frühhumanismus.

7 Janota (vgl. Anm. 1), S. 462 f.

8 Parallel setzt sich auch die Versliteratur fort, wie der fast zeitgleich geschriebene *Wernigeroder Alexander* bezeugt. Vgl. Dieter Welz, 'Der große Alexander'. In: ²*VL* 3 (1981), Sp. 281.

9 Karin Schneider, 'Buch von Troja I'. In: ²*VL* 1 (1978), Sp. 1100 und 11 (2004), Sp. 300; Volker Zapf, 'Elsässisches Trojabuch'. In: *Deutsches Literatur-Lexikon 5* (vgl. Anm. 2), Sp. 1143–1145. [Bearbeitungen der *Historia destructionis Troiae* finden sich auch anderswo in Westeuropa; in Frankreich, England und den Niederen Landen fand allerdings vor allem die Bearbeitung Raoul Lefèvres Verbreitung; vgl. die Beiträge von Besamusca und Willaert, S. 72–74, sowie De Bruijn, S. 95–101, in diesem Band).]

10 Vgl. Karin Schneider, 'Buch von Troja nach Guido de Columnis'. In: ²*VL* 1 (1978), Sp. 1101–1104; Hans-Hugo Steinhoff, 'Mair, Hans von Nördlingen'. In: ²*VL* 5 (1985), Sp. 1180–1183; Mike Malm, 'Mair von Nördlingen, Hans'. In: *Deutsches Literatur-Lexikon. Das Mittelalter, Bd. 3: Reiseberichte und Geschichtsschreibung*. Hg. v. Wolfgang Achnitz. Berlin, Boston 2011, Sp. 475–477.

11 Gisela Kornrumpf, 'Meister Wichwolt'. In: *Killy*² 12 (2011), S. 367f; Volker Zapf, 'Meister Wichwolt'. In: *Deutsches Literatur-Lexikon 3* (vgl. Anm. 10), Sp. 510–514; Peter H. Andersen, 'Wigbolds Alexanderbuch – Eine Pioniertat'. In: *Eulenspiegel trifft Melusine* (vgl. Anm. 3), S. 183–200.

Alexander des Johannes Hartlieb folgt, dem ein außerordentlicher Erfolg beschieden war.[12]

Vorwiegend handelt es sich bei den Prosabearbeitungen antiker Stoffe um einen Kulturtransfer aus der mittellateinischen Literatur, ihre Übersetzer waren *Litterati*, d. h. sie gehörten der Schicht der lateinisch Gebildeten an.[13] Allen diesen frühen Bearbeitern ist das Bemühen um Historisierung des Stoffes gemeinsam; der *Alexander* dient bei Hartlieb und Wichwolt als Fürstenspiegel; ebenfalls in den Prosabearbeitungen vom *Buch von Troja*[14] werden Darstellungen von Minne und Rittertum, wie sie zuvor noch Konrads *Trojanerkrieg* prägten, stark zurückgedrängt und „die historische Faktizität der Erzählung in den Mittelpunkt" gerückt.[15]

Wie werden die neuen Prosabearbeitungen antiker Stoffe nun im Druckzeitalter aufgenommen? Als erfolgreichster Text unter den neuen Prosabearbeitungen erweist sich Hartliebs *Alexander*, der sich mit 20 Handschriften und 11 (9) Drucken bereits bis 1500 einer außerordentlichen Beliebtheit erfreute.[16] Keiner der übrigen Texte kommt auch nur entfernt an diesen Publikumserfolg heran. Von den zahlreichen Trojabuch-Versionen, die im 15. Jahrhundert auf uns gekommen sind, werden nur zwei verlegt: eine oberdeutsche Druckfassung, die auf einer Kompilation des *Elsässischen Trojabuchs* mit der Bearbeitung der *Historia destructionis Troiae* durch Hans Mair aus Nördlingen basiert. Sie wird bis 1500 in sieben Inkunabeln (Erstausgabe: Augsburg 1474) überliefert.[17] Eine

---

12 Klaus Grubmüller, 'Hartlieb, Johannes'. In: ²*VL* 3 (1981), Sp. 480–496 und 11 (2004), Sp. 589 f.; Werner Röcke, 'Hartlieb, Johannes'. In: *Killy*² 12 (2011), S. 35 f.

13 Hartlieb war *doctor der erzenie* und Leibarzt des bayerischen Herzogs, für den er den *Alexander* nach Guido de Columnis übersetzte. Hans Mair aus Nörtlingen, Ratsherr, Spitalpfleger und auswärtiger Rechtsvertreter der Stadt, war ein gebildeter Jurist, während Wichwolt, wie die Bezeichnung *meister* und die selbständige Benutzung mehrerer lateinischer Quellen nahelegt, offenbar den Magistertitel erworben hatte.

14 Vgl. Volker Zapf, 'Buch von Troja nach Guido de Columnis'. In: *Deutsches Literatur-Lexikon 5* (vgl. Anm. 2), Sp. 1275–1277. Hinzu kommen noch drei Bearbeitungen, die zu großen Teilen auf Konrads Trojanerkrieg basieren.

15 Zapf (Anm. 14).

16 http://www.handschriftencensus.de/werke/1910; GW 883a–890. Zwei Drucke sind nicht nachweisbar.

17 Die Augsburger Drucke fallen durch verschiedene Redaktionen auf. Vgl. Clemens Alfen, Petra Flochler und Elisabeth Lienert, 'Deutsche Trojatexte des 12.–16. Jhs., Repertorium'. In: *Die deutsche Trojaliteratur des Mittelalters und der frühen Neuzeit. Materialien und Untersuchungen*. Hg. v. Horst Brunner. Wiesbaden 1990 (Wissensliteratur im Mittelalter 3), S. 104–111; GW 7233–7239. Zwei weitere Straßburger Drucke sind Postinkunabeln aus der Zeit nach 1500 (GW6, Sp. 802a = VD16 H 5679 und VD16 H 5680).

anonyme niederdeutsche Druckfassung der *Historia* des Guido de Columnis wurde im 15. Jahrhundert zweimal verlegt.[18]

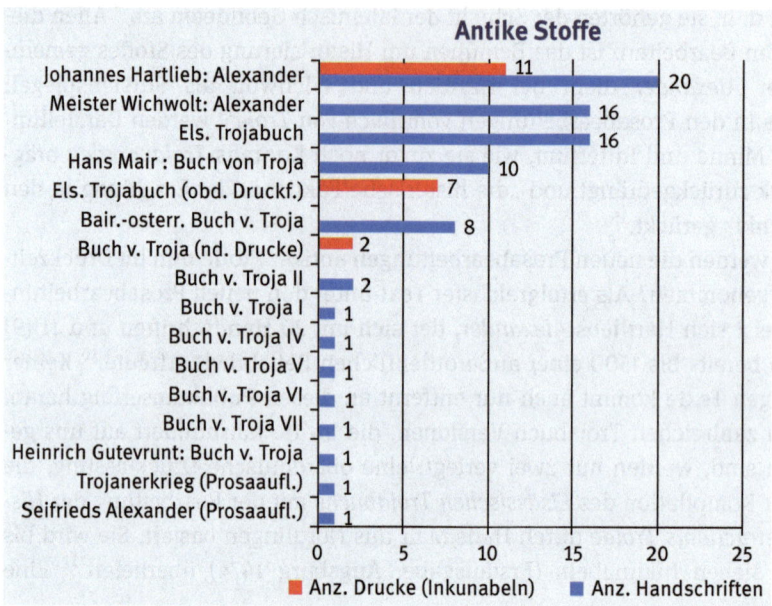

Antike Stoffe

Johannes Hartlieb: Alexander	11 / 20
Meister Wichwolt: Alexander	16
Els. Trojabuch	16
Hans Mair : Buch von Troja	10
Els. Trojabuch (obd. Druckf.)	7
Bair.-osterr. Buch v. Troja	8
Buch v. Troja (nd. Drucke)	2
Buch v. Troja II	2
Buch v. Troja I	1
Buch v. Troja IV	1
Buch v. Troja V	1
Buch v. Troja VI	1
Buch v. Troja VII	1
Heinrich Gutevrunt: Buch v. Troja	1
Trojanerkrieg (Prosaaufl.)	1
Seifrieds Alexander (Prosaaufl.)	1

0   5   10   15   20   25

■ Anz. Drucke (Inkunabeln)   ■ Anz. Handschriften

3 Französisch-burgundische Stoffe

Neben historisch-antiken Stoffen, die vorzugsweise nach mittellateinischen Quellen bearbeitet wurden, sind es vor allem französische Werke, die als Vorlage frühneuhochdeutscher Prosabearbeitungen dienten. Am Beginn stehen auch hier wieder ‚historisch verbürgte' Stoffe, nämlich ältere Texte der Chanson de Geste, deren Helden dem Sagenkreis Karls d. Gr. angehören. Ebenfalls die zahlreichen Entlehnungen aus der jüngeren französischen Erzählliteratur lassen bevorzugt Themen des ritterlichen Heidenkampfes und der Kreuzzugsthematik erkennen. Abgesehen von einer niederdeutschen Bearbeitung von *Gerart von Rossiliun*, die allerdings nur fragmentarisch in einer ostfälischen Handschrift (um 1400)

---

18 [Lübeck: Lukas Brandis], 1477/78 (GW 7240); [Magdeburg: Moritz Brandis], 1495 (GW 7242).

erhalten blieb,[19] setzt der Prosaroman ab den dreißiger Jahren des 15. Jahrhunderts zunächst mit Bearbeitungen der Gräfin Elisabeth von Nassau-Saarbrücken ein, die zu einem eng mit Frankreich verbundenen höfischen Kulturraum zählt.[20] Offenbar nach einer in Versen geschriebenen Vorlage[21] verfasste Elisabeth den Prosazyklus von *Herpin*, Königin *Sibille*, *Loher und Maller* sowie *Hug Scheppel*, wobei die Texte wahrscheinlich schon in der französischen Handschrift „in einer genealogisch begründeten zyklischen Einheit vorgelegen haben."[22] Überliefert sind die Romane erst nach dem Tod Elisabeths in reich bebilderten Prachtcodices, von denen allein drei ihr Sohn, Johann III. von Saarbrücken „anlässlich seines Eintritts in den Ritterorden *de Croissant* nach 1455"[23] in Auftrag gab; ihre Tochter, Margarethe von Rodemachern, besaß die Heidelberger Handschrift 1012 mit *Loher und Maller*,[24] Margarethe von Savoyen eine Bilderhandschrift von

---

19 Hamburg, SUB, Cod. germ. 77 (ehem. Werningerode, Gräfl. Stolbergsche Bibliothek). Wann die Dichtung entstanden ist, bleibt ganz ungewiss.
20 Elisabeths Verfasserschaft gilt als umstritten, in jedem Fall sind die Romane aber in ihrer engsten Umgebung entstanden. Zu Elisabeth von Nassau-Saarbrücken und ihrem Kulturraum vgl. Wolfgang Haubrichs und Hans-Walter Herrmann, unter Mitw. v. Gerhard Sauder (Hg.), *Zwischen Deutschland und Frankreich. Elisabeth von Lothringen, Gräfin von Nassau-Saarbrücken*. St. Ingbert 2002; Bruno Jahn, 'Elisabeth'. In: *Deutsches Literatur-Lexikon 5* (vgl. Anm. 2), Sp. 1494–1505.
21 Von der frz. Vorlage, die Elisabeth von ihrer Mutter, Margarethe von Vaudemont-Joinville, für ihre Übersetzungen besaß, ist einzig zu *Lohier et Malart* ein Blatt aufgetaucht, das als Aktenumschlag des Nassauischen Staatsarchivs überlebt hat und sich heute in Wiesbaden, HStA, Abt. 1105, Nr. 40 befindet. Farbabb. in Eva Horváth und Hans-Walter Storck (Hg.), *Von Rittern, Bürgern und von Gottes Wort*. Hamburg 2002 (Schriften aus dem Antiquariat Günther, Hamburg, 2), Nr. 30; Textabdruck und Schwarz-Weiß-Abb. in Ute von Bloh, Kurt Gärtner und Michael Heintze, '*Lohier et Malart – Loher und Maller*: Vorschläge zu einer Edition des Epos'. In: *Zwischen Deutschland und Frankreich* (vgl. Anm. 20), S. 427–458, hier 432 und Abb. 30.
22 Hans-Hugo Steinhoff, 'Elisabeth von Nassau-Saarbrücken'. In: ²*VL* 2 (1980), Sp. 482–488; Wolfgang Haubrichs, 'Die vier Prosahistorien Elisabeths – Skizzierung ihres Inhalts'. In: *Zwischen Deutschland und Frankreich* (vgl. Anm. 20), S. 11–16; Ute von Bloh, *Ausgerenkte Ordnung*. *Vier Prosaepen aus dem Umkreis der Gräfin Elisabeth von Nassau-Saarbrücken: Herzog Herpin, Loher und Maller, Huge Scheppel, Königin Sibille*. Tübingen 2002 (MTU 119); Ute von Bloh (Hg.), *Loher und Maller. Kritische Edition eines spätmittelalterlichen Prosaepos*. Berlin 2013 (TMA 50); Bernd Bastert (Hg.), *Herzog Herpin. Kritische Edition eines spätmittelalterlichen Prosaepos*. Berlin 2014 (TMA 51). Ute von Bloh und Bernd Bastert, *Loher und Maller – Herzog Herpin: Kommentar und Erschließung*. Berlin 2017 (TMA 55).
23 Peter Jörg Becker, 'Elisabeth von Nassau-Saarbrücken: Herzog Herpin'. In: *Aderlass und Seelentrost. Die Überlieferung deutscher Texte im Spiegel Berliner Handschriften und Inkunabeln*. Hg. v. Peter Jörg Becker und Eef Overgaauw. Mainz 2003, S. 135–137, hier 135 (Kat. Nr. 63).
24 Zu den Handschriften, ihrem Buchschmuck und Besitzern vgl. vor allem die Beiträge von Wolfgang Haubrichs, 'Kurze Forschungsgeschichte zum literarischen Werk Elisabeths'. In: *Zwischen Deutschland und Frankreich* (vgl. Anm. 20), S. 17–48, hier S. 34–38; Hans-Walther Storck, 'Die handschriftliche Überlieferung der Werke

Herzog Herpin aus der Werkstatt Ludwig Henfflins.[25] Von Elisabeths Romanen wurde nur *Hug Scheppel* noch am Ende der Inkunabelzeit gedruckt, allerdings in einer stark gekürzten Bearbeitung, die als *Ein lieplich lesen vnd ein // warhafftige Hystorie*[26] im Jahr 1500 auf den Markt kam.[27] Mit Ausnahme der *Königin Sibille*, die nicht in die Druckwerkstätten gelangte, wurden die übrigen Werke im 16. Jahrhundert mehrfach verlegt.[28]

Einen beachtlichen Erfolg erzielte bereits im 15. Jahrhundert der Roman *Pontus und Sidonia*, dessen Stofftradition auf die ältere anglo-normanischen Chanson *Horn et Rimenhild* zurückreicht, von Geoffrey de la Tour Landry aber noch vor 1400 in den französischen Roman *Ponthus et la belle Sidoyne* umgearbeitet wurde.[29] Auf ihm basieren drei deutschsprachige Prosafassungen, wovon die älteste, stark gekürzte Berner Bearbeitung (C) noch in der Mitte des 15. Jahrhunderts entstanden ist. Während diese sich nur unikal in einer Handschrift des Berner Ratsherrn Kaspar von Mülinen (1481–1538) erhalten hat,[30]

Elisabeths von Nassau-Saarbrücken und die malerische Ausstattung der Handschriften'. In: *Zwischen Deutschland und Frankreich* (vgl. Anm. 20), S. 591–606; sowie Eva Wolff, 'Die Sprache der Bilder. Bild-Erzählung in den Handschriften der Romane der Elisabeth von Nassau-Saarbrücken'. In: *Zwischen Deutschland und Frankreich* (vgl. Anm. 20), S. 591–622 (mit Farbabb.); Wolfgang Haubrichs, 'Mahl und Krieg. Die Erzählung der Adelskultur in den Texten und Bildern des Hamburger *Huge Scheppel* der Elisabeth von Lothringen, Gräfin von Nassau-Saarbrücken'. In: *Eulenspiegel trifft Melusine* (vgl. Anm. 3), S. 201–216 und Abb. (meist in Farbe) 1–14; Horváth und Storck (vgl. Anm. 21), Farbabb. Nr. 31 und 33.

25 Heidelberg UB, Cpg 152. Vgl. Karin Zimmermann, *Die Codices Palatini germanici in der Universitätsbibliothek Heidelberg (Cod. Pal. Germ. 1–181)*. Wiesbaden 2003, S. 332–333; Maria Effinger und Kerstin Losert (Hg.), *Mit schönen figuren. Buchkunst im deutschen Südwesten*. Heidelberg 2014, S. 72–74 (Farbabb. Nr. 38); Digitalisat: http://digi.ub.uni-heidelberg.de/digi lit/cpg152.

26 Titelblatt des Hamburger Exemplars des Erstdrucks abgebildet bei Horváth und Storck (vgl. Anm. 21), Nr. 34.

27 Angefertigt hat sie der ehemalige Saarbrücker Bedienstete und Schreiber Conrad Heyndörffer. Vgl. Haubrichs (vgl. Anm. 24), S. 19.

28 Vgl. Gerhard Sauder, 'Die Rezeption der Prosaromane Elisabeths von Nassau-Saarbrücken – Vom "Volksbuch" bis zur Romantik'. In: *Zwischen Deutschland und Frankreich* (vgl. Anm. 20), S. 569–589 (m. Abb.); ergänzend Jahn (vgl. Anm. 20), Sp 197 f. Zur Straßburger Ausgabe des *Huge Scheppel* von 1537 (VD16 H 5855) vgl. Effinger und Losert (vgl. Anm. 25), S. 99 f. (Abb. 54).

29 Vgl. Xenia von Ertzdorff, *Romane und Novellen des 15. und 16. Jahrhunderts in Deutschland*. Darmstadt 1989, S. 72–75; Mario Müller, 'Pontus und Sidonia'. In: *Deutsches Literatur-Lexikon 5* (vgl. Anm. 2), Sp. 1575–1598.

30 Bern, Burgerbibl., Ms. Mül. 619, S. 1–85. Vgl. Reinhard Hahn, '*Pontus und Sidonia* in der Berner Fassung'. In: *Daphnis* 32 (2003), S. 289–350; Kristina Streun, 'Pontus und Sidonia (C)'.

wurde die Bearbeitung (A), die der Gemahlin Sigmunds von Tirol, Eleonore von Schottland, zugewiesen wird,[31] auch im Druck verbreitet. Erstmals in einer Gothaer Handschrift von 1465 (Cod. Chart. A 590) bezeugt, ist sie die einzige Fassung, die von 1483 bis 1600 mindestens siebzehnmal verlegt wurde. Die B-Fassung, die A nahesteht, jedoch ausschmückender erzählt, wird in fünf Handschriften tradiert, die überwiegend aus Adelsbibliotheken stammen und den Prosaroman teils mit älteren Versepen wie Pleiers *Tandareis und Flordibel* oder *Friedrich von Schwaben*, teils mit dem älteren *Prosa-Lancelot* überliefern.[32] Eine reich illustrierte Handschrift (Heidelberg, UB, Cpg 142) gab 1474 Margarethe von Savoyen, die Gemahlin Ulrichs von Württemberg, wiederum in der Werkstatt Ludwig Henfflins in Auftrag[33]; darüber hinaus ist für die Bibliothek Mechthilds von der Pfalz durch Püterichs Ehrenbrief (1462) schon früh eine Abschrift von *Pontus und Sidonia* bezeugt.[34]

Ebenfalls in Bern überträgt 1456 der zur städtischen Führungsschicht zählende Thüring von Ringoltingen die Feengeschichte *Melusine* in deutsche Prosa,[35] die im Basler Erstdruck mit den Worten eingeleitet wird: *Dis ouentúrlich bůch bewiset* [...] *von einer frowen genant Melusina* [...]/ *Do by ma[n] briffen mag/* [...] *das die hystory wor vnd an ir selber also ist.*[36] Gewidmet hat Thüring seinen Roman dem Markgrafen Rudolf IV. von Hachberg-Rötteln, der

---

In: ²*VL* 11 (2004), Sp. 1259 f.; Müller (vgl. Anm. 29), Sp. 1577–1579 (http://www.handschriften census.de/19648).

31 Zur Verfasserfrage siehe den neusten Forschungsbericht bei Müller (vgl. Anm. 29), insb. Sp. 1582 ff.

32 Xenia von Ertzdorff, 'Pontus und Sidonia'. In: ²*VL* 7 (1989), Sp. 780–782; Müller (vgl. Anm. 29), Sp. 1577 f.

33 Zimmermann (vgl. Anm. 25), S. 313f (Digitalisat: http://digi.ub.uni-heidelberg.de/diglit/cpg142).

34 Vgl. Volker Zapf, 'Püterich von Reichertshausen'. In: *Deutsches Literatur-Lexikon 5* (vgl. Anm. 2), Sp. 1664–1669; *Faks. Bayerische Staatsbibliothek, Cgm 9220*. Mit einer Einf. v. Klaus Grubmüller und einer Beschr. v. Ulrich Montag. München 1999 (Patrimonia 154). Der Hinweis auf *Pontus und Sidonia* befindet sich in Str. 99.

35 Jan-Dirk Müller, 'Thüring von Ringoltingen'. In: ²*VL* 9 (1995), Sp. 908–914; Mike Malm, 'Thüring von Ringoltingen'. In: *Deutsches Literatur-Lexikon 5* (vgl. Anm. 2), Sp. 1598–1604; Thüring von Ringoltingen, *Melusine* (1456). Nach dem Erstdruck Basel: Richel um 1473–1474 hg. v. André Schnyder in Verb. mit Ursula Rautenberg. Bd. II, Kommentar und Aufsätze. Wiesbaden 2006; Jean-Claude Mühlethaler und André Schnyder (Hg.), *550 Jahre dt. Melusine. Couldrette und Thüring von Ringoltingen*. Bern 2008 (Beitr. der wiss. Tagung der Universitäten Bern und Lausanne).

36 Zitiert nach dem Faks. (Ex. Karlsruhe, BLB, St. Peter pap. 23, BL. 1a), in Thüring von Ringoltingen, *Melusine* (Anm. 35), Bd. 1, S. 5.

großen Einfluss am burgundischen Hof besaß und somit ein wichtiger politischer Bündnisgenosse Berns in den fünfziger und sechziger Jahren des 15. Jahrhunderts war. Als Vorlage diente dem Berner Ratsherrn und späterem Schultheiß eine von Coudrette für die Grafen von Parthenay um 1400 geschriebene Versfassung, die er jedoch in Prosa umsetzte, um den Wahrheitsgehalt der Geschichte zu unterstreichen.[37]

Thürings *selczene vnd gar wunderliche fremde hystorie,*[38] in deren Mittelpunkt Melusine, die Ahnherrin des Kreuzfahrergeschlechts Lusignan, und die erfolgreichen Heidenkämpfe ihrer Söhne stehen, war ein außergewöhnlicher Erfolg beschieden. Bis 1500 wurde der Roman schon in 17 Handschriften und 11 Drucken verbreitet, denen bis ins 19. Jahrhundert noch mindestens 60 Ausgaben folgten.[39] Hingegen blieb einer anonymen zeitgenössischen Berner Bearbeitung des französischen Prosaromans *Cleomades* ein vergleichbarer Erfolg versagt.[40] Auch die *Ystoire du vaillant chevalier Pierre, filz du conte de proivence, et la belle Maguelone* wird in Deutschland erst durch die *Schöne Magelone* Veit Warbecks bekannt, der sie 1524 für den sächsischen Kronprinzen bearbeitete und die ab 1535 in zahlreichen Auflagen des 16. und 17. Jahrhunderts verbreitet wurde.[41] Eine ältere anonyme Prosafassung, die vielleicht noch im letzten Viertel des 15. Jahrhunderts entstanden ist, blieb hingegen nur

---

37 Zu den vielfältigen Beglaubigungsstrategien, denen sich Thüring in der *Melusine* bedient vgl. demnächst meinen Aufsatz 'Rekontextualisierung des Wissens. *Res fictae* und *res factae* im vormodernen Roman am Beispiel von Thürings *Melusine*'. In: *Enzyklopädisches Erzählen und vormoderne Romanpoetik.* Hg. v. Mathias Herweg, Johannes Klaus Kipf und Dirk Werle (Wolfenbütteler Forschungen) [im Druck].
38 Thüring von Ringoltingen, *Melusine* (Anm. 35), Bd. 1, S. 5.
39 Vgl. Martina Backes, *Fremde Historien. Untersuchungen zur Überlieferungs- und Rezeptionsgeschichte französischer Erzählstoffe im deutschen Mittelalter.* Tübingen 2004 (Hermaea 103), S. 103–112; ergänzend: Tina Terrahe, 'Eine neue Hs. der *Melusine* Thürings von Ringoltingen'. In: *ZfdA* 138 (2009), S. 50–52. Eine Dokumentation der gesamten Drucküberlieferung ist durch Hans-Jörg Künast und Ursula Rautenberg in Vorbereitung. Forschungsbericht in: Hans-Jörg Künast und Ursula Rautenberg, 'Typographie und Leseweisen. Überlegungen zu den *Melusine*-Ausgaben der Frankfurter Druckoffizinen [...]'. In: *Eulenspiegel trifft Melusine* (vgl. Anm. 3), S. 341–359, hier S. 341–343.
40 Der Roman ist nur fragmentarisch in einer einzigen Handschrift der Berner Burgerbibliothek (Mss. hist. helv. VII. 81) zusammen mit der Berner Chronik und der Chronik Jacob Twingers von Königshofen überliefert. Vgl. Volker Zapf, 'Cleomades'. In: *Deutsches Literatur-Lexikon 5* (vgl. Anm. 2), Sp. 1573–1575; http://www.handschriftencensus.de/20865.
41 Vgl. Hans-Hugo Steinhoff, 'Magelone'. In: ²*VL* 5 (1985), Sp. 1142–1148; Volker Zapf, 'Warbeck'. In: *Deutsches Literatur-Lexikon 5* (vgl. Anm. 2), Sp. 2050–2055.

unikal in einer Handschrift von 1525 erhalten.[42] Ebenfalls der Roman *Paris und Vienna*,[43] der von der Liebe des *vramen riddere* Paris zu Vienna, der Tochter des Dauphins, erzählt und in Frankreich, England, den Niederlanden und Italien sehr erfolgreich war, ist nur in einer niederdeutschen Bearbeitung auf uns gekommen, die 1488 von Gerhard Leeu in Antwerpen gedruckt wurde, der ein Jahr zuvor auch die niederländische und französische Fassung herausgebracht hatte. Diesen Drucken sind die 26 Holzschnitte für die niederdeutsche Ausgabe entnommen, die dem sog. „Meister von Harlem" zugesprochen werden.[44]

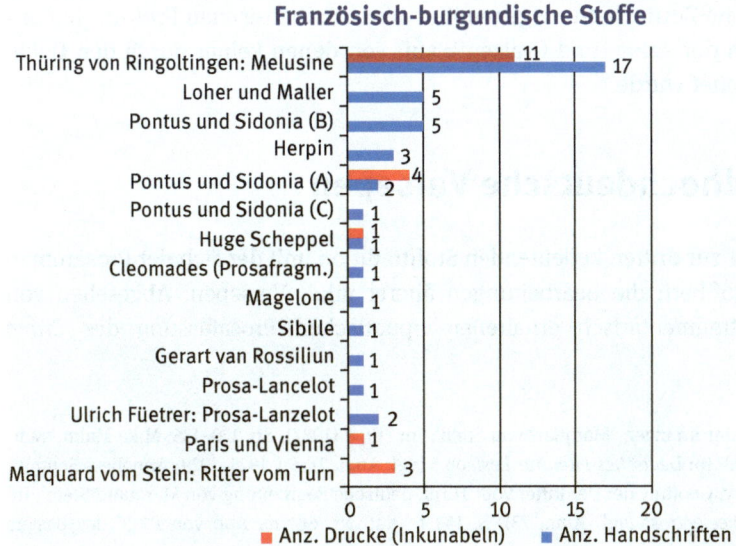

Französisch-burgundische Stoffe

Thüring von Ringoltingen: Melusine — 11 — 17
Loher und Maller — 5
Pontus und Sidonia (B) — 5
Herpin — 3
Pontus und Sidonia (A) — 4 / 2
Pontus und Sidonia (C) — 1
Huge Scheppel — 1 / 1
Cleomades (Prosafragm.) — 1
Magelone — 1
Sibille — 1
Gerart van Rossiliun — 1
Prosa-Lancelot — 1
Ulrich Füetrer: Prosa-Lancelot — 2
Paris und Vienna — 1
Marquard vom Stein: Ritter vom Turn — 3

0   5   10   15   20

■ Anz. Drucke (Inkunabeln)   ■ Anz. Handschriften

Hingegen war der Erzählsammlung *Der Ritter vom Turn*, die der württembergische Landvogt von Mömpelgard, Marquart von Stein, nach dem *Livre du chevalier de la Tour Landry pour l'enseignement de ses filles* im späten 15. Jahrhundert verfasste, ein rascher Erfolg beschieden. Noch drei Inkunabeln tradieren

---

42 *Piro de Prouenze und Magelonna* (jetzt: Krakau, BJ, Berol. Mgq 1579). Zum Forschungsstand siehe Steinhoff (vgl. Anm. 41), Sp. 1144; Volker Zapf, 'Magelone'. In: *Deutsches Literatur-Lexikon 5* (vgl. Anm. 2), Sp. 1881–1884.
43 Ertzdorff (vgl. Anm. 29), S. 62.
44 Jürgen Meier, 'Paris und Vienna'. In: ²*VL* 7 (1989), Sp. 306–309; Mike Malm, 'Paris und Vienna'. In: *Deutsches Literatur-Lexikon* 5 (vgl. Anm. 2), Sp. 1901–1904; GW 12699 (Digitalisat: http://pds.lib.harvard.edu/pds/view/30971723).

ab 1493 das Werk, das im Basler Erstdruck mit 46 künstlerisch hochwertigen Holzschnitten nach Vorlagen Albrecht Dürers ausgestattet wurde. Im 16. Jahrhundert erlebte der *Ritter vom Turn* neun weitere Ausgaben.[45]

Wie die meisten deutschen Prosafassungen antiker Stoffe erreichten von den zahlreichen Prosaauflösungen, die der älteren Chanson de Geste und der jüngeren französischen Erzähltradition entlehnt wurden, nur wenige die Druckoffizinen der Inkunabelzeit. Mit Abstand erweist sich hier Thürings *Melusine* als erfolgreichster Roman, der bis ins 19. Jahrhundert immer wieder verlegt wurde. Verglichen mit den Druckauflagen, die vor allem die Prosabearbeitungen von Werken der jüngeren französischen Erzähltradition erzielten, fällt in Deutschland die große Zurückhaltung gegenüber den altfranzösischen Prosazyklen aus dem Bereich der Artus- und Gralsepik auf, von denen keiner durch den Buchdruck verbreitet wurde.[46]

4 Mittelhochdeutsche Versepen

Kommen wir zur dritten bedeutenden Stofftradition, mit der sich der Prosaroman vor 1500 profiliert: die Bearbeitungen älterer mhd. Versepen. Abgesehen von einer nur fragmentarisch erhaltenen ripuarischen Prosafassung des *Crane*

---

45 Hans-Joachim Kreutzer, 'Marquart von Stein'. In: ²*VL* 6 (1987), Sp. 129–135; Mike Malm, 'Marquart von Stein'. In: *Deutsches Literatur-Lexikon* 5 (vgl. Anm. 2), Sp. 1925–1929; Anneliese Schmitt, 'La Tour-Landry, Geoffrey de: Der Ritter vom Turm, deutsche Bearbeitung von Marquard Stein'. In: *Aderlass und Seelentrost* (vgl. Anm. 23), S. 143 f. (Kat. Nr. 66) m. Abb von B1 3ʳ des Baslers Erstdrucks.

46 Der *Prosa-Lancelot*, dessen erster Teil fragmentarisch schon um 1250 in Deutschland überliefert ist, wurde offenbar vor 1470 am Heidelberger Hof (P = Cpg 147) fortgesetzt. Neben dem Kurfürsten Friedrich I. käme auch seine Schwester, Mechtild von der Pfalz, als Auftraggeberin in Frage, da sie gemäß Püterichs 'Ehrenbrief' mehrere Lancelot-Handschriften besessen hat (Zimmermann (vgl. Anm. 25), S. 324; Martina Backes, *Das literarische Leben am kurpfälzischen Hof zu Heidelberg im 15. Jahrhundert. Ein Beitrag zur Gönnerforschung des Spätmittelalters*, Tübingen 1992, S. 168, Anm. 197). Eine nahezu vollständige Bearbeitung, die auch die Lücke in P füllt, erfolgte erst im 16. Jh. Am Münchner Hof verfasste Ulrich Füetrer im 15. Jh. eine kürzende Bearbeitung des *Prosa-Lancelot*, der er wenig später auch eine strophische Fassung folgen ließ (vgl. Kurt Nyholm, 'Füetrer, Ulrich'. In: ²*VL* 2 (1980), Sp. 999–1007; Mike Malm, 'Fuetrer'. In: *Deutsches Literatur-Lexikon* 5 (vgl. Anm. 2), Sp. 1867–1873). Noch später ist eine deutsche Bearbeitung des *Tristan en prose* nachzuweisen. Die wörtliche Übersetzung, die der Gruppe C der frz. Tradition angehört, ist nur trümmerhaft in einer Handschrift des 16. Jh. auf uns gekommen (vgl. Hans-Hugo Steinhoff, 'Tristan'. In: ²*VL* 9 (1995), Sp. 1060 f.; Florian Altenhöfer, 'Tristan'. In: *Deutsches Literatur-Lexikon 5* (vgl. Anm. 2), Sp. 1966). [Vgl. für die Verbreitung gedruckter Artusromane in Westeuropa den Beitrag von Montorsi in diesem Band, S. 167–188.]

Bertolds von Holle[47] wurden zwei oberdeutsche Prosaromane offenbar unmittelbar für den Buchdruck geschaffen: *Tristrant und Isalde* nach Eilharts *Tristrant* (Erstdruck: Augsburg, Anton Sorg, 1484) und *Herr Wigoleis vom Rade* nach dem Versroman Wirnts von Grafenberg (Erstdruck: Augsburg Johann Schönsperger, d. Ä, 1493). Beide haben eine beachtliche Wirkungsgeschichte bis in die Romantik erfahren und 1807 Joseph Görres zu seiner Schrift *Die deutschen Volksbücher* veranlasst. Eine stark gekürzte Prosaauflösung des Versromans *Wilhelm von Österreich* Johanns von Würzburg liegt bis 1500 in zwei Handschriften und zwei Augsburger Drucken von 1481 und 1491 vor.[48]

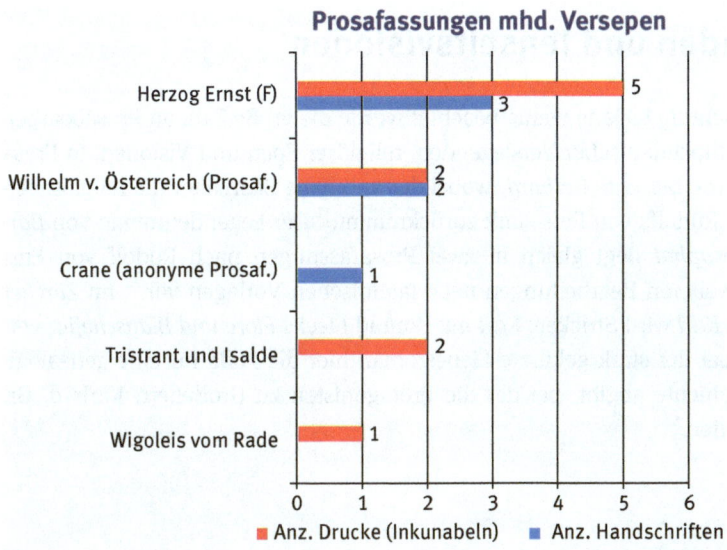

Prosafassungen mhd. Versepen

Einen Sonderfall innerhalb der Rezeption mhd. Epen stellt die anonyme Prosabearbeitung des *Herzog Ernst* (Fassung F) dar, die nicht nach dem mhd. Text,

---

47 Vgl. Joachim Heinzle, *Wandlungen und Neuansätze im 13. Jahrhundert. Geschichte der deutschen Literatur von den Anfängen bis zum Beginn der Neuzeit.* Bd. 2, T. 2. Tübingen ²1994, S. 113 f. Der Text ist nur unikal überliefert (Darmstadt, LUB, Hs. 2667: Jh.; rip.). Digitalisat: http://tudiget.ulb.tu-darmstadt.de/show/Hs-2667.
48 Vgl. Cora Dietl, 'Wilhelm von Österreich'. In: ²*VL* 10 (1999), Sp. 1114–1116; Volker Zapf, 'Wilhelm von Österreich'. In: *Deutsches Literatur-Lexikon 5* (vgl. Anm. 2), Sp. 1785–1787. Aus dem 16. Jh. ist nur eine späte Handschrift (Karlsruhe, LB, Cod. Donaueschingen 153) und das Titelblatt eines Druckes (vor 1550) erhalten.

sondern der lateinischen Bearbeitung des Werks erfolgte. Neben drei Handschriften, von denen zwei den *Herzog Ernst* mit der *Historia Hierosolymitana* verbinden, wird der Text seit ca. 1476 auch gedruckt (fünf Inkunabeln und zahlreiche Ausgaben im 16. Jahrhundert).[49] Textsymbiosen mit *Schildbergers Reisebuch* oder *Brandans Meerfahrt* indizieren, dass der Roman vor allem als Reise- und Orientbuch geschätzt wurde. Eine weitere Umarbeitung erfährt der Text dann in den stark gekürzten Ausgaben des 16. Jahrhunderts, die den Roman auf die phantastische Orientreise reduzierten. In dieser Form überlebte der Stoff bis in unsere Tage.[50]

5 Legenden und Jenseitsvisionen

Von der Forschung bislang wenig beachtet wurde die große Zahl an Prosabearbeitungen mittelhochdeutscher Verslegenden, religiöser Epen und Visionen. In Prosa übersetzt wurde *Der gute Gerhard*, wobei der anonyme Bearbeiter die religiöse Argumentation Rudolfs von Ems stark zurücknimmt.[51] Der Legendenroman von *Barlaam und Josaphat* liegt gleich in zwei Prosafassungen nach Rudolf von Ems sowie zwei weiteren Bearbeitungen nach lateinischen Vorlagen vor.[52] Im *Zürcher Buch vom hl. Karl* wird Strickers *Karl* mit Konrad Flecks *Flore und Blanscheflur* verbunden, wobei der stark gekürzte Liebesroman hier die Folie für eine genealogische Vorgeschichte abgibt, bei der die Protagonisten zu Großeltern Karls d. Gr. gemacht werden.[53]

---

49 Vgl. Volker Zapf, 'Herzog Ernst'. In: *Deutsches Literatur-Lexikon 5* (vgl. Anm. 2), Sp. 154 f. und 158; ergänzend: GW 12534, 12535, 12537–12539.
50 Vgl. Peter Hacks, *Das Volksbuch von Herzog Ernst*, Uraufführung 1967. Zur reichen Rezeptionsgeschichte des *Prosa-Herzog Ernst*, vgl. Zapf, 'Herzog Ernst' (Anm. 49), S. 154 f.
51 *Von Kaiser Otto dem Rotten und dem guoten Gerhard zu Köln*. Vgl. Rudolf Benzinger et al. (Hgg.), *Der gute Gerhard Rudolf von Ems in einer anonymen Prosaauflösung [...]*. Berlin 2001 (DTM 81).
52 Eine obd. und rip. Fassung liegen vor, wobei die obd. Bearbeitung eine vollständige Übersetzung aus dem *Speculum historiale* des Vincent von Beauvais ist und in einer Handschrift (Berlin, SB, mgq 1147; 150 Bll.) sowie zwei illustrierten Augsburger Drucken vor 1500 verbreitet wurde (GW 3398 und 3399). Vgl. Christine Stöllinger-Löser, 'Barlaam und Josaphat'. In: ²*VL* 11 (2004), Sp. 215–219, hier Sp. 216 f.
53 Karl-Ernst Geith, 'Zürcher Buch vom heiligen Karl'. In: ²*VL* 10 (1999), Sp. 1597–1600 und 11 (2004), Sp. 1697; Christine Stridde, 'Zürcher Buch vom heiligen Karl'. In: *Deutsches Literatur-Lexikon 5*, Sp. 1781–1783.

Prosaauflösungen finden sich im 15. Jahrhundert von Hartmanns *Grego-rius*,[54] Wolframs *Willehalm*,[55] dem *Georg* Reinbots von Durne,[56] Konrads *Ale-xius*,[57] dem *Münchner Oswald*[58] sowie *Sente Reinolt* (Reinolt von Montalban), der einer mittelniederländischen Vorlage folgte und stofflich eng mit den *Hai-monskindern* verbunden ist, die im 16. Jahrhundert gedruckt wurden.[59] Mit

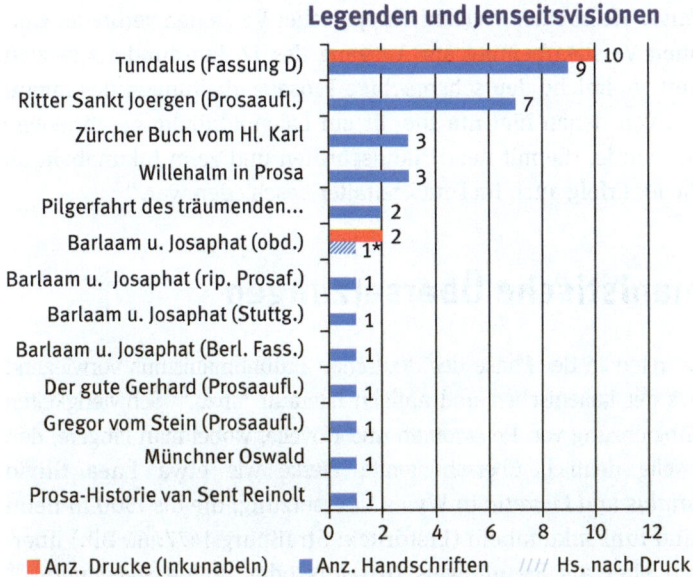

Legenden und Jenseitsvisionen

---

54 Literarische Würdigung der legendarischen Prosaerzählung, insb. auch der Heidelberger Fassung vom *Hl. Georg auf dem Stein* im Cpg 119, bei Von Ertzdorff (vgl. Anm. 29), S. 10–12; Bernward Plate, *Gregorius auf dem Stein, Frühneuhochdeutsche Prosa (15. Jh.) nach dem mittel-hochdeutschen Versepos Hartmanns von Aue*. Darmstadt 1983 (Texte zur Forschung 39).

55 Holger Deifuß, *Hystoria von dem wirdigen ritter sant Wilhelm. Krit. Edition und Untersuchung einer frühneuhochdeutschen Prosauflösung*. Frankfurt 2005 (Germ. Arbeiten zu Sprache und Kulturgesch. 45). Vgl. dazu die Rezension von Christoph Gerhardt. In: *ZfdA* 136 (2007), S. 263–271; Christoph Gerhardt, 'Willehalm (Prosaroman)'. In: ²*VL* 10 (1999), Sp. 1151–1154; Konrad Reinhold, 'Willehalm'. In: *Deutsches Literatur-Lexikon 5* (vgl. Anm. 2), Sp. 1783 f.

56 Markus Schmitz, *Die legent vnd dz leben des hochgelobten manlichen ritters sant joergen. Kritische Neuedition und Interpretation einer alemannischen Prosalegende des heiligen Georg im 15. Jh.*. Berlin 2013 (TMA 49); Stridde (vgl. Anm. 53), Sp. 1782.

57 Hans-Friedrich Rosenfeld, 'Alexius [Nachtrag]'. In: ²*VL* 11 (2004), Sp. 61–62.

58 Volker Zapf, 'Oswald'. In: *Deutsches Literatur-Lexikon 5* (vgl. Anm. 2), Sp. 1260.

59 Vgl. Hartmut Beckers, 'Reinolt von Montalban'. In: ²*VL* 7 (1989), Sp. 1208–1214, hier 1213f; Katharina Philipowski, 'Reinolt von Montelban'. In: *Deutsches Literatur-Lexikon 5* (vgl. Anm. 2), Sp. 1605–1608, hier 1606.

Ausnahme der oberdeutschen *Barlaam*-Druckfassung, von der sich zwei Inkunabeln erhalten haben, gelangten die übrigen Prosafassungen nicht zum Druck, sondern verblieben in der Manuskriptkultur, soweit sie nicht in stark gekürzten Bearbeitungen in Legendensammlungen integriert und z. B. in *Der Heiligen Leben* zum Abdruck kamen.[60]

Auf eine außerordentliche Resonanz stieß im Mittelalter die Jenseitsvision vom *Ritter Tundalus*, die in einer Vielzahl europäischer Versionen verbreitet war. Neben einer frühen Versbearbeitung am Ausgang des 12. Jahrhunderts setzten im 15. Jahrhundert zahlreiche deutschsprachige Prosabearbeitungen des lateinischen Textes ein, von denen hier nur die für ein Laienpublikum geschriebene Fassung D erfasst wurde, die mit neun Handschriften und zehn Inkunabeln ab 1483 ein beachtlicher Erfolg auch im Druckzeitalter beschieden war.[61]

6 Frühhumanistische Übersetzungen

Als letzte Gruppe treten in der Phase des deutschen Frühhumanismus vorwiegend Übersetzungen aus der italienischen und antiken Literatur hinzu.[62] Schwierigkeiten bereitet hier die Abgrenzung von Prosaroman und Novelle, wobei man längere, den Umfang der Novelle deutlich überschreitende Werke wie etwa Enea Silvio Piccolominis *Eurialus und Lucretia* in Wyles Übersetzung, die bis 1500 in neun Handschriften und fünf Inkunabeln (Erstdruck: Straßburg 1477: 66 Bll.) überliefert ist,[63] wohl eher als Steinhöwels *Griseldis* oder Wyles *Sigismunda*,[64]

---

60 So wurde z. B. *Gregorius auf dem Stein* in *Der Heiligen Leben* gedruckt. Vgl. Klaus Gantert, 'Der Heiligen Leben'. In: *Aderlass und Seelentrost* (vgl. Anm. 23), S. 218–221 (Kat. Nr. 112) mit Abb.
61 Vgl. Nigel Palmer, 'Tundalus'. In: ²*VL* 9 (1995), Sp. 1142–1146, hier 1142 f. (Fassung D); Nigel Palmer, *Visio Tnugdali. The German and Dutch Translations and Their Circulation in the Later Middle Ages*. München 1982 (MTU 76). Fassung D: Hss. (S. 71 f.) und Drucke (S. 278 ff.); Christine Stridde, 'Tundalus'. In: *Deutsches Literatur-Lexikon. Das Mittelalter, Bd. 2: Das geistliche Schrifttum des Spätmittelalters*. Hg. v. Wolfgang Achnitz. Berlin, Boston 2011, Sp. 787–791.
62 Zur frühhumanistischen Übersetzungsliteratur vgl. die Ergebnisse des Marburger Repertorium (MRFH): http://www.mrfh.de; ferner Bertelsmeier-Kierst, 'Übersetzen' (vgl. Anm. 2).
63 Vgl. Aeneas Silvius Piccolomini (Pius II) and Niklas von Wyle, *The Tale of Two Lovers Eurialus and Lucretia*. Ed. by E. J. Morrall. Amsterdam 1988 (Amsterdamer Publikationen zur Sprache und Literatur 77), S. 44; MRFH 42103.
64 Von den kürzeren Texten (Erstdrucke: 10–12 Bll.) wurde die *Griseldis* in 12 Hss. und 15 Inkunabeln (vgl. MRFH 43503), Wyles *Sigismunda*-Novelle in 5 Hss. und 12 Drucken (vgl. MRFH 42104) bis 1500 tradiert.

die Müller[65] und Schnyder[66] noch in das Corpus der Prosaromane aufgenommen haben, der großepischen Form zurechnen kann. Einen Grenzfall stellen Novellen- und Erzählsammlungen dar, die durch eine Rahmenhandlung (z. B. *Decameron*) oder Vita (z. B. *Aesop*) eine Makrostruktur aufweisen und damit in gewisser Weise noch „romanhaft"[67] genannt werden können.

Überraschend viele der im Frühhumanismus entstandenen Werke gelangen noch im 15. Jahrhundert in die Druckoffizinen, wobei sich Übersetzer wie z. B. der Ulmer Stadtarzt Heinrich Steinhöwel schon früh um eine fruchtbare Zusammenarbeit mit dem neuen Buchdruckergewerbe bemüht haben. Seine eigenen Übersetzungen wie auch Werke anderer frühhumanistischer Autoren ließ er ab 1473 bei Johann Zainer in Ulm verlegen, der in den siebziger Jahren des 15. Jahrhunderts ein literarisch anspruchsvolles und innovatives Buchsortiment in deutscher Sprache herausbrachte, zu dem neben Wyles *Sigismunda* und Steinhöwels *Griseldis*, die großen Boccaccio-Übersetzungen, Arigos *Decameron* und Steinhöwels Bearbeitung der *claris mulieribus*, sowie der *Aesop* gehörten.

Von diesen größeren Übersetzungen erweist sich mit Abstand Steinhöwels *Aesop* als der erfolgreichste Text der Inkunabelzeit. Das Werk erlebte 15 oberdeutsche Druckauflagen, von denen sich noch unmittelbar zwei weitere Bearbeitungen, der Kölner und Magdeburger *Aesop* ableiten, die ebenfalls zum Druck gelangten.[68] Hingegen blieb den großen Boccaccio-Übertragungen im 15. Jahrhundert ein vergleichbarer Erfolg im neuen Medium des gedruckten Buches versagt, Steinhöwels *Erlauchte Frauen* erlebten drei Ausgaben und zwei kürzende Bearbeitungen bzw. Teilveröffentlichungen,[69] das umfangreiche *Decameron* (Ulmer Erstdruck: 398 Bll.) nur zwei Drucke bis 1500, wurde aber im 16. Jahrhundert, als die Bücherpreise deutlich fielen, zahlreich verlegt.[70] Die bei Johann Zainer gedruckten Werke Steinhöwels erzielten mit ihren qualitätsvollen

---

65 Jan-Dirk Müller, 'Augsburger Drucke von Prosaromanen im 15. und 16. Jahrhundert'. In: *Augsburger Buchdruck und Verlagswesen. Von den Anfängen bis zur Gegenwart.* Hg. v. Helmut Glier und Johannes Janota. Wiesbaden 1997, S. 337–352, hier 341 f.

66 Schnyder, 'Corpus' (Anm. 3), S. 550.

67 Gerhard Dicke, 'Steinhöwel'. In: ²*Vl* 9 (1995), Sp. 258–278, hier Sp. 271. [Vgl. für den ‚romanhaften' Charakter des *Aesop* auch den Beitrag von De Bruijn in diesem Band, S 101–103).]

68 Zu Steinhöwels *Aesop* vgl. MRFH 43407; zum Kölner *Aesop* vgl. MRFH 43409; und zum Magdeburger *Aesop* vgl. MRFH 43410.

69 Gesamtausgaben: Ulm 1474, Augsburg 1479 und Straßburg 1488. Der Nachdruck Johann Zainers von 1476 enthält nur die Holzschnitte mit Bildbeischriften, der Mancz-Druck aus Blaubeuren nur das Kap. über Semiramis. Vgl. MRFH 43405.

70 Erstdruck: Ulm 1476–1477, dem 1490 die erste illustrierte Ausgabe Anton Sorgs folgte (vgl. MRFH 40401).

Holzschnitten europaweite Resonanz und wurden später für französische, niederländische und spanische Ausgaben kopiert. Beliebt war auch Steinhöwels literarisches Erstlingswerk *Apollonius*, der in sechs Handschriften und sieben Inkunabeln tradiert wurde,[71] sowie das *Buch der Weisheit*, das Antonius von Pforr nach der mittellateinischen Sammlung *Directorium humane vitae* des Johann von Capua für den württembergischen Grafen, Eberhard im Barte, übersetzte. Die Sammlung moralischer Fabeln und Geschichten wurde bereits bis 1500 in neun Handschriften und sieben Inkunabeln verbreitet.[72]

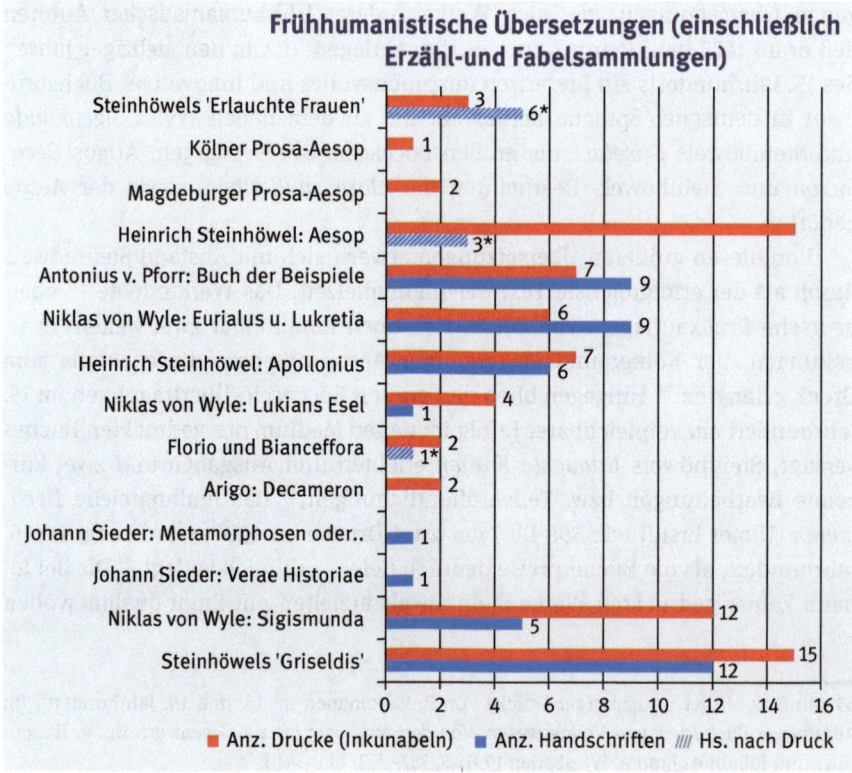

Frühhumanistische Übersetzungen (einschließlich Erzähl- und Fabelsammlungen)

---

71 Tina Terrahe, *Heinrich Steinhöwels Apollonius. Edition und Studien.* Berlin, Boston 2013 (Frühe Neuzeit 179), S. 106–126; MRFH 43502.

72 Volker Zapf, 'Antonius von Pforr'. In: *Deutsches Literatur-Lexikon* 5 (vgl. Anm. 2), Sp. 1839–1844, hier 1841 f.; Ulrike Bodemann, 'Anton von Pforr, *Buch der Beispiele der alten Weisen*'. In: *Katalog der Illustrierten Handschriften*, Bd. 2, Lfg. 5, 1996, S. 360–392 (mit Abb. der Hss. und Drucke); Friedemar Geissler, 'Die Drucke des Buches der Beispiele der alten Weisen'. In: *Beiträge zur Inkunabelkunde 3.* F. 3 (1967), S. 18–46; http://www.handschriftencensus.de/werke/611; GW M13190, M13178, M13180, M13181, M13184, M13187, M13192.

Die ebenfalls für Eberhard im Barte angefertigte Übersetzung von Lukians *Esel*, die Niklas von Wyle nach der lateinischen Vorlage Poggio Bracciolinis verfasste, erlebte bis 1500 immerhin vier Auflagen (Erstdruck: um 1477) und eine Druckabschrift.[73] Erst spät kam die anonyme Bearbeitung *Florio und Bianceffora* nach Boccaccios *Filocolo* zum Druck, die 1499 in Metz auf den Markt gebracht wurde und 1500 bereits eine zweite Auflage erlebte. Der Liebesroman avancierte im 16. Jahrhundert rasch zum ‚Bestseller‘.[74]

Offenbar konnten, so müssen wir aus den Überlieferungszahlen schließen, vor allem diejenigen Werke rasch hohe Auflagen erzielen, die auf eine lange Stofftradition im Mittelalter (*Aesop, Apollonius, Buch der Weisheit*) oder bereits auf eine reiche Handschriftentradierung vor der Drucklegung (*Melusine, Eurialus und Lukretia, Griseldis*) zurückblicken konnten. Hingegen wurden die großen Boccaccio-Übertragungen wohl doch als zu neuartig empfunden, um als Unterhaltungsbuch auf dem gedruckten Buchmarkt unmittelbar Fuß zu fassen. Versagt blieb der Erfolg auch den Werken Johann Sieders, obwohl er für sehr prominente Auftraggeber, den kurfürstlichen Kanzler Johann Dalberg und Kaiser Maximilian I., zwei hellenistische Romane übersetzte, den *Asinus Aureus* des Apuleius und die *Verae Historiae* Lukians, die als frühste Repräsentanten des pikaresken und phantastisch-utopischen Romans in Deutschland gelten können.[75] Erst 1538 wurde der *Guldin Esel* im Auftrag von Sieders Stiefbruder mit Unterstützung Kaiser Ferdinands in einer reich illustrierten Ausgabe (Augsburg: Alexander Weißenhorn, 1538) mit Holzschnitten des Hans Schäufele gedruckt,[76] während die *Verae Historiae* nur im Widmungsexemplar Johanns von Dalberg handschriftlich überlebten.

7 Regionale Unterschiede

Nachdem wir uns so einen kursorischen Überblick über den Bestand an Werken der neuen Erzählprosa, ihren Stofftraditionen und ihrer Überlieferungsdichte

---

73 Vgl. MRFH 42115.

74 Vgl. *Florio und Bianceffora. Ein gar schone hystori der hochen lieb des kuniglichen fursten Florio vnnd von seyner lieben Bianceffora*. Nachdr. der Ausgabe Metz 1499. Mit einen Nachw. v. Renate Noll-Wiemann. Hildesheim, New York 1975 (Deutsche Volksbücher in Faksimiledrucken, A. 3); Silke Schünemann, *Florio und Bianceforra (1499) – Studien zu einer literarischen Übersetzung*, Tübingen 2005 (Frühe Neuzeit 106); MRFH 0012 (http://ww.mrfh.de/0012).

75 Vgl. Franz Josef Worstbrock, 'Sieder, Johann'. In: *VL Deutscher Humanismus* 2 (2013), Sp. 896–902; MRFH 0034 (http://www.mrfh.de/0034).

76 Augsburg: Alexander Weißenhorn, 1538. Abb: http://mrfh.de/abbildung.php?id=1279; Digitalisat: http://archive.org/details/apulgedichtevoneinemguldeneselsub (Göttinger Ex.).

verschafft haben, sollen – fokussiert auf den Prosaroman – grundlegende Unterschiede zwischen der Manuskriptkultur und dem neu einsetzenden Buchdruck festgehalten werden. Zunächst überrascht die große Dichte der Handschriftenproduktion, die auf dem Gebiet des Prosaromans zu beobachten ist. Ihr Anteil übersteigt das Druckaufkommen bis 1500 noch bei weitem: 265 Handschriften stehen 125 Druckauflagen gegenüber, d. h. mehr als doppelt so oft wurden Handschriften abgeschrieben als Drucke verlegt. Vergleicht man damit das Verhältnis von Handschriften und Inkunabelauflagen, das über das MRFH für die Gesamtzahl der frühhumanistischen Übersetzungen ermittelt werden konnte, so wird der Unterschied besonders deutlich. Das hohe Handschriftenaufkommen spricht dafür, dass nicht nur die Versliteratur, sondern in großem Maße auch die neue Gattung des Prosaromans zunächst noch stark im höfischen Milieu verankert blieb und Adelsbibliotheken weiterhin eine vorrangige Rolle bei der Verbreitung der Texte im 15. Jahrhundert spielten.

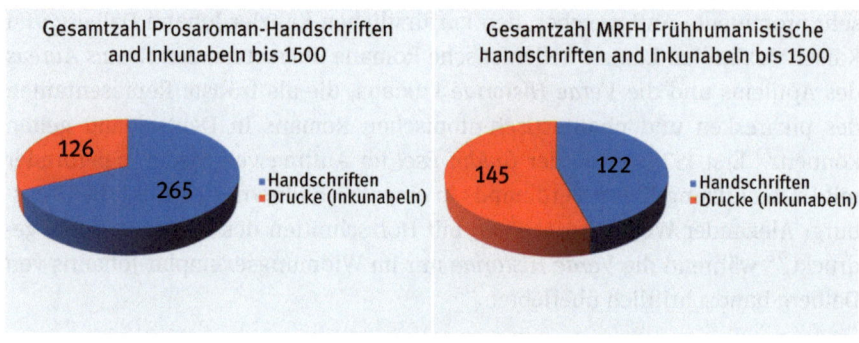

Auffällig bleibt auch die große Vielfalt an Einzelfassungen in der Handschriftentradition des 15. Jahrhunderts. So haben sich beispielsweise zum Trojabuch zwölf Fassungen in der Manuskriptkultur erhalten, während sich auf dem gedruckten Buchmarkt oftmals nur eine einzige Fassung durchsetzt, oder es gibt sprachlich klar abgegrenzte Räume, für die wie z. B. beim *Buch von Troja* je eine oberdeutsche und niederdeutsche Druckfassung auf den Markt kommt. Meistens geht jedoch den niederdeutschen Auflagen eine oberdeutsche Drucktradition voraus. So basieren die niederdeutschen Inkunabeln u.a. von Hartliebs *Alexander* (Erstausgabe 1472) 1477–78, *Die sieben weisen Meister* (Erstdruck 1473) oder Thürings *Melusine* (Erstdruck 1474) 1478 auf oberdeutschen Ausgaben. Nur wenn die Vorlage dem niederländisch-burgundischen Raum entlehnt wurde, wie z. B. bei der niederdeutschen Druckausgabe von *Paris und Vienna*, die Gerhard Leeu 1488 in Antwerpen druckte, geht der niederdeutsche Raum voran bzw. etabliert sich eine singuläre Drucktradition im Norden.

Im oberdeutschen Raum lässt sich vor 1500 noch eine deutliche Zweiteilung in Druckorte mit durchgeführter neuhochdeutscher Diphthongierung (Zentren: Augsburg, Nürnberg) und den Druckorten mit Beibehaltung der alten Längen (Zentren: Straßburg, Ulm, Basel) beobachten.[77] Beide Räume verfügten alsbald über eigene Vertriebsnetze, bei denen von Straßburg, Ulm oder Basel aus der alemannisch-schwäbische Raum, einschließlich der Schweiz, sowie die mittelrheinischen Gebiete beliefert wurden, während Drucker aus Augsburg und Nürnberg den ostschwäbischen, bairisch-österreichischen sowie den fränkisch-ostmitteldeutschen Raum mit Büchern versorgten.[78]

Bemerkenswert ist aber nicht nur die sprachlich-geographische Zäsur, sondern die deutschsprachigen Drucke aus dem Südwesten unterscheiden sich auch im Layout deutlich von den Augsburger Inkunabeln. Augsburg war führend in der deutschsprachigen Buchproduktion und spezialisierte sich, abgesehen von Bibeln und dem breiten Strom religiöser Gebrauchsliteratur, auf unterhaltende Prosa, deren Markenzeichen zunehmend kleinformatige Holzschnitte wurden, wobei man bei weniger umfangreichen Werken bereits in der Inkunabelzeit zum Quartformat überging.[79] Während die Augsburger Drucke auf dem Sektor der unterhaltenden Prosa somit alsbald ein eigenes Profil entwickelten, blieben die Drucke aus den südwestdeutschen Metropolen (Basel, Ulm und Straßburg) in ihrem Layout viel stärker der Handschriftenkultur verhaftet, die sich gerade am Oberrhein, in der Schweiz und in Schwaben bevorzugt an französischen und burgundisch-flämischen Vorbildern orientierte.

Nicht selten scheinen den dort ansässigen Inkunabeldruckern Handschriften aus Adelsbibliotheken vorgelegen zu haben, aus denen sie aufwendige Elemente wie heraldischen Buchschmuck, Rankenbordüren und die Bildvorlagen für ihre Holzschnitte entlehnten. So benutzte Conrad Fyner für die Uracher Erstausgabe (um 1481) vom *Buch der Weisheit*, die er mit 128 Holzschnitten aufwendig

---

77 Im 16. Jahrhundert ändert sich dies, weil auch alemannische und westdeutsche Drucker, vor allem unter dem Konkurrenzdruck der ostmd. Bibelausgaben, schreibsprachlich die Diphthongierung durchführen.

78 Gut belegt z. B. bei der Drucküberlieferung der *Melusine* oder beim *Decameron*. Vgl. Christa Bertelsmeier-Kierst, *Griseldis in Deutschland. Studien zu Steinhöwel und Arigo*. Heidelberg 1988 (GRM-Beiheft 8), S. 68.

79 Vgl. Müller (vgl. Anm. 65); Hans-Jörg Künast, *Getruckt zu Augspurg: Buchdruck und Buchhandel zwischen 1468 und 1555*. Tübingen 1997 (Studiana Augustana 8). [Siehe für die Benutzung des Quartformats in England den Beitrag von Boffey (Seite 138), für die Verwendung des Folioformats bei französischen Artusromanen den Beitrag von Montorsi (Seite 174) und für das Oktavformat in Dänemark den Beitrag von Richter (Seite 330) in diesem Band.]

illustrieren ließ,[80] als Vorlage Miniaturen aus der Heidelberger Handschrift (Cpg 466), die aus der unmittelbaren Umgebung des württembergischen Hofes, vielleicht aus dem Besitz von Eberhards Schwägerin, Margarethe von Savoyen, stammt.[81] Noch anspruchsvoller gestaltete 1483 Lienhart Holl die Ulmer Erstausgabe vom *Buch der Weisheit*, deren Holzschnitte Lilli Fischel „als Meisterwerke

Antonius von Pforr : Buch der Beispiele der alten Weisen

Heidelberg, UB, Cpg 84, 1474/75
aus dem Besitz Eberhards von
Württemberg (im Barte)

Ulm, Lienhart Holl, 1483
Holzschnitte nach dem Manuskript
Eberhards im Barte

---

80 Peter Amelung, *Der Frühdruck im deutschen Südwesten. 1473–1500. Eine Ausstellung der Württembergischen Landesbibliothek Stuttgart*. Bd. I: Ulm. Stuttgart 1979, Kat. Nr. 141, Abb. 218, 221 und 223.
81 Vgl. Mathias Miller und Karin Zimmermann, *Die Codices Palatini germanici in der Universitätsbibliothek Heidelberg (Cod. Pal. germ. 304–495)*. Wiesbaden 2007, S. 500 f.; Effinger und Losert (vgl. Anm. 25), S. 58–60 und Abb. 30; Bodeman (vgl. Anm. 72): Digitalisat: http://digi.ub.uni-heidelberg.de/diglit/cpg466.

deutscher Graphik und des ulmischen Stils"[82] bezeichnete.[83] Holl ersetzte die halbseitigen Illustrationen der Fyner-Ausgaben durch ganzseitige Holzschnitte, deren Vorlagen unmittelbar dem Heidelberger Codex (Cpg 84) entnommen wurden, dessen aufwendige, im burgundisch-niederländischen Stil angefertigte Miniaturen weitgehend dem für Eberhard von Württemberg etwas früher angefertigten Pergamentcodex (Chantilly, Musée Condé, Ms. 460) entsprechen und entweder für Graf Eberhard selbst oder seine Mutter, die Erzherzogin Mechthild von der Pfalz, verfasst wurde, in deren Besitz sich der Cpg 84 offenbar später befand.[84] Ein kleiner Teil der Auflage wurde darüber hinaus in Holls Erstausgabe auf Pergament gedruckt.[85] Auch für die Ulmer Ausgabe von Heinrich Steinhöwels *Erlauchten Frauen* (1473/74), deren künstlerisch hochwertige Holzschnitte „auf französisch-burgundische Vorbilder zurückgehen",[86] wurde die Widmungsvorrede an Eleonore von Schottland, die Gemahlin Sigmunds von Tirol, in einigen Exemplaren auf Pergament gedruckt.

Im Südwesten behielt man darüber hinaus noch Normalfolio als Standarddruckformat bei, das ebenfalls in der Handschriften-Produktion die Regel war.[87] Bei besonders repräsentativen Drucken konnte aber auch für Werke der erzählenden Prosa das sog. ‚Königsformat' verwendet werden, wie der Basler Erstdruck vom *Ritter vom Turn* im Auftrag Johann Bergmanns von Olpe mit seinem beeindruckenden Format (42 x 29 cm) demonstriert.[88] Dieses Format war zuvor ein Markenzeichen der Bilderhandschriften Diepold Laubers in Hagenau gewesen, der vor allem für Konrads *Trojanerkrieg* und seine *Historienbibeln* dieses Überformat wählte. Das für Maximilian I. geschriebene *Ambraser Heldenbuch*, eine Sammlung mittelhochdeutscher Versepik, wird im frühen 16. Jahrhundert nochmals an diese Tradition anknüpfen.

Wie diese Beispiele erhellen, orientierte sich die anspruchsvolle Inkunabelproduktion im Südwesten noch deutlich am Handschriftenpublikum, dessen Geschmack nachhaltig durch die Manuskriptkultur Frankreichs und Burgunds im

---

82 Lilli Fischel, *Bilderfolgen des frühen Buchdruck. Studien zur Inkunabel-Illustration in Ulm und Straßburg.* Konstanz, Stuttgart 1963, S. 63–91, hier 91.

83 Zu den Ulmer Ausgaben Holls: Amelung (vgl. Anm. 80), Nr. 141 (m. Abb. 216, 217 und 219), Nr. 142 (m. Abb. 220, 222, 224 und 225).

84 Vgl. Zimmermann (vgl. Anm. 25), S. 213 f.; Effinger und Losert (Anm. 25), S. 32 f., 36 f. und Abb. 2, 12 f.; Bodemann (vgl. Anm. 72); Digitalisat: http://digi.ub.uni-heidelberg.de/diglit/cpg84.

85 Amelung (vgl. Anm. 80), S. 297.

86 Amelung (vgl. Anm. 80), S. 76.

87 Backes (vgl. Anm. 39), S. 118.

88 Vgl. Schmitt (vgl. Anm. 45) und Peter Jörg Becker, 'Diepold Lauber'. In: *Aderlass und Seelentrost* (vgl. Anm. 23), S. 130–135, ins. Nr. 62.

15. Jahrhundert geprägt wurde. Die aufwendig gestalteten Inkunabeln aus Basel, Ulm oder Straßburg dürften somit um ein Vielfaches teurer als vergleichbare Druckexemplare aus Augsburg gewesen sein und sprachen ausschließlich die vermögendsten Käuferschichten aus dem Adel und den Eliten der Metropolen an. Unter den ‚Massen' war diese Literaturproduktion also auch in der Inkunabelzeit noch lange nicht ‚zuhause' und dies zeigt einmal mehr, wie irreführend der Begriff des ‚Volksbuchs' ist, wenn er bereits auf die Inkunabelzeit angewendet wird, wo das gedruckte Buch noch mit dem handschriftlichen konkurrierte und man vor allem im Südwesten durch kostbaren Buchschmuck Elemente der Manuskriptkultur im Wiegendruck konservierte. Erst im Laufe des 16. Jahrhunderts wird sich dann speziell auf dem Gebiet der unterhaltenden Prosa das Buch als Massenerzeugnis auch für breitere städtische Schichten durchsetzen.

8 Fazit

Noch wenig wurde für den aufkommenden Buchmarkt die Frage untersucht, wie sich der mediale Wandel auf die Texte und die sie begleitenden Paratexte auswirkte. Es fällt auf, dass gerade Augsburger Drucke schon relativ früh Bearbeitungstendenzen zeigen, wie sie dann im Bereich der Erzählprosa im Laufe des 16. Jahrhunderts in großem Stil für gedruckte Erzeugnisse üblich werden. So wurde in Steinhöwels *Apollonius* nach dem Erstdruck 1471 bei Günter Zainer der Reimprolog mit dem kunstvollen Akrostichon bereits im nachfolgenden Druck Johann Bämlers und allen weiteren Ausgaben unterdrückt, weil man ihn offenbar als „veraltet oder unpassend für das intendierte Publikum früher deutscher Druckprosa" empfand.[89] Nur in der vom Autor überwachten und vermutlich mitfinanzierten Ulmer Erstausgabe wird Steinhöwels *Aesop* zweisprachig gesetzt, während die nachfolgenden Augsburger Drucker, offenbar aus marktrelevanten Gründen, den Text nur noch einsprachig, auf Latein oder Deutsch, verlegten. Anton Sorg versah 1490 seine Augsburger Ausgabe des *Decameron* nicht nur mit absatzfördernden Holzschnitten, sondern entfernte stillschweigend auch die Novelle VII,10, um vermutlich der Kritik kirchlicher Kreise zuvorzukommen. Er leitete damit einen Prozess ein, bei dem vor allem in Ausgaben des 16. Jahrhunderts der einheitliche Kunstcharakter des *Decameron* mehr und mehr zerstört wurde, indem die Drucker Passagen nach Gutdünken strichen oder fremde Geschichten hinzufügten und ab der Ausgabe von 1535 die Rahmenhandlung fast vollständig unterdrückten, so dass das Werk sich in den Druckausgaben des 16. Jahrhunderts den

---

89 Terrahe, *Apollonius* (Anm. 71), S. 142.

herkömmlichen Schwanksammlungen annäherte.[90] Auch für das *Buch der Weisheit* oder den *Ritter vom Turn*, die beide im Südwesten beeindruckende Prachtausgaben bis 1500 erlebten, lassen sich ähnliche Eingriffe beobachten und es wäre eine lohnende Aufgabe, diese Veränderungen literarischer Texte im frühen Buchdruck des 15. und 16. Jahrhunderts systematisch zu untersuchen. Die oft angemerkten ‚Trivialisierungstendenzen' im frühneuhochdeutschen Prosaroman zeigen sich m.e. verstärkt in den direkt für den Buchmarkt hergestellten Texten, etwa in den anonym in Augsburg verlegten Prosafassungen von *Tristrant und Isalde* und *Herr Wigoleis vom Rade*. Ebenso lässt sich beobachten, dass in den Druckauflagen nicht selten Werke anonym erscheinen, denen in der handschriftlichen Tradierung noch Angaben zum Autor oder Widmungsempfänger in Vorreden vorausgingen. Um diese, teils gravierenden Veränderungen durch den frühen Buchdruck sichtbar zu machen, bedarf es einer umfassenden Untersuchung, die nicht nur die Frühdrucke, sondern auch die handschriftliche Tradierung der Texte eingehend berücksichtigen müsste. Erst auf diesem Fundament können die mediengeschichtlichen Veränderungen im Druckzeitalter eingehend dokumentiert und die Auswirkungen auf die deutschsprachige Literatur in Gänze erfasst werden.

Bibliografie

Achnitz, Wolfgang, 'Das Feld der literarischen Kleinformen im Mittelalter'. In: *Deutsches Literatur-Lexikon: Das Mittelalter, Bd. 5: Epik*. Hg v. Wolfgang Achnitz. Berlin, Boston 2013, S. XXVII–XXXVIII.

Aeneas Silvius Piccolomini (Pius II) and Niklas von Wyle, *The Tale of Two Lovers Eurialus and Lucretia*. Ed. by E.J. Morrall. Amsterdam 1988 (Amsterdamer Publikationen zur Sprache und Literatur 77).

Andersen, Peter H., 'Wigbolds Alexanderbuch – Eine Pioniertat'. In: *Eulenspiegel trifft Melusine. Der frühneuhochdeutsche Prosaroman im Licht neuer Forschungen und Methoden*. Hg. v. Catherine Drittenbass und André Schnyder. Amsterdam, New York 2010 (Chloe 42), S. 183–200.

Amelung, Peter, *Der Frühdruck im deutschen Südwesten. 1473–1500.. Eine Ausstellung der Württembergischen Landesbibliothek Stuttgart*. Bd. I. Ulm. Stuttgart 1979.

Alfen, Clemens, Petra Flochler und Elisabeth Lienert, 'Deutsche Trojatexte des 12.–16. Jhs., Repertorium'. In: *Die deutsche Trojaliteratur des Mittelalters und der frühen Neuzeit. Materialien und Untersuchungen*. Hg. v. Horst Brunner. Wiesbaden 1990 (Wissensliteratur im Mittelalter 3), S. 104–111.

Altenhöfer, Florian, 'Tristan'. In: *Deutsches Literatur-Lexikon: Das Mittelalter, Bd. 5: Epik*. Hg. v. Wolfgang Achnitz. Berlin, Boston 2013, Sp. 1966.

---

90 Vgl. Bertelsmeier-Kierst, *Griseldis* (Anm. 78), S. 174 f.

Backes, Martina, *Das literarische Leben am kurpfälzischen Hof zu Heidelberg im 15. Jahrhundert. Ein Beitrag zur Gönnerforschung des Spätmittelalters.* Tübingen 1992.
Backes, Martina, *Fremde Historien. Untersuchungen zur Überlieferungs- und Rezeptionsgeschichte französischer Erzählstoffe im deutschen Mittelalter.* Tübingen 2004 (Hermaea 103).
Bastert, Bernd (Hg.), *Herzog Herpin: Kritische Edition eines spätmittelalterlichen Prosaepos.* Berlin 2014 (TMA 51).
Becker, Peter Jörg, 'Diepold Lauber'. In: *Aderlass und Seelentrost. Die Überlieferung deutscher Texte im Spiegel Berliner Handschriften und Inkunabeln.* Hg. v. Peter Jörg Becker und Eef Overgaauw. Mainz 2003, S. 130–135.
Becker, Peter Jörg, 'Elisabeth von Nassau-Saarbrücken: Herzog Herpin'. In: *Aderlass und Seelentrost. Die Überlieferung deutscher Texte im Spiegel Berliner Handschriften und Inkunabeln.* Hg. v. Peter Jörg Becker und Eef Overgaauw. Mainz 2003, S. 135–137.
Beckers, Hartmut, 'Reinolt von Montalban'. In: [2] *VL* 7 (1989), Sp. 1208–1214.
Benzinger, Rudolf et al. (Hgg.), *Der gute Gerhard Rudolf von Ems in einer anonymen Prosaauflösung und die lateinische und deutsche Fassung der Gerold-Legende Albrechts von Bonstetten. Nach den Handschriften Reg. O 157 und Reg. O 29a und b im Thüringischen Hauptstaatsarchiv Weimar.* Berlin 2001 (DTM 81).
Bertelsmeier-Kierst, Christa, *Griseldis in Deutschland. Studien zu Steinhöwel und Arigo.* Heidelberg 1988 (GRM-Beiheft 8).
Bertelsmeier-Kierst, Christa, 'Zur Rezeption des lateinischen und volkssprachlichen Boccaccio im deutschen Frühhumanismus'. In: *Giovanni Boccaccio in Europa. Studien zu seiner Rezeption in Spätmittelalter und Früher Neuzeit.* Hg. v. Achim Aurnhammer und Rainer Stillers. Wiesbaden 2014 (Wolfenbütteler Abh. zur Renaissanceforschung 31), S. 131–154.
Bertelsmeier-Kierst, Christa, 'Erzählen in Prosa. Zur Entwicklung des deutschen Prosaromans bis 1500'. In: *ZfdA* 143 (2014), S. 141–165.
Bertelsmeier-Kierst, Christa, 'Übersetzen im deutschen Frühhumanismus. Ergebnisse des MRFH zur Einbürgerung humanistischer und antiker Autoren bis 1500'. In: *Humanistische Antikenübersetzung und frühneuzeitliche Poetik in Deutschland (1450–1620).* Hg. v. Regina Töpfer, Johannes Klaus Kipf und Jörg Robert. Berlin, Boston 2017 (Frühe Neuzeit 211), S. 125–150.
Bertelsmeier-Kierst, Christa, 'Rekontextualisierung des Wissens. *Res fictae* und *res factae* im vormodernen Roman am Beispiel von Thürings *Melusine*'. In: *Enzyklopädisches Erzählen und vormoderne Romanpoetik.* Hg. v. Mathias Herweg, Johannes Klaus Kipf und Dirk Werle (Wolfenbütteler Forschungen) [im Druck].
Bloh, Ute von, *Ausgerenkte Ordnung. Vier Prosaepen aus dem Umkreis der Gräfin Elisabeth von Nassau-Saarbrücken: Herzog Herpin, Loher und Maller, Huge Scheppel, Königin Sibille.* Tübingen 2002 (MTU 119).
Bloh, Ute von, Kurt Gärtner und Michael Heintze, '*Lohier et Malart – Loher und Maller*: Vorschläge zu einer Edition des Epos'. In: *Zwischen Deutschland und Frankreich. Elisabeth von Lothringen, Gräfin von Nassau-Saarbrücken.* Hg. v. Wolfgang Haubrichs und Hans-Walter Herrman, unter Mitw. v. Gerhard Sauder. St. Ingbert 2002, S. 427–458.
Bloh, Ute von (Hg.), *Loher und Maller: Kritische Edition eines spätmittelalterlichen Prosaepos.* Berlin 2013 (TMA 50).
Bloh, Ute von und Bernd Bastert, *Loher und Maller – Herzog Herpin: Kommentar und Erschließung.* Berlin 2017 (TMA 55).

Bodemann, Ulrike, 'Anton von Pforr, *Buch der Beispiele der alten Weisen*'. In: *Katalog der Illustrierten Handschriften*, Bd. 2, Lfg. 5, 1996, S. 360–392.

Cramer, Thomas, 'Aspekte des höfischen Romans im 14. Jahrhundert'. In: *Zur deutschen Literatur und Sprache des 14. Jahrhunderts. Dubliner Colloquium 1981*. Hg. v. Walter Haug, Timothy R. Jackson und Johannes Janota. Heidelberg 1983, S. 208–220.

Deifuß, Holger, *Hystoria von dem wirdigen ritter sant Wilhelm. Kritische Edition und Untersuchung einer frühneuhochdeutschen Prosaauflösung*. Frankfurt 2005 (Germ. Arbeiten zu Sprache und Kulturgesch. 45).

Dicke, Gerhard, 'Steinhöwel'. In: ^{2} *Vl* 9 (1995), Sp. 258–278.

Dietl, Cora, 'Wilhelm von Österreich'. In: ^{2} *VL* 10 (1999), Sp. 1114–1116.

Effinger, Maria und Kerstin Losert (Hg.), *Mit schönen figuren. Buchkunst im deutschen Südwesten*. Heidelberg 2014.

Ertzdorff, Xenia von, *Romane und Novellen des 15. und 16. Jahrhunderts in Deutschland*. Darmstadt 1989.

Ertzdorff, Xenia von, 'Pontus und Sidonia'. In: ^{2} *VL* 7 (1989), Sp. 780–782.

Faks. Bayerische Staatsbibliothek, Cgm 9220. Mit einer Einf. v. Klaus Grubmüller und einer Beschr. v. Ulrich Montag. München 1999 (Patrimonia 154).

Fischel, Lilli, *Bilderfolgen des frühen Buchdruck. Studien zur Inkunabel-Illustration in Ulm und Straßburg*. Konstanz, Stuttgart 1963.

Florio und Bianceffora. Ein gar schone hystori der hochen lieb des kuniglichen fursten Florio vnnd von seyner lieben Bianceffora. Nachdr. der Ausgabe Metz 1499. Mit einen Nachw. v. Renate Noll-Wiemann. Hildesheim, New York 1975 (Deutsche Volksbücher in Faksimiledrucken, A. 3).

Gantert, Klaus, 'Der Heiligen Leben'. In: *Aderlass und Seelentrost. Die Überlieferung deutscher Texte im Spiegel Berliner Handschriften und Inkunabeln*. Hg. v. Peter Jörg Becker und Eef Overgaauw. Mainz 2003, S. 218–221.

Geissler, Friedemar, 'Die Drucke des Buches der Beispiele der alten Weisen'. In: *Beiträge zur Inkunabelkunde 3*. F. 3 (1967), S. 18–46.

Geith, Karl-Ernst, 'Zürcher Buch vom heiligen Karl'. In: ^{2} *VL* 10 (1999), Sp. 1597–1600 und 11 (2004), Sp. 1697.

Gerhardt, Christoph, 'Willehalm (Prosaroman)'. In: ^{2} *VL* 10 (1999), Sp. 1151–1154.

Gerhardt, Christoph, Rez. zu: Holger Deifuß, *Hystoria von dem wirdigen ritter sant Wilhelm*. In: *ZfdA* 136 (2007), S. 263–271.

Grubmüller, Klaus, 'Hartlieb, Johannes'. In: ^{2} *VL* 3 (1981), Sp. 480–496 und 11 (2004), Sp. 589–590.

Hahn, Reinhard, '*Pontus und Sidonia* in der Berner Fassung'. In: *Daphnis* 32 (2003), S. 289–350.

Haubrichs, Wolfgang und Hans-Walter Herrmann, unter Mitw. v. Gerhard Sauder (Hg.), *Zwischen Deutschland und Frankreich. Elisabeth von Lothringen, Gräfin von Nassau-Saarbrücken*. St. Ingbert 2002.

Haubrichs, Wolfgang, 'Kurze Forschungsgeschichte zum literarischen Werk Elisabeths'. In: *Zwischen Deutschland und Frankreich. Elisabeth von Lothringen, Gräfin von Nassau-Saarbrücken*. Hg. v. Wolfgang Haubrichs und Hans-Walter Herrman, unter Mitw. v. Gerhard Sauder. St. Ingbert 2002, S. 17–48.

Haubrichs, Wolfgang, 'Die vier Prosahistorien Elisabeths – Skizzierung ihres Inhalts'. In: *Zwischen Deutschland und Frankreich. Elisabeth von Lothringen, Gräfin von Nassau-

Saarbrücken. Hg. v. Wolfgang Haubrichs und Hans-Walter Herrman, unter Mitw.
v. Gerhard Sauder. St. Ingbert 2002, S. 11–16.

Haubrichs, Wolfgang, 'Mahl und Krieg. Die Erzählung der Adelskultur in den Texten und
Bildern des Hamburger *Huge Scheppel* der Elisabeth von Lothringen, Gräfin von Nassau-
Saarbrücken'. In: *Eulenspiegel trifft Melusine. Der frühneuhochdeutsche Prosaroman im
Licht neuer Forschungen und Methoden*. Hg. v. Catherine Drittenbass und André
Schnyder. Amsterdam, New York 2010 (Chloe 42), S. 201–216.

Heinzle, Joachim, *Wandlungen und Neuansätze im 13. Jahrhundert. Geschichte der deutschen
Literatur von den Anfängen bis zum Beginn der Neuzeit*. Bd. 2, T. 2. Tübingen ²1994.

Horváth, Eva und Hans-Walter Storck (Hg.), *Von Rittern, Bürgern und von Gottes Wort*.
Hamburg 2002 (Schriften aus dem Antiquariat Günther, Hamburg, 2).

Jahn, Bruno, 'Elisabeth'. In: *Deutsches Literatur-Lexikon: Das Mittelalter, Bd. 5: Epik*. Hg.
v. Wolfgang Achnitz. Berlin, Boston 2013, Sp. 1494–1505.

Janota, Johannes, *Orientierung durch volkssprachliche Schriftlichkeit (1280/
90–1380/90). Geschichte der deutschen Literatur von den Anfängen bis zum Beginn der
Neuzeit*. Hg. v. Joachim Heinzle. Band III.1 Tübingen 2004.

Kocher, Ursula, *Boccaccio und die deutsche Novellistik. Formen der Transposition italienischer
"novelle" im 15. u. 16. Jahrhundert*. Amsterdam 2005.

Kornrumpf, Gisela, 'Meister Wichwolt'. In: *Killy²* 12 (2011), S. 367–368.

Kreutzer, Hans-Joachim, 'Marquart von Stein'. In: *² VL* 6 (1987), Sp. 129–135.

Künast, Hans-Jörg, *Getruckt zu zu Augspurg: Buchdruck und Buchhandel zwischen 1468 und
1555*. Tübingen 1997 (Studiana Augustana 8).

Künast, Hans-Jörg und Ursula Rautenberg, 'Typographie und Leseweisen. Überlegungen zu
den *Melusine*-Ausgaben der Frankfurter Druckoffizinen[. . .]'. In: *Eulenspiegel trifft
Melusine. Der frühneuhochdeutsche Prosaroman im Licht neuer Forschungen und
Methoden*. Hg. v. Catherine Drittenbass und André Schnyder. Amsterdam, New York 2010
(Chloe 42), S. 341–359.

Malm, Mike, 'Mair von Nördlingen, Hans'. In: *Deutsches Literatur-Lexikon. Das Mittelalter, Bd.
3: Reiseberichte und Geschichtsschreibung*. Hg. v. Wolfgang Achnitz. Berlin, Boston 2011,
Sp. 475–477.

Malm, Mike, 'Fuetrer'. In: *Deutsches Literatur-Lexikon: Das Mittelalter, Bd. 5: Epik*. Hg.
v. Wolfgang Achnitz. Berlin, Boston 2013, Sp. 1867–1873.

Malm, Mike 'Paris und Vienna'. In: *Deutsches Literatur-Lexikon: Das Mittelalter, Bd. 5: Epik*.
Hg. v. Wolfgang Achnitz. Berlin, Boston 2013, Sp. 1901–1904.

Malm, Mike, 'Marquart von Stein'. In: *Deutsches Literatur-Lexikon: Das Mittelalter, Bd. 5: Epik*.
Hg. v. Wolfgang Achnitz. Berlin, Boston 2013, Sp. 1925–1929.

Malm, Mike, 'Thüring von Ringoltingen'. In: *Deutsches Literatur-Lexikon: Das Mittelalter, Bd. 5:
Epik*. Hg. v. Wolfgang Achnitz. Berlin, Boston 2013, Sp. 1598–1604.

Meier, Jürgen, 'Paris und Vienna'. In: *² VL* 7 (1989), Sp. 306–309.

Miller, Mathias und Karin Zimmermann, *Die Codices Palatini germanici in der
Universitätsbibliothek* Heidelberg *(Cod. Pal. germ. 304–495)*. Wiesbaden 2007.

Mühlethaler Jean-Claude und André Schnyder (Hg.), *550 Jahre dt. Melusine. Couldrette und
Thüring von Ringoltingen*. Bern 2008 (Beitr. der wiss. Tagung der Universitäten Bern und
Lausanne).

Müller, Jan-Dirk, 'Volksbuch/Prosaroman im 15./16. Jahrhundert – Perspektiven der
Forschung.' In: *Internationales Archiv für Sozialgeschichte der Literatur: Sonderheft
Forschungsreferate* 1 (1985), S. 1–128.

Müller, Jan-Dirk, 'Thüring von Ringoltingen'. In: [2] VL 9 (1995), Sp. 908–914.

Müller, Jan-Dirk, 'Augsburger Drucke von Prosaromanen im 15. und 16. Jahrhundert'. In: Augsburger Buchdruck und Verlagswesen. Von den Anfängen bis zur Gegenwart. Hg. v. Helmut Glier und Johannes Janota. Wiesbaden 1997, S. 337–352.

Müller, Jan-Dirk, 'Prosaroman'. In: Reallexikon der deutschen Literaturwissenschaft 3 (2003), S. 174–177.

Müller, Mario, 'Pontus und Sidonia'. In: Deutsches Literatur-Lexikon: Das Mittelalter, Bd. 5: Epik. Hg. v. Wolfgang Achnitz. Berlin, Boston 2013, Sp. 1575–1598.

Nyholm, Kurt, 'Füetrer: Ulrich'. In: [2] VL 2 (1980), Sp. 999–1007.

Palmer, Nigel, Visio Tnugdali. The German and Dutch Translations and Their Circulation in the Later Middle Ages. München 1982 (MTU 76).

Palmer, Nigel, 'Tundalus'. In: [2] VL 9 (1995), Sp. 1142–1146.

Philipowski, Katharina, 'Reinolt von Montelban'. In: Deutsches Literatur-Lexikon: Das Mittelalter, Bd. 5: Epik. Hg. v. Wolfgang Achnitz. Berlin, Boston 2013, Sp. 1605–1608.

Plate, Bernward, Gregorius auf dem Stein, Frühneuhochdeutsche Prosa (15. Jh.) nach dem mittelhochdeutschen Versepos Hartmanns von Aue. Darmstadt 1983 (Texte zur Forschung 39).

Reinhold, Konrad, 'Willehalm'. In: Deutsches Literatur-Lexikon: Das Mittelalter, Bd. 5: Epik. Hg. v. Wolfgang Achnitz. Berlin, Boston 2013, Sp. 17283–1784.

Röcke, Werner, 'Hartlieb, Johannes'. In: Killy[2] 12 (2011), S. 35–36.

Rosenfeld, Hans-Friedrich, 'Alexius [Nachtrag] '. In: [2] VL 11 (2004), Sp. 61–62.

Rubini Messerli, Luisa, Boccaccio deutsch. Die Dekameron-Rezeption in der deutschen Literatur (15.–17. Jahrhundert). Amsterdam 2012 (Chloe 45).

Sauder, Gerhard, 'Die Rezeption der Prosaromane Elisabeths von Nassau-Saarbrücken – Vom "Volksbuch" bis zur Romantik'. In: Zwischen Deutschland und Frankreich. Elisabeth von Lothringen, Gräfin von Nassau-Saarbrücken. Hg. v. Wolfgang Haubrichs und Hans-Walter Herrmann, unter Mitw. v. Gerhard Sauder. St. Ingbert 2002, S. 569–589.

Schmitt, Anneliese, 'La Tour-Landry, Geoffrey de: Der Ritter vom Turm, deutsche Bearbeitung von Marquard Stein'. In: Aderlass und Seelentrost. Die Überlieferung deutscher Texte im Spiegel Berliner Handschriften und Inkunabeln. Hg. v. Peter Jörg Becker und Eef Overgaauw. Mainz 2003, S. 143–144.

Schmitz, Markus, Die legent vnd dz leben des hochgelobten manlichen ritters sant joergen. Kritische Neuedition und Interpretation einer alemannischen Prosalegende des heiligen Georg im 15. Jh.). Berlin 2013 (TMA 49).

Schneider, Karin, 'Buch von Troja nach Guido de Columnis'. In: [2] VL I (1978), Sp. 1101–1104.

Schneider, Karin, 'Buch von Troja I'. In: [2] VL 1 (1978), Sp. 1100 und [2] VL 11 (2004), Sp. 300.

Schnyder, André, 'Der deutsche Prosaroman des 15. und 16. Jahrhunderts'. In: Eulenspiegel trifft Melusine. Der frühneuhochdeutsche Prosaroman im Licht neuer Forschungen und Methoden. Hg. v. Catherine Drittenbass und André Schnyder. Amsterdam, New York 2010 (Chloe 42), S. 11–39.

Schnyder, André, 'Das Corpus der frühneuhochdeutschen Prosaromane: Eine tabellarische Übersicht als Problemaufriss'. In: Eulenspiegel trifft Melusine. Der frühneuhochdeutsche Prosaroman im Licht neuer Forschungen und Methoden. Hg. v. Catherine Drittenbass und André Schnyder. Amsterdam, New York 2010 (Chloe 42), S. 545–556.

Schünemann, Silke, Florio und Biancefforra (1499) – Studien zu einer literarischen Übersetzung. Tübingen 2005 (Frühe Neuzeit 106).

Steinhoff, Hans-Hugo, 'Elisabeth von Nassau-Saarbrücken'. In: [2] VL 2 (1980), Sp. 482–488.

Steinhoff, Hans-Hugo, 'Magelone'. In: [2] *VL* 5 (1985), Sp. 1142–1148.

Steinhoff, Hans-Hugo, 'Mair, Hans von Nördlingen'. In: [2] *VL* 5 (1985), Sp. 1180–1183.

Steinhoff, Hans-Hugo, 'Tristan'. In: [2] *VL* 9 (1995), Sp. 1060–11061.

Streun, Kristina, 'Pontus und Sidonia (C)'. In: [2] *VL* 11 (2004), Sp. 1259–1260.

Stöllinger-Löser, Christine, 'Barlaam und Josaphat'. In: [2] *VL* 11 (2004), Sp. 215–219.

Storck, Hans-Walther, 'Die handschriftliche Überlieferung der Werke Elisabeths von Nassau-Saarbrücken und die malerische Ausstattung der Handschriften'. In: *Zwischen Deutschland und Frankreich. Elisabeth von Lothringen, Gräfin von Nassau-Saarbrücken.* Hg. v. Wolfgang Haubrichs und Hans-Walter Herrmann, unter Mitw. v. Gerhard Sauder. St. Ingbert 2002, S. 591–606.

Stridde, Christine, 'Tundalus'. In: *Deutsches Literatur-Lexikon. Das Mittelalter, Bd. 2: Das geistliche Schrifttum des Spätmittelalters.* Hg. v. Wolfgang Achnitz. Berlin, Boston 2011, Sp. 787–791.

Stridde, Christine, 'Zürcher Buch vom heiligen Karl'. In: *Deutsches Literatur-Lexikon: Das Mittelalter, Bd. 5: Epik.* Hg. v. Wolfgang Achnitz. Berlin, Boston 2013, Sp. 1781–1783.

Terrahe, Tina, 'Eine neue Handschrift der *Melusine* Thürings von Ringoltingen'. In: *ZfdA* 138 (2009), S. 50–52.

Terrahe, Tina, *Heinrich Steinhöwels Apollonius. Edition und Studien.* Berlin, Boston 2013 (Frühe Neuzeit 179).

Thüring von Ringoltingen, *Melusine* (1456). Nach dem Erstdruck Basel: Richel um 1473/1474 hg. v. André Schnyder in Verb. mit Ursula Rautenberg. Bd. II, Kommentar und Aufsätze. Wiesbaden 2006.

Welz, Dieter, 'Der große Alexander'. In: [2] *VL* 3 (1981), Sp. 281.

Wolff, Eva, 'Die Sprache der Bilder. Bild-Erzählung in den Handschriften der Romane der Elisabeth von Nassau-Saarbrücken'. In: *Zwischen Deutschland und Frankreich. Elisabeth von Lothringen, Gräfin von Nassau-Saarbrücken.* Hg. v. Wolfgang Haubrichs und Hans-Walter Herrmann, unter Mitw. v. Gerhard Sauder. St. Ingbert 2002, S. 591–622.

Worstbrock, Franz Josef, 'Sieder, Johann'. In: *VL Deutscher Humanismus* 2 (2013), Sp. 896–902.

Zapf, Volker, 'Meister Wichwolt'. In: *Deutsches Literatur-Lexikon. Das Mittelalter, Bd. 3: Reiseberichte und Geschichtsschreibung.* Hg. v. Wolfgang Achnitz. Berlin, Boston 2011, Sp. 510–514.

Zapf, Volker, 'Antonius von Pforr'. In: *Deutsches Literatur-Lexikon: Das Mittelalter, Bd. 5: Epik.* Hg. v. Wolfgang Achnitz. Berlin, Boston 2013, Sp. 1839–1844.

Zapf, Volker, 'Buch von Troja nach Guido de Columnis'. In: *Deutsches Literatur-Lexikon: Das Mittelalter, Bd. 5: Epik.* Hg. v. Wolfgang Achnitz. Berlin, Boston 2013, Sp. 1275–1277.

Zapf, Volker, 'Cleomades'. In: *Deutsches Literatur-Lexikon: Das Mittelalter, Bd. 5: Epik.* Hg. v. Wolfgang Achnitz. Berlin, Boston 2013, Sp. 1573–1575.

Zapf, Volker, 'Elsässisches Trojabuch'. In: *Deutsches Literatur-Lexikon: Das Mittelalter, Bd. 5: Epik.* Hg. v. Wolfgang Achnitz. Berlin, Boston 2013, Sp. 1143–1145.

Zapf, Volker, 'Herzog Ernst'. In: *Deutsches Literatur-Lexikon: Das Mittelalter, Bd. 5: Epik.* Hg. v. Wolfgang Achnitz. Berlin, Boston 2013, Sp. 149–165.

Zapf, Volker, 'Magelone'. In: *Deutsches Literatur-Lexikon: Das Mittelalter, Bd. 5: Epik.* Hg. v. Wolfgang Achnitz. Berlin, Boston 2013, Sp. 1881–1884.

Zapf, Volker, 'Oswald'. In: *Deutsches Literatur-Lexikon: Das Mittelalter, Bd. 5: Epik.* Hg. v. Wolfgang Achnitz. Berlin, Boston 2013, Sp. 1260.

Zapf, Volker, 'Püterich von Reichertshausen'. In: *Deutsches Literatur-Lexikon: Das Mittelalter, Bd. 5: Epik*. Hg. v. Wolfgang Achnitz. Berlin, Boston 2013, Sp. 1669–1669.

Zapf, Volker, 'Warbeck'. In: *Deutsches Literatur-Lexikon: Das Mittelalter, Bd. 5: Epik*. Hg. v. Wolfgang Achnitz. Berlin, Boston 2013, Sp. 2050–2055.

Zapf, Volker, 'Wilhelm von Österreich'. In: *Deutsches Literatur-Lexikon: Das Mittelalter, Bd. 5: Epik*. Hg. v. Wolfgang Achnitz. Berlin, Boston 2013, Sp. 1785–1787.

Zimmermann, Karin, *Die Codices Palatini germanici in der Universitätsbibliothek* Heidelberg *(Cod. Pal. Germ. 1–181)*. Wiesbaden 2003.

Bart Besamusca and Frank Willaert

Continuities and Discontinuities in the Production and Reception of Middle Dutch Narrative Literature

Abstracts: In this article, we argue that in the development of Middle Dutch narrative literature three stages can be distinguished. In the first phase, indicated in this contribution as 'Middle Dutch narrative literature in manuscripts', authors of romances stuck to verse instead of prose, and stopped writing these texts after the middle of the fourteenth century. Between *c.* 1400 and *c.* 1470, Middle Dutch romances were only read in the eastern part of the Low Countries, in aristocratic circles, and not in Flanders or Brabant, the central parts of the region. The second phase, indicated as 'Holland', witnessed the reintroduction of Middle Dutch narrative literature by means of the printing press around 1470. In small towns located in the northern parts of the Low Countries, early printers produced prose narratives that had a strong didactic bias. These texts were adaptations of both Latin sources and Middle Dutch verse texts available in manuscript copies. The output of these printers included, in addition, editions of well-known verse narratives. The third phase, indicated as 'Antwerp', started with the shift of the production of printed texts from Holland to the metropolis of Antwerp in the 1480s. Antwerp printers looked for appealing sources outside of the Low Countries and adapted their material in order to attract both readers who were interested in new texts and readers who preferred texts which belonged to an established literary tradition.

Dans cet article, nous tâchons de démontrer que la littérature narrative en moyen néerlandais s'est développée en trois étapes. Dans la première phase, que nous avons appelée 'littérature narrative moyen néerlandaise transmise par manuscrits', les auteurs rédigeaient leurs romans en vers et non en prose, et ils arrêtèrent d'en produire vers le milieu du quatorzième siècle. Entre *c.* 1400 et *c.* 1470, les romans en moyen néerlandais n'étaient lus que dans des milieux aristocratiques situés dans les régions orientales des anciens Pays-Bas; par contre, dans le comté de Flandre et le duché du Brabant, ils paraissent être tombés dans l'oubli. La seconde étape, que nous appelons 'La Hollande', voit la réintroduction, à partir de 1470 environ, de textes narratifs en moyen néerlandais mais uniquement en tant que livres imprimés. Dans plusieurs petites villes situées dans le Nord des anciens Pays-Bas, des pionniers de l'imprimerie produisaient des textes narratifs en prose à forte tendance didactique. Ces textes étaient des adaptations de sources latines aussi bien que de textes néerlandais en vers, disponibles sous forme manuscrite. Ces imprimeurs produisaient, en

Note: We would like to thank Elisabeth de Bruijn, Hubert Meeus, Wim Blockmans and Paul Wackers for their comments on earlier versions of this article and Annika van Bodegraven for her assistance.

Bart Besamusca, Utrecht University
Frank Willaert, University of Antwerp

outre, des éditions de textes narratifs en vers qui étaient restés bien connus. La troisième étape, intitulée 'Anvers', commence avec le transfert, dans les années 1480, de la production de textes imprimés de la Hollande vers la ville d'Anvers. Les imprimeurs anversois étaient constamment à l'affût de sources attrayantes en dehors des Pays-Bas, et adaptaient ces matériaux d'une telle façon qu'ils pouvaient intéresser aussi bien des lecteurs à la recherche de nouveaux textes que des lecteurs préférant des textes appartenant à une tradition littéraire bien établie.

In this article, we present some observations on the development of Middle Dutch narrative literature during the transitional period from manuscript to print. We will point out continuities and discontinuities, starting in the thirteenth century and ending around the middle of the sixteenth century. We have identified three successive stages: Middle Dutch narrative literature in manuscripts, printed Middle Dutch narrative literature in Holland and, lastly, printed Middle Dutch narrative literature in Antwerp. These stages will be discussed below in three sections. In each of these sections, we will take into account the interplay between Dutch and non-Dutch (German, French and, where appropriate, English) narrative literature.

1 Middle Dutch Narrative Literature in Manuscripts

Although we subscribe to a long and established scholarly tradition when using the term 'Middle Dutch' in this article, it should be noted that it may imperil an adequate understanding of the literary situation in the medieval Low Countries. Two problems stand out. Firstly, the term suggests a clear-cut boundary between Dutch and German, whereas in the Middle Ages the Germanic dialects written between the North Sea and the Alps were perceived as a linguistic continuum.[1] Secondly, the term makes us all too easily forget the regional diversity within the literary landscape that we identify today with the territories where Dutch is the main language.[2] In this context, we may note that an often forgotten border that really mattered for narrative literature in Middle Dutch is the river Scheldt, which, until the Treaty of Cambrai (the so-called 'Ladies' Peace'), in 1529, separated the greater part of the county of Flanders, still part of the kingdom of

---

1 Luc de Grauwe, 'Das historische Verhältnis deutsch-niederländisch "revisited". Zur Nicht-Existenz von Einheitsarealen im Sprachbewußtsein des Mittelalters und der beginnenden Neuzeit'. In: *ABäG* 35 (1992), p. 191–205.
2 Frank Willaert, *De ruimte van het boek. Literaire regio's in de Lage Landen tijdens de middeleeuwen*. Leiden 2010 (Negentiende Bert van Selm-lezing).

France, from the rest of the Low Countries, which belonged to the German Empire. Arthurian romances and narratives featuring Charlemagne and his vassals, either indigenous texts or translations from Old French sources, seem mainly to have been produced in the county of Flanders, during the thirteenth and the beginning of the fourteenth centuries.[3] Apart from a few exceptions, most of the Dutch narratives composed in the duchy of Brabant do not belong to these two types of texts. Moreover, they mostly date from the first half of the fourteenth century and often deal with themes that were appropriated into Brabantine (legendary) history.[4] This does not mean, however, that Arthurian and Charlemagne romances were unknown in Brabant: Flemish narratives seem to have been eagerly imported into the territories east of the river Scheldt.[5] The opposite is not the case: Flanders seems to have ignored the Middle Dutch literary production from elsewhere almost entirely, including romances.[6]

---

3 See the survey in Bram Caers, 'Een *buchelin inn flemische*. Over ontstaan en verspreiding van de ridderepiek in de Nederlanden (ca. 1150–1450)'. In: *TNTL* 127 (2011), p. 223–251, here p. 225–226. The following titles, listed by Caers, are Arthurian romances that originated in Flanders: *Wrake van Ragisel, Ferguut, Perchevael, Lanceloet en het hert met de witte voet, Walewein, Lantsloot vander Haghedochte, Queeste van den Grale, Arturs doet, Lanceloet, Moriaen, Riddere metter mouwen*. Caers also lists the following epics concerning Charlemagne and his Peers in Flanders: *Floovent, Renout van Montalbaen, Roelantslied, Vlaamse Aiol, Karel ende Elegast, Ogier van Denemarken I* and *II, Geraert van Viane, Madelgijs* and *Huge van Bordeeus*. For the classification of these narratives as Charlemagne epics, see Bart Besamusca, *Repertorium van de Middelnederlandse Karelepiek. Een beknopte beschrijving van de handschriftelijke en gedrukte overlevering*. Utrecht 1983. For the dates of origin of all these and other chivalric epics, see Bram Caers and Mike Kestemont, 'Over de datering van de Middelnederlandse ridderepiek'. In: *Verslagen en Mededelingen van de Koninklijke Academie voor Nederlandse Taal- en Letterkunde* 121 (2011), p. 1–59.
4 This is clearly the case with the epics *Godevaert metten baerde* and the *Grimbergsche oorlog* (Remco Sleiderink, '"Une si belle histoire de nos propres seigneurs." La noblesse brabançonne et la littérature en néerlandais (première moitié du XIVe siècle)'. In: *Le Moyen Âge* 113 (2007), p. 549–567, esp. p. 555–557) and has also been argued with reference to the very successful *Heinric en Margriete van Limborch* (Remco Sleiderink, *De stem van de meester. De hertogen van Brabant en hun rol in het literaire leven (1106–1430)*. Amsterdam 2003 (Nederlandse literatuur en cultuur in de middeleeuwen 25), p. 111–112). Other Brabantine narratives from the first half of the fourteenth century include a translation of the *Chastelaine de Vergi, Cassamus* (based on the *Vœux du paon*), *Florimont*, a prose translation of the *Lancelot propre* and Lodewijk van Velthem's translation of the *Suite-Vulgate du Merlin*.
5 Willaert (see note 2), p. 18–21; Caers (see note 3), p. 234–238 and 241–244.
6 Willaert (see note 2), p. 22–25; Caers (see note 3), p. 241.

As far as narrative texts are concerned, the northern parts of the Low Countries feature only works by Jacob van Maerlant. In the second half of the thirteenth century, members of the comital family of Holland-Zeeland and associated aristocrats commissioned this Flemish cleric to write a number of verse romances: *Alexanders geesten* (*c.* 1260), a translation of the *Alexandreis* by Walter of Châtillon, the *Historie vanden Grale/Merlijn* (*c.* 1261), an adaptation of French prose versions of the *Joseph d'Arimathie* and *Merlin* by Robert de Boron, the Arthurian romance of *Torec* (*c.* 1262), based on the now lost Old French *Torrez ou le chevalier du cercle d'or*, and the *Historie van Troyen* (*c.* 1264), based on the *Roman de Troie* by Benoît de St. Maure, followed by an adaptation of Virgil's *Aeneid*. According to Frits van Oostrom, who published a groundbreaking monograph on Jacob van Maerlant, all these works, however diverse they might be, are the result of the wishes of the tutors of the future count Floris V – who had become fatherless when only two years old – to provide him with appropriate role models, combining chivalric and princely virtues (Alexander, Arthur, Torec, Eneas), and to inculcate a sense of his royal lineage into him – as his father William II had not only been count of Holland and Zeeland, but also king of the Romans.[7] With the exception of *Torec*, the aforementioned works can only be considered romances in one particular sense, as Maerlant had clearly intended to write trustworthy historical accounts. Later in his career, when he discovered the existence of Geoffrey of Monmouth's *Historia regum Britanniae* and Vincent of Beauvais' *Speculum historiale*, which he translated into Dutch, he felt cheated by the unreliable fantasies of these "scone Walsche valsche poeten, die meer rimen dan si weten".[8]

Nearly all Middle Dutch romances were composed between 1200 and *c.* 1350.[9] Many fourteenth-century narratives differ from the earlier ones in that they are generally quite long, feature many characters, have a complicated

---

7 Frits van Oostrom, *Maerlants wereld*. Amsterdam 1996, p. 324: "[Maerlants] vroege werk [...] staat voor een groot deel in het teken van het koningschap: alle verhalen handelen over jonge edellieden op weg naar majesteit."
8 *Jacob van Maerlant's Spiegel historiael, met de fragmenten der later toegevoegde gedeelten bewerkt door Philip Utenbroeke en Lodewijc van Velthem*. Ed. by M. de Vries and E. Verwijs. Vol. 3. Leiden 1863, p. 204 (IV, book I, cap. XXIX, 27–28). Translation: "these beguiling French poets, who versify beyond their competence". See Van Oostrom (see note 7), p. 319 and 337.
9 Caers and Kestemont (see note 3), p. 16–38. The early exceptions are Veldeke's *Eneas*, the Limburg *Aiol*, *Floyris ende Blantseflur* and *Henric ende Claredamie*, which all originated in the eastern part of the Low Countries, and possibly *Wisselau* and *Nevelingenlied*, that are mostly thought to have originated in the duchy of Brabant.

narrative structure, tend toward 'realism', do not eschew superlatives and exaggerations and make use of very diverse sources.[10] Examples include *Heinric en Margriete van Limborch, Seghelijn van Jherusalem, Hughe van Bordeeus* (Huon de Bordeaux), Lodewijk van Velthem's *Merlijn* Continuation, *Madelgijs* and *Ogier van Denemerken*. It is striking that many of these titles (but not necessarily the same texts) were to reappear in the age of print.

In contrast to what happened in France, the writing of Middle Dutch romances in the Low Countries seems to have come to a complete standstill by the middle of the fourteenth century. In this respect, the Dutch literary development is not unlike the German one where, after the first decades of the fourteenth century, even earlier than in Middle Dutch, no new romances were written for almost a century.[11] By the end of the

---

10 An Faems, 'De Middelnederlandse late ridderepiek: "bleeke spookgestalten" krijgen kleur'. In: *Ene andre tale. Tendensen in de Middelnederlandse late ridderepiek.* Ed. by An Faems and Marjolein Hogenbirk. Hilversum 2012 (Middeleeuwse Studies en Bronnen 131), p. 11–36, especially p. 17–19.

11 For courtly romance, see Thomas Cramer, 'Aspekte des höfischen Romans im 14. Jahrhundert'. In: *Zur deutschen Literatur und Sprache des 14. Jahrhunderts. Dubliner Colloquium 1981.* Ed. by Walter Haug, Timothy R. Jackson and Johannes Janota. Heidelberg 1983 (Reihe Siegen 45), p. 208–220. Middle High German courtly romance comes to a provisional end with a series of narratives that all deal with dynastic issues and are aimed at an aristocratic readership: Ulrich von Etzenbach's *Wilhelm von Wenden* (1287) (written for King Wenceslas II of Bohemia), the anonymous *Reinfried von Braunschweig* (after 1291), Johann von Würzburg's *Wilhelm von Österreich* (1314) (possibly written for the Dukes Leopold and Frederick of Austria), Heinrich von Neustadt's *Apollonius von Tyrlant* (after 1291) and *Lohengrin* (1280–1290) for the house of Habsburg (see Mathias Herweg, 'Herkommen und Herrschaft: Zur Signatur der Spätausläufer des deutschen Versromans um 1300'. In: *Archiv für das Studium der neueren Sprachen und Literaturen* 156 (2004), p. 241–287). Equally directed towards an aristocratic readership was Claus Wisse's, Philipp Colin's and Samson Pine's *Rappoltsteiner Parzifal* (1331/1336), a compilation of Wolfram's *Parzival* and of predominantly literal translations of the French *Perceval* Continuations, supplemented by materials taken from various manuscripts of Chrétien de Troyes' *Perceval*, commissioned by Ulrich V or VI or VII of the Alsatian dynasty of Rappoltstein (Bernd Bastert, 'Late Medieval Summations. *Rappoltsteiner Parzifal* and Ulrich Füetrer's *Buch der Abenteuer'*. In: *The Arthur of the Germans. The Arthurian Legend in Medieval German and Dutch Literature.* Ed. by W.H. Jackson and S. Ranawake. Cardiff 2000, p. 166–180, especially p. 167–172). Whether the anonymous *Friedrich von Schwaben* (after 1314) should be added to this group of romances is unclear, as this romance may only date from the beginning of the fifteenth century. This romance was almost certainly commissioned by a Swabian dynasty, possibly that of the Württemberger (see Beate Kellner, 'Literarische Kontexte und pragmatische Bezugsfelder im spätmittelalterlichen Roman *Friedrich von Schwaben'*. In: *Dialoge. Sprachliche Kommunikation in und zwischen Texten im deutschen Mittelalter.* Ed. by Nikolaus Henkel, Martin H. Jones and Nigel F. Palmer.

century, however, German romances seem to have got a second wind. Although some of them were written in verse, prose became the dominant form, as had already been the case in France for more than 150 years.[12] As

---

Hamburger Colloquium 1999. Tübingen 2003, p. 135–158, here p. 156–157, n. 70). In several respects, all these romances seem to bear resemblances to the Middle Dutch *Heinric en Margriete van Limborch* (Brabant, *c.* 1300) (cf. Herweg, (see above), p. 250, n. 27). As far as Carolingian epics are concerned, there is the Ripuarian *Karlmeinet* (*c.* 1320–1350), which compiles several shorter narratives and episodes taken from Latin and Dutch chronicles into a *vita poetica Caroli Magni* (Hartmut Beckers, 'Die *Karlmeinet*-Kompilation: Eine deutsche *vita poetica Karoli Magni* aus dem frühen 14. Jahrhundert'. In: *Cyclification. The Development of Narrative Cycles in the Chansons de Geste and the Arthurian Romances*. Ed. by Bart Besamusca, Willem P. Gerritsen, Corry Hogetoorn and Orlanda S.H. Lie. Amsterdam et al. 1994, p. 113–117), possibly also the Middle Low German *Gerart van Rossiliun* which is however difficult to date (thirteenth or fourteenth century?) (see e.g. Danielle Buchinger, 'Rezeption der chanson de geste in Spätmittelalter'. In: *Wolfram-Studien XI. Chansons de geste in Deutschland*. Ed. by Joachim Heinzle, L. Peter Johnson and Gisela Vollman-Profe. Schweinfurter Kolloquium 1988. Berlin 1989, p. 86–106, especially p. 87–94).

12 On the rise of prose and the decline of verse romances in French literature, see e.g. Francis Gingras, *Le Bâtard conquérant. Essor et expansion du genre romanesque au Moyen Âge*. Paris 2011 (Nouvelle bibliothèque du moyen âge 106), p. 353–377. French prose romances up to 1500 are inventoried by Brian Woledge, *Bibliographie des romans et nouvelles en prose française antérieurs à 1500*. Genève 1975 [1954] (Société de publications romanes et françaises 42) and *Bibliographie des romans et nouvelles en prose française antérieurs à 1500*. Supplément 1954–1975. Genève 1975 (Publications romanes et françaises 130). On prosification in French literature, the essential monograph is still Georges Doutrepont, *Les Mises en prose des épopées et des romans chevaleresques du XIVe au XVIe siècle*. Bruxelles 1939 (Académie royale de Belgique. Classe des lettres et des sciences morales et politiques. Mémoires, vol. 40). The inventory of French prosifications in this book (p. 19–314) is meanwhile superseded by Maria Colombo Timelli et al. (eds), *Nouveau Répertoire de mises en prose (XIVe-XVIe siècle)*. Paris 2014 (Textes littéraires du moyen âge 30). On French verse romances in the later Middle Ages, see Jean-Claude Mühlethaler, 'Vers statt Prosa. Schreiben gegen den Strom im Frankreich des ausgehenden Mittelalters'. In: *Eulenspiegel trifft Melusine. Der frühneuhochdeutsche Prosaroman im Licht neuer Forschungen und Methoden*. Ed. by Catherine Drittenbass and André Schnyder. Akten der Lausanner Tagung von 2. bis 4. Oktober 2008. Amsterdam 2010 (Chloe 42), p. 163–182. On the revival of High German verse romances in the second half of the fifteenth century, see Ute von Bloh, 'Anders gefragt: Vers oder Prosa? "Reinolt von Montalban" und andere Übersetzungen aus dem Mittelniederländischen im Umkreis des Heidelberger Hofes'. In: *Wolfram-Studien XIV. Übersetzen im Mittelalter*. Ed. by Joachim Heinzle, L. Peter Johnson and Gisela Vollmann-Profe. Cambridger Kolloquium 1994. Berlin 1996, p. 265–293; on prose romances in German, see Christa Bertelsmeier-Kierst, 'Erzählen in Prosa. Zur Entwicklung des deutschen Prosaromans bis 1500'. In: *ZfdA* 143 (2014), p. 141–165. From 1393 up to 1500, Bertelsmeier-Kierst counts 10 romances in verse and 68 romances in prose, both in manuscript and in print.

in French literature, prose made these narratives more authoritative, pretending to present the reader with 'true' history.[13] In the case of prosifications, retelling the old stories in a new form and modernizing their language was also a way of making them more readable and more enjoyable.[14]

In contrast with the German state of affairs, no new Dutch romances, neither in verse nor in prose, were produced between the middle of the fourteenth century and the last decades of the fifteenth century. Furthermore, prosifications of verse texts are strikingly absent, although prose flourished in Middle Dutch religious and didactic literature. As a matter of fact, with the exception of one, very poorly preserved, translation of the French Prose *Lancelot*, Dutch authors (and their audiences) seem to have considered prose unsuitable for narrative texts.[15] One explanation for this phenomenon may be that the immense prestige of Jacob van Maerlant did not incite late medieval authors to re-tell old verse texts in prose, as his verse translations of the *Historia scholastica* and the *Speculum historiale* had shown that truth and rhyme could go together.[16] A second, and in our view more fundamental, explanation is that in Flanders and in Brabant, interest in Middle Dutch narrative literature seems to have waned altogether. Although in the second half of the fourteenth century, manuscripts containing romances were still produced

---

13 Jan-Dirk Müller, 'Volksbuch/Prosaroman im 15./16. Jahrhundert – Perspektiven der Forschung'. In: *Internationales Archiv für Sozialgeschichte der Literatur: Sonderheft Forschungsreferate* 1 (1985), p. 1–128, here p. 15–25, where, however, other factors (e.g. aural reception, silent reading, the preferences of patrons, linguistic evolutions, distrust of *ornatus* in general etc.) also are taken in consideration. On the relationship between prose and 'truth' on the one and "romans, rimes et mensonges" on the other hand in French, see the fine-tuned discussion in Gingras (see note 12), p. 361–364.

14 On the necessity to modernize verse romances in Old French for fifteenth-century readers, see Doutrepont, *Mises en prose* (note 12), p. 388–396; see also Gingras (see note 12), p. 373–377 on the pleasure taken in what in the *Romance of Perceforest* is called "beaux parlers d'armes et d'amours".

15 See Bart Besamusca, 'The Prevalence of Verse in Medieval Dutch and English Arthurian Fiction'. In: *Journal of English and Germanic Philology* 112 (2013), p. 461–474. The Prose *Lancelot* was translated at least three times into Middle Dutch (but see also below, p. 65). The only prose translation is preserved in three fragments, that all belonged to the same manuscript (Orlanda S.H. Lie, *The Middle Dutch Prose Lancelot. A Study of the Rotterdam Fragments and their Place in the French, German, and Dutch* Lancelot en prose *Tradition*. Amsterdam, Oxford, New York 1987 (Middelnederlandse Lancelotromans 3); Bart Minnen and Geert Claassens, 'De *Roman van Lancelot* in Middelnederlands proza. Het fragment-Wezemaal'. In: *TNTL* 121 (2005), p. 169–183).

16 On Maerlant's attitude towards the problematical relationship between verse and truth, see Van Oostrom, (see note 7), p. 410–411.

and still appeared in inventories, this is no longer the case beyond the turn of the fifteenth century.[17] By then, even though we cannot rule out that older manuscripts were still read, narrative literature seems to have completely disappeared from the sphere of interest of the Dutch reading public in Flanders and in Brabant.[18] Concerning the county of Holland and the prince-bishopric of Utrecht, we do not have any proof that there ever was, after Maerlant, a significant reception of romances before the introduction of the printing press.[19]

Why, then, did the production of narrative literature and of manuscripts containing romances come to a complete standstill in Flanders and Brabant in the later Middle Ages? In a recent article, Wim Blockmans has addressed this issue for Flanders in particular. He points out that from the beginning of the

---

17 See the important survey of epic manuscripts by Jan Willem Klein, '"Het getal zijner jaren is onnaspeurlijk". Een herijking van de dateringen van de handschriften en fragmenten met Middelnederlandse ridderepiek'. In: *TNTL* 111 (1995), p. 1–23, here p. 16. Dutch chivalric literature also appears in some fourteenth-century inventories: *Een bouc van Oegiere* (Oger the Dane), *Seghelijn Ysenbaert* and possibly *een dic bouc van Alexanders parabelen* (Maerlant's *Alexanders geesten*?) in the 1389 inventory of the estate of the Ghent citizen John Wasselins (*Corpus catalogorum Belgii. The Medieval Booklists of the Southern Low Countries*. Ed. by Albert Derolez. Vol. 3: *Counts of Flanders. Provinces of East Flanders, Antwerp and Limburg*. Brussel 1999, p. 120). One late but very interesting testimony of interest taken in chivalric literature written in Dutch is that of the influential nobleman John VI of Gistel († 1417), the last of his kin, who, according to an inventory written between 11 February and 20 April 1417, possessed among others *I bouc van Perchevaul, I bouc van Karle Marteel, I bouc van den grave van Sint Gillis* (a Dutch (?) adaptation of the chanson de geste *Élie de Saint-Gilles* (?)) and *een dietsch bouc sprekende van ystorien van Ingeland ende van den ruddere metten leeuwe ende andren* (a book in Dutch about the history of England (Geoffrey of Monmouth's *Rerum Britanniae historiae* (?) and, without any doubt, a lost translation of Chrétien's *Yvain*). Of course, these manuscripts may have been quite old already by the time they were inventoried. On this booklist, see Hanno Wijsman, *Luxury Bound. Illustrated Manuscript Production and Noble and Princely Book Ownership in the Burgundian Netherlands (1400–1550)*. Turnhout 2010 (Burgundica 16), especially p. 351–353.
18 An exception would be *Reynaerts historie*, if we accept Amand Berteloot's view that this Flemish sequel of *Van den vos Reynaerde* was composed between 1430 and 1460. See his 'Zur Datierung von *Reynaerts historie*'. In: *Sprache in Vergangenheit und Gegenwart. Beiträge aus dem Institut für Germanistische Sprachwissenschaft der Philipps-Universität Marburg*. Ed. by Wolfgang Brandt. Marburg 1988, p. 26–31.
19 The animal epic forms an interesting exception though: one manuscript of *Van den vos Reynaerde*, the so-called Dyck MS (Münster, UL, N.R. 381), was written in Eastern Holland or in Utrecht between 1330–1360 (see below); of both manuscripts of *Reynaerts historie*, one was copied about 1470 in the western part of the Netherlands, possibly in Utrecht (Brussels, KBR, 14601), the other one, which is only preserved in fragments, in Holland in the year 1477 (The Hague, Royal Library, 75 B 7).

fourteenth century onwards, the growing divide between the counts and their cities and the emancipation of the latter brought about the rise of a specifically urban literary culture, with little interest in narrative texts.[20] It is conceivable that a comparable evolution took place in Brabant half a century later. Whereas in the first half of the century several narrative texts were created that glorified the unity of the citizenry of Brabant around its Duke John III (see above p. 51), the marriage, in 1351, of the only heiress, Joan of Brabant, with Wenceslaus of Luxemburg, while beneficial to French literature (Jean Froissart, for example, wrote his romance *Meliador*, so he states, "a la requeste et contemplacion de monseigneur Wincelaus"), did not encourage important literary projects in Dutch.[21] As in Flanders, the Dutch literary space in Brabant seems to have been filled mainly with what we may call urban literature, with an emphasis either on religious, didactic, historical or instructional texts or on short literary ones, that were suitable for performances by professional reciters.[22]

Consequently, in the course of the second half of the fourteenth century, the literary dividing line between Flanders and Brabant seems to vanish, or, to be more precise, to move eastward, at least as far as narrative literature is concerned. Although Middle Dutch narrative texts were no longer copied in the central regions of the Low Countries (i.e. Flanders and Brabant) in the fifteenth century, they were eagerly read, copied and sometimes adapted in territories further to the east, from Lower-Saxony and the Meuse-and-Rhine area to Heidelberg. We will illustrate this phenomenon by discussing the manuscript dissemination of some of the most important Middle Dutch narratives in the course of the fifteenth century.

At the end of the fifteenth century, an inhabitant of Borgloon in the Dutch speaking part of the prince-bishopric of Liège jotted down the *Roelantslied*, an early thirteenth-century Flemish adaptation of the famous *Chanson de Roland*,

---

20 Wim Blockmans, 'Contingentie van literaire milieus.' In: *Het Gruuthusehandschrift. Literatuur, muziek, devotie rond 1400*. Ed. by Frank Willaert, Jos Koldeweij and Johan Oosterman. Internationaal congres Brugge, 25–27 april 2013. Gent 2015, p. 19–39, here p. 27–28.
21 This does not mean that Dutch was entirely absent from the ducal court, however. In 1371, the language of the ducal accounts changed from Latin to Dutch, not French. Alongside German and French, Dutch-speaking literary artists too, like Augustijnken, performed before the duke and his household. See Sleiderink, *De stem van de meester* (note 4), p. 123–126. On the growing importance of French literature at the ducal court during the reign of Wenceslaus and on the duke's special relationship with Jean Froissart, see p. 126–133. On the special interest the ducal couple took in Arthurian literature, see p. 131.
22 For this characterisation of the Dutch literary scene in Flanders, see Blockmans, (see note 20), p. 31.

in a multi-text codex (now Amsterdam, UB, MS I A 24[1]), that he had started to compile for his personal use.[23] While all other (Flemish and Brabantine) copies of this text came into being in the fourteenth century, the detail that more than a century later a reader still took an interest in this text may possibly be explained by the fact that he resided no more than fifty kilometers west from Aachen. In this region the prevailing image of Charlemagne was that of God's instrument on earth, a restorer of God's justice and a foe of the heathens.[24] This portrayal may also explain why, a century earlier, the Ripuarian compiler of the *Karlmeinet* Compilation decided to include the short narrative *Karel ende Elegast* in his *vita poetica* of the Emperor. After all, this short tale illustrates to perfection the special protection that Charlemagne enjoyed on the part of God.[25] A comparable explanation may be given for the Middle German

---

23 Jos Biemans, Hans Kienhorst, Willem Kuiper and Rob Resoort (eds), *Het handschrift-Borgloon. Hs. Amsterdam, Universiteitsbibliotheek (UvA), I A 24 l, m, n.* Hilversum 2000 (Middeleeuwse verzamelhandschriften uit de Nederlanden 5), p. 87–139. According to the editors (p. 15–20), the Borgloon manuscript was a heterogeneous collection for personal use, realized at different moments during the last quarter of the fifteenth century. The same manuscript also contained the narrative *Jonathas ende Rosafiere*, which some scholars consider as a (religious) chivalric romance, others as a Marian legend, or something in between. On this issue, see An Faems, 'Jonathas ende Rosafiere: (religieuze) ridderroman of Mariamirakel?'. In: *Queeste* 7 (2000), p. 97–112, who advances sound arguments in favour of the second option (a miracle of Mary).
24 See Bernd Bastert, '*Verus apostolus sicut Saxonia et Fresonia atque Westphalia*. Karl der Große in der Literatur der *Nideren Lande*'. In: *ZfdPh* 122 (2003), Sonderheft: *Regionale Literaturgeschichtsschreibung. Aufgaben, Analysen und Perspektiven*. Ed. by Helmut Tervooren and Jens Haustein, p. 74–80. See also Bernd Bastert, *Helden als Heilige*. Chanson de geste-*Rezeption im deutschsprachigen Raum*. Tübingen, Basel 2010 (Bibliotheca Germanica 54), p. 336–356. On the Middle Dutch *Roelantslied*, see H. van Dijk, *Het Roelantslied. Studie over de Middelnederlandse vertaling van het Chanson de Roland, gevolgd door een diplomatische uitgave van de overgeleverde teksten*. 2 vols. Utrecht 1981.
25 Bernd Bastert, 'Heiliger, Hochzeiter, Heidenschlächter. Die Karlmeinet-Kompilation zwischen Oberdeutschland und den *Nideren Landen*'. In: *Schnittpunkte. Deutsch-Niederländische Literaturbeziehungen im späten Mittelalter*. Ed. by Angelika Lehmann-Benz, Ulrike Zellmann and Urban Küsters. New York etc. 2003 (Studien zur Geschichte und Kultur Nordwesteuropas 5), p. 125–143, especially p. 140, where *Karel ende Elegast* and the *Roelandslied* are both mentioned in one and the same breath. It is tempting to connect this interpretation with the fact that the only manuscript of the *Karlmeinet* was kept in the convent of the discalced Carmelites in Cologne. However, as this convent was only founded in 1613, we do not know anything about the commissioner or the first owner of the Cologne manuscript (see Frank Fürbeth, 'Der "Karlmeinet": Vita poetica oder Vita historica Caroli Magni? Zur Differenz von textimmanenter und textexterner Kohärenz'. In: *Texttyp und Textproduktion in der deutschen Literatur des Mittelalters*. Ed. by Elisabeth Andersen, Manfred Eikelmann and Anne Simon. Berlin, New York 2005 (Trends in Medieval Philology 7), p. 217–234, here p. 219.

adaptation of *Karel ende Elegast*, probably dating from the first half of the fifteenth century.[26]

Various other Middle Dutch narratives made their way eastward during the course of the fifteenth century. Somewhere in the Lower Rhine area, about 1415, a scribe copied the mid-fourteenth century Flemish crusade romance *Seghelijn van Jherusalem*; around 1430, this copy was included in a multi-text codex mainly devoted to "courtly love and courtly virtue" (Berlin, SB, mgf 922). It is striking, but not unusual in this area without linguistic boundaries, that the scribe or his patron did not deem it necessary to adapt the Flemish language of his exemplar to the local dialect.[27] We know nothing about the users of this manuscript, but an aristocratic readership seems probable.

We are better informed about manuscript Burgsteinfurt, Fürst zu Bentheimsche Schloßbibliothek, 28, produced around 1422, that preserves Jacob van Maerlant's *Historie van den Grale* and *Merlijns boec*, followed by the *Merlijn* Continuation by Lodewijk van Velthem. At the end of Velthem's text (fol. 229ra), the second of the two scribes mentions the name of the manuscript's first owner: Count Everwin I of Bentheim († 1454). This is followed by a list of other books belonging to the count, among which "twe nye boke van lantslotte vnde eyn olt boek van lantslotte, ... Jtem van allexander... jtem de markgreue willem jtem perceuale".[28] Whether these books were also adaptations of Middle Dutch works, we do not know. It is of course tempting to connect them with works like the three (very probably even five, see below p. 65) translations of the Prose *Lancelot*, Maerlant's *Alexanders geesten*, one of the Charlemagne romances about *Willem van Oringen* (an adaptation of the *Moniage Guillaume*), or the romance of *Perchevael* (a translation of Chrétien's

---

26 *Karel ende Elegast und Karl und Ellegast*. Ed. and transl. by Bernd Bastert, Bart Besamusca and Carla Dauven-van Knippenberg. Münster 2005 (Bibliothek mittelniederländischer Literatur 1), p. 195–197 and 208.

27 The miscellany Berlin mgf 922 contains texts in dialects, which in secondary literature are defined as Flemish, Brabantian, Low Rhenish, Central West German, Middle Rhenish, Moselle and Rhine Franconian, Bavarian etc.

28 *Jacob van Maerlants Historie van den Grale und Boek van Merline*. Nach der Steinfurter Handschrift herausgegeben von Timothy Sodmann. Köln, Wien 1980 (Niederdeutsche Studien 26), p. 425. On the date of this list, see p. 32.

Conte du Graal), but identifications with other (Middle High German) works are equally possible.[29]

Maerlant was much appreciated in what is nowadays the Dutch-German border region. Around 1400, his *Alexanders geesten*, which, as we have just noted, may have figured in the Bentheim library, was copied in the Lower Rhine area and (slightly) adapted to the local dialect. In 1664, this manuscript (now Munich, BSB, Cod. germ. 41) was in the possession of the Duke of Berg in Düsseldorf.[30] About three quarters of a century later, a Lower Rhenish adaptation of Maerlant's *Historie van Troyen* was copied at the initiative of the nobleman Wessel IV van den Loe (1443–1509), who inhabited Schloß Wissen near Kevelaer. The manuscript, written in the local dialect, was kept there for centuries until it was sold to the Royal Library in Brussels in 1973 (MS IV 927).[31] It is worth pointing out that the three Maerlant manuscripts mentioned here are the only ones that have transmitted *Alexanders geesten, Historie vanden Grale / Merlijns boec* and *Historie van Troyen* to us in their entirety. Without the interest of 'German' noblemen, these works by Flanders' most prolific medieval author would have come down to us in the form of fragments only.[32]

---

29 In *Le Moniage Guillaume*, William of Orange is mostly called "Guillaumes le marcis" (G. Kalff, *Middelnederlandsche epische fragmenten met aanteekeningen*. Groningen 1885 (Bibliotheek van Nederlandsche letterkunde 38), p. 102). On the cycle of Guillaume d'Orange in Middle Dutch, see Hans Kienhorst, 'Fragment van een onbekende Middelnederlandse roman over Willem van Oringen'. In: *TNTL* 114 (1998), p. 125–137. As, however, "markgreue willem" is followed by "perceuale", it seems more probable that Wolfram's *Willehalm* and *Parzival* are meant here. In the booklist of Count Otto VII (1434–1494) and Count Frederick II (1434–1503) of Hoya-Bruchhausen (Lower Saxony), both titles, followed by (pseudo-)Wolfram's *(Jüngerer) Titurel*, are mentioned in exactly the same order. See Hartmut Beckers, '*Desse boke de horn den greve van der hoien vnde sint altomale dudesk*. Ein Versuch zur literarhistorischen Identifizierung des Handschriftenbestandes einer niedersächsischen Adelsbibliothek des späten 15. Jahrhunderts'. In: *Niederdeutsches Wort* 16 (1976), p. 126–143, here p. 137–138, who arrives at the same conclusion.
30 J. Deschamps, *Middelnederlandse handschriften uit Europese en Amerikaanse bibliotheken. Tentoonstelling ter gelegenheid van het honderdjarig bestaan van de Koninklijke Zuidnederlandse Maatschappij voor Taal- en Letterkunde en Geschiedenis. Catalogus.* Brussel, Koninklijke Bibliotheek Albert I, 24 okt.–24 dec. 1970, 2nd ed. Leiden 1972, p. 31–32.
31 J. Deschamps and H. Mulder, *Inventaris van de Middelnederlandse handschriften van de Koninklijke Bibliotheek van België.* Vol. 1. Brussel 1998, p. 55–56.
32 The fragments are described in Hans Kienhorst, *De handschriften van de Middelnederlandse ridderepiek. Een codicologische beschrijving.* Vol. 1. Deventer 1988, p. 8–13 (*Alexanders geesten*), p. 140–143 (only fragments of Velthem's *Merlijn* Continuation are known so far) and p. 196–210 (*Historie van Troyen*).

Maerlant had conceived his texts as trustworthy historical accounts. Nevertheless, the texts that he himself had – or would have – dismissed as mendacious trifles, also seem to have found an eager reception in the Meuse-Rhine-area. One of the two complete manuscripts of the famous thirteenh-century beast epic *Vanden vos Reynaerde*, though copied in the eastern part of Holland or in Utrecht between 1330–1360, came into the possession of Count William I of Limburg-Broich in 1430 at the latest and was kept in his Schloß Dyck, until it was bought by the University of Münster in 1991 (UB, N.R. 381).[33] We do not know the late fifteenth-century (Cologne?) commissioner of a fragmentarily preserved Ripuarian manuscript (Cologne, Historisches Archiv, Best. 7010 W 322 and Berlin, SB, Hdschr. 398) of the (Flemish) *Parthonopeus van Blois* and this also holds true for his or her fellow country(wo)man from (the neighbourhood of) Aix-la-Chapelle, who several decades earlier, around 1420–1430, had a copy (Brussels, KBR, 18231) made of the early fourteenth century Brabantine *Heinric en Margriete van Limborch*.[34] An early owner of this codex, however, must have been Wirich VI, count of Daun zu Oberstein (1415/1420–1501), who lived in the southern part of the Eifel and whose

---

33 Everardus A. Overgaauw, 'Die Dycksche Handschrift. Ihre Entdeckung, Herkunft, Datierung und früheren Besitzer'. In: *Die Dycksche Handschrift*. Ed. by Bertram Haller and Hans Mühl. Berlin, Münster 1992, p. 40–58; Eef Overgaauw, *Die mittelalterlichen Handschriften der Universitäts- und Landesbibliothek Münster*. Wiesbaden 1996, p. 152–154.
34 *Parthonopeus*: Helmut Tervooren, 'Zur Rezeption mittelniederländischer Literatur in Köln: ein neues Bruchstück des "Parthonopeus"'. In: *Rheinische Vierteljahrsblätter* 49 (1985), p. 92–116; and '"Parthonopeus von Blois" (ripuar. Fragment)'. In: ²*VL* 7 (1989), cols 315–316; *Margriete van Limborch: Roman van Heinric en Margriete van Limborch*, uit-gegeven volgens het Brusselse handschrift. Ed. by Rob Meesters. Amsterdam, Antwerpen 1951. On the place of origin of this manuscript, see Hartmut Beckers, '*Der püecher hau-bet, die von der tafelrunde wunder sagen*. Wirich von Stein und die Verbreitung des "Prosa-Lancelot" im 15. Jh.'. In: *Wolfram-Studien IX. Schweinfurter 'Lancelot'-Kolloquium 1984*. Ed. by Werner Schröder. Berlin 1986, p. 17–44, here p. 29; and Thomas Klein, 'Die Rezeption mittelniederländischer Versdichtungen im Rheinland und Augustijns "Herzog von Braunschweig"'. In: *Die spätmittelalterliche Rezeption niederländischer Literatur im deutschen Sprachgebiet (ABäG 47 1997)*. Ed. by Rita Schlusemann and Paul Wackers, p. 78–107, here p. 90–91; Rita Schlusemann, *Schöne Historien. Niederländische Romane im deutschen Spätmittelalter und in der frühen Neuzeit*. Berlin, Boston 2016 (Frühe Neuzeit, 203), p. 259–260 mentions a number of hypothetical commissioners of this Ripuarian manuscript.

first name is mentioned on fol. 147rb, under the last column of the text.[35] Through friendly and marital relationships, the manuscript must have landed in the important library of the counts of Manderscheid-Blankenheim.[36] On fol. 147v, an owner's mark informs us that the manuscript was in the possession of Cuno (1444–1489), junior count (*jonggrave*) of Manderscheid and count of Blankenheim in 1474.[37] This transfer does not surprise us, as the lords of Daun maintained close relations with the counts of Manderscheid-Blankenheim so that three other manuscripts once possessed by Wirich also found their way into their library.[38]

---

35 For a reproduction: see Meesters (see note 34), p. LII. Meesters' suggestion that the statement "Que remede" above Wirich's name indicates that Wirich would have corrected his copy, is wrong:"Que remede" is Wirich's French motto "That it may help". On Wirich VI as booklover, see Beckers, *Der püecher haubet* (note 34), p. 26–36 and Hartmut Beckers, 'Literarische Interessenbildung bei einem rheinischen Grafengeschlecht um 1470/80: Die Blankenheimer Schloßbibliothek'. In: *Literarische Interessenbildung im Mittelater. DFG-Symposion 1991*. Ed. by Joachim Heinzle. Stuttgart, Weimar 1993 (Germanistische Symposien. Berichtsbände 14), p. 5–20, here p. 13 and 16.

36 On the close ties between Wirich of Daun and the counts, especially Cuno, of Manderscheid-Blankenheim, see Beckers, *Der püecher haubet* (note 34), p. 29–30; Hartmut Beckers, 'Handschriften mittelalterlicher deutscher Literatur aus der ehemaligen Schloßbibliothek Blankenheim'. In: *Die Manderscheider. Eine Eifeler Adelsfamilie. Herrschaft – Wirtschaft – Kultur*. Katalog zur Ausstellung. Blankenheim, Gildehaus 4. Mai– 29. Juli 1990, Manderscheid, Kurhaus 16. August – 11. November 1990. Köln 1990, p. 57–82, here p. 64; Hartmut Beckers, 'Literarische Interessenbildung' (note 35), p. 15–17; Rita Schlusemann, 'Literarische Beziehungen als Quelle für buchhistorische Fragen. Die fränkischen Rheinlande in der zweiten Hälfte des 15. Jahrhunderts'. In: *Sources for the History of Medieval Books and Libraries*. Ed. by Rita Schlusemann, Jos M.M. Hermans and Margriet Hoogvliet. Groningen 2000, p. 95–107, here p. 101; and Schlusemann, *Schöne Historien* (note 34), p. 260–262. On the library of Blankenheim, see Beckers' article 'Literarische Interessenbildung' (note 35) as well as his contribution to the exhibition catalogue mentioned earlier in this footnote.

37 For a reproduction, see Meesters (see note 34), p. LIV. Cuno of Manderscheid-Blankenheim probably lay at the origin of the Blankenheim library, the development of which does not seem to have started before 1471 (Beckers, *Literarische Interessenbildung* (note 35), p. 12).

38 This relates to the Moselle-Franconian *Willehalm*-codex K (Cologne, Hist. Archiv der Stadt, Bestand 7010 (W) 357), to the Moselle-Franconian compilation based on the *Tafel vanden kersten ghelove* (1404) by the Holland Dominican Dirc van Delf (Darmstadt, Universitäts- und Landesbibliothek, 2667) and possibly also to the richly illustrated codex Z, dated 28 August 1286, of the Old French *Lancelot en prose* (Bonn, UB, S 526) (Beckers, *Der püecher haubet* (note 34), p. 27–33). As the latter manuscript probably did not come in Wirich's hands until 1495, it may only have entered the Blankenheim library after his death in 1501 (see Irmgard Fischer, 'Beschreibung der Handschrift S 526 der Universitätsbibliothek Bonn'. In: *Lancelot en prose. Farbmikrofische-Edition der Handschrift Bonn, Universitätsbibliothek, Handschrift S 526*. München 1992, p. 26–30, here p. 29).

Wirich also played an important role in the literary life at the palatine court in Heidelberg under Frederick I the Victorious (reigned 1449–1476) and his successor Philip the Upright (reigned 1476–1508) as well as at the court of Frederick's sister, Archduchess Mechthild of Austria (1419–1482), in Rottenburg.[39] This certainly involved the Rhenish-Franconian rendition ('Umschreibung') of the Middle Dutch Charlemagne romance *Malagis* and possibly also Johann of Soest's *Kinder von Limburg* (1479), an adaptation of *Heinric en Margriete van Limborch* made at the request of Philip the Upright, Mechthild's nephew.[40] In both cases it is conceivable that these Heidelberg works were based on texts that (had) belonged to Wirich's library; Johann of Soest's adaptation was at any rate based on a manuscript that is very close to (but not identical with) the Brussels manuscript.[41] Whether two

---

39 On literary life at the Heidelberg and Rottenburg courts under Frederick, Philipp and Mechthild, see Martina Backes, *Das literarische Leben am kurpfälzischen Hof zu Heidelberg im 15. Jahrhundert. Ein Beitrag zur Gönnerforschung des Spätmittelalters*. Tübingen 1992 (Hermaea 68), especially p. 114–171 and 185–190.

40 The Rhenish Franconian language of the Charlemagne romances discussed here and in the next paragraphs is in fact little more than a superficial veneer on the original Middle Dutch, which remains clearly discernable. On this question, see e.g. Martin J. Schubert, 'Nederlands-Duitse betrekkingen op het gebied van taal en literatuur in de late Middeleeuwen. Over de manier waarop *Malagis, Ogier* en *Reinolt* vertaald zijn'. In: *Van Madelgijs tot Malagis. Een bundel opstellen verzameld n.a.v. de tachtigste verjaardag van Gilbert de Smet*. Ed. by Georges de Schutter and Jan Goossens. Gent 2002, p. 53–64. In the case of *Ogier von Dänemark*, it seems even more appropriate to speak of an (almost unreadable) German copy of a Middle Dutch text: see Amand Berteloot, 'Gewollt oder nicht gekonnt? Oder erst gar nicht gewollt? Der Heidelberger "Ogier von Dänemark"'. In: *ZfdPh* 130 (2011), Sonderheft: *Dialog mit den Nachbarn. Mittelniederländische Literatur zwischen dem 12. und dem 16. Jahrhundert*. Ed. by Helmut Tervooren, Bernd Bastert and Frank Willaert, p. 193–201.

41 Schlusemann, 'Literarische Beziehungen' (note 36), p. 102–103. In the famous *Ehrenbrief*, which Jakob Püterich von Reichertshausen sent to the archduchess in 1462, he mentions the presence, in her library, of *Malagis, Rainhart* (= *Reinolt*) and *Margareth von Lünburg* (*Der Ehrenbrief des Pütrich von Reichertshausen*. Ed. by Fritz Behrend and Rudolf Wolkan. Weimar 1920, stanza 98–99). The latter title may refer to the Middle Dutch or Ripuarian manuscript which Johann von Soest would use later for his adaptation. Although Schlusemann (p. 105, n. 37) is of the opinion that Püterich's mention of *Malagis* and *Reinout* cannot relate to Heidelberg, UB, Cpg 340, but should concern the Dutch (or Ripuarian) exemplar, we would not consider this impossible, as a dating of this manuscript, based on the watermarks, to the early sixties is conceivable and even plausible (cf. *Der deutsche Malagis. Nach den Heidelberger Handschriften Cpg 340 und Cpg 315*. Ed. by Annegret Haase, Bob W.Th. Duijvestijn, Gilbert A.R. de Smet and Rudolf Bentzinger. Berlin 2000 (Deutsche Texte des Mittelalters 82), p. XV; see also Bob Duijvestijn, 'Madelgijs, zwerftocht van een epische stof'. In: *Van Madelgijs tot Malagis. Een bundel opstellen n.a.v. de tachtigste verjaardag van Gilbert de Smet*. Ed. by Georges de Schutter and Jan Goossens. Gent 2002, p. 23–34, here p. 31, who qualifies his previous position on this issue (Bob Duijvestijn, 'Niederländische Dichtung in

other renditions of Middle Dutch Charlemagne romances, *Reinolt von Montelban* and *Ogier von Dänemark*, were equally based on manuscripts that were procured by Wirich VI of Daun, we do not know, but we should not exclude this possibility.

Malagis was considered a prequel to *Reinolt von Montelban* and the two texts were accordingly copied together, and in that order, probably at the request of Archduchess Mechthild (Heidelberg, UB, Cpg 340), about 1465.[42] However, as she seems to have presented her son Eberhard V the Bearded, Count of Württemberg (reigned 1459–1496), with this manuscript, she had new copies made of both works, but now in individual manuscripts (Cpg 315 and Cpg 399 respectively) around 1480.[43]

In his famous 'Ehrenbrief' of 1462 to the Archduchess, Jakob Püterich von Reichertshausen calls Wirich vom Stein "der püecher haubet (…), die von der tafelrunde wunder sagen".[44] It has been suggested that Wirich may very well have been the purveyor of the exemplar of the – at that time still lacking – second part

---

der Privatbücherei der Pfalzgräfin Mechthild (1418/19–1482)'. In: *Miscellanea neerlandica. Opstellen voor dr. Jan Deschamps ter gelegenheid van zijn zeventigste verjaardag*. Ed. by Elly Cockx-Indestege and Frans Hendrickx. Vol. 2. Leuven 1987, p. 251–261, here p. 254–256).

42 Hartmut Beckers, 'Frühneuhochdeutsche Fassungen niederländischer Erzähliteratur im Umkreis des pfalzgräflichen Hofes zu Heidelberg um 1450/80'. In: Cockx-Indestege and Hendrickx (note 41), p. 237–249, here, p. 239. According to Bob Duijvestijn, ('Niederländische Dichtung' (note 41), p. 255), Heidelberg, UB, Cpg 340 should be considered either as an autograph or as a first copy of the rough version of the rendition.

43 On the library of Eberhard V the Bearded, see R. Cermann, 'Die Bibliothek Herzog Eberhards im Bart von Württemberg (1445–1496)'. In: *Scriptorium* 51 (1997), p. 30–50 (on Cpg 340, p. 39–40). Several scholars (e.g. Beckers, 'Frühneuhochdeutsche Fassungen' (note 42), p. 239; Duijvestijn, 'Niederländische Dichtung' (note 41), p. 255) are of the opinion that Mechthild gave this manuscript to her son as a wedding present, as it bears his motto (*Attempto*) and the year of his marriage with Barbara Gonzaga of Mantua (1474). We should bear in mind, however, that almost all books that were in Eberhard's possession at that moment, bear his motto and the year 1474 (Cermann, p. 39).

44 Behrend and Wolkan (see note 41), stanza 76. Transl.: "the 'head' of the books that tell about the marvels of the Round Table". The translation of this verse is not without problems. According to Beckers ('*Der püecher haubet*' (note 34), p. 42–45), the line may be corrupt and should accordingly be translated as:"to him belongs [*im … ist* instead of *er … ist*] the best of all the books that tell of the marvels of the round table". Or Püterich may erroneously have considered Wirich to be the author of the *Prosa Lancelot* and may have meant:"he is the maker of the most prominent book on the marvels of the round table".

of the three-partite *Prosa-Lancelot*.[45] According to a hypothesis by Harmut Beckers, this part was translated, around 1470, from an unknown Dutch exemplar, in order to realize the famous, lavishly illuminated manuscript of the *Prosa-Lancelot* (Heidelberg, UB, Cpg 147).[46] As this translation, and consequently its Middle Dutch exemplar, did not completely link up with the older part 1, however, a second attempt was made, the so-called *Karrensuite*, after the completion of Cpg 147 and before 1476, on the basis of a booklet that the Heidelberg translator claims to have found *inn flemische*.[47] The only manuscript of the *Karrensuite* (Cologne, Hist. Archiv der Stadt, Best. 7020 (W*) 46) was soon to end up in the library of the counts of Blankenheim-Manderscheid. If Beckers' proposal is correct, this would once more underscore the close relationships that existed between Wirich VI of Daun, the counts of Manderscheid-Blankenheim and the

---

45 The first part of the German *Prosa-Lancelot* is commonly dated in the thirteenth century: it comprises the *Lancelot propre* but breaks off in the middle of the *Suite de la Charrette*; the third part was translated in the fourteenth century and corresponds with the *Queste del Saint Graal* and the *Mort le Roi Artu*; the second part, finally, was probably translated in Heidelberg about 1470 and starts with the *Agravain*, so that there remained a lacuna with regard to the *Suite de la Charrette*. For two fairly recent states of the art, see Fritz Peter Knapp, '10.4. Der deutsche "Prosa-Lancelot"'. In: *Höfischer Roman in Vers und Prosa*. Ed. by René Pérennec and Elisabeth Schmid. Berlin, New York 2010 (Germania Litteraria Mediaevalis Francigena 5), p. 415–424, here p. 415–416, and Katja Rothstein, *Der mittelhochdeutsche Prosa-Lancelot. Eine entstehungs- und überlieferungsgeschichtliche Untersuchung unter besonderer Berücksichtigung der Handschrift Ms. allem. 8017–8020*. Frankfurt am Main etc. 2007 (Kultur, Wissenschaft, Literatur. Beiträge zur Mittelalterforschung 15), p. 12–15.

46 Beckers, '*Der püecher haubet*' (note 34), p. 36–39; H.B., 'Frühneuhochdeutsche Fassungen' (note 42), p. 245–246; Schlusemann, *Schöne historien* (note 34), p. 273. The hypothesis that the second part of the *Prosa-Lancelot* is based on a Dutch exemplar is, however, not beyond all doubt: see the literature mentioned in Rita Schlusemann, 'The Late-Medieval German Reception of Dutch Arthurian Literature in Heidelberg and Blankenheim'. In: *King Arthur in the Medieval Low Countries*. Ed. by Geert H.M. Claassens and David F. Johnson. Leuven 2000, p. 97–111 (Mediaevalia Lovaniensia 1, 28), here p. 102–103 and the discussion of this question in Rothstein (see note 45), p. 24–26 and 156–159.

47 Beckers, '*Der püecher haubet*' (note 34), p. 39–40 and 'Frühneuhochdeutsche Fassungen' (note 42), p. 246–247; Schlusemann, 'Literarische Beziehungen' (note 36), p. 97–100 and 'The Late-Medieval German Reception' (note 46), p. 103–106. The 'Flemish' exemplar was at any rate not one of the three extant Middle Dutch translations of the *Lancelot propre*: see Orlanda S.H. Lie, 'The Flemish Exemplar of Ms.W. f°46* Blankenheim, a Fifteenth-Century German Translation of the *Suite de la Charrette*'. In: *Arturus Rex. Vol. 2 Actus Conventus Lovaniensis 1987*. Ed. by Willy van Hoecke, Gilbert Tournoy, and Werner Verbeke. Leuven 1991 (Mediaevalia Lovaniensia 1/17), p. 404–418.

Palatine princes in and around Heidelberg in the second half of the fifteenth century.[48]

Assuming that the manuscript tradition of Middle Dutch romances offers a reliable picture of their reception in the course of the fifteenth century, we can safely conclude that at that time Dutch narratives were exclusively read east of Flanders and Brabant: from the region of Münster along the Meuse, Moselle and Rhine-area to Heidelberg. The majority of the commissioners and owners of these manuscripts were members of the aristocracy. The Dutch literary scene in Brabant and Flanders, on the contrary, seems to have been dominated, as far as secular literature was concerned, by commoners who only had a limited interest in these long narratives. Chivalric literature did exist in the Low Countries, but it was exclusively Francophone. With the rise of the Burgundian dynasty, not only the dukes themselves (among whom chiefly Philip the Good), but also the high nobility and a limited number of officers (mostly laymen without an academic title, ennobled or belonging to the middle nobility) took to an abundant production of narrative literature in French, consisting of new romances such as *L'Histoire des Sires de Gavre* or *Olivier de Castille* and prosifications of older narratives about heroes such as Alexander, Jason, Hercules, Charlemagne, Girart de Roussillon and Geoffrey of Bouillon.[49] When, for example, Philip the Good died in 1467, no less than one third of his library consisted of chivalric romances, Charlemagne epics and courtly poetry, genres which also found a place in the book collections of the higher nobility

---

48 Beckers, *Der pücher haubet* (note 34), p. 41, 'Frühneuhochdeutsche Fassungen' (note 42), p. 247 and 'Literarische Interessenbildung' (note 35), p. 15; Schlusemann, 'Literarische Beziehungen' (note 36), 'The Late-Medieval German Reception' (note 46), p. 105 and *Schöne Historien* (note 34), p. 262–265. See however Rothstein (see note 45), p. 60, 123–127, 131–132, 147–148 and 165–166, who doubts Beckers' hypothesis that the *Karrensuite* originated in Heidelberg and was meant to (partially) fill the gap between the first and second part of the *Prosa-Lancelot*.
49 Georges Doutrepont, *La littérature française à la cour des ducs de Bourgogne. Philippe le Hardi – Jean sans Peur – Philippe le Bon – Charles le Téméraire*. Paris 1909, in part. p. 1–186 and p. 482–485; Georges Doutrepont, *Les Mises en prose* (note 12), p. 414–441; Wijsman (see note 17), p. 505–507; Céline van Hoorebeeck, *Livres et lectures de fonctionnaires des ducs de Bourgogne (ca 1420–1520)*. Turnhout 2014 (Texte, Codex et Contexte 16), p. 318; Céline van Hoorebeeck, 'Les lectures "romanesques" des officiers des ducs de Bourgogne (ca 1420–1520)'. In: *Le romanesque aux XIVe et XVe siècles*. Ed. by Danièle Bohler. Bordeaux 2009, p. 257–268. On the political dimensions of several of these Burgundian narratives, see Yvon Lacaze, 'Le Rôle des traditions dans la genèse d'un sentiment national au 15e siècle. La Bourgogne de Philippe le Bon'. In: *Bibliothèque de l'École des Chartes* 129 (1971), p. 303–385.

and, – albeit to a far lesser extent – of a number of ducal officers in the Low Countries.[50] In this way, narrative literature contributed to the efforts to integrate and unite the political and bureaucratic elites surrounding the Burgundian dynasty. The (Dutch-speaking) Flemish and Brabantine citizens, however, do not seem to have participated in a meaningful way in that aspect of the 'Burgundianisation' of cultural life.[51] The outdated Middle Dutch narrative literature, once so blooming, seems to have fallen into oblivion in these territories for many decades when, in the seventies of the fifteenth century, the first printers started publishing literary texts in the vernacular.

To summarize, four features that seem characteristic for the literary tradition in the Low Countries should be listed:

1. In the thirteenth and fourteenth centuries, there was a deep rift between the Flemish and Brabantine production of romances in Middle Dutch. Flemish narratives were successful east of the river Scheldt, but the reverse was not the case: literature produced east of the river Scheldt did not penetrate the county of Flanders.

2. In Flemish narratives, Arthurian and Charlemagne traditions dominate. This phenomenon may be related to literary production in French, as several Arthurian, especially Grail romances (e.g. *Perceval* and at least two *Continuations*) and some Charlemagne epics (especially some "epics of revolt") seem to have originated in Flanders. The Brabantine literary production seems to have focused on local themes, characters and materials. As far as the production (but not the reception) of Arthurian literature is concerned, Brabant and the other regions near the river Rhine seem to have been "une terre anti-Arthurienne", both for Dutch and for French-speaking authors.[52]

3. From the middle of the fourteenth century onwards, the production of lengthy romances came to a standstill, both in Flanders and in Brabant. In

---

50 Van Hoorebeeck, *Livres et lectures* (see note 49), p. 117; and 'Les lectures "romanesques"' (see note 49), p. 259.

51 One could apply with still more justice to the Flemish and Brabantine citizenry Céline Van Hoorebeeck's remark about the all in all limited success of Burgundian literature among the ducal officers: "En grossissant le trait, on pourrait dire que la diffusion de la littérature bourguignonne qu'on retrouve à foison dans les collections de la haute noblesse ne s'est pas faite en circuit fermé mais presque. On touche là aux limites d'un mouvement d'intégration par la culture" (Van Hoorebeeck, *Livres et lectures* (note 49), p. 319).

52 Cf. Philippe Walter, 'Tout commence par des chansons... (Intertextualités lotharingiennes)'. In: *Styles et valeurs. Pour une histoire de l'art littéraire au moyen âge*. Ed. by D. Poirion. Paris 1990, p. 187–209, here p. 197; Willaert, *De ruimte* (note 2), p. 18.

contrast to developments in French and German literature, the prose form remained very marginal and older narratives were not prosified.

4. From 1400 onwards, narrative literature was no longer read in the central territories of the Low Countries. The Northern Low Countries, with the important exception of Zeeland during Maerlant's stay there, did not participate at all in the production and the reception of narrative literature. At the dawn of vernacular printing in the Low Countries, a complete void reigned in what are now the Dutch-speaking territories for at least three quarters of a century. A fifteenth century amateur of Middle Dutch narrative literature would have been better advised to look for a kindred spirit in some castle in Westphalia, Cologne or Heidelberg, than trying to find one in the Low Countries.

2 Holland

A striking discontinuity can be observed in the county of Holland in the last decades of the fifteenth century. There and then, Middle Dutch romances appear on stage in spite of their almost complete absence, both in terms of production and reception, in that region in the past. This phenomenon is accompanied by two crucial changes in the production of narrative texts. Middle Dutch romances are now mainly written in prose, in contrast to the preceding verse texts, and are printed instead of copied by hand.

The first printers of vernacular texts were mainly active in the northern cities of the Low Countries, like Gouda, Delft, Haarlem, Utrecht and Zwolle.[53] These places seem to have provided enterprising printers with opportunities for making a living, in contrast to the financially and culturally more developed Flemish and Brabantine towns. In these latter, the Chambers of Rhetoric dominated the literary scene and an infrastructure of professional scribes was able to provide the audience with the texts that interested them.[54]

As far as Middle Dutch romances were concerned, printers in the Holland towns Gouda, Delft and Haarlem seem to have been well aware of texts that

---

53 For overviews, see *De vijfhonderdste verjaring van de boekdrukkunst in de Nederlanden. Catalogus*. Brussel 1973; Peter M.H. Cuijpers, *Teksten als koopwaar: vroege drukkers verkennen de markt. Een kwantitatieve analyse van de productie van Nederlandstalige boeken (tot circa 1550) en de 'lezershulp' in de seculiere prozateksten*. Nieuwkoop 1998, p. 71–79.
54 See Herman Pleij, 'De betekenis van de beginnende drukpers voor de ontwikkeling van de Nederlandse literatuur in Noord en Zuid'. In: *Spektator* 21 (1992), p. 227–263.

would sell well.[55] As a matter of fact, quite a number of their editions correspond with romances that were printed elsewhere in Europe in the same period. Examples include the Dutch *Appollonius van Thyro*, which was published in Delft, supposedly by Christiaen Snellaert, in 1493 (ISTC ia00924600; GW 2285), and the *Vier Heemskinderen*, which appeared in Gouda, maybe produced by the so-called 'Printer of the *Chevalier déliberé*' (ISTC ia01433700; GW 12486), after 1489. The French romance about Appollonius was printed by Louis Cruse in Geneva around 1482 as *Romant de Appollin roy de thir* (ISTC ia00924800 GW 2279) and *Les quatre fils Aymon* may have been published by Guillaume le Roy in Lyon about 1482–1485 (ISTC ia01432800; GW 3133).[56] The same titles show up in German literature in the early period of print. In Augsburg, Günther Zainer published Heinrich Steinhöwel's *Die histori des königes Appolonii regis Tyri* in 1471 (ISTC ia00925000; GW 2273). Using a Dutch printed prose text, Johann Koelhoff the Younger published the story about the four 'Heimschen kynderen' in Cologne in 1493 (ISTC ia01434000; GW 3140).[57] In England, William Caxton printed a translation of the French Lyon print of *Les quatre fils Aymon* in 1490–1491 under the title *The foure sonnes of Aimon* (ISTC ia01434500; GW3141).[58]

The early printers in Holland rarely translated their romances from another vernacular text, instead preferring to adapt existing Latin or Middle Dutch texts they could easily lay their hands on. Gerard Leeu's production of romances during his activities in Holland may serve as an example.[59] His *Historie van Alexander* (ISTC ia00400900; GW 891), published in Gouda in 1477, is the oldest text in the corpus of printed Middle Dutch romances. Its source was the Alexander part of a Brabantine Bible translation, the so-called *Bible translation*

---

55 Early printers in Utrecht and Zwolle were particularly interested in religious texts, doubtless under the influence of the spiritual reform movement Devotio Moderna.

56 According to Sarah Baudelle-Michels, *Les quatre fils Aymon* was published in Lyon by the Imprimeur de l'*Abuzé en Court* between 1483 and 1485. See her '*Renaut de Montauban* ou *Les Quatre Fils Aymon* (prose vulgate)'. In: *Nouveau Répertoire de mises en prose (XIVe-XVIe siècle)* Ed. by Maria Colombo Timelli et al. Paris 2014, p. 699–716, here p. 710.

57 On Johann Koelhoff the Younger's edition and the Dutch source, see Beate Weifenbach, 'Johann Koelhoff der Jüngere: Die *Vier Heymschen Kynderen*. Die Bedeutung der Kölner Inkunabel aus dem Jahre 1493 für die Drucktradition von Haimonskindertexten in Deutschland'. In: *ABäG* 51 (1999), p. 169–193, here p. 174, 180–181.

58 See Baudelle-Michels (see note 56), p. 713. See also Janet M. Cowen, 'Die mittelenglischen Romane um Karl den Großen'. In: *Karl der Große in den europäischen Literaturen des Mittelalters. Konstruktion eines Mythos*. Ed. by Bernd Bastert. Tübingen 2004, p. 163–182, here p. 179–181.

59 See Koen Goudriaan et al. (eds), *Een drukker zoekt publiek. Gheraert Leeu te Gouda 1477–1484*. Delft 1993.

of 1360. This portion of the text concerning Alexander was based on two texts by the above-mentioned Flemish author Jacob van Maerlant, the *Spiegel histo-riael* and *Alexanders geesten*, and Petrus Comestor's *Historia scholastica.*[60] Leeu's *Historie van Alexander* met with much success, as it was printed four times between 1477 and 1491: one time by Leeu himself in Gouda and three times in Delft, by Jacob Jacobszoon van der Meer and Mauricius Yemantszoon (1479) and Chistiaen Snellaert (1488 and 1491).[61]

In 1479, Leeu printed the *Historie van Troyen* (ISTC ic00775500; GW 7243), which is a translation in Dutch of the *Historia destructionis Troiae* by Guido de Columnis. The Dutch text was completed by the addition of a prosification of Jacob van Maerlant's verse adaptation of Virgil's *Aeneid*, that originally served as the final part of Maerlant's widely read *Historie van Troyen.*[62] Work by Maerlant was also used for Leeu's *Destructie van Jherusalem*, printed in 1482 (ISTC ij00488500; GW M08652). This text is a prosification of Maerlant's verse translation of Flavius Josephus' *De Bello Judaico.*[63] The Flemish poet had com-posed this text, called the 'Wrake van Jerusalem' (Revenge on Jerusalem) in sec-ondary literature, to complete his renowned *Rijmbijbel*, which is a verse translation of Petrus Comestor's *Historia Scholastica.*[64]

In that same year, 1479, Leeu produced two other narrative texts based on Latin or Middle Dutch sources. His *Seven wisen van Rome* (ISTC is00450100; GW 12876) was translated from the *Historia septem sapientum Rome*, a Latin prose adaptation of a French source.[65] Leeu's Latin source was probably printed in Cologne by the printer of Augustine's *De fide* before 1473 (ISTC

---

60 See S.S. Hoogstra, *Proza-bewerkingen van het Leven van Alexander den Groote in het Middelnederlandsch.* 's-Gravenhage 1898, p. CXII–CXV.
61 See Bart Besamusca, 'De geschiedenis van Alexander de Grote in vier vroege drukken'. In: *Jaarboek voor Nederlandse boekgeschiedenis* 22 (2015), p. 123–140.
62 See W.P. Gerritsen, 'Een onbekende prozaversie van Maerlants *Aeneis*-bewerking'. In: *Miscellanea Neerlandica. Opstellen voor dr. Jan Deschamps ter gelegenheid van zijn zeventigste verjaardag.* Ed. by Elly Cockx-Indestege and Frans Hendrickx. Vol. 2. Leuven 1987, p. 163–174.
63 See Willem Kuiper, '*Die Destructie van Jherusalem* in handschrift en druk'. In: *Voortgang, jaarboek voor de neerlandistiek* 25 (2007), p. 67–88, here p. 83–84.
64 For Maerlant's translation of the *De Bello Judaico*, see Petra Berendrecht, *Proeven van be-kwaamheid. Jacob van Maerlant en de omgang met zijn Latijnse bronnen.* Amsterdam 1996 (Nederlandse literatuur en cultuur in de Middeleeuwen 14), p. 117–137. For the *Rijmbijbel*, see Jaap van Moolenbroek and Maaike Mulder (eds), *Scolastica willic ontbinden. Over de Rijmbijbel van Jacob van Maerlant.* Hilversum 1991.
65 Before 1500, Leeu's edition was reprinted at least three times: Delft, J.J. Van der Meer, 1483 (ISTC is00450150; GW 12877); Gouda, printer of *Teghen die strael der minnen*, 1484 or later (ISTC is00450200; GW 12878); Delft, J.J. Van der Meer or Ch. Snellaert, 1488–1491 (ISTC is00450300; GW 12879).

is00446000; GW 12847).[66] A Middle Dutch text was used to produce the *Hystorie van Reynaert die vos* (ISTC ir00135800; GW 12725). Probably a reprint of an edition that was published before 1479, also by Leeu, this text is a prosification of the verse text *Reynaerts historie*. It is likely that Leeu had this work close at hand, since the two manuscripts in which this text has come down to us were copied in Utrecht and Holland in the 1470s.[67] It is significant that Leeu wanted to avoid the impression that this tale was too frivolous and departed too far from the truth. In his prologue, he stressed the text's didactic character, calling Reynaert's adventures "parabolen" (parables), that contain "veel schoen leren ende merckelike punten" (many good lessons and noteworthy points).[68]

We know of only two verse romances that appeared in print in Holland in this early period: the long fourteenth-century romance *Seghelijn van Jherusalem*, printed in Delft between 1483 and 1485 by Jacob Jacobsz. van der Meer (ISTC is00366400; GW 12790), and the short romance *Karel ende Elegast*, printed for the first time by Gherardus De Leempt in the city of Den Bosch between 1484 and 1488 (ISTC ic00204650; GW 12600). Both romances were quite

---

66 For an overview, see Fred de Bree, 'Gheraert Leeu als drukker van Nederlands verhalend proza'. In: *Een drukker zoekt publiek. Gheraert Leeu te Gouda 1477–1484*. Ed. by Koen Goudriaan et al. Delft 1993, p. 61–80, here p. 63–69.

67 See *Reynaerts historie*. Ed. and transl. by Rita Schlusemann and Paul Wackers. Münster 2005 (Bibliothek mittelniederländischer Literatur 2), p. 416–418.

68 Hans Rijns (ed.), *De gedrukte Nederlandse Reynaerttraditie. Een diplomatische en synoptische uitgave naar de bronnen vanaf 1479 tot 1700*. Hilversum 2007 (Middeleeuwse studies en bronnen 100), p. 12. The word 'punten', points, is often used in didactic and edifying texts: see Wim van Anrooij,' "Poenten" in de Middelnederlandse letterkunde. Een geledingssysteem in het zakelijke en discursieve vertoog'. In: Wim van Anrooij et al., *Al t'Antwerpen in die stad. Jan van Boendale en de literaire cultuur van zijn tijd*. Amsterdam 2002, p. 65–80 and 166–168. For Leeu's prologue, see Herman Pleij, 'Over betekenis en belang van de leesinstructie in de gedrukte proza-Reynaert van 1479'. In: Herman Pleij, Joris Reynaert et al., *Geschreven en gedrukt. Boekproductie van handschrift naar druk in de overgang van Middeleeuwen naar Moderne tijd*. Gent 2004, p. 207–232. Pleij (p. 225) rejects Janet Coleman's claim that (Caxton's translation of) Leeu's prologue' should be taken in a satirical vein; see her *Public Reading and the Reading Public in Late Medieval England and France*. Cambridge 1996, p. 217–218. Caxton used the Dutch prosification of *Reynaerts historie* to produce his *History of reynard the fox* (ISTC ir00137000; GW 12728) in 1481. For a study of Caxton's translation, see Rita Schlusemann, *Die hystorie van reynaert die vos und The history of reynaerd the fox. Die spätmittelalterlichen Prosabearbeitungen des Reynaert-Stoffes*. Frankfurt am Main 1991. For the printed Dutch tradition, see Paul Wackers, 'The Printed Dutch Reynaert Tradition: From the Fifteenth to the Nineteenth Century'. In: *Reynard the Fox. Social Engagement and Cultural Metamorphoses in the Beast Epic from the Middle Ages to the Present*. Ed. by Kenneth Varty. New York, Oxford 2000, p. 73–103.

succesful, as they were reprinted several times until far into the sixteenth century.[69] It is difficult to tell why they were not prosified. According to Herman Pleij, De Leempt's *Karel ende Elegast* was meant as a schoolbook.[70] While De Leempt's printing list indeed featured several schoolbooks in Latin and two Latin-Dutch dictionaries, there is no firm evidence that *Karel ende Elegast* was really meant for schooling. The fact that later editions of *Karel ende Elegast* feature a short epilogue dealing with the life and virtues of Charlemagne may indicate that this short tale was thought fit for use in the classroom. As far as *Seghelijn van Jherusalem* is concerned, however, its sheer length (more than 12.000 lines) makes this hypothesis highly improbable.

The two verse romances share a strong religious bias. In both texts, the main character is subjected to God's mysterious ways. Seghelijn has even been characterized as a *miles christianus* and his story has a hagiographic slant to it.[71] It is conceivable that the strong Christian features of *Karel ende Elegast* and *Seghelijn van Jherusalem* made them attractive for printers whose production was geared towards moralizing and religious texts.[72]

Whereas most of the printers in Holland who produced romances made use of source texts in Dutch and Latin, the Haarlem printer Jacob Bellaert was the exception. Like most of his colleagues, he printed devotional texts, but he also ventured to produce Dutch translations from French, more precisely Burgundian texts.[73] These books share some characteristics with the Burgundian editions printed by his Bruges colleague Colard Mansion: luxurious lay-out and high liter-

69 For *Karel ende Elegast*, see Bart Besamusca, Hans van Dijk (eds), Thea Summerfield (transl.), '*Karel ende Elegast*'. In: *Olifant* 26 (2011), p. 51–165, here p. 52–53. On the *Seghelijn* editions, see Jef Schaeps' contribution in the present volume, p. 297–324.

70 Herman Pleij, *Het gevleugelde woord. Geschiedenis van de Nederlandse literatuur 1400–1560*. Amsterdam 2007, p. 466.

71 See Geert H.M. Claassens, '"Doe leefde hi soe heilichlike". *Seghelijn van Jherusalem* tussen ridderepiek en hagiografie,' In: *Ene andre tale. Tendensen in de Middelnederlandse late ridderepiek*. Ed. by An Faems and Marjolein Hogenbirk. Hilversum 2012 (Middeleeuwse Studies en Bronnen 131), p. 195–212.

72 See Rob Resoort, 'Het raadsel van de rijmdrukken'. In: *Nederlandse Letterkunde* 3 (1998), p. 309–326, here p. 339.

73 For overviews, see *De vijfhonderdste verjaring* (see note 53), p. 286–287; Wilma Keesman, 'Jacob Bellaert en Haarlem'. In: *Haarlems Helicon. Literatuur en toneel te Haarlem vóór 1800*. Ed. by E. K. Grootes. Hilversum 1993, p. 27–48; Saskia Bogaart, *Geleerde kennis in de volkstaal. Van den proprieteyten der dinghen (Haarlem 1485) in perspectief*. Hilversum 2004, p. 47–56.

ary quality.[74] Aristocratic purchasers of his books could fit their coat of arms in an empty escutcheon that was part of Bellaert's printer's mark.[75] Between 10 December 1483 and 5 May 1485, Bellaert published the *Historie van Jason* (ISTC il00111000; GW M17467), a Dutch translation of Raoul Lefèvre's *Histoire de Jason*, and on 5 May 1485, he printed the *Vergaderinge der historien van Troyen* (ISTC il00116000; GW M17453), a translation of the *Recueil des histoires de Troies* by the same French author.[76] Both editions feature a woodcut with a representation of the author offering his book to his patron Philip the Good: the coat of arms hanging on a tree behind the duke probably points to Claes van Ruyven (*c.* 1446–1492), who held a number of important positions in the city of Haarlem and the surrounding region (Kennemerland) between 1471 until his violent death in 1492 and was as such an important representative of the Burgundian dynasty in Holland.[77] If Van Ruyven supported Bellaert, it is improbable that his sponsorship was sufficient to keep Bellaert's business afloat.[78] The number of potential buyers of his luxurious and capital-intensive products must

---

74 See *De vijfhonderdste verjaring* (see note 53), p. 212–239; Ludo Vandamme, 'Colard Mansion et le monde du livre à Bruges'. In: *Le berceau du livre imprimé, autour des incunables*. Ed. by Pierre Aquilon and Thierry Claerr. Turnhout 2010, p. 177–186; Renaud Adam, 'Colard Mansion, passeur de textes?'. In: *Le Roman français dans les premiers imprimés* Ed. by Anne Schoysman and Maria Colombo Timelli. Paris 2016 (Rencontres 147), p. 11–24; Evelien Hauwaerts, Evelien de Wilde and Ludo Vandamme (eds), *Colard Mansion. Incunabula, Prints and Manuscripts in Medieval Bruges*. S. l. 2018.

75 Keesman, 'Jacob Bellaert en Haarlem' (note 73), p. 35–36.

76 See Wilma Keesman, *De eindeloze stad. Troje en Trojaanse oorsprongsmythen in de (laat) middeleeuwse en vroegmoderne Nederlanden*. Hilversum 2017 (Middeleeuwse studies en bronnen 159), p. 51–57. Some time later, between 24 December 1485 and 12 August 1486, Bellaert also printed the French sources of both editions (ISTC il00110950, GW M17455 and ISTC il00113500, GW M17434). These editions are the only French titles that Bellaert produced. For these editions, he made use of French editions printed by William Caxton in Bruges or Ghent *c.* 1476–1477 (*Histoire de Jason*) and *c.* 1474–1475 (*Recueil*). See Lotte Hellinga, *Texts in Transit: Manuscript to Proof and Print in the Fifteenth Century*. Leiden 2014, p. 312–313, 326, 347–360, and Lotte Hellinga, 'William Caxton and Colard Mansion'. In: *Colard Mansion. Incunabula, Prints and Manuscripts in Medieval Bruges* (note 74), p. 63–71, here p. 65 and 69.

77 Keesman, 'Jacob Bellaert en Haarlem' (note 73), p. 41–43 and Keesman, *De eindeloze stad* (note 76), p. 54–56.

78 For local patronage of regional presses in France, see Malcolm Walsby, 'The Vanishing Press: Printing in Provincial France in the Early Sixteenth Century'. In: *The Book Triumphant: Print in Transition in the Sixteenth and Seventeenth Centuries*. Ed. by Malcolm Walsby and Graeme Kemp. Leiden, Boston 2011, p. 97–111, here p. 106–111. For a comparable case of aristocratic patronage of a printed edition of a Burgundian literary text in Holland, see Susie Speakman Sutch, 'De Gouda-editie van *Le Chevalier délibéré*. Een boek uitgegeven in eigen beheer'. In: Herman Pleij, Joris Reynaert et al., *Geschreven en gedrukt. Boekproductie van*

have been far too small.[79] Bellaert's last edition, the Dutch translation of Guillaume de Digulleville's *Le Pèlerinage de la vie humaine* (ISTC ig00638000; GW 11851), appeared on 20 August 1486 and then we lose track of him. It is generally assumed that he had to stop his activities due to bankruptcy.

It is evident that by the end of the 1480s, the small towns in Holland did not offer enough opportunities for printers to keep their businesses alive. One printer, Gerard Leeu, knew this all too well. In 1484, he had already decided to leave Gouda and after trying his luck in Bruges for a short time, opted for the rapidly expanding city of Antwerp.[80]

Many printers in Holland printed titles that we also find in neighbouring literatures at the same time. In order to have a better idea of the specific profile of the production in Holland, we list here the French production of romances (first editions only) until 1490, based on the overview by Giovanni Matteo Roccati.[81] In bold we indicate the French titles that have approximately the same content as editions printed in Holland. None of these Dutch editions, however, are translations from the French, except the texts that have *L'histoire de Jason* and *Le Recueil des histoires de Troie* as their source.

Strikingly, but not surprisingly, almost all the French, and in particular the chivalric romances, are absent from the Holland production. The only possible exception seems to be *Les quatre fils Aymon*: the Dutch edition, printed in Gouda in 1489 or later (ISTC ia01433700; GW 12486), is, however, not based on a French source, but on a very popular Middle Dutch verse adaptation from the thirteenth century. With the exception of the two Bellaert titles, all the other Dutch titles are adaptations of Latin or Middle Dutch texts. They have a strong didactic bias, teaching history, morals or both.

---

handschrift naar druk in de overgang van Middeleeuwen naar Moderne tijd. Gent 2004, p. 137–155.

79 An additional explanation for the disappearance of Bellaert's printing press may be that the potential buyers of his books had easy access to editions printed elsewhere because of the presence of local booksellers. For these booksellers in provincial France, see Walsby (see note 78), p. 102–106. For printed German romances, a large aristocratic audience seems to have existed. See the article by Bertelsmeier-Kierst in the present volume, p. 17–47.

80 For Leeu in Bruges and Antwerp, see Goudriaan et al. (see note 59) and Anne Rouzet, *Dictionnaire des imprimeurs, libraires et éditeurs des XVe et XVIe siècles dans les limites géographiques de la Belgique actuelle.* Nieuwkoop 1975, p. 121–123.

81 Giovanni Matteo Roccati, 'Le roman dans les incunables. L'impact des stratégies éditoriales dans le choix des titres imprimés.' In: *Le Roman français dans les premiers imprimés.* Ed. by Anne Schoysman and Maria Colombo Timelli. Paris 2016 (Rencontres 147), p. 95–126, here p. 122–123.

1474	Bruges/Ghent?	Caxton	*L'histoire de Jason*
1474	Bruges/Ghent?	Caxton	*Le recueil des histoires de Troyes*
1477	Lyon	Le Roy	*Pierre de Provence et la belle Maguelonne I*
1477	**Lyon**	**Philippi-Reinhart**	**La Destruction de Troye**
1478	Genève	Steinschaber	*Fierabras*
1478	Genève	Steinschaber	*Histoire de la belle Mélusine*
1478	Lyon	Le Roy	*Baudoin*
1478	Bruges	Mansion	*L'Abusé en Court*
1479	Genève	Dujardin	*Ponthus et la belle Sidoine*
1479	**Genève**	**Steinschaber**	**Destruction de Jérusalem (Vengeance de nostre seigneur)**
1479	Lyon	Huss	*Pierre de Provence et la belle Maguelonne II*
1479	Lyon	Le Roy	*Clamadès*
1480	Lyon	Le Roy	*Paris et Vienne*
1482	**Lyon**	**Cruse**	**Le Roman de Apollin roy de Thir**
1482	**Genève**	**Cruse**	**La patience de Griseldis**
1482	Genève	Cruse	*Olivier de Castille et Artus d'Algarbe*
1482	**Lyon**	**Le Roy**	**Les quatre fils Aymon**
1483	Lyon	Le Roy	*Eneydes*
1487	Abbeville	Gérard	*Le triumphe des neuf preux*
1487	Lyon	Le Roy	*Le livre des faits d'armes de Bertrand du Guesclin*
1488	Paris	du Pré	*Lancelot du Lac 2*
1488	Rouen	Le Bourgeois	*Lancelot du Lac 1*
1489	Lyon	Maillet	*Valentin et Orson*

1489	Paris	Le Rouge	*Les Sept sages romains*
1489	Rouen	Le Bourgeois	*Le roman du noble et vaillant Chevalier Tristan*
1490	Lyon		*Euriale et Lucresse*

Listing the production of Dutch romances in the northern Low Countries until *c.* 1490 results in the following overview (< means "or later"):

1477	Gouda	Leeu	*Alexander*
1479	Gouda	Leeu	*Reynaert-prose*
1479	**Gouda**	**Leeu**	***Seven wise mannen van Rome***
1479	**Gouda**	**Leeu**	***Historien van Troyen* (G.de Col.)**
1482	**Gouda**	**Leeu**	***Destructie van Jherusalem***
1483<	**Haarlem**	**Bellaert**	***Jason* (Lefèvre)**
1483<	Delft	Van der Meer	*Seghelijn van Jherusalem*
1484<	's-Hertogenbosch	De Leempt	*Karel ende Elegast*
1484<	Gouda	Printer *Strael der minnen*	*Strael der minnen* (pseudo-Petrarca)
1485	**Haarlem**	**Bellaert**	***Vergaderinge van Troyen* (Lefèvre)**
1486	Gouda	Printer *Godevaert*	*Godevaert van Boloen*
1486<	Gouda	van Ghemen	*Julius Caesar*
1489<	**Gouda**	**Printer *Chevalier délibéré***	***Heemskinderen***
1493	**Delft**	**Snellaert**	***Apollonius van Tyro***

It is interesting to note which titles do not occur, or do so much later, in the French corpus. The Dutch production in the northern part of the Low Countries has a strong tendency towards history, in particular history concerning heroes from the past, such as Alexander, Charlemagne, Godefroi de Bouillon and Julius Caesar. In most cases, these texts are based on sources that were considered highly reliable, such as Latin chronicles (*Godevaert, Caesar*) and the History Bible (*Alexander*). The short text on Charlemagne (*Karel ende Elegast*) may be an exception, but has a strong moralizing bias and would be explicitly linked with the life and virtues of Charlemagne in later Antwerp editions. This bias is also present in three quite luxurious Gouda editions, *Godevaert van Boloen* (1486; ISTC ig00317000; GW 12573), *Julius Caesar* (1486; ISTC ic00029500; GW 5879) and *De vier Heemskinderen* (1490; ISTC ia01433700; GW 12486), which may have been commissioned by a wealthy patron.[82] Furthermore, the Prose *Reynaert* was presented by Leeu as a didactic text, as a parable that informed its readers about human morality. Love does not hold a prominent place, except in the pseudo-Petrarch novella *Strael der minnen* (after 1484; ISTC ip00399700; GW M31678), which does, however, promote fidelity in marriage and consequently has a strong moralizing tendency.

3 Antwerp

It is well documented that the initial flourishing of the printing press in the northern parts of the Low Countries was followed by a period in which Antwerp was the centre of book production. This transition took place in the 1480s. In the decade between 1470 and 1480, there was no production of printed books in Antwerp.[83] Then, the state of affairs changed rapidly. Four cities, Antwerp, Leuven, Deventer and Zwolle, produced almost ninety percent of the Latin titles up to 1550. About 42 percent of these editions came from the Antwerp printing presses. The city was also dominant in the market of printed books in Dutch. In the period up to the middle of the sixteenth century, 55 percent of these titles appeared in Antwerp. Minor rivals were Delft and Leiden. The generally accepted explanation for this transition from Holland to Antwerp is that due to its

---

82 Speakman Sutch (see note 78) p. 141–152 suggests that the patron of at least two of these works, *Godevaert van Boloen* and *De vier Heemskinderen*, as well as of a French edition of *Le Chevalier délibéré* by Olivier de la Marche (after 31 October 1489; ICTS il00029010, GW M16748) may be identified with Jan van Cats, bailiff in Gouda for Mary of Burgundy and brother-in-law of Claes van Ruyven, whom we have already met as a patron of the Haarlem printer Jacob Bellaert. Sutch's hypothesis is, however, a risky one, as Jan van Cats must have died in 1488–1489, while *Le Chevalier délibéré* and *De vier Heemskinderen* were printed after 31 October 1489 and in 1490, respectively. On the printers' patrons in Gouda, see also Jan Willem Klein, 'Ghescreven ofte gheprent. Aspecten van de (Goudse) middeleeuwse boekproductie'. In: Herman Pleij, Joris Reynaert et al., *Geschreven en gedrukt. Boekproductie van handschrift naar druk in de overgang van Middeleeuwen naar Moderne tijd*. Gent 2004, p. 67–83, here p. 72–76.
83 For an overview, see Cuijpers (see note 53), p. 71–72.

strategic position at the Scheldt estuary and its extensive infrastructure of bankers, merchants, authors, typesetters and potential readers, this Brabantine city provided the near-ideal circumstances for commercial book production.[84] For our purposes, it is interesting that the shift from north to south had an impact on the production of Middle Dutch romances.

Clearly aware of economic developments and opportunities, Gheraert Leeu moved his print shop from Gouda, where he had been active since 1477, to Antwerp in the summer of 1484. Starting with the Latin-Dutch dictionary *Gemmula vocabulorum* (ISTC iv00332500; GW M51159), he produced here at least 159 editions until his untimely death in December 1492.[85] In 1487, his first Antwerp romances appeared. On May 15 of that year, the printing of the *Histoire du chevalier Paris et de la belle Vienne* (ISTC ip00112800; GW 12686) was completed, followed by the publication of its Dutch translation, the *Historie van Parijs ende Vienna* (ISTC ip00113800; GW 12700). This adventurous love story enjoyed great popularity, as is attested by five French editions after the *editio princeps* of 1480 by Guillaume Le Roy (Huss 1485, Leeu 1487, Meslier 1491, Trepperel 1498 and 1499[86]), a Low German version, published by Leeu in 1488 (ISTC ip00115200; GW 12699), an English version produced by Leeu in 1492 (ISTC ip00113600; GW 12692) and three reprints of the Dutch text, published in Antwerp by Leeu about 1492 (ISTC ip00114500; GW 12701), by Govaert Bac about 1495 (ISTC ip00115000; GW 12702) and by Henrick Eckert van Homberch in 1510 (NK 1090).[87]

In producing the *Historie van Parijs ende Vienna*, Leeu continued a practice of Jacob Bellaert, because he printed a Middle Dutch translation of a contemporary French source. Whereas the Haarlem printer was exceptional in this respect, as we noted earlier, Leeu seems to have paved the way for the

---

84 See Francine de Nave, 'Een typografische hoofdstad in opkomst, bloei en verval'. In: *Antwerpen, verhaal van een metropool*. Ed. by J. Van der Stock. Gent, 1993, p. 87–95. See also Rita Schlusemann, 'Buchmarkt in Antwerpen am Anfang des 16. Jahrhunderts'. In: *Laienlektüre und Buchmarkt im späten Mittelalter*. Ed. by Thomas Kock and Rita Schlusemann. Frankfurt am Main 1997, p. 33–59.

85 See *Inventaris van incunabelen gedrukt te Antwerpen 1481–1500*. Antwerpen 1982 (Publikaties van de stadsbibliotheek en het archief en museum voor het Vlaamse cultuurleven 1), p. 45–67.

86 See Roccati (see note 81), p. 119.

87 For a comparative study of the international *Paris et de la belle Vienne* tradition, see Baukje Finet-van der Schaaf, 'Les incunables français, néerlandais, allemand et anglais de *L'histoire du très vaillant chevalier Paris et de la belle Vienne, fille du dauphin* et leur rapport à la tradition française manuscrite du récit'. In: *L'épopée romane. Actes du XVe congrès international Rencesvals. Poitiers, 21–27 août 2000*. 2 vols. Ed. by Gabriel Bianciotto and Claudio Galderisi. Poitiers 2002, p. 825–836.

production in Antwerp of Dutch romances based on contemporary French sour-
ces. In the period up to about 1500 a number of editions testify to this trend.
While Leeu himself published *Meluzine* in 1491 (ISTC ij00218420; GW 12665),[88]
Jan van Doesborch produced *Buevijn van Austoen* in 1504 (NK 1085).[89]

A slightly more complicated example is provided by the Antwerp printer
Roland van den Dorpe, who published the *Destructie van Troyen* between 1497
and 1500 (ISTC ih00281000; GW 12522). This text is based on both Dutch and
French sources. Van den Dorpe mixed two texts that were printed in Holland
and have been mentioned before: Leeu's *Historie van Troyen* and Bellaert's
Vergaderinge der historien van Troyen. In addition, he renewed the text tradition
by adding a translation of Louis de Beauvau's French rendition of Boccaccio's *Il
Filostrato* and presenting the amorous dialogues between Troilus and Briseida
in the form of verse passages.[90] These lyrical insertions developed into
a literary fashion, mainly under the influence of Jan van Doesborch, who took
over the printing house of the widow of Roland van den Dorpe in 1501.[91]

A particularly instructive example in this context is the *Destructie van
Jherusalem*, which was probably printed by Willem Vorsterman about 1505 (NK
4430). The source text for this production could have been the *Destructie van
Jherusalem* (ISTC ij00488500; GW M08652) which Leeu published in Gouda in
1482 (supra). However, Vorsterman seems to have ignored Leeu's edition in favour of a translation of a French source, the highly popular *Destruction de
Jérusalem*, also called *La Vengeance de nostre seigneur*.[92] There was, apparently,
a growing awareness among printers that there was a market, in particular in the
economically and culturally more emancipated southern regions of the Low

---

88 For *Meluzine*, see Johan H. Winkelman, *De staart van Meluzine*. Amsterdam 2000; Lydia
Zeldenrust, 'Serpent or Half-Serpent? Bernhard Richel's *Melusine* and the Making of a Western
European Icon'. In: *Neophilologus* 100 (2016), p. 19–41; Lydia Zeldenrust, 'The Lady with the
Serpent's Tail: Hybridity and the Dutch *Meluzine*'. In: *Melusine's Footprint: Tracing the Legacy
of a Medieval Myth*. Ed. by Misty Urban, Deva F. Kemmis and Melissa Ridley Elmes. Leiden
2017 (Explorations in Medieval Culture 4), p. 132–145. For the French source, see Luc.
Debaene, *De Nederlandse volksboeken. Ontstaan en geschiedenis van de Nederlandse prozaromans, gedrukt tussen 1475 en 1540*. 2nd ed. Hulst 1977, p. 119–120.
89 For the French source of *Buevijn van Austoen*, see P.J.A. Franssen, *Tussen tekst en publiek.
Jan van Doesborch, drukker-uitgever en literator te Antwerpen en Utrecht in de eerste helft van
de zestiende eeuw*. Amsterdam 1990, p. 52.
90 See Keesman, *De eindeloze stad* (note 76), p. 57–61.
91 See Elisabeth de Bruijn, 'Das Spiel der Stimmen. Performative Verspassagen in einigen
niederländischen Prosaromanen (ca. 1500–1540)'. In: *Stimme und Performanz in der mittelalterlichen Literatur*. Ed. by Monica Unzeitig, Nine Miedema and Angela Schrott. Berlin 2017,
p. 133–154.
92 See Roccati (see note 81), p. 116–117.

Countries, that included buyers who wanted to be acquainted with fashionable French romances, such as *Paris et Vienne* and *Mélusine*, but were unable to read them, or preferred to read them in their own language. Bellaert had been searching in vain for this type of consumer of romances some years earlier.

The printing of translations of contemporary French romances continued in the first half of the sixteenth century. Examples of this trend include *Olyvier van Castillen* (NK 3170), printed by Van Homberch about 1510,[93] *Robrecht de Duyvel*, published by Michiel Hillen van Hoochstraten in 1516,[94] and *Peeter van Provencen* (NK 3171), produced by Willem Vorsterman about 1517. Their French counterparts circulated since 1477 (*Pierre et Maguelonne*), 1482 (*Olivier de Castille*) and 1496 (*Robert le Diable*).[95] The recently discovered edition of *Galien Rethore*, published by Willem Vorsterman somewhere between *c.* 1504 and *c.* 1543, fits this category: the Dutch text is based on a French source, published by Anthoine Vérard in 1500 (or a later edition).[96]

This appreciation of non-Dutch popular romances extended to vernaculars other than French. This development is attested, for example, by two Antwerp texts in the corpus of Middle Dutch printed romances which are based on English sources. These English texts were both printed by Wynkyn de Worde.[97] In 1528, Michiel van Hoochstraaten published *Van den jongen geheeten Jacke* (NK 1087), a translation of *The Frere and the Boye* (*c.* 1510). Around 1540, Symon Cock produced the *Historie van Merlijn* (NK 3169), which is a translation of De Worde's *A lytel treatyse of ye byrth and prophecye of Marlyn* (first edition *c.* 1499).[98] However, publishers did not only draw on English source texts. In or

---

93 According to Luc. Debaene, the Dutch *Olyvier van Castillen* is based on both the French and the Castilian prose romance, see his 'Nederlandse prozaromans en Spaanse "Libros de caballerias"'. In: *Liber alumnorum Prof. Dr. E. Rombauts, aangeboden ter gelegenheid van zijn vijfenzestigste verjaardag en zijn dertigjarig hoogleraarschap*. Leuven 1968, p. 129–144, here p. 133–139. However, Elisabeth de Bruijn convincingly demonstrates that the Dutch translation had a French romance as its model. See *Queeste* 25 (2018), p. 67–86.
94 See Cuijpers (see note 53), p. 290. See also *Robrecht de duyvel*. Ed. by Rob Resoort. Muiderberg 1980.
95 See Roccati (see note 81), p. 108, 112.
96 See Elisabeth de Bruijn, '*Galien Rethore* herontdekt'. In: *Madoc* 31 (2017), p. 75–82.
97 For Wynkyn de Worde, see the articles by Boffey, p. 125–141, and Sánchez-Martí, p. 143–166, in the present volume.
98 On *Jacke*, *Merlijn* and their English translations, see Elisabeth de Bruijn, 'To Content the Continent. The Dutch Narratives *Merlijn* and *Jacke* Compared to Their English Counterparts'. In: *TNTL* 133 (2017), p. 83–108. A third example could be *Helias* (NK 3172), published by Jan van Doesborch around 1520–1530. However, it is uncertain whether this romance is based on the French *Genealogie avecques les Gestes* (1499) by Pierre Desrey (first edition: Le Noir 1504) or on the English *Helyas, Knight of the Swanne* (first edition: De Worde, 1512). See Elisabeth de

before 1518, Jan van Doesborch must have printed a rendition of the Low German *Historie van tween kopluden* (*c.* 1495), which is only preserved in a 1531 edition by Willem Vorsterman (*Frederick van Jenuen*, NK 1086).[99] The latter also used a Spanish edition for his *Sibilla* (NK 3173), published around 1538.[100] It is safe to conclude that Antwerp printers were internationally orientated in their search for romance material in the vernacular.

The printers' keen eyes for romances which were appreciated by audiences outside of the Low Countries did not prevent them from publishing local material that had proven its attractiveness in the past. Regularly, they produced Middle Dutch romances which were transmitted in manuscripts and/or printed editions earlier on. Around 1517, for example, Jan van Doesborch printed *Floris ende Blancefloer* (NK 3160), based on the thirteenth-century verse text by the Flemish poet Diederic van Assenede. Some years later, in 1521, Van Doesborch published two romances, *Jason* and *Hercules* (NK 3164), which could be bought as a set and separately.[101] These texts are adaptations of Bellaert's texts about these classical heroes, printed in 1484–1485.[102] A prominent example of this continuity is provided by *Margariete van Limborch* (NK 3168), which Willem Vorsterman produced in 1516. It is a long prose text, based on the lengthy verse romance *Heinric en Margriete van Limborch* which we mentioned earlier.[103] Vorsterman's willingness to publish this voluminous folio edition indicates that homegrown romances still attracted readers in the first half of the sixteenth century.

Bruijn, 'Reculer pour mieux sauter: de bronnenproblematiek en de literaire eigenheid van de Middelnederlandse *Helias'*. In: *Verslagen en Mededelingen van de Koninklijke Academie voor Nederlandse Taal- en Letterkunde* 126 (2016), p. 227–263.

99 Debaene, *De Nederlandse volksboeken* (see n. 88), p. 87; Franssen (see n. 87), p. 67 en 105; Rita Schlusemann, 'Wechselseitige niederdeutsch/niederländische Literaturbeziehungen in der frühen gedruckten Erzähldichtung. Mit einer Edition des Magdeburger Drucks der *Historie van twen kopluden* (um 1495)'. In: *Jahrbuch des Vereins für niederdeutsche Sprachforschung* 125 (2002), p. 97–130, here p. 112, n. 46.

100 See Bart Besamusca, 'Willem Vorsterman's *Sibilla*: the Dutch Story of Charlemagne's Repudiated Wife'. In: *L'imaginaire courtois et son double*. Ed. by Giovanna Angeli and Luciano Formisano. Napoli 1992, p. 245–254; and Baukje Finet-van der Schaaf, 'Le roman en prose néerlandais de la reine Sibille et son modèle espagnol: *La Hystoria de la Reyna Sebilla'*. In: *Charlemagne in the North: Proceedings of the Twelfth International Conference of the Société Rencesvals*. Ed. by Philip E. Bennett, Anne Elisabeth Cobby and Graham A. Runnalls. Edinburgh 1993, p. 31–43.

101 See Bart Besamusca, 'Raoul Lefèvre in Dutch: Two 1521 Editions of the Antwerp Printer Jan van Doesborch'. In: *Journal of the Early Book Society* 20 (2017), p. 219–232.

102 See Bart Besamusca, 'Tekst en beeld in twee drukken van Jan van Doesborch: *Van Jason ende Hercules* en *Die historie van den stercken Hercules'*. In: *SpdL* 59 (2017), p. 1–34.

103 For a recent study, see Schlusemann, *Schöne Historien* (note 34).

Striking is the endurance of verse texts in the Antwerp production of local Middle Dutch romances. The corpus of Middle Dutch printed romances includes five texts which were reprinted in verse, despite the strong tendency to apply the prose form to printed romances. The short verse text *Karel ende Elegast*, which was published in Holland twice in the period 1484–1488, was reprinted in Antwerp four times before 1540.[104] The other printed verse texts are the verse *Reynaert* published by Leeu in Antwerp around 1487 (ISTC ir00136300; GW 12727),[105] *Jonathas ende Rosafiere*, which dates from around 1505 (NK 3165),[106] the *Strijt van Roncevale*, which incorporates lines from the *Roelantslied*, the Middle Dutch *Chanson de Roland*, and was published by Vorsterman about 1520 (NK 3907),[107] and finally *Seghelijn van Jherusalem*. This verse romance of no less than twelve thousand lines was reprinted in Antwerp at least four times.[108]

Parijs ende Vienna and *Seghelijn van Jherusalem* nicely illustrate the Antwerp reception of Middle Dutch romances. The printers who were active in this city in the period between *c.* 1480 and *c.* 1540 reckoned with varying literary tastes. There were readers who appreciated the printers' invitation to get acquainted with romances that were *en vogue* in the surrounding linguistic areas. Other readers, or the same ones at different moments, preferred the good old stories which had come down to them in earlier printed editions.

4 Conclusion

In this article, we have distinguished three stages in the development of Middle Dutch narrative literature. We have argued that each of these phases has its own defining characteristics. In the first phase, the manuscript period up to around

---

104 These editions are 's-Hertogenbosch: De Leempt, 1484–1488 (ISTC ic00204650; GW 12600); Delft: Van der Meer or Snellaert, 1487–1488 (ISTC ic00204700; GW 12601); Antwerp: Bac, 1493–1498 (ISTC ic00204750; GW 12602); Antwerp: Bac, 1496–1498 (ISTC ic00204760; GW 12604); Antwerp: Lettersnider, 1498 (ISTC ic00204770; GW 12603); Antwerp: Van Berghen or Van Doesborch, *c.* 1530 (NK 3166). The place of production of the *Karel ende Elegast* edition kept in Saint-Petersburg is unknown, see A.M. Duinhoven and G.A. van Thienen, 'Een onbekende druk van de *Karel ende Elegast* in Leningrad'. In: *TNTL* 106 (1990), p. 1–14.
105 Note that, as mentioned earlier, Leeu printed the *prose* version in Gouda nearly a decade earlier.
106 On this romance, see note 23. The text was reprinted twice between 1510 and 1515. See Faems (see note 23), p. 97–98, n. 6.
107 See Van Dijk (see note 24), p. 44–155.
108 See the article by Schaeps in the present volume, p. 297–324. For the printing of English verse romances, see the contributions by Boffey, p. 125–141, and Sánchez-Martí, p. 143–166.

1470, it is striking that, in contrast to French, English and German literature, the writing of romances seems to have stopped after the middle of the fourteenth century. Moreover, the prose form, so enthusiastically adopted by French authors, was almost completely ignored by Middle Dutch writers, as is shown by the absence of prosifications of verse romances in this period. Furthermore, a reception gap of almost three quarters of a century is clearly identifiable after around 1400. Middle Dutch romances were no longer read in Flanders and Brabant, the central parts of the Low Countries. They remained popular, however, in aristocratic milieus located in the eastern parts of the Low Countries and further eastwards.

The second stage in the development of Middle Dutch narrative literature is characterized by the introduction of printed texts. The early printers not only reintroduced Middle Dutch romances, they also adopted the prose form for these texts. Located in small towns in the northern parts of the Low Countries, they produced texts which were mainly Middle Dutch adaptations of Latin sources and Middle Dutch verse texts that circulated in manuscript copies. In contrast to their colleagues who printed French texts, the early printers of Middle Dutch texts preferred romances that had a strong didactic bias. Noteworthy is the continued production of verse texts, such as *Karel ende Elegast* and *Seghelijn van Jherusalem*, in this period.

Driven by commercial motives, the printing of Middle Dutch romances shifted from Holland to the metropolis of Antwerp in the 1480s. This is, in our view, the start of the third stage in the development of Middle Dutch narrative literature. This shift is surely not a unique case. A comparable transition took place in France. The production of French narrative literature began in cities such as Bruges, Genève and Lyons, before definitively moving to Paris around 1490.[109] The printers of English romances were right from the start located in London / Westminster.[110] The production of German romances seems to deviate from this pattern, because they were produced in a number of equally important printing centres, such as Augsburg, Basel, Cologne, Nürnberg and Straßburg.

It is noteworthy, furthermore, that in this third stage, the printers who produced Middle Dutch romances were more internationally orientated towards other vernaculars in their search for appealing sources. This international, in

---

109 See Roccati (see note 81), p. 108–113. On the concentration of printing in a small number of major cities in France, England and the Low Countries, see Andrew Pettegree, 'Centre and Periphery in the European Book World'. In: *Transactions of the Royal Historical Society*, 6th Series, 18 (2008), p. 101–128.

110 See Jordi Sánchez-Martí, 'The Printed History of the Middle English Verse Romances'. In: *Modern Philology* 107 (2009), p. 1–31, especially p. 11. See also his article in the present volume, p. 143–166.

particular French, orientation of the Antwerp printers is shared by their English and German colleagues.[111] Finally, printers in Antwerp adapted their material for a market which included readers who were attracted by new romances and readers who favoured texts that were part of an established literary tradition. We see the same happening in France and Germany.[112] English readers seem to have preferred prose and verse romances which had English antecedents.[113]

Bibliography

Adam, Renaud, 'Colard Mansion, passeur de textes?'. In: *Le Roman français dans les premiers imprimés*. Ed. by Anne Schoysman and Maria Colombo Timelli. Paris 2016 (Rencontres 147), p. 11–24.

Anrooij, Wim van, '"Poenten" in de Middelnederlandse letterkunde. Een geledingssysteem in het zakelijke en discursieve vertoog'. In: Wim van Anrooij et al., *Al t'Antwerpen in die stad. Jan van Boendale en de literaire cultuur van zijn tijd*. Amsterdam 2002 (Nederlandse literatuur en cultuur in de middeleeuwen 24), p. 65–80 and 166–168.

Backes, Martina, *Das literarische Leben am kurpfälzischen Hof zu Heidelberg im 15. Jahrhundert. Ein Beitrag zur Gönnerforschung des Spätmittelalters*. Tübingen 1992 (Hermaea 68).

Bastert, Bernd, 'Late Medieval Summations. *Rappoltsteiner Parzifal* and Ulrich Füetrer's *Buch der Abenteuer*'. In: *The Arthur of the Germans. The Arthurian Legend in Medieval German and Dutch Literature*. Ed. by W.H. Jackson and S. Ranawake. Cardiff 2000, p. 166–180.

Bastert, Bernd, '*Verus apostolus sicut Saxonia et Fresonia atque Westphalia*. Karl der Große in der Literatur der *Nideren Lande*'. In: *Zeitschrift für deutsche Philologie* 122 (2003), Sonderheft: *Regionale Literaturgeschichtsschreibung. Aufgaben, Analysen und Perspektiven*. Ed. by Helmut Tervooren and Jens Haustein, p. 74–80.

Bastert, Bernd, 'Heiliger, Hochzeiter, Heidenschlächter. Die Karlmeinet-Kompilation zwischen Oberdeutschland und den *Nideren Landen*'. In: *Schnittpunke. Deutsch-Niederländische Literaturbeziehungen im späten Mittelalter*. Ed. by Angelika Lehmann-Benz, Ulrike Zellmann and Urban Küsters. New York etc. 2003 (Studien zur Geschichte und Kultur Nordwesteuropas 5), p. 125–143.

Bastert, Bernd, *Helden als Heilige*. Chanson de geste-*Rezeption im deutschsprachigen Raum*. Tübingen, Basel 2010 (Bibliotheca Germanica 54).

111 See the contributions by Boffey (p. 134) and Bertelsmeier-Kierst (p. 22–28) in the present volume. For William Caxton's preference for French source material, see Jordi Sánchez-Martí, 'The Printed Transmission of Medieval Romance from William Caxton to Wynkyn de Worde, 1473–1533'. In: *The Transmission of Medieval Romance: Metres, Manuscripts and Early Prints*. Ed. by Ad Putter and Judith A. Jefferson. Cambridge 2018, p. 170–190.
112 See Roccati (see note 81) and the article by Bertelsmeier-Kierst in the present volume, p. 17–47.
113 See Jordi Sánchez-Martí, 'The Printed History' (note 110) and 'The Printed Transmission' (note 111) and his article in the present volume, p. 143–166.

Baudelle-Michels, Sarah, '*Renaut de Montauban* ou *Les Quatre Fils Aymon* (prose vulgate)'. In: *Nouveau Répertoire de mises en prose (XIVᵉ-XVIᵉ siècle)*. Ed. by Maria Colombo Timelli et al. Paris 2014 (Textes littéraires du moyen âge 30), p. 699–716.

Beckers, Hartmut, '*Desse boke de horn den greve van der hoien vnde sint altomale dudesk*. Ein Versuch zur literarhistorischen Identifizierung des Handschriftenbestandes einer niedersächsischen Adelsbibliothek des späten 15. Jahrhunderts'. In: *Niederdeutsches Wort* 16 (1976), p. 126–143.

Beckers, Hartmut, '*Der püecher haubet, die von der tafelrunde wunder sagen*. Wirich von Stein und die Verbreitung des "Prosa-Lancelot" im 15. Jh.'. In: *Wolfram-Studien* IX. *Schweinfurter 'Lancelot'-Kolloquium 1984*. Ed. by Werner Schröder. Berlin 1986, p. 17–44.

Beckers, Hartmut, 'Frühneuhochdeutsche Fassungen niederländischer Erzählliteratur im Umkreis des pfalzgräflichen Hofes zu Heidelberg um 1450/80'. In: *Miscellanea neerlandica. Opstellen voor dr. Jan Deschamps ter gelegenheid van zijn zeventigste verjaardag*. Ed. by Elly Cockx-Indestege and Frans Hendrickx. Vol. 2. Leuven 1987 (Miscellanea Neerlandica 2), p. 237–249

Beckers, Hartmut, 'Handschriften mittelalterlicher deutscher Literatur aus der ehemaligen Schloßbibliothek Blankenheim'. In: *Die Manderscheider. Eine Eifeler Adelsfamilie. Herrschaft – Wirtschaft – Kultur*. Katalog zur Ausstellung. Blankenheim, Gildehaus 4. Mai– 29. Juli 1990, Manderscheid, Kurhaus 16. August – 11. November 1990. Köln 1990, p. 57–82.

Beckers, Hartmut, 'Literarische Interessenbildung bei einem rheinischen Grafengeschlecht um 1470/80: Die Blankenheimer Schloßbibliothek'. In: *Literarische Interessenbildung im Mittelater. DFG-Symposion 1991*. Ed. by Joachim Heinzle. Stuttgart, Weimar 1993 (Germanistische Symposien. Berichtsbände 14), p. 5–20.

Beckers, Hartmut, 'Die *Karlmeinet*-Kompilation: Eine deutsche *vita poetica Karoli Magni* aus dem frühen 14. Jahrhundert'. In: *Cyclification. The Development of Narrative Cycles in the Chansons de Geste and the Arthurian Romances*. Ed. by Bart Besamusca, Willem P. Gerritsen, Corry Hogetoorn and Orlanda S.H. Lie. Amsterdam et al. 1994, p. 113–117.

Berendrecht, Petra, *Proeven van bekwaamheid. Jacob van Maerlant en de omgang met zijn Latijnse bronnen*. Amsterdam 1996 (Nederlandse literatuur en cultuur in de Middeleeuwen 14).

Berteloot, Amand, 'Zur Datierung von *Reynaerts historie*'. In: *Sprache in Vergangenheit und Gegenwart. Beiträge aus dem Institut für Germanistische Sprachwissenschaft der Philipps-Universität Marburg*. Ed. by Wolfgang Brandt. Marburg 1988, p. 26–31.

Berteloot, Amand, 'Gewollt oder nicht gekonnt? Oder erst gar nicht gewollt? Der Heidelberger "Ogier von Dänemark"'. In: *ZfdPh* 130 (2011), Sonderheft: *Dialog mit den Nachbarn. Mittelniederländische Literatur zwischen dem 12. und dem 16. Jahrhundert*. Ed. by Helmut Tervooren, Bernd Bastert and Frank Willaert, p. 193–201.

Bertelsmeier-Kierst, Christa, 'Erzählen in Prosa. Zur Entwicklung des deutschen Prosaromans bis 1500'. In: *ZfdA* 143 (2014), p. 141–165.

Besamusca, Bart, *Repertorium van de Middelnederlandse Karelepiek. Een beknopte beschrijving van de handschriftelijke en gedrukte overlevering*. Utrecht 1983.

Besamusca, Bart, 'Willem Vorsterman's *Sibilla*: the Dutch Story of Charlemagne's Repudiated Wife'. In: *L'imaginaire courtois et son double*. Ed. by Giovanna Angeli and Luciano Formisano. Napoli 1992, p. 245–254.

Besamusca, Bart, 'The Prevalence of Verse in Medieval Dutch and English Arthurian Fiction'. In: *Journal of English and Germanic Philology* 112 (2013), p. 461–474.

Besamusca, Bart, 'De geschiedenis van Alexander de Grote in vier vroege drukken'. In: *Jaarboek voor Nederlandse boekgeschiedenis* 22 (2015), p. 123–140.

Besamusca, Bart, 'Raoul Lefèvre in Dutch: Two 1521 Editions of the Antwerp Printer Jan van Doesborch'. In: *JEBS* 20 (2017), p. 219–232.

Besamusca, Bart, 'Tekst en beeld in twee drukken van Jan van Doesborch: *Van Jason ende Hercules* en *Die historie van den stercken Hercules*'. In: *SpdL* 59 (2017), p. 1–34.

Besamusca, Bart, Hans van Dijk (eds), Thea Summerfield (transl.), '*Karel ende Elegast*'. In: *Olifant* 26 (2011), p. 51–165.

Biemans, Jos, Hans Kienhorst, Willem Kuiper and Rob Resoort (eds), *Het handschrift-Borgloon*. Hs. Amsterdam, Universiteitsbibliotheek (UvA), I A 24 *l, m, n*. Diplomatische editie. Hilversum 2000 (Middeleeuwse verzamelhandschriften uit de Nederlanden 5).

Blockmans, Wim, 'Contingentie van literaire milieus.' In: *Het Gruuthusehandschrift. Literatuur, muziek, devotie rond 1400*. Ed. by Frank Willaert, Jos Koldeweij and Johan Oosterman. Internationaal congres Brugge, 25–27 april 2013. Gent 2015, p. 19–39.

Bloh, Ute von, 'Anders gefragt: Vers oder Prosa? "Reinolt von Montalban" und andere Übersetzungen aus dem Mittelniederländischen im Umkreis des Heidelberger Hofes'. In: *Wolfram-Studien* XIV. *Übersetzen im Mittelalter*. Ed. by Joachim Heinzle, L. Peter Johnson and Gisela Vollmann-Profe. Cambridger Kolloquium 1994. Berlin 1996, p. 265–293.

Bogaart, Saskia, *Geleerde kennis in de volkstaal*. Van den proprieteyten der dinghen *(Haarlem 1485) in perspectief*. Hilversum 2004.

Bree, Fred de, 'Gheraert Leeu als drukker van Nederlands verhalend proza'. In: *Een drukker zoekt publiek. Gheraert Leeu te Gouda 1477–1484*. Ed. by Koen Goudriaan et al. Delft 1993, p. 61–80.

Bruijn, Elisabeth de, 'Reculer pour mieux sauter: de bronnenproblematiek en de literaire eigenheid van de Middelnederlandse *Helias*'. In: *Verslagen en Mededelingen van de Koninklijke Academie voor Nederlandse Taal- en Letterkunde* 126 (2016), p. 227–263.

Bruijn, Elisabeth de, 'Das Spiel der Stimmen. Performative Verspassagen in einigen niederländischen Prosaromanen (ca. 1500–1540)'. In: *Stimme und Performanz in der mittelalterlichen Literatur*. Ed. by Monica Unzeitig, Nine Miedema and Angela Schrott. Berlin 2017, p. 133–154.

Bruijn, Elisabeth de, '*Galien Rethore* herontdekt'. In: *Madoc* 31 (2017), p. 75–82.

Bruijn, Elisabeth de, 'To Content the Continent. The Dutch Narratives *Merlijn* and *Jacke* Compared to Their English Counterparts'. In: *TNTL* 133 (2017), p. 83–108.

Buchinger, Danielle, 'Rezeption der chanson de geste in Spätmittelalter'. In: *Wolfram-Studien* XI. *Chansons de geste in Deutschland*. Ed. by Joachim Heinzle, L. Peter Johnson and Gisela Vollman-Profe. Schweinfurter Kolloquium 1988. Berlin 1989, p. 86–106.

Caers, Bram, 'Een *buchelin inn flemische*. Over ontstaan en verspreiding van de ridderepiek in de Nederlanden (ca. 1150–1450)'. In: *TNTL* 127 (2011), p. 223–251.

Caers, Bram and Mike Kestemont, 'Over de datering van de Middelnederlandse ridderepiek'. In: *Verslagen en Mededelingen van de Koninklijke Academie voor Nederlandse Taal- en Letterkunde* 121 (2011), p. 1–59.

Cermann, R., 'Die Bibliothek Herzog Eberhards im Bart von Württemberg (1445–1496)'. In: *Scriptorium* 51 (1997), p. 30–50.

Claassens, Geert H.M., '"Doe leefde hi soe heilichlike". *Seghelijn van Jherusalem* tussen ridderepiek en hagiografie,' In: *Ene andre tale. Tendensen in de Middelnederlandse late ridderepiek*. Ed. by An Faems and Marjolein Hogenbirk. Hilversum 2012 (Middeleeuwse Studies en Bronnen 131), p. 195–212.

Coleman, Janet, *Public Reading and the Reading Public in Late Medieval England and France*. Cambridge 1996.

Colombo Timelli, Maria et al. (eds), *Nouveau Répertoire de mises en prose (XIVe-XVIe siècle)*. Paris 2014 (Textes littéraires du moyen âge 30).

Corpus catalogorum Belgii. The Medieval Booklists of the Southern Low Countries. Ed. by Albert Derolez. Vol. 3: *Counts of Flanders. provinces of East Flanders, Antwerp and Limburg*. Brussel 1999.

Cowen, Janet M., 'Die mittelenglischen Romane um Karl den Großen'. In: *Karl der Große in den europäischen Literaturen des Mittelalters. Konstruktion eines Mythos*. Ed. by Bernd Bastert. Tübingen 2004, p. 163–182.

Cramer, Thomas, 'Aspekte des höfischen Romans im 14. Jahrhundert'. In: *Zur deutschen Literatur und Sprache des 14. Jahrhunderts*. Ed. by Walter Haug, Timothy R. Jackson and Johannes Janota. Dubliner Colloquium 1981. Heidelberg 1983 (Reihe Siegen 45), p. 208–220.

Cuijpers, Peter M.H., *Teksten als koopwaar: vroege drukkers verkennen de markt. Een kwantitatieve analyse van de productie van Nederlandstalige boeken (tot circa 1550) en de 'lezershulp' in de seculiere prozateksten*. Nieuwkoop 1998.

Debaene, Luc., 'Nederlandse prozaromans en Spaanse "Libros de caballerias"'. In: *Liber alumnorum Prof. Dr. E. Rombauts, aangeboden ter gelegenheid van zijn vijfenzestigste verjaardag en zijn dertigjarig hoogleraarschap*. Leuven 1968, p. 129–144.

Debaene, Luc., *De Nederlandse volksboeken. Ontstaan en geschiedenis van de Nederlandse prozaromans, gedrukt tussen 1475 en 1540*. 2nd ed. Hulst 1977.

Deschamps, J., *Middelnederlandse handschriften uit Europese en Amerikaanse bibliotheken. Tentoonstelling ter gelegenheid van het honderdjarig bestaan van de Koninklijke Zuidnederlandse Maatschappij voor Taal- en letterkunde en Geschiedenis*. Brussel, Koninklijke Bibliotheek Albert I, 24 okt.–24 dec. 1970. *Catalogus*, 2nd ed. Leiden 1972.

Deschamps, J. and H. Mulder, *Inventaris van de Middelnederlandse handschriften van de Koninklijke Bibliotheek van België*. Vol. 1. Brussel 1998.

Der deutsche Malagis. Nach den Heidelberger Handschriften Cpg 340 und Cpg 315. Ed. by Annegret Haase, Bob W.Th. Duijvestijn, Gilbert A.R. de Smet and Rudolf Bentzinger. Berlin 2000 (Deutsche Texte des Mittelalters 82).

Dijk, H. van, *Het Roelantslied. Studie over de Middelnederlandse vertaling van het Chanson de Roland, gevolgd door een diplomatische uitgave van de overgeleverde teksten*. 2 vols. Utrecht 1981.

Doutrepont, Georges, *La littérature française à la cour des ducs de Bourgogne. Philippe le Hardi – Jean sans Peur – Philippe le Bon – Charles le Téméraire*. Paris 1909.

Doutrepont, Georges, *Les Mises en prose des épopées et des romans chevaleresques du XIVe au XVIe siècle*. Bruxelles 1939 (Académie royale de Belgique. Classe des lettres et des sciences morales et politiques. Mémoires, vol. 40).

Duijvestijn, Bob, 'Niederländische Dichtung in der Privatbücherei der Pfalzgräfin Mechthild (1418/19–1482)'. In: *Miscellanea neerlandica. Opstellen voor dr. Jan Deschamps ter gelegenheid van zijn zeventigste verjaardag*. Ed. by Elly Cockx-Indestege and Frans Hendrickx. Vol. 2. Leuven 1987, (Miscellanea Neerlandica 2), p. 251–261.

Duijvestijn, Bob, 'Madelgijs, zwerftocht van een epische stof'. In: *Van Madelgijs tot Malagis. Een bundel opstellen n.a.v. de tachtigste verjaardag van Gilbert de Smet*. Ed. by Georges de Schutter and Jan Goossens. Gent 2002, p. 23–34.

Duinhoven, A.M. and G.A. van Thienen, 'Een onbekende druk van de *Karel ende Elegast* in Leningrad'. In: *TNTL* 106 (1990), p. 1–14.

Der Ehrenbrief des Pütrich von Reichertshausen. Ed. by Fritz Behrend and Rudolf Wolkan. Weimar 1920.

Faems, An, '*Jonathas ende Rosafiere*: (religieuze) ridderroman of Mariamirakel?'. In: *Queeste 7* (2000), p. 97–112.

Faems, An, 'De Middelnederlandse late ridderepiek: "bleeke spookgestalten" krijgen kleur'. In: *Ene andre tale. Tendensen in de Middelnederlandse late ridderepiek*. Ed. by An Faems and Marjolein Hogenbirk. Hilversum 2012 (Middeleeuwse Studies en Bronnen 131), p. 11–36.

Finet-van der Schaaf, Baukje, 'Le roman en prose néerlandais de la reine Sibille et son modèle espagnol: *La Hystoria de la Reyna Sebilla*'. In: *Charlemagne in the North: Proceedings of the Twelfth International Conference of the Société Rencesvals*. Ed. by Philip E. Bennett, Anne Elisabeth Cobby and Graham A. Runnalls. Edinburgh 1993, p. 31–43.

Finet-van der Schaaf, Baukje, 'Les incunables français, néerlandais, allemand et anglais de *L'histoire du très vaillant chevalier Paris et de la belle Vienne, fille du dauphin* et leur rapport à la tradition française manuscrite du récit'. In: *L'épopée romane. Actes du XVᵉ congrès international Rencesvals. Poitiers, 21–27 août 2000*. 2 vols. Ed. by Gabriel Bianciotto and Claudio Galderisi. Poitiers 2002, p. 825–836.

Fischer, Irmgard, 'Beschreibung der Handschrift S 526 der Universitätsbibliothek Bonn'. In: *Lancelot en prose. Farbmikrofische-Edition der Handschrift Bonn, Universitätsbibliothek, Handschrift S 526*. München 1992, p. 26–30.

Franssen, P.J.A., *Tussen tekst en publiek. Jan van Doesborch, drukker-uitgever en literator te Antwerpen en Utrecht in de eerste helft van de zestiende eeuw*. Amsterdam 1990.

Fürbeth, Frank, 'Der "Karlmeinet": Vita poetica oder Vita historica Caroli Magni? Zur Differenz von textimmanenter und textexterner Kohärenz'. In: *Texttyp und Textproduktion in der deutschen Literatur des Mittelalters*. Ed. by Elisabeth Andersen, Manfred Eikelmann and Anne Simon. Berlin, New York 2005 (Trends in Medieval Philology 7), p. 217–234.

Gerritsen, W.P., 'Een onbekende prozaversie van Maerlants *Aeneis*-bewerking'. In: *Miscellanea Neerlandica. Opstellen voor dr. Jan Deschamps ter gelegenheid van zijn zeventigste verjaardag*. Ed. by Elly Cockx-Indestege and Frans Hendrickx. Vol. 2. Leuven 1987 (Miscellanea Neerlandica 2), p. 163–174.

Gingras, Francis, *Le Bâtard conquérant. Essor et expansion du genre romanesque au Moyen Âge*. Paris 2011 (Nouvelle bibliothèque du moyen âge 106).

Goudriaan, Koen et al. (eds), *Een drukker zoekt publiek. Gheraert Leeu te Gouda 1477–1484*. Delft 1993.

Grauwe, Luc de, 'Das historische Verhältnis deutsch-niederländisch 'revisited'. Zur Nicht-Existenz von Einheitsarealen im Sprachbewußtsein des Mittelalters und der beginnenden Neuzeit'. In: *ABäG* 35 (1992), p. 191–205.

Hauwaerts, Evelien, Evelien de Wilde and Ludo Vandamme (eds), *Colard Mansion. Incunabula, Prints and Manuscripts in Medieval Bruges*. S.l. 2018.

Hellinga, Lotte, *Texts in Transit: Manuscript to Proof and Print in the Fifteenth Century*. Leiden 2014.

Hellinga, Lotte, 'William Caxton and Colard Mansion'. In: *Colard Mansion. Incunabula, Prints and Manuscripts in Medieval Bruges*. Ed. by Evelien Hauwaerts, Evelien de Wilde and Ludo Vandamme. S.l. 2018, p. 63–71.

Herweg, Mathias, 'Herkommen und Herrschaft: Zur Signatur der Spätausläufer des deutschen Versromans um 1300'. In: *Archiv für das Studium der neueren Sprachen und Literaturen* 156 (2004), p. 241–287.

Hoogstra, S.S., *Proza-bewerkingen van het Leven van Alexander den Groote in het Middelnederlandsch*. 's-Gravenhage 1898.

Hoorebeeck, Céline van, 'Les lectures "romanesques" des officiers des ducs de Bourgogne (ca 1420–1520)'. In: *Le romanesque aux XIVe et XVe siècles*. Ed. by Danièle Bohler. Bordeaux 2009, p. 257–268.

Hoorebeeck, Céline van, *Livres et lectures de fonctionnaires des ducs de Bourgogne (ca 1420–1520)*. Turnhout 2014 (Texte, Codex et Contexte 16).

Inventaris van incunabelen gedrukt te Antwerpen 1481–1500. Antwerpen 1982 (Publikaties van de stadsbibliotheek en het archief en museum voor het Vlaamse cultuurleven 1).

Jacob van Maerlants Historie van den Grale und Boek van Merline. Nach der Steinfurter Handschrift herausgegeben von Timothy Sodmann. Köln, Wien 1980 (Niederdeutsche Studien 26).

Jacob van Maerlants Spiegel historiael, met de fragmenten der later toegevoegde gedeelten bewerkt door Philip Utenbroeke en Lodewijc van Velthem. Ed. by M. de Vries and E. Verwijs. Vol. 3. Leiden 1863.

Kalff, G., *Middelnederlandsche epische fragmenten met aanteekeningen*. Groningen 1885 (Bibliotheek van Nederlandsche letterkunde 38).

Karel ende Elegast und Karl und Ellegast. Ed. and transl. by Bernd Bastert, Bart Besamusca and Carla Dauven-van Knippenberg. Münster 2005 (Bibliothek mittelniederländischer Literatur 1).

Keesman, Wilma, 'Jacob Bellaert en Haarlem'. In: *Haarlems Helicon. Literatuur en toneel te Haarlem vóór 1800* Ed. by E.K. Grootes. Hilversum 1993, p. 27–48.

Keesman, Wilma, *De eindeloze stad. Troje en Trojaanse oorsprongsmythen in de (laat) middeleeuwse en vroegmoderne Nederlanden*. Hilversum 2017 (Middeleeuwse studies en bronnen 159).

Kellner, Beate, 'Literarische Kontexte und pragmatische Bezugsfelder im spätmittelalterlichen Roman *Friedrich von Schwaben*'. In: *Dialoge. Sprachliche Kommunikation in und zwischen Texten im deutschen Mittelalter*. Ed. by Nikolaus Henkel, Martin H. Jones and Nigel F. Palmer. Hamburger Colloquium 1999. Tübingen 2003, p. 135–158.

Kienhorst, Hans, *De handschriften van de Middelnederlandse ridderepiek. Een codicologische beschrijving*. 2 vols. Deventer 1988.

Kienhorst, Hans, 'Fragment van een onbekende Middelnederlandse roman over Willem van Oringen'. In: *TNTL* 114 (1998), p. 125–137.

Klein, Jan Willem, '"Het getal zijner jaren is onnaspeurlijk". Een herijking van de dateringen van de handschriften en fragmenten met Middelnederlandse ridderepiek'. In: *TNTL* 111 (1995), p. 1–23.

Klein, Jan Willem, 'Ghescreven ofte gheprent. Aspecten van de (Goudse) middeleeuwse boekproductie'. In: Herman Pleij, Joris Reynaert et al., *Geschreven en gedrukt. Boekproductie van handschrift naar druk in de overgang van Middeleeuwen naar Moderne tijd*. Gent 2004, p. 67–83.

Klein, Thomas, 'Die Rezeption mittelniederländischer Versdichtungen im Rheinland und Augustijns "Herzog von Braunschweig"'. In: *Die spätmittelalterliche Rezeption niederländischer Literatur im deutschen Sprachgebiet* (ABäG 47 1997). Ed. by Rita Schlusemann and Paul Wackers, p. 78–107.

Knapp, Fritz Peter, '10.4. Der deutsche "Prosa-Lancelot"'. In: *Höfischer Roman in Vers und Prosa*. Ed. by René Pérennec and Elisabeth Schmid. Berlin, New York 2010 (Germania Litteraria Mediaevalis Francigena 5), p. 415–424.

Kuiper, Willem, '*Die Destructie van Jherusalem* in handschrift en druk'. In: *Voortgang, jaarboek voor de neerlandistiek* 25 (2007), p. 67–88.

Lacaze, Yvon, 'Le Rôle des traditions dans la genèse d'un sentiment national au 15e siècle. La Bourgogne de Philippe le Bon'. In: *Bibliothèque de l'École des Chartes* 129 (1971), p. 303–385.

Lie, Orlanda S.H., *The Middle Dutch Prose Lancelot. A Study of the Rotterdam Fragments and their Place in the French, German, and Dutch Lancelot en prose Tradition*. Amsterdam, Oxford, New York 1987 (Middelnederlandse Lancelotromans 3).

Lie, Orlanda S.H., 'The Flemish Exemplar of Ms.W. f°46* Blankenheim, a Fifteenth-Century German Translation of the *Suite de la Charrette*'. In: *Arturus Rex. Vol. 2 Actus Conventus Lovaniensis 1987*. Ed. by Willy van Hoecke, Gilbert Tournoy and Werner Verbeke. Leuven 1991 (Mediaevalia Lovaniensia 1/17), p. 404–418.

Margriete van Limborch: Roman van Heinric en Margriete van Limborch, uitgegeven volgens het Brusselse handschrift. Ed. by Rob Meesters. Amsterdam, Antwerpen 1951.

Minnen, Bart and Geert Claassens, 'De *Roman van Lancelot* in Middelnederlands proza. Het fragment-Wezemaal'. In: *TNTL* 121 (2005), p. 169–183.

Moolenbroek, Jaap van and Maaike Mulder (eds), *Scolastica willic ontbinden. Over de Rijmbijbel van Jacob van Maerlant*. Hilversum 1991.

Mühlethaler, Jean-Claude, 'Vers statt Prosa. Schreiben gegen den Strom im Frankreich des ausgehenden Mittelalters'. In: *Eulenspiegel trifft Melusine. Der frühneuhochdeutsche Prosaroman im Licht neuer Forschungen und Methoden*. Ed. by Catherine Drittenbass and André Schnyder. Akten der Lausanner Tagung von 2. bis 4. Oktober 2008. Amsterdam 2010 (Chloe 42), p. 163–182.

Müller, Jan-Dirk, 'Volksbuch/Prosaroman im 15./16. Jahrhundert – Perspektiven der Forschung'. In: *Internationales Archiv für Sozialgeschichte der Literatur: Sonderheft Forschungsreferate* 1 (1985), p. 1–128.

Nave, Francine de, 'Een typografische hoofdstad in opkomst, bloei en verval'. In: *Antwerpen, verhaal van een metropool*. Ed. by J. Van der Stock. Gent, 1993, p. 87–95.

Oostrom, Frits van, *Maerlants wereld*. Amsterdam 1996.

Overgaauw, Everardus A., 'Die Dycksche Handschrift. Ihre Entdeckung, Herkunft, Datierung und früheren Besitzer'. In: *Die Dycksche Handschrift*. Ed. by Bertram Haller and Hans Mühl. Berlin, Münster 1992, p. 40–58.

Overgaauw, Eef, *Die mittelalterlichen Handschriften der Universitäts- und Landesbibliothek Münster*. Wiesbaden 1996.

Pettegree, Andrew, 'Centre and Periphery in the European Book World'. In: *Transactions of the Royal Historical Society*, 6th Series, 18 (2008), p. 101–128.

Pleij, Herman, 'De betekenis van de beginnende drukpers voor de ontwikkeling van de Nederlandse literatuur in Noord en Zuid'. In: *Spektator* 21 (1992), p. 227–263.

Pleij, Herman, 'Over betekenis en belang van de leesinstructie in de gedrukte proza-Reynaert van 1479'. In: Herman Pleij, Joris Reynaert et al., *Geschreven en gedrukt. Boekproductie van handschrift naar druk in de overgang van Middeleeuwen naar Moderne tijd*. Gent 2004, p. 207–232.

Pleij, Herman, *Het gevleugelde woord. Geschiedenis van de Nederlandse literatuur 1400–1560*. Amsterdam 2007.

Resoort, Rob, 'Het raadsel van de rijmdrukken'. In: *Nederlandse Letterkunde* 3 (1998), p. 309–326.

Reynaerts historie. Ed. and transl. by Rita Schlusemann and Paul Wackers. Münster 2005 (Bibliothek mittelniederländischer Literatur 2).

Rijns, Hans (ed.), *De gedrukte Nederlandse Reynaerttraditie. Een diplomatische en synoptische uitgave naar de bronnen vanaf 1479 tot 1700*. Hilversum 2007 (Middeleeuwse Studies en Bronnen 100).

Robrecht de duyvel. Ed. by Rob Resoort. Muiderberg 1980.

Roccati, Giovanni Matteo, 'Le roman dans les incunables. L'impact des stratégies éditoriales dans le choix des titres imprimés'. In: *Le Roman français dans les premiers imprimés*. Ed. by Anne Schoysman and Maria Colombo Timelli. Paris 2016 (Rencontres 147), p. 95–126.

Rothstein, Katja, *Der mittelhochdeutsche Prosa-Lancelot. Eine entstehungs- und überlieferungsgeschichtliche Untersuchung unter besonderer Berücksichtigung der Handschrift Ms. allem. 8017–8020*. Frankfurt am Main etc. 2007 (Kultur, Wissenschaft, Literatur. Beiträge zur Mittelalterforschung 15).

Rouzet, Anne, *Dictionnaire des imprimeurs, libraires et éditeurs des XVe et XVIe siècles dans les limites géographiques de la Belgique actuelle*. Nieuwkoop 1975.

Sánchez-Martí, Jordi, 'The Printed History of the Middle English Verse Romances'. In: *Modern Philology* 107 (2009), p. 1–31.

Sánchez-Martí, Jordi, 'The Printed Transmission of Medieval Romance from William Caxton to Wynkyn de Worde, 1473–1533'. In: *The Transmission of Medieval Romance: Metre, Manuscripts and Early Prints*. Ed. by Ad Putter and Judith Jefferson. Cambridge 2018, p. 170–190.

Schlusemann, Rita, *Die hystorie van reynaert die vos und The history of reynaerd the fox. Die spätmittelalterlichen Prosabearbeitungen des Reynaert-Stoffes*. Frankfurt am Main 1991.

Schlusemann, Rita, 'Buchmarkt in Antwerpen am Anfang des 16. Jahrhunderts'. In: *Laienlektüre und Buchmarkt im späten Mittelalter*. Ed. by Thomas Kock and Rita Schlusemann. Frankfurt am Main 1997, p. 33–59.

Schlusemann, Rita, 'Literarische Beziehungen als Quelle für buchhistorische Fragen. Die fränkischen Rheinlande in der zweiten Hälfte des 15. Jahrhunderts'. In: *Sources for the History of Medieval Books and Libraries*. Ed. by Rita Schlusemann, Jos M.M. Hermans and Margriet Hoogvliet. Groningen 2000, p. 95–107.

Schlusemann, Rita, 'The Late-Medieval German Reception of Dutch Arthurian Literature in Heidelberg and Blankenheim'. In: *King Arthur in the Medieval Low Countries*. Ed. by Geert H.M. Claassens and David F. Johnson. Leuven 2000 (Mediaevalia Lovaniensia 1, 28), p. 97–111.

Schlusemann, Rita, 'Wechselseitige niederdeutsch/niederländische Literaturbeziehungen in der frühen gedruckten Erzähldichtung. Mit einer Edition des Magdeburger Drucks der *Historie van twen kopluden* (um 1495)'. In: *Jahrbuch des Vereins für niederdeutsche Sprachforschung* 125 (2002), p. 97–130.

Schlusemann, Rita, *Schöne Historien. Niederländische Romane im deutschen Spätmittelalter und in der frühen Neuzeit*. Berlin, Boston 2016 (Frühe Neuzeit, 203).

Schubert, Martin J., 'Nederlands-Duitse betrekkingen op het gebied van taal en literatuur in de late Middeleeuwen. Over de manier waarop *Malagis, Ogier* en *Reinolt* vertaald zijn.' In: *Van Madelgijs tot Malagis. Een bundel opstellen verzameld n.a.v. de tachtigste verjaardag van Gilbert de Smet*. Ed. by Georges de Schutter and Jan Goossens. Gent 2002, p. 53–64.

Sleiderink, Remco, *De stem van de meester. De hertogen van Brabant en hun rol in het literaire leven (1106–1430)*. Amsterdam 2003 (Nederlandse literatuur en cultuur in de middeleeuwen 25).

Sleiderink, Remco, "Une si belle histoire de nos propres seigneurs." La noblesse brabançonne et la littérature en néerlandais (première moitié du XIVe siècle)'. In: *Le Moyen Âge* 113 (2007), p. 549–567.

Speakman Sutch, Susie, 'De Gouda-editie van *Le Chevalier délibéré*. Een boek uitgegeven in eigen beheer'. In: Herman Pleij, Joris Reynaert et al., *Geschreven en gedrukt. Boekproductie van handschrift naar druk in de overgang van Middeleeuwen naar Moderne tijd*. Gent 2004, p. 137–155.

Tervooren, Helmut, 'Zur Rezeption mittelniederländischer Literatur in Köln: ein neues Bruchstück des "Parthonopeus"'. In: *Rheinische Vierteljahrsblätter* 49 (1985), p. 92–116.

Tervooren, Helmut, '"Parthonopeus von Blois" (ripuar. Fragment)'. In: ²*VL* 7 (1989), col. 315–316.

Vandamme, Ludo, 'Colard Mansion et le monde du livre à Bruges'. In: *Le berceau du livre imprimé, autour des incunables*. Ed. by Pierre Aquilon and Thierry Claerr. Turnhout 2010, p. 177–186.

De vijfhonderdste verjaring van de boekdrukkunst in de Nederlanden. Catalogus. Brussel 1973.

Wackers, Paul, 'The Printed Dutch Reynaert Tradition: From the Fifteenth to the Nineteenth Century'. In: *Reynard the Fox. Social Engagement and Cultural Metamorphoses in the Beast Epic from the Middle Ages to the Present*. Ed. by Kenneth Varty. New York, Oxford 2000, p. 73–103.

Walsby, Malcolm, 'The Vanishing Press: Printing in Provincial France in the Early Sixteenth Century'. In: *The Book Triumphant: Print in Transition in the Sixteenth and Seventeenth Centuries*. Ed. by Malcolm Walsby and Graeme Kemp. Leiden, Boston 2011, p. 97–111.

Walter, Philippe, 'Tout commence par des chansons… (Intertextualités lotharingiennes)'. In: *Styles et valeurs. Pour une histoire de l'art littéraire au moyen âge*. Ed. by D. Poirion. Paris 1990, p. 187–209.

Weifenbach, Beate, 'Johann Koelhoff der Jüngere: Die *Vier Heymschen Kynderen*. Die Bedeutung der Kölner Inkunabel aus dem Jahre 1493 für die Drucktradition von Haimonskindertexten in Deutschland'. In: *ABäG* 51 (1999), p. 169–193.

Wijsman, Hanno, *Luxury Bound. Illustrated Manuscript Production and Noble and Princely Book Ownership in the Burgundian Netherlands (1400–1550)*. Turnhout 2010 (Burgundica 16).

Willaert, Frank, *De ruimte van het boek. Literaire regio's in de Lage Landen tijdens de middeleeuwen*. Leiden 2010 (Negentiende Bert van Selm-lezing).

Winkelman, Johan H., *De staart van Meluzine*. Amsterdam 2000.

Woledge, Brian, *Bibliographie des romans et nouvelles en prose française antérieurs à 1500*. Genève 1975 [1954] (Société de publications romanes et françaises 42).

Woledge, Brian, *Bibliographie des romans et nouvelles en prose française antérieurs à 1500*. Supplément 1954–1975. Genève 1975 (Publications romanes et françaises 130).

Zeldenrust, Lydia, 'Serpent or Half-Serpent? Bernhard Richel's *Melusine* and the Making of a Western European Icon'. In: *Neophilologus* 100 (2016), p. 19–41.

Zeldenrust, Lydia,'The Lady with the Serpent's Tail: Hybridity and the Dutch *Meluzine*'. In: *Melusine's Footprint: Tracing the Legacy of a Medieval Myth*. Ed. by Misty Urban, Deva F. Kemmis and Melissa Ridley Elmes. Leiden 2017 (Explorations in Medieval Culture 4), p. 132–145.

Elisabeth de Bruijn

The Southern Appeal: Dutch Translations of French Romances (*c.* 1484–*c.* 1540) in a Western European Perspective

Abstracts: French literature was by far the most important source of inspiration for the transla-tion, adaptation and creation of medieval romances in other Western European languages. Although this is already well-established for the manuscript period, the importance of French subject matter after the advent of printing merits further research. This article deals with the early printed transmission of Dutch romances translated from the French until *c.* 1540. It sheds light on some chronological developments in the reception of these romances in the Low Countries by focusing on the publishers' lists of a number of printers as well as on the texts' longevity. Additionally, this article adopts a synchronic view: in order to understand the international appeal of some works, other Western European translations of these titles are also taken into consideration. It turns out that Dutch and English publishers show an interest in similar French subject matter. However, the Dutch editions reveal a higher degree of inter-ference with the text: they tend to make use of multiple sources, remove the names of histori-cal agents involved in the creation of the romances, or include dramatic and lyrical verses, suggesting the influence of rhetoricians and thereby indicating a more urban public.

La littérature française était de loin la plus importante source d'inspiration pour la traduction, l'adaptation et la création de romans médiévaux dans les autres langues de l'Europe occidentale. Cette primauté, désormais largement étudiée pour les siècles des traductions manuscrites, se sera prolongée après l'introduction de l'imprimerie. Le present article interroge donc la transmis-sion imprimée, à ce jour toujours bien moins explorée, de romans néerlandais traduits du français avant c. 1540. Nous nous concentrons pour l'essentiel sur une collection de fonds d'im-primeurs ainsi que sur la longévité des textes, qui devraient nous permettre de jeter une nouvelle lumière sur la réception de ces romans dans les anciens Pays-Bas. S'y ajoute une perspective synchronique: afin de mieux comprendre le rayonnement international de certains textes, nous avons également pris en consideration d'autres traductions dans des langues de l'Europe occi-dentale. Il s'avère notamment que des imprimeurs néerlandais et anglais s'intéressent plus d'une fois à des sources françaises similaires. Néanmoins, les éditions néerlandaises témoignent d'un degré bien plus élevé d'interventions dans le texte: elles ont tendance à faire usage d'une multitude de sources, à éliminer les noms de personnes impliquées dans la création des romans, ou à inclure des passages lyriques ou dramatiques en vers, ce qui suggère l'intervention de rhétoriqueurs et une reception des ces textes dans des milieux citadins.

Note: I am grateful to Bart Besamusca, Jordi Sánchez-Martí and Frank Willaert for their valuable comments and suggestions.

Elisabeth de Bruijn, University of Antwerp

Throughout the Middle Ages, France profoundly influenced literary life in Western Europe. Most notably, it was the cradle of numerous vernacular (chivalric) romances, many of which inspired translations or adaptions in other European languages. The lion's share of medieval Dutch romances from the manuscript period was translated from or modelled on romances of French origin.[1] The first Dutch romances that appeared in the age of print, however, were no translations from the French, but works that were already known through Dutch manuscripts or that were translated from Latin sources.[2] While romances of French origin came into favour after the move of Gheraert Leeu from Gouda to Antwerp in 1484, they did not manage to outnumber the originally Dutch romances and by no means dominated the market.[3] Moreover, publishers seem to have become more and more aware of narrative literature that was *en vogue* in other European languages. As compared to other vernaculars, however, France continued to be the number one supplier of romance subject matter in the period from *c.* 1484 – *c.* 1540. This leads to the question which French romances were considered marketable enough to compete with the group of originally Dutch romances and the increasing number of translations from other vernaculars. This article focuses on the printed transmission of Dutch romances translated from the French. It discusses their subsequent publishers – most importantly Jacob Bellaert, Gheraert Leeu and Willem Vorsterman –, considering the way they fitted into the respective publishers' list as well as the texts' longevity. The chronological discussion of the romances helps to assess developments in their reception in the Low Countries. Many of these romances also found their way into other (Western European) languages in the first decades after the advent of print. These translations are taken into consideration as well, as they allow for an examination of their contemporary international appeal and offer insight into those features that are characteristic of the Dutch editions.

---

1 For a recent overview see Johan Oosterman, 'Franse en Nederlandse letterkunde in middeleeuws Vlaanderen'. In: *Literaire bruggenbouwers tussen Nederland en Frankrijk. Receptie, vertaling en cultuuroverdracht sinds de Middeleeuwen.* Ed. by Maaike Koffeman, Alicia Montoya and Marc Smeets. Amsterdam 2017, p. 29–47.
2 See the contribution by Besamusca and Willaert in the present volume, p. 49–92. See also Luc. Debaene, *De Nederlandse volksboeken. Ontstaan en geschiedenis van de Nederlandse prozaromans, gedrukt tussen 1475 en 1540.* 2nd ed. Hulst 1977, p. 302–318.
3 Debaene, *De Nederlandse volksboeken* (note 2), p. 328–329.

1 The Beginning: Jacob Bellaert

The first to have printed narratives translated from the French was Jacob Bellaert. Somewhere between 10 December 1483 and 5 May 1485 he published an edition of the *Historie van Jason*,[4] soon followed by the *Vergaderinge der historien van Troyen*, which is dated 5 May 1485.[5] The two texts were translated after the French *Histoire de Jason* (*editio princeps* Bruges or Ghent?, *c.* 1476)[6] and the *Recueil des histoires de Troyes* (*editio princeps* Bruges or Ghent?, *c.* 1474–1475)[7] respectively. Interestingly, Bellaert also published editions of these French texts, *Jason* probably between 24 December 1485 and 12 August 1486[8] and the *Recueil* somewhere between 24 December 1485 and 25 July 1486.[9] Bellaert's publisher's list indicates only three active years of printing, between 10 December 1483 and 20 August 1486, in which he published some 18 editions. Except for the previously mentioned *Jason* and the *Recueil* these are all in Dutch, comprising also other translations "of texts which belonged to the courtly literature of the dukes of Burgundy".[10]

Little is known of Bellaert's personal and professional life. There are several indications that he worked for – or perhaps in collaboration with – Gheraert Leeu, who started a printing business in Gouda, in the Northern Low Countries, in 1477.[11] For reasons that are still subject to speculation Bellaert began his own business in Haarlem, some 50 kilometres north of Gouda.[12] While Leeu had published a Troy edition already in 1479 (the *Historien van Troyen*, based on the authoritative version of Guido de Columnis), both Bellaert's *Jason* and his

---

4 ISTC il00111000; GW M17467.
5 ISTC il00116000; GW M17453.
6 ISTC il00110930. In her contribution to the catalogue of the recent Bruges exhibition 'Haute Lecture by Colard Mansion', Lotte Hellinga gives the dates 1476–1477, see: Lotte Hellinga 'William Caxton and Colard Mansion'. In: *Colard Mansion. Incunabula, Prints and Manuscripts in Medieval Bruges*. Ed. by Evelien Hauwaerts, Evelien de Wilde and Ludo Vandamme. Gent 2018, p. 63–69 (p. 69).
7 ISTC il00113000. For the possible date and place of printing and for the identity of the printer (possibly David Aubert for William Caxton?), see Lotte Hellinga, 'William Caxton, Colard Mansion, and the Printer in Type 1'. In: *Bulletin du Bibliophile* 2011, p. 86–114, an article republished in Lotte Hellinga, *Incunabula in Transit. People and Trade*. Leiden 2018, p. 286–322.
8 ISTC il00110950; GW M17455.
9 ISTC il00113500; GW M17434.
10 Lotte Hellinga, *Texts in Transit. Manuscript to Proof and Print in the Fifteenth Century*. Leiden 2014, p. 323.
11 See Hellinga, *Texts in Transit* (note 10), p. 324.
12 Wilma Keesman, 'Jacob Bellaert en Haarlem'. In: *Haarlems Helicon. Literatuur en toneel te Haarlem vóór 1800*. Ed. by E.K. Grootes. Hilversum 1993, p. 28–30.

Vergaderinge were translated after the Burgundian versions by Raoul Lefèvre.[13] Lefèvre's retellings of the mythological stories date back to *c.* 1460 (*Histoire de Jason*) and *c.* 1464 (*Recueil des histoires de Troyes*) and were dedicated to duke Philip the Good.[14] In contrast with the extravagantly illuminated manuscripts of the time, the unillustrated *editiones principes* of the *Recueil* and *Jason* make a sober impression. Bellaert's editions of *Jason* and the *Vergaderinge*, on the other hand, are described as 'elitist' and 'luxurious'.[15] With their large folio-format, their two columns and their large woodcuts, they are indeed reminiscent of the lavish Burgundian codices, as well as of the printed editions of his Bruges colleague Colard Mansion.[16] That Bellaert's editions targeted an aristocratic clientele is demonstrated by the blank coat of arms in his printer's mark, which allowed owners to fill it out with their own coat of arms by means of an *ex libris* (Fig. 1).[17] That Bellaert could also rely on aristocratic patronage is demonstrated by the opening woodcut used for both the *Vergaderinge* and the *Jason*, which depicts the coat of arms of the prominent Haarlem family Van Ruyven in the background (Fig. 2).[18]

The translator of the *Vergaderinge der historien van Troyen* made a very close translation of the French *Recueil*.[19] Moreover he literally translated the incipit and prologue that present Duke Philip the Good as the instigator of the French work. The reference to "Roelof die Smit" (the Dutch translation of Raoul Lefèvre) in the incipit and Raoul's portrayal in the opening woodcut, presenting his work to Philip the Good, also alludes to the Burgundian origin of the work. Instead of

---

13 These Burgundian reworkings of Lefèvre also go back to the *Historia destructionis Troiae*, see Wilma Keesman, *De eindeloze stad. Troje en Trojaanse oorsprongsmythen in de (laat)middel-eeuwse en vroegmoderne Nederlanden*. Hilversum 2017, p. 47–49.

14 Hellinga, *Texts in Transit* (note 10), p. 305.

15 *De vijfhonderdste verjaring van de boekdrukkunst in de Nederlanden. Catalogus.* Brussel 1973, p. 286; Wilma Keesman, 'Jacob Bellaert en Haarlem' (note 12), p. 35.

16 Keesman, *De eindeloze stad* (note 13), p. 54.

17 Keesman, 'Jacob Bellaert en Haarlem' (note 12), p. 35–36.

18 Keesman, 'Jacob Bellaert en Haarlem' (note 12), p. 41–43.

19 According to Willem Kuiper, some words can only be understood if one knows the French source text, as in the case of *kinderen* ('to child') as a translation of *enfanter* ('to give birth'). However, contrary to what Kuiper states, the verb does exist in Dutch (there are several attestations in the sixteenth century and the verb *kinden* also exists in Low German). See the introduction to Willem Kuiper's online edition 'Die vergaderinge der historien van Troyen'. In: *Bibliotheek van de Middelnederlandse letterkunde. Nieuwe digitale reeks*. Ed. by Willem Kuiper. Amsterdam 2008–2016 (URL: http://cf.hum.uva.nl/dsp/scriptamanent/bml/Vergaderinge_der_historien_van_Troyen/Vergaderinge_der_historien_van_Troyen.html). The verb *kinderen* is found on fol. F2v of Bellaert's 1485 edition, see the facsimile of the copy in the Lessing Rosenwald collection in Washington (Incun. 1485. L 43) (URL: http://hdl.loc.gov/loc.rbc/Rosenwald.0487.1).

Fig. 1: Printer's mark in the *Vergaderinge der historien van Troyen* (Haarlem: Bellaert, 1485), fol. z5r. Washington, Library of Congress, Incun. 1485. L 43.

Fig. 2: Opening woodcut of the *Vergaderinge der historien van Troyen* (Haarlem: Bellaert, 1485), fol. a1v. Washington, Library of Congress, Incun. 1485. L 43.

looking for new markets, Bellaert seems to have preferred seeking entry into aristo-cratic circles. The idea that this is what led to his downfall is widely accepted. While it is also possible that Bellaert stopped printing after 1486 because of other reasons (e.g. moving, illness, decease), there are indications that he either overes-timated the market for his expensive products or that he underestimated the competition. There are indications that the economic climate in Haarlem was bad at the time and that people were less inclined to spend money on luxuri-ous books.[20] But it is even more conceivable that the northern elite, probably less affected by the economy, was limited in size and scope and that the mar-ket for expensive books was quickly saturated. The fact that the last two books Bellaert printed were French versions of the *Jason* and the *Recueil*, can also be taken two ways: either his Dutch versions were relatively successful or he acknowledged his misjudgement and tried to make up for it by starting to print for the French-speaking market.[21] The lack of an afterlife of the Dutch *Vergaderinge*, as opposed to its French counterparts, rather points toward the second possibility.

The isolated position of the Dutch *Vergaderinge* becomes even more telling when compared to the transmission of the French *Recueil* and the English *Recuyell* (Table 1). In the Low Countries, Bellaert's *Vergaderinge* and his *Jason* only had an afterlife in the shape of Jan van Doesborch's reworkings *Van Jason ende Hercules* and *Die historie vanden stercken Hercules*, where the romances were stripped of their Burgundian appearance.[22] The afterlife of Van Doesborch's edi-tions as well as the rise of other Troy narratives indicates that the Low Countries did not lose their interest in the history of Troy as such but only in Bellaert's ver-sion of it. By contrast, Coldiron observes with respect to the French transmission that "[t]he splendidly produced, very finely and heavily illustrated Lyon editions witness that the Burgundian *Recueil* was, even in France, territory worth seizing and re-seizing".[23] The English *Recuyell* – which was probably printed by William Caxton in Flanders and is the first book known to have been printed in the English language – was reprinted several times in the sixteenth and seventeenth

---

20 Saskia Bogaart, *Geleerde kennis in de volkstaal. Van den proprieteyten der dinghen (Haarlem 1485) in perspectief.* Hilversum 2004, p. 49–50.

21 Keesman, *De eindeloze stad* (note 13), p. 57.

22 See below. Besides, the only late-medieval Troy narrative that really seems to have had sig-nificant success was the *Destructie van Troyen* (Antwerp: Van den Dorpe, *c.* 1496–1500), also discussed below, see Keesman, *De eindeloze stad* (note 13), p. 61.

23 A.E.B. Coldiron, *Printers without Borders. Translation and Textuality in the Renaissance.* Cambridge 2015, p. 40.

Table 1: Printed transmission of the *Recueil* in French, English and Dutch before 1600.

French edition Recueil des histoires de Troye	English edition The Recuyell of the Historyes of Troy	Dutch edition Vergaderinge van Troyen
	[Flanders, possibly Ghent], [1473–74]	
[Bruges or Ghent?, 1474–75]		
Haarlem: [J. Bellaert], 1485–86		Haarlem: [J. Bellaert], 1485
Lyon: Topié-Heremberck, 1490		
Lyon: Maillet, 1494		
Paris: Vérard, 1494		
	London: De Worde, 1502	
	London: De Worde, 1503	
Paris: Le Noir, 1508		
Lyon: Saccon, 1510		
Lyon: du Ry, 1529		
Paris: Le Noir, s.d.		
Paris: Janot – Le Noir, 1532		
Lyon: de Harsy, 1544		
	London: W. Copland, 1553	
	London: Creede-Simmes, 1596–97	

centuries and it coexisted with other Troy stories.[24] Interestingly, both the quite literally translated content of the French original and the 'Burgundian framing' in the paratext of Caxton's translation persisted in the sixteenth and seventeenth reprints of the English text, indicating not only an interest in the Trojan, but also in the Burgundian past.[25] While there was an interest in Burgundian manuscripts in the Low Countries, a similar fascination for Burgundian-style printed books has not been attested. This could explain why Bellaert's edition

---

24 One of these titles was, unsurprisingly, Chaucer's *Troilus and Criseyde*, printed for the first time by Caxton in 1483 (STC 5094). The English *Jason* was only reprinted once by Gheraert Leeu in 1492 (STC 15384).

25 In her paragraph 'Troys for England (via Burgundy): reprinting lost empires' Coldiron, *Printers without Borders* (note 23) states: "Although its own empire fell by 1478, medieval Burgundy remained vibrant in England throughout the sixteenth and seventeenth centuries [...] in art, furniture, tapestries, clothing, and design." (p. 43–44). She even uses the term 'Troy-gundy' (p. 45) to denote both the ancient-Trojan culture and the frame of the medieval-Burgundian culture through which the fall of Troy was mediated: "Troy lost, Burgundy lost: but both are long and carefully preserved, ever in terms of each other, in the printers' black-letter paratexts on generations of readers' shelves" (p. 46).

failed to gain a foothold. This lack of interest in the Low Countries was apparently found at all social levels, whereas the Burgundian framing in England seems to have appealed to different layers of society, including the higher aristocracy, the gentry, merchants and clerics.[26] Considering the status of French in Dutch elite circles, it is conceivable that those who were attracted by the Burgundian version of the history of Troy might just as well have read it in French. In fact, the prestige of the French language probably obstructed the blossoming of Burgundian literature in Dutch.

2 Exploring the Market: Gheraert Leeu

Unlike Bellaert, Gheraert Leeu must have anticipated the demise of the printing business in the Northern Low Countries in good time. Although Leeu had run a rather successful company in Gouda since 1477, he decided to move his printing house to Antwerp in 1484.[27] In the following years, this strategical location with its rich hinterland allowed him to print books for the international market. His editions mainly included devotional works and school books, in Dutch and Latin. In 1485 he printed his first Dutch narrative in Antwerp: *Esopus*.[28] This version of the text did not just consist of a collection of fables, but it also included the so-called 'vita' of Aesop.[29] Whereas the few narrative texts which Leeu had published in Gouda had Dutch or Latin sources, his Antwerp *Esopus* was translated from another vernacular. In the

---

26 Yu-Chiao Wang, 'Caxton's Romances and Their Early Tudor Readers'. In: *Huntington Library Quarterly* 67 (2004), p. 173–188. In view of Bellaert's Burgundian orientation it is interesting that "Caxton did not consider the connections to the Burgundian court sufficient for an English market; he did not dedicate *The History of Jason* to Margaret [Duchess of Burgundy, EdB] but rather to the Prince of Wales" (p. 174).

27 For an introduction to Leeu see Koen Goudriaan, 'Inleiding'. In: *Een drukker zoekt publiek. Gheraert Leeu te Gouda 1477–1484.* Ed. by Koen Goudriaan et al. Gouda 1993, p. 3–11.

28 ISTC ia00116900; GW 374. For a brief analysis of this publisher's list see Koen Goudriaan, 'Een drukker en zijn markt. Gheraert Leeu (Gouda 1477 – Antwerpen 1492/3)'. In: *Madoc* 6 (1992), p. 194–205.

29 In contrast to the mere collections of fables, this version of *Esopus* has a narrative structure and thus meets the criteria of our research corpus (see p. 4 of the Introduction). The different national philologies seem to hold different views on the genre of *Esopus*. The story does not usually appear in studies on English or French romance. However, in the German tradition, *Esopus* is sometimes included in collections of prose 'romances'; see, for instance, the contribution by Bertelsmeier-Kierst in the present volume, p. 33 and Christa Bertelsmeier-Kierst, 'Erzählen in Prosa. Zur Entwicklung des deutschen Prosaromans bis 1500'. In: *ZfdA* 143 (2014), p. 141–165.

prologue Leeu indicates that he translated the text from Julien Macho's French *Esope* (Lyon: Huss and Schabeller, 1484).[30] However, it has been demonstrated that his illustrations as well as some textual details are derived from Steinhöwel's Latin edition of the text (Straßburg: Knoblochtzer, *c.* 1481), which was taken from his bilingual Latin-German edition (Ulm: Zainer, *c.* 1476/77).[31]

Leeu's assessment of the benefit/risk ratio must have taken into account the fact that the French edition had already been printed in Lyon three times in the period 1480–1484, while Steinhöwel's German text was by then printed no less than nine times.[32] Moreover, in 1484 Caxton had taken his chances by publishing an English translation of Macho's *Esope*.[33] The success of *Esopus* in France and in Germany, as well as the initiative of his English colleague, may have convinced Leeu that he played a safe hand with his Dutch edition of the text. What makes the businessman stand out, however, is that he not merely introduced a successful text into a new market in the shape of a slavish translation from the French (like Caxton), but the fact that his edition was the result of careful compilation. On top of that, Leeu tailored his edition to his Dutch audience by inserting explanations, doublets, (rhymed) proverbs and translations of Latin passages, which are missing in the French editions.[34] In contrast with Macho and Steinhöwel, Leeu left out some anecdotes on adultery, featuring women who outsmart men. As these passages do appear in Leeu's Latin *Esopus* edition of 1486, it is believed that they were not deemed appropriate for his vernacular audience.[35] This example shows that Leeu carefully adjusted his editions in targeting different audiences. The

---

30 See fol. Aij recto. The *editio princeps* was published in 1480 by Phillipi and Reinhardi in Lyon. However, Beate Hecker, *Julien Macho, Esope. Eingeleitet und herausgegeben nach der Edition von 1486.* Hamburg 1982, p. LV, has shown that Leeu used the 1484 edition.

31 Gerd Dicke, *Heinrich Steinhöwels 'Esopus' und seine Fortsetzer. Untersuchungen zu einem Bucherfolg der Frühdruckzeit.* Tübingen 1994, p. 120 and Paul Wackers, 'Gheraert Leeu as a Printer of Fables and Animal Stories'. In: *Reinardus, Yearbook of the International Reynard Society* 20 (2007–2008), p. 128–152 (especially p. 146).

32 See for the French editions ISTC ia00118200; ia00118250 and ia00118300. For the German editions see 'Heinrich Steinhöwel, *Aesop*'. In: MRFH (URL: https://www.mrfh.de/werke.php?werk_id=10&wahl=textzeugen).

33 ISTC ia00117500; GW 376.

34 *Het leven en de fabels van Esopus.* Ed. by Hans Rijns and Willem van Bentum. Hilversum 2016, p. 32–33.

35 *Het leven en de fabels van Esopus* (see note 34), p. 33–34.

Dutch *Esopus* was reprinted repeatedly up to the 19th century and as such represents one of the few early printed romances that stood the test of time.[36]

Only two French editions of *Paris et Vienne* were printed before Leeu himself published another French edition of the text in 1487,[37] possibly following the example of his insular colleague William Caxton, who had published an English edition in 1485.[38] Unlike Caxton, Leeu included 25 large, unique woodcuts, which he had especially made for this romance. Leeu's French edition was most likely at the basis of the Dutch translation of the text, which he also published in 1487 and which was the first Dutch chivalric romance Leeu printed in Antwerp.[39] In 1488 Leeu tried his luck with a Low German version of the text, *Paris und Vienna*.[40] After the death of William Caxton early in 1492, Leeu did not hesitate to "fill the gap left by Caxton, and in June 1492 he published two books for the English market, significantly two romances, namely *Jason* and *Paris*" (Table 2).[41] Leeu did not have the chance to further develop his market strategies in England, however, due to his sudden death in December of the same year.

For his English edition of *Paris and Vienne* Leeu reprinted the translation made by Caxton using an English type, but he included the series of woodcuts he used for his Dutch, French and Low German editions and he adjusted the lay-out to make it look like his continental editions.[42] On the Continent he provided his French-speaking customers with a French version different from the ones provided by Le Roy and Huss, nevertheless using a French type. The Dutch translation is so close to the French that a common French source is assumed: deviations are mainly found at the level of detail and reveal an overall

---

36 It is one of the 23 titles that are considered the 'canon of volksboeken' on the basis of their transmission up to 1900; see Peter Cuijpers, *Van Reynaert de Vos tot Tijl Uilenspiegel. Op zoek naar een canon van volksboeken, 1600–1900.* Zutphen 2014, p. 146.

37 ISTC ip00112800; GW 12686.

38 ISTC ip00113500; GW 12691.

39 ISTC ip00113800; GW 12700.

40 ISTC ip00115200; GW 12699.

41 Jordi Sánchez-Martí, 'The Printed Transmission of Medieval Romance from William Caxton to Wynkyn de Worde, 1473–1533'. In: *The Transmission of Medieval Romance: Metres, Manuscripts and Early Prints.* Ed. by Ad Putter and Judith A. Jefferson. Cambridge 2018, p. 170–190 (quote on p. 180), who also provides additional arguments that Leeu attempted to extend his market into England.

42 Gabriele Diekmann-Dröge, '*Paris und Vienna* in Antwerpen. Der mittelniederdeutsche Frühdruck aus der Offizin Gheraert Leeus'. In: *Niederdeutsches Wort* 26 (1986), p. 55–76 (here p. 57). The inclusion of the woodcuts required seven additional subscriptions, which correspond to the Dutch subscriptions and not to the French or Low German ones, see p. 64.

Table 2: Printed transmission of *Paris et Vienne* in French, English, Dutch and Low German before 1600.

French edition *Paris et Vienne*	English edition *Paris and Vienne*	Dutch edition *Parijs ende Vienna*	Low German edition *Paris unde Vienna*
[Lyon: Le Roy, 1480]			
[Lyon: Huss, 1485]	Westminster: Caxton, 1485		
Antwerp: Leeu, 1487		**Antwerp: Leeu, 1487**	
			Antwerp: Leeu, 1488
Paris: Meslier, [1491]		**Antwerp: Leeu, [1491–92]**	
	Antwerp: Leeu, 1492		
		Antwerp: G. Bac, [1493–95]	
Paris: Trepperel, [1498]			
Paris: Trepperel, [1499]			
Paris: Meslier, [*c.* 1500]			
	London: De Worde, 1501–04?		
Paris: Le Noir, 1502	London: De Worde, 1501–04?		
		Antwerp: [Homberch], 1510	
Paris: Nourry, 1520			
Paris: Trepperel, [*c.* 1525]			
Paris: Lotrian, [*c.* 1530]			
Paris: Moderne [c. 1540]		[Antwerp: J./Wid. van Liesveldt, *c.* 1540]	
[Lyon: Chaussard Frères 1554]			
Paris: Bonfons, [s.d.]			
Paris: Calvarin, [s.d.]			
Lyon: Rigaud, 1596			
Troyes: Oudot, [s.d.]			

tendency of the Dutch translator to use more concise phrasings.[43] Notwithstanding Leeu's efforts to exploit new markets, no reprints are known of the Low German edition of *Paris und Vienna*. The Dutch edition is known to have been reprinted once by Leeu himself and three times by other publishers, the last time around 1540. Although there are indications that the story of Paris and Vienna was still known in England in the late sixteenth century, no reprints of Caxton's edition were transmitted besides the one by Leeu and the two by De Worde of shortly after 1500.[44] This contrasts with the extreme popularity of *Paris et Vienne* in France and Italy.[45] Despite the story's European outreach, *Paris et Vienne* did not become the bestseller in the Germanic language areas that Leeu must have hoped for – at least not in terms of reprints. Perhaps its distinct 'medieval' chivalric character prevented the story from becoming a success over time to the same extent that it was across borders.

Around the year 1393 Jean d'Arras wrote his *Histoire de Mélusine*, a prose text that was to become one of the most popular late medieval romances in French-speaking territories.[46] The German prose adaptation by Thüring von Ringoltingen, based on the verse reworking by the French author Coudrette

---

43 Diekmann-Dröge (see note 42), p. 65–66, who also points out one exceptional omission that does affect the content: unlike Leeu's other versions, his French edition has one column of text in which the fate of Paris and Vienna is compared to that of another famous couple: Bueve de Hantone and Jusiana. The *editio princeps* of the French *Bueve de Hantone* was only published by Vérard in 1499 and the Dutch translation in 1504; see below. For Leeu's Low German edition a Dutch source similar to – but not identical with – the 1487 edition must have been used (p. 67). Singularities of the Low German edition as compared to the other Leeu editions are of a marginal character too.

44 These indications are a performance by the boys of Westminster School in 1572 and a licence, which was transferred in 1586; see Helen Cooper, 'Going Native: the Caxton and Mainwaring Versions of Paris and Vienne'. In: *Travel and Prose Fiction in Early Modern England*. Ed. by Nandini Das, special number of *The Yearbook of English Studies* 41 (2011), p. 21–34 (p. 21). It was only Matthews Mainwaring's entirely rewritten version of 1628 that seems to have sparked a renewed interest in the story in the seventeenth century, see p. 21.

45 See *Paris e Vienna, romanzo cavalleresco*. Ed. by Anna Maria Babbi. Padova 1991, p. 29–55 for the French transmission and p. 57–121 for the Italian transmission. Printed editions of the prose version are also found in Catalan, Spanish and Latin (p. 129–138), while verse adaptations exist in Yiddish, Swedish, Armenian, Russian and Rumanian (p. 139–153).

46 At least 13 fifteenth-century manuscripts, 6 incunabula and 15 sixteenth-century editions testify to the story's rich afterlife in France; Lydia Zeldenrust, *Mutations of an Animal-Human Hybrid Monster: The Western European Mélusine Translations (c. 1400–1600)*. Doctoral thesis Queen Mary University of London 2015, p. 242–245 provides a list with the French manuscripts and printed editions up to *c.* 1600.

entitled the *Roman de Parthenay*, has been equally popular.[47] By the time Leeu published his edition of the Dutch *Meluzine*,[48] which is dated 9 February 1491, the story had already been available in 4 French and 10 German editions, not to mention the many manuscripts in both languages. Leeu's translation for the most part goes back to Jean d'Arras' *Histoire de Mélusine*.[49] It has been shown recently, however, that the Dutch edition also inserts episodes that are only found in the *Roman de Parthenay*, thus being the only European translation that is based on both French versions.[50] Interestingly, the episodes in Leeu's edition are accompanied by three woodcuts that seem to be modelled after those found in German incunabula, indicating that the episodes from the *Roman de Parthenay* were mediated through a German edition that Leeu used to complement his French example.[51] This demonstrates that Leeu's edition is not a mere rendition of the French, but, again, the result of careful compilation. Perhaps Leeu aimed at publishing the most complete version possible of the Melusine story, or perhaps his demonstrable close connections with German publishers (as in the case of *Esopus*) could have simply provided him with materials and woodcuts.[52] In this respect, Lydia Zeldenrust's suggestion that the episodes from the *Roman de Parthenay* "were inserted not to tell a more complete story than that of the two French romances, but to complete the story told by the German *Melusine* images" is worthy of consideration.[53]

However, it would be wrong to assume that Leeu was only driven by the wish to present his audience with an edition that was the result of mere collation. The Dutch translator steers clear of an all too slavish translation and – unlike Bellaert – avoids the use of French idiom.[54] Moreover, Leeu shows his own signature in the lay-out of his *Meluzine* by opting for a presentation in two columns instead of one, by inserting several woodcuts different from Steinschaber's

---

47 The German version was transmitted in 17 manuscripts, 11 incunabula and 20 sixteenth-century editions; Zeldenrust (see note 46), p. 247–250.

48 ISTC ij00218420; GW 12665.

49 The orthography of names suggests that Leeu's edition has Steinschaber's *editio princeps* as its source: Bob Duijvestijn, 'Der niederländische Prosaroman von Meluzine; eine Orientierung'. In: *Melusine. Actes du Colloque du Centre d'Études Médiévales de l'Université de Picardie Jules Verne, 13 et 14 Janvier 1996*. Ed. by Danielle Buschinger and Wolfgang Spiewok. Greifswald 1996, p. 37–50 (p. 42).

50 Zeldenrust (see note 46), p. 141.

51 It is also important to note that the *Roman de Parthenay* was not printed in French; Zeldenrust (see note 46), p. 157.

52 Zeldenrust (see note 46), p. 157.

53 Zeldenrust (see note 46), p. 157.

54 Duijvestijn (see note 49), p. 44–45.

edition and by taking over woodcuts from his *Paris et Vienne* editions.[55] Another singularity of the Dutch *Meluzine* is that the text is significantly shorter than its French counterpart due to the avoidance of repetitive elements and descriptive details. Most importantly, however, is the elimination of references to the patron (Duke de Berry), the dedicatee (Marie de Bar) and the supplier of source materials (the count of Salisbury) in the Dutch prologue.[56] These elements rather seem to have been of importance in the printed tradition of the French and German versions of the text, many of which were owned by members of the nobility. Aristocratic ownership can also be assumed for the independently made English prose and verse translations, which refer to French commissioners as well as the "Erle of Salesbury".[57] As for the Castilian *Melosina*, which preserves the dedication to the Duke of Berry, it is known that Margaret of Austria owned a copy of the 1489 edition, while the now-lost Castilian edition of 1512 as well as the 1526 one are dedicated to an unspecified princess.[58] Although the afterlife of the English *Recuyell* makes clear that the aristocratic appearance of an edition does not automatically imply an aristocratic readership, it is reasonable to assume that the element of genealogy so characteristic to the Melusine story appealed to members of the nobility. At the risk of taking the reverse argument too far, the lack of attested aristocratic ownership of Middle Dutch romances accords with the tendency to eliminate names of historical agents in Dutch romances (examples of which are given below).[59] The Dutch *Meluzine* was reprinted twice in

---

55 Ina Kok, *Woodcuts in Incunabula Printed in the Low Countries*. 4 vols. Houten 2013, p. 233 and Zeldenrust (see note 46), p. 146.

56 Although the names of Duke Jean de Berry (patron of *Histoire de Mélusine*) and the Lord of Parthenay (patron of *Roman de Parthenay*) are mentioned in the highly abridged epilogue, their appearance there lacks every contextualization and therefore makes a rather alienating impression; Zeldenrust (see note 46), p. 154–155.

57 Zeldenrust (see note 46), p. 175 and 198–199. Both English translations are completely preserved in manuscript (which in itself points to an upper-class audience). Fragments are known of a printed version that is attributed to Wynkyn de Worde; see STC 14648.

58 Zeldenrust (see note 46), p. 115–116 and 121.

59 Rob Resoort, 'De presentatie van drukwerk in de volkstaal in de Nederlanden tot 1501: waar zijn de auteurs, vertalers en opdrachtgevers? Een verkenning'. In: *Geschreven en gedrukt. Boekproductie van handschrift naar druk in de overgang van Middeleeuwen naar moderne tijd.* Ed. by Herman Pleij, Joris Reynaert et al. Gent 2004, p. 177–206, observes that references to authors and translators are preserved in about 12,5% of the Dutch incunabula, especially in the domain of 'artes' [non-literary] texts and devotional works. References to the names of French authors/translators are found in some cases (Raoul Lefèvre in the *Vergaderinge* and Julien Macho in *Esopus*), while the names of Dutch translators are usually unknown. More research on Dutch authors, translators and commissioners is needed, especially for the post–1500 period.

Antwerp, by Van Homberch in 1510 and by Verdussen in 1602.[60] In view of the immense popularity of *Melusine* in Germany and France, it is remarkable that in English and Dutch territories the romance appears to have been even less popular than *Paris et Vienne*.

3 A New Aesthetics: Roland van den Dorpe and Jan van Doesborch

Not much is known about Roland van den Dorpe, who only published ten – mainly devotional and exclusively Dutch – editions between *c.* 1496 and *c.* 1500.[61] Significantly, his only popular romance was a Troy narrative: the *Destructie van Troyen*, which cannot be dated more accurately.[62] While the title page suggests that the Trojan war and the love between Troylus and Briseda are equally important, the explicit ("Hier es voleyndt die historie vander amoruesheyt van Troylus ende van Briseda. ende oeck kortelijc ouerlopen die destructie van troyen") emphasizes the love of Troilus and Briseda, while the destruction of Troy is more of a side issue.[63] In this shift of focus, the edition differs from the 'historiographical' adaptation of Guido de Columnis' *Historia destructionis Troiae* published by Leeu in 1479 and the 'Burgundian' version published by Bellaert in 1485.[64] In Van den Dorpe's edition, the parts on the Trojan war are compiled from the texts published by Leeu and Bellaert, but the story of Troylus and Briseda is taken from Boccaccio's *Il Filostrato*, which was probably known to Van den Dorpe through the French translation by Louis de Beauvau: the *Roman de Troyle*.[65] Interestingly, the *Roman de Troyle* did not make it into print.[66]

---

60 USTC 436815 (the edition by Verdussen is not catalogued).
61 Anne Rouzet, *Dictionnaire des imprimeurs, libraires et éditeurs des XVᵉ et XVIᵉ siècles dans les limites géographiques de la Belgique actuelle*. Nieuwkoop 1975, p. 57–58; *Vijfhonderdste verjaring* (see note 15), p. 506.
62 ISTC ih00281000; GW 12522.
63 "Here ends the history of the love of Troylus and of Briseda and also briefly touched upon the destruction of Troy" (my translation).
64 Note that Leeu again used two sources for his edition, as he completed his translation of Guido de Columnis by parts of Maerlant's adaptation of the *Aeneis*; see the contribution by Besamusca and Willaert in this volume, p. 70.
65 Keesman, *De eindeloze stad* (note 13), p. 57.
66 ARLIMA lists 14 manuscripts of Louis de Beauvau's *Roman de Troyle*: https://www.arlima.net/il/louis_de_beauvau.html.

While the episodes from the *Roman de Troyle* were translated into verse, the prose form was used for the parts on the Trojan war. This alternation of prose and verse passages is a technique attested for the first time in the *Destructie van Troyen*, but which would turn out to become typical for a great number of Dutch romances in the period up to *c.* 1540.[67] It differs from the *prosimetrum* style, also represented in two French editions by Gheraert Leeu, for several reasons.[68] First, the mix of both forms does not result from the use of both a prose and a verse source text, but the verses appear to have been written especially for the romance. Second, in many romances the verse passages are preceded by speech headings that give them the impression of a dramatic text. Third, in several romances the verses take the shape of *refreinen*, a form of stanzaic poetry that was cultivated by *rederijkers* (Rhetoricians), members of the organized Chambers of Rhetoric. *Rederijkers* dominated literary life in the Southern Low Countries and were also responsible for the production and performance of theatre plays, some titles of which correspond to those of prose romances. It is likely that *rederijkers* were in some way involved in the composition of the verse passages in Middle Dutch romances.

Verse passages in prose romances did not only enliven the text but also helped to visualize the story in the minds of the reader.[69] Whether it was for the verse passages or not, Van den Dorpe must have thought that his *Destructie van Troyen* would appeal to his audience, even though no French printed edition of the *Roman de Troyle* existed that could provide him with an estimate of his chances.[70] Indeed, of the three Troy narratives in the Low Countries only the *Destructie van Troyen* could be considered to have been 'successful' judging by

---

[67] For an overview see Elisabeth de Bruijn, 'Das Spiel der Stimmen. Performative Verspassagen in einigen niederländischen Prosaromanen (ca. 1500–1540)'. In: *Stimme und Performanz in der mittelalterlichen Literatur*. Ed. by Monica Unzeitig, Nine Miedema and Angela Schrott. Berlin 2017, p. 133–154 (p. 133, note 1) and Luc. Debaene, 'Rederijkers en prozaromans'. In: *De gulden passer* 27 (1949), p. 1–23.

[68] These editions are *Van den drie blinden danssen* (1482) and *Doctrinael des tijts* (1486), translations of Pierre Michault's *La dance des aveugles* and *Doctrinal du temps* respectively.

[69] See Dirk Coigneau, 'Drama in druk, tot circa 1540'. In: *Spel en spektakel. Middeleeuws toneel in de Lage Landen*. Ed. by Hans van Dijk and Bart Ramakers. Amsterdam 2001 (Nederlandse literatuur en cultuur in de Middeleeuwen 23), p. 201–214 and 352–359. See also De Bruijn, 'Das Spiel der Stimmen' (note 67).

[70] According to Willem Kuiper, 'Briseïda. De identiteit van een 'middeleeuws' romanpersonage'. In: *Simulacrum, het eigentijdse tijdschrift voor kunst en cultuur*, themanummer Identiteit, 12 (2004), p. 17–19, the edition was aimed at an audience of young adults in the vicinity of Antwerp.

the number of reprints.[71] While innovations within the text and its presentation could have contributed to its popularity, the historical circumstances might at least have been equally important. It has been demonstrated that the citizens of Antwerp had traditionally shown an interest in its assumed Trojan descent and it is beyond doubt that the city itself offered ideal conditions for commercial success.[72] Yet the belief in a Trojan descent seems to have been an international phenomenon and the hegemony of Antwerp does not explain the continuing interest in only one of the many available Troy stories. Illustrative in this case is that in France and Germany, the interest in new 'humanist' sources of the Troy legend (e.g. Dares and Dictys or Homeros) coincides with the end of the printed transmission of the stories based on Guido de Columnis around 1540.[73] In the Low Countries and England, humanist works were published from the second half of the sixteenth century onwards, but they did not shove aside the existing Troy stories.[74] This reminds us that the life of certain text versions was strongly determined by local interests and traditions.

In the case of Van den Dorpe, the persistent interest in the *Destructie van Troyen* can also be explained by means of the effective market strategies of his successor, Jan van Doesborch, who took over the printing business from Van den Dorpe's widow around 1501. The first prose romance he published was *Buevijn van Austoen* in 1504.[75] It was a highly abbreviated translation from the French *Bueve de Hantone* (*editio princeps* Paris: Vérard, 1499), which had by then been put into print three times.[76] Being reprinted only once by Adriaen van Berghen in 1511,[77] the Dutch translation appears to have been somewhat less successful than the French prose version or the English version in verse, which was transmitted in both manuscript and print.[78] The fact that not only Van Doesborch's *Buevijn*

---

71 The *Destructie van Troyen* was reprinted in Antwerp by Van Doesborch between 1508–1515 (USTC 436813), by Vorsterman in 1541 (USTC 441931), by Roelants in 1556 (not catalogued) and by Van Ghelen between 1569–1582 (not catalogued); see Keesman, *De eindeloze stad* (note 13), p. 61, note 109, who also lists the transmission in the seventeenth, eighteenth and nineteenth centuries.

72 Keesman, *De eindeloze stad* (note 13), p. 64–65 and p. 63 respectively.

73 Keesman, *De eindeloze stad* (note 13), p. 70.

74 As we have seen, the Burgundian *Recuyell* continued to be popular in England; see also Keesman, *De eindeloze stad* (note 13), p. 70.

75 USTC 436691.

76 ISTC ib01275100. See for the sixteenth-century French transmission USTC 26022; 39048; 62906; 55584; 80018.

77 USTC 436832.

78 See for the sixteenth-century English transmission STC 1987; 1987.5; 1988; 1988.2; 1988.4; 1988.6; 1988.8; 1989; 1990.

and his reprint of the *Destructie van Troyen* (*c.* 1508–1515), but the majority of his romances are characterized by the insertion of verses, indicates that it was Van Doesborch who conventionalized this technique.[79]

Another interesting facet of his publisher's strategy is that Van Doesborch was not so much concerned with what was going on in France. Approximately one third of his editions was published in English, showing a clear orientation towards the English market.[80] Almost two decades after Leeu's demise, Van Doesborch thus seems to have realized the westward expansion of the printing business that Leeu had in mind. And similar to Leeu, Van Doesborch attempted to immediately cash in by publishing an English and a Dutch edition of the same text.[81] It is telling that his English edition of, for instance, *Frederyke of Jennen* (1518) lacks the verse passages with speech headings that we find in *Frederick van Jenuen* (*c.* 1518). Even the speech headings in the so-called 'reading drama' *Mariken van Nieumeghen* (probably printed by Van Doesborch before *c.* 1515) have disappeared in the English reworking *Mary of Nemmegen* (*c.* 1515), which is entirely in prose. This underlines the assumption that the interpolation of verses was to a large extent conventional and that Van Doesborch must have been acquainted with literary traditions in England as well as on the Continent. It has been argued that Van Doesborch maintained close connections with Caxton's successor Wynkyn de Worde (active from 1492 until his death in about 1534–1535).[82] Originating from the Continent, De Worde had grown to be one of the most prolific English printers of that time, his publisher's list comprising about forty romances.[83] It is likely that Van Doesborch's contacts with De Worde helped him to assess the market oversees.

Van Doesborch's relation with De Worde as well as the evidence suggesting that the technique of compilation was no exception in the creation of early printed romances make it difficult to determine if the source of Van Doesborch's Swan Knight story *Helias*,[84] printed in the second decade of the sixteenth century, has been Pierre Desrey's French *Genealogie avecques les gestes* (*editio princeps*

---

79 De Bruijn, 'Das Spiel der Stimmen' (note 67), p. 153. Many of Van Doesborch's prose romances were published by later printers. However, as Van Doesborch had by then already published English translations of these romances, for which a Dutch source can be assumed, the *editiones principes* of these sources are ascribed to Van Doesborch; see P.J.A. Franssen, 'Jan van Doesborch (?–1536), Printer of English texts'. In: *Quaerendo* 16 (1986), p. 259–280.

80 Franssen, 'Jan van Doesborch' (note 79).

81 Franssen, 'Jan van Doesborch' (note 79).

82 P.J.A. Franssen, *Tussen tekst en publiek. Jan van Doesborch, drukker-uitgever en literator te Antwerpen en Utrecht in de eerste helft van de zestiende eeuw.* Amsterdam 1990, p. 47.

83 See the contribution by Jordi Sánchez-Martí in this volume, p. 143–166.

84 USTC 436920.

Paris: J. Petit, *c.* 1500) or the English *Knight of the Swanne* (London: W. de Worde, 1512).[85] In any case, it is interesting that the English and French editions are very much alike, whereas the Dutch text is again highly abbreviated – except for the inserted verse passages. Only a fragment of Van Doesborch's edition of *Helias* has survived, but a seventeenth-century edition is considered to be a quite literal rendition. If its prologue already existed in Van Doesborch's edition, it does not refer to any of the historical actors mentioned in the dedication of the French source: King Louis XII and his uncle, Engelbrecht of Cleves, count of Nevers, who are said to be descended from the Swan Knight.[86] The translator of the English *Knight of the Swanne*, Robert Copland, remodels the prologue in such a way that now his beneficiary, Duke Edward of Buckingham, becomes a linear descendant of the Swan Knight. In contrast to the French and English versions, the Dutch edition does not contain any reference allowing for a possible situation in an aristocratic environment.

It has recently been shown that Van Doesborch applied a market strategy similar to his Dutch-English parallel productions in the case of *Van Jason ende Hercules* (8 November 1521) and *Die historie vanden stercken Hercules* (12 December 1521).[87] As pointed out above, the sources of Van Doesborch's editions were Bellaert's *Jason* and the *Vergaderinge der historien van Troyen* respectively. Both editions were stripped of their 'Burgundian' shell in that they are highly abbreviated, centred on action and sensation and provided with a more extensive illustrative programme.[88] Although *Van Jason ende Hercules* and *Die historie vanden stercken Hercules* were published separately, both the illustrations on the title pages and several (cross)references in the text promote

85 The philological evidence is not conclusive, although arguments in favour of a French source are somewhat stronger. But even in the case of a French source, it is likely that Van Doesborch had at least taken notice of De Worde's English 1512 edition of the *Knight of the Swanne*, while the latter could also have provided Van Doesborch with a French edition, see Elisabeth de Bruijn, 'Reculer pour mieux sauter: de bronnenproblematiek en de literaire eigenheid van de Middelnederlandse *Helias*'. In: *Verslagen en Mededelingen van de Koninklijke Academie voor Nederlandse Taal- en Letterkunde* 126 (2016), p. 227–263.

86 F. Suard, 'Pierre Desrey et *La Généalogie de Godefroy de Bouillon*'. In: *Les épopées de la croisade*. Ed. by K.H. Bender and H. Kleber. Special issue of *Zeitschrift für französische Sprache und Literatur* 11 (1987), p. 151–162 (p. 154).

87 USTC 410164; Bart Besamusca, 'Raoul Lefèvre in Dutch: Two 1521 Editions of the Antwerp Printer Jan van Doesborch'. In: *Journal of the Early Book Society* 20 (2017), p. 219–232.

88 Bart Besamusca, 'Tekst en beeld in twee drukken van Jan van Doesborch: *Van Jason ende Hercules* en *Die historie van den stercken Hercules*'. In: *Spiegel der Letteren* 59 (2017), p. 1–34.

the purchase of the editions as a set.[89] This market strategy was also attested in the case of some editions published by De Worde, from whom Van Doesborch might have learned the approach.[90] In the *Historie van den stercken Hercules* Van Doesborch moreover adds a reference to an edition that has the third destruction of Troy and the love of Troylus and Briseda as its theme, thereby including his *c.* 1508–1515 edition of the *Destructie van Troyen* in his sales strategy.[91]

4 Individual Cases: Hendrik Eckert van Homberch and Michiel Hillen van Hoochstraten

The publisher's list of Hendrik Eckert van Homberch contains devotional works in Latin and Dutch, ancient works, Bibles, scholarly and didactic works and a few chivalric romances.[92] Nothing in his publisher's list indicates a particular interest in works of French origin. Significantly, Eckert van Homberch reprinted all three of Leeu's Antwerp romances discussed above: *Esopus*[93] in 1498 and both *Parijs ende Vienna* and *Meluzine* in 1510.[94] Supposedly in the same year he also published *Olyvier van Castillen*,[95] which is the first known Dutch edition of the text and which was reprinted in Antwerp by Jan van Ghelen in 1576.[96] The Dutch edition of *Olyvier* thus did not have a spectacular afterlife, nor did the English and German editions of the text.[97] This sharply contrasts with the popularity of the story in France and – perhaps not surprisingly – in "Olivier's

---

89 Besamusca, 'Raoul Lefèvre in Dutch' (note 87).

90 Besamusca, 'Raoul Lefèvre in Dutch' (note 87), p. 226–227.

91 Besamusca, 'Raoul Lefèvre in Dutch' (note 87), p. 227.

92 Rouzet (see note 61), p. 60.

93 ISTC ia00117000; GW 00375.

94 USTC 436801 and USTC 436815. Eckert van Homberch also reprinted *Seghelijn van Jherusalem* twice, see the contribution of Jef Schaeps in this volume, p. 297–324.

95 USTC 436819.

96 USTC 430519.

97 One English edition is known to have been printed by Wynkyn de Worde in 1518. A license to print the story was given to Thomas East on the 12th of March, 1582, but no copy of an edition is known; see *The History of Oliver of Castile*. Ed. by Robert Edmund Graves. London 1898. The German version goes back to a translation made by Wilhelm Ziely, which was printed by Adam Petri in 1521 (USTC 66894) and 1521/1522 (USTC668941), significantly in Basel, not far from Geneva, where the *editio princeps* was published.

fictional fatherland" Spain, where it was repeatedly reprinted in the course of the sixteenth century.[98]

The French *Olivier* has a prologue in which Philippe Camus is mentioned as the author of the text and count Jean II de Croÿ, count of Chimay, as its beneficiary. References like these encouraged Ana Pairet to assess developments of self-naming and self-representation of historical agents in the editorial tradition of *Olivier* and *Melusine*, both texts with a rich transmission.[99] She observed that the prologue of the Spanish translation reproduces the names of both the beneficiary and the author (even though presented as the 'translator') as found in the French *Olivier*. It is telling that this historical framing is precisely what is missing in the Dutch edition. Contrary to what we find in research literature, the translator of the Dutch *Olyvier* did not make use of a Spanish source for his translation, but only used a French example.[100] He made an even more literal translation of the French prologue than his Castilian colleague, but with one exception: the proper names of the author Philippe Camus (presented as the translator) and instigator Jean II de Croÿ, preserved in the Castilian translation, are replaced by '.N.', the commonly-used abbreviation of 'Nomen'. This is without a doubt the most extreme example of the Dutch disinterest in preserving those names that allude to a story's aristocratic origin.

> Ic .N. hopende inder gracien godes hebbe begrepen dese teghenwoerdighe hystorie te translateren ende ouer te setten vanden walsche in duytsche ter begherten ende beuelen van .N.
>
> (I, .N., trusting in the grace of God, have taken it upon me to translate and render the present story from French into Dutch, at the request and order of N.)

---

98 See for the quote: Ana Pairet, 'Medieval Bestsellers in the Age of Print: *Melusine* and *Olivier de Castille*'. In: *The Medieval Author in Medieval French Literature*. Ed. by Virginie Greene. New York 2006, p. 189–204 (p. 193). For the French incunabula see ISTC ia01178650; ia01178700; ia01178750; ia01178800; ias01178850; ia01178870 and for the sixteenth-century transmission USTC 49881; 64879; 55753; 55944; 49233. See for the Spanish transmission ISTC ia01180000 and USTC 347670; 347671; 347672; 347673; 338115; 344662; 350748; 338116; 350959; 346600; 337881; 351163.

99 Pairet (see note 98).

100 A publication on the French source of the Dutch *Olyvier*, 'De Nederlandstalige druk van *Olyvier van Castillen* (circa 1510). Een ongewoon getrouwe vertaling' was recently published in *Queeste. Journal of medieval literature in the Low Countries* (2018), p. 67–86. It shows that *Olyvier* was entirely translated from an edition close to the French edition of *c.* 1491–1492 and not – as was believed in the research – after the 1482 edition complemented by a Spanish source. Both the Spanish and the Dutch editions are thus translated following the French edition of *c.* 1491–1492.

Although Van Homberch's contemporary, Michiel Hillen van Hoochstraten, was the most prolific publisher of the early sixteenth century, the printing of romances does not seem to have been the latter's primary concern. The prose romance *Robrecht de Duyvel* occupies a rather isolated place in Van Hoochstraten's publisher's list. His edition, dated 1516, was only discovered shortly before 1980, but its existence had been deduced from several sixteenth- and seventeenth-century indices, one of them mentioning a 1543 edition by Jacob van Liesvelt.[101] The Dutch translation closely corresponds with the French prose edition of the text, but it also has variants that are found in the English prose edition only (as was the case with *Helias*), making it difficult to assess the genesis of the text.[102] It is noteworthy that *Olivier de Castille* and *Robert le Diable*, both published in Dutch around or shortly after 1510, met with great popularity in Spain, where translations from the French had difficulties to compete with originally Castilian romances.[103] There does not seem to be any reason for the fact that the Dutch translations of *Olivier de Castille* and *Robert le Diable* were printed shortly after the Spanish editions other than that both romances were highly popular in France, that they contain 'new' – that is to say fifteenth-century prosifications of – romances and that early sixteenth-century editions also existed in English, indicating a European appeal. Both in the Low Countries and in England, however, their popularity did not last.

5 The Later Years: Willem Vorsterman and Two Decades of Decline

The four publications of Willem Vorsterman that go back to a French source pale into insignificance with respect to the scope of his publisher's list, which

---

101 *Robrecht de Duyvel*. Ed. by Rob Resoort. Muiderberg 1980, p. 24.
102 More research into the source of the Dutch edition is needed, see Franssen, *Tussen tekst en publiek* (note 82), p. 44. See for the French incunabula transmission ISTC ir00202900; ir00202920; ir00202925; ir00202930; ir00202940; and for the transmission in the sixteenth century (10 editions) Mariagrazia Ricci, 'Robert le Diable'. In: *Nouveau Répertoire de mises en prose (XIVᵉ–XVIᵉ siècle)*. Ed. by Maria Colombo Timelli et al. Paris 2014, p. 753–760. For the transmission in England, see STC 21070; 21071; 21071.5, all printed between *c.* 1500–1517.
103 Daniel Eisenberg, *Romances of Chivalry in the Spanish Golden Age*. Newark, Delaware 1982, indicates "that the foreign romances of chivalry available in translation were tangential works, having lost whatever influence they may have had in Castile in the fifteenth or earlier centuries" (URL: http://www.cervantesvirtual.com/obra-visor/romances-of-chivalry-in-the-spanish-golden-age-0/html/ffcd58ce-82b1-11df-acc7-002185ce6064_37.html). For the transmission in Spain, see USTC 347782; 343558; 351106; 351144; 343234; 348851.

comprises over 400 titles. Among his romances we find adaptations based on Dutch manuscript texts, namely *Margariete van Limborch* (1516), *Strijt van Roncevale* (*c.* 1520) and *Hughe van Bordeus* (*c.* 1540), but also translations from the Low German *Frederick van Jenuen* (1531, probably first printed by Van Doesborch before 1518) and from the originally Spanish romance *Sibilla* (*c.* 1538). Vorsterman is often said to have had a clear business sense.[104] It may not surprise that he printed mainly those narratives that had demonstrable success. The first translation from an originally French romance he published was his *c.* 1505 edition of the *Destructie van Jherusalem*,[105] reprinted by himself around 1525[106] and by Jacob or Widow Van Liesveldt around 1540.[107] It is noteworthy that Gheraert Leeu had already published another version of the *Destructie van Jherusalem* in 1482, using Jacob van Maerlant's rhymed *Wrake van Jherusalem*, which in turn goes back to Flavius Josephus' *De bello judaico*.[108] Interestingly, Vorsterman did not use this 'historiographical' version of the text but chose the originally French 'romantic, naïve, popular history', *La Vengeance de nostre seigneur*, instead.[109] His publisher's decision parallels that of Van den Dorpe, who also left Leeu's historiographical edition of the *Destructie van Troyen* aside and published a 'modernized' edition of the story that enjoyed continued popularity.

Vorsterman's *c.* 1517 edition of *Peeter van Provencen*[110] (translated after the French *Pierre de Provence*) was published around the same time as *Olivier de*

---

104 Yves Vermeulen, *Tot profijt en genoegen. Motiveringen voor de produktie van Nederlandstalige gedrukte teksten 1477–1540*. Groningen 1986, p. 129.

105 USTC 441789.

106 USTC 410390.

107 USTC 410390.

108 Willem Kuiper, 'Die *Destructie van Jherusalem* in handschrift en druk'. In: *Voortgang, jaarboek voor de neerlandistiek* 25 (2007), p. 67–88 (p. 84). This was also observed by Willy Braekman, *Die destructie vander stat van Jherusalem. Een Vlaams Volksboek, naar het uniek exemplaar van de Antwerpse druk van Willem Vorsterman (c. 1525)*. Brugge 1984, p. 6–7.

109 See for the quotation *Die destructie vander stat van Jherusalem. Een Vlaams Volksboek, naar het uniek exemplaar van de Antwerpse druk van Willem Vorsterman (ca. 1525)*. Ed. by Willy Braekman. Brugge 1984, p. 6 (my translation). Future research should reveal if the edition published by Vorsterman goes back to a handwritten version of the *Vengeance de nostre seigneur*, as suggested by Willem Kuiper's introduction, 'Die Destructie van Jherusalem'. In: *Bibliotheek van Middelnederlandse Letterkunde, nieuwe digitale reeks*. Ed. by Willem Kuiper 2008–2016 (URL: http://cf.hum.uva.nl/dsp/scriptamanent/bml/Destructie_van_Jherusalem/Destructie_van_Jherusalem.html), or an early printed edition, as accepted by Braekman (p. 8). More research into the transmission of the *Vengeance* is necessary but complex, not least because the lack of uniform titles of the printed *Vengeance*.

110 USTC 436967.

Castille and *Robert le Diable*. There is no evidence that the story ever made it into print in England. The sixteenth-century Spanish translation enjoyed considerable popularity, but it was in Germany that the text was most enthusiastically welcomed, as is shown by the number of reprints of Veit Warbeck's German translation in the course of the sixteenth century and after.[111] It was not, however, until 1535 that the *editio princeps* of this German edition was printed, indicating that Vorsterman only relied on the success of the French edition when he printed the first European translation of the story. His *Peeter van Provencen* edition is a literal translation from the French, with the exception of 28 inserted *refreinen*, which is the highest number found in a sixteenth-century prose romance.[112] These *refreinen* reappear in the edition's 1565 Antwerp reprint by Claes vanden Wouwere, but they are missing in three other late sixteenth-century editions, in which the French and Dutch versions of the story are printed side by side.[113] It is likely that these bilingual editions of *Peeter van Provencen* served as school books, arguably because their "well-known and highly appreciated subject matter" was found suitable for children in the Low Countries so as to learn French.[114] Despite its quite innocent content, the Spanish intellectual Juan Luis Vives, who lived in the Southern Low Countries, mentions *Peeter van Provencen* in his *De institutione foeminae christianae* (1524) as one of the books that could harm the education of young girls, thereby confirming that the work was at least partially aimed at a youthful readership.[115]

After the publication of *Peeter of Provencen* in *c.* 1517, no new Dutch romances of French origin seem to have been published up to around 1540, neither by Vorsterman nor by other publishers. Also in general, the number of 'volksboeken' published in the 20s and 30s of the sixteenth century is significantly

---

111 The appendix to *Pierre de Provence et la Belle Maguelonne*. Ed. by Anna Maria Babbi. Soveria Mannelli 2003, p. 276–278 lists seven Castilian editions and no fewer than 31 German editions for the sixteenth century.

112 Pierre Vinck, 'Het volksboek Die Historie van Peeter van Provencen ende die schoone Maghelone van Napels'. In: *Jaarboek De Fonteine* 27 (1976–1977), p. 3–45. The source of the edition has been a corrupt version of the so-called French 'C' version, printed for the first time around 1485 in Lyon (p. 26).

113 The 1565 edition is not catalogued in the USTC. The bilingual editions were printed by Jan van Waesberghe in 1560 (USTC 59081 and 63951) and 1587 (USTC 79810).

114 Rob Resoort, 'Een proper profitelijc boec. Eind vijftiende en zestiende eeuw'. In: *De hele Bibelebontse berg. De geschiedenis van het kinderboek in Nederland en Vlaanderen van de middeleeuwen tot heden*. Ed. by Nettie Heimeriks and Willem van Toorn. Amsterdam 1989, p. 41–103 (p. 71).

115 Resoort, 'Een proper profitelijc boec' (note 114), p. 59.

lower than in the previous two decades. Works that do appear in this period include reprints of earlier romances as well as romances translated from other languages, such as English (*Jacke*, Antwerp: Hillen van Hoochstraten, 1528), Low German (*Frederick van Jenuen*, Antwerp: Vorsterman, 1531, but probably first printed by Van Doesborch before 1518) and, for the first time, Spanish (*Turias ende Floreta*, Brussels: Van der Noot, 1523; *Sibilla*, Antwerp: Vorsterman, c. 1538). The wider international orientation is one possible explanation for the decline of translations from originally French romances. More 'literary' explanations can be sought in the changes of literary taste or the appeal of other genres than romances. Economically speaking, it could also have been possible that the market was saturated in some way. Previous research has shown that the number of copies increased in the period up to 1540 but this does not mean that the demand grew accordingly.[116] Furthermore, the early sixteenth century witnessed the first waves of censorship and the humanist offensive against fictional stories – notably the Spanish humanist Vives who explicitly mentions some Dutch romances as poisonous reading. On a much more practical level, one should be aware of the fact that the printing of romances was strongly connected to certain individuals, such as Leeu and Van Doesborch and as such dependent on the initiative of those who applied themselves to romances – and those who could afford them. This trend is also visible in Germany, France and perhaps most noticeably, England, where the supply of romances decreases after De Worde's passing until William Copland renewed production in the mid-1550s.[117]

Somewhere around 1540, Vorsterman published his edition of de *Verloren sone*, a translation from the French *L'Enfant Prodigue par personnaiges*, which resembles contemporary romances in its formal presentation.[118] The content of the story is abbreviated to such an extent that it only makes up half of the French verse text. A remarkable feature is that the Dutch translation does adopt the verse form of its example but inserts prose sections at the beginning of each

---

116 According to Peter Cuijpers, *Teksten als koopwaar. Vroege drukkers verkennen de markt: een kwantitatieve analyse van de productie van Nederlandstalige boeken (tot circa 1550) en de 'lezershulp' in de seculiere prozateksten*. Nieuwkoop 1998, p. 53, the average print run of 300 copies in 1480 gradually increased to an average of 500 in 1540. Little is known, however, about the demand.

117 See the contribution of Sánchez-Martí in the present volume, p. 143–166.

118 USTC 410388. It is still under debate if the French text was printed by Alain Lotrian around 1529 or by Jean Janot and the widow of Jean Trepperel between 1510 and 1517, see An Faems, 'De verloren sone: een parabel *int langhe*'. In: *Vechten met de engel. Herschrijven in de Nederlandstalige literatuur*. Ed. by Ben van Humbeeck, Valerie Rousseau and Cin Windey. Antwerp 2009, p. 185–206 (p. 191).

chapter to smooth the transition between the chapters.[119] The result of this procedure is a romance that is characterized by the mix of prose and verse that audiences in the Low Countries were accustomed to.[120]

The last known translation from the French published by Vorsterman is *Galien Rethore*, which was only brought to academic notice in the spring of 2016, when it was sold at auction. Though the date of the edition is described in the auction catalogue as "before 1540?", it cannot be determined any further than the active years of Vorsterman between *c.* 1504 and *c.* 1543.[121] A transcription of the Dutch edition, published synoptically along with Antoine Vérard's *editio princeps* from around 1500, has been published online by Willem Kuiper.[122] His initial findings about the translation indicate that the text is highly abbreviated, leaving out everything that does not directly relate to the adventures of the protagonist.[123] It shows signs of expurgation as well, arguably because the translation was aimed at an audience of young adults (something Kuiper also assumes for many other Dutch romances).[124] In contrast with his French source, Vorsterman's edition is illustrated with many woodcuts, covering both columns of the folio edition. This presentation calls for further study, especially in the light of Vorsterman's other romance editions, the majority of which are in quarto. Notwithstanding the general decrease of folio editions in the course of the sixteenth century, the format was used in Claes van den Wouwere's 1564 edition of *Ponthus en Sydonie* as well as in Jan van Ghelen's 1576 reprint of *Olyvier van Castillen*. Both publishers preferred smaller formats for other works in this period. Apparently, in their editions of medieval romance material they applied conventional schemes – and even used the by then outdated folio format – which may have provided the audience with a sense of identifiability and familiarity.

---

119 Faems (see note 118), p. 193.

120 De Bruijn, 'Das Spiel der Stimmen' (note 67), p. 151.

121 Elisabeth de Bruijn, '*Galien Rethore* herontdekt'. In: *Madoc* 31 (2017), p. 75–82. In handwritten notes by the edition's former owner, Willy Braekman, the edition is dated *c.* 1520–1525, but no motivation for this dating is given. Both the edition and the notes are preserved in the Hendrik Conscience Heritage Library in Antwerp.

122 Willem Kuiper, '*Galien Rethore*: de editie'. In: *Neerlandistiek. Online tijdschrift voor taal- en letterkundig onderzoek* (March 23, 2018) (URL: http://www.neerlandistiek.nl/2017/02/galien-rethore-de-editie/).

123 Willem Kuiper, '*Galien Rethore* online'. In: *Neerlandistiek. Online tijdschrift voor taal- en letterkundig onderzoek* (March 23, 2018) (URL: http://www.neerlandistiek.nl/2016/12/galien-rethore-on-line/).

124 Kuiper, '*Galien Rethore*: de editie' (note 122).

6 Conclusion

In the era of print, some translations were initially made from French romances. However, the orientation of Dutch publishers gradually became wider and they also used source texts from other centres of European literature. The editions by Gheraert Leeu indicate that his printing business had been international rather than Francophone already at an early stage, both in its input (e.g. the use of a Latin Knoblochtzer edition for his *Esopus*) and in its output (shown by his *Paris et Vienne* editions in Low German and – after Caxton's demise – in English). Jan van Doesborch's romance production had been predominantly oriented towards the English market, whereas Willem Vorsterman published romances of various European origins. The Low Countries seem to have discovered their new South in the late 20s of the sixteenth century, when the first works of Spanish origin were translated. Notably, almost all romances of French origin that did appear in the Low Countries were texts with international appeal, meaning that if a translation was published in Dutch, it had most likely also been published in English, Spanish or, to a lesser extent, German. Only Roland van den Dorpe seems to have deviated from this rule by using a manuscript of the *Roman de Troyle* to complement his edition of the *Destructie van Troyen*. In their choice of French materials, the Low Countries often sided with England, in that printers on both sides of the Channel showed an interest in the French *Recueil, Jason, Esopus, Paris et Vienne, Melusine, Bueve de Hantone*, the Swan Knight, *Olivier de Castille* and *Robert le Diable*. Many of these originally French stories were either not printed in Germany, or they drew on different versions of the text (as in the case of *Esopus, Meluzine* and *Pierre de Provence*).

Despite the fact that the Dutch adaptations often go back to the same French sources as the Spanish or English translations, they show their own signature in the way they appropriate the material. As a rule, Dutch translations of French romances are shorter than their French examples because they are abbreviated, whether a little or very much so. Many of these abbreviations result in a plain, understandable translation that would appeal to a youthful audience, as was suggested for many of the discussed romances.[125] The fact that all discussed romances (with the exception of the *Verloren sone*) appear on early seventeenth-century lists of censored school books indicates that a century later, young adults constituted an important share of these romances' readership. Another characteristic of the Dutch translations is the tendency to interfere with the text. In the incunabula period, Leeu's *Esopus, Melusine* and *Paris*

---

125 Resoort, 'Een proper profitelijc boec' (note 114), p. 43–72.

et Vienne editions as well as Van den Dorpe's *Destructie van Troyen* testify to the trend to combine texts from multiple sources, while many romances published between *c.* 1500–1540 insert verse passages, which come in the shape of *refreinen* or dramatic dialogues. This contrasts with English translations of French sources, which "tended to be strictly faithful to their originals".[126] The verse passages, which are most likely composed by *rederijkers*, offer the most concrete clue for situating many Dutch prose romances in an urban middle class environment. It is tempting to connect this to the highly puzzling Dutch tendency to remove the names of the historical actors involved in the French originals. In the surrounding territories, printed romances were still suffused with the spirit of the stories' aristocratic origin and many chivalric narratives enjoyed a continued interest in the late sixteenth century. The lack of reprints of stories like *Parijs ende Vienna, Olyvier van Castillen, Peeter van Provencen* and *Galien Rhetore* in the Low Countries, on the other hand, suggests that medieval chivalric romances fell out of favour when a new era was born.

Bibliography

Bertelsmeier-Kierst, Christa, 'Erzählen in Prosa. Zur Entwicklung des deutschen Prosaromans bis 1500'. In: *ZfdA* 143 (2014), p. 141–165.

Besamusca, Bart, 'Raoul Lefèvre in Dutch: Two 1521 Editions of the Antwerp Printer Jan van Doesborch'. In: *Journal of the Early Book Society* 20 (2017), p. 219–232.

Besamusca, Bart, 'Tekst en beeld in twee drukken van Jan van Doesborch: *Van Jason ende Hercules* en *Die historie van den stercken Hercules*'. In: *Spiegel der Letteren* 59 (2017), p. 1–34.

Bogaart, Saskia, *Geleerde kennis in de volkstaal*. Van den proprieteyten der dinghen *(Haarlem 1485) in perspectief*. Hilversum 2004.

Braekman, Willy, *Die destructie vander stat van Jherusalem. Een Vlaams Volksboek, naar het uniek exemplaar van de Antwerpse druk van Willem Vorsterman (c. 1525)*. Brugge 1984.

Bruijn, Elisabeth de, 'Reculer pour mieux sauter: de bronnenproblematiek en de literaire eigenheid van de Middelnederlandse *Helias*'. In: *Verslagen en Mededelingen van de Koninklijke Academie voor Nederlandse Taal- en Letterkunde* 126 (2016), p. 227–263.

Bruijn, Elisabeth de, 'Das Spiel der Stimmen. Performative Verspassagen in einigen niederländischen Prosaromanen (ca. 1500–1540)'. In: *Stimme und Performanz in der mittelalterlichen Literatur*. Ed. by Monica Unzeitig, Nine Miedema and Angela Schrott. Berlin 2017.

Bruijn, Elisabeth de, '*Galien Rethore* herontdekt'. In: *Madoc* 31 (2017), p. 75–82.

---

[126] Helen Cooper, 'Prose Romances'. In: *A Companion to Middle English Prose*. Ed. by A.S.G. Edwards. Cambridge 2014, p. 215–229 (p. 221–222).

Bruijn, Elisabeth de, 'De Nederlandstalige druk van *Olyvier van Castillen* (circa 1510). Een ongewoon getrouwe vertaling'. In: *Queeste. Journal of medieval literature in the Low Countries* 25 (2018), p. 67–86.

Coigneau, Dirk, 'Drama in druk, tot circa 1540'. In: *Spel en spektakel. Middeleeuws toneel in de Lage Landen*. Ed. by Hans van Dijk and Bart Ramakers. Amsterdam 2001 (Nederlandse literatuur en cultuur in de Middeleeuwen 23), p. 201–214 and 352–359.

Coldiron, A.E.B., *Printers without Borders. Translation and Textuality in the Renaissance*. Cambridge 2015.

Cooper, Helen, 'Going Native: the Caxton and Mainwaring Versions of Paris and Vienne'. In: *Travel and Prose Fiction in Early Modern England*. Ed. by Nandini Das, special number of *The Yearbook of English Studies* 41 (2011), p. 21–34.

Cooper, Helen, 'Prose Romances'. In: *A Companion to Middle English Prose*. Ed. by A.S.G. Edwards. Cambridge 2014, p. 215–229.

Cuijpers, Peter, *Teksten als koopwaar. Vroege drukkers verkennen de markt: een kwantitatieve analyse van de productie van Nederlandstalige boeken (tot circa 1550) en de 'lezershulp' in de seculiere prozateksten*. Nieuwkoop 1998.

Cuijpers, Peter, *Van Reynaert de Vos tot Tijl Uilenspiegel. Op zoek naar een canon van volksboeken, 1600–1900*. Zutphen 2014.

Debaene, Luc., 'Rederijkers en prozaromans'. In: *De gulden passer* 27 (1949), p. 1–23.

Debaene, Luc., *De Nederlandse volksboeken. Ontstaan en geschiedenis van de Nederlandse prozaromans, gedrukt tussen 1475 en 1540*. 2nd ed. Hulst 1977.

Dicke, Gerd, *Heinrich Steinhöwels 'Esopus' und seine Fortsetzer. Untersuchungen zu einem Bucherfolg der Frühdruckzeit*. Tübingen 1994.

Diekmann-Dröge, Gabriele, '*Paris und Vienna* in Antwerpen. Der mittelniederdeutsche Frühdruck aus der Offizin Gheraert Leeus'. In: *Niederdeutsches Wort* 26 (1986), p. 55–76.

Duijvestijn, Bob, 'Der niederländische Prosaroman von Meluzine; eine Orientierung'. In: *Melusine. Actes du Colloque du Centre d'Études Médiévales de l'Université de Picardie Jules Verne, 13 et 14 Janvier 1996*. Ed. by Danielle Buschinger and Wolfgang Spiewok. Greifswald 1996.

Eisenberg, Daniel, *Romances of Chivalry in the Spanish Golden Age*. Newark, Delaware 1982.

Faems, An, 'De verloren sone: een parabel *int langhe*'. In: *Vechten met de engel. Herschrijven in de Nederlandstalige literatuur*. Ed. by Ben van Humbeeck, Valerie Rousseau and Cin Windey. Antwerp 2009, p. 185–206.

Franssen, P.J.A., 'Jan van Doesborch (?–1536), Printer of English texts'. In: *Quaerendo* 16 (1986), p. 259–280.

Franssen, P.J.A., *Tussen tekst en publiek. Jan van Doesborch, drukker-uitgever en literator te Antwerpen en Utrecht in de eerste helft van de zestiende eeuw*. Amsterdam 1990.

Goudriaan, Koen, 'Een drukker en zijn markt. Gheraert Leeu (Gouda 1477 – Antwerpen 1492/3)'. In: *Madoc* 6 (1992), p. 194–205.

Goudriaan, Koen, 'Inleiding'. In: *Een drukker zoekt publiek. Gheraert Leeu te Gouda 1477–1484*. Ed. by Koen Goudriaan et al. Gouda 1993, p. 3–11.

Hecker, Beate, *Julien Macho, Esope. Eingeleitet und herausgegeben nach der Edition von 1486*. Hamburg 1982.

Hellinga, Lotte, *Texts in Transit. Manuscript to Proof and Print in the Fifteenth Century*. Leiden 2014.

Hellinga, Lotte, 'William Caxton and Colard Mansion'. In: *Colard Mansion. Incunabula, Prints and Manuscripts in Medieval Bruges*. Ed. by Evelien Hauwaerts, Evelien de Wilde and Ludo Vandamme. Gent 2018, p. 63–69.

Lotte Hellinga, 'William Caxton, Colard Mansion, and the Printer in Type 1'. In: *Bulletin du Bibliophile* 2011, p. 86–114 [republished in Lotte Hellinga, *Incunabula in Transit. People and Trade*. Leiden 2018, p. 286–322].

The History of Oliver of Castile. Ed. by Robert Edmund Graves. London 1898.

Keesman, Wilma, 'Jacob Bellaert en Haarlem'. In: *Haarlems Helicon. Literatuur en toneel te Haarlem vóór 1800*. Ed. by E.K. Grootes. Hilversum 1993, p. 27–48.

Keesman, Wilma, *De eindeloze stad. Troje en Trojaanse oorsprongsmythen in de (laat)-middeleeuwse en vroegmoderne Nederlanden*. Hilversum 2017.

Kok, Ina, *Woodcuts in Incunabula Printed in the Low Countries*. 4 vols. Houten 2013.

Kuiper, Willem, 'Briseïda. De identiteit van een 'middeleeuws' romanpersonage'. In: *Simulacrum, het eigentijdse tijdschrift voor kunst en cultuur*, themanummer Identiteit, 12 (2004), p. 17–19.

Kuiper, Willem, 'Die *Destructie van Jherusalem* in handschrift en druk'. In: *Voortgang, jaarboek voor de neerlandistiek* 25 (2007), p. 67–88.

Kuiper, Willem, 'Die Destructie van Jherusalem'. In: *Bibliotheek van Middelnederlandse Letterkunde, nieuwe digitale reeks*. Ed. by Willem Kuiper 2008–2016 (URL: http://cf.hum. uva.nl/dsp/scriptamanent/bml/Destructie_van_Jherusalem/Destructie_van_Jherusalem. html).

Kuiper, Willem, 'Die vergaderinge der historien van Troyen'. In: *Bibliotheek van de Middelnederlandse letterkunde. Nieuwe digitale reeks*. Ed. by Willem Kuiper. Amsterdam 2008–2016 (URL: http://cf.hum.uva.nl/dsp/scriptamanent/bml/Vergaderinge_der_histor ien_van_Troyen/Vergaderinge_der_historien_van_Troyen.html).

Kuiper, Willem, '*Galien Rethore*: de editie'. In: *Neerlandistiek. Online tijdschrift voor taal- en letterkundig onderzoek* (March 23, 2018) (URL: http://www.neerlandistiek.nl/2017/02/ga lien-rethore-de-editie/).

Kuiper, Willem, '*Galien Rethore* online'. In: *Neerlandistiek. Online tijdschrift voor taal- en letterkundig onderzoek* (March 23, 2018) (URL: http://www.neerlandistiek.nl/2016/12/ga lien-rethore-on-line/).

Het leven en de fabels van Esopus. Ed. by Hans Rijns and Willem van Bentum. Hilversum 2016.

Oosterman, Johan, 'Franse en Nederlandse letterkunde in middeleeuws Vlaanderen'. In: *Literaire bruggenbouwers tussen Nederland en Frankrijk. Receptie, vertaling en cultuuroverdracht sinds de Middeleeuwen*. Ed. by Maaike Koffeman, Alicia Montoya and Marc Smeets. Amsterdam 2017, p. 29–47.

Pairet, Ana, 'Medieval Bestsellers in the Age of Print: *Melusine* and *Olivier de Castille*'. In: *The Medieval Author in Medieval French Literature*. Ed. by Virginie Greene. New York 2006, p. 189–204.

Paris e Vienna, romanzo cavalleresco. Ed. by Anna Maria Babbi. Padova 1991.

Pierre de Provence et la Belle Maguelonne. Ed. by Anna Maria Babbi. Soveria Mannelli 2003.

Resoort, Rob, 'Een proper profitelijc boec. Eind vijftiende en zestiende eeuw'. In: *De hele Bibelebontse berg. De geschiedenis van het kinderboek in Nederland en Vlaanderen van de middeleeuwen tot heden*. Ed. by Nettie Heimeriks and Willem van Toorn. Amsterdam 1989, p. 41–103.

Resoort, Rob, 'De presentatie van drukwerk in de volkstaal in de Nederlanden tot 1501: waar zijn de auteurs, vertalers en opdrachtgevers? Een verkenning'. In: *Geschreven en gedrukt. Boekproductie van handschrift naar druk in de overgang van Middeleeuwen naar moderne tijd.* Ed. by Herman Pleij, Joris Reynaert et al. Gent 2004, p. 177–206.

Ricci, Mariagrazia, 'Robert le Diable'. In: *Nouveau Répertoire de mises en prose (XIVe–XVIe siècle).* Ed. by Maria Colombo Timelli et al. Paris 2014, p. 753–760.

Robrecht de Duyvel. Ed. by Rob Resoort. Muiderberg 1980.

Rouzet, Anne, *Dictionnaire des imprimeurs, libraires et éditeurs des XVe et XVIe siècles dans les limites géographiques de la Belgique actuelle.* Nieuwkoop 1975.

Sánchez-Martí, Jordi, 'The Printed Transmission of Medieval Romance from William Caxton to Wynkyn de Worde, 1473–1533'. In: *The Transmission of Medieval Romance: Metres, Manuscripts and Early Prints.* Ed. by Ad Putter and Judith A. Jefferson. Cambridge 2018, p. 170–190.

Suard, F., 'Pierre Desrey et *La Généalogie de Godefroy de Bouillon*'. In: *Les épopées de la croisade.* Ed. by K.H. Bender and H. Kleber. Special issue of *Zeitschrift für französische Sprache und Literatur* 11 (1987), p. 151–162.

Vermeulen, Yves, *Tot profijt en genoegen. Motiveringen voor de produktie van Nederlandstalige gedrukte teksten 1477–1540.* Groningen 1986.

De vijfhonderdste verjaring van de boekdrukkunst in de Nederlanden. Catalogus. Brussel 1973.

Vinck, Pierre, 'Het volksboek Die Historie van Peeter van Provencen ende die schoone Maghelone van Napels'. In: *Jaarboek De Fonteine* 27 (1976–1977), p. 3–45.

Wackers, Paul, 'Gheraert Leeu as a Printer of Fables and Animal Stories'. In: *Reinardus, Yearbook of the International Reynard Society* 20 (2007–2008), p. 128–152.

Wang, Yu-Chiao, 'Caxton's Romances and Their Early Tudor Readers'. In: *Huntington Library Quarterly* 67 (2004), p. 173–188.

Zeldenrust, Lydia, *Mutations of an Animal-Human Hybrid Monster: The Western European Mélusine Translations (c. 1400–1600).* Doctoral thesis Queen Mary University of London 2015.

Julia Boffey
The Printing of English Narratives in Wynkyn de Worde's Later Career

Abstracts: In the course of his long career, the London printer Wynkyn de Worde produced editions of English narratives of different kinds. Although these constitute a relatively small part of his total output, they nonetheless suggest that he took some interest in developing titles involving romance and "merry jest", and his attention to these genres in the early and middle part of his career has been the subject of productive scholarship. This essay surveys evidence from the later years of de Worde's career. It investigates the extent to which he concerned himself with new titles or with reprints of works of this kind and looks for signs of experimentation in the ways they were presented (taking account of title-pages and the provision of woodcuts, for example). It pays particular attention to the *novelle* and jests, as well as to indications that the printing of some of these English tales were in response to particular circumstances.

Au cours de sa longue carrière, l'imprimeur londonien Wynkyn de Worde a produit des éditions de plusieurs genres narratifs anglais. Bien que ceux-ci ne constituent qu'une partie relativement restreinte de sa production totale, il semble néanmoins que l'imprimeur londonien ait vraiment tenté de constituer un fonds composé de romans et de contes à rire. L'attention que Wynkyn de Worde a portée à ces genres au début et au milieu de sa carrière a déjà fait l'objet de recherches abondantes. Cet article étudie les dernières années de sa carrière. En particulier, il tente de discerner dans quelle mesure de Worde est lui-même responsable du choix de nouveaux titres ou de titres à réimprimer, et décrit aussi dans quelle mesure l'imprimeur londonien a introduit des innovations au niveau de la présentation (les pages de titre ou les gravures sur bois, par exemple). L'article consacre beaucoup d'attention aux *novelle* et aux histoires comiques, et à des signes qui pourraient indiquer que l'impression de certains textes s'est faite en réponse à des circonstances particulières.

Wynkyn de Worde had a long career as one of England's major early printers. Starting work with William Caxton at Westminster, he took on Caxton's business after his death in 1492 and evidently remained actively at work until his own death in 1534/5.[1] This career of over forty years, during the

---

[1] N. F. Blake, 'Wynkyn de Worde: the Early Years'. In: *Gutenberg Jahrbuch* (1971), p. 62–69; N. F. Blake, 'Wynkyn de Worde: the Later Years'. In: *Gutenberg Jahrbuch* (1972), p. 128–138; Mary C. Erler, 'Wynkyn de Worde's Will: Legatees and Bequests'. In: *The Library*, 6th ser., 10 (1988), p. 107–121. His connection with Caxton was made prominent in most of the printers' marks he used (see the examples in R. B. McKerrow, *Printers' and Publishers' Devices in England and*

Julia Boffey, Queen Mary University of London

early part of which (in 1501) he moved the business from Westminster to the city of London, saw the printing of around 850 titles.[2] Although this figure includes multiple editions of some titles, especially significant in the case of schoolbooks which went through many editions, it is still a striking total; and still more so if, as has been calculated, around 70% of the works he printed were put in print by him for the first time. The books he printed included many works a long way from narrative literature: not just the grammars and schoolbooks in which he came to specialize, but also indulgences, works for priests and treatises of spiritual instruction; many of these were Latin works. His total output includes only somewhere around forty to fifty titles that fall into the category of 'narrative literature' in the vernacular, in prose or verse.[3] But for over four decades Wynkyn de Worde was one of the main printers of such materials in England, with an output in this area rivalled only by that of Richard Pynson[4]; and his innovations in this field were significant.

The activities of De Worde's early years as a printer, including innovations made in the fields of type and woodcut illustration, have been exhaustively documented by Lotte Hellinga.[5] Some of the preoccupations of his first decades in London, after 1501, are explored in Martha Driver's work on the appearance of the books he printed, particularly his experiments with the design possibilities of the printed page and with the commercial potential of illustration and other design features.[6] Driver notes De Worde's cultivation of a 'brand' through the standardization of certain features of his books and his ready exploitation of factotum figures

---

Scotland, 1485–1640. London 1913). [For De Worde, see also the contribution by Sánchez-Martí in the present volume, p. 143.]

2 This figure is derived from the information given in STC Vol. III, p.187–189, and is necessarily approximate (it includes reprinted titles and books printed for De Worde by others or using his types, for example). For analyses of De Worde's overall output, some of which are based on outdated assessments of the total number of books he printed, see H. S. Bennett, English Books & Readers 1475 to 1557. Cambridge 1970 [1952], p. 190–192; James Moran, Wynkyn de Worde: Father of Fleet Street. Ed. by Lotte Hellinga and Mary C. Erler, with a preface by John Dreyfus. London 2003 [1976], p. 48–49; and Lotte Hellinga, William Caxton and Early Printing in England. London 2010, p. 131–155.

3 For the purposes of this discussion, 'narrative literature' is taken to include romances in prose and verse; entertaining stories, variously comic and exemplary; novelle in English. Categories that have been excluded are dream visions (by authors including Chaucer, Lydgate, Skelton, Hawes and Neville), debates and love complaints.

4 On Pynson, see Pamela Neville-Sington, 'Pynson, Richard (c.1449–1529/30)'. In: ODNB, online ed., Jan 2008 [http://0-www.oxforddnb.com.catalogue.libraries.london.ac.uk/view/article/22935].

5 See Moran, Wynkyn de Worde (note 2), p. 182–229.

6 Martha W. Driver, The Image in Print: Book Illustration in Late Medieval England and its Sources. London 2004, p. 77–114.

in the forms of title-page that he favoured. Work by other scholars on De Worde's printing of English romances during these years has fleshed out the detail of De Worde's strategies in relation to these particular narratives, a 'line' which he seems quite deliberately to have developed in his first two decades in business and to the design of which he clearly paid attention.[7] Carol Meale has written of the "continuing vitality" of the romance genre among the many works printed by De Worde, noting that the number of times that he reprinted individual romances attests to "a lively demand amongst the readers and buyers of books".[8]

Most studies of the works printed by De Worde have concentrated on the early and middle part of his career, perhaps partly in order to clarify the new directions he took after Caxton's death, and to ascertain how his preoccupations differed from those of Richard Pynson, London's other major printer during the first decades of the sixteenth century. Certainly De Worde's most energetic cultivation of new markets seems to have taken place in the years before 1520, particularly with his publication of Latin schoolbooks by authors like John Stanbridge and Robert Whittinton; and these years also saw the first appearances of most of the Middle English narratives he printed – romances, verse narratives and short narrative 'jests' (comic stories, in prose and in verse) of various kinds. To some extent the range of works published in the years after 1520 until his death in 1535 might reasonably be characterized as unadventurous, dominated by reprints of established successes like the schoolbooks, which Lotte Hellinga has seen as a "cash crop" forming "a very significant proportion of his total output".[9] But even though the number of narrative works published between 1520 and 1535 is not great, it is worth reviewing the degree to which these works do or do not replicate patterns established earlier in de Worde's working life and inspecting features of their presentation to see how elements of design may have played into their production and marketing. Such a review can serve to highlight the particularities of readers' tastes in narrative literature at this point and help to determine the extent to which these might have undergone changes over the course of De Worde's long career.

---

7 See especially Carol M. Meale, 'Caxton, de Worde and the Publication of Romance in Late Medieval England'. In: *The Library* 6th ser., 14 (1992), p. 283–298; Jordi Sánchez-Martí, 'The Printed History of Middle English Verse Romances'. In: *Modern Philology* 107 (2009), p. 1–31; and Jordi Sánchez-Martí, 'Illustrating the Middle English Verse Romances'. In: *Word and Image* 27 (2011), p. 90–102.

8 Meale, *Caxton* (note 7), p. 298.

9 Hellinga (see note 2), p. 153.

Works of narrative literature printed by De Worde between 1520 and 1535 fall into three main categories. First are the reprints of romances, in both prose and verse, which De Worde had already published before 1520. These include *Sir Bevis of Hampton* (verse; [1500], STC 1987; [*c*.1500], STC 1987.5; [1533?], STC 1988.6); *The Knyght of the swanne* or *Helyas* (prose; 1512, STC 7571; *c*. 1522, STC 7571.5); *Capystranus* (verse; *c*. 1515, STC 14649; [?1527], STC 14649.5; [1530?], STC 14650); *Kynge Rycharde cuer du lyon* (verse; 1509, STC 21007; 1528, STC 21008); *The dystruccyon of Iherusalem* (prose; [1510?], STC 14518; 1528, STC 14519); Malory, *Le Morte Darthur* (prose; 1498, STC 802; 1529, STC 803); *ye byrth & prophecye of Marlyn* (verse; 1499, STC 17840.7; 1510, STC 17841; 1529, STC 17841.3). Clearly these must have counted as reliable favourites of some kind and attention will be given below to the extent to which certain of them were revised or updated in any way as they were reprinted across the course of time.

In the second category are romances that were printed by De Worde for the first time in the years between 1520 and 1535, or which survive only in editions assigned on some form of evidence to these years. This group of works includes two which were printed only by De Worde and thus will merit some attention: *Undo youre dore*, also known in later editions as *The Squire of Low Degree* (verse; [*c*. 1520], STC 23111.5), and *The life of Ipomydon* (verse; [*c*. 1522], STC 5732.5; [*c*. 1527], STC 5733). A further 'new' romance for De Worde in these years, *Sir Tryamour* (verse; 1530, STC 24302), had been previously printed by Pynson and is accordingly slightly different. The third category of English narrative works printed by De Worde between 1520 and 1535 includes the tried and tested non-romance favourites the *Gesta romanorum* (prose; previously printed by De Worde [*c*.1502], STC 21286.2; [*c*. 1510], STC 21286.3; [*c*. 1515], STC 21286.5; [*c*. 1525], STC 21286.7) and *Reynard the Fox* (prose; *c*. 1525, STC 20192a), previously printed by Pynson ([1494], STC 20921; [before 1506], STC 20921.5), from Caxton's translation; two verse *novelle* based on stories by Boccaccio, in versions made by William Walter and apparently printed for the first time: *ye hystory of Tytus & Gesyppus* (1525, STC 3184.5) and *The amerous hystory of Guystard and Sygysmonde* (1532, STC 3183.5); and finally a small clutch of short comic tales: *Les faictz merueilleux de virgille* (French prose; *c*. 1520, STC 24827.5); Skelton's *The Tunning of Elinor Rumming* (verse; [*c*.1521], STC 22611.5); *a mery iest of the mylner of Abyngdon* (verse; 1532–34: STC 78) and *a lytell propre ieste called cryste crosse me spede* (verse; *c*. 1534, STC 14546.5). These last two sorts of work – *novelle* and comic tales – will also come under scrutiny in what follows.

Before embarking on detailed study of all these titles there are some general observations to be made about what survives from these years of De

Worde's career. Probably the most important of these points is one that relates to the survival patterns of all early books, which are inevitably patchy and may well be unrepresentative. Even what survives is often fragmentary, sometimes lacking first and last leaves which might have carried crucial information about matters like publication dates or authorship, and in some cases so depleted as to constitute very little in the form of hard evidence. All of this makes it something of a challenge to trace patterns or continuities or new departures, although one point that might be made about the English narratives printed by De Worde between 1520 and 1535 is that long works of 'literary' verse by authors like Chaucer and Lydgate are absent (at earlier points De Worde had printed Chaucer's *Canterbury Tales* and *Troilus and Criseyde* and Lydgate's *Siege of Thebes*, but he seems to have been uninterested in new editions). Another complicating feature of De Worde's later career is the increasing evidence for forms of collaboration with other printers, ventures which have the effect of blurring the outlines of what might have been his own initiatives during these years. The association of some vernacular narratives with De Worde's name may in fact owe more to the energies of collaborators like Robert Copland, who certainly shaped some texts for publication even if not suggesting them as new initiatives. Of the works listed in the paragraph above, at least three have associations of some kind with Copland: *Ipomydon, The Knyght of the swanne* and *The amerous hystory of Guystard and Sygysmonde.*[10] Some of the younger printers acquiring business in London in the 1520s and 1530s had worked with De Worde or collaborated with him and their own ventures into the printing of English narratives may owe more than is now apparent to lost De Worde editions: John Skot, who had connections of some kind with De Worde, printed *The hystory of syr Isembras c.* 1530 (verse; STC 14280.5, frag.) and *The jest of Sir Gawaine c.* 1528 (verse; STC 11691a.3) and *c.* 1530 (verse; STC 11691a.5, this time in collaboration with John Butler, who had also worked for De Worde)[11]; after De Worde's death one of his former apprentices, John Byddell, produced his

---

10 For the verse by Copland added to *Ipomydon* and *Guystard and Sygysmonde*, see Mary C. Erler (ed.), *Robert Copland: Poems*. Toronto 1993, p. 76–77, 149–159. On his role in *Ipomydon*, see Jordi Sánchez-Martí, 'Wynkyn de Worde's Editions of *Ipomydon*: A Reassessment of the Evidence'. In: *Neophilologus* 89 (2005), p. 153–163; and Jordi Sánchez-Martí, 'Robert Copland and *The Lyfe of Ipomydon*'. In: *Notes and Queries* 55 (2008), p. 139–142.

11 On Skot and Butler, see STC Vol. III, p. 156 and p. 33; and Peter W. M. Blayney, *The Stationers' Company and the Printers of London 1501–1557*. 2 vols, Cambridge 2013, p. 179–180.

own edition of *Adam Bell* (verse; 2 June 1536, STC 1806), printed at least once earlier in De Worde's career around 1505.[12]

1 Reprinting Romances

Rycharde cuer du lyon and Malory's *Morte Darthur* are examples of substantial romances printed by De Worde both early and late in his career. Comparison of the surviving editions offers the opportunity to assess the amount of energy that went into updating these works over time and to investigate evidence of any experimentation with how they were presented, in terms of their size and paratextual apparatus. Their treatment illustrates a mixture of continuities and innovation. *Rycharde*, a metrical romance, was printed by De Worde in 1509 (STC 21007) and again in 1528 (STC 21008), on both occasions in quarto. The title-pages and colophons of the two editions are almost identical, apart from the fact that De Worde styles himself in the earlier one "printer to the king's mother" (Henry VII's mother, Lady Margaret Beaufort, died on 29 June 1509, and for a period before this point De Worde took the opportunity of stressing his connection with her in colophons to the works he printed).[13] The layout of the text is similar in both editions and the same woodcuts are used throughout, mostly in the same order – although there is one change, perhaps because a cut had gone missing.[14] A woodcut of travelers in a ship used in the 1509 edition was replaced in the 1528 edition with a slightly different version of this scene, a cut used for a number of works after its first appearance in Hawes's *Pastime of Pleasure*, also printed for the first time in 1509. There is no particular evidence of innovation or experimentation here: rather a pragmatic 'patching up' to keep a tried and tested product looking as it looked before.

The second edition of Malory's *Morte Darthur* suggests a more alert awareness of what might be commercially attractive. De Worde's first edition of this work, printed in 1498, was one of the big folio-sized volumes produced while his business was still at Westminster: its substantial text derived from Caxton's edition of 1485 and De Worde's innovation in 1498 was to enhance it with

---

12 On Byddell see STC Vol. III, p. 35; and Blayney (see note 11), p. 285–286. The printer responsible for an edition of *Syr Degore* (verse; [*c*. 1535], STC 6470.5) has not been identified.
13 See A. S. G. Edwards and Carol M. Meale, 'The Marketing of Printed Books in Late Medieval England'. In: *The Library* 6th ser., 15 (1993) p. 95–124.
14 See Edward Hodnett, *English Woodcuts 1480–1535*. Oxford 1973 [1935], no. 1109.

a number of woodcuts (STC 802).[15] The later edition, printed in 1529 (STC 803), remained folio-sized, unusually for this stage in De Worde's career, but also involved a number of changes. The text was modernized and the syntax on occasion changed; most, but not all of the woodcuts from the earlier edition were used and a number of new ones (some of which appear in other works printed by De Worde around this time) were pressed into service. It would be fair to say that De Worde must have regarded this as a premium product and one worth taking care to update. The 1529 edition was also given an unusual and florid full-page version of De Worde's printer's device.[16] In addition, rather differently from most of the romances printed at this period by De Worde and others, the *Morte Darthur* was attributed to a named author. Thomas Malory had included his own name in the final section of the work and the printer's colophon draws attention to the fact that "this noble and ioyous boke" was "reduced into Englysshe by the moost wel dysposed knyght afore named".

Most of the romances printed by De Worde were presented without information about authorship – no doubt because these tended to be works of some antiquity, whose authors were simply unknown. Only in the case of the *c.* 1522 edition of *The Knyght of the swanne* or *Helyas*, which survives in fragmentary form (STC 7571.5), is there likely to have been some indication of the human agency by which the work came into being. If the *c.* 1522 edition followed the model of De Worde's earlier one, dated 6 February 1512 (STC 7571), it probably included a "Prologue of ye translatour" supplied by De Worde's associate Robert Copland, in which Copland explains that the prose translation (called a "hystory") was commissioned by Edward Stafford, third duke of Buckingham, "lynyally ... dyscended" from the family of Helyas the swan-knight and that he was "cohorted" by De Worde to make a translation from "a true approued" French, printed copy.

The factors which might have prompted De Worde to revisit romances that he had already printed at an earlier point in his career are mostly obscure. *The Knyght of the swanne* may conceivably have acquired a new topical relevance after 17 May 1521, when Edward Stafford, commissioner of its translation, was executed on the orders of Henry VIII after being tried for treason, but the STC date of its reprinting is approximate (*c.* 1522) and does not allow for useful speculation.[17] Since most of these reprinted romances cannot be

---

15 Hodnett (see note 14), p. 14, 77, 91; D. Thomas Hanks Jr., 'Caxton, de Worde and Malory's *Morte Darthur*'. In: *Reviewing 'Le Morte Darthur': Texts and Contexts, Characters and Themes,* ed. by K. S. Whetter and Raluca L. Radulescu. Woodbridge 2005 (Arthurian Studies 60), p. 27–48.
16 McKerrow (see note 1), no. 46.
17 See C. S. L. Davies, 'Stafford, Edward, third duke of Buckingham (1478–1521)'. In: ODNB, online ed., Jan 2008 [http://0-www.oxforddnb.com.catalogue.libraries.london.ac.uk/view/article/26202].

assigned to specific dates it is hard to relate them to particular circumstances, but it is possible that the *c.* 1527 reprinting of *Capystranus* (STC 14649.5), the elaborated story of an Italian soldier-saint who led Christian troops against Ottoman forces at the siege of Belgrade in 1456, may have responded to a heightened sense of threat from the east: Suleiman the Magnificent had won the battle of Mohacs in Hungary in 1526 and went on to lead the siege of Vienna in 1529. This context may also have suggested the reprinting of the crusading romance *Kynge Rycharde cuer du lyon* (STC 21008) and of the historical prose romance *The dystruccyon of Iherusalem* around 1528 (STC 14519).[18] Since Malory's *Morte* concludes with the departure on crusade of the few Arthurian knights left after Arthur's death it is just about possible to interpret its reprinting as associated with the same set of circumstances; but in this case perhaps another prompt was at work: folio editions of the English works were being produced by other printers – the verse romance *King Alexander* by Richard Faques in (1525?) (STC 321) and many of Chaucer's works, in three volumes, by Richard Pynson in 1526 (STC 5086, STC 5088, STC 5096) – and the production of a new folio-sized edition of the *Morte Darthur* may have seemed a shrewd commercial move.

2 New Romances Printed 1520–1535

The new titles printed by De Worde between 1520 and 1535, insofar as it is possible to determine these, would seem to include only two romances, both in what by this stage may have been the slightly old-fashioned form of verse: *The life of Ipomydon*, in two editions (*c.* 1522, STC 5732.5; *c.* 1527, STC 5733) and *Undo youre dore* (*The Squire of Low Degree; c.* 1520, STC 23111.5). *Ipomydon* was not in itself new – versions survive in fifteenth-century manuscript copies – but one particular text was evidently made available to De Worde by a London mercer, John Colyns, who acquired it in 1517.[19] Study of the manuscript (London, British Library MS Harley 2252) and of the surviving fragments of the printed editions, suggests that Colyns's copy was prepared for De Worde's printshop by Robert Copland, who added an envoy, at some point between 1517 and about 1524; a date of *c.* 1527 has been proposed for

---

18 This prose text of the *dystruccyon*, first printed by de Worde in 1510(?) and reprinted by Pynson in 1513(?), was apparently translated from a French original: see R. E. Lewis, N. F. Blake and A. S. G. Edwards, *Index of Printed Middle English Prose*. New York 1985, no. 241.
19 This is the B version of *Ipomydon* (BL MS Harley 2252).

the second edition.[20] This is an unusual example of a work which seems to have recommended itself for printing through the simple factor of availability: an acquaintance had a manuscript copy which could be temporarily lent for the printer's use.

The decision to print *Undo youre dore* (*The Squire of Low Degree*) is more of a mystery. No sources are known, no manuscript copy of the work has survived and there is no trace of other early printed editions, although it was to be among the romances given a new lease of life by William Copland in the mid-sixteenth century and appears from references made to it in booksellers' records and other works from *c.* 1520 onwards to have been reasonably well known.[21] It is a curious narrative, different in many ways from other contemporary romances in both verse and prose: it has a disjointed plot, a seemingly disproportionate concern with the material benefits of social advancement and a slightly off-colour preoccupation with the heroine's seven-year worship of a mummified body she supposes to be that of her lost lover. In formal terms, too, it takes romance in unusual directions, devoting much space to dialogue. There may be grounds for supposing that its printing was some kind of experiment on De Worde's part, a testing of the market for romance of a generically innovative mode. The paratextual material that accompanies it in fact makes it look more like a courtly dialogue than a romance. Its title-page employs a woodcut of a richly dressed man receiving a token from a richly-dressed woman; the image is surmounted by a banderole in which appear the words "here begynneth vndo your dore", as if the central moment in the narrative will be a conversation between the two.[22] The colophon also rounds the work off with the words "thus endeth undo your doore", adding only afterwards "other wise / called the squyer of lowe degre". Other uses of the woodcut, in De Worde's editions of Stephen Hawes's *Comforte of Lovers* ([1515], STC 12942.5), Chaucer's *Troylus and Cresyde* (1517, STC 5095) and in the curious alliterative poem *The iiii leues of the truelove* (1510?, STC 15345), devotional rather than secular, do not suggest that the image carried associations with the range of

---

20 Carol M. Meale, 'Wynkyn de Worde's Setting-Copy for *Ipomydon*'. In: *Studies in Bibliography* 35 (1982), p. 156–171. Sanchez-Martí, *Editions of* Ipomydon (note 10) proposes a reversal of what has been supposed to be the order in which the editions were printed.
21 See further Julia Boffey and A. S. G. Edwards, '*The Squire of Low Degree* and the Penumbra of Romance Narrative in the Early Sixteenth Century'. In: *Romance Rewritten. The Evolution of Middle English Romance A Tribute to Helen Cooper*'. Ed. by Elizabeth Archibald, Megan Leitch and Corinne Saunders. Cambridge 2018, p. 229–240.
22 Hodnett (see note 14), no. 1009.

romances invoked within *The Squire of Low Degree*.[23] And the woodcut on the verso of the title-page appears elsewhere not in romance narratives but in a satire and a dream-vision: De Worde's edition of Copland's verse translation of *The Fyftene Joyes of maryage* (1509, STC 15258; fragments of an earlier edition, STC 15257.5 are dated [*c.* 1507]) and Berthelet's edition of Lydgate's *Temple of glasse* ([1529?]; STC 17034).

3 Prose Narratives, Verse *novelle*, 'Merry Jests'

Alongside the sporadic reprinting and printing of romances in the years from 1520 to 1535, De Worde issued a variety of other vernacular narratives, in both prose and verse. Some of these seem to constitute responses to ventures made by continental printers and testify to an evident awareness of what was being printed in other continental centres and most probably bought in London in imported copies. Van Doesborch had been printing prose works of this kind in Antwerp for the English market: *Frederick of Jennen* in 1518 (STC 11361), *Mary of Nemmegen* probably in the same year (STC 17557) and *The parson of Kalenborowe* possibly a little later (*c.* 1520, STC 14894.5).[24] Also around 1518, he printed *the lyfe of Virgilius and of his deth and many maruayles that he dyd by whychcraft* (STC 24828): a work which also existed in French versions such as one printed by Guillaume Nyverd between 1500 and 1519 and another by Jacques Nyverd after 1514. De Worde did not miss the opportunity to get on this bandwagon. He had already produced his own edition of *Frederick of Jennen* (1517?, STC 11361a) and around 1520 he involved himself in a Parisian collaboration on a French-language version of the life of Virgil entitled *Les faictz merveilleux de virgille* (STC 24827.5). It was printed in octavo, in Paris, "pour Jean sainct Denis" and presumably also for De Worde, since it carries his device. No English version survives among books printed by De Worde, but the fact that William Copland was able to print the work in English in 1562? (STC 24829), at a point when he was reprinting other of De Worde's narratives and romances, may mean that he had access to a translation later printed by De Worde of which all trace is now lost.

Certain other narratives seem to have recommended themselves for publication on the basis of commercial success in continental editions. Two separate

---

23 Hodnett (see note 14), no. 1120. The speech scrolls contain text only in *The iiii Leues of truelove*: [woman:] "holde this a token y yyve [yvvye?]" and [man:] "for your sake I shall it take". Copland's edition reproduces the title-page woodcut but not the one on the verso.
24 [For Van Doesborch, see also the contribution by De Bruijn in the present volume, p. 110–113.]

tales from Boccaccio's *Decameron*, translated into English verse by William Walter, probably come into this category. *Ye hystory of Tytus & Gesyppus* survives in an edition from 1525 (STC 3184.5) and *The amerous hystory of Guystard and Sygysmonde* from 1532 (STC 3183.5). Possibly because the two stories were considered slightly higher-status texts than other kinds of narrative, it was seen fit to include some information about their translator. According to the title-pages of the two *novelle* and the other of his works printed by De Worde, *The spectacle of louers … a lytell contrauers dyalogue bytwene loue and councell* ([1533?], STC 25008), he was "somtyme servaunte to syr Henry Marney knyght chaunceler of the duchy of Lancastre". It would be useful to know more about Walter, but little biographical information has survived.[25] Marney (1447–1523) was a member of the privy council under Henry VII and Henry VIII and had interests in both Essex and London, where his first wife was a daughter of an alderman and merchant taylor and a member of a prominent family.[26] His servant William Walter may have had London connections of his own and it is possible that an acquaintance with Robert Copland, who had been providing translations for De Worde since *c.* 1505, first brought him to the printer's notice: Copland supplied a verse framework for Walter's *Guystarde* translation of *c.* 1533.[27]

The title-pages of both *Tytus and Gesyppus* and *Guystarde and Sygysmonde* proclaim that the English versions are translated from Latin rather than from Boccaccio's Italian. Likely sources have been identified in Latin prose versions of the stories made respectively by Filippo Beroaldo (*Mythica historia de Tito Gisippoque*) and Leonardo Bruni, also known as Leonardo Aretino (*De duobus amantibus Guiscardo et Sigismunda*).[28] It is worth noting that the Latin versions of both stories circulated independently outside the context of either the

---

25 A. S. G. Edwards, 'Walter, William (*fl. c.*1525–1533)'. In: ODNB, online ed., Jan 2008 [http://0-www.oxforddnb.com.catalogue.libraries.london.ac.uk/view/article/28641].)

26 James P. Carley, 'Marney, Henry, first Baron Marney (1456/7–1523)'. In: ODNB, online ed., Jan 2008 [http://0-www.oxforddnb.com.catalogue.libraries.london.ac.uk/view/article/70724].

27 A William Walter was admitted as clerk of the Exchequer in April 1524 (London, The National Archives SP 46/139/fo171) and in 1498 a William Walter, citizen and grocer of London, with his wife Ellen, claimed a debt from Humphrey Medwall, citizen and goldmith (TNA C 241/275/334). For details of Copland's biography, see Erler, *Copland* (note 10), Introduction.

28 See *Early English Versions of the Tales of Guiscardo and Ghismonda and Titus and Gisippus from the Decameron*. Ed. by H. G. Wright. London 1937 (Early English Text Society, 205), where the earliest printing of the *Mythica historia* is dated 1491, in the context of *Orationes et poemata* (Bologna; GW 4144), and the first independent edition of the story *c.* 1498 (Leipzig; GW 4501). There is some further brief discussion in Guyda Armstrong, *The English Boccaccio: A History in Books*. Toronto 2013, p. 163–164.

Decameron or of other works by their Latin translators. Both went through a number of continental editions and the story of Guystard and Sigismond had an especially wide circulation, since it became available in a translation by Beroaldo as well as in Bruni's version.[29] De Worde's editions paid some attention to giving these stories visual appeal. The title-page of *Tytus and Gysippus* presents some factotum figures, here labelled with banderoles, who appear countless times in De Worde's books, doing service not just for narratives but also for interludes and plays, dialogues and debates, misogynist works and treatises of various kinds.[30] The four cuts in *Guystarde and Sygysmonde,* the later of the two works to be printed, may have been specially made for this narrative, since they do not appear in other of De Worde's books and are closely tied to the substance of the text.[31]

Rather different from these more up-market narratives are the short comic tales in verse that De Worde printed between 1520 and 1535, adding to a line which he seems to have been quite keen to develop after his move from Westminster to Fleet Street: works falling into this category from the decade after the move include *The smith that forged him a new dame* ([c. 1505], STC 22653.5), *a lytell geste of Robyn hode* ([1506?], STC 13689) and *a mery geste of the frere and the boye* ([1510–13], STC 14522). De Worde was not the only printer to issue works of this kind – Robin Hood narratives and other comic tales were produced sporadically by Pynson and others – but De Worde's special interest is perhaps demonstrated in his association with a greater range of titles. Relevant to the date limits of this discussion are *a mery iest of the mylner of Abyngdon* ([1532–4?], STC 78) and *a lytell propre ieste called cryste crosse me spede* ([1534?], STC 14546.5). *Cryste crosse me spede*, of which only two leaves survive, recounts the substance of a gossips' feast in an ale-house and is one of a number of comic anti-feminist pieces, sometimes in the form of complaint or dialogue rather than narrative, among De Worde's publications.[32] *The mylner of Abyngdon* is a slightly more sophisticated *fabliau*; described on its title-page as "a mery iest / of the mylner of Abyngton with his / wyfe and his doughter and / two poore scholers of / Cambridge", it is essentially a reworking of the tale of the Reeve from Chaucer's *Canterbury Tales*. The action is given a new setting (Abingdon in Cambridgeshire rather than Trumpington) and Chaucer's

---

29 USTC lists 115 editions.

30 Driver (see note 6), p. 49–75.

31 Hodnett (see note 14), no. 927a–d*.

32 See Julia Boffey, 'Wynkyn de Worde and Misogyny in Print'. In: *Chaucer in Perspective: Middle English Essays in Honour of Norman Blake*. Ed. by Geoffrey Lester. Sheffield 1999, p. 236–251.

pentameter couplets are replaced with twelve-line tail rhyme stanzas. Certain elements of the narrative are given new twists: the two students are brothers, for example, and they search for wheat to alleviate their widowed mother's poverty; and at the end of the tale the thieving miller, unlike his counterpart in Chaucer's story, appears to regret his actions.[33] Although Chaucer's name is not mentioned in the surviving portion of this tale, its relationship to the Reeve's Tale would have been clear to anyone acquainted with *The Canterbury Tales* and was perhaps assumed to be one of its 'mery' qualities.

The mylner of Abyngdon suggests possible intersections between higher and lower status reading matter that are often overlooked in discussions of premodern culture predicated on the notion of distinct audiences for 'elite' and 'popular' literature. Such intersections may also be evident in De Worde's printing of John Skelton's *The Tunning of Elinor Rumming* (1521?, STC 22611.5), a verse account of the goings-on in the premises of a fearsome female brewer and tavern-keeper. In both content and spirit this piece anticipates *Cryste crosse me spede* and like that it probably took the shape of a small single-gathering pamphlet or booklet. The edition attributed to De Worde survives only in seriously depleted form,[34] but a full text is preserved in a collection of Skelton's verse printed *c.* 1545 (STC 22598), where its scabrous humour is thrown into relief by a series of witty Latin colophons. In this and other later editions Skelton's authorship is made plain at both the start and end of the poem ("per Skelton laureat", "Quod Skelton Laureat", "*Laureati Skeltonidis in despectu malignantium distichon*"), but the fragmentary nature of the edition attributed to De Worde means that it is now impossible to know whether or not such phrases were present in it. De Worde did not miss opportunities to mention authors' names, drawing attention to the "preclared and famous clerke Geffray Chaucer" on the title-page of his 1530 edition of *The Parliament of Fowls*, for example (STC 5092),[35] and naming Stephen Hawes and William Neville in his editions of their works (Hawes's *Example of Vertue*, 1530, STC 12947; Neville's *Castell of Pleasure*, [1530], STC 18475), but Skelton's *Tunning of Elinor Rumming* is unusual among "mery jests" for its connection with a named

---

33 The final leaf is missing from the single surviving copy.

34 See R. S. Kinsman, 'Eleanor Rediviva: Fragments of an Edition of Skelton's *Elynour Rummyng*, ca. 1521'. In: *Huntington Library Quarterly* 18 (1955), p. 315–327.

35 The *Parliament*, perhaps newly designed for this edition, gives prominence to Chaucer's name on the title-page and draws attention to his status as *auctor* with an author-woodcut used mainly elsewhere by De Worde on Latin grammars: see Hodnett (see note 14), no. 926. Rastell's 1525? edition of the poem (STC 5091.5) had rather differently used a woodcut of a bird and some eggs (Hodnett (see note 14), no. 2286).

author; and mostly with works of this kind De Worde (like other printers) was unconcerned to supply details of authorship or source.

4 Narratives in Context

The slightly odd assortment of works discussed in the category above – prose narratives, verse *novelle*, 'merry jests' – has its own point to make in the larger context of the output of De Worde's later career. By this point a pattern seems to have been established of reprinting works that were to hand and only occasionally taking any new initiatives. Such new moves as were made in relation to narratives usually involved texts that were short: *Ipomydon* stands out as an unusual departure. Practices in relation to size of book and paratextual apparatus tended to be conservative. In the earlier part of his career, during the years when he seems to have actively wanted to establish a market for verse romances and to build on Caxton's established success with prose romance, De Worde printed a number of long verse romances incorporating many woodcuts (some newly designed, others from stock) as attractive features. In his final decade, although the illustration of the 1529 Malory suggests a degree of continuing interest, he was seemingly less concerned with this aspect of marketing and design innovation. Among narrative works whose title-pages survive, factotum figures are much in evidence. Even in works for which new cuts might have been supplied, such as *Guystarde and Sygysmonde*, the labour involved would hardly have been extensive. The "mery jest" of the *Mylner of Abyngdon* has a title-page woodcut which does not survive in any other contexts, but it simply depicts a mill, with no people visible, and could well have been found somewhere in existing stock.[36]

Like most of the books de Worde printed, works of narrative literature appeared by this stage almost always in quarto-sized editions: the 1529 edition of Malory stands out as one of very few folio-sized books printed at this stage in his career,[37] and *Les faictz merveilleux de virgille* as an unusual experiment in

36 Hodnett (see note 14), no. 879.
37 De Worde seems to have opted for quarto at an early stage, for example reducing the prose romance *Paris and Vienne* to this format in 1505 (STC 19207a and 19208) in comparison with the folio-sized editions printed by Caxton (1485, STC 19206) and Leeu (1492, STC 19207). William Bonde's *Pilgrimage of perfection*, (23 February 1531, STC 3278) is one of the few other folio-sized books printed in De Worde's later career. [For the preference for octavo in Denmark, see the contribution by Richter in the present volume, p. 330. For French Arthurian romances in folio, see the article by Montorsi, p. 174. For German preferences, see the contribution by Bertelsmeier-Kierst, p. 37.]

octavo (a format occasionally used for grammars, such as Lily, *de octo oratio-nis*, STC 15601.7, schoolbooks like Terence, *Vulgaria*, STC 23908, and for various Latin handbooks for priests). The preference for quarto was presumably determined in part by economic factors, but it may also reflect the fact that this is a 'saleable' size of book, easy for purchasers to hold and read. Few of de Worde's narratives from these years have significant paratextual apparatus of any kind and in layout they are strikingly simple, especially in comparison with his much more complicatedly conceived schoolbooks and grammars.[38] Some small degree of effort may have gone into the generic distinctions that might be signaled in the words used on the title-pages or in colophons to narrative works. Like other early printers, de Worde used "history" of a number of the romances and narratives he printed, very occasionally diversifying into "treatise".[39] "Mery jest" is used rather more specifically, though, as if this was somehow felt to be a more distinct category. From earlier in de Worde's career the term is used of *How the plowman learned his paternoster* ([c. 1510], STC 20034), *a lytell geste of Robyn hode* ([1506?], STC 13689) and *the frere and the boye* ([c. 1510], STC 14522); and from the period under consideration here also of *Cryste crosse me spede* and *The mylner of abyngdon*.

Statistics suggest that narratives formed only a small proportion of De Worde's output during these years. This discussion has made particular reference to eighteen works, a small number of which were printed more than once during the period 1520–1535. STC figures indicate that the total number of editions printed by De Worde during this period (sometimes in collaboration with others) reaches well over 300. Narrative works thus constituted only a very small part of regular business – barely one title a year – most of which was by this stage taken up with grammars and schoolbooks of various kinds, some of which went through multiple successive editions. De Worde may have retained an interest in printing narrative literature in the final decade or so of his career, but he was hardly actively seeking to develop new initiatives in this area. The works of this kind that he brought into print for the first time during these years are short works of the "mery jest" kind and *novelle* like the Boccaccio translations. He seems not to have wanted by this stage to venture seriously into Chaucer and Lydgate, printing only short works by each. He was happy to reprint the works of Stephen Hawes, with whom he probably had personal connections earlier in career; and he perhaps printed William Neville because

---

38 See, for example, his editions of Robert Whittinton's *Verborum praeterita & supina* (1521, STC 25558 and many reprints up until 1533).

39 The 1510 edition of STC 17841.3, *ye byrth & prophecy of Merlin* calls it a "treatise" but because the 1529 edition is fragmentary it is not possible to know if the term was repeated there.

Neville worked with Copland and Copland had edited the earlier edition. De Worde apparently responded to 'prods' of various kinds: perhaps printing *The Parliament of Fowls* because Rastell had printed it and because Pynson had brought out a whole volume of Chaucer's minor poems; printing Malory's *Morte Darthur* for the second time in 1529, in folio, because Faques had recently printed a long new romance, *King Alexander*, in a folio edition (1525? STC 321). Although his own energies may have flagged slightly in his later years in relation to English narrative works, it is nonetheless striking that a number of his associates – people who had worked for and with him, or used his types – helped to start their own businesses with the printing of short romances and jests: exactly the kinds of work which De Worde had at an earlier stage helped to put on the map in printed form. The commercial attractions of these works continued to be recognized.

Bibliography

Armstrong, Guyda, *The English Boccaccio: A History in Books*. Toronto 2013.

Bennett, H. S., *English Books & Readers 1475 to 1557*. Cambridge 1970 [1952].

Blake, N. F., 'Wynkyn de Worde: the Early Years'. In: *Gutenberg Jahrbuch* (1971), p. 62–69.

Blake, N. F., 'Wynkyn de Worde: the Later Years'. In: *Gutenberg Jahrbuch* (1972), p. 128–138.

Blayney, Peter W. M., *The Stationers' Company and the Printers of London 1501–1557*. 2 vols, Cambridge 2013.

Boffey, Julia, 'Wynkyn de Worde and Misogyny in Print'. In: *Chaucer in Perspective: Middle English Essays in Honour of Norman Blake*. Ed. by Geoffrey Lester. Sheffield 1999, p. 236–251.

Boffey, Julia and A. S. G. Edwards, '*The Squire of Low Degree* and the Penumbra of Romance Narrative in the Early Sixteenth Century'. In: *Romance Rewritten. The Evolution of Middle English Romance. A Tribute to Helen Cooper*. Ed. by Elizabeth Archibald, Megan Leitch and Corinne Saunders. Cambridge 2018, p. 229–240.

Carley, James P., 'Marney, Henry, first Baron Marney (1456/7–1523)'. In: ODNB, online ed., Jan 2008 [http://0-www.oxforddnb.com.catalogue.libraries.london.ac.uk/view/article/70724].

Davies, C. S. L., 'Stafford, Edward, third duke of Buckingham (1478–1521)'. In: ODNB, online ed., Jan 2008 [http://0-www.oxforddnb.com.catalogue.libraries.london.ac.uk/view/article/26202].

Driver, Martha W., *The Image in Print: Book Illustration in Late Medieval England and its Sources*. London 2004.

Edwards, A. S. G. and Carol M. Meale, 'The Marketing of Printed Books in Late Medieval England'. In: *The Library* 6th ser., 15 (1993), p. 95–124.

Edwards, A. S. G., 'Walter, William (*fl. c.*1525–1533)'. In: ODNB, online ed., Jan 2008 [http://0-www.oxforddnb.com.catalogue.libraries.london.ac.uk/view/article/28641].

Erler, Mary C., 'Wynkyn de Worde's Will: Legatees and Bequests'. In: *The Library*, 6th ser., 10 (1988), p. 107–112.

Hanks, D. Thomas Jr., 'Caxton, de Worde and Malory's *Morte Darthur*'. In: *Reviewing 'Le Morte Darthur': Texts and Contexts, Characters and Themes*. ed. by K. S. Whetter and Raluca L. Radulescu. Woodbridge 2005 (Arthurian Studies 60), p. 27–48.

Hellinga, Lotte, *William Caxton and Early Printing in England*. London 2010.

Hodnett, Edward, *English Woodcuts 1480–1535*. Oxford 1973 [1935].

Kinsman, R. S., 'Eleanor Rediviva: Fragments of an Edition of Skelton's *Elynour Rummyng*, ca. 1521'. In: *Huntington Library Quarterly* 18 (1955), p. 315–327.

Lewis, R. E., N. F. Blake and A. S. G. Edwards, *Index of Printed Middle English Prose*. New York 1985.

McKerrow, R. B., *Printers' and Publishers' Devices in England and Scotland, 1485–1640*. London 1913.

Meale, Carol M., 'Wynkyn de Worde's Setting-Copy for *Ipomydon*'. In: *Studies in Bibliography* 35 (1982), p. 156–171.

Meale, Carol M., 'Caxton, de Worde and the Publication of Romance in Late Medieval England'. In: *The Library* 6th ser., 14 (1992), p. 283–298.

Moran, James, *Wynkyn de Worde: Father of Fleet Street*.Ed. by Lotte Hellinga and Mary C. Erler, with a preface by John Dreyfus. London 2003 [1976].

Neville-Sington, Pamela, 'Pynson, Richard (*c.*1449–1529/30)'. In: ODNB, Oxford 2004; online ed., Jan 2008 [http://0-www.oxforddnb.com.catalogue.libraries.london.ac.uk/view/article/22935].

Robert Copland: Poems.Ed. by Mary C. Erler. Toronto 1993.

Sánchez-Martí, Jordi, 'Wynkyn de Worde's Editions of *Ipomydon*: A Reassessment of the Evidence'. In: *Neophilologus* 89 (2005), p. 153–163.

Sánchez-Martí, Jordi, 'Robert Copland and *The Lyfe of Ipomydon*'. In: *Notes and Queries* 55 (2008), p. 139–142.

Sánchez-Martí, Jordi, 'The Printed History of Middle English Verse Romances'. In: *Modern Philology* 107 (2009), p. 1–31.

Sánchez-Martí, Jordi, 'Illustrating the Middle English Verse Romances'. In: *Word and Image* 27 (2011), p. 90–102.

Wright, H.G. (ed.), *Early English Versions of the Tales of Guiscardo and Ghismonda and Titus and Gisippus from the Decameron*. London 1937 (Early English Text Society, 205).

Jordi Sánchez-Martí

The Publication of English Medieval Romances after the Death of Wynkyn de Worde, 1536–1569

Abstracts: Wynkyn de Worde was the main promoter of printing English medieval romances, the publication of which ceased in the years following his death. This article suggests that the ideological influence of the Reformation, which condemned all chivalric literature for its alleged affinity with Catholicism, was responsible for the neglect of the genre. Medieval romances did not emerge again until 1553, the year when a Catholic monarch, Queen Mary I, succeeded to the throne. Aware that the change of monarch would immediately entail a change in the ideological context, the printer William Copland was hoping to bring the English medieval romances back into vogue and, in 1553, printed two romances. In the following years he collaborated with other printers in the publication of this medieval corpus for a new generation of readers. With an output of twenty-one editions up until *c.* 1565, Copland was instrumental in reviving the printed medieval romances even though the genre slid once more into oblivion after his death.

Wynkyn de Worde war der wichtigste Druckerverleger für englische mittelalterliche Romane, deren Publikation in den Jahren nach seinem Tod stagnierte. Dieser Beitrag zeigt, dass der ideologische Einfluss der Reformation, die die ritterlich-höfische Literatur wegen ihrer Affinität zum Katholizismus verurteilte, für die stiefmütterliche Behandlung des Genres verantwortlich war. Die mittelalterlichen Romane kamen erst 1553 wieder auf, dem Jahr, in dem eine katholische Monarchin, Königin Mary I., den Thron bestieg. Aus dem Bewusstsein heraus, dass ein neuer Monarch ziemlich schnell eine Änderung des ideologischen Kontexts nach sich ziehen würde, hegte der Drucker William Copland die Hoffnung, englische mittelalterliche Romane wieder populär machen zu können, und er druckte 1553 zwei Romane. In den Folgejahren arbeitete er mit anderen Druckern zusammen, indem er dieses mittelalterliche Corpus für eine neue Lesergeneration auf den Markt brachte. Bis etwa 1565 veröffentlichte er 21 Drucke, sodass Copland für die Wiederbelebung der mittelalterlichen Romane sehr wichtig war, obwohl das Genre nach seinem Tod erneut in Vergessenheit geriet

1 Introduction

Romance was the most popular genre of secular literature in late medieval England. The ample manuscript record that has come down to us together

Jordi Sánchez-Martí, University of Alicante

with the large variety of romance narratives preserved attests to the genre's popularity.[1] The advent of the printing press, however, completely altered England's literary landscape and, despite the genre's popularity and long-lasting tradition, printers initially neglected it. Although English medieval romance initially failed to make a successful transition from manuscript to print, it was not because William Caxton, the first English printer, was uninterested in it, since the first work he chose to print in English – namely, the *Recuyell of the histories of Troy* (1473)[2] – is actually a romance and, besides, he printed another eight romances from his Westminster premises. Yet, Caxton devoted his energies to promoting the printed dissemination of a romance canon different from the English traditional romances, which were mostly in verse form. Instead he favoured the literary fashions from the continent, thus printing mostly his own translations of French prose romances, perceived as more sophisticated, marketing them to the upper classes. It was not until Caxton's death in 1492 that English printers started to realize the need to target their products to a more socially diverse class of customers. Wynkyn de Worde, who worked for Caxton and inherited his business, was endowed with a deeper commercial instinct than his master and soon gravitated towards the publication of the English popular verse romances, precisely the literary corpus Caxton had neglected. Throughout his career as a printer De Worde published approximately forty Middle English romances, comprising traditional English works in verse and translations of continental romances in prose. The apparent commercial success of this line of business attracted other printers that also wanted to profit from the customers' interest in this literary corpus. As a result, about sixty editions of English medieval romances were printed between 1497 and 1535.

The production of printed romances until the death of De Worde in 1535 has been the object of detailed scholarly scrutiny, among other reasons because it affects the activity of Caxton, the English print pioneer, and De Worde, the

---

1 For an overview of the medieval English romances, see J. Burke Severs (gen. ed.), *A Manual of the Writings in Middle English, 1050–1500*. Ed. by Mortimer J. Donovan et al. Vol. 1: *Romances*. New Haven 1967. For the manuscript tradition, see Gisela Guddat-Figge, *Catalogue of Manuscripts Containing Middle English Romances*. Munich 1976.
2 See Lotte Hellinga (ed.), *Printing in England in the Fifteenth Century: E. Gordon Duff's Bibliography with Supplementary Descriptions, Chronologies, and a Census of Copies*. London 2009, no. 242.

most prolific of all the early English printers.[3] By contrast, critics have been less inclined to explore the printed transmission of the English romances in the years following De Worde's demise, focussing mainly on specific issues. A. S. G. Edwards has studied William Copland's role in the printed dissemination of the English romances between *c.* 1550 and *c.* 1565, roughly the same period that has occupied Edward Wilson-Lee in an article that explores the possible provincial distribution of the printed romances that, he argues, encouraged the reemergence of the genre.[4] Jennifer Fellows has discussed the printed circulation of the Middle English romances in a book chapter that centres on only five romance works, analysing mainly their textual history.[5] Finally, I have also touched on the topic as part of a study devoted exclusively to the romances in verse form.[6]

The purpose of this essay is to offer a comprehensive overview of the publication of medieval romances in England between 1536, the year after Wynkyn de Worde – the first promoter of the English traditional romances – died, until 1569,[7] when William Copland – the leading figure in the second wave of romance printing – passed away. To do so I will examine the extant bibliographical evidence and combine this information with our knowledge of the English socio-historical context, the dynamics affecting the book trade itself and the activity of

---

3 See Carol M. Meale, 'Caxton, de Worde, and the Publication of Romance in Late Medieval England'. In: *The Library*, 6th ser., 14 (1992), p. 283–298; Tracy Adams, 'Printing and the Transformation of the Middle English Romance'. In: *Neophilologus* 82 (1998), p. 291–310; Yu-Chiao Wang, 'Caxton's Romances and Their Early Tudor Readers'. In: *Huntington Library Quarterly* 67 (2004), p. 173–188; Jordi Sánchez-Martí, 'The Printed History of the Middle English Verse Romances'. In: *Modern Philology* 107 (2009), p. 1–31; Alison Wiggins, 'Romance in the Age of Print'. In: *The Romance of the Middle Ages*. Ed. by Nicholas Perkins and Alison Wiggins. Oxford 2012, p. 121–149. Relevant information is also provided in Ronald S. Crane, *The Vogue of Medieval Chivalric Romance During the English Renaissance*. Menasha, Wisconsin 1919 and Lotte Hellinga, *William Caxton and Early Printing in England*. London 2010. See also my chapter 'The Printed Transmission of Medieval Romance from William Caxton to Wynkyn de Worde, 1473–1535'. In: *The Transmission of Medieval Romance: Metres, Manuscripts and Early Prints*. Ed. by Ad Putter and Judith A. Jefferson. Cambridge 2018, p. 170–190. [See also the article by Boffey in the present volume, p. 125–141.]
4 A.S.G. Edwards, 'William Copland and the Identity of Printed Middle English Romance'. In: *The Matter of Identity in Medieval Romance*. Ed. by Phillipa Hardman. Cambridge 2002, p. 139–147; Edward Wilson-Lee, 'Romance and Resistance: Narratives of Chivalry in Mid-Tudor England'. In: *Renaissance Studies* 24 (2010), p. 482–495.
5 Jennifer Fellows, 'Printed Romance in the Sixteenth Century'. In: *A Companion to Medieval Popular Romance*. Ed. by Raluca L. Radulescu, Cory James Rushton. Cambridge 2009 (Studies in Medieval Romance 10), p. 67–78.
6 Sánchez-Martí, 'Printed History' (note 3), p. 12–19.
7 For biographical information, see N. F. Blake, 'Worde, Wynkyn de (*d.* 1534/5)'. In: ODNB. Vol. 60, p. 295–298.

individual printers involved in the publication of medieval romances. By so doing I hope to reconstruct the evolution of the printed history of romance during the central part of the sixteenth century, when England was ruled successively by Henry VIII, Edward VI, Mary I and Elizabeth I. Denoting the genre's adaptability to the changing historical circumstances, romances achieved printed continuity during the second half of the sixteenth century, in contrast with the majority of English medieval literature, attracting a large clientele and bringing financial gains to printers.[8] The versatility of romance goes back to the Middle Ages, when it was apt to be transmitted orally and in manuscript format,[9] and was reinforced in the print era as the genre adjusted to the demands of the new technology.

2 Medieval Romance during the English Reformation, 1536–1553

De Worde's demise signaled the end of an era in the publication of the Middle English romances and must have left an important gap in the book trade. On the other hand, it opened up new business opportunities for other printers. As Blayney remarks, we find that up until 1542 "one retired printer return[ed] to the fray, one provincial printer relocate[d] to London, and no fewer than thirteen new master printers set up in the metropolitan area".[10] Nonetheless, it is surprising that no printer made any attempt to fill the gap left by De Worde in the market of printed romances, as Gheraert Leeu did right after Caxton's death by printing two romance works from Antwerp.[11] It seems reasonable to assume

---

8 As stated by A. S. G. Edwards and Julia Boffey, 'Literary Texts'. In: *Cambridge History of the Book in Britain*. Ed. by Lotte Hellinga and J. B. Trapp. Vol. 3. Cambridge 1999, p. 563: "Apart from Chaucer, few Middle English works or authors seem to have found an audience after the first half of the sixteenth century". For the printed continuity of English medieval literature, see Julia Boffey, 'From Manuscript to Print: Continuity and Change'. In: *A Companion to the Early Printed Book in Britain, 1476–1558*. Ed. by Vincent Gillespie and Susan Powell. Cambridge 2014, p. 13–26.
9 For the oral transmission of the genre in late medieval England, see Ad Putter, 'Middle English Romances and the Oral Tradition'. In: *Medieval Oral Literature*. Ed. by Karl Reichl. Berlin, Boston 2012 (De Gruyter Lexikon), p. 335–351.
10 Peter W. M. Blayney, *The Stationers' Company and the Printers of London, 1501–1557*. Vol. 1. Cambridge 2013, p. 389.
11 They are *The History of Jason* (STC 15384) and *Paris and Vienne* (STC 19207), printed in June 1492. See Gerard van Thienen and John Goldfinch (ed.), *Incunabula Printed in the Low Countries: A Census*. Nieuwkoop 1999, nos 1418 and 1695.

that the best candidates to take over De Worde's role in commercially exploiting the English medieval romances should be the London printers who printed these works in the years previous to his death; that is, those printers who tried to compete with De Worde for the market of English romances at the beginning of the 1530s, namely, John Skot, Peter Treveris and John Mitchell. We need to understand why they failed to take advantage of their hypothetically favourable position and circumstances. Skot printed the first extant edition of *Jeste of Sir Gawaine* in 1528(?) and of *Sir Isumbras* in *c.* 1530.[12] Having probably received his training from De Worde, Skot must have maintained some connection with the manuscript culture that enabled him to introduce at least one new romance title that was never printed before.[13] Skot's personal circumstances changed dramatically when he became involved in the publication of the controversial book Edward Bocking, a Benedictine monk, wrote about his spiritual protegée Elizabeth Barton, known as the Holy Maid of Kent. Bocking, Barton and four accomplices were hanged at Tyburn on 20 April 1534, whereas Skot saved himself by means of a "Confessyion", preserved in a memorandum written by Thomas Cromwell in his own hand.[14] After this episode Skot printed only seven books and ended his career in 1537, without sufficient time and conditions to take over the printing of medieval romances. In 1528(?) too, the printer Peter Treveris issued an edition of *Eglamour of Artois* for Richard Bankes and, like Skot, an edition of *Sir Isumbras* in *c.* 1530.[15] His career ended about 1532 and he "probably died in the mid-1530s".[16] Finally, John Mitchell also printed two

---

12 STC 11691a.3 and 14280.5, respectively.

13 For biographical information, see Janet Ing Freeman, 'Skot, John (*fl.* 1521–1537)'. In: ODNB. Vol. 50, p. 888; E. Gordon Duff, *A Century of the English Book Trade.* London 1905, p. 149; Henry R. Plomer, *Wynkyn de Worde and His Contemporaries from the Death of Caxton to 1535: A Chapter in English Printing.* London 1925, p. 213–215. For Skot's links with De Worde, see Blayney (see note 10), vol. 1, p. 179 and Tamara Atkin and A. S. G. Edwards, 'Printers, Publishers and Promoters to 1558'. In: Gillespie and Powell (see note 8), p. 40–41. Although Skot's edition of *Jeste of Sir Gawaine*, printed for John Butler (cf. Plomer p. 222), is the earliest to have survived, the presence of the items "syr Jsambras" and "syr hisemmbras" in the ledger of a printer in 1520 suggests that a previous edition existed, possibly published by De Worde; see F. Madan, 'Day-Book of John Dorne, Bookseller in Oxford, A.D. 1520'. In: *Collectanea* 1, pt. 3 (1885), p. 117, no. 1137 and p. 137, no. 1788.

14 See Ethan H. Shagar, 'Bocking, Edward (*d.* 1534)'. In: ODNB. Vol. 6, p. 389–390 and Alan Neame, *The Holy Maid of Kent: The Life of Elizabeth Barton, 1506–1534.* London 1971. Blayney (see note 10), vol. 1, p. 326, provides the text of Cromwell's memorandum.

15 STC 7542.5 and 14280.7, respectively.

16 N. F. Blake, 'Treveris, Peter (*fl.* 1525–1532)'. In: ODNB. Vol. 55, p. 347. See also Duff (see note 13), p. 158–159; Plomer (see note 13), p. 218–221; and Atkin and Edwards (see note 13), p. 36. Note that the STC tentatively assigns his edition of *Eglamour* to John Rastell. Instead,

verse romances, namely, *Jeste of Sir Gawaine* and *Sir Lamwell*, the two in 1531(?), right before relocating to Canterbury.[17] Mitchell carried on printing until his death in 1556, but the commercialization of medieval romances was probably less viable from the countryside, outside the capital's more dynamic distribution channels.

In light of the adverse circumstances surrounding each one of the three London printers who issued six editions of verse romances between 1528(?) and 1531(?), it seems understandable that they failed to capitalise on De Worde's death and expand their publication of romance texts. Likewise, the printer and publisher John Butler, despite having financed two editions of *Jeste of Sir Gawaine* as mentioned above, was not in a position to take the place of De Worde either, since he stopped printing in 1531.[18] The only printer who was engaged in the publication of romances before De Worde died and whose career continued normally afterwards was Richard Bankes. It is significant, however, that Bankes did not finance the publication of any additional verse romance, a clear indication that the public perception of this literary corpus changed and its commercial value diminished. Moreover, out of the fifteen printers who set up in the metropolitan area after De Worde's death, only one of them tried his luck with the English romances. It was Thomas Petyt, who started printing in 1536 and published a reprint of *Jeste of Sir Gawaine* in c. 1540(?).[19] Blayney has commented that one of Petyt's defining characteristics in his early years as a printer was "his preference for letting others establish a book's vendibility

---

I now follow Blayney (see note 10), vol. 2, p. 1040, who attributes it to Treveris. Bankes worked as a printer between 1523 and 1526 and thereafter acted as a publisher until 1539, when he started printing books again until 1546; see Blayney (see note 10), vol. 1, p. 180–83, 423–29; Duff (see note 13), p. 7–8; and Plomer (see note 13), p. 215–216.

17 STC 11691a.5 and 15187, respectively. The STC (vol. 3, Addenda and Corrigenda) dates the two editions to 1530–1532(?), but I follow the more approximate date suggested by Blayney (see note 10), vol. 2, p. 1046, 1048. Note that Mitchell's edition of *Jeste of Sir Gawaine* was printed for John Butler; cf. Blayney (see note 10), vol. 1, p. 282–283. For biographical information, see Janet Ing Freeman, 'Mitchell, John (d. 1556)'. In: ODNB. Vol. 38, p. 408–409. For an assessment of Mitchell's printing career, see Julia Boffey, 'John Mychell and the Printing of Lydgate in the 1530s'. In: *Huntington Library Quarterly* 67 (2004–2005), p. 251–260. See also E. Gordon Duff, *The English Provincial Printers, Stationers and Bookbinders to 1557*. Cambridge 1912, p. 117–119. For Butler, see note 188.

18 See Blayney (see note 10), vol. 1, p. 197–198; and Duff, *English Book Trade* (note 13), p. 19–20.

19 STC 11691a.7. It is, therefore, inaccurate that "No romances printed between 1530 and 1554 survive", as states Wilson-Lee (see note 4), p. 482. Another three romances were printed between 1550 and 1553, as will be shown below, and four between 1531 and 1533.

before reprinting it",[20] thus suggesting that the previous editions of *Jeste* were sufficiently successful to warrant its being reprinted, despite the unfavourable cultural and political environment, as will be discussed below. Petyt's *Jeste* is an isolated case, a one-off edition intended to make a quick profit, so we can imply that his commitment to the genre was limited and occasional. Similarly, the 1550(?) edition of *Eglamour of Artois*,[21] produced by John Walley, one of the major publishers of the mid-sixteenth century, can also be considered as another oddity, since it was not part of a commercial strategy to reprint the corpus of romances. Walley's real purpose was to reap financial benefit from a work that had not been reprinted since 1528(?).[22]

It seems, therefore, that after De Worde's death printers were not interested in competing for his market share of printed romances, as if the genre were no longer perceived as commercially attractive. Consequently, from 1535 onwards this literary corpus seemed doomed to disappear, since only the odd edition, like Petyt's and Walley's, appeared in the following fifteen years and there was no indication that this medieval genre could once more fill the stalls of early modern booksellers. The inability of the printers who had competed with De Worde in the early 1530s to continue printing romances in 1536 and after does not suffice to explain why other printers did not grasp this seemingly ideal opportunity. The causes for this apparent lack of interest in printing medieval romances, therefore, seem to lie elsewhere and to be related to the changes in the political and religious context brought by the Reformation in the mid-1530s. All activities that could be somehow associated with the old religion, the authority of the Pope and the life in monasteries and abbeys became suspicious. Soon the detractors of chivalric literature started to align the corpus of English medieval romances with the decadence of the old order. In 'A Declaration of the Faith, and a Justification of the Proceedings of King Henry VIII. in matters of Religion', signed in 1539, we read, "Englishmen have now [...] the Holy Bible and New Testament in their Mother Tongue, instead of the old fabulous

---

20 Blayney (see note 10), vol. 1, p. 401. For more information, see Duff, *English Book Trade* (note 13), p. 120–121; and Alexandra Gillespie, 'Petyt, Thomas (*b.* in or before 1494, *d.* 1565/6)'. In: ODNB. Vol. 43, p. 962–963.

21 STC 7542.7.

22 Cf. Blayney (see note 10), vol. 2, p. 660–661. For more information on Walley, see Duff, *English Book Trade* (note 13), p. 164. For a description of his edition of *Eglamour*, see *Sir Eglamour of Artois*. Ed. by Frances E. Richardson. London 1965 (Early English Text Society, Original Series 256), p. xiv; and Joseph Ames, *Typographical Antiquities or The History of Printing in England, Scotland, and Ireland*. Ed. by Thomas Frognall Dibdin. Vol. 4. Hildesheim 1969 [1810–1819], p. 275, no. 2290.

and phantasticall books, of the 'Table round', 'Launcelot du Lac', 'Huon de Bourdeux', 'Bevy of Hampton', 'Guy of Warwick', &c., and such other whose unpure filth and vain fabulosity the light of God has abolished utterly".[23] By condemning romances, both in verse and in prose, as corrupt and immoral, this excerpt promotes a new literary horizon, free of such kind of impurities, but closer to God and revealed truth, since the people themselves were able to access the word of God directly in English. This kind of statement contributed to convey the impression that medieval romance was a cultural product of the old order and an instrument for disseminating the values of Catholic ideology. A leading exponent of this deprecatory discourse against chivalric literature was the English humanist Roger Ascham, as is best illustrated by the comments he made in his *Toxophilus*, published in 1545:

> In our fathers tyme nothing was red, but bookes of fayned cheualrie, wherin a man by redinge, shuld be led to none other ende, but onely to manslaughter and baudrye. Yf any man suppose they were good ynough to passe the time with al, he is decyued. For surelye vayne woordes doo woorke no smal thinge in vayne, ignoraunt and younge mindes … These bokes (as I haue heard say) were made the moste parte in Abbayes and Monasteries, a very lickely and fit fruite of suche an ydle and blynde kinde of lyuynge.[24]

Using moral arguments to inveigh against chivalric literature, as Ascham does here, was not something new in England, since similar reasons were cited as early as the fourteenth century, for instance in the anonymous *Speculum Vitae*, which alludes to the *vanyte* (line 48) that infects medieval romance.[25] What is different in Ascham's attitude is that he related his moralising criticism to contemporary events and provided ideological justification for the Protestant Reform implemented by the Henrician parliament, in particular for the Dissolution of the Monasteries Acts of 1536 and 1539.[26] This political and religious dimension to Ascham's message may have rendered it more effective socially, since the genre

---

23 In: Jeremy Collier (ed.), *An Ecclesiastical History of Great Britain*. Vol. 9. London 1841 [1708–1714], p. 162–174, here 163; quoted in Alex Davis, *Chivalry and Romance in the English Renaissance*. Cambridge 2003 (Studies in Renaissance Literature 11), p. 8.

24 *Toxophilus*. In: Roger Ascham, *English Works*. Ed. by William Aldis Wright. Cambridge 1904, p. XIV–XV; for a similar line of argument, see his posthumously published *The Scholemaster*. In: *English Works*. Ed. by William Aldis Wright. Cambridge 1904, p. 230–231. For bibliographical information, see Rosemary O'Day, 'Ascham, Roger (1514/5–1568)'. In: ODNB. Vol. 2, p. 588–594.

25 See *Speculum Vitae: A Reading Edition*. Ed. by Ralph Hanna. Oxford 2008 (Early English Text Society, Original Series 331), p. 6.

26 Cf. 27 Hen. 8, c. 28 and 31 Hen. 8, c. 13; see G. R. Elton (ed.), *The Tudor Constitution: Documents and Commentary*. 2nd ed. Cambridge 1982, nos 186, 188.

would be perceived as unsavoury, suspect and potentially dangerous in the context of the English Reformation. It seems natural that printers grew cautious and were disinclined to print a literary corpus that allegedly connoted the values of that reviled period when "Papistrie ... couered and ouerflowed all England".[27]

3 Printing Romances during the Reign of Mary I, 1553–1558

With the accession to the throne of the Catholic Queen, Mary I, in 1553, the political situation changed dramatically and had direct consequences for the book-trade in general and the publication of romances in particular. During Mary's reign the publication of religious books experienced a sharp downtrend and by 1558 was reduced to less than half the percentage of religious works published in a typical year from the preceding Edwardian period.[28] Besides, as the pendulum of religious opinion swung to favour the promotion of Catholic ideas, the publication of medieval romances was no longer frowned upon as politically incorrect and could be resumed without the printers' fearing legal and commercial consequences.[29] It is no surprise then that, during the reign of the Catholic queen, the publication of romances flourished once again, with ten separate editions printed in the entire Marian period.

After the coronation of Mary I, one of the printers that decided to revise his publication policy was William Copland, who until that point had been routinely engaged in the printing of reformist materials, including editions of Tyndale's biblical translations and writings and texts such as *The Faule of the Romyshe Churche* and *A Godly Dyalogue & Dysputacion betwene Pyers Plowman*,

---

27 Roger Ascham, *The Scholemaster* (see note 244), p. 230; cf. Helen Cooper, *The English Romance in Time: Transforming Motifs from Geoffrey of Monmouth to the Death of Shakespeare.* Oxford 2004, p. 38. For the humanist attack against romance, including Ascham's, see Davis (see note 23), p. 1–19; and James Wade, 'Penitential Romance after the Reformation'. In: *Medieval into Renaissance: Essays for Helen Cooper.* Ed. by Andrew King and Matthew Woodcock. Cambridge 2016, p. 92–94.

28 See John N. King, 'The Book-Trade under Edward VI and Mary I'. In: Hellinga and Trapp (ed.) (see note 8), p. 164–178. The statistical information appears in tabular form on p. 176–178. See also Blayney (see note 10), vol. 2, p. 831–835.

29 Medieval romances offered "a market for popular literature inoffensive to the Catholic regime", as Wilson-Lee (see note 4), p. 487, states. For the new regulations of the book-trade introduced during Queen Mary's reign, see Blayney (see note 10), vol. 2, p. 825–831.

and a Popysh Preest. [30] The reversion of the political and religious attitudes to
a pre-Reformation state, however, compelled Copland to abandon this line of
business and find alternative sources of textual matter. One of the genres
Copland explored was medieval romance and in 1553, the same year of Mary's
inauguration, he put two romance narratives on the market, namely, an edition
of the substantial prose *Recuyell* in folio and a shorter one of the verse *Guy of
Warwick* in quarto.[31] These editions heralded the beginning of a resurgence of
the publication of medieval romances that benefitted from Copland's new-
found enthusiasm for the genre. His strong commitment to it is best illustrated
by the volume of his romance output – approximately 21 editions, twelve in
verse and nine in prose –, the variety of works – 16 – and the length of time –
13 years, between 1553 and *c.* 1565.[32] Considering the chronological concentration of this activity, Copland's commitment is comparable in intensity to, and
even greater than, De Worde's, whose nearly forty editions were spread over
approximately thirty-five years. It seems natural to conceive, as Edwards suggests, that De Worde offered "the only possible model from whom Copland
could have derived, perhaps via Robert Copland [i.e., his father], his sense of
the commercial potentiality of the romance form".[33] It can be no coincidence
that such resolve to print the Middle English romances should come from
a printer whose father had been an assistant to Wynkyn de Worde, for whom
he translated two prose romances – *Kynge Appollyn of Thyre* (1510) and *Helyas*
(1512)[34] – and composed an envoi to De Worde's edition of *Ipomydon*, published
as late as 1532.[35] With his active involvement in the publication of medieval

---

30 See respectively STC 24451 (1548?), 24459 (1549), 21306 (*c.* 1550), 19903 and 19903.5 (1550).
31 STC 15378 and 12541.5, respectively. Note that the *Recuyell* had not been printed again since
De Worde published it in 1503 (STC 15376–77); this date is based on Blayney (see note 10), vol. 2,
p. 1048. For a bibliographical description of Copland's *Recuyell*, see Ames (see note 22), vol. 3,
p. 133–135, no. 886. *Guy of Warwick* had not been issued since Richard Pynson and De Worde
printed separate editions (STC 12540–41) at the end of the fifteenth century.
32 Edwards (see note 4), p. 139, counts a total of "twenty-two separate editions of thirteen romances". For biographical information, see H. R. Tedder, 'Copland, William (*d.* 1569)'. Rev. by
Mary C. Erler. In: ODNB. Vol. 13, p. 336. For more information, see Duff, *English Book Trade*
(note 13), p. 32–33; and Blayney (see note 10), vol. 2, p. 611–613.
33 Edwards (see note 4), p. 142.
34 STC 708.5 and 7571, respectively. Note that the only copy of *Kynge Appollyn* contains quires
printed in 1532–34; see Joseph J. Gwara, 'Robert Copland and *The Judgement of Love*'. In:
Studies in Bibliography 59 (2015), p. 101, no. 40.
35 STC 5733. This date is suggested by Joseph J. Gwara. 'Three Forms of w and Four English
Printers: Robert Copland, Henry Pepwell, Henry Watson, and Wynkyn de Worde'. In: *PBSA* 106
(2012), p. 218. An earlier edition was published *c.* 1522 (STC 5732.5), although it is preserved in
fragmentary form and is missing the envoi. For a discussion, see Jordi Sánchez-Martí, 'Wynkyn

romances during the first three decades of the century, Robert represents the necessary link between his master Wynkyn and his heir William, between the model of commercial publication of romances and his emulator.

Table 1: Prose romances printed between 1536 and 1569.[36]

Year	Title	Printer	Format	STC
1553	Recuyell of the histories of Troy	W. Copland	fol.	15378
1554	Four sons of Aymon	W. Copland for T. Petyt	fol.	1010
1554	Four sons of Aymon	W. Copland for J. Walley	fol.	1011
1554	Four sons of Aymon	W. Copland for R. Toy	fol.	1011.5
1555	Valentyne and Orson	W. Copland for J. Walley	4°	24571.7
1557	Malory, Morte Darthur	W. Copland	fol.	804
c.1553–60?	Huon of Burdeux (?)	W. Copland (?)	fol.(?)	—
c.1560?	Helyas	W. Copland	4°	7572
1560?	Arthur of Little Britain	W. Copland for R. Redborne	fol.	807
1560?	Arthur of Little Britain	W. Copland	fol.	807.5
1562?	Virgilius	W. Copland	4°	24829
c.1565	Valentyne and Orson	W. Copland	4°	24572

Robert must have transmitted his knowledge of, and experience with, medieval romances to William as part of his son's training before the latter inherited his father's business in 1547. Although we can assume that William was intimately familiar with the printed tradition of the English romances,[37] it is strange that he made no attempt to commercially exploit this corpus before 1553. His

---

de Worde's Editions of *Ipomydon*: A Reassessment of the Evidence'. In: *Neophilologus*, 89 (2005), 153–63; and Gwara, 'Three Forms of w' (note 35), p. 196, no. 47. For biographical information on Robert Copland, see his *Poems*. Ed. by Mary C. Erler. Toronto 1993, p. 3–10; F. C. Francis, *Robert Copland: Sixteenth-Century Printer and Translator*. Glasgow 1961; and Mary C. Erler, 'Copland, Robert (*fl.* 1505–1547)'. In: ODNB. Vol. 13, p. 334–336.

36 There is evidence to suggest that Lord Berners's *Huon of Burdeux*, whose *editio princeps* dates from *c.* 1515 (STC 13998.5), was printed again between 1545 and 1561; see Joyce Boro, 'The Textual History of *Huon of Burdeux*: A Reassessment of the Facts'. In: *Notes and Queries*, n.s. 48 (2001), p. 233–237. Since the fashion for medieval prose romances reemerged in 1553–1560, it seems safe to narrow down the publication date of *Huon* to this range of years and conjecturally attribute it to Copland.

37 Gwara, 'Three Forms of w' (see note 35), p. 196, no. 47, has connected William's "reprints of older material" with some of the shop copies of texts, including romances, that were in Robert's possession. Considering that most of William's editions of verse romances can be

avoidance of publishing romances is indicative that between 1536 and the early part of 1553 there must have been some kind of tacit ban on the genre among printers, who were reluctant to cultivate this literary corpus owing to the powerful discourse that associated romances with Catholic ideology and their authorship with monks, "as I haue heard say", as Ascham comments.

Between 1554 and 1558, as he was working from the family premises at the Sign of the Rose Garland in Fleet Street, William Copland printed romance works in the following years: 1554, *Four sons of Aymon* (prose); 1555, *Eglamour* (verse),[38] *Valentyne and Orson* (prose); 1556, *Knight of Curtesy* (verse)[39]; 1557, Malory's *Morte Darthur*.[40] In 1554 the printers Thomas Petyt, Robert Toy and John Walley formed a publishing partnership and commissioned Copland to print the sizeable *Four sons of Aymon*, which appeared with three variant colophons, one for each publisher.[41] It seems likely that Walley, who had printed *Eglamour* in 1550, played an active role in promoting this partnership to continue cultivating the romance genre, but in this case wanted to reduce the risk involved in the publication of such a lengthy work. In 1555 Walley, once again, engaged Copland to print another prose romance, *Valentyne and Orson*, this time without the participation of any other publisher, thus suggesting that the

---

traced back to De Worde (cf. Sánchez-Martí, 'Printed History' (note 3), p. 17, no. 47), it seems reasonable to think that William had easy access to early editions.

38 STC 7543.

39 STC 24223.

40 Cf. Edwards (see note 4), p. 144. For locating Copland's premises, see Blayney (see note 10), vol. 2, p. 970–973, 985–986, map 1, no. 102. For bibliographical information of all the Middle English prose romances published between 1536 and 1569, see table 1. Descriptions for the following editions can be found in Ames (see note 22): *Aymon* (vol. 3, p. 137–143, no. 889), *Eglamour* (vol. 3, p. 167, no. 926), *Knight of Curtesy* (vol. 3, p. 168, no. 927), *Morte Darthur* (vol. 3, p. 143, no. 891). For *Valentyne*, see Arthur Dickson, *Valentine and Orson: A Study in Late Medieval Romance*. New York 1929, p. 286; for more on his *Knight of Curtesy*, see Elizabeth McCausland, '*The Knight of Curtesy and the Fair Lady of Faguell*': *A Study of the Date and Dialect of the Poem and Its Folklore Origins*, Northampton, Mass. 1922 (Smith College Studies in Modern Languages 4, no. 1), p. vii. On Copland's romance publication during the Marian period, see also Yu-Chiao Wang, 'William Copland's and Thomas East's Promotional Strategies for the *Morte Darthur*: A Study of the Origins, Forms, and Contexts of Their Title Pages'. In: *JEBS* 6 (2003), p. 80–81.

41 Note that Petyt's shop was next door to Toy's in St Paul's Churchyard. On Toy, see Blayney (see note 10), vol. 2, 815–816; Duff, *English Book Trade* (note 13), p. 158; and the information in the ODNB entry on his son: Ian Gadd, 'Toy, Humphrey (*b.* in or before 1537, *d.* 1577)'. In: ODNB. Vol. 55, p. 174. Note that this was not the first time the three publishers collaborated in co-publishing projects; in 1551 they were part of a syndicate that had the Great Bible printed by Nicholas Hill (STC 2083–2086.5).

edition of *Four sons of Aymon* elicited a good market response.[42] In so doing Copland gained confidence that this form of narrative literature remained commercially attractive and resumed his own line of romance publication, started in 1553, with a new reprint of *Eglamour*, only five years after Walley's.[43] The following year he produced the first edition of the Middle English *Knight of Curtesy* and in 1557 a reprint of Malory's Arthuriad, which had not been printed since De Worde's second edition of 1529.[44] Copland's contribution to the printing of romances during the first half of the decade suggests that initially he exercised caution, first, by sounding the market in 1553 with two editions of a prose and a verse romance and, next, by avoiding financial risk in 1554–1555, when he printed two long prose romances at the request of others.[45] Certain of the genre's potentialities, from then onwards Copland, on his own initiative, implemented a commercial strategy for supplying the market with English medieval romances.

4 Competition and the Publication of Romance in the Early Elizabethan Period, 1558–1569

Towards the end of the 1550s, not only were readers and customers attracted to the genre, but also other printers, who saw in this literary corpus an opportunity to make easy economic gains. In one of the first meetings of the newly incorporated Stationers' Company, sometime between 19 July 1557 and 9 July 1558, the printer John King obtained a licence to print *The Jeste of Sir Gawaine* and *Sir*

---

42 In these years Copland collaborated with Walley by printing for him the New Testament (1550; STC 2861) and Stephen Hawes's *Pastime of Pleasure* (1555; STC 12952).

43 STC 7543. Note that, on purely textual grounds, D. J. Curnow and Ad Putter, 'Textual and Familial Relationships: The Place of the Michigan Fragment in the Evolution of *Sir Eglamour*'. In: *People and Texts: Relationships in Medieval Literature. Studies presented to Erik Kooper*. Ed. by Thea Summerfield and Keith Busby. Amsterdam, New York 2007 (Costerus New Series 166), p. 57, offer the improbable view that Walley's edition descends from Copland's second edition of the romance of *c.* 1565 (STC 7544.5). For a description of Copland's *Eglamour* of 1555, see Richardson (see note 22), p. xiii. For a list of all verse romances printed in the 1550s and 1560s, see Sánchez-Martí, 'Printed History' (note 3), p. 13, table 2.

44 STC 803.

45 Wilson-Lee (see note 4) seems to be suggesting just the opposite by stating that during the Marian period, "Although a few of the shorter romances were printed for other publishers, almost all of the more ambitious projects identified Copland as the sole printer and publisher" (p. 486).

Lamwell.[46] A fragment of King's edition of the latter has come down to us, probably printed in 1558 from his printing house in Creed Lane, before he moved to
Paul's Cross Churchyard in 1559.[47] In a later session of the Company, held between 10 July 1558 and 10 July 1559, Thomas Marshe was licensed to print another Middle English verse romance, namely, *Bevis of Hampton*.[48] Marshe, whose
name appears associated with King for the publication of three books in 1554,[49]
had some business dealings with Copland, who that same year printed a book
for him.[50] In the Company's meeting of 10 June 1560, John King applied for
a licence to print two more verse romances, namely, *The Squyr of Low Degre* and
Sir Degare.[51] The last attempt by Copland's competitors to break into the market
of medieval romances took place on 11 May 1561, when John Tisdale received
a licence to print *Bevis*, although he never produced such an edition.[52]

Copland's competitors' choice of texts suggests that they were interested in
putting on the market solely popular verse romances, a product that they felt
was potentially more lucrative and financially less risky than the longer prose
romances. All the romance works licensed between 1557 and 1561 had been previously printed, though not reissued since De Worde died.[53] King and Marshe
became aware of this corpus's commercial value and wanted to capitalise on it,
but acted with prudence when selecting their forthcoming titles. In order to
avoid being perceived as deliberately encroaching on Copland's business, they
chose to get licences for verse texts not printed by Copland, who appeared
more concerned with and focussed on publishing prose romances. In addition

46 See Edward Arber (ed.), *A Transcript of the Registers of the Company of Stationers of London 1554–1640 A.D.* Vol. 1. New York: 1950 [1875–1894], p. 79. For information on King, see Duff, *English Book Trade* (see note 13), p. 86.
47 STC 15187.5. The dating 1558(?) is suggested by Blayney (see note 10), vol. 2, p. 1048; the STC gives 1560. For the two premises of King, see Blayney, vol. 2, p. 978–979 and map 3 (p. 996), no. 17 (p. 1000).
48 See Arber (see note 46), vol. 1, p. 95. For information on Marshe, see Blayney (see note 10), vol. 2, p. 783–784; and Duff, *English Book Trade* (note 13), p. 100.
49 STC 3366, 10989a.5, 22599.
50 STC 22602.5.
51 Arber (see note 46), vol. 1, p. 128.
52 Arber (see note 46), vol. 1, p. 156. For information on Tisdale, see Ames (see note 22), vol. 4, p. 345–353; Blayney (see note 10), vol. 2, p. 794–795; Duff, *English Book Trade* (note 13), p. 156; and H. R. Tedder, 'Tisdale, John (*b*. 1530/31–*d*. in or after 1563)'. In: ODNB. Rev. by Anita McConnell. Vol. 54, p. 839.
53 Except for *Squyr of Low Degre* (1520?; STC 23111.5), all the other licensed romances were printed for the last time during the first half of the 1530s: *Bevis* (1533?; STC 1988.6); *Degare* (1535?; STC 6470.5); *Jeste* (1531?; STC 11691a.5); *Lamwell* (1531?; STC 15187).

they also took the precaution of going through the official channels established by the Stationers' Company, perhaps anticipating Copland's resentment.

Indeed, Copland must have perceived his competitors' moves as a threat to his dominant position, to his stranglehold on the market of printed romances, and decided to retaliate. Disregarding the Company's regulations, Copland reacted promptly by putting on the market from his new premises at the Three Crane Wharf in the Vintry an edition of *Bevis of Hampton* and *Squyr of Low Degre* in 1560(?),[54] precisely two of the romance texts for whose publication his rivals received a licence. Although it might seem surprising that Copland, one of the original members of the Stationers' Company, flouted the newly introduced licence system, we need to bear in mind that in the early years of the Company his conduct was not entirely unusual.[55] If Copland intended to dissuade King and Marshe from bringing out their editions of *Bevis* and *Squyr*, he certainly contrived to do so and, in addition, sent a strong message to these and other potential rivals. Not only did Copland assert himself as the sole and legitimate owner of the moral rights to print this genre, but he also showed how he was willing to confront anyone who challenged this claim. As a result, Tisdale desisted from using his licence, while Copland remained the only printer who issued romances until his death, without any printer challenging his exclusivity on the genre.[56]

---

54 STC 1988.8 and 23112, respectively. These editions are described in Jennifer Fellows, 'The Middle English and Renaissance *Bevis*: A Textual Survey'. In: *'Sir Bevis of Hampton' in Literary Tradition*. Ed. by Jennifer Fellows and Ivana Djordjevic. Cambridge 2008 (Studies in Medieval Romance 8), p. 111, no. 9 and *The Squyr of Lowe Degre: A Middle English Metrical Romance*. Ed. by William Edward Mead. Boston 1904, p. xi–xii. See also Ames (see note 22), vol. 3, p. 165–167 (no. 924) and p. 164 (no. 921) respectively. For locating Copland's premises, see STC, vol. 3, p. 255, under S.9. Copland worked from this address until 1562. Wilson-Lee (see note 4), p. 486, understands Copland's relocation here as indication "that his books were finding lucrative markets outside London"; however, we lack sufficient evidence to suggest that he was more successfully marketing his editions of romances among provincial customers.

55 For the presence of Copland's name in the Company's charter of 1557, see Blayney (see note 10), vol. 2, p. 1017, line 62. Note that from early on we have evidence that Copland was fined for ignoring the licence system: e.g. between 10 July 1558 and 10 July 1559, Copland "for pryntinge of *a pronostication* of NOSTERDAMUS withoute lycense and for mysbehavynge hym selfe before the master and Wardyns was fyned at iij^s iiij^{d}" (Arber (see note 46), vol. 1, p. 101). For more information on the licensing system, see W. W. Greg, *Some Aspects and Problems of London Publishing between 1550 and 1650*. (The Lyell Lectures) Oxford 1956.

56 In fact, no printer applied for a licence to publish a romance until a meeting of the Stationers' Company that took place between 22 July 1568 and 22 July 1569, when Copland was already dead or had ended his career. Thomas Purfoot then received licence to print three verse romances: *Bevis*, *Generides* and *Richard Coeur de Lion*; see Arber (see note 46), vol. 1, p. 389. On Purfoot, see Blayney (see note 10), vol. 1, p. 513 and vol. 2, p. 809–810.

Fig. 1: *Sir Degare* (J. King, 1560). Oxford, Bodleian Library, University of Oxford, 4° C 39 Art. Seld. (3), title page. By permission.

Additionally, Copland also applied more subtle tactics to establish his superiority in the market of printed romances, as becomes apparent when his edition of *Bevis* is compared with John King's *Sir Degare*, both issued in 1560.[57] King's *Degare* is a modest production containing no illustration apart from the one on the title page.[58] Still, King's edition reproduces the caption-like rubrics that appear in De Worde's *editio princeps* of the same romance (1512) for the purpose of providing an interpretation of the five woodcuts illustrating it.[59] King had no access to the original cuts, was unwilling to take the trouble to enhance the text's presentation, but retained the rubrics, probably without fully understanding their original function in De Worde's edition. By contrast, Copland's *Bevis* presents a complete illustrations programme that is revealing, first, because all the images are made reusing or copying woodcuts created in the early part of the sixteenth century, thus supporting the idea that Copland had easy access to the editions produced and the materials used by English printers from previous generations; and secondly, because this is the first illustrated edition of a Middle English verse romance to be printed since De Worde's death.[60] Although Edwards argues that Copland decided to include illustrations in his edition of

---

57 STC 1988.8 and 6472, respectively. I am inclined to believe that King printed *Degare* some months before Copland published his *Bevis* and *Squyr* in the same year. Nonetheless, we do not know whether King was preparing to compete with Copland, since he died in 1561.

58 For a description of this edition, see Ames (see note 22), vol. 4, p. 338–339, no. 2434*. For the image on the title page, see fig. 1. This was used previously in William Copland's 1555 edition of Hawes's *Pastime of Pleasure* (see note 42), sig. c2r; see Ruth Samson Luborsky and Elizabeth Morley Ingram, *A Guide to English Illustrated Books, 1536–1603*. Vol. 1. Tempe, Ariz. 1998 (Medieval & Renaissance Texts & Studies 166), p. 431–432.

59 STC 6470. The rubrics appear on sig. B1^v, B4^r, C2^r, D1^v and D4^v; for the illustrations in De Worde's *Sir Degare*, see the discussion in Jordi Sánchez-Martí, 'Illustrating the Printed Middle English Verse Romances, *c.*1500–*c.*1535'. In: *Word & Image* 27 (2011), p. 95–97.

60 With regards to the use of illustrations, Copland made a clear distinction between verse and prose romances. Except for his edition of *Recuyell*, all the other prose romances he printed are richly illustrated: *Four sons of Aymon*, 23 cuts; *Valentyne and Orson*, 47 cuts in 1555, 43 cuts in *c.* 1565; *Morte Darthur*, 26 cuts; *Helyas*, 21 cuts; *Arthur of Little Britain*, 25 cuts; *Virgilius*, 10 cuts. Descriptions of the images in these editions are available in Luborsky and Ingram (see note 58), arranged by STC number in vol. 1. For a description of the woodcuts in Copland's *Bevis*, see Luborsky and Ingram, vol. 1, p. 81. Edwards's statement that "Copland's cuts [in *Bevis*] have no relation to the single earlier illustrated edition, by Pynson" (see note 4, p. 143) is inaccurate. Woodcut no. 1 (sig. C3^v, Hod. 1939) appears on Pynson's edition (STC 1988) on sig. B6^r; no. 3 (I4^v, Hod. 1940) was previously used by Pynson on sig. F6^v; and no. 4 (K1^v, Hod. 1941) appears on sig. G2^r in Pynson's. For a facsimile reproduction of nos 1 and 3, see Sánchez-Martí (see note 59), fig. 4 and 5; for no. 4, see Alison Wiggins and Rosalind Field (ed.), *Guy of Warwick: Icon and Ancestor*. Cambridge 2007 (Studies in Medieval Romance 4), plate 12. Additionally, Edwards (see note 4) also contends that the woodcuts in Copland's

Bevis because probably he "saw *Bevis* as in some way a special case, possibly a hot seller that warranted a variation from his norm",[61] it seems unsafe to assume this was the case, because *Bevis* had not been printed for more than twenty-five years, since De Worde's edition of 1533 (see note 53). If Copland was convinced that the book could become 'a hot seller', he would not have waited for seven years to print it. Still, the illustrations surely made an impact on the book's sales, since Copland reissued the romance about 1565.

The year 1560 proved to be a turning point in Copland's strategy. While continuing with his usual line of business by producing richly illustrated editions of two lengthy prose romances,[62] Copland also faced direct competition from other London printers, whom he fought off by putting two verse romances on the market. As Edwards suggests, "It seems that Copland came to feel that the primary market demand was for verse romances and aimed towards the end of his career to flood it".[63] From then on Copland turned his energy to exploiting the metrical romances, as if in beating off his competitors he awakened to the commercial value this medieval corpus still carried in Elizabethan England. From his new premises at Lothbury, opposite St Margaret's Church, Copland printed two prose romances in quarto, namely, the short *Virgilius* and a reprint of *Valentyne and Orson*,[64] whereas he issued six verse romances, four of which

---

Bevis "have at best a tenuous applicability to any point in the narrative" (p. 143). I have argued to the contrary elsewhere (see note 59), p. 90–92.

61 Edwards (see note 4), p. 143.

62 They are *Helyas*, originally translated from French by his father Robert, and Lord Berners's *Arthur of Little Britain*. Descriptions can be found in Ames (see note 22): *Helyas* (vol. 3, p. 152–56, no. 907); *Arthur* (vol. 4, p. 190–192, no. 2123). Note that Copland produced two variant editions of *Arthur*, one of them printed for Robert Redborne (described in Ames, see note 22), a London bookseller; see Duff, *English Book Trade* (note 13), p. 131.

63 Edwards (see note 4), p. 144.

64 For locating his printing house, see STC, vol. 3, p. 250, under H.9. Descriptions are provided in Ames (see note 22): *Virgilius* (vol. 3, p. 171, no. 935), *Valentyne* (vol. 3, p. 163–164, no. 920). While Edwards (see note 4), p. 139, no. 1, excludes *Virgilius* from his discussion of romances, Copland's choice of woodcuts suggests that he was probably marketing this work as a romance, because some of those cuts were typically used in illustrated editions of medieval romances; woodcut no. 2 (sig. A2^r, Hod. 1122) appears in *Arthur*'s title page; no. 3 (A3^r, Hod. 912) in *Valentyne* (G1^v), *Arthur* (B5^r) and *Helyas* (I2^v); no. 5 (B3^r, Hod. 936; see fig. 2): although Copland did not use this cut elsewhere, it appears only in the editions of the prose romance *Dystruccion of Jherusalem* printed by De Worde (1510?, STC 14518; 1528, STC 14519) and Pynson (1513?; STC 14517). Moreover, in 1575 Robert Langham mentions 'Virgyls lyfe' among the romances owned by Captain Cox; see Robert Langham, *A Letter*. Ed. by R. J. P. Kuin. Leiden 1983 (Medieval and Renaissance Texts 2), p. 53. Note that George R. Keiser also considers *Virgilius* as a romance; see his chapter 'The Romances'. In: *Middle English Prose: A Critical Guide to Major Authors and*

were reprints of previous editions he himself had already published, namely, *Bevis, Eglamour, Guy* and *Sir Triamour*,[65] a clear sign that, despite the genre's Catholic associations and the prevalent Protestant ideology, the Middle English romances remained popular among Elizabethan readers.

5 Conclusion

Between 1536 and 1569 English printers brought out approximately twenty-seven separate editions of medieval romances, excluding variant editions. The early part of this period was affected by the ideological changes brought about by the Reformation, which contributed to the romance genre's effective neglect and public avoidance. After the coronation of a Catholic monarch in 1553, however, nothing prevented printers from publishing romances once again and soon these went on sale at London's bookshops, a tendency that was allowed to continue after Elizabeth I came to the throne. While various printers played a part in restoring medieval romances to their previous place in the book market, William Copland stands out for his active role in the publication of some twenty-two separate editions. In fact, he displayed a proprietorial attitude to the corpus of romances and, after the coronation of Elizabeth, felt he held de facto exclusive rights to print them. Had Copland not enjoyed a virtual monopoly on the genre, it seems probable that more romances would have been printed, particularly in the 1560s. The actions of his few competitors at the end of the 1550s influenced Copland in his choice of texts, since until that moment he seemed more partial to publishing prose romances. In the 1560s he almost abandoned that line of business and centred his attention on the romances in verse, with which Copland obtained a better market response. The public's

---

Genres. Ed. by A. S. G. Edwards. New Brunswick 1984, p. 271–289. Copland bought a licence to print *Virgilius* in 1561–1562; see Arber (see note 46), vol. 1, p. 178.

65 STC 1989, 7544.5, 12542 and 24303.3, respectively. The edition of *Bevis* is described in Fellows (see note 54), p. 11; *Eglamour* in STC; *Guy* in Ames (see note 22), vol. 3, p. 167, no. 925 and Ronald S. Crane, 'The Vogue of *Guy of Warwick* from the Close of the Middle Ages to the Romantic Revival'. In: *PMLA* 30 (1915), p. 129–130, no. 8.; and *Triamour* in Egerton Brydges (ed.), *The British Bibliographer* 1 (1810), p. 62, no. 4 and Luborsky and Ingram (see note 58), vol. 1, p. 713. Another edition should be added to this list, since Jill Whitelock, Head of Special Collections at Cambridge University Library, has recently identified an early printed fragment in the library as belonging to a new *Bevis* edition, now CUL 5000.d.144. This edition was most likely printed by Copland during the second half of the 1560s. I am grateful to Dr. Whitelock for sharing with me the evidence and her note 'An Unrecorded Printing of *Bevis of Hampton*: A Fragment in Cambridge University Library', which was in preparation at the time of writing.

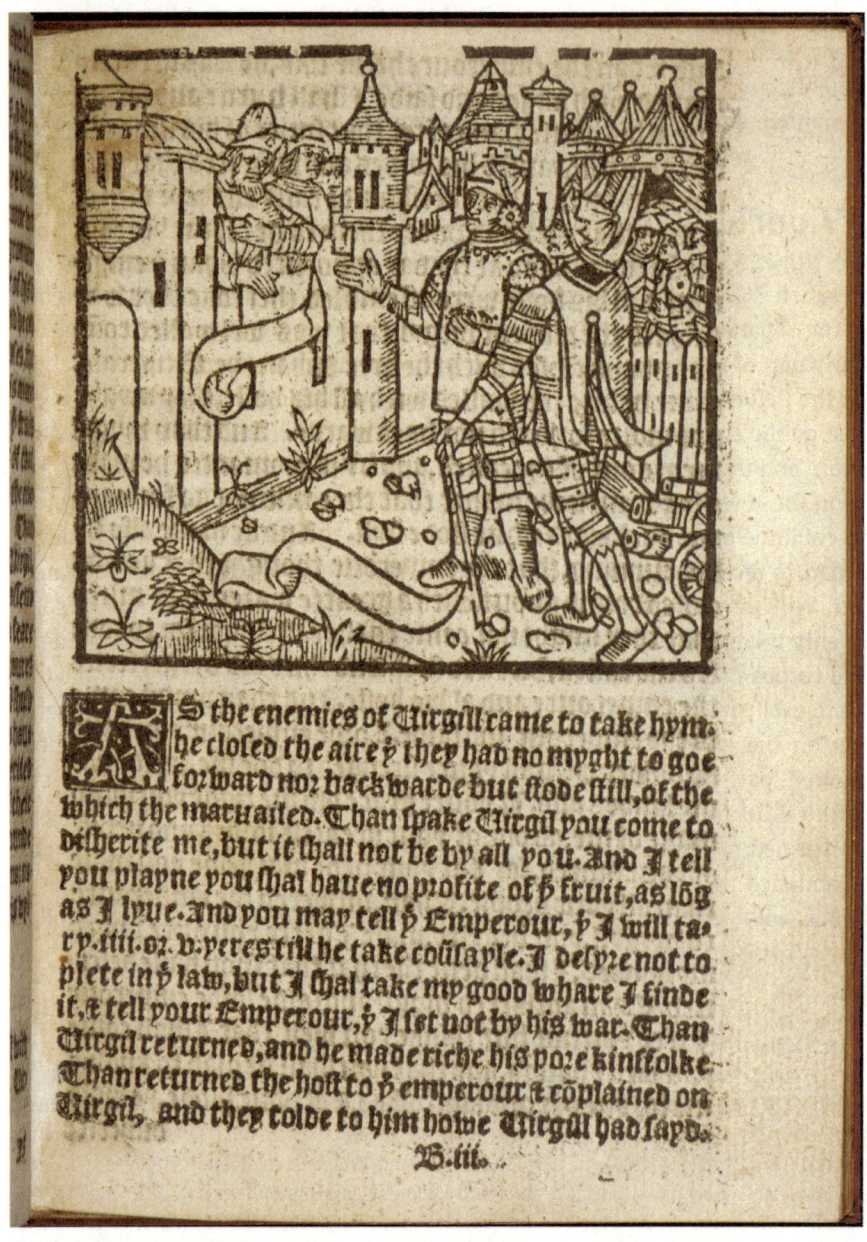

S the enemies of Virgill came to take hym:
he closed the aire ŷ they had no myght to goe
forward nor backwarde but stode still, of the
which the maruailed. Than spake Virgil you come to
disherite me, but it shall not be by all you. And I tell
you playne you shal haue no profite of ŷ fruit, as lōg
as I lyue. And you may tell ŷ Emperour, ŷ I will ta-
ry iiii. or v. yeres till he take coūsayle. I desyre not to
plete in ŷ law, but I shal take my good whare I finde
it, & tell your Emperour, ŷ I set not by his war. Than
Virgil returned, and he made riche his pore kinsfolke.
Than retturned the host to ŷ emperour & cōplained on
Virgil, and they tolde to him howe Virgul had sayd.
B.iii.

Fig. 2: *The Lyfe of Virgilius* (W. Copland, 1562?), Hod. 936. London, British Library, C.21.c.35, sig. B3ʳ. © The British Library Board.

preference for the verse romances had a parallel in the number of reissues printed from *c.* 1555 to *c.* 1569 – a total of eight verse romances for only one in prose – and shows a historical continuity in the literary taste of late medieval and early modern English readers of romances. With his strategy Copland used up the commercial value of the genre, among other reasons because the catalogue of romances he could offer remained almost unchanged since the manuscript and incunabular periods. Never did the genre of medieval romance appear again in print as a literary corpus, whereas only the odd edition was produced before the end of the century. Copland's death in 1569, therefore, marks the virtual end to the printed dissemination of the medieval English romances.[66]

Bibliography

Adams, Tracy, 'Printing and the Transformation of the Middle English Romance'. In: *Neophilologus* 82 (1998), p. 291–310.

Ames, Joseph, *Typographical Antiquities or The History of Printing in England, Scotland, and Ireland* Ed. by Thomas Frognall Dibdin. 4 vols. Hildesheim 1969 [1810–1819].

Arber, Edward (ed.), *A Transcript of the Registers of the Company of Stationers of London 1554–1640 A.D.* 5 vols. New York 1950 [1875–1894].

Ascham, Roger, *The Scholemaster*. In: Roger Ascham, *English Works*. Ed. by William Aldis Wright. Cambridge 1904 (Cambridge English Classics), p. 171–302.

Ascham, Roger, *Toxophilus*. In: Roger Ascham, *English Works*. Ed. by William Aldis Wright. Cambridge 1904 (Cambridge English Classics), pp. vii–xx, 1–119.

Atkin, Tamara and A. S. G. Edwards, 'Printers, Publishers and Promoters to 1558'. In: *A Companion to the Early Printed Book in Britain, 1476–1558*. Ed. by Vincent Gillespie and Susan Powell. Cambridge 2014, p. 27–44.

Blake, N. F., 'Treveris, Peter (*fl.* 1525–1532)'. In: ODNB. Vol. 55, p. 347.

Blake, N. F., 'Worde, Wynkyn de (*d.* 1534/5)'. In: ODNB. Vol. 60, p. 295–298.

Blayney, Peter W. M., *The Stationers' Company and the Printers of London, 1501–1557*. 2 vol. Cambridge 2013.

Boffey, Julia, 'John Mychell and the Printing of Lydgate in the 1530s'. In: *Huntington Library Quarterly* 67 (2004/2005), p. 251–260.

Boffey, Julia, 'From Manuscript to Print: Continuity and Change'. In: *A Companion to the Early Printed Book in Britain, 1476–1558*. Ed. by Vincent Gillespie, Susan Powell. Cambridge 2014, p. 13–26.

Boro, Joyce, 'The Textual History of *Huon of Burdeux*: A Reassessment of the Facts'. In: *Notes and Queries*, n.s., 48 (2001), p. 233–237.

Brydges, Egerton (ed.), *The British Bibliographer* 1 (1810).

---

66 Research for this chapter was funded in part by the Spanish Ministry of Economy and Competitiveness (ref. FFI2015–70101-P).

Collier, Jeremy (ed.), *An Ecclesiastical History of Great Britain*. London 1841 [1708–1714], vol. 9, p. 162–174 ('A Declaration of the Faith, and a Justification of the Proceedings of King Henry VIII. in matters of Religion').

Cooper, Helen, *The English Romance in Time: Transforming Motifs from Geoffrey of Monmouth to the Death of Shakespeare*. Oxford 2004.

Copland, Robert *Poems*. Ed. by Mary C. Erler. Toronto 1993.

Crane, Ronald S., 'The Vogue of *Guy of Warwick* from the Close of the Middle Ages to the Romantic Revival'. In: *PMLA* 30 (1915), p. 125–194.

Crane, Ronald S., *The Vogue of Medieval Chivalric Romance During the English Renaissance*. Menasha, Wis. 1919.

Curnow, D. J. and Ad Putter, 'Textual and Familial Relationships: The Place of the Michigan Fragment in the Evolution of *Sir Eglamour*'. In: *People and Texts: Relationships in Medieval Literature. Studies presented to Erik Kooper*. Ed. by Thea Summerfield and Keith Busby. Amsterdam, New York 2007 (Costerus New Series 166), p. 51–66.

Davis, Alex, *Chivalry and Romance in the English Renaissance*. Cambridge 2003 (Studies in Renaissance Literature 11).

Dickson, Arthur, *Valentine and Orson: A Study in Late Medieval Romance*. New York 1929.

Duff, E. Gordon, *A Century of the English Book Trade*. London 1905.

Duff, E. Gordon, *The English Provincial Printers, Stationers and Bookbinders to 1557*. Cambridge 1912.

Edwards, A. S. G., 'William Copland and the Identity of Printed Middle English Romance'. In: *The Matter of Identity in Medieval Romance*. Ed. by Phillipa Hardman. Cambridge 2002, p. 139–147.

Edwards, A. S. G. and Julia Boffey, 'Literary Texts'. In: *The Cambridge History of the Book in Britain*. Ed. by Lotte Hellinga and J. B. Trapp. Vol. 3. Cambridge 1999, p. 555–575.

Elton, G. R. (ed.), *The Tudor Constitution: Documents and Commentary*. 2nd ed. Cambridge 1982.

Erler, Mary C., 'Copland, Robert (*fl.* 1505–1547)'. In: ODNB. Vol. 13, p. 334–336.

Fellows, Jennifer, 'Printed Romance in the Sixteenth Century'. In: *A Companion to Medieval Popular Romance*. Ed. by Raluca L. Radulescu, Cory James Rushton. Cambridge 2009 (Studies in Medieval Romance 10), p. 67–78.

Fellows, Jennifer, 'The Middle English and Renaissance *Bevis*: A Textual Survey'. In: *'Sir Bevis of Hampton' in Literary Tradition*. Ed. by Jennifer Fellows and Ivana Djordjevic. Cambridge 2008 (Studies in Medieval Romance 8), p. 80–113.

Francis, F. C., *Robert Copland: Sixteenth-Century Printer and Translator*. Glasgow 1961.

Freeman, Janet Ing, 'Mitchell, John (*d.* 1556)'. In: ODNB. Vol. 38, p. 408–409.

Freeman, Janet Ing, 'Skot, John (*fl.* 1521–1537)'. In: ODNB. Vol. 50, p. 888.

Gadd, Ian, 'Toy, Humphrey (*b.* in or before 1537, *d.* 1577)'. In: ODNB. Vol. 55, p. 174–175.

Gillespie, Alexandra, 'Petyt, Thomas (*b.* in or before 1494, *d.* 1565/6)'. In: ODNB. Vol. 43, p. 962–963.

Greg, W. W., *Some Aspects and Problems of London Publishing between 1550 and 1650*. Oxford 1956 (The Lyell Lectures).

Guddat-Figge, Gisela, *Catalogue of Manuscripts Containing Middle English Romances*. Munich 1976.

Gwara, Joseph J., 'Three Forms of w and Four English Printers: Robert Copland, Henry Pepwell, Henry Watson, and Wynkyn de Worde'. In: *PBSA* 106 (2012), p. 141–230.

Gwara, Joseph J., 'Robert Copland and *The Judgement of Love*'. In: *Studies in Bibliography* 59 (2015), p. 85–113.

Hellinga, Lotte (ed.), *Printing in England in the Fifteenth Century: E. Gordon Duff's Bibliography with Supplementary Descriptions, Chronologies, and a Census of Copies*. London 2009.

Hellinga, Lotte, *William Caxton and Early Printing in England*. London 2010.

Keiser, George R., 'The Romances'. In: *Middle English Prose: A Critical Guide to Major Authors and Genres*. Ed. by A. S. G. Edwards. New Brunswick 1984, p. 271–289.

King, John N., 'The Book-Trade under Edward VI and Mary I'. In: *The Cambridge History of the Book in Britain*. Ed. by Lotte Hellinga, J. B. Trapp. Vol. 3. Cambridge 1999, p. 164–178.

Langham, Robert, *A Letter*. Ed. by R. J. P. Kuin. Leiden 1983 (Medieval and Renaissance Texts 2).

Luborsky, Ruth Samson and Elizabeth Morley Ingram, *A Guide to English Illustrated Books, 1536–1603*. 2 vols. Tempe, Ariz. 1998 (Medieval & Renaissance Texts & Studies 166).

Madan, F., 'Day-Book of John Dorne, Bookseller in Oxford, A.D. 1520'. In: *Collectanea* 1, pt. 3 (1885), p. 73–177.

McCausland, Elizabeth, '*The Knight of Curtesy and the Fair Lady of Faguell*': A Study of the Date and Dialect of the Poem and Its Folklore Origins. Northampton, Mass. 1922 (Smith College Studies in Modern Languages 4, no. 1).

Meale, Carol M., 'Caxton, de Worde, and the Publication of Romance in Late Medieval England'. In: *The Library*, 6th ser., 14 (1992), p. 283–298.

Neame, Alan, *The Holy Maid of Kent: The Life of Elizabeth Barton, 1506–1534*. London 1971.

O'Day, Rosemary, 'Ascham, Roger (1514/5–1568)'. In: *ODNB*. Vol. 2, p. 588–594.

Plomer, Henry R., *Wynkyn de Worde and His Contemporaries from the Death of Caxton to 1535: A Chapter in English Printing*. London 1925.

Putter, Ad, 'Middle English Romances and the Oral Tradition'. In: *Medieval Oral Literature*. Ed. by Karl Reichl. Berlin, Boston 2012 (De Gruyter Lexikon), p. 335–351.

Sánchez-Martí, Jordi, 'Wynkyn de Worde's Editions of *Ipomydon*: A Reassessment of the Evidence'. In: *Neophilologus* 89 (2005), p. 153–163

Sánchez-Martí, Jordi, 'The Printed History of the Middle English Verse Romances'. In: *Modern Philology* 107 (2009), p. 1–31.

Sánchez-Martí, Jordi, 'Illustrating the Printed Middle English Verse Romances, *c*.1500–*c*.1535'. In: *Word & Image* 27 (2011), p. 90–102.

Sánchez-Martí, Jordi, 'The Printed Transmission of Medieval Romance from William Caxton to Wynkyn de Worde, 1473–1535'. In: *The Transmission of Medieval Romance: Metres, Manuscripts and Early Prints*. Ed. by Ad Putter and Judith A. Jefferson. Cambridge 2018, p. 170–190.

Severs, J. Burke (gen. ed.), *A Manual of the Writings in Middle English, 1050–1500*. Ed. by Mortimer J. Donovan et al. Vol. 1: Romances. New Haven 1967.

Shagar, Ethan H, 'Bocking, Edward (*d.* 1534)'. In: *ODNB*. Vol. 6, p. 389–390.

Sir Eglamour of Artois. Ed. by Frances E. Richardson. Oxford 1965 (Early English Text Society, Original Series 256).

Speculum Vitae: A Reading Edition. Ed. by Ralph Hanna. 2 vols. Oxford 2008 (Early English Text Society, Original Series 331–332).

The Squyr of Lowe Degre: A Middle English Metrical Romance. Ed. by William Edward Mead. Boston, Mass. 1904.

Tedder, H. R., 'Copland, William (*d.* 1569)'. Rev. by Mary C. Erler. In: *ODNB*. Vol. 13, p. 336.

Tedder, H. R., 'Tisdale, John (*b.* 1530/31–*d.* in or after 1563)'. Rev. by Anita McConnell. In: ODNB. Vol. 54, p. 839.

Thienen, Gerard van and John Goldfinch (ed.), *Incunabula Printed in the Low Countries: A Census*. Nieuwkoop 1999.

Wade, James, 'Penitential Romance after the Reformation'. In: *Medieval into Renaissance: Essays for Helen Cooper*. Ed. by Andrew King and Matthew Woodcock. Cambridge 2016, p. 91–106.

Wang, Yu-Chiao, 'William Copland's and Thomas East's Promotional Strategies for the *Morte Darthur*: A Study of the Origins, Forms, and Contexts of Their Title Pages'. In: *JEBS* 6 (2003), p. 77–92.

Wang, Yu-Chiao, 'Caxton's Romances and Their Early Tudor Readers'. In: *Huntington Library Quarterly* 67 (2004), p. 173–188.

Wiggins, Alison, 'Romance in the Age of Print'. In: *The Romance of the Middle Ages*. Ed. by Nicholas Perkins and Alison Wiggins. Oxford 2012, p. 121–149.

Wiggins, Alison and Rosalind Field (ed.), *Guy of Warwick: Icon and Ancestor*. Cambridge 2007 (Studies in Medieval Romance 4).

Wilson-Lee, Edward, 'Romance and Resistance: Narratives of Chivalry in Mid-Tudor England'. In: *Renaissance Studies* 24 (2010), p. 482–495.

Francesco Montorsi
Production éditoriale et diffusion des récits arthuriens en France (XVe–XVIe siècles)

Abstracts: This contribution studies the influence of the printing presses on the fifteenth- and sixteenth-century dynamics of a well-defined literary medieval genre, the French Arthurian romance, a corpus consisting of eleven texts first published between 1488 and 1530. The study sheds light particularly on some aspects of both the production and reception of these texts by answering questions such as: Which titles were selected by the printer from within the Arthurian genre? Which printers have been active protagonists in the textual transmission? In which editorial centres? What does their editorial production curve look like? Which kinds of readers bought these books? Towards the end, the study produces two comparative analyses in order to better grasp the peculiar characters of Arthurian editions, both in the French context and the wider European setting. First, French Arthurian publications are quantitatively compared with other medieval romances published in France. Second, the French Arthurian texts are compared to those published in other European countries in the sixteenth century.

La contribution étudie l'influence de l'imprimerie sur la dynamique d'un genre médiéval bien défini, le roman arthurien français. Ce corpus se compose de onze textes, dont les premières éditions s'échelonnent entre 1488 et 1530. L'étude éclaircit certains aspects de la production éditoriale et de la réception de ces textes en répondant à plusieurs questions. Quels titres ont été sélectionnés par l'imprimerie ? Quels imprimeurs ont été les agents principaux de la transmission textuelle ? Dans quels centres d'édition ? Comment se présente la courbe de production de ce domaine éditorial ? Quels types de lecteurs ont lu ces textes ? La dernière partie de la contribution propose deux analyses comparatives visant à révéler les particularités propres à l'édition arthurienne, à la fois en France et en Europe. En premier lieu, les éditions arthuriennes françaises sont comparées quantitativement aux éditions de romans médiévaux non-arthuriens qui paraissent en France à la même époque. En second lieu, les textes arthuriens français sont confrontés avec les éditions arthuriennes qui paraissent dans d'autres pays de l'espace européen au XVIe siècle.

Analyser les effets de l'imprimerie dans la production et la réception de la littérature aux XVe et XVIe siècles est un exercice qui peut être utilement accompli à partir d'une étude de cas, portant sur un genre littéraire ou un corpus de texte défini. Les textes arthuriens imprimés en France semblent se

Francesco Montorsi, Université de Zurich

prêter à un travail de ce type. Il s'agit d'un groupe de récits qui ne sont pas excessivement nombreux, qui présentent une homogénéité formelle et de contenu et dont la critique s'est attaché à élucider l'histoire.[1]

Notre contribution va étudier le passage à l'imprimé de ces textes en privilégiant les aspects liés à la production et à la diffusion éditoriale: le rôle des imprimeurs-libraires, la sélection des titres opérée par les presses, le lectorat auquel on s'adresse. Afin de mieux comprendre la spécificité propre au corpus qui met en scène les chevaliers de la Table Ronde, la diffusion du récit arthurien est comparée à celle des autres romans d'origine médiévale. Enfin nous mettons en parallèle la situation arthurienne française avec les expériences éditoriales des autres espaces où le roi Arthur a reçu l'honneur des presses.

1 La continuité de l'imprimé arthurien

Aux XVe et XVIe siècles, onze romans arthuriens médiévaux passent dans l'ère typographique. Dans l'ordre chronologique de parution, ce sont: *Lancelot* (Rouen et Paris, 1488, USTC 27606), *Tristan* (Paris, 1489, USTC 27596), *Artus de Bretagne* (Lyon, 1493, USTC 70845), *Merlin* (Paris, 1498, USTC 38121), *Gyron* (Paris, s.d., *c.* 1503, USTC 26047), *Giglan* (Paris, s.d., entre 1512 et 1519, seul exemplaire conservé à Göttingen, sub, fab III, 1327 inc), *Saint Graal* (Paris, 1516, USTC 47273), *Ysaïe le Triste* (Paris, s.d., *c.* 1522, USTC 26469), *Méliadus* (Paris, 1528, USTC 27701), *Perceforest* (Paris, 1528, USTC 372) et *Perceval* (Paris, 1530, USTC 27598). On ajoutera trois cas particuliers qui ne concernent pas des éditions de manuscrits mais des réfections et qui à ce titre, ne nous occuperont pas: le remaniement du *Tristan* par Jean Maugin (Paris, 1554, USTC 27446), l'abrègement du *Lancelot* par l'imprimeur Benoît Rigaud (Lyon, 1591, USTC

---

1 Sur les romans arthuriens passés à l'imprimé voir Jane Taylor, *Rewriting Arthurian Romance in Renaissance France. From Manuscript to Printed Book.* Cambridge 2014; Cedric E. Pickford, 'Les éditions imprimées de romans arthuriens en prose antérieurs à 1600'. In: *Bulletin bibliographique de la Société internationale arthurienne* 13 (1961), p. 99–109; Philippe Ménard, 'La réception des romans de chevalerie à la fin du Moyen Âge et au XVIe siècle'. In: *Bulletin bibliographique de la Société internationale arthurienne* 49 (1997), p. 234–273. Il existe désormais des études pour chaque imprimé arthurien, certains disposant d'une bibliographie nourrie (voir les recensements annuels du *Bulletin bibliographique de la Société internationale arthurienne*). Le pionnier dans ce domaine, Cedric Pickford, a fait paraître les fac-similés de plusieurs romans (*Tristan, Lancelot, Merlin, Gyron, Méliadus, Saint Graal*).

27608), ainsi que l'extraction du *Perceforest* parue sous le nom de *Chevalier doré* (Paris, 1541, USTC 37790).

À cette époque il n'existe pas de romans arthuriens en vers imprimés.[2] Cette particularité reflète le panorama globale de l'édition de romans médiévaux à la Renaissance où les récits en vers sont des cas extraordinaires (*Romant de Richart filz de Robert le Diable* et le *Romant du duc Guillaume*, imprimés une et deux fois). La plus grande partie des récits arthuriens imprimés aux XVe et XVIe siècles ont été originellement écrits en prose, mais deux sont des mises en prose. *Giglan*[3] est une adaptation du *Bel inconnu* de Renaut de Beaujeu et du *Jaufré* provençal. Le *Saint Graal* est, quant à lui, une prosification tardive réunissant six récits, dont une mise en prose du *Conte du Graal* de Chrétien de Troyes et trois continuations.[4]

Certaines absences peuvent être remarquées. Les romans arthuriens en vers d'après Chrétien de Troyes ne sont représentés indirectement que par les versions prosifiées du *Bel Inconnu* et de *Jaufré*. Quant à Chrétien de Troyes lui-même, aucun de ses romans n'est imprimé à part la mise en prose déjà citée du *Conte du Graal*, par ailleurs morceau d'une plus vaste compilation.

Dans le processus de sélection des œuvres arthuriennes, l'imprimerie a reproduit les habitudes existantes plutôt qu'elle n'a favorisé la redécouverte de textes oubliés ou la création de nouvelles formes. Les textes passés à l'imprimé sont ces textes qu'on copiait, vendait et lisait encore au XVe siècle.[5] Des récits

---

2 Le *Chevalier au lion* de Sala, transmis par un seul manuscrit, n'a pas dépassé la tradition manuscrite, cf. l'édition de Pierre Servet. Paris 1996.

3 Sur ce texte voir, en dernier lieu, les articles de Sergio Cappello, 'Le passage à l'imprimé des mises en prose de romans. *Giglan* et *Guillaume de Palerne* "a l'enseigne de l'escu de France"', p. 69–84 et Sylvie Lefèvre, '*Giglan* et Claude Platin entre Lyon et Paris. Des livres imprimés à Internet: la lente métamorphose d'un dossier". In: *Pour un nouveau répertoire des mises en prose. Romans, chansons de geste, autres genres*. Éd. par Maria Colombo Timelli, Barbara Ferrari et Anne Schoysman. Paris 2014, p. 195–212.

4 Le roman est composé de: l'*Elucidation* et *Bliocadran* (deux prologues), le *Conte du Graal*, la *Première Continuation*, la *Deuxième Continuation*, la *Continuation* de Manessier. Pour une introduction au texte, on lira Maria Colombo Timelli, '*La Tresplaisante et recreative hystoire du trespreulx et vaillant chevallier Perceval le Galloys...* (1530), mise en prose tardive du "cycle" du Graal'. In: *Le Moyen Français* 64 (2009), p. 13–54; ainsi que Taylor (voir note 1), p. 119–146.

5 Ménard (voir note 1), p. 236, remarque que 26 manuscrits du *Lancelot en prose* et environ une vingtaine du *Tristan en prose* ont été copiés au XVe siècle, pour certains même au XVIe siècle. Le répertoire de Brian Woledge est un utile point de départ pour apprécier la présence de manuscrits tardifs: *Bibliographie des romans et nouvelles en prose française antérieurs à 1500*. Genève 1975.

non répandus à la même époque comme les romans de Chrétien[6] ou les romans en vers du XIIIe siècle[7] n'ont pas eu l'honneur de l'impression. Certes il existe deux ouvrages qui adaptent en prose des textes médiévaux pour la diffusion imprimée. Il ne faudrait néanmoins pas surestimer l'aspect novateur de ces opérations. Le phénomène de la mise en prose constitue une activité d'*aggiornamento* littéraire et traduction intralinguistique qui, commencée au XIVe siècle en Bourgogne, se poursuit plus tard dans les ateliers d'imprimerie.[8]

Le rôle conservateur de l'imprimerie dans le processus de sélection des titres arthuriens a été produit par deux facteurs somme toute assez banals: les libraires ont édité les textes dont la vente semblait plus facile, ce qui a encouragé la diffusion de livres en circulation. De plus, ils ont eu tendance à imprimer des textes pour lesquels ils disposaient d'exemplaires manuscrits, plutôt que des textes d'accès malaisé et dont la diffusion était désormais restreinte, tels les romans de Chrétien de Troyes.

2 Courbe de production, libraires, centres éditoriaux

Le passage des manuscrits à l'imprimé[9] est un phénomène qui s'étale entre 1488 et 1530 dû essentiellement à l'initiative de deux imprimeurs parisiens, Antoine Vérard, entre 1488–1489 et *c.* 1506 et plus tard, Galliot Du Pré, entre 1516 et 1530.

---

6 Keith Busby, Terry Nixon, Alison Stones et Lori Walters (éd.), *Les manuscrits de Chrétien de Troyes*. 2 vols. Amsterdam 1993.

7 À l'exception du *Méliador* de Froissart (deuxième moitié du XIVe siècle), les romans arthuriens en vers ont été écrits entre 1200 et 1280. La diffusion de ces textes auprès du lectorat a été, déjà à l'époque de leur composition, mince, voir Richard Trachsler, *Les romans arthuriens en vers après Chrétien de Troyes*. Roma 1997, p. 21 et 25–31.

8 Maria Colombo Timelli, Barbara Ferrari et Anne Schoysman (éd.), *Nouveau Répertoire de mises en prose (XIVe–XVIe siècle)*. Paris 2014. Parmi les proses qui ne sont connues que par des imprimés figurent *Mabrian* (s.d., vers 1525, USTC 95074), *Florimont* (1528, USTC 49958), *Guillaume de Palerne* (s.d., entre 1527 et 1530, USTC 53705), *Richard sans peur* (s.d., vers 1528, USTC 83795) et *Meurvin* (1540, USTC 37782).

9 Pour un panorama chronologique du passage à l'imprimé des romans médiévaux, on renvoie à Sergio Cappello, 'Répertoire chronologique des premières éditions des romans médiévaux français aux XVe et XVIe siècles'. In: *Est Ovest: lingue, stili, società. Studi in ricordo di Guido Barbina*. Éd. par Giampaolo Borghello. Udine 2001, p. 167–186.

Lancelot paraît en 1488 grâce à l'association de Jean le Bourgeois, à Rouen, et Jean Du Pré, à Paris (et avec le concours anonyme, suivant certains,[10] d'Antoine Vérard). Ce dernier est à l'origine de plusieurs éditions *princeps* de récits médiévaux,[11] dont trois arthuriens. C'est lui qui, après avoir donné le jour à *Tristan* en 1489 imprime en 1498 les trois volumes du *Merlin* et, plus tard, vers 1503[12] *Gyron le Courtois*. En 1493 paraît *Artus de Bretagne*, un récit qui aura une carrière éditoriale tout à fait différente de celle des autres romans arthuriens, à la fois en raison de son succès durable et de ses débuts lyonnais, chez Jean de la Fontaine.

C'est Galliot Du Pré qui prend la suite de Vérard dans la publication de textes inédits, souvent en association avec d'autres libraires. En 1516, une association composée par Du Pré, Michel Le Noir et Jean Petit, publie le *Saint Graal*. *Ysaïe le Triste* est, quant à lui, édité vers 1522 par Pierre Vidoue et Du Pré. En 1528, ce dernier fait imprimer le *Méliadus de Leonnoys* et le *Perceforest* et publie, deux ans plus tard, en association avec Jean Logis et Jean Saint-Denis, le *Perceval*. La seule exception à cette vague d'éditions *princeps* qui relèvent de l'atelier de Galliot Du Pré est *Giglan*, imprimé entre 1512 et 1519, dans l'atelier de la Veuve Jean Trepperel.[13]

À l'exception du *Perceval* – dernier roman passé, en 1530, à l'imprimé – les récits arthuriens ont tous été réimprimés au moins une fois (Figure 1). Le texte le plus publié est *Artus de Bretagne*, qui bénéficie, au long du XVIe siècle, d'un nombre d'impressions, 16, qui dépasse de loin celui des autres romans (à lui seul, il comptabilise le 28% des éditions totales). Cet ouvrage dont la matière est hétérodoxe par rapport aux ,classiques' arthuriens a sans doute joui aussi d'un public différent, moins restreint socialement, par rapport à d'autres romans de la Table Ronde. Dans le classement des textes les plus édités suivent

---

10 Cedric E. Pickford, 'Antoine Vérard, éditeur du *Lancelot* et du *Tristan*'. In: *Mélanges de langue et littérature françaises du Moyen Âge offerts à Charles Foulon*. 2 vols. Rennes 1980, I, p. 277–285.

11 En plus des romans arthuriens, signalons les éditions *princeps* du *Jouvencel* (1493, USTC 70951), de *Galien Rhetoré* (1500, USTC 53862), *Beufve d'Anthonnes* (s.d., entre 1499 et 1503, USTC 70952) et *Doolin de Mayence* (1501, USTC 26008).

12 Le *Gyron* est daté par Cedric E. Pickford de vers 1501 (voir *Gyron le Courtoys*, London 1977). Nous suivons ici la datation proposée par Brigitte Moreau, *Inventaire chronologique des éditions parisiennes du XVIe siècle. 1531–1535*. Vol. 4. Abbeville 1992.

13 La démonstration de la priorité chronologique de cette édition sans date a été faite par Cappello, 'Le passage' (note 3).

Merlin et *Tristan* (7 éditions), *Giglan* et *Lancelot du Lac* (6 éditions), *Ysaïe le Triste* (4 éditions), *Gyron le Courtois* (3 éditions), *Méliadus de Leonnoys, Perceforest, Saint Graal* (chacun avec 2 éditions).

Fig. 1: Les éditions de romans arthuriens en France.

Lancelot, 6 éditions	Rouen et Paris, Jean le Bourgeois et Jean Du Pré, 1488, USTC 27606
	Paris, Antoine Vérard, 1494, USTC 71230
	Paris, Antoine Vérard, 1504 [daté par l'imprimeur, par erreur, de 1494], USTC 47285
	Paris, Michel Le Noir, 1513, USTC 49390
	Paris, Michel Le Noir, 1520, USTC 47183
	Paris, Philippe Le Noir et Jean Petit, 1533, USTC 23173
Tristan, 7 éditions	Paris, Antoine Vérard, 1489, USTC 27596
	Paris, Antoine Vérard, s.d. [ante 1496], USTC 71497
	Paris, Antoine Vérard, s.d. [*c.* 1499], USTC 71498
	Paris, Antoine Vérard, s.d. [*c.* 1506], USTC 8320
	Paris, Michel Le Noir et Jean Petit, 1514, USTC 88740
	Paris, Michel Le Noir, 1520, USTC 26435
	Paris, Denis Janot, 1533, USTC 27597
Artus de Bretagne, 16 éditions	s. l. [Lyon], s. n. [Jean de la Fontaine], 1493, USTC 70845
	Lyon, s. n. [Michel Topié], 1496, USTC 70846
	Paris, Michel Le Noir, 1502, USTC 30255
	Paris, Michel Le Noir, 1509, USTC 64432
	Paris, [Veuve Trepperel et/ou Jean Janot], [entre 1512 et 1522] (édition sans exemplaire attesté)
	Paris, Michel Le Noir, 1514, USTC 49894
	Lyon, Olivier Arnoullet, s.d. [entre 1517 et 1567], USTC 49458
	Paris, Veuve J. Trepperel, s.d. [*c.* 1525], USTC 72798
	Paris, Alain Lotrian, s.d. [*c.* 1531], USTC 73010
	Paris, Alain Lotrian et Denis Janot, s.d. [*c.* 1533], USTC 59316
	Paris, Pierre Sergent, s.d. [entre 1533–1547], USTC 76153
	Paris, Jean Bonfons, s.d. [entre 1547–1566], USTC 29430
	Paris, Jean Bonfons, s.d. [entre 1547–1566] (1 ex. à München, BSB, Res/4 P.o.gall. 48, voir Cappello note 18)
	Paris, Jean Bonfons, s.d. [entre 1547–1566], USTC 29434
	Lyon, Olivier Arnoullet, 1556, USTC 60581
	Paris, Nicolas Bonfons, 1584, USTC 29119

Merlin, 7 éditions	Paris, Antoine Vérard, 1498, USTC 38121
	Paris, Antoine Vérard, s.d. [*c.* 1503], MacFarlane n° 173[14]
	Paris, Michel Le Noir, 1505, USTC 26095
	Rennes, Caen, Rouen, Jean Macé, Michel Angier et Richard Massé, s.d. [entre 1507 et 1518], USTC 55750
	Paris, Veuve J. Trepperel et Jean Janot, s.d. [entre 1512 et 1519], USTC 55694
	Paris, Philippe Le Noir, 1526, USTC 6975
	Paris, Philippe Le Noir, 1528, USTC 47146
Gyron le Courtois, 3 éditions	Paris, Antoine Vérard, s.d. [*c.* 1503], USTC 26047
	Paris, Jean Petit et Michel Le Noir, s.d. [*c.* 1516], USTC 26336
	Paris, Michel Le Noir, 1519, USTC 26394
Giglan, 6 éditions	Paris, s. n. (veuve Trepperel et Jean Janot), s.d. [entre 1512 et 1519] (un ex. à Göttingen, sub, fab III, 1327 inc)
	Lyon, s. n. (Claude Nourry), s.d. [entre 1512 et 1530], USTC 88797
	Lyon, Claude Nourry, 1530, USTC 55789
	Lyon, Gilles et Jacques Huguetan, 1539, USTC 79974
	Lyon, Olivier Arnoullet, s.d. [entre 1530 et 1567], USTC 80041
	Paris, Nicolas Chrestien, s.d. [entre 1547 et 1557] (édition sans exemplaire attesté)
Saint Graal, 2 éditions	Paris, Jean Petit, Galliot Du Pré et Michel Le Noir, 1516, USTC 47273
	Paris, Philippe Le Noir, 1523, USTC 27595
Ysaïe le Triste, 4 éditions	Paris, Pierre Vidoue et Galliot Du Pré, s.d. [*c.* 1522], USTC 26469
	Paris, Philippe Le Noir, s.d. [*c.* 1528], USTC 55607
	Paris, Alain Lotrian, s.d. [*c.* 1531], USTC 73041
	Paris, Jean Bonfons, s.d. [entre 1547 et 1566], USTC 55821
Méliadus de Leonnoys, 2 éditions	Paris, Galliot Du Pré, 1528, USTC 27701
	Paris, Denis Janot, 1533 [1532 ancien style], USTC 31119
Perceforest, 2 éditions	Paris, Galliot Du Pré, 1528, USTC 372
	Paris, Gilles de Gourmont, Philippe Le Noir et François Regnault, 1531–1532, USTC 47140
Perceval, 1 édition	Paris, Jean Logis, Jean Saint Denis et Galliot Du Pré, 1530, USTC 27598

14 John Macfarlane, *Antoine Vérard*. London 1900.

Les lieux des 56 impressions sont les suivants: 1 édition à Rouen / Paris, 1 édition à Rennes / Caen / Rouen, 8 éditions à Lyon et 46 éditions à Paris. S'il est vrai que, au XVIe siècle, Paris produit chaque année environ trois fois plus de livres que Lyon,[15] cela veut dire que la production arthurienne se concentre à Paris encore plus que le reste de l'édition française (82% pour Paris et 14% pour Lyon). Le rôle central joué par la capitale pourrait être lié au public ciblé par ces romans, la noblesse et la riche bourgeoisie de Robe ayant davantage résidence à Paris. Cela pourrait ne pas relever du hasard que les huit impressions lyonnaises concernent deux livres, *Artus de Bretagne* et *Giglan*, qui ont touché un public moins socialement restreint que celui d'autres imprimés arthuriens. L'édition de Rennes / Caen / Rouen est, quant à elle, un *Merlin* imprimé en *in-quarto*, un format moins somptueux et moins cher que les *in-folio* parisiens traditionnels.[16]

À Paris, les imprimeurs qui diffusent la littérature arthurienne sont: Antoine Vérard, Philippe Le Noir, Michel Le Noir, Galliot Du Pré, Alain Lotrian, Denis Janot, Jean Bonfons, la veuve Trepperel et Jean Petit (sont ici évoqués seulement ces imprimeurs qui publient deux éditions au moins). À Lyon, nous trouvons Jean de la Fontaine, Michel Topié, Olivier Arnoullet, Claude Nourry et Gilles et Jacques Huguetan. Le 23 ou 25% des textes (14 sur 56), a été imprimée par une association d'imprimeurs, phénomène particulièrement fréquent à Paris. Ce chiffre est cohérent avec les résultats d'une étude sur les éditions parisiennes des années 1530.[17] On trouve seulement une fois à Lyon une association d'imprimeurs, une fois à Rouen (mais avec Paris) et une fois pour l'édition partagée entre Rennes, Caen et Rouen.

Les plus grands passeurs de textes sont les Parisiens. Entre 1502 et 1520, Michel Le Noir imprime onze romans, dont la presque totalité, 10, sont des rééditions. Suivent Antoine Vérard, avec 9 éditions entre 1489 et *c.* 1506 (dont 3 *princeps*), Philippe Le Noir avec 6 éditions entre 1523 et 1533 (toutes des

---

15 Henri-Jean Martin, 'Classements et conjonctures'. In: *Histoire de l'édition française.* Vol. 1, *Le livre conquérant. Du Moyen Âge au milieu du XVIIe siècle*. Éd. par Roger Chartier et Henri-Jean Martin. Paris 1983, p. 429–457, part. p. 443.
16 Ceci étant cette explication sociologique peut être nuancée lorsqu'on sait que le livre imprimé parisien circule largement dans d'autres régions de France, voir Graham A. Runnals, 'The Book Market in Early Sixteenth-Century France (as seen through Fernando Colon's Collection of French Books)'. In: *Early Book Society Newsletter*, 2nd ser., I (1996), p. 3–5.
17 Selon les calculs d'Annie Charon-Parent, un tiers des éditions parisiennes recensées par Brigitte Moreau entre 1530 et 1535 font l'objet de partages, cf. 'Associations dans la librairie parisienne du XVIe siècle'. In: *L'Europe et le livre. Réseaux et pratiques du négoce de librairie, XVIe–XIXe siècles*. Éd. par Frédéric Barbier, Sabine Juratic et Dominique Varry. Paris 1996, p. 17–30.

rééditions), Galliot Du Pré, avec 5 éditions entre 1516 et 1530 (toutes des *princeps*). Les Lyonnais qui ont imprimé le plus sont Olivier Arnoullet, avec 2 rééditions du *Giglan* et une d'*Artus de Bretagne*, toutes non datées, et Claude Nourry, qui imprime deux fois *Giglan* vers 1530 et à une date non précisée.

Au prix de quelques approximations en raison des éditions non datées,[18] nous élaborons une courbe symbolisant les impressions des récits arthuriens sur des périodes de cinq ans (Figure 2):

Pendant la première phase éditoriale (entre 1485 et 1504), dominée par Antoine Vérard, les romans sont imprimés à hauteur de 2 à 4 tous les cinq ans. S'ensuit une phase (1505 à 1529) marquée par les réimpressions de Le Noir (1502–1520) et les *princeps* de Galliot Du Pré (1516–1530), où est publié un nombre accru de textes, autour d'un titre par an. Le créneau de 1530–1534 constitue le pic de production avec neuf titres. Immédiatement après, l'édition arthurienne s'écroule: deux titres pour les ans 1535–1539, un pour 1540–1544, un pour 1545–1549, deux pour 1550–1554, trois pour 1555–1559, un pour 1560–1564. Suite à cette date, la seule réimpression sera l'*Artus de Bretagne* de 1584.[19]

Dans les années 1530 se situe la disgrâce du roman arthurien. Après 1533, plus aucune édition n'existe de ces romans, tels *Tristan* ou *Lancelot*, qui avaient

---

18 Dans le cas des éditions sans date mais datables, nous suivons en général les répertoires connus, en particulier l'*Inventaire chronologique des éditions parisiennes du XVIe siècle* publié par Brigitte Moreau à partir des fiches de Philippe Renouard (voir note 12). Pour *Artus de Bretagne* et *Giglan*, qui présentent le plus grand nombre d'éditions non datées, nous suivons les renseignements fournis par Sergio Cappello, 'Les éditions d'Artus de Bretagne au XVIe siècle'. In: *Artus de Bretagne. Du manuscrit à l'imprimé (XIVe–XIXe siècles)*. Éd. par Christine Ferlampin-Acher. Rennes 2015, p. 153–186 et Cappello, 'Le passage' (note 3). Une édition qui dispose d'une fourchette de datation de moins de 10 ans est insérée dans le créneau qui correspond le mieux à l'approximation (par ex. *Giglan*, s.d., entre 1512 et 1519→1515–1519). Là où la fourchette de datation est de 10 ans ou plus, nous attribuons un laps temporel de manière quelque peu arbitraire. Un critère de bons sens que nous avons suivi est d'espacer dans le temps les impressions non datées d'un imprimeur tel que J. Bonfons. Ci-après nos approximations: *Merlin*, Macé, Angier et Massé, entre 1507–1518→1510–1514; *Artus*, Veuve Trepperel et/ou Janot, entre 1512 et 1522→1515–1519; *Giglan*, Nourry, entre 1512 et 1530→1520–1524 (cette édition est sans doute postérieure à celle de la veuve Trepperel et/ou Janot, entre 1512 et 1519); *Artus*, Sergent, entre 1533 et 1547→1535–1539; *Artus*, Arnoullet, entre 1517 et 1567→1540–1544 (cette édition est sans doute antérieure à celle imprimée par le même Arnoullet en 1556); *Giglan*, Arnoullet, entre 1530 et 1567→1545–1549; *Giglan*, Chrestien, entre 1547 et 1557→ 1550–1554; *Artus*, J. Bonfons, entre 1547 et 1566→1550–1554; *Ysaïe le Triste*, J. Bonfons, entre 1547 et 1566→1555–1559; *Artus*, J. Bonfons, entre 1547–1566→1555–1559; *Artus*, Paris, J. Bonfons, entre 1547–1566→1560–1564.
19 De cette édition existe un fac-similé: *Artus de Bretagne*. Éd. par Nicole Cazauran et Christine Ferlampin-Acher. Paris 1996.

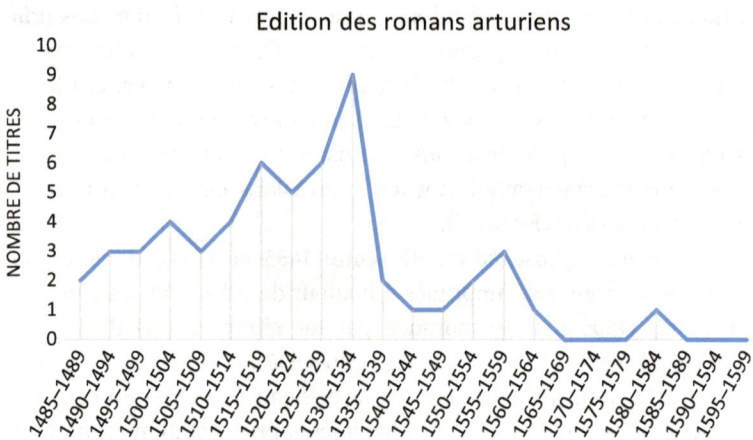

Fig. 2: La courbe de production des romans arthuriens.

fait les délices de générations de lecteurs sans interruption depuis le début du XIIIᵉ siècle. L'insuccès n'épargne que les textes hétérodoxes, les romans arthuriens de la fin du Moyen Âge tels *Ysaïe le Triste* ou *Artus de Bretagne* ou le remaniement tardif de *Giglan*, publiés selon des formats qui ne s'adressent plus aux élites mais à un large public.

Il faut souligner que la disgrâce des récits arthuriens ne trouve pas de correspondance avec l'édition globale française, qui continue à croître jusqu'au début des guerres de religion.[20] L'infortune ne trouve pas de correspondance non plus avec les impressions des proses épiques ou des romans d'aventures, qui continuent à être rééditées tout au long du siècle, pour certaines même au-delà. Cette infortune a par contre son parallèle dans d'autres phénomènes d'abandons éditoriaux. Vers les années 1530/1540, la librairie française délaisse la publication d'autres pans des lettres médiévales: traductions (de la Bible, des textes antiques), ouvrages historiques comme les *Grandes chroniques de France* (ou *Chroniques de Saint-Denis*), textes littéraires tels le *Roman de la Rose* ou les *Cent nouvelles nouvelles*, etc. Ce tournant éditorial, qui incarne en un sens la fin du Moyen Âge, reflète l'abandon d'anciennes traditions et l'adoption d'autres formes et valeurs littéraires de la part du public cultivé. Dans le cas des récits arthuriens, ceux-ci sont en partie remplacés par les romans renaissants tels l'*Amadis* ou le *Roland furieux*, qui sont traduits à

---

20 Emmanuel Le Roy Ladurie, 'Une histoire sérielle du livre (XVᵉ–XXᵉ siècles)'. In: *Histoire, économie et société* 14/1 (1995), p. 3–24.

partir des années 1540 et qui jouissent dès leur apparition d'un fulgurant succès.[21]

3 La composition du lectorat

Les préfaces des romans arthuriens s'adressent aux nobles (aux „tresexcellentz, belliqueulx, invictissimes et insuperables heroes françoys" dans *Perceforest*). Suivant un ancien motif, elles proclament que la lecture des chevaleries sert à „exciter et esmouvoir les cueurs [...] à glorieusement et vertueusement vivre" (Tristan).[22]

Formulations topiques certes, mais qui correspondent pourtant à une certaine réalité socio-culturelle. À une époque où l'on cherche dans la littérature des exemples de vie et où les modèles éducatifs humanistes ne se sont pas encore imposés, les romans de chevalerie participent de l'éducation littéraire de ces classes aristocratiques qui tirent leurs privilèges et leur honneur de la participation aux activités guerrières. Selon le témoignage d'un de ses contemporains, François Ier encourageait les nobles de la cour à puiser un miroir de vie dans les romans de chevalerie:

---

21 Michel Simonin, 'La disgrâce d'Amadis'. In: *Studi francesi* 82 (1984), p. 1–35; Luce Guillerm, *Sujet de l'écriture et traduction autour de 1540*. Paris 1988; *Les Amadis en France au XVIe siècle*. Paris 2000 (Cahiers du Centre V.-L. Saulnier 17). À propos du succès des nouveaux récits de chevalerie, voir le témoignage du traducteur Allègre, qui parmi les lectures des grands, cite en 1556 les nouveaux romans renaissants: „Ce non obstant en la plus part de ce fleurissant royaume de France, on ne voit gueres autres livres es maisons des grands, qu'Amadis, Philocopes, et Rolands, qui ne chantent qu'armes, amours, et mensonges: et soubs l'escorce de quelque beau parler, incitent l'homme de sa nature menteur et voluptueux, à s'aliener du tout de verité et vertu: ne rapportant autre fruict de la longue lecture de ces fables (qui occupent la meilleure partie du peu de temps que vivons) que de contrefaire le beau langaige", *Decade contenant les vies des Empereurs* (Paris: Michel de Vascosan, 1556, ff. *iiir°–v°*), ainsi qu'à une époque plus tardive, les propos de François de La Noue, *Discours politiques et militaires*. Éd. par Frank Edmund Sutcliffe. Genève, Paris 1967, p. 162. [Sur la disgrâce de certains genres, dont le roman arthurien, dans les années 1530, voir aussi la discussion sur le fonds de Galliot du Pré dans la contribution de Van Hemelryck et Delsaux à ce volume, en particulier p. 196–223.]

22 Plusieurs exemples se lisent dans Nicole Cazauran, 'Les romans de chevalerie en France: entre exemple et récréation'. In: Le roman de chevalerie au temps de la Renaissance. Éd. par Marie-Thérèse Jones-Davies. Paris 1987 (Centre de recherches sur la Renaissance, 12), p. 29–48. Sur le lectorat du roman arthurien voir les observations de Taylor (voir note 1), p. 49–53 et Ménard (voir note 1), p. 254–257. [Sur les lectorats des traductions de romans chevaleresques français traduits en néerlandais et en anglais, voir la contribution de De Bruijn à ce volume, p. 93–124; sur le public des romans allemands, voir la contribution de Bertelsmeier-Kierst, p. 17–47; sur la clientèle de Galliot du Pré, voir aussi Van Hemelryck et Delsaux, p. 223–230.]

> Au contraire j'ay ouy racompter autresfois à un grand seigneur, de ses plus favoris, que [v°] quand il s'en faisoit lire en sa chambre [les romans de chevalerie], il ammonestoit les gentils-hommes là presens de les manier aucunesfois en leurs maisons, leur remonstrant par sa royalle eloquence que sous l'ecorce de ces joyeuses narrations y gisoit de bonnes instructions morales pour la noblesse, en exaulsant les vertueux faits et blasmant les vicieux. [...] Puis leur affermoit que mieux ils gousteroient les enseignemens des meurs parmy ceste douce volupté de comptes plaisans et heroiques que dedans les autheurs des Ethiques, epineux, secs et ethiques [...].[23]

Le roi chevalier était d'ailleurs connu pour ses lectures chevaleresques, dont certains moralistes, tel Jean Thenaud, auraient voulu le détourner, lui ainsi que les autres nobles.[24]

Les données historiques relatives à la diffusion des récits arthuriens confirment largement ces témoignages littéraires. À cette époque le coût de la main d'œuvre est peu important et le papier, matériau cher, compte, avec l'éventuelle reliure, pour la plus grande partie du prix de revient du livre.[25] La dimension du livre – le nombre de pages et la taille du volume – constitue donc la variable fondamentale du prix. Or un certain nombre de récits arthuriens sont de vastes ouvrages, qui ont été imprimés exclusivement en grand format: *Lancelot, Tristan, Gyron, Méliadus, Perceforest, Perceval, Saint Graal*. Des livres français acquis par Fernand Colomb, le fils de Christophe, le plus onéreux est le *Perceforest* acheté en 1535,[26] dont les trois tomes reliés lui ont coûté 1 écu d'or, une somme beaucoup

---

23 Suivant le témoignage de Jacques Gohory dans *Le Treizieme Livre d'Amadis de Gaule* (Paris, Lucas Breyer: 1571, f. a iii r° et v°), „À l'illustre et vertueuse Catherine de Clermont Contesse de Rectz".

24 „[...] ung livre du Triumphe des Vertuz [...] qui pourra servir ou temps de vostre tresmagnifique sejour de quelque passetemps et d'un romant [i.e. „pourra remplacer un roman"], ouquel l'on pourra trop myeulx proffiter que en autres plusieurs qui sont plains de fables, mensonges, amours deshonnestes et folles fantasies, dont maintes nobles maisons sont plaines, par la lecture desquelz l'on n'est en fin meilleur, plus sçavant ou vertueux, ains au contraire", Jean Thenaud, *Le triumphe des vertuz*, 1er traité, *Le triumphe de prudence*. Éd. par Titia J. Schuurs Janssen et René E. V. Stuip. Genève 1996, 'Epître dédicatoire', p. 3. L'épître dédicatoire est adressée à la mère de François Ier, Louise de Savoie. Les manuscrits de présentation de l'ouvrage, datant de 1517–1518, auraient été offerts à Louise et à son fils (voir p. lxii de l'introduction).

25 Jeanne Veyrin-Forrer, 'Fabriquer un livre au XVIe siècle'. In: *Histoire de l'édition française* (note 15), p. 279–301; Graham A. Runnalls, 'La vie, la mort, les livres de l'imprimeur-libraire parisien Denis Janot'. In: *Revue belge de philologie et d'histoire* 78 (2000), p. 797–851; et Henri-Jean Martin, *Le livre français sous l'Ancien Régime*. Paris 1987, 'Comment mesurer un succès littéraire. Le problème des tirages', p. 209–223.

26 Fernand Colomb avait l'habitude d'inscrire au dernier feuillet de tout livre acheté le lieu, la date d'acquisition, le prix de chaque volume en monnaie du pays, voir Jean Babelon, *La bibliothèque française de Fernand Colomb*. Paris 1913, part. p. ix et, pour le *Perceforest*, n° 168,

plus grande que celle dépensée pour d'autres romans et qui équivaut à autour de vingt journées de travail pour un ouvrier du bâtiment non spécialisé.[27]

Les prix des *in-folios* arthuriens étaient donc seulement accessibles aux classes les plus aisées, les nobles, mais aussi une catégorie sociale dont l'ascension est fulgurante au XVIe siècle, la Robe, c'est-à-dire ces familles dont les membres siègent dans un parlement du royaume, administrent la justice ou les finances dans une cour. Il n'est pas surprenant que parmi les acheteurs de romans arthuriens se trouvent, à côté de la classe aristocratique, des représentants de cette nouvelle élite. En effet, ses affiliés représentent les plus gros possesseurs de livres au cours du siècle.[28] Des huit occurrences du *Gyron* signalés par Alexander Schutz dans son inventaire des bibliothèques privées parisiennes, trois relèvent de l'aristocratie, les autres cinq de la Robe.[29] Des douze occurrences du *Tristan*, 5 concernent l'aristocratie et 6 des gens de justice (plus une profession inconnue).[30]

Les groupes marchands et artisans étaient parfois, mais plus rarement, des possesseurs de romans arthuriens. En 1533 et en 1546 à Amiens une Marie Le Scellier, femme d'un marchand, et l'apothicaire Jean Boucquet ont un *Merlin* (qui a été imprimé, on le rappelle, en *in-quarto*). Toujours à Amiens, le même Jean Boucquet et le marchand Nicolas Gouger possèdent un *Saint Graal*. Par ailleurs, ces lecteurs moins aisés ont sans doute augmenté lorsque certains romans se sont

---

p. 160–161. [Sur le format des livres produits respectivement au sud-ouest de l'Allemagne et à Augsbourg, voir les remarques de Bertelsmeier-Kierst dans ce volume, p. 37. Sur le format des livres produits au Danemark et en Angleterre, voir Richter, p. 330 et Boffey, p. 138.]

27 Micheline Baulant, 'Prix et salaires à Paris au XVIe siècles. Sources et résultats'. In: *Annales. Économies, sociétés, civilisations* 31/5 (1976), p. 954–995, part. p. 981. Un écu d'or équivaut à 3 livres, soit 60 sols (1 livre = 20 sols = 240 deniers). Entre 1538 et 1542, un manœuvre du bâtiment (c'est-à-dire un ouvrier manuel pas ou peu qualifié) mettait vingt jours à gagner cette somme. Pour un maçon, il en fallait dix.

28 Selon les statistiques d'Alexander H. Schutz, *Vernacular Books in Parisian Private Libraries of the 16th Century According to the Notarial Inventories.* Chapel Hill 1955, p. 6, les hommes de justice composent environ la moitié des possesseurs de bibliothèques parisiennes.

29 Schutz (voir note 28). Pour les 5 lecteurs provenant de la bourgeoisie de Robe, il s'agit d'un conseiller du roi, de la femme d'un conseiller de chambre du roi, de la femme d'un avocat en la cour du Parlement, d'un ancien prévôt, d'un receveur des amendes du parlement de Paris. Pour les inventaires du XVIe siècle, on aura recours aussi à Roger Doucet, *Les bibliothèques parisiennes du XVIe siècle.* Paris 1956; Albert Labarre, *Le livre dans la vie amiénoise du XVIe siècle. L'enseignement des inventaires après décès (1503–1576).* Paris, Louvain 1971. Sur les gens de Robe au XVIe siècle, voir Georges Huppert, *Bourgeois et gentilshommes. La réussite sociale en France au XVIe siècle.* Paris 1982 [Chicago 1977]; Donald R. Kelley, *Foundations of Modern Historical Scholarship. Language, Law, and History in the French Renaissance.* New York, London 1970, p. 242–245 et p. 274.

30 Un conseiller du roi dans la chambre des comptes, deux échevins, un avocat au Parlement, un notaire au Parlement, un secrétaire des finances.

frayé un chemin dans les formats portatifs. Malheureusement, ces éditions à prix et volume réduits ont péri plus rapidement que les grands formats et ont aussi laissé moins de trace dans les inventaires, qui négligeaient parfois de les priser.[31] La raison du succès de récits tels qu'*Ysaïe le Triste, Giglan* et surtout *Artus de Bretagne*, publiés en des formats *in-quarto*, réside précisément dans la capacité de s'adresser à un ample lectorat. Si *Artus de Bretagne* n'avait pas bénéficié de cette audience, il n'aurait pas été édité par des imprimeurs populaires comme Nicolas Bonfons en 1584 et surtout Nicolas Oudot en 1628 – unique cas de roman médiéval arthurien à être passé dans le catalogue de la Bibliothèque Bleue.[32]

4 Analyse comparative du corpus arthurien (récits chevaleresques français et autres traditions européennes)

Si on multiplie le nombre d'éditions arthuriennes – 56 pour 11 œuvres[33] – par les tirages alors courants,[34] on pourra avoir une idée du nombre de livres à sujet arthurien ayant circulé en France entre 1480 et la fin du XVIe siècle. Ces chiffres font apprécier l'extraordinaire impact que l'imprimerie a eu sur la diffusion de la matière arthurienne.

Cette augmentation exponentielle des livres ne doit pas faire oublier que le corpus arthurien a joui, par rapport à d'autres textes, d'une moindre faveur, qui s'est manifestée par un nombre réduit de titres et par des rééditions moins

---

31 Dans les inventaires étudiés par Schutz, *Artus de Bretagne*, imprimé 16 fois au XVIe siècle, est enregistré moins de fois (3) que le *Méliadus* (4), qui a eu deux éditions seulement. Sur la tendance à ne pas signaler les livres de peu de valeur, voir Schutz (voir note 28), p. 10–11 et Labarre (voir note 29), p. 211–212.

32 Alfred Felix Morin, *Catalogue descriptif de la Bibliothèque bleue*. Genève 1974, n° 576. Il existe aussi des éditions de la Bibliothèque Bleue du *Chevalier Doré*.

33 Voir *supra* le tableau. En ce qui concerne les réfections arthuriennes modernes jusqu'à la fin du XVIe siècle: le *Nouveau Tristan* a été imprimé 4 fois, le *Chevalier doré* 3, alors que le *Lancelot* de Benoît Rigaud n'a jamais été réédité.

34 Autour de 500 pour les incunables. Pour les ouvrages du XVIe siècle, on recense les opinions suivantes: entre 600 et 1250 pour Veyrin-Forrer (voir note 25), p. 281; entre 1000 et 1500 pour Lucien Febvre et Henri-Jean Martin, *L'apparition du livre*. Paris 1971, p. 307–311; de 700 à 1500 pour Annie Charon-Parent, *Les métiers du livre à Paris au XVIe siècle (1535–1560)*. Genève 1974, p. 141. Le tirage moyen des exemplaires de Christophe Plantin est de 1250 exemplaires alors que pour des œuvres plus recherchées il arrive à 2000/2500, voir Leon Voet, *The Golden Compasses*. Vol. 2. Amsterdam, London, New York 1969–1972, p. 169.

fréquentes. Richard Cooper a évalué à 14% la part arthurienne dans l'ensemble de la production des romans médiévaux chevaleresques,[35] derrière les récits portant sur la matière antique (16%), les romans d'aventure (30%) ainsi que les mises en prose des chansons de geste (30%).

Les autres romans de chevalerie sont bien plus souvent imprimés que les récits arthuriens, ce qui est particulièrement vrai pour les proses épiques, telles que *Fierabras* (appelé plus tard les *Conqueste du grand roy Charlemagne*), imprimé au moins 30 fois et les *Quatre fils Aymon*, imprimé au moins 33 fois, aux XVe et XVIe siècles. Le premier livre d'*Amadis*, chef-de-file de ces romans renaissants[36] qui semblent avoir remplacés les récits arthuriens dans les bibliothèques des grands, a été imprimé huit fois en l'espace d'environ 20 ans.[37]

Par ailleurs, plusieurs ouvrages médiévaux largement diffusés ont traversé tout le XVIe siècle. Certains récits (*Fierabras, Quatre fils Aymon, Paris et Vienne* et *Pierre de Provence* entre autres) ont été même intégrés, au siècle suivant, dans le catalogue de Bibliothèque Bleue, en poursuivant leur succès auprès d'un public populaire. Quant aux romans renaissants, ils ont bénéficié eux aussi d'un cycle d'édition plus ample que le groupe arthurien. Les *Amadis, Roland* et Cie ont été imprimés en trois vagues d'édition: 1540–1556, 1570–1590 et 1615–1630.

Le roman arthurien en France a donc été un genre peu représenté par rapport à d'autres récits médiévaux. De plus, sa fortune a été très rapide et s'est concentrée auprès d'un public plus socialement restreint que pour d'autres textes. Ce relatif insuccès doit être compris à l'intérieur du contexte éditorial et culturel français mais il peut être situé aussi dans le cadre plus général de l'édition européenne. En effet, les différents pays produisent peu d'impressions arthuriennes, ainsi que le montre le tableau suivant recensant la production arthurienne jusqu'en 1560 (Figure 3).

---

35 Richard Cooper, 'Outline Bibliography of Works on Chivalry Published in France before 1600'. In: *Chivalry in the Renaissance*. Éd. par Sidney Anglo. Woodbridge 1990, p. 193–238. En raison de l'ampleur du sujet, ces statiques sont inévitablement entachées de quelques erreurs et il est assuré que le roman arthurien représente une portion encore inférieure de l'ensemble. En ce qui concerne la liste de récits arthuriens fournie par Cooper, il faudra en retrancher *Clériadus et Méliadice* ainsi que le *Gauvain* imprimé à Strasbourg en 1540 (le texte, aujourd'hui perdu, serait en allemand). Pour les proses épiques, il faudra augmenter la liste à partir des données fournies par François Suard, *Guillaume d'Orange. Étude du roman en prose*. Paris 1979, p. 541–543.

36 Francesco Montorsi, *L'apport des traductions de l'italien dans la dynamique du récit de chevalerie (1490–1550)*. Paris 2015, p. 53–56 et 63–66 et Cooper (voir note 35). Sur les *Amadis* au XVIe siècle, voir *supra* n. 21.

37 *Amadis de Gaule. Livre I. Traduction Herberay Des Essarts*. Éd. par Michel Bideaux. Paris 2006, p. 93–100.

Fig. 3: Les romans arthuriens en Europe (1470–1560)[38]

En castillan	*El baladro del sabio Merlin con sus profecías*, 1498, USTC 333516 *Libro del esforçado cavallero don Tristan de Leonis*, 1501, USTC 347851 *La demanda del sancto Grial*, 1515, USTC 343001 *El baladro del sabio Merlin. Primera parte de la demanda del sancto Grial*, 1535, USTC 338111
En italien	*Vita [ou Historia] di Merlino*, 1480 [=1481] USTC 993023 *Libro de bataglie de Tristano, Galasso e de la reina Isotta*, 1492, USTC 990351 Evangelista Fossa, *Libro novo de lo Innamoramento di Galvano, c.* 1505/1509, USTC 830447 Niccolò degli Agostini, *Il primo libro dell'innamoramento di messer Tristano e di madonna Isotta*, 1515, USTC 807981 Niccolò degli Agostini, *Il secondo e terzo libro di Tristano*, 1520, USTC 807989 Niccolò degli Agostini, *Lo inamoramento de messer Lancilotto e di madonna Genevra*, 1521, USTC 807990 Niccolò degli Agostini, *Libro terzo e ultimo dell'innamoramento di Lancilotto e Ginevra*, 1526, USTC 807991 Luigi Alamanni, *Gyrone il Cortese*, 1548, USTC 153977 *La dilettevole historia del valorosiss. Parsaforesto*, 1558–1559, USTC 801034 *Gli egregi fatti del gran re Meliadus*, 1558–1560, USTC 804076
En anglais	Thomas Malory, *La Morte d'Arthour*, 1485, USTC 500105 *A little treatise of the birth and prophecy of Merlin, c.* 1499 (?), USTC 516092 *Golagros and Gawane*, 1508, USTC 500984 *Jeaste of sir Gawain, c.* 1528, USTC 502051 *The treatise of sir Lamwell, c.* 1530–32 (?), USTC 516319 Lord Berner, *The history of Arthur of Lytell Brytaine, c.* 1555, USTC 505696
En allemand	*Parzival*, 1477, USTC 749908 *Titurel*, 1477, USTC 749909 *Tristrant und Isalde*, 1484, USTC 749458 *Wigoleis vom Rade*, 1493, USTC 749897
En néerlandais	*Historie van Merlijn, c.* 1540, USTC 438077

---

38 Nous relevons les textes parus la première fois entre 1470 et 1560 et excluons donc les quelques productions qui paraissent entre 1561 et la fin du siècle. Les ouvrages exclus sont l'abrègement du *Lancelot* par l'imprimeur Benoît Rigaud (1591), deux ouvrages originaux anglais tels que *Chinon of England* de Christopher Middleton (1597) et *Tom a Licoln* de Richard Johnson (1599), ainsi que deux textes italiens, l'*Avarchide* de Luigi Alamanni poème épique d'inspiration classique mais de sujet arthurien (1570, posthume) et *I primi quattro canti del Lancillotto* d'Erasmo da Valvasone (1580).

Le maigre butin de la production éditoriale en dehors de la France est composé, d'après nos recherches, de 25 romans. Un seul texte a paru dans l'aire néerlandophone. Les récits arthuriens imprimés sont au nombre de quatre en Espagne,[39] ainsi qu'en Allemagne. La Table Ronde a plus de circulation en Angleterre, où on trouve six textes, et encore davantage, de manière quelque peu surprenante, en Italie avec dix romans. La France, avec ses 13 textes arthuriens, compte finalement, en nombre de titres, pour un tiers de la production éditoriale européenne.

La constatation d'une faible présence d'Arthur se fait encore plus criante lorsqu'on examine la part relative du corpus arthurien dans l'ensemble chevaleresque, ou romanesque, de chaque pays. Les quatre textes du corpus espagnol s'opposent aux 45 titres chevaleresques imprimés entre 1496 et 1602 qu'Eisenberg et Marín Pina ont recensés dans leur *Bibliografía de los libros de caballerías castellanos*, un travail qui ne recense pas les ouvrages traduits d'autres langues.[40] Les deux romans en prose écrits en allemand s'insèrent dans un corpus prosaïque d'au moins 50 textes imprimés aux XVe et XVIe siècle.[41] En Italie, les récits arthuriens sont une goutte dans le *mare magnum* de la narration chevaleresque, qui contient plusieurs dizaines d'items et qui est composée de nombreux récits carolingiens (dont les chefs-d'œuvre de Pulci, Boiardo, l'Arioste), de traductions intégrales des sagas castillanes, ainsi que de continuations originales de ces

---

39 En nous conformant aux usages de la critique espagnole, nous ne considérons pas *Tristán el Joven* comme un roman arthurien. Ce texte est une adaptation et continuation anonyme du récit tristanien qui retrace, entre autres, les aventures des enfants de Tristan et Yseut. Le roman est considéré par la critique comme un *libro de caballerías*, à l'instar des *Amadis*. Par exemple, Daniel Eisenberg et María Carmen Marín Pina, qui excluent les romans arthuriens de leur relevé, traitent du *Tristán el Joven* dans leur répertoire, *Bibliografía de los libros de caballerías castellanos*. Zaragoza 2000, p. 435–439. Ce roman a été traduit en italien en 1555 sous le titre d'*Opere magnanime dei due Tristani*.

40 Eisenberg et Marín Pina (voir note 39).

41 Bodo Gotzkowsky, '*Volksbücher*'. *Prosaromane, Renaissancenovellen, Versdichtungen und Schwankbücher. Bibliographie der deutschen Drucke*. 2 vols. Baden-Baden 1991–1994 (nous considérons tous les sous-genres étudiés par Gotzkowsky sauf les ‚Schwanksammlungen', recueils de récits brefs; par ailleurs la notice ‚Troja-romane' fait état de trois différents textes). Des études ultérieures, qui prennent en compte aussi les textes restés manuscrits et font d'autres choix définitoires, élargissent la liste de Gotzkowsky, voir Christa Bertelsmeier-Kierst, 'Erzählen in Prosa. Zur Entwicklung des deutschen Prosaromans bis 1500'. In: *ZfdA* 143 (2014), p. 141–165; André Schnyder, 'Das Corpus der frühneuhochdeutschen Prosaromane: Eine tabellarische Übersicht als Problemaufriss'. In: *Eulenspiegel trifft Melusine. Der frühneuhochdeutsche Prosaroman im Licht neuer Forschungen und Methoden*. Akten der Lausanner Tagung von 2. bis 4. Oktober 2008. Éd. par Catherine Drittenbass et André Schnyder. Amsterdam 2010 (Chloe 42), p. 545–556.

dernières.[42] En Grande Bretagne les récits arthuriens constituent un cinquième du corpus métrique anglais,[43] alors que la part arthurienne dans l'ensemble des romans en prose de ce pays est encore plus réduite.[44]

Dans le domaine arthurien les succès sont donc rares. Si on ne considère que les romans qui ont bénéficié d'au moins cinq éditions, chiffre peu impressionnant, nous avons deux textes pour l'Allemagne (*Tristrant und Isalde* et *Wigoleis*), tandis qu'en Espagne, en Italie et Angleterre un seul texte, à chaque fois, touche ou dépasse cette frontière (*Tristán de Leonís, Vita di Merlino, La Morte d'Arthour*). La très grande majorité de textes imprimés en dehors de la France, 18 sur 25, ne connaît qu'un ou deux tirages,[45] signe du peu de faveur que suscite l'édition arthurienne. Dans le cas italien la proportion est de neuf sur dix.

5 Conclusions

L'histoire des effets de l'imprimerie sur la littérature arthurienne est faite à la fois de phénomènes de continuité et de rupture. La tradition des récits de la Table Ronde se déploie à cheval de l'invention de Gutenberg sans que celle-ci

---

42 La référence bibliographique reste, malgré son ancienneté, Gaetano Melzi et Paolo Antonio Tosi, *Bibliografia dei romanzi di cavalleria in versi e in prosa italiani*. Milano 1865³. Sur l'histoire de la *Bibliografia* de Melzi et Tosi, ainsi que sur l'absence d'un répertoire moderne, cf. Neil Harris, 'Marin Sanudo, Forerunner of Melzi'. In: *La Bibliofilia* 95 (1993), p. 1–37. L'article d'Harris contient aussi d'importants renseignements sur les premiers romans chevaleresques imprimés en Italie. Sur les récits chevaleresques espagnols, ou d'inspiration espagnole, publiés en Italie, voir l'étude d'Anna Bognolo, Giovanni Cara et Stefano Neri, *Repertorio delle continuazioni italiane ai romanzi cavallereschi spagnoli*. Ciclo di Amadis di Gaula. Roma 2013 (en particulier la contribution de Stefano Neri, p. 85–139, 'Il romanzo cavalleresco spagnolo in Italia'), ainsi que l'analyse pionnière d'Henry Thomas, *Spanish and Portuguese Romances of Chivalry. The Revival of the Romance of Chivalry and its Extension and Influence abroad*. Cambridge 1920, p. 180–199.
43 Jordi Sánchez-Martí, 'The Printed History of the Middle English Verse Romances'. In: *Modern Philology* 107 (2009), p. 1–31, répertorie 18 romans métriques médiévaux imprimés, dont trois de sujet arthurien (*Golagros and Gawane* étant exclu du relevé de Sánchez-Martí en raison de sa provenance écossaise).
44 Les romans arthuriens en prose sont *La Morte d'Arthour* et *Arthur of lytell Brytaine*. Une liste de romans chevaleresque, en prose et en vers, imprimés aux XVᵉ et XVIᵉ siècles se trouve dans Ronald J. Crane, *The Vogue of Medieval Chivalric Romance During the English Renaissance*. Menasha, Wisconsin, 1919.
45 Les textes qui ont été imprimés plus que deux fois sont: *Tristán de Leonís; Tristrant und Isalde; Wigoleis; Vita di Merlino; La Morte d'Arthour; A little treatise of the birth and prophecy of Merlin* et *The Jeaste of Sir Gawain*.

introduise de changements significatifs dans la sélection des textes. Copiés à la main ou composés sur la table du typographe, ce sont toujours les mêmes récits qui sont lus à la fin du XVe siècle. Pour la plupart parisiens, les imprimeurs s'adressent surtout aux secteurs les plus aisés du lectorat, la noblesse et les gens de Robe, à une époque où les gestes des chevaliers servent de modèles éducatifs pour les hautes classes.

Un changement radical prend place au début des années 1530. Après une croissance de la courbe de production, qui culmine dans le pic de 1530–1534, les lecteurs abandonnent les récits arthuriens. Pendant un bref laps de temps, les différents romans cessent soudainement d'être imprimés. Il s'agit, dans plusieurs cas, de la dernière étape d'une transmission qui durait sans solution de continuité depuis plus de deux siècles. Cette crise éditoriale n'a pas d'équivalence avec la production d'autres récits médiévaux, en premier lieu les récits épiques, qui continuent à être édités en France tout au long du XVIe siècle et parfois même au-delà. Elle trouve en revanche un parallèle dans d'autres phénomènes d'abandon éditorial, qui à la même époque frappent des pans entiers des lettres médiévales.

L'infortune éditoriale de la Table Ronde française peut être comprise dans le cadre européen. Au XVIe siècle, dans tous les pays européens, assez rares sont les récits arthuriens imprimés. Ceux qui le sont ont souvent peu de succès de public. Même en Angleterre, malgré l'œuvre de Thomas Malory, le XVIe siècle est l'époque d'un ‚roi disparaissant',[46] au moins dans le domaine de la narration longue. Ainsi, dans ce contexte de pauvreté éditoriale, la librairie française représente le lieu où les romans de la Table Ronde ont le plus de succès, tout au moins avant la rupture décisive des années 1530.

Bibliographie

Amadis de Gaule. Livre I. Traduction Herberay Des Essarts. Éd. par Michel Bideaux. Paris 2006.
Les Amadis en France au XVIe siècle. Paris 2000 (Cahiers du Centre V.-L. Saulnier 17).
Artus de Bretagne. Éd. par Nicole Cazauran et Christine Ferlampin-Acher. Paris 1996.
Babelon, Jean, *La bibliothèque française de Fernand Colomb*. Paris 1913.
Baulant, Micheline, ‘Prix et salaires à Paris au XVIe siècles. Sources et résultats'. In: *Annales. Économies, sociétés, civilisations* 31 (1976), p. 954–995.

---

46 ‚Disappearing king' est le titre de la partie consacrée au XVIe siècle dans l'article de Rob Gossedge et Stephen Knight, 'The Arthur of the Sixteenth to Nineteenth Centuries'. In: *The Cambridge Companion to Arthurian Legend*. Éd. par Elizabeth Archibald et Ad Putter. Cambridge 2009, p. 103–119, part. p. 103–105.

Bertelsmeier-Kierst, Christa, 'Erzählen in Prosa. Zur Entwicklung des deutschen Prosaromans bis 1500'. In: *ZfdA* 143 (2014), p. 141–165.

Bognolo, Anna, Giovanni Cara et Stefano Neri, *Repertorio delle continuazioni italiane ai romanzi cavallereschi spagnoli. Ciclo di* Amadis di Gaula. Roma 2013.

Busby, Keith, Terry Nixon, Alison Stones et Lori Walters (éd.), *Les manuscrits de Chrétien de Troyes*. 2 vols. Amsterdam 1993.

Cappello, Sergio, 'Répertoire chronologique des premières éditions des romans médiévaux français aux XVe et XVIe siècles'. In: *Est Ovest: lingue, stili, società. Studi in ricordo di Guido Barbina*. Éd. par Giampaolo Borghello. Udine 2001, p. 167–186.

Cappello, Sergio, 'Le passage à l'imprimé des mises en prose de romans. *Giglan* et *Guillaume de Palerne* "a l'enseigne de l'escu de France"'. In: *Pour un nouveau répertoire des mises en prose. Romans, chansons de geste, autres genres*. Éd. par Maria Colombo Timelli, Barbara Ferrari et Anne Schoysman. Paris 2014, p. 69–84.

Cappello, Sergio, 'Les éditions d'Artus de Bretagne au XVIe siècle'. In: *Artus de Bretagne. Du manuscrit à l'imprimé (XIVe–XIXe siècles)*. Éd. par Christine Ferlampin-Acher. Rennes 2015, p. 153–186.

Cazauran, Nicole, 'Les romans de chevalerie en France: entre exemple et récréation'. In: *Le roman de chevalerie au temps de la Renaissance*. Éd. par Marie-Thérèse Jones-Davies. Paris 1987 (Centre de recherches sur la Renaissance, 12), p. 29–48.

Charon-Parent, Annie, *Les métiers du livre à Paris au XVIe siècle (1535–1560)*. Genève 1974.

Charon-Parent, Annie, 'Associations dans la librairie parisienne du XVIe siècle'. In: *L'Europe et le livre. Réseaux et pratiques du négoce de librairie, XVIe–XIXe siècles*. Éd. par Frédéric Barbier, Sabine Juratic et Dominique Varry. Paris 1996, p. *17–30*.

Colombo Timelli, Maria, 'La *Tresplaisante et recreative hystoire du trespreulx et vaillant chevallier Perceval le Galloys...* (1530), mise en prose tardive du "cycle" du Graal'. In: *Le Moyen Français* 64 (2009), p. 13–54.

Colombo Timelli, Maria, Barbara Ferrari et Anne Schoysman (éd.), *Nouveau Répertoire de mises en prose (XIVe–XVIe siècle)*. Paris 2014.

Cooper, Richard, 'Outline Bibliography of Works on Chivalry Published in France before 1600'. In: *Chivalry in the Renaissance*. Éd. par Sidney Anglo. Woodbridge 1990, p. 193–238.

Crane, Ronald J., *The Vogue of Medieval Chivalric Romance During the English Renaissance*. Menasha, Wisconsin, 1919.

Doucet, Roger, *Les bibliothèques parisiennes du XVIe siècle*. Paris 1956.

Eisenberg, Daniel et María Carmen Marín Pina, *Bibliografía de los libros de caballerías castellanos*. Zaragoza 2000.

Febvre, Lucien et Henri-Jean Martin, *L'apparition du livre*. Paris 1971.

Gossedge, Rob et Stephen Knight, 'The Arthur of the Sixteenth to Nineteenth Centuries'. In: *The Cambridge Companion to Arthurian Legend*. Éd. par Elizabeth Archibald et Ad Putter. Cambridge 2009, p. 103–119.

Gotzkowsky, Bodo, '*Volksbücher*'. *Prosaromane, Renaissancenovellen, Versdichtungen und Schwankbücher. Bibliographie der deutschen Drucke*. 2 vols. Baden-Baden 1991–1994.

Guillerm, Luce, *Sujet de l'écriture et traduction autour de 1540*. Paris 1988.

Gyron le Courtoys. Éd. par Cedric E. Pickford. London 1977.

Harris, Neil, 'Marin Sanudo, Forerunner of Melzi'. In: *La Bibliofilia* 95 (1993), p. 1–37.

Huppert, Georges, *Bourgeois et gentilshommes. La réussite sociale en France au XVIe siècle*. Paris 1982 [Chicago 1977].

Kelley, Donald R., *Foundations of Modern Historical Scholarship. Language, Law, and History in the French Renaissance*. New York, London 1970.

Labarre, Albert, *Le livre dans la vie amiénoise du XVIᵉ siècle. L'enseignement des inventaires après décès (1503–1576)*. Paris, Louvain 1971.

de La Noue, François, *Discours politiques et militaires*. Éd. par Frank Edmund Sutcliffe. Genève, Paris 1967.

Lefèvre, Sylvie, '*Giglan* et Claude Platin entre Lyon et Paris. Des livres imprimés à Internet: la lente métamorphose d'un dossier'. In: *Pour un nouveau répertoire des mises en prose. Romans, chansons de geste, autres genres*. Éd. par Maria Colombo Timelli, Barbara Ferrari et Anne Schoysman, Paris 2014, p. 195–212.

Le Roy Ladurie, Emmanuel, 'Une histoire sérielle du livre (XVᵉ–XXᵉ siècles)'. In: *Histoire, économie et société* 14/1 (1995), p. 3–24.

Macfarlane, John, *Antoine Vérard*. London 1900.

Martin, Henri-Jean, 'Classements et conjonctures'. In: *Histoire de l'édition française.Vol. 1, Le livre conquérant. Du Moyen Âge au milieu du XVIIᵉ siècle*. Éd. par Roger Chartier et Henri-Jean Martin. Paris 1983, p. 429–457.

Martin, Henri-Jean, *Le livre français sous l'Ancien Régime*. Paris 1987.

Melzi, Gaetano et Paolo Antonio Tosi, *Bibliografia dei romanzi di cavalleria in versi e in prosa italiani*. Milano 1865³.

Ménard, Philippe, 'La réception des romans de chevalerie à la fin du Moyen Âge et au XVIᵉ siècle'. In: *Bulletin bibliographique de la Société internationale arthurienne* 49 (1997), p. 234–273.

Montorsi, Francesco, *L'apport des traductions de l'italien dans la dynamique du récit de chevalerie (1490–1550)*. Paris 2015.

Moreau, Brigitte, *Inventaire chronologique des éditions parisiennes du XVIᵉ siècle. 1531–1535*. Vol. 4. Abbeville 1992.

Morin, Alfred Felix, *Catalogue descriptif de la Bibliothèque bleue*. Genève 1974.

Pickford, Cedric E., 'Les éditions imprimées de romans arthuriens en prose antérieurs à 1600'. In: *Bulletin bibliographique de la Société internationale arthurienne* 13 (1961), p. 99–109.

Pickford, Cedric E., 'Antoine Vérard, éditeur du *Lancelot* et du *Tristan*'. In: *Mélanges de langue et littérature françaises du Moyen Âge offerts à Charles Foulon*. 2 vols. Rennes 1980, I, p. 277–285.

Runnalls, Graham A., 'La vie, la mort, les livres de l'imprimeur-libraire parisien Denis Janot'. In: *Revue belge de philologie et d'histoire* 78 (2000), p. 797–851.

Runnals, Graham A., 'The Book Market in Early Sixteenth-Century France (as seen through Fernando Colon's Collection of French Books)'. In: *Early Book Society Newsletter*, 2nd ser., I (1996), p. 3–5.

Sala, Pierre, *Chevalier au lion*. Éd. par Pierre Servet. Paris 1996.

Sánchez-Martí, Jordi, 'The Printed History of the Middle English Verse Romances'. In: *Modern Philology* 107 (2009), p. 1–31.

Schnyder, André, 'Das Corpus der frühneuhochdeutschen Prosaromane: Eine tabellarische Übersicht als Problemaufriss'. In: *Eulenspiegel trifft Melusine. Der frühneuhochdeutsche Prosaroman im Licht neuer Forschungen und Methoden*. Akten der Lausanner Tagung von 2. bis 4. Oktober 2008. Éd. par Catherine Drittenbass et André Schnyder. Amsterdam 2010 (Chloe 42),p. 545–556.

Schutz, Alexander H., *Vernacular Books in Parisian Private Libraries of the 16th Century According to the Notarial Inventories*. Chapel Hill 1955.

Simonin, Michel, 'La disgrâce d'Amadis'. In: *Studi francesi* 82 (1984), p. 1–35.

Suard, François, *Guillaume d'Orange. Étude du roman en prose*. Paris 1979.

Taylor, Jane, *Rewriting Arthurian Romance in Renaissance France. From Manuscript to Printed Book*. Cambridge 2014.

Thenaud, Jean, *Le triumphe des vertuz*, 1er traité, *Le triumphe de prudence*. Éd. par Titia J. Schuurs Janssen et René E. V. Stuip. Genève 1996.

Thomas, Henry, *Spanish and Portuguese Romances of Chivalry. The Revival of the Romance of Chivalry and its Extension and Influence abroad*. Cambridge 1920.

Trachsler, Richard, *Les romans arthuriens en vers après Chrétien de Troyes*. Roma 1997.

Veyrin-Forrer, Jeanne, 'Fabriquer un livre au XVIe siècle'. In: *Histoire de l'édition française. Vol. 1, Le livre conquérant. Du Moyen Âge au milieu du XVIIe siècle*. Éd. par Roger Chartier et Henri-Jean Martin. *Paris 1983*, p. 279–301.

Voet, Leon, *The Golden Compasses*. 2 vols. Amsterdam, London, New York 1969–1972.

Woledge, Brian, *Bibliographie des romans et nouvelles en prose française antérieurs à 1500*. Genève 1975.

Olivier Delsaux et Tania Van Hemelryck

L'édition imprimée des textes médiévaux en langue française au début du seizième siècle. Le cas de Galliot du Pré (1512–1560)

Abstracts: This article investigates the editorial policy of one of the major sixteenth-century French publishers: Galliot du Pré (1512–1560), well-known by medieval specialists for his publication of Clément Marot's edition of François Villon's poetry and for his first editions of *Perceval* of *Meliadus de Leonnoys*. This study, which focuses on texts written by authors who lived before the beginning of Galliot du Pré's career, is grounded on a new and extensive survey of evidence from two domains: on the one hand, Galliot du Pré's surviving editions, and, on the other hand, a quite exceptional and still underexploited testimony, the posthumous inventory of Galliot du Pré's private library and bookshop. Our analysis relies on the study of the preserved books (texts, authors, titles, privileges, prologues, layout, etc.) and on the context of their publication, that is to say, the historical and political context surrounding their publication, their circulation and their usage. More generally, we intend to understand *when, how* and *why* Galliot du Pré, who specialized in the publication of books for sale to lawyers and civil servants, also became invested in the sometimes quite risky promotion of French medieval literature.

Cet article vise à explorer la politique éditoriale d'un des principaux libraires du XVIe siècle français: Galliot du Pré (1512–1560), bien connu des médiévistes pour sa publication des Œuvres poétiques de François Villon éditées par Clément Marot et pour ses éditions *princeps* de *Perceval* et de *Meliadus de Leonnoys*. Cette étude, centrée sur les textes écrits par des auteurs morts avant le début de la carrière de Galliot du Pré, est basée sur une nouvelle étude exhaustive de deux types de témoignages: d'une part, les éditions conservées de Galliot du Pré; d'autre part, un document rare et encore sous-exploité: l'inventaire après-décès de la bibliothèque de Galliot du Pré et de sa *librairie*. Notre analyse se fonde sur l'étude des livres conservés (textes, auteurs, titre, privilège, prologues, mise en page, mise en texte, etc.) et sur l'étude du contexte de leur diffusion, c'est-à-dire le contexte historique et politique entourant leur publication, leur circulation et leur consommation. De manière générale, nous chercherons à comprendre *quand, comment* et *pourquoi* Galliot du Pré, spécialisé dans la publication de textes aisément vendables aux hommes du Parlement et de la Chancellerie, a également investi dans la publication et la promotion de textes littéraires français médiévaux, entreprise qui pouvait parfois comporter des risques.

Olivier Delsaux et Tania Van Hemelryck, UCLouvain

1 Problématique et mise en contexte[1]

Le libraire-éditeur et marchand de livres parisien Galliot du Pré, actif de 1512 jusqu'à sa mort en 1561,[2] est bien connu des historiens du livre et des historiens de la littérature en moyen français, en particulier pour ses éditions *princeps* de romans arthuriens tels que *Perceval*[3] ou *Meliadus de Leonnoys*,[4] ou encore pour ses éditions de versions ‚revues et corrigées' de

---

1 Dans les transcriptions des textes du seizième siècle, nous avons résolu les abréviations, distingué *i* de *j*, *u* de *v*, *à* de *a*, *où* de *ou*, accentué les *e* fermés en fin de mot et introduit une ponctuation moderne. Dans les transcriptions des pages de titre, les termes imprimés en rouge sont rendus par des caractères italiques tandis que les variations de casse et les marques de ponctuation sont maintenues telles qu'elles apparaissent.

2 Paul Delalain, *Notice sur Galliot du Pré, libraire parisien de 1512 à 1560*. Paris 1890; Paul Delalain, *Notice complémentaire sur Galliot du Pré, libraire parisien de 1512 à 1560*. Paris 1891; Arthur Tilley, 'A Paris Bookseller – Galliot du Pré'. In: *Studies in the French Renaissance*. Cambridge 1922, p. 168–218; Madeleine Connat, 'Galliot Dupré et sa famille: documents inédits'. In: *Bibliothèque d'Humanisme et Renaissance* 4 (1944), p. 427–435; Annie Charon-Parent, *Les métiers du livre à Paris au XVIe siècle (1535–1560)*. Genève 1974 (EPHE. Sciences historiques et philologiques. Histoire et civilisation du livre 6); Annie Charon-Parent, 'Aspects de la politique éditoriale de Galliot Du Pré'. In: *Le Livre dans l'Europe de la Renaissance. Actes du XXVIIIe Colloque international d'études humanistes de Tours [juillet 1985]*. Éd. par Pierre Aquilon et Henri-Jean Martin. Paris 1988, p. 54–67; Annie Charon-Parent, 'Du Pré, Galliot'. In: *Dictionnaire encyclopédique du livre*. Éd. par Pascal Fouché, Daniel Péchoin, Philippe Schuwer et al. T. 1. Paris 2002, p. 836–837.

3 Il s'agit d'une compilation de trois textes ayant le Graal comme thème principal: l'*Histoire du saint Graal* (du cycle Vulgate); le *Perlesvaus*; de longs extraits de la *Queste del saint Graal*; un court fragment explicatif du *Lancelot en prose*. Sur ce texte, voir, entre autres, Jean Tilley, 'Sur le Perceval en prose de 1530'. In: *Fin du Moyen Âge et Renaissance. Mélanges de Philologie française offerts à Robert Guiette*. Anvers 1961, p. 233–247; Pierre Servet, 'D'un Perceval l'autre. La mise en prose du *Conte du Graal* (1530)'. In: *L'œuvre de Chrétien de Troyes dans la littérature française – Réminiscences, résurgences et réécritures*. Éd. par Claude Lachet. Lyon 1997, p. 197–210; Maria Colombo Timelli, '*Perceval le Galloys* (1530), première "traduction" moderne du cycle du Graal'. In: *'Un paysage choisi'. Mélanges de linguistique française offerts à Leo Schena*. Éd. par Giovanna Bellati et Leo Schena. Turin, Paris 2007, p. 119–128; Maria Colombo Timelli, '*La Tresplaisante et recreative hystoire du trespreulx et vaillant chevallier Perceval le Galloys...* (1530), mise en prose tardive du "cycle" du Graal'. In: *Le Moyen Français* 64 (2009), p. 13–54; Jane H.M. Taylor, *Rewriting Arthurian Romance in Renaissance France. From Manuscript to Printed Book*. Woodbridge 2014, p. 119–146.

4 Barbara Wahlen, *L'écriture à rebours. Le Roman de Meliadus du XIIIe au XVIIIe siècle*. Genève 2010 (Publications romanes et françaises 252), en part. p. 296–334; Sophie Albert, 'Recycler Meliadus: la réception de l'identité héroïque dans l'imprimé *Meliadus de Leonnoys* (1528)'. In: *Cahiers de recherches médiévales et humanistes* 24 (2012), p. 487–503 (aussi disponible en ligne: URL: http://crm.revues.org/12961; DOI: 10.4000/crm.12961, consulté le 20 juillet 2017).

‚classiques' médiévaux tels que le *Roman de la Rose*,[5] Alain Chartier ou François Villon.[6] Cependant, la majorité des études parues à ce jour sur les libraires-éditeurs de la première moitié du seizième siècle ont adopté une perspective monographique, centrée sur l'étude de l'édition d'un texte ou d'un groupe de textes en particulier.[7] Si une approche précise et limitée est légitime pour rendre compte de certains processus de l'histoire du livre,[8] elle tend par définition à isoler le corpus étudié du reste de sa production

[Sur Galliot du Pré en tant qu'imprimeur de romans arthuriens, voir la contribution de Montorsi dans ce volume, en particulier p. 170–177.]

5 Bernard Weinberg, 'Guillaume Michel dit de Tours. The Editor of the 1526 *Roman de la Rose*'. In: *Bibliothèque d'Humanisme et Renaissance* 11 (1949), p. 72–85; Stephen G. Nichols, 'Marot, Villon et le *Roman de la Rose*. A Study in the Language of Creation and Re-creation'. In: *Studies in Philology* 63 (1966), p. 141–142; Philippe Frieden, 'Le *Roman de la Rose*, de l'édition aux manuscrits'. In: *Perspectives médiévales* [en ligne] 34 (2012) (URL: http://peme.revues.org/ 290; DOI: 10.4000/peme.290, consulté le 20 juillet 2017); Martine Lefèvre, 'La production imprimée: lectures et postérité du *Roman de la rose*'. In: *Le Roman de la rose. L'art d'aimer au Moyen Âge*. Éd. par Nathalie Coilly et Marie-Hélène Tesnière. Paris 2014, p. 157–158.

6 Voir, entre autres, Madeleine Lazard, 'Clément Marot éditeur et lecteur de Villon'. In: *Cahiers de l'Association internationale des études françaises* 32 (1980), p. 7–20; Jacqueline Cerquiglini-Toulet, 'Clément Marot et la critique littéraire et textuelle: du bien renommé au mal imprimé Villon'. In: *Clément Marot "prince des poètes françois", 1496–1996. Actes du Colloque international de Cahors en Quercy, 21–25 mai 1996*. Éd. par Gérard Defaux et Michel Simonin. Paris 1997 (Colloques, congrès et conférences sur la Renaissance 8), p. 157–164; Pierre Chiron, 'L'édition des *Œuvres* de Villon annotée par Clément Marot, ou comment l'autorité vient au texte'. In: *Littératures classiques* 64 (2007), *La note d'autorité. Aperçus histo-riques (XVIᵉ–XVIIIᵉ s.)*, p. 33–51; Claude Thiry, 'Marot, éditeur de Villon'. In: *Villon entre mythe et poésie. Actes du colloque organisé les 15, 16 et 17 décembre 2006 à la Bibliothèque historique de la Ville de Paris*. Éd. par Jean Dufournet et Marcel Faure. Paris 2011 (Colloques, congrès et conférences sur le Moyen Âge 9), p. 281–290.

7 Outre les études déjà citées, Cristian Bratu, 'Denis Sauvage: the Editing of Medieval Chronicles in Sixteenth-century France'. In: *Studies in Medieval and Renaissance History*, 3rd Series, 7 (2010), p. 255–278; Jean Dufournet, 'Denis Sauvage et Commynes. La première édition des *Mémoires*'. In: *Convergences médiévales. Épopée, lyrique, roman. Mélanges offerts à Madeleine Tyssens*. Éd. par Nadine Henrard, Paola Moreno et Martine Thiry-Stassin. Bruxelles 2001 (Bibliothèque du Moyen Âge 19), p. 161–171; Tania Van Hemelryck, 'Du *Perceforest* manu-scrit à l'imprimé de Galliot du Pré (1528). Un long fleuve tranquille?'. In: *Le Roman français dans les premiers imprimés*. Paris 2016 (Rencontres 147 / Civilisation médiévale 17), p. 159–174; Jean Balsamo, 'La collection des anciens poètes français de Galliot du Pré (1528–1533)'. In: *L'analisi linguistica e letteraria* 8 (2000), p. 179–194.

8 Sur cette question, Roger Chartier, 'Préface'. In: *Les usages de l'imprimé, 15ᵉ–19ᵉ siècle*. Éd. par Roger Chartier. Paris 1987, p. 8.

et à décontextualiser, désémantiser et démotiver bon nombre de paramètres textuels, péritextuels et matériels.[9]

C'est pourquoi, dans le cadre d'un projet de recherche financé par l'Université catholique de Louvain, nous avons souhaité étudier la *politique éditoriale* de Galliot du Pré dans une perspective résolument transversale, quantitative et comparative. Une telle ambition nécessite de revenir sur la notion de *politique éditoriale*. Nous proposons de la définir, au départ des pratiques d'édition moderne,[10] comme la stratégie et les choix primordiaux d'un éditeur sur son programme d'édition. De façon schématique, on peut identifier quatre lignes de force de toute politique éditoriale:

1   la recherche d'auteurs ou de textes;
2   la recherche d'un thème ou d'une spécialisation;
3   la recherche de formes éditoriales, visibles dans la mise en œuvre du livre;
4   la prise en considération du contexte historique comme élément favorable à la réception et à la diffusion des livres.

Actuellement, les études sur les politiques éditoriales des libraires et éditeurs du seizième siècle se limitent le plus souvent à étudier les points 1 et 2, c'est-à-dire les *auteurs/textes* et les *thèmes* de prédilection d'un éditeur-libraire. Ainsi,

---

9 Sur cette question, Ezio Ornato, 'L'évaluation quantitative des stratégies éditoriales. Problèmes méthodologiques et techniques'. In: Chiara Ruzzier, Xavier Hermand et Ezio Ornato, *Les stratégies éditoriales à l'époque de l'incunable: le cas des anciens Pays-Bas.* Turnhout 2012, p. 133–203 (p. 135).
10 Philippe Schuwer, 'Politique éditoriale'. In: *Dictionnaire encyclopédique du livre.* Éd. par Pascal Fouché, Daniel Péchoin et Philippe Schuwer et al. T. 3. Paris 2011, p. 303–304; Philippe Schuwer, *Traité pratique d'édition.* Paris 1997. Sur l'emploi de cette notion au XVIe siècle, voir les travaux d'A. Charon-Parent (note 2); Domique Coq, 'Les débuts de l'édition en langue vulgaire en France. Publics et politiques éditoriales'. In: *Gutenberg-Jahrbuch* (1982), p. 59–72; Michel Simonin, 'Peut-on parler de politique éditoriale au XVIe siècle? Le cas de Vincent Sertenas, libraire du Palais'. In: *Le Livre dans l'Europe de la Renaissance. Actes du XXIIIe colloque international d'Études humanistes de Tours.* Éd. par Pierre Aquilon et Henri-Jean Martin. Paris 1988, p. 264–281; Gérard Morisse, 'Pour une approche de l'activité de Sébastien Gryphe, libraire-imprimeur lyonnais du XVIe siècle'. In: *Revue française d'histoire du livre* 126–127 (2005–2006), p. 13–68; Brigitte Ouvry-Vial et Anne Réach-Ngô (éd.), *L'acte éditorial. Publier à la Renaissance et aujourd'hui.* Paris 2010 (Études et essais sur la Renaissance 89); Jean-Paul Pittion, *Le livre à la Renaissance. Introduction à la bibliographie historique et matérielle.* Turnhout 2013 (Nugae humanisticae sub signo Erasmi 15), p. 295–297; Anne Réach-Ngô, 'L'écriture éditoriale à la Renaissance. Pour une herméneutique de l'imprimé'. In: *Communication et Langages* 154 (2007), p. 41–57; Chiara Ruzzier, Xavier Hermand et Ezio Ornato, *Les stratégies éditoriales à l'époque de l'incunable: le cas des anciens Pays-Bas.* Turnhout 2012 (Bibliologia. Elementa ad librorum studia pertinentia 33).

l'étude de la politique éditoriale française de Galliot du Pré est majoritairement limitée au décompte des livres qu'il a publiés et s'y trouve souvent résumée – pour ce qui est de la littérature – à sa prédilection pour les romans de chevalerie, les livres d'histoire et les traductions d'autorités latines.

Comment, concrètement, approcher ces quatre lignes de force de la politique éditoriale d'un libraire-éditeur ancien? Il nous semble que l'on peut distinguer, d'une part, les approches qui partent du *livre* et, d'autre part, celles qui partent du *contexte* qui entoure la production et la circulation du livre.

Pour ce qui est de la *première approche*, centrée sur le *livre*, elle est généralement réduite à la question ‚Que publie-t-il?' et au recensement quantitatif des livres conservés et mentionnés dans les bases de données et catalogues modernes du type *Universal Short Title Catalogue*[11] ou *La Base des éditions parisiennes du 16e siècle.*[12] Un tel recensement, aujourd'hui réalisable plus aisément qu'avant – mais pas pour autant sans biais et sans risques[13] – peut conduire à une cartographie utile du nombre de textes publiés, de leur type et de la fréquence de leur réédition. Cette approche immédiate de la politique éditoriale est la plus fréquente aujourd'hui.

Toujours dans cette approche réalisée au départ des livres conservés, il nous semble autant, sinon plus, essentiel de répondre à la question ‚Comment publie t-il?' et d'étudier la mise en forme textuelle et péritextuelle de cette politique éditoriale, c'est-à-dire la forme dans laquelle un libraire permet, voire conditionne, à un lecteur de s'approprier un texte.[14] D'une part, la version du texte qu'il offre au lecteur et qui a pu être revue, corrigée, actualisée et/ou modernisée... D'autre part, le péritexte qui l'accompagne et qui est le plus souvent une intervention de l'éditeur: titre, prologues allographes, tables, manchettes. Une telle approche d'une œuvre au sein d'un dispositif textuel et matériel neuf est couramment mise en œuvre à l'occasion de l'étude d'une œuvre ou d'un genre,[15] mais, pour

---

11 www.ustc.ac.uk/, consulté le 20 juillet 2017.

12 http://bp16.bnf.fr [reprend les notices de l'*Inventaire chronologique des éditions parisiennes du 16e siècle*, 1972–2004], consulté le 20 juillet 2017.

13 Voir Ruzzier, Hermand et Ornato (voir note 10).

14 Sur cette question, voir Donald F. McKenzie, *Bibliography and the Sociology of Texts.* Cambridge 1999; Roger Chartier, *La main de l'auteur et l'esprit de l'imprimeur: XVIe–XVIIIe siècle.* Paris 2015, p. 14–15.

15 Voir, par exemple, Trung Tran, 'Le texte illustré au XVIe siècle, stratégie éditoriale ou création littéraire?'. In: *L'acte éditorial. Publier à la Renaissance et aujourd'hui.* Éd. par Brigitte Ouvry-Vial et Anne Réach-Ngô. Paris 2010 (Études et essais sur la Renaissance 89), p. 59–88; Anne Réach-Ngô, 'La mise en recueil des narrations à la Renaissance ou l'art de la bibliothèque portative'. In: *L'acte éditorial*, p. 125–148; Anne Réach-Ngô, 'Performance et

l'ensemble de la production médiévale d'un libraire de textes français, elle n'a été que trop peu mise en œuvre; l'on rappellera le travail inaugurant de Mary Beth Winn pour ce qui est d'Antoine Vérard.[16]

Quant à la *seconde approche*, celle tournée vers le contexte de production et de circulation du livre, elle est beaucoup plus aléatoire pour les éditeurs de textes français des quinzième et seizième siècles, pour lesquels on n'a pas nécessairement conservé, par exemple, une correspondance abondante, un catalogue de vente, des actes de comptabilité.[17] Dans le cas de Galliot, l'on dispose de l'inventaire après décès des livres conservés à son domicile et dans sa boutique au Palais,[18] établi par les libraires Jean Macé et Gilles Corrozet. Malgré la rareté de ce type de documents pour les libraires de textes français,[19] jusqu'ici, cet inventaire n'a fait l'objet d'aucune édition et *a fortiori* d'aucune exploitation systématique. Seule A. Charon-Parent a utilisé cet inventaire, mais de façon partielle.[20]

Cet inventaire offre un aperçu non plus seulement des livres *publiés* par Galliot du Pré, mais des livres qu'en 1561, il avait en stock à son domicile et qu'il proposait à la vente dans sa boutique du Palais – et dans la publication

---

paratextes éditoriaux à la Renaissance'. In: *Textes en performance*. Éd. par Ambroise Barras et Éric Eigenmann. Genève 2006, p. 183–197; Anne Réach-Ngô, *L'Écriture éditoriale à la Renaissance. Genèses et promotion du récit sentimental français (1530–1560)*. Genève 2013.

16 Mary B. Winn, *Anthoine Vérard, Parisian Publisher (1485–1512). Prologues, Poems and Presentations*. Genève 1997 (Travaux d'Humanisme et renaissance 313); *Le Moyen Français* 69 (2011), *Antoine Vérard*. Éd. par Paola Cifarelli, Maria Colombo Timelli et Anne Schoysman. Voir également Sergio Cappello, 'Les éditions de romans de Jean II Trepperel'. In: *Raconter en prose. XIVe–XVIe siècle*. Éd. par Paola Cifarelli, Maria Colombo Timelli, Matteo Milani et Anne Schoysman. Paris 2017, p. 121–145.

17 Sur ces questions, voir, par exemple, Claire Lesage, Ève Netchine et Véronique Sarrazin, *Catalogues de libraires 1473–1810*. Paris 2006; Annie Charon, Claire Lesage et Ève Netchine, *Le livre entre le commerce et l'histoire des idées. Les catalogues de libraires (XVe – XIXe siècle)*. Paris 2001.

18 Paris, Archives nationales, Minutier central des notaires de Paris, LXXIII, 43, 12 IV 1561. Le Palais était le siège du Parlement, de la cour des comptes, de la cour des monnaies, mais aussi un lieu public où étaient installées des boutiques, dont celles des libraires dans la Grand'Salle, cf. *Infra*.

19 Graham Runnalls, 'La vie, la mort et les livres de l'imprimeur-libraire parisien Jean Janot d'après son inventaire après décès (17 février 1522 n. st.)'. In: *Revue belge de philologie et d'histoire* 78 (2000), p. 797–851.

20 Et vraisemblablement sans revenir à l'inventaire original, comme l'attesterait le fait que les renvois se font par page alors que le document original est, en réalité, folioté. Du reste, la plupart du temps, les données fournies (titre, nombre d'exemplaire, montant prisé) le sont sans que le texte original de l'inventaire ne soit explicitement cité.

desquels Galliot du Pré n'était pas intervenu (*a fortiori* pour des titres publiés avant le début de ses activités). Pour cette dernière catégorie (les livres offerts à la clientèle), l'on peut légitimement supposer que ceux-ci ont fait l'objet d'un choix délibéré du libraire parmi les titres disponibles alors à Paris. Pour les livres présents à son domicile, comme dans toute bibliothèque, ancienne ou moderne, leur présence ne suit pas nécessairement un choix de Galliot, en particulier pour ce qui est des livres qu'il a hérités de son père Jean du Pré ou des livres qu'il a pu acquérir lors de ventes ‚groupées' du fonds de libraires récemment décédés.[21]

Dans cette même perspective du contexte de la vie après la publication du livre, il est nécessaire d'étudier la circulation et la consommation effective des livres publiés et/ou vendus par Galliot sur la base des mentions de ses livres dans les inventaires du seizième siècle et des marques de possession et de lecture dans les exemplaires conservés. Une telle approche, qui constitue un projet de recherche à part entière, offrirait un éclairage tout à fait novateur sur le profil de ses clients et sur leurs usages de ses livres et, *in fine*, sur la transition entre la fin du Moyen Âge et le début des Temps modernes.

C'est donc selon cette double perspective, *dans* le livre et *autour* du livre, que nous avons étudié la politique éditoriale de Galliot du Pré et ce au départ du corpus des textes français écrits par des auteurs morts avant que Galliot ne commence à publier, soit en 1512. Un tel focus nous permettait de sélectionner la majorité du corpus médiéval, à l'exception de quelques figures à cheval et, du reste, réputées difficiles à classer telles que Jean Lemaire de Belges ou Guillaume Cretin, et d'ainsi répondre à l'une de nos questions de recherche: déterminer si Galliot et ses contemporains eurent le sentiment d'une rupture entre la production ‚moderne' et la production ‚ancienne' et d'ainsi valider le sentiment des chercheurs que Galliot aurait été particulièrement intéressé par la littérature médiévale. Surtout, le choix de travailler sur les publications d'auteurs morts nous permettait de travailler sur un corpus ‚neutralisé' en termes d'intentionnalité du texte et du péritexte puisque l'éditeur est désormais seul aux commandes et l'auteur n'intervient *de facto* plus dans la mise en forme du texte.

Parmi les textes d'auteurs morts avant 1512, nous nous sommes concentrés sur les textes ‚littéraires' – en excluant les textes professionnels et à vocation

---

21 L'on rappellera que par exemple à la mort d'Antoine Augereau en 1534, Galliot du Pré acquiert le fonds de sa librairie (Jeanne Veyrin-Forrer, 'Antoine Augereau, graveur de lettres, imprimeur et libraire parisien (1534)'. In: *La lettre et le texte. Trente années de recherches sur l'histoire du livre*. Éd. par Jeanne Veyrin-Forrer. Paris 1987, p. 3–50, appendice 3, p. 39–41).

pratique (par ex. les très nombreux textes juridiques ou administratifs) ou les pièces occasionnelles et de circonstances relevant de l'actualité. Nous désirions, en effet, comprendre les voies par lesquelles Galliot, libraire juré de l'université, actif au centre névralgique de l'activité juridique de Paris et de ce fait avant tout spécialisé et réputé pour la production de textes administratifs et juridiques de l'extrême contemporain, a été amené à publier, par ailleurs, des textes qui relèvent, selon nos critères modernes, de la littérature. Dans cette optique, nous voudrions d'emblée suggérer l'hypothèse que le choix des textes littéraires médiévaux à publier et la façon dont ils furent présentés au public témoignent d'un ciblage de Galliot, non sur le public universitaire et élitiste de la rive gauche, mais sur le public ‚local' des serviteurs de l'État et des hommes de justice qui fréquentaient son échoppe, au départ pour se fournir en textes de lois.

2 Première approche: les livres publiés par Galliot

À partir des catalogues et bases de données actuellement disponibles,[22] nous avons recensé tous les livres publiés par Galliot du Pré de textes français littéraires écrits par des auteurs morts avant 1512. Cela représente 60 éditions[23]; pour donner un ordre de grandeur/de comparaison: Galliot a publié 330 éditions, dont 180 en français.[24]

2.1 Aperçu quantitatif

Que peut-on retirer d'une approche quantitative globale de ces publications? Le graphique ci-dessous représente la proportion d'éditions de textes antérieurs à 1512 par rapport au total des 180 éditions de textes littéraires français publiées par Galliot (Figure 1).

---

22 USTC; *BP16 – Bibliographie des éditions parisiennes du 16ᵉ siècle*; Andrew Pettegree et al. (éd.), *French Vernacular Books. Books Published in the French Language before 1601.* Leiden 2007.
23 N'ont pas été retenus les doublons de ces bases et les éditions sans exemplaire survivant, p. ex. USTC 94516 (Arnoul Gréban), USTC 51628 (Guillaume Alexis), USTC 72840 (*La genealogie des tres chrestiens roys de France*).
24 Sur ces évaluations, Charon-Parent (note 2); Balsamo, 'La collection' (note 7).

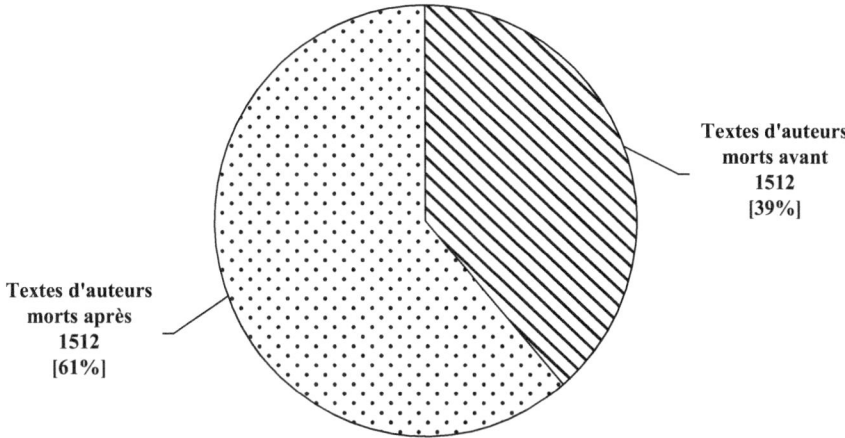

Fig. 1: – Éditions de textes littéraires français publiées par Galliot du Pré.

La part d'éditions de textes ‚anciens' n'est pas négligeable pour un libraire actif jusqu'en 1561. Néanmoins, pour déterminer si ces données témoignent d'un intérêt personnel et particulier pour cette littérature, il faudrait pouvoir confronter cette proportion avec celle d'autres libraires parisiens de l'époque.

Dans les 60 éditions de textes littéraires français ‚médiévaux' publiés par Galliot, nous avons distingué trois catégories: les *éditions princeps*, les auto-rééditions et les rééditions (Figure 2).

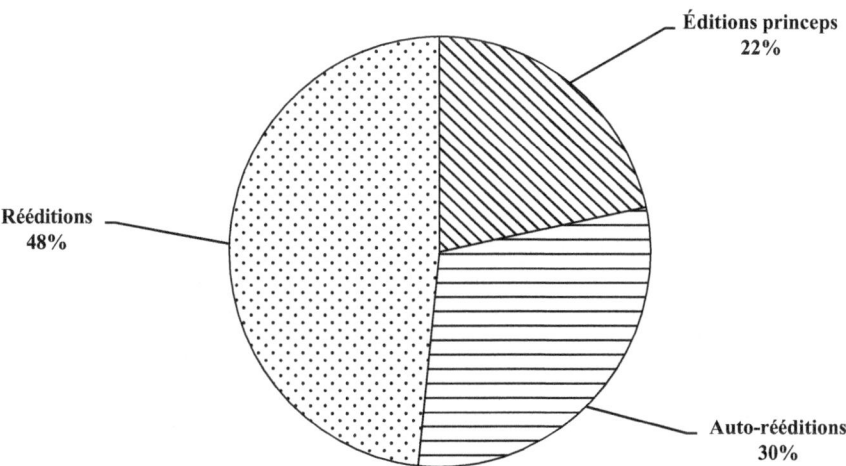

Fig. 2: – Éditions de textes littéraires français d'auteurs morts avant 1512 publiées par Galliot du Pré.

Parmi les 60 éditions, seules 13 (22 %) sont des éditions *princeps*, c'est-à-dire que Galliot du Pré est le premier à imprimer l'œuvre, prenant davantage le risque de ne pas rencontrer un public. C'est le cas pour le *Temple de Boccace* de George Chastelain (1517), la traduction des *Chroniques de Hainaut* de Jacques de Guise par Jean Wauquelin (1531), le roman de *Perceforest* (1531) ou le roman en prose d'*Ysaïe le Triste* (1522).

Dans les 47 éditions qui restent, 18 (30 %) sont des cas d'*auto-rééditions*, c'est-à-dire des cas où Galliot republie un texte qu'il a déjà publié auparavant: une telle réédition limitait les risques et les frais inhérents à la fabrication du livre; c'est le cas, par exemple, pour les *Mémoires* de Philippe de Commynes, qu'il édite 5 fois entre 1524 et 1561 (1524, 1525, 1546, 1552, 1561) ou les *Annales de France* de Nicole Gilles, qu'il publie 7 fois entre 1525 et 1553 (1525, 1527, 1538, 1547, 1549, 1552, 1553). Ces cas témoignent indéniablement de ‚succès de librairie‘, du moins à l'aune de nos critères modernes de ‚best-seller‘.

Enfin, 29 (48 %) sont des cas de *rééditions* de textes que d'autres libraires ont publiés auparavant, par exemple les œuvres poétiques d'Alain Chartier (1526) ou le *Roman de la Rose* de Jean de Meun et Guillaume de Lorris (1526).[25]

Ce troisième graphique présente, dans la diachronie de la carrière de Galliot, les éditions de textes d'auteurs mort avant 1512, en distinguant toujours éditions princeps, auto-rééditions et rééditions (Figure 3).

Le graphique rend compte du fait que le sommet de sa publication de textes en français d'auteurs du quinzième siècle se situe entre 1525 et 1532, témoignant avant tout, sinon plus, de l'investissement de Galliot dans ce corpus spécialisé médiéval, plus que du succès de ces éditions. L'on peut également observer qu'après 1531, Galliot du Pré ne publie plus d'édition *princeps* d'une œuvre du quinzième siècle, hormis la *Chronique* de Jean de Roye en 1558.[26] À partir de 1531,

---

25 Il s'agit souvent de textes dont l'édition (directement) antérieure a été publiée par Antoine Vérard. C'est le cas du *Compendium hystoriale* d'Henri Romain (1528 [Paris: Vérard, 1509 (USTC 57453)]), des *Epistres d'Ovide* traduites par Octovien de Saint-Gelais (1528 [Vérard, 1500, 1502, 1505 (USTC 38477, 55657, 64880)]), de la traduction française de Flavius Josephus (1530 [Paris: Vérard, 1492 (USTC 71201)]), de l'*Alexandre* de Quinte-Curce par Vasque de Lucène (1530 [Paris: Vérard, 1500 (USTC 71309)]), du *Miroir historial* par Jean de Vignay (1531 [Vérard, 1495–1496 (USTC 37416)]).

26 Sans d'ailleurs que le péritexte de cette édition signale l'ancienneté du texte: „La cronique du treschrestien et victorieux roy Loys unziesme du nom (que Dieu absolve) avec plusieurs histoires advenues tant es pays de France, Angleterre, que Flandres et Artois, puis l'an mil quatre cens soixante et un, jusq'en l'an mil quatre cens quatre vingtz et trois" (exemplaire Lyon, BM, 319199, page de titre) [...] „faire imprimer et vendre la presente histoire, intitulée l'abregé des faictz dignes de memoire du roy Loys unziesme du nom" (privilège, fol. a¹ r°).

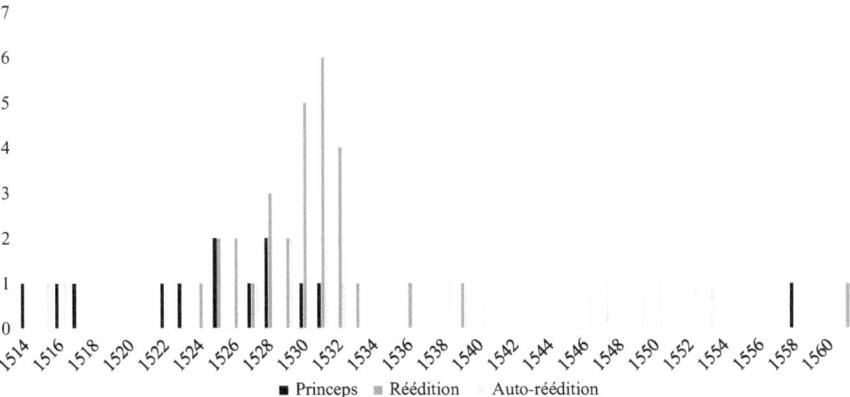

Fig. 3: – Éditions de textes littéraires français d'auteurs morts avant 1512 publiées par Galliot du Pré.

il se limitera à rééditer les textes dont il a lui-même publié l'édition *princeps*; qui plus est, il s'agit des textes d'auteurs morts récemment (c'est-à-dire au seizième siècle): les historiens Philippe de Commynes (1511) et Nicole Gilles (1503).

Ce ralentissement brutal, en 1530, de la publication d'œuvres ‚médiévales‘ n'est peut-être pas anodin. L'on pourrait croire que cette baisse correspond à un désintérêt de Galliot pour la littérature du Moyen Âge et à une volonté de publier des œuvres ‚modernes‘.[27] Cependant, si l'on considère la production totale d'éditions de textes littéraires français publiés par Galliot, l'on observe que les courbes des éditions de textes du fonds ancien (i.e. d'auteurs de textes français morts avant 1512) et de textes du fonds moderne (i.e. d'auteurs de textes français morts à partir de 1512) se superposent et qu'il n'y a pas, sur ce point en tout cas, de distinction entre fonds ‚moderne‘ et fonds ‚ancien‘ (Figure 4).

L'on peut y observer ce même effort de publication de textes en français dans les années 1525–1532. Ce pic est-il purement conjoncturel? Serait-il lié à un afflux de capital chez Galliot ou à la baisse de régime des autres imprimeurs sur la place parisienne? Est-il légitime de penser qu'en 1530 Galliot ait voulu participer à la promotion du nouveau modèle culturel et linguistique que défendait le

---

[27] Galliot confirmerait là une tendance générale dans les *politiques éditoriales*, qui sont souvent cycliques et constituent une „succession d'initiatives réussies ou avortées, d'avancées et de régressions" plus qu'une politique continue et parfaitement cohérente (Schuwer, 'Politique éditoriale' (note 10)). [Sur la baisse d'éditions de romans arthuriens au cours des années 1530, voir l'article de Montorsi dans ce volume, p. 170–177.]

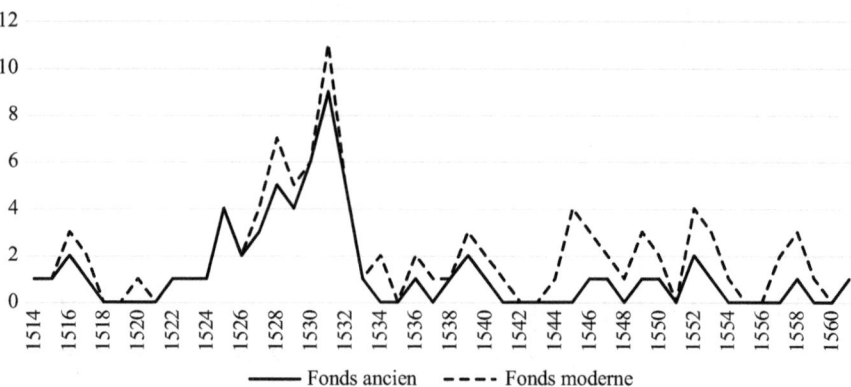

Fig. 4: – Éditions de textes littéraires français publiées par Galliot du Pré.

roi de France François Ier, avec la fondation du Collège des lecteurs royaux par Guillaume Budé (1530), l'Édit de Villers-Cotterêts (1539) – qui officialisait l'emploi du français pour toutes les activités administratives et juridiques – et divers projets de traduction de textes de l'Antiquité ou de textes humanistes italiens ou castillans?[28] Galliot est, en effet, bien partie prenante de ce mouvement puisque c'est lui qui obtient le privilège pour la publication de l'Édit de Villers-Cotterêts.[29]

Un simple recensement des éditions conservées permet également de dégager la typologie des textes qu'il a publiés.

Ce graphique (Figure 5) distribue l'ensemble des textes publiés par Galliot en fonction de la date de rédaction du texte (sur la base des moitiés de siècle)[30] et du type de texte, en distinguant de façon sommaire *roman, lyrisme, théâtre,*

---

28 Sur ce mouvement, voir, entre autres, Paul Chavy, 'Les traductions humanistes au début de la Renaissance française: traductions médiévales, traductions modernes'. In: *Canadian Review of Comparative Literature* 1981, p. 284–306; Luce Guillerm, *Sujet de l'écriture et traduction autour de 1540.* U. de Lille III 1988, thèse de doctorat inédite; Véronique Duché-Gavet, 'Le statut du traducteur (1526–1554)'. In: *Travaux de littérature* 20 (2007), *Le statut littéraire de l'écrivain.* Éd. par Lise Sabourin, p. 202–214; Roberto Crescenzo, 'Louis Le Roy et le statut de traducteur des Anciens au XVIe siècle'. In: *Travaux de literature* 20 (2007), p. 215–227; Jean Balsamo, 'La première génération des traducteurs de l'italien en français (1500–1535)'. In: *Passeurs de textes II. Gens du livre et gens de lettres à la Renaissance.* Éd. par Chiara Lastraioli et al. Tours 2014, p. 15–31.
29 *Ordonnances royaulx sur le faict de la justice et abbreviation des proces...* [avec privilège], Paris, vend Galliot du Pré, 1539; exemplaire consulté Paris, BnF, Vélins 979 USTC 45283.
30 1re moitié du XIIIe siècle (13_1); 2e moitié du XIIIe siècle (13_2); 1re moitié du XIVe siècle (14_1); 2e moitié du XIVe siècle (14_2); 1re moitié du XVe siècle (15_1); 2e moitié du XVe siècle (15_2).

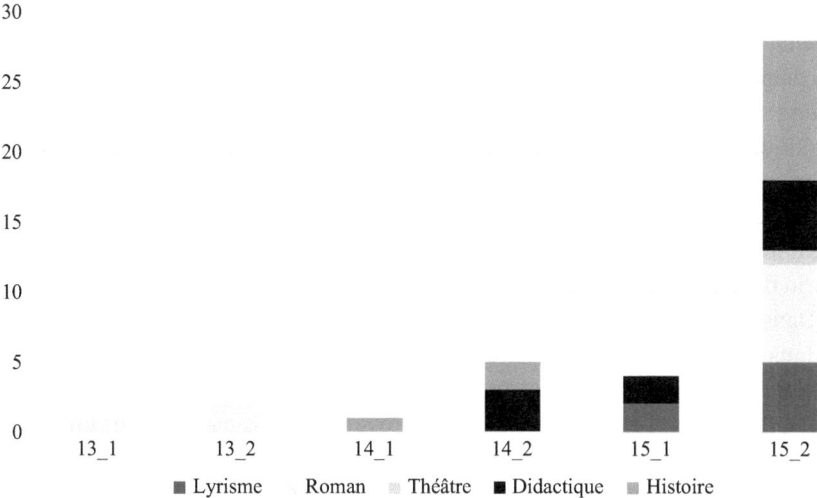

Fig. 5: – Éditions de textes littéraires français d'auteurs morts avant 1512 publiées par Galliot du Pré.

texte didactique, histoire.[31] L'on constate, d'une part, un intérêt particulier pour l'histoire et, d'autre part, assez logiquement, que Galliot publie surtout des textes récents, de la seconde moitié du quinzième siècle. Néanmoins, il ne faut pas perdre de vue que ce graphique ne reprend que les titres *publiés* par Galliot; Galliot vendait d'autres titres dans sa boutique (cf. *infra*). Par ailleurs, il est à noter que l'intérêt d'une telle approche typologique reste limité tant que l'on ne peut pas la comparer avec celle d'autres imprimeurs, par exemple celle de son contemporain Vincent Sertenas.[32]

Enfin, il reste à souligner que certaines éditions publiées par Galliot du Pré semblent répondre à des circonstances historiques précises, qui témoignent d'une stratégie éditoriale guidée par des critères extra-littéraires et extra-philologiques, tout en illustrant également les processus de renouvellement de la littérature médiévale.

---

31 Pour des typologies plus fines de textes contemporains, voir Hanno Wijsman, *Luxury Bound. Illustrated Manuscripts Production and Noble and Princely Book Ownership in the Burgundian Netherlands (1400–1550)*. Turnhout 2010 (Burgundica 16); Chiara Ruzzier, Xavier Hermand et Ezio Ornato (note 10); Céline Van Hoorebeeck, *Livres et lectures des fonctionnaires des ducs de Bourgogne (ca 1420–1520)*, Turnhout 2014 (Texte, Codex et Contexte 16).
32 Voir Simonin (voir note 10).

Ainsi, la publication en 1531 des encore très ‚médiévales' *Chroniques de Hainaut*, dans la traduction française que Jean Wauquelin réalisa au milieu du quinzième siècle pour le duc de Bourgogne Philippe le Bon,[33] peut nous paraître incongrue au vu de l'horizon d'attente, à la fois historique et esthétique, de la génération de François Ier; cependant, cette édition pourrait être mise en rapport avec la signature de la Paix de Cambrai le 3 août 1529, qui mit fin à la crise entre François Ier et Charles Quint, conflit dû à la non-restitution du duché de Bourgogne par François Ier prévue par le Traité de Madrid de janvier 1526.

Dans un tel contexte, la publication en 1531 des *Chroniques de Hainaut* s'ancre dans une logique opportuniste de service au roi, plus que dans une logique philologique ou littéraire, tout en permettant à la clientèle parlementaire de Galliot, *a priori* au courant de la politique royale, de se renseigner sur l'histoire de ce territoire à l'origine de la discorde; l'édition est donc une réponse opportuniste de publication pour écouler un texte médiéval qui ne sera pas republié par la suite.

Un autre cas éclaire également cette stratégie de choix en fonction de critères extra-littéraires et extra-philologiques; il illustre également les processus de renouvellement de la littérature médiévale. En septembre 1520, Galliot publie l'édition *princeps* de la nouvelle traduction, par Guillaume Michel de Tours, des *Vies de douze Cesars* de Suétone (qualifiée de „nouvellement translatez" sur la page de titre).[34] Pourtant, Galliot disposait d'exemplaires (publiés par Vérard en 1490 et 1500)[35] de l'adaptation médiévale de Suétone que sont les *Fais des Romains,* qui constituait un ouvrage à succès depuis sa compilation au treizième siècle.[36] Galliot pouvait donc à peu de frais la vendre ou la faire réimprimer. Cependant, une traduction centrée sur Suétone tombait plus à

---

33 Sur la tradition imprimée de ce texte, voir Pierre Cockshaw et Christiane Van den Bergen-Pantens, *Les Chroniques de Hainaut ou les Ambitions d'un Prince Bourguignon.* Bruxelles 2000; Tania Van Hemelryck, 'La ou les traductions françaises des *Annales historie illustrium principum Hanonie* de Jacques de Guise? L'éclairage de la tradition manuscrite'. In: *Le Moyen Français* 51–52–53 (2003), *Traduction, dérimation, compilation. La phraséologie.* Éd. par Giuseppe Di Stefano et Rose M. Bidler, p. 613–625.

34 *Des faictz et gestes des douze Cesars* [avec privilège]. Paris: Pierre Vidoué pour Galliot du Pré, 1520 (USTC 26460), exemplaire consulté Vienne, ÖNB, 54 E 17.

35 „1 Lucain, Suetonne et Saluste fol. Virard" [Vérard, 1490, 1500 (USTC 71258, 54066)] (fol. 16r); „1 Lucain Suetoine et Saluste fol. grand Virard" [Vérard, 1500, 2° (USTC 54066 ?)] (fol. 45r).

36 Sur ce texte, voir, entre autres, Gabrielle Spiegel, *Romancing the Past. The Rise of Vernacular Prose Historiography in Thirteenth-Century France.* Berkeley 1993; Catherine Croizy-Naquet, *Écrire l'histoire romaine au début du XIIIe siècle. L'Histoire ancienne et les Faits des Romains.* Paris 1999.

propos dans le contexte historique de 1520. En effet, en juin de cette année, François Ier commanda, en guise de cadeaux diplomatiques pour la rencontre du Camp du Drap d'or (destinée à parachever la négociation des alliances entre la France et l'Angleterre), trois manuscrits à Jean Bourdichon, contenant une version anonyme librement inspirée de la vie des douze Césars. En septembre de la même année, Galliot reçoit le privilège du roi de France pour publier la traduction de Suétone par Guillaume Michel, s'ancrant dans une logique opportuniste de service au roi,[37] plus que dans une logique philologique ou littéraire.

Son travail de publication et de vente des œuvres poétiques de François Villon est également illustratif de sa politique éditoriale, soucieuse d'utiliser toutes les opportunités et en adéquation avec l'actualité, cette fois ‚littéraire', de son temps. Ainsi, en 1532, il publie la première édition de Villon en lettres romaines – les précédentes éditions étaient en lettres gothiques[38] – à laquelle il adjoint entre autres les *Repues franches*, ensemble de récits apocryphes qui exploitent la légende du poète parisien disparu en janvier 1463.[39] Il est intéressant de noter que jusque-là les *Repues franches* furent imprimées de manière isolée, notamment par Jean Trepperel, jusqu'à ce que Galliot décide de les associer judicieusement avec les œuvres de François Villon en 1532. Pourtant, dès l'année suivante, en 1533, il publie l'édition de Villon par le poète et humaniste Clément Marot, qui vise justement à éclipser les éditions précédentes, dont celle de Galliot du Pré lui-même.[40] La concurrence de

---

37 Le contexte historique de 1520 semble avoir imprégné le péritexte. Le prologue qui ouvre l'imprimé („Proesme capital") et qui s'adresse à Charles IV de Bourbon – le *je* n'y est pas nécessairement le traducteur, mais pourrait être Galliot – inscrit nettement la traduction dans la perspective d'une édification politique et morale des princes français grâce aux auteurs de l'Antiquité. Charles y est présenté comme „l'un des plus constans et fermes pilliers de la coronne de France, soubstenant la statue de toute bonne conduicte, bon conseil et protection du peuple gallicane" (fol. a^2 v°).

38 Sur la tradition textuelle de François Villon, François Villon, *Testament / Lais / Poésies diverses*. Éd. par Jean Rychner et Albert Henry, Genève 1974–1977 (Textes littéraires français 207, 208, 239, 240); Jean Rychner, 'Observations sur les textes incunables du *Testament* de Villon. I. L'édition de Jean Dupré, Lyon, vers 1490'. In: *Études de langue et de littérature du Moyen Âge offertes à Félix Lecoy* par ses collègues, ses élèves et ses amis. Paris 1973, p. 529–539; Jean Rychner, 'Observations sur les textes incunables du *Testament* de Villon. II. L'édition de Germain Bineaut, Paris, 1490'. In: *Mélanges de linguistique et de philologie et littérature médiévales offerts à Monsieur Paul Imbs*. Éd. par Robert Martin et Georges Straka. Strasbourg 1973 (Travaux de linguistique et de littérature 11/1), p. 615–620. Voir également les références de la note 6.

39 Sur ce texte, *Le recueil des repues franches de maistre François Villon et de ses compagnons*. Éd. par Jelle Koopmans et Paul Verhuyck. Genève 1995 (Textes littéraires français 455).

40 L'impression a été confiée à Louis Blaubloom dit Cyaneus (voir Balsamo, 'La collection' (note 7)).

l'édition Marot est directement visible dans l'inventaire de Galliot puisqu'en 1561, il lui reste ‚en stock' plus de 180 exemplaires de l'édition de 1532[41]; de l'édition Marot, il n'en reste que 37, dont la mention suit directement dans l'inventaire du domicile.[42] Galliot a saisi l'opportunité de publier le travail philologique de Clément Marot – ce que soulignent d'ailleurs le titre „Les œuvres de Françoys Villon de Paris, reveues et remises en leur entier" ainsi que le privilège et le prologue[43] –, poète qui incarnait par excellence le renouveau de la littérature française[44] et portait le titre de „valet de chambre du roi", qualité mise en évidence par la page de titre et qui, comme Marot le fera pour son *Adolescence clémentine*, entend faire lire le ‚vrai Villon'.

2.2 La mise en forme péritextuelle

Toujours dans une perspective orientée vers le *livre*, nous voudrions considérer à présent la question de la mise en forme péritextuelle des œuvres publiées par Galliot, en considérant les phénomènes récurrents et particulièrement significatifs relevés principalement dans deux lieux emblématiques du péritexte: la page de titre et le prologue allographe.[45]

---

41 „180 François Villon, lettre romaine, des premiers [?] 8° petit papier" (fol. 41v); néanmoins, un „Villon vieil" sera vendu dans la boutique parmi les „Livres in 8° doré sur la tranche".

42 „7 François Villon corrigez par Marot" (fol. 41v).

43 „Si en Villon on treuve encor à dire, / S'il n'est reduict ainsi qu'ay pretendu, / moy tout seul en soyt le blasme, sire, / qui plus y ay travaillé qu'entendu." (quatrain d'ouverture, exemplaire Paris, BnF, Rés. Y^e 1297, fol. A^2 r°); „reveues, corrigees et restituees à leur vraye intelligence" (privilège); „Entre tous les bons livres imprimez de la langue françoise, ne s'en veoit ung si incorrect ne si lourdement corrompu que celluy de Villon et m'esbahy [...] comment les imprimeurs de Paris, et les enfans de la ville, n'en ont eu plus grant soing [...] tant y ay trouvé de broillerie en l'ordre des coupletz et des vers, en mesure, en langaige, en la ryme, en la raison, que je ne sçay duquel je doy plus avoir pitié, ou de l'œuvre ainsi oultrement gastee, ou de l'ignorance de ceulx qui l'imprimerent. Et, pour vous en faire preuve, me suys advisé, lecteurs, de vous mettre icy ung des coupletz incorrectz du mal imprimé Villon, qui vous sera exemple et tesmoing d'ung grant nombre d'autres autant broillez et gastez que luy [...] Qui est celluy qui vouldroit nyer le sens n'en estre grandement corrompu? Ainsi, pour vray, l'ay je trouvé aux vieilles impressions, et encorez pis aux nouvelles." (prologue de Marot, fol. a^3 r°–v°).

44 Voir, entre autre, Gérard Defaux, *Le Poète en son jardin. Étude sur Clément Marot et 'L'Adolescence clémentine'*. Paris 1996; Frank Lestringant, *Clément Marot, de 'L'Adolescence clémentine' à 'L'Enfer'*. Padova 1998.

45 Sur ce terme, voir Gérard Genette, *Seuils*. Paris 1987 (Poétique), p. 265–266.

2.2.1 La page de titre

La page de titre constitue un lieu essentiel dans la stratégie éditoriale d'un libraire[46]; la mise en valeur du titre est certes liée à l'usage de tailles de fontes et de styles de caractères particuliers et distinctifs, voire d'encre rouge, mais elle est également liée aux mots utilisés, soit de tout ce qui constitue la *grammaire du titre* au sein de ce qu'Anne Réach-Ngô nomme l',écriture éditoriale'.[47]

Prenons le cas de l'édition en 1525 du recueil intitulé de façon programmatique *Traictez singuliers*, où Galliot publie des pièces de deux auteurs médiévaux bourguignons de la fin du quinzième siècle, George Chastelain et Jean Molinet, encadrées par celles de deux auteurs contemporains toujours vivants, Jean Lemaire de Belges et Guillaume Cretin (Figure 6):

> *Traictez singuliers* contenus ou present opuscule.
> *Les trois comptes* intitulez de *Cupido* et de *Atropos* dont le premier fut inventé par *Seraphin poete italien*.
> Le *second et tiers* de l'invention de maistre *Jehan Le maire* et a esté ceste oeuvre fondee affin de retirer les gens de folles amours.
> *Les epitaphes* de *Hector et Achilles* avec le jugement de *Alexandre le Grand* composees par *George Chastelain* dit *l'aventurier*.
> Le temple de *Mars* faict et composé par *J. Molinet*.
> Plusieurs *chantz royaulx / Balades / Rondeaulx et Epistres* composees par feu de bonne memoire maistre *Guillaume cretin* nagueres chantre de la saincte chapelle du *palais*.

---

46 Voir, entre autres, Jean Vial, 'Formules publicitaires dans les premiers livres français'. In: *1500–1900. Gutenberg-Jahrbuch* 1958, p. 149–154; Jean-François Gilmont et Alexandre Vanautgaerden (éd.), *La page de titre à la Renaissance*. Turnhout 2008; Dominique Coq, 'Les incunables: textes anciens, textes nouveaux'. In: *Histoire de l'édition française. Tome 1. Le livre conquérant. Du Moyen Âge au milieu du XVIIe siècle*. Éd. par Martin Henri-Jean, Chartier Roger et Vivet Jean-Pierre. Paris 1983, p. 203–227; Dominique Coq, 'Les politiques éditoriales des premiers imprimeurs parisiens et lyonnais (1470–1485)'. In: *Legenda aurea: sept siècles de diffusion*. Éd. par Brenda Dunn-Lardeau. Montréal 1986; Danièle Sansy, 'Texte et image dans les incunables français'. In: *Médiévales* 22–23 (1992), p. 48–70, en part. p. 52–64; Margaret McFadden Smith, *The Title Page. Its Early Development 1460–1510*. London 2000; Mathilde Thorel, 'Pratiques de l'intitulation au XVIe siècle'. In: Ouvry-Vial et Réach-Ngô (éd.), 'L'Acte éditorial' (note 10), p. 165–183.
47 Anne Réach-Ngô, 'L'écriture éditoriale' (note 10). [Sur la stratégie éditoriale derrière les titres et les pages de titre des *libros de caballerias* espagnols, voir la contribution de Syrovy dans ce volume, p. 351–374.]

⸿ Traictez singu-
liers contenus au present opuscule.

⸿ Les trois comptes intitulez de Cupido et de
Atropos/ dont le premier fut inuente par Sera-
phin poete Italien.

⸿ Le second a tiers de linuention de maistre Je-
han le maire ꝗ a este ceste oeuure fondee affin de
retirer les gens de folles amours.

⸿ Les epitaphes de Hector ꝗ Achilles auec le iu
gement de Alexandre le grand/ composees par
George chastelain dit lauenturier.

⸿ Le teple de mars fait ꝗ copose par J. molinet.

⸿ Plusieurs chantz royaulx/ Balades/ Ron-
deaulx et Epistres composees par feu de bonne
memoire maistre Guillaume cretin nagueres
chantre de la saincte chappelle du Palais.

⸿ Lapparition du feu mareschal de Chabanes
faicte ꝗ composee par ledit Cretin.

⸿ Il se Bend a Paris en la grant salle du
Palais en la boutique de Galliot du pre.

⸿ Auec priuilege.

1525.

Fig. 6: – Page de titre des *Traictez singuliers* (1525) © Munich, BSB.

L'apparition du feu mareschal de *Chabannes* faicte & composee par ledit *Cretin*.

Il se vend a *Paris* en la grant salle du *Palais* en la boutique de *Galliot du pré*.

Avec privilege

(exemplaire Munich, BSB, P.o.gall. 2142)

Compte tenu de la longueur et du caractère très descriptif du titre, l'encre rouge met en évidence des éléments susceptibles d'allécher le client de Galliot, par exemple les figures exemplaires archicélèbres de Cupido, d'Hector, d'Achilles et d'Alexandre le Grand, mais surtout les noms des auteurs. Dans cette perspective, les noms de Lemaire et de Cretin, auteurs de la seconde génération des ‚Grands Rhétoriqueurs' servent vraisemblablement d'appât et d'argument de vente, pour un auteur de la première génération, comme George Chastelain, qui se faisait rare dans les éditions imprimées.[48]

Un même phénomène de mise en évidence de syntagmes, jouant ici sur la référence à des succès de librairie, est observable pour l'édition *princeps* des *Chroniques de Hainaut* par Jean Wauquelin en 1531, où les mentions „illustrations de Gaule" et „grande cité de Belges" sont imprimées en rouge afin, peut-être, de susciter une association avec les *Illustrations* de Jean Lemaire de Belges publiées la même année par Galliot (Figure 7).

$ *Le premier volume des*
Illustrations de la *Gaulle Belgique* / antiquitez du pays de
Haynnau / et de la grand cité de Belges : a present dicte *Ba*
vay / *dont procedent les chaussees de Brunehault. Et*
de plusieurs princes qui ont regné / et fondé plusieurs
villes et citez dudit pays / et aultres choses sin
gulieres / *et dignes de memoire* / advenues
durant leurs regnes / jusques au duc
Philippes de Bourgongne /
dernier decedé .

(exemplaire Paris, BnF, Rés. M 219)

Pour ce qui touche à la syntaxe du titre, une autre manière d'attirer le chaland consiste à utiliser des termes spécifiques susceptibles de mettre en valeur l'auteur et/ou l'œuvre publiés. Par exemple, l'on voit Galliot associer le nom de

---

48 Le privilège de l'édition princeps du *Temple de Boccace* par Galliot du Pré le précise d'ailleurs: „à grande difficulté ledict suppliant a recouvert la coppie dudict livre et que les fraitz d'icelluy sont faictz et a esté ledict livre veu et corrigé" (exemplaire Vienne, ÖNB, 18 C 10).

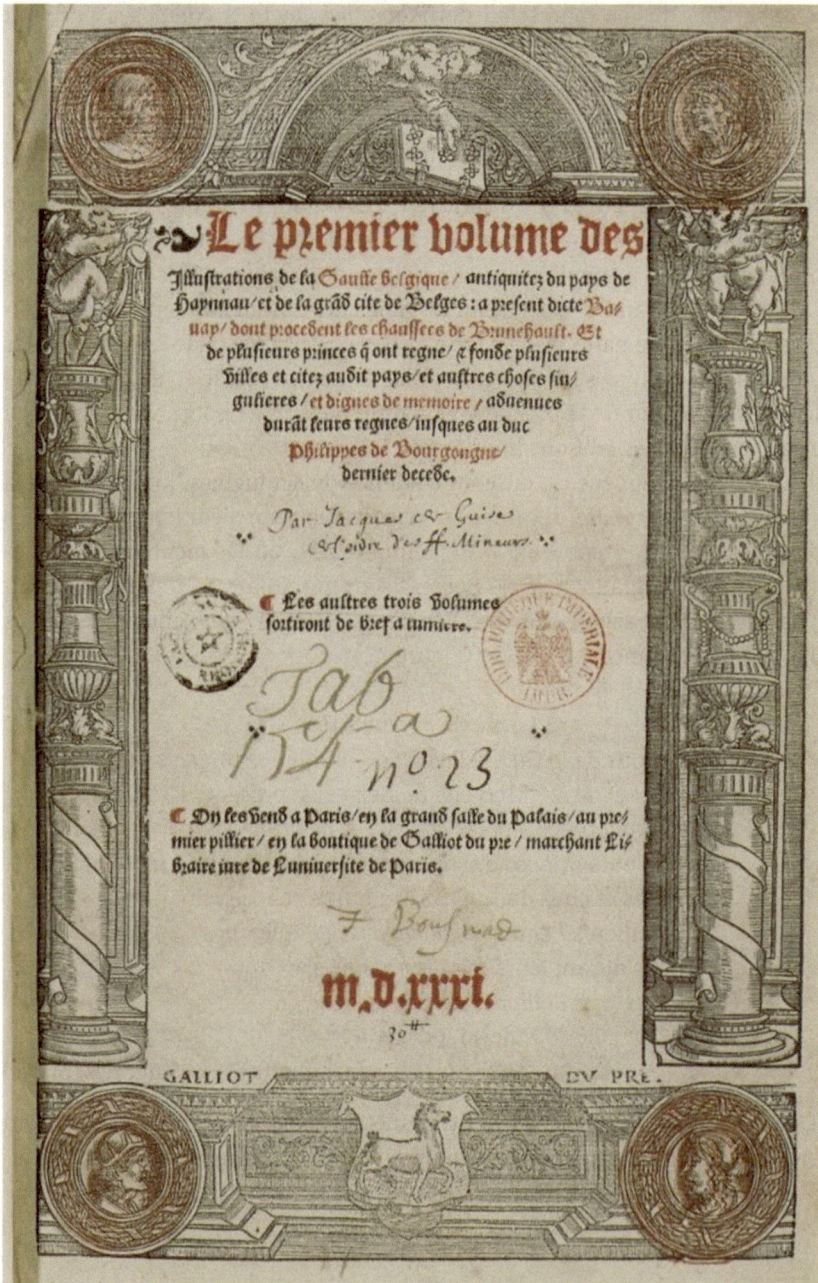

Fig. 7: – Page de titre des *Chroniques de Hainaut* de Jean Wauquelin (1531) © Paris, BnF.

l'auteur avec celui de figures politiques d'autorités *a priori* plus connues de l'acheteur potentiel de sa boutique que certains auteurs édités. Ainsi, en est-il de Martin le Franc, qualifié de „secrétaire du feu pape Felix V" (1530),[49] de Nicole Gilles, „en son vivant indiciaire et secretaire du roy et contreroleur de son tresor" (1525),[50] ou encore de Guillaume de Tignonville, „chevalier conseiller et chambellan du roi" (1531).[51]

Les deux éditions des œuvres d'Alain Chartier que Galliot fait imprimer entre 1526 et 1529, mais dans des formats et caractères différents, témoignent du caractère conscient de l'usage de la titulature sur la page de titre, qui apparaît dès lors comme un élément constitutif de la 'grammaire du péritexte liminaire' chez Galliot du Pré.

Dans la première édition des œuvres complètes et révisées d'Alain Chartier, Galliot ajoute, par rapport aux éditions antérieures des œuvres de Chartier (comme celle due à Philippe Le Noir[52] en 1523), la précision du statut de l'auteur: „secretaire du feu roy Charles septiesme"; lorsqu'il la rééditera, en 1529 au format octavo, il sera contraint, pour respecter l'économie du format, de supprimer des éléments de son titre à rallonge de 1526, mais il maintiendra ce qui paraît être un argument de vente (Figures 8 et 9):

LES FAICTZ ET DICTZ DE FEU
De bonne memoire Maistre Alain Chartier en son vivant Secretaire
Du feu roy Charles septiesme Du nom. Nouvellement im
primé / reveu et corrigé oultre les precedentes impressions / et
divisé par chapitres pour plus facillement comprendre
le contenu en iceulx Adjousté le Debat du gras
et du maigre / que n'auroit encores esté impri

---

49 Exemplaire Paris, BnF, Rés. Y^e 4031.

50 Exemplaire Paris, Arsenal, Fol. H 1606. „secretaire du roy et contrerolleur de son tresor" (1538, page de titre, exemplaire Vienne, ÖNB, 58 K 38); „en son vivant secretaire, indiciaire du roy et contrerolleur de son thresor" (1549, page de titre, exemplaire Paris, Arsenal, Fol. H 1609). Une désignation similaire apparaît sur la page de titre de l'édition *princeps* de la traduction de trois oraisons de Cicéron „par Estiene le Blanc, conseiller du roy et contrerolleur general de son espargne" (1534, exemplaire Munich, BSB, 4 A.lat.b. 214 k).

51 Exemplaire Paris, BnF, Rés. R 1721.

52 „*SEnsuyvent les* faictz & dictz de *maistre Alain* chartier contenant en soy douze livres dont les noms sont en la table cy aprés. *Qui traictent de plusieurs choses touchans les* guerres faictes par les angloys et aultres ennemis. Avec la *genealogie des Roys de France avec le breviere des Nobles* le livre de Reveillematin et aultres livres joyeulx *comme pourrez ouyr* cy aprés" (Paris, Philippe le Noir, 1523 [exemplaire Paris, Bibl. de l'ENS, Lettres Ulm Rés. XV-X L F p 238 c 8°]).

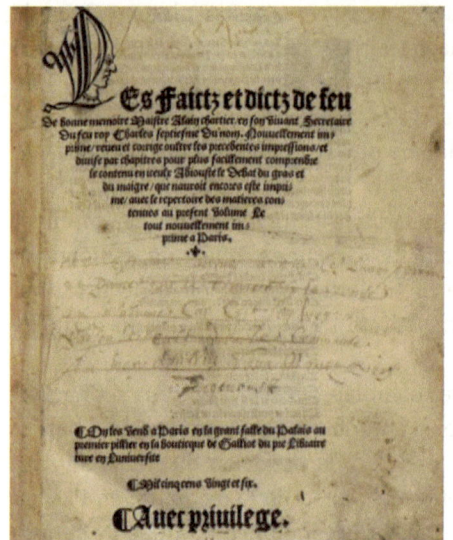 

Fig. 8 et 9: – Pages de titre des éditions de 1526
et de 1529 des œuvres d'Alain Chartier.
[reproductions sont à une échelle différente]
© Munich, BSB.

> mé, avec le repertoire des matieres con
> tenues au present volume. Le
> tout nouvellement im
> primé à Paris.
> . $.

(Paris, Galliot du Pré, 1526, titre, Munich, BSB, 2 P.O. gall. 7)

> $ *LES ŒUVRES* $
> *feu maistre Alain Chartier en son*
> *vivant Secretaire du feu roy Char*
> *les septiesme du non. Nouvelle*
> *ment imprimees, reveues et*
> *corrigiees oultre les pre*
> *cedentes impressions.*

(1529, titre [Alain Chartier réécrit en noir], exemplaire Munich, BSB, P.O. gall. 373)

L'on soulignera ici qu'en 1529 Galliot choisit le terme d'œuvres, terme sans doute plus moderne – selon nos premiers sondages, il s'agirait de la première utilisation du terme sur une page de titre pour désigner le livre imprimé d'un écrivain français, sur le modèle des traductions des *opera* d'écrivains latins qualifiées d',œuvres'[53] – que le très médiéval binôme *faictz et dictz* utilisé en 1526; surtout, le terme d'*œuvres* pourrait viser à suggérer la promotion d'un geste auctorial de rassemblement cohérent d'œuvres diverses similaire à celui alors construit et affiché par des auteurs contemporains tels que Clément Marot[54] – à moins d'y voir un geste plus simplement éditorial et bassement commercial d'un éditeur désireux de vendre les œuvres complètes d'un auteur à des lecteurs possédant déjà quelques textes de l'auteur. L'édition de 1532 des œuvres poétiques de François Villon par Galliot du Pré est également la première de la tradition imprimée de cet auteur à s'intituler *œuvres*: „Les œuvres de maistre Françoys Villon"; le privilège de l'édition de 1533, revue par Clément Marot, précise d'ailleurs que Galliot était désireux de „faire imprimer et vendre les œuvres de feu Françoys Villon" (fol. a[4] r°).

Cette recherche d'attractivité par le biais de la page de titre se confirme par l'usage d'adjectifs vantant les qualités ‚divertissantes' des textes anonymes, essentiellement médiévaux et majoritairement narratifs, que Galliot publie; il s'agit d'adjectifs courants dans les pages de titre des textes français des années 1520–1530 et, plus globalement, dans les textes littéraires produits à cette époque[55]:

lequel traicte de plusieurs matieres <u>recreatives</u> (*Sainct Greaal* 1516, exemplaire Paris, BnF, Rés. Y^2 23);

histoyre moult <u>plaisante</u> et <u>delectable</u> (*Ysaïe le triste* 1522, exemplaire Paris, BnF, Rés. Y^2 72);

Histhoire singuliere et fort <u>recreative</u> (*Mabrien* 1525, exemplaire Paris, BnF, Rés. M Y^2 896);

Hystoire moult <u>recreative</u> et <u>delectable</u> (*Philippe de Madien* 1527, exemplaire Paris, BnF, Rés. Y^2 161);

---

53 Voir la traduction anonyme (faussement attribuée à Laurent de Premierfait) d'œuvres morales de Sénèque *Les euvres de Senecque translateez de latin en françoys* (Paris: Antoine Vérard, [c. 1500] USTC 71469), la traduction des *Commentaires* de César *Les oeuvres et brefves exposicions de Julius Cesar* (Paris: Michel Le Noir, 1517 USTC 29056) ou celle des œuvres majeures de Virgile *Les œuvres de Virgille translatees de latin en françoys* (Paris: Nicolas Cousteau pour Galliot du Pré, 1529 USTC 24233).

54 Sur la notion d'œuvres chez Clément Marot, voir François Rigolot, 'Clément Marot et l'émergence de la conscience littéraire à la Renaissance'. In: *La Génération Marot. Poètes français et néo-latins (1510–1550), Actes du Colloque international de Baltimore, 5–7 décembre 1996*. Éd. par Gérard Defaux. Paris 1997, p. 21–34 (p. 21). Voir aussi Nancy Regalado, 'Gathering the Works: The "Œuvres de Villon" and the Intergeneric Passage of the Medieval French Lyric into Single-Author Collections'. In: *L'Esprit créateur* 33 (1993), p. 87–100.

55 François Cornilliat, *'Or ne mens'. Couleurs de l'éloge et du blâme chez les 'Grands Rhétoriqueurs'*. Paris 1994.

Histoire singuliere et recreative (*Meliadus* 1528, exemplaire Paris, BnF, Rés. Y^2 354);

La *treselegante*, delicieuse, *melliflue* et tresplaisante *hystoire* du tresnoble *victorieux* et excellentissime roy *Perceforest* (*Perceforest* 1528, exemplaire Chantilly, BC, XII H 19);

livre *plaisant, copieux et habondant en sentences* (Martin le Franc, *Le Champion des dames* 1530, exemplaire Paris, BnF, Rés. Y^e 4031);

Tresplaisante et recreative hystoire (*Perceval* 1530, exemplaire Vienne, ÖNB, 23490 C);

oeuvre curieux et moult recreatif (*Sidrac* 1531, exemplaire Gand, BU, Rés. 1551) [nous soulignons].

De façon plus globale, si l'on considère la page de titre des 60 éditions de textes français d'auteurs morts avant 1512 publiées par Galliot du Pré, l'on peut observer que plus de la moitié qualifient le *livre* de ‚nouveau' (au sens de‚depuis peu' et non de ‚à nouveau') (Figure 10):

- soit parce qu'il est dit „nouvellement imprimé", comme pour *Ysaïe le Triste* en 1522[56];
- soit parce qu'il est dit „nouvellement revu et corrigé", comme pour les œuvres d'Alain Chartier en 1526[57];
- soit parce qu'il est dit „nouvellement/depuis additionné" du récit des événements qui se sont déroulés entretemps, comme les *Annales de France* de Nicole Gilles en 1525[58];

---

56 „Histoyre moult plai||sante et delectable / nouvelle||ment Imprimee à Paris ." (page de titre, exemplaire Paris, BnF, Rés. Y^2 72). Sur les imprimés de ce texte, Gabriel Bianciotto, 'Le roman d'*Isaïe le Triste*: les imprimés'. In: *Ensi firent li ancessor. Mélanges de philologie médiévale offerts à Marc-René Jung*. Éd. par Luciano Rossi, Christine Jacob-Hugon et Ursula Bähler. Alessandria 1996, p. 623–639.

57 „Le tout nouvellement imprimé à Paris" (1526, titre, Paris, BnF, Rés. Y^e 34).

58 „Les treselegantes || Tresveridiques et copieuses Annalles Des trespreux / tresno||bles / treschrestiens et tresexcellens moderateurs des belliqueu||ses Gaules . Depuis la triste desolation de la tresinclyte et tres||fameuse cité de Troye Jusques au regne du trevertueux roy || François à present regnant . Compilees par feu treseloquent et || noble Hystoriographe en son vivant indiciaire et secretaire du || Roy et Contreroleur de son tresor maistre Nicole Gilles jusques || au temps de tresprudent et victorieux roy Loys unziesme . Et depuis additionnees selon les modernes hystoriens jusques en L'an || Mil cinq cens et vingt ." (page de titre, exemplaire Paris, Arsenal, Fol. H 1606).

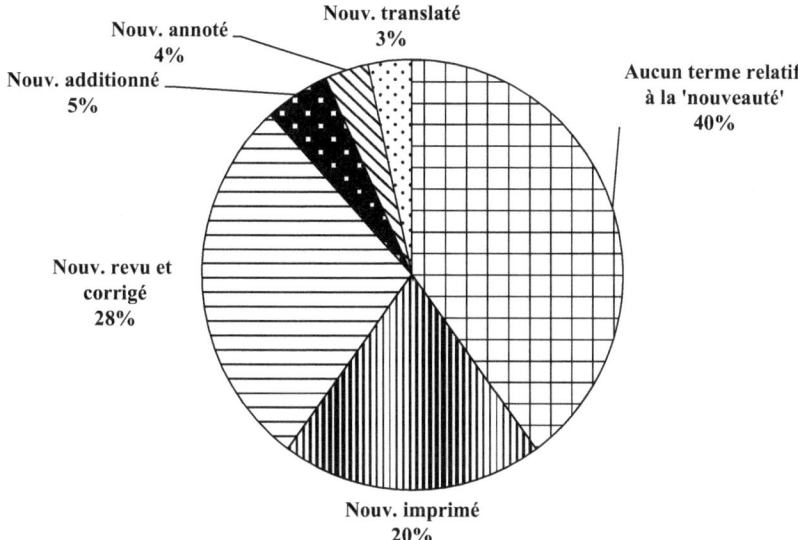

Fig. 10: – Titre des éditions de textes littéraires d'auteurs morts avant 1521.

– soit parce qu'il est dit „nouvellement/à present annoté", comme pour le Flavius Josephus de 1532 (où cette qualité est mise en évidence à l'encre rouge sur la page de titre)[59];
– soit parce qu'il est dit „nouvellement translaté", comme pour le *Compendium historial* d'Henri Romain.[60]

Seulement 40% des livres publiés ne reprennent pas les termes ‚nouvellement', ‚à present' ou ‚depuis' dans leur page de titre. Cela semble confirmer que l'argument de nouveauté fait partie des stratégies éditoriales de Galliot du Pré, indépendamment parfois de la vérité philologiquement établie. Ainsi, la traduction du *De remediis utriusque Fortunae* de Pétrarque est identifiée comme

---

59 „*L'histoire* escripte pre‖mierement en Grec par *Josephus le Juif / autheur ‖ tresnoble et ancien* Et en aprés mise en *La‖tin* dont elle a esté depuys faicte ‖ *Françoyse . Conte‖nant* les guer‖res qui ‖ furent au pays de *Judee* puys ‖ le temps que la *Cité de Hierusa‖lem* fut premiere-ment prinse par le *Roy ‖ Antyochus* [...] *Elle est à present notee ‖* à la marge des accordances de la Bible ‖ et d'ung aultre *historiographie ancien ‖ nommé Egesippus*. Le tout bien à propos / et par *merveilleuse di‖ligence*" (page de titre, exemplaire Paris, Arsenal, Fol. H 684).

60 „COMPENDIUM ‖ Hystorial des polices des Empires / Royaulme ‖ et choses publicques . Nouvellement trans‖laté de latin en François" (Paris, Arsenal, 4° H 743). Sur la tradition tex-tuelle de ce texte, voir Laurence Dupré La Tour, 'La traduction manuscrite du *Compendium Historial* d'Henri Romain'. In: *Revue d'histoire des textes* 5 (1977), p. 137–168.

„nouvellement imprimé" sur la page de titre et „nouvellement translaté de latin en françois" dans le colophon (fol. 174d), alors que Galliot se contente, en réalité, de publier la traduction réalisée en 1370 par Jean Daudin pour le roi Charles V.[61]

Sur les 13 éditions princeps publiées par Galliot, seules huit présentent une revendication commerciale de la nouveauté dans le titre (qualifiant le plus souvent le processus d'impression)[62]; dans une seule, Galliot souligne dans le titre qu'il s'agit d'une édition *princeps*: l'*Hystoire du sainct Greaal* – compilation de l'*Estoire del Saint Graal* et du *Perlesvaus* – publiée en 1516, dont le titre précise „lesquelz livres ne furent jamais imprimez jusques à present". Notre notion moderne d'édition *princeps* n'est donc ni pertinente ni opératoire et en tout cas moins importante que celle de ‚nouveauté', tendant à souligner un rapport à la chronologie et au temps historique différents du nôtre.

Comme nous l'avons déjà signalé, les rééditions sont nombreuses chez Galliot et se justifient toujours péritextuellement dès la page de titre, car la réédition de Galliot propose au lecteur:

- une actualisation du texte; c'est le cas des textes historiographiques auxquels est ajoutée la mention des derniers évènements advenus entre la date de rédaction/la date de dernière publication et la date de la présente publication, par exemple pour les *Annales de France* de Nicole Gilles en 1525 (édition *princeps*): „et De‖puis additionnees selon les modernes hystoriens jusques en L'an ‖ Mil cinq cens et vingt" (page de titre, Paris, Arsenal, Fol. H 1606)[63];

---

61 Paris, BnF, Rés. R 543, fol. CLXXIIII v°. Sur cette traduction, Léopold Delisle, 'Anciennes traductions françaises du traité de Pétrarque sur les remèdes de l'une et l'autre fortune'. In: *Notices et extraits des manuscrits de la Bibliothèque nationale et autres bibliothèques* 34 (1891), p. 273–304; Nicholas Mann, 'La fortune de Pétrarque en France. Recherches sur le *De remediis*'. In: *Studi-francesi* 37 (1969), p. 1–15; Sandrine-Hériché Pradeau, 'La traduction du *De remediis utriusque fortunae* de Pétrarque par Jean Daudin: la rhétorique et la contrariété'. In: *Traduire au XIVe siècle. Évrart de Conty et la vie intellectuelle à la cour de Charles V*. Éd. par Joëlle Ducos et Michèle Goyens. Paris 2015, p. 267–292.

62 „Ensemble aussi plusieurs additions des choses advenues es temps ‖ et regnes des Treschrestiens Roys de France Charles VIII, que Die (sic lire "Dieu") absoule . Et Loys XII ‖ de ce nom à present regnant" (Robert Gaguin, *Chroniques*, 1514, titre); „lesquelz livres ne furent jamais ‖ imprimez jusques à present" (*L'hystoire du sainct Greaal*, 1516, titre); „nouvellement imprimee à Paris" (*Ysaïe le triste*, 1522); „nouvellement imprimé" (traduction du *De remediis* de Pétrarque, 1523); „Et de‖puis additionnees selon les modernes hystoriens jusques en l'an ‖ mil cinq cens et vingt" (Nicole Gilles, *Annales*, 1525); „Et nouvellement imprimé à Paris" (*Mabrian*, 1525); „nouvellement imprimee à Paris" (*Meliadus de Leonnoys*, 1528); „non au paravant imprimé" (*Perceval le Galloys*, 1530).

63 L'*Avis au lecteur* qui ouvre le volume précise: „par inadvertance, negligence ou autrement des correcteurs compositeurs ou imprimeurs d'icelluy livre ont esté delaissez et obmis à castiger,

- l'ajout d'un texte inédit à des œuvres complètes; c'est le cas pour le *Debat du gras et du maigre* ajouté à l'édition de Chartier en 1526: „adjousté le debat du gras et ‖ du maigre / que n'auroit [sic] encores esté imprimé" (page titre, Paris, BnF, Rés. Y^e 34) ou celui des *Lunettes des Princes* de Jean Meschinot, publiées „ensemble plusieurs additions et ballades" (1528, page de titre, Vienne, ÖNB, BE 5 T 47);
- une révision sur le texte latin; c'est le cas pour la publication collective d'œuvres morales de Cicéron (dans des traductions de Laurent de Premierfait, J. Colin ou David Miffant): „Le tout diligemment reveu corrigé et amendé selon le latin" (1539, page de titre, Munich, BSB, A.lat.b. 568) ou celle de l'*Alexandre* de Quinte Curse par Vasque de Lucène: „*Translaté* de latin en fran‖çoys / *et puis nagueres* reveu ‖ et concordé avec Plutarque / Justin et autres ‖ aucteurs" (1530, page de titre, Vienne, ÖNB, 51 O 7)[64];
- une annotation continue; c'est le cas pour l'édition de 1530 de la traduction de Tite Live par Pierre Bersuire: „Et en ensuyvant les faictz dudit Tytus Livius au‖ cunes addicions de plusieurs grans historiographes / si comme ‖ Orose, Saluste, Suetone et Lucain" (page de titre, Gand, UB, BIB.HIST.004972 v.1) ou pour le *Roman de la Rose*: „Cy est le Romant de la roze / Ou tout l'art damour est enclose / Histoires et auctoritez / Et maintz beaulx propos usitez / Qui a esté nouvellement / Corrigé suffisantement / Et cotté à l'avantaige / Com on voit en chascune page" (1526, page de titre, Munich, BSB, 2° P.o. gall. 24 d);
- un péritexte facilitant la lecture et la consultation, comme l'ajout d'un découpage en chapitres; c'est le cas pour l'édition des œuvres d'Alain Chartier et celle des *Mémoires* de Philippe de Commynes: „divisé par chapitres pour plus facillement comprendre le contenu en iceulx" (Alain Chartier, 1526, page de titre, Paris, BnF, Rés. Y^e 34); „nouvellement reveue et corrigée avec la table des chapitres contenuz en ladicte cronique" (Philippe de Commynes, 1524, page de titre, Gand, BU, Rés. 1551).

Encore une fois, il serait nécessaire, pour saisir l'impact et la finalité de ce type de qualificatifs de pousser plus loin l'analyse des titres des textes français imprimés, afin d'en dégager la grammaire de base, dans la diachronie du seizième siècle (notamment en lien avec les aspects techniques, typographiques

---

corriger et reformer aucunes petites faultes, vices ou erreurs estans en la copie originelle sur laquelle a esté imprimé cedit livre et signalement touchant aucunes dates des annés courans; pour lesquelz vices, faultes ou erreurs congnoistre et iceulx corriger fault noter ce qui s'ensuyt." (fol. 3^r°.) Voir également l'édition des *Grandes Chroniques* de Robert Gaguin en 1514.

64 Sur ce texte et sa version imprimée, Robert Bossuat, 'Vasque de Lucène, traducteur de Quinte-Curce (1468)'. In: *Bibliothèque d'Humanisme et Renaissance* 8 (1946), p. 197–245.

et matériels), mais aussi les déclinaisons particulières, fruits des stratégies éditoriales de chaque imprimeur-libraire.

Malgré tout, parfois, dans le cas d'auto-rééditions, on ne constate pas de modification ou de plus-value ‚textuelle' ou ‚péritextuelle' majeure, mais l'adoption de nouvelles caractéristiques matérielles, telles que le format, la taille et la police de caractère. C'est le cas de ses versions révisées du *Roman de la Rose* et des *Œuvres* d'Alain Chartier publiées en 1526, que Galliot réédite toutes deux en 1529 chez Pierre Vidoué dans un format de poche et en lettres romaines, poursuivant ainsi le déploiement de ses stratégies éditoriales. Galliot voulait peut-être susciter l'achat d'une nouvelle édition, certes d'un texte déjà possédé par le futur acheteur, mais dans une autre facture, tout à fait novatrice pour un texte français médiéval. Un autre objectif de Galliot en 1529 était peut-être de susciter l'achat d'une collection complète de petits livres de poche de textes français. En effet, comme Jean Balsamo l'a déjà montré,[65] de 1528 à 1531, Galliot publie avec Pierre Vidoué une petite dizaine de livres in 8° en lettres romaines. Ces livres contiennent majoritairement des textes ‚anciens': outre Jean Lemaire de Belges, les *Lunettes des Princes* de Jean Meschinot (*c.* 1460); les *Epistres* d'Ovide par Octovien de Saint-Gelais (*c.* 1498); le *Roman de la Rose*; Alain Chartier; les *Offices* de Cicéron par David Miffant (*c.* 1500); le *Champion des dames* de Martin le Franc (*c.* 1440); le *Sidrac* (2e moitié du 13e s.); les *Dictz moraux des philosophes*, traduction par Guillaume de Tignonville du *Liber philosophorum moralium antiquorum* attribué à Guillaume de Conches (*c.* 1402). Il s'agit d'ouvrages dont on connaît le succès par ailleurs ou dont le titre était en lui-même attractif, comme pour le *Sidrac* ou les *Dictz moraulx*:

MILQUATRE VINGTZ
et quatre *demandes* avec les
Solutions et *Responses*
tous propoz, oeuvre
curieux et moult
recreatif, selon le saige *Sidrach* (1531, exemplaire Gand, UB, Rés. 1551)

LES DICTZ
Moraulx des Philosophes, transla
tez de latin en *Françoys* par noble
homme *Messire* Guillaume
de Tignonville cheva
lier conseiller et cham
bellan du *Roy* .

---

65 Balsamo, 'La collection' (note 7).

Les dictz des saiges .

Le secret des secretz de *Aristote*. (1531, exemplaire Paris, BnF, Rés. R 1721)

Galliot adapte donc un fonds ancien et déjà publié aux goûts nouveaux, avec un cumul de nouveautés, tant celle de la forme que celle revendiquée sur la page de titre, qui comprend fréquemment l'adjectif ,nouveau' ou l'adverbe ,nouvellement':

"nouvellement reveues et corrigees" (Octovien de Saint-Gelais, traduction des *Epîtres* d'Ovide, 1528, page de titre, Paris, BnF, Rés. P Y^C 719);

"de nouveau composees" (Jean Meschinot, *Les lunettes des princes*, 1528, page de titre, Vienne, ÖNB, BE 5 T 47);

"nouvellement imprimees, reveues et corrigiees oultre les precedentes impressions" (Alain Chartier, 1529, page de titre, Vienne, ÖNB, 58 L 17);

"reveu et corrigé oultre les precedentes impressions" (*Le Roman de la Rose*, 1529, page de titre, Munich, BSB, P.O.gall. 1288);

"nouvellement imprimé" (*Le Champion des dames*, 1530, page de titre, Paris, BnF, Rés. Y^e 4031);

"nouvellement reveues et corrigees oultre les precedentes impressions" (Jean Lemaire de Belges, *Illustrations*, 1531, page de titre, Paris, BnF, Rés. M 219).

Galliot a pu chercher à susciter l'achat de plusieurs de ces volumes similaires, voire de toute la collection.

2.2.2 Les prologues allographes

Contrairement à la pratique d'Antoine Vérard, qui privilégie la modification du prologue de l'auteur et la substitution de sa figure de libraire à celle de l'auteur,[66] Galliot du Pré privilégie l'ajout de prologues allographes où l'énonciateur se positionne clairement comme celui qui a édité un texte déjà disponible – sans qu'il soit toujours possible d'identifier, derrière le *je*, le libraire Galliot ou le réviseur effectif du texte. Sur la vingtaine de prologues

---

66 Winn (voir note 16). Sur ces questions, voir aussi Anne Réach-Ngô (éd.), *Créations d'atelier. L'éditeur et la fabrique de l'œuvre*. Paris 2014; Anne Réach-Ngô, 'Instances et stratégies éditoriales à la Renaissance: de la fabrique du livre à la fabrication de l'auteur'. In: *La fabrication de l'auteur*, dir. par Marie-Pier Luneau et Josée Vincent (dir.), *La fabrication de l'auteur*. Québec 2010, p. 333–362; Cynthia J. Brown, *Poets, Patrons, and Printers. Crisis of Authority in Late Medieval France*. London 1995; Adrian Amstrong, *Technique and Technology. Script, Print, and Poetics in France 1470–1550*. Oxford 2000 (Oxford Modern Languages and Literature Monographs).

allographes de textes français d'auteurs morts avant 1512, il n'y a qu'un seul cas où l'énonciateur prend la place de l'auteur du texte publié. Effectivement, l'édition de 1530 de la traduction des *Antiquités judaïques* de Flavius Josèphe reprend le prologue du traducteur qui ouvrait l'édition Vérard et où ce dernier se présentait comme le traducteur offrant son œuvre à „vous, Charles, par la grace de Dieu, roy de France huytisme de ce nom" et rappelait les autres traductions qu'il avait offertes au souverain; chez Galliot, le texte est identique, mais s'adresse désormais à „vous, Françoys, par la grace de Dieu, roy de France".

Il n'est pas anodin que nous soyons en 1530, année de la fondation du Collège des trois langues. Galliot cherche, rapidement et à peu de frais, à se positionner, vis-à-vis du roi, comme un spécialiste de la littérature française, qui soutient l'entreprise de traduction et qui reprend le flambeau du libraire serviteur des princes qu'était Vérard.

De la bataille judaique Antoine Vérard 1492 (ex. Paris, BnF, Rés. H 10, fol. a¹ r° [nous soulignons])	L'histoire escripte premierement en grec par Josephus le Juif Galliot du Pré 1530 (Gand, UB, BIB.HIST.004972, fol. a¹ v° [nous soulignons])
à l'honneur aussi et reverence de la souveraine royalle magesté de vous, *Charles, par la grace de Dieu, roy de France huytisme de ce nom,* après la translation du livre que fist Paoul Orose, lequel *vous ay translaté* depuis n'a gueres [...] je me suis mys à translater les sept livres que fist Josephus intitulez de la bataille judaïque, affin de poursuyvre la matiere des juifz commencee en Orose	à l'honneur aussi et reverence de la souveraine royalle majesté de vous *Françoys par la grace de Dieu, roy de France de ce nom,* après la translation du livre que feist Paoul Orose, lequel *vous ay translaté* de puis n'a gueres [...] je me suis mys à translater les sept livres que feist Josephus intitulez de la bataille Judaïque affin de poursuyvre la matiere des Juifz commencee en Orose

Une dizaine de prologues allographes insistent sur le caractère ,viel', ,ancien', ,antique' de la langue du texte médiéval imprimé, avec un souci de rassurer le lecteur en précisant la plupart du temps qu'un travail éditorial a été réalisé et que le texte est désormais accessible puisqu'il a été révisé et récrit en „commun langaige vulgaire" (*Ysaïe le Triste,* 1522),[67] en „bon vulgaire françoys" (*Mabrien,* 1525)[68]) et en „nostre vulgaire françoys" (*Perceval le*

---

[67] „bien m'a semblé chose convenable et de raison rediger par escript et reformer en commun langaige vulgaire l'hystoire du tresvaillant et preux chevalier *Isaye le Triste*" (*Proesme capital de ce present volume,* Paris, BnF, Rés. Y2 72, fol. a² r°).

[68] „lequel auroit à grans fraitz faict traduyre de vieil et ancien langaige, en vulgaire françoys, et icelluy imprimer" (privilège, exemplaire Paris, BnF, Rés. M Y² 896); „nouvellement reduict

Galloys, 1530)[69] et non plus en „mauvais et trop ancien langaige sentant son inveteré commencement et origine de parler" (*Roman de la Rose*, 1526)[70] ou en „fort, non acoustumé et estrange [françoys]" (*Perceval*, 1530). La publication de *Mabrien* en 1525 met en lumière, aux trois endroits stratégiques du péritexte (dans la page de titre, dans le privilège et dans la préface aux humbles lecteurs), cet effort de distanciation par rapport à un état de langue considéré comme différent:

> „Le tout traduict de vieil langaige en vulgaire françoys" (titre, exemplaire Paris, BnF, Rés. M Y[2] 896);
>
> „[…] lequel auroit à grans fraitz faict traduyre de vieil et ancien langiage, en vulgaire françoys et icelluy imprimer" (privilège);
>
> „[…] nouvellement reduict de vieil langaige corrumpu en *bon* vulgaire françoys" (*Prologue du present livre aulx humbles lecteurs*, col. a[2] d [nous soulignons]).

Il est à noter qu'à partir de 1533, cette langue ‚vieille' n'est plus corrigée. Par exemple, dans l'„Avis de l'Imprimeur au lecteur" de l'édition 1553 des *Annales* de Nicole Gilles, il est précisé: „Quant au stile et maniere d'escrire de l'auteur, qui à la verité sent un peu son vieillard, il fit grande conscience d'y rien changer afin de laisser voir aux lecteurs la difference qu'il y a entre les antiques et modernes."[71]

De même, dans la révision des *Mémoires* de Philippe de Commynes par Denis Sauvage, le réviseur précise:

> je n'ay voulu mettre en texte ny en marge certains vieux mots et quelques phrases, ou manieres de parler, presque autant aagees, qui se rencontrent au vieil Exemplaire, ayant le plussouvent, *chastoy* pour *chastiment*, *Venu que fut* pour *Quand il fut venu* et leurs semblables, comme pareillement je n'ay voulu en oster quelques autres, qui se pourroyent mieux dire maintenant, pour ne faire trop de compte de l'antiquité et pour ne la desestimer aussi plus que de raison, mais bien ay je mis, sur la marge, l'interpretation de telles

---

de vieil langaige corrumpu en bon vulgaire françoys pour la delectacion et passe temps de plusieurs qui de livre liront" (*Prologue du present livre aulx humbles lecteurs*, fol. a[2] r°).

69 „Et parce que le langaige dudict Mennessier ne de son predecesseur n'est en usaige en nostre vulgaire françoys, mais fort, non acoustumé et estrange, je, pour satiffaire aux desirs, plaisirs et voulontez des princes, seigneurs et aultres, suyvans la maternelle langue de France, ay bien voulu m'employer à traduire et mectre de rithme en prose familiere les faictz et vie dudict vertueux chevallier Perceval, en ensuyvant au plus prés selon ma possibilité et pouair le sens de mes predecesseurs translateurs, comme ay trouvé par leur escript." (*Prologue*, Paris, BnF, Rés. Y[2] 74, fol. a[1] d).

70 Prologue allographe intitulé „Preambule du livre" (Munich, BSB, 2° P.O. gall. 24 d, fol. $[2] v°).

71 „L'imprimeur aux lecteurs" (Vienne, ÖNB, 58 A 19, fol. a[2] r°).

rencontres qui pourroyent aucunement arrester celuy qui n'auroit beaucoup hanté la langue françoyse (*Advertissement aux lecteurs*, 1552, fol. a³ r°).

En 1533 déjà, dans son édition des œuvres de François Villon, Clément Marot, affirmait dans son prologue allographe: „Et pour ce, comme j'ay dit, que je n'ay touché à son antique façon de parler, je vous ay exposé sur la marge avecques les annotacions, ce qui m'a semblé le plus dur à entendre, laissant le reste à voz promptes intelligences" (fol. a⁵ r°).

Ces témoignages semblent montrer que Galliot était désireux de participer au mouvement de promotion de la langue française, comme le montrait déjà son investissement dans la littérature française à la fin des années 1520; l'on rappellera également que Galliot a publié Guillaume Budé, Jean Marot, Jacques Pelletier du Mans... et qu'il est le premier à éditer les traductions de Thucydide et de Xénophon de Claude de Seyssel et ses prologues inaugurant la politique culturelle de François Iᵉʳ.[72]

Autre exemple: en 1536, Galliot publie une version révisée et actualisée de la *Mer des histoires*, adaptation française du *Rudimentum noviciorum*,[73] la présentant dans le prologue allographe („Aux humbles lecteurs en l'emendation de l'œuvre")[74] comme un lourd travail de rafraîchissement et d'amplification d'un texte écrit sous Louis XI, traduit, en français, sous Charles VII, maintes fois réimprimé et désormais révisé et actualisé, par lui, jusqu'au règne du roi régnant, François Iᵉʳ:

J'ay faict, de nouveau, reimprimer ceste dicte hystoire qui fut en l'an mil CCCC LXXV, faicte premierement latine soubz l'empire de Federic troisiesme du nom et regnant sur les

---

[72] Paul Chavy, 'Les Traductions Humanistes de Claude de Seyssel'. In: *L'humanisme français au début de la Renaissance. Colloque international de Tours*. Éd. par André Stegman. Paris 1973, p. 361–376; Gianni Mombello, 'Claude de Seyssel: un esprit modéré au service de l'expansion française'. In: *Culture et pouvoir au temps de l'Humanisme et de la Renaissance*. Éd. par Louis Terreaux. Genève 1978, p. 71–122.

[73] Sur la tradition française de ce texte, Theodor Schwarz, *Über den Verfasser und die Quellen des 'Rudimentum novitiorum'*. Rostock 1888; Edith A. Wright, '*La Mer des Hystoires*, Paris 1488'. In: *Boston Public Library* 11 (1959), p. 59–74; Robert Brun, '*La Mer des histoires* de Pierre Le Rouge offerte à Charles VIII'. In: *Humanisme actif. Mélanges d'art et de littérature offerts à Julien Cain*. Vol. 2. Paris 1968, p. 191–197; *La Mer des hystoires, traduction française du 'Rudimentum noviciorum'*. Éd. par Nelly Sciardis. Paris 2004.

[74] Voir également le privilège: „puis ung an ença ait recouvert ung livre long temps a imprimé [sic] duquel l'on ne pouoit plus recouvrer [...] lequel à grant diligence auroit par gens sçavans faict veoir et corriger et cocter au marge les passages singuliers estans en icelluy, aussi faict mettre la dacte des temps tant puis l'an du monde [...] jusques à present [...] en la fin duquel auroit faict mettre et adjousté ce qui auroit esté faict digne de memoire [...] extraict de plusieurs aucteurs tant latins que françois" (privilège).

François Loys unziesme [...] laquelle, depuis, pour sa magnificence et singularité, fut tra-
duicte de latin en françois regnant en France Charles huytiesme, par ung natif du pays de
Beauvoysin. Et, pour decorer une chose si riche, ay faict rafreschir et ampliffier les chapitres d'aucunes substances qui y estoient deffaillantes, noter les choses dignes de memoire
au marge, accorder les aages et temps, cocter les dactes selon les vrayes computations,
veriffier et reveoir la table et indice à la verité et en fin additionner et augmenter oultre
les precedentes impressions les evenemens merveilleux et grandes fortunes du regne du
treschrestien roy de France Françoys premier de ce nom, jusques à present mil cinq cens
XXXVI, le tout en beaulx caracteres et impression correcte, reveue et corrigee diligemment
par gens de lettres et congnoissance, au moyen que en ladicte hystoire, qui pour le grant
fruict qui y est caché *a esté plusieurs fois imprimee*, y avoit beaucoup de choses depravees
et supposees (Paris, BnF, Rés. G 226, fol. §² v).

Galliot se présente comme un homme soucieux de ‚decorer' un patrimoine
doublement français – par sa langue et par son soutien de figures d'autorité
royales – au bénéfice du „treschrestien roy de France Françoys premier de ce
nom", dans une mise en forme qui s'inscrit dans la politique de défense et d'illustration du français et dans une posture philologique, définie de façon positive („le tout en beaulx caracteres et impression correcte, reveue et corrigee
diligemment par gens de lettres") et négative („y avoit beaucoup de choses depravees et supposees").

Au-delà de ces caractérisations de la langue du texte publié, il n'y a que
quelques cas où l'ancienneté du texte soit mise en évidence dans la page de
titre. *Perceforest* est désigné comme des „anciennes croniques", dans une for-
mulation topique qui vise évidemment à appuyer leur authenticité (1528).[75] Les
prologues des romans *Meliadus de Leonnoys* (1528) et l'*Histoire du Graal* (1516)
justifient la publication de ces éditions *princeps* en précisant que le texte n'a
jamais été imprimé auparavant, désignation relativement neutre et qui s'inscrit
dans la logique de nouveauté revendiquée sur la page de titre[76]; *Ysaïe le Triste*
(1522), qu'il est inconnu du public moderne et qu'il constitue de ce fait une histoire „quasi du tout nouvelle".[77]

---

75 Van Hemelryck, 'Du *Perceforest* manuscrit' (note 7).

76 „de long temps ne fust venu le livre es mains des desirans lecteurs [...]" (*Meliadus,
Prologue de ce present volume*, Paris, BnF, Rés. Y² 354, fol. a² v°).

77 „pour l'augmentation du reliefvement de voz esperitz fatigués et atenués des autres livres
lyre, pour les matieres et propos tant de fois leutz et revisez, tellement qu'ilz sont ja extimez
vieulx et anciens, ce que n'est pas l'hystoire que vous presente, selon mon advis et oppinion
de plusieurs, car elle me semble quasi du tout nouvelle, consideré que ceulx de present et
temps moderne ne la veirent jamais" (*Ysaïe le triste, Proesme capital de ce present volume*,
Paris, BnF, Rés. Y² 72, fol. a² r°).

À ce propos, il serait utile d'approfondir l'étude de l'évolution sémantique du mot *moderne* pour déterminer si, dans les cas présentés chez Galliot, le mot qualifie simplement ce qui est contemporain ou s'il renvoie déjà à une époque historique précise, considérée comme distincte du Moyen Âge qui précède.[78]

Dans le cas où le texte publié par Galliot avait déjà été publié auparavant, parfois amplement, il justifie son édition par la qualité philologique de la version qu'il a voulu offrir au lecteur. Outre le cas de l'édition Clément Marot des œuvres de Villon en 1533 déjà évoqué, où l'initiative du travail d'édition revient sans doute autant, sinon plus, au poète et à son mécène royal, l'on notera le cas dans deux œuvres majeures du Moyen Âge français qu'il publie en 1526: Alain Chartier et le *Roman de la Rose*. Le péritexte des deux éditions reprend un message et des formulations similaires: le texte circulait déjà – avant cette „moderne saison" –, mais corrompu et de ce fait peu lisible et appréciable:

> Et si on disoit d'aventure que le livre a esté par long temps, devant ceste moderne saison, veu et regardé, je le concede, toutteffois, il estoit mal correct et tronqué en divers lieux, en sorte que les sentences estoient demeurees imparfaictes, tant par la faulte, negligence ou non sçavoir des imprimeurs que d'aultres, lesquelz se sont ingerez et entremis le vouloir corriger. (Alain Chartier, prologue allographe, Paris, BnF, Rés. Ye 34, col. a² d)
>
> reintegrer et en son entier remettre le livre qui par long temps devant ceste moderne saison tant a esté de tous gens d'esprit estimé que bien l'a daigné chascun veoir et tenir au plus hault anglet de sa librairie pour les bonnes sentences, propos et ditz naturelz et moraulx qui dedans sont mis et inserez [...] Cestuy livre present a esté au par avant par la faulte, comme je croy, des imprimeurs, assez mal correct ou, par advanture, de ceulx qui ont baillé le double pour l'imprimer, car l'un et l'autre peult estre cause de son incorrection. [...] (*Roman de la Rose*, prologue allographe *Preambule du livre*, Munich, BSB, 2° P.O. gall. 24 d, fol. $² v°).

Comme on le voit, le péritexte du *Roman de la Rose* incrimine plus explicitement les imprimeurs antérieurs. L'édition fournie par Galliot y remédie par des corrections et également une division en chapitres:

> Pour ceste cause, a esté ledit livre puis peu de temps corrigé, reveu et divisé par chapitres pour plus facile congnoissance des matieres dedans contenues et inserees (Alain Chartier, *ibidem*);
>
> pour laquelle chose restituer en meilleur estat et plus expediente forme pour l'intelligence des lecteurs et auditeurs [...] l'ay corrigé au moins mal que j'ay pu, y adjoustant les quottations des plus principaulx notables et auctoritez venant à propos [...] qui nouvellement l'a faict imprimer après avoir veu sa correction, tant du mauvais et trop ancien

---

[78] Voir quelques pistes de réflexion, dans Georges Matoré, 'Le temps au XVIᵉ siècle'. In: *L'Information grammaticale* 32 (1987), p. 3–8 et *Modernités* 5 (1994), *Ce que modernité veut dire*. Éd. par Yves Vadé.

langaige sentant son inveteré commencement et origine de parler, que de l'imparfaicte quantité des mettres, touts quasi corrompuz (*Roman de la Rose*, ibidem).

Les prologues allographes ne justifient guères la publication d'un texte ancien. L'utilité et l'édification ou la récréation du lecteur semblent être les principales motivations – ce qui rejoint là les justifications les plus traditionnelles des prologues des textes littéraires de la fin du Moyen Âge et du début de la Renaissance.[79] Galliot avance cet argument, tant dans un privilège comme celui du *Perceforest*[80] que dans un prologue allographe, comme celui des *Œuvres* de Chartier[81] ou celui du *Roman de la Rose*.[82]

3 La circulation et la consommation des livres

Passons à l'approche de la politique éditoriale de Galliot du Pré sous l'angle de la circulation et de la consommation, par le biais de l'inventaire après décès, qui livre un instantané de sa pratique éditoriale en 1561, mais aussi de la configuration d'une boutique de libraire du Palais dans la deuxième moitié du seizième siècle.

3.1 La boutique

L'inventaire conservé à Paris aux Archives Nationales est constitué de 70 folios listant 3175 entrées, soit 39417 volumes et 238 rames; pour chaque édition

---

79 Voir, par exemple, Laurence Harf-Lancner et Emmanuel Baumgartner, *Seuils de l'œuvre dans le texte médiéval*. Paris 2002; Pascale Mounier, *Le roman humaniste. Un genre novateur français (1532–1564)*. Paris 2007, p. 165–207.

80 „ […] a recouvert les anciennes croniques et histoires d'Angleterre, faitz et gestes du noble roy Perceforest, jadis faitz et compilléz pour l'instruction et exercice des armes; lesdictes histoires aornées et decorées de plusieurs belles sentences et auctoritéz à l'edification de ceulx qui les vouldront voir et lyre." (Paris, BnF, Rés. Y² 28, fol. a² r°).

81 „Doncques, cela veu et premedité, bonne et juste raison a esté vous presenter, O vous, nobles lecteurs et auditeurs, ce present livre, contenant les œuvres de feu Maistre Alain Charretier, en son vivant secretaire du feu roy Charles septiesme, car il est autant ou plus prouffitable pour ung chascun bon chrestien introduyre que livre qu'on puisse lire en langaige françois et vulgaire pour les matieres tresutiles dedans icelluy contenues, dignes et singulieres, tant en prose qu'en rime" (Paris, BnF, Rés. Y^e 34, col. a² d).

82 „les choses dignes de memoire pour leur proffit et utilité soient a demeure perpetuellement sans estre du tout assopies par trop longue saison et labilité de temps caduc et transitoire" (prologue allographe, Munich, BSB, 2° P.O. gall. 24 d).

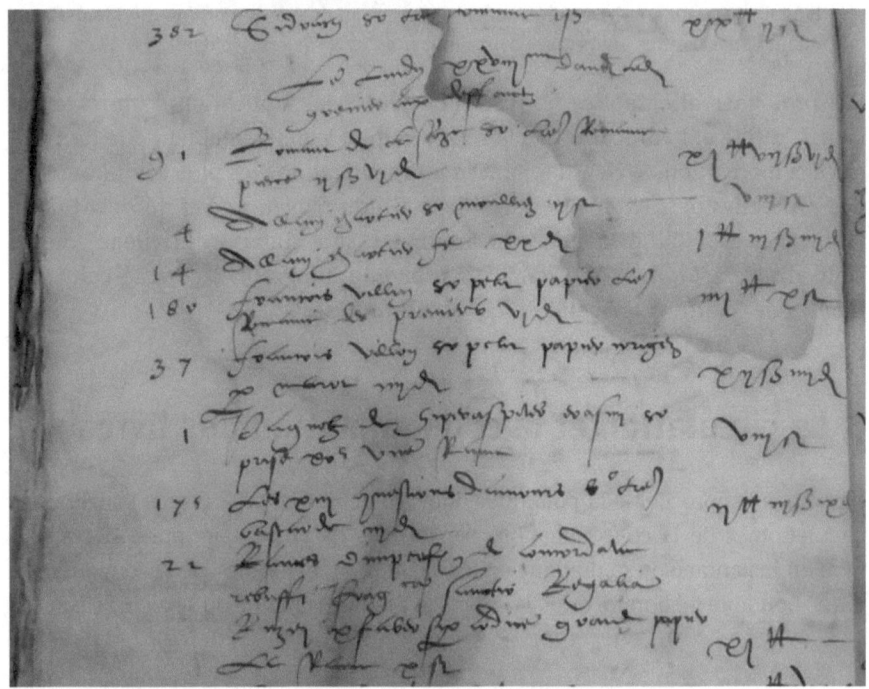

Fig. 11: Inventaire après décès des livres de Galliot du Pré (Paris, AN, Minutier central des notaires de Paris, LXXIII, 43, 12 IV 1561, fol. 41v) © Paris, AN.

recensée, sont notés le titre, de façon souvent très laconique, le format, le nombre d'exemplaires encore présents au domicile ou dans la boutique et la somme à laquelle le tout a été prisé (Figure 11); parfois, est précisé le lieu d'édition et/ou l'éditeur, étant donné que Galliot du Pré vendait également des livres „achetés en gros chez des marchands parisiens ou acquis lors de la dispersion d'une bibliothèque particulière ou d'un fonds de librairie".[83]

Ces différentes informations cumulées permettent, dans certains cas, d'identifier précisément l'édition dans les répertoires actuels, mais dans d'autres, il n'est même pas possible d'identifier le texte ou la version du texte (par exemple, dans la langue originale ou en traduction), soit que les données reprises dans l'inventaire soient inexactes, soit que l'identification moderne des formats soit erronée, soit encore que l'édition notifiée n'ait pas été conservée.

---

83 Charon-Parent (voir note 2).

L'inventaire a recensé les livres de Galliot en deux endroits: à son domicile et à sa boutique du Palais. Pour ce qui est de son domicile, les stocks conservés à ce moment-là ont été recensés pièce par pièce. Comme dans toute bibliothèque, on peut repérer des groupements, souvent liés à l'origine du livre. Par exemple, les livres publiés par Vérard ou les livres de confrères imprimés hors de Paris (à Lyon, Rouen ou Poitiers par exemple). Le nombre d'exemplaires de Vérard est interpelant: à son domicile, Galliot conserve environ deux-cents exemplaires de 20 éditions mentionnées telles quelles comme des Vérard dans l'inventaire, auxquelles il faut ajouter les dizaines d'éditions où il est très plausible qu'il s'agisse d'une édition Vérard:

4 Triumphes de Peatracque fol. Verard [Vérard, 1514, 2° (USTC 26261)] (fol. 3v)

41 Seneque des motz dorés 8 letre bastarde [Vérard, [1491], 2° (USTC 71470 ?)] (fol. 4v)

1 Pistilles [*sic*] des epistres 4 et evangilles V grans volumes Virard [Vérard, 1504, 2° (USTC 26063)] (fol. 4v)

4 Bocace des dames fol. Verard [Vérard, 1493, 2° (USTC 38114)] (fol. 4v)

9 Le pelerinaige de l'home fol. Verard [Vérard, 1512, 2° (USTC 13279)] (fol. 4v)

1 Postiles Verard fol. imparfaicts prisés X s. une rame [Vérard 1498, 1504, 1511, 1512] (fol. 4v)

II pacqués 26 Le sejour d'honneur 4° Verard [Vérard, 1503, 1519] (fol. 5v)

2 Jardin de santé, l'un de Philippe le noyr, l'autre de Verarde l'ung faut de titre Prisez ensemble [Vérard, [1499], 2° (USTC 51000)] (fol. 6v)

1 Lucain, Suetonne et Saluste fol. Virard [Vérard, 1490, 1500 (USTC 71258, 54066)] (fol. 16r)

1 Les Gestes romaines imparfaits fol. Verard [Vérard, 1500, 1508 (USTC 71039, 26142] (fol. 16r)

1 Josephus de la Bataille judaicque grand Verrard aultre lyvre reliez [Vérard, 1492, 2° (USTC 71201)] (fol. 16r)

1 Triumphes Petrarcque fol. Virard [Vérard, 1514, 2° (USTC 26261)] (fol. 16r)

1 Ortus sanitatis en françois impression de Verard fol. [Vérard, [1499], 2° (USTC 51000)] (fol. 18r)

1 IIIIme volume Vincent historial [Vérard, 1495, 2° (USTC 47491 ?)] (fol. 22r)

1 Lancelot du Lac III volume Virard relié en boys [Vérard, 1494, 2° (USTC 71227 ?)] (fol. 44r)

1 Boccace des nobles malheureux Virard viel reliure [Vérard, 1494, [1506], 2° (USTC 79157, 38117, 8316)] (fol. 44r)

1 Second volume de la mer des hystoires Vivrard grand reliure [Vérard, 1517, 2° (USTC 52841)] (fol. 44r)

1 Terence en françois Verard reliure [Vérard, 1499, 2° (USTC 71486)] (fol. 44r)

117 Sejour d'honneur Verard 4° [Vérard, 1503, 1519, 4° (USTC 8304, 1032)] (fol. 44r)

10 Rational des divins offices fol. [Vérard, 1503, 2° (USTC 6866)] (fol. 44v)

26 Epistres saint Paul glosees [?] Verard fol. [Vérard, 1504, 1508, 2° (USTC 64770, 6536)] (fol. 44v)

6 Tresor de noblesse 4° [Vérard, 1506, 4° (USTC 8317 ?)] (fol. 44v)

1 Guion le courtoys grand Virard [Vérard, 1501, [1503], 2° (USTC 24200, 26047)] (fol. 45r)

1 Lucain Suetoine et Saluste fol. grand Virard [Vérard, 1500, 2° (USTC 54066 ?)] (fol. 45r).

L'inventaire nous offre également un éclairage quantitatif sur l'écoulement des stocks et les invendus de Galliot, dont une large partie a été entreposée dans „le grenier aux deffaitz" (fol. 41v) à côté des livres abîmés ou incomplets. Vu que les tirages moyens de l'époque oscillaient entre 800 et 1000 exemplaires,[84] les 382 exemplaires restants du *Sidrach* de 1531 (fol. 41v), mais également les 453 exemplaires du *Champion des dames* de 1530 (fol. 35r) ou les 430 exemplaires des *Ditz moraux des philosophes* de 1531 (fol. 40r) – livres faisant partie de la petite collection d'anciens textes mise au point par Galliot (cf. *supra*) – laissent penser qu'en 1561, ces textes, publiés après 1530 et dont le contenu et la forme étaient encore très ancrés dans la culture médiévale, n'eurent pas de succès ou en tout cas moins de succès que les textes médiévaux publiés avant 1530 absents de l'inventaire, comme le *Sainct Greaal* de 1516, *Ysaïe le Triste* de 1522, *Mabrien* de 1527 et dont il a vraisemblablement écoulé – ou détruit ? – tout le stock avant 1561. D'ailleurs, les textes dont Galliot gardait encore des stocks importants ne furent plus imprimés ensuite, que ce soit par Galliot ou par un autre. Malgré tout, Galliot ne ‚lâchait' pas totalement ses publications et il vendait encore dans sa boutique des *Champion des dames* (fol. 55r [dorés sur la tranche]) et des *Dictz moraux* (fol. 66v [reliés en parchemin]).

Il est également intéressant d'observer que Galliot disposait à son domicile d'un stock important de textes médiévaux qui ne figurent pas dans sa boutique et dont il est possible de penser qu'il ait choisi de ne plus les vendre. Ainsi, de deux textes d'esthétique très médiévale qui apparaissent à son domicile, mais nulle part dans la boutique: les 117 exemplaires du *Sejours d'honneur* d'Octovien de Saint-Gelais („117 Sejour d'honneur Verard 4°" fol. 44r [1503 ou 1519 USTC 8304 et 1032]) ou les cinquante *Arrets d'amour* de Martial d'Auvergne („50 Les LII arrest d'amours 8°", fol. 8v [nombreux imprimés]). Par contre, pour des textes conservés dans moins de dix

---

84 Coq, 'Les débuts' (note 10).

exemplaires, il est difficile de tirer argument de leur absence de la boutique; l'un des exemplaires a pu être récemment vendu; l'on peut penser à *Ogier le Dannoys* (4 ex. „4° Lyon" [fol. 20r]), *Galien le Restoré* (6 ex. „4° Lyon" [fol. 20r]) et *Giglan* (1 ex. „4° Lyon" [fol. 20r]), qui apparaissent d'ailleurs groupés à son domicile.

L'inventaire prise également sa boutique. On reste assez mal informé sur la configuration précise des deux étals dont il disposait au Palais. Certes, on dispose de gravures du Palais, mais elles sont plus tardives.[85] Tout ce que l'on sait, c'est que la Grande Salle du Palais, centre de l'administration de la justice, est une galerie marchande, où l'on trouvait merciers et marchands de mode à côté des étals de libraires. Dans cet environnement, les libraires trouvaient dans la masse des fonctionnaires de l'État arpentant le lieu, à la fois des producteurs et des consommateurs de texte.

En 1561, la boutique de Galliot comprenait 1358 exemplaires, parmi lesquels 351 exemplaires de textes littéraires, répartis entre 64 exemplaires pour le Moyen Âge et 299 exemplaires d'auteurs morts après 1512 (Figure 12).

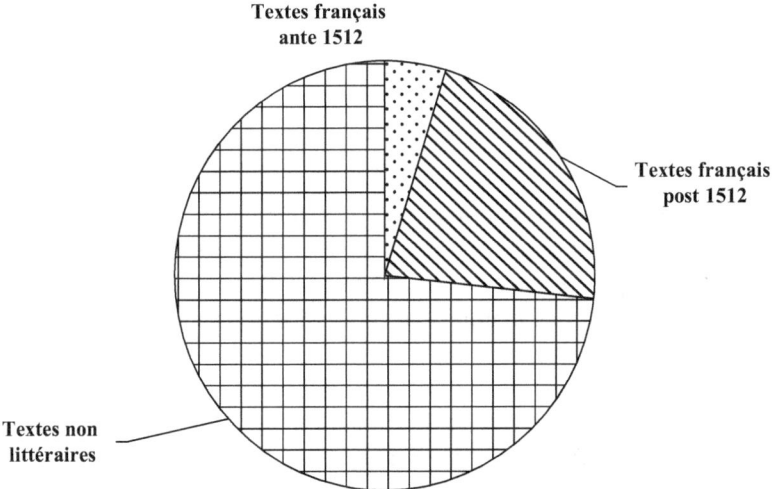

Textes français ante 1512

Textes français post 1512

Textes non littéraires

Fig. 12: – Exemplaires prisés dans la boutique de Galliot du Pré en 1561.

---

85 Androuet du Cerceau, *Les plus excellens bastimens de France* (Paris 1576); Abraham Bosse, *La Galerie du Palais* (vers 1638), en ligne (http://expositions.bnf.fr/bosse/grand/158. htm, consulté le 20 juillet 2017); Eugène Viollet-le-Duc, *Dictionnaire raisonné de l'architecture française du XIe au XVIe siècle*. Paris [1860?], s.v. „Palais"; J. Guérout, *Le Palais de la Cité à Paris des origines à 1417. Essai topographique et archéologique*, 1949 [extrait de *Paris et Ile-de-France. Mémoires* 1 (1949–1953)].

L'inventaire de la boutique classe les livres en fonction de leur format et de leur finition (doré sur tranche, relié, sur vélin, etc.); comme dans l'inventaire du domicile, l'on peut parfois observer des groupements de textes médiévaux comme la séquence *Roman de la Rose – Champion des Dames –* François Villon dans la section „Livres in 8° doré sur la tranche" (fol. 55r).

Les éditions parisiennes de textes français du Moyen Âge que Galliot vendait, mais qu'il n'avait pas lui-même publiées étaient souvent des Vérard, se présentaient donc dans des mises en forme encore anciennes, ne fût-ce que par l'emploi de lettres gothiques. L'on constate également que ces livres exogènes (une vingtaine) n'entraient pas en concurrence avec sa production, mais venaient l'étoffer soulignant qu'imprimer ne sert pas tant à se faire un nom qu'une fortune... Par exemple, Galliot vend les traductions françaises de plusieurs œuvres de Boccace,[86] alors que de Boccace, il n'a publié que les *treize elegantes demandes d'amours* (1530), qui n'est pas visible dans l'inventaire de sa boutique; il vend différentes versions des *Triomphes* de Pétrarque,[87] tandis qu'il n'a publié que ses *Remedes de l'une et l'autre fortune* (1523/1524 [22 exemplaires à son domicile, fol. 4r; aucun dans sa boutique]).

3.2 Les possesseurs

Toujours selon l'angle de la réception et de la consommation, une dernière approche de la politique éditoriale de Galliot du Pré peut être envisagée par le prisme des premiers possesseurs de ses éditions, à découvrir sur la base des mentions d'inventaires et des marques de possession présentes sur les exemplaires conservés.

Sur ce point, l'inventaire de 1561 est particulièrement intéressant, car il mentionne, à la fin, après l'inventaire de la boutique, une quinzaine de livres, „aux armes du Capitaine Poullain estans au logis":

---

86 „1 Flamette" (fol. 56v „Livres in 8° doré sur la tranche"); „1 Decameron de Boccace letre italique françois" (fol. 57v „Livres in 8° dorez sur la tranche"); „2 Decameron de Boccace françois" (fol. 60r „Livres en 16° en veau non dorez"); „2 Decameron de Boccacce françois" (fol. 65r „Livres in 4° reliez en parchemin"); „1 Philocoppe de Boccace françois" (fol. 67v „Livres in 8° reliez en velin"); „1 Bocace des nobles malheureux" (fol. 51v „Grandz vellins reliez en veau").

87 "1 Triumphes de Petrarcque françois" (fol. 50r, „Grandz vellins reliez en veau" [Vérard, 1514 ?]); "1 Triumphes de Petracque in 16° françois" (fol. 60r, „Livres en 16° en veau non dorez" [de Marnef, 1545 ou Groulleau 1554 ?]); „1 Triumphes de Petrarcque françois" (fol. 66v, „Livres in 16° reliez en parchemin" [de Marnef, 1545 ou Groulleau 1554 ?]).

Livres aux armes du capitaine Poullain estans au logis

1	Miroir de redemption humaine
1	Les regnardz traversans
1	Les 3ᵉ et 5ᵉ d'Amadis de Gaulle in folio[88]
1	Jardin de plaisance
1	Pelerinage de l'homme relié avec celuy de l'ame[89]
1	Espinette du jeune prince
1	Heures en ryme françoise
1	La nef des foz[90]
1	Rethoricque de Fabri
1	Sommaire historial / La sallade et Guy de Warwich reliez ensemble [70v]
1	Les cent histoires de Troyes[91]
1	Romant de la Roze en prose
1	Huon de Bordeaux
1	Verger d'honneur [Octovien de Saint-Gelais]
1	Petrarcque des Remedes de Fortune [trad. par Jean Daudin, Galliot du Pré, 1523]
1	Epistres moralles[92]
1	Poesie de Charles de Sainte Marche (fol. 70r–v).

On peut identifier le "capitaine Poullain" à Antoine Escalin des Aimars (1498–1578), dit le capitaine "Paulin" ou "Polin" (ci-après "Polin"), baron de La Garde-Adhémar (Tricastin puis Drôme), diplomate et ambassadeur au service de François Iᵉʳ, qui le chargea de missions, notamment en Italie et en Turquie.[93]

---

88 „1 Amadis en plus de XII volumes fol." (domicile, fol. 22r), „Quatre livres de Amadis fol." (domicile, fol. 25r).

89 „9 Le pelerinaige de l'homme" (domicile, fol. 4v); „1 Le pellerin de la vye humaine fol." (domicile, fol. 6r); „3 pacquez Le pelerinaige de l'homme fol." (domicile, fol. 44v).

90 "7 Nef des folz Lion 4°" (domicile, fol. 11r); "Nef des folz" (boutique, fol. 52v, „Livres in 4° reliez en veau").

91 "1 Recueil des histoires de Troye Lyon 4°" (domicile, fol. 15r); "7 Recueil des histoires de Troye Lyon 4°" (domicile, fol. 16v); "1 Recueil des histoires de Troye" (boutique, fol. 52r, „Livres in 4° reliez en veau").

92 "1 Epistres moralles fol." (domicile, fol. 22r); "2 Epistres morales Poictiers" (domicile, fol. 49r, „Grandz vellins reliez en veau").

93 Adrien Richer, *Vies de Jacques Cassard et du capitaine Paulin*. Avignon 1817; François de la Chenaye-Desbois, *Dictionnaire de la noblesse contenant les généalogies, l'histoire (...)*, t. VI, 2ᵉ éd., Paris 1773, *s.v*; Yann Bouvier, 'Antoine Escalin des Aimars (1498?–1578) de la Garde-Adhémar au siège de Nice: le parcours d'un ambassadeur de François Iᵉʳ'. In: *Recherches régionales. Alpes-Maritimes et contrées limitrophes* 48 (2007), p. 73–100.

Il s'agit soit d'un stock de livres, commandé par Polin et dont Galliot fournissait les exemplaires avec des reliures personnalisées; cependant, seul un petit nombre de ces livres apparaissent, par ailleurs, au domicile de Galliot ou dans sa boutique. Soit il s'agit d'un stock de livres appartenant au capitaine Polin et qui aurait été mis en dépôt chez Galliot, peut-être à la suite de sa destitution en 1557. La moitié du stock de livres destinés ou appartenant à Polin est constituée de textes médiévaux.

Pour étoffer cette approche, dans le cas précis de Galliot du Pré, il faudrait envisager des campagnes systématiques de consultation de l'ensemble des exemplaires conservés de chaque édition de Galliot. Par exemple, on peut noter que l'exemplaire de la BnF de l'*Histoire du sainct Greaal* de 1516 a été possédé par Jean Ballesdens.[94] Celui-ci était avocat au Parlement de Paris au deuxième tiers du dix-septième siècle.[95] Certes, Ballesdens n'est pas l'acheteur et le premier possesseur du livre, mais cela constitue un indice d'un réseau de consommation dans les milieux de robe de la Cité, que Galliot a ciblé dans sa politique éditoriale.

Il faudrait également approfondir l'étude des destinataires des vélins de Galliot du Pré, dont l'identification de certains pourrait conforter son désir de toucher, également, et comme l'avait fait Vérard, un public nobiliaire. L'on notera ici l'exemplaire enluminé, sur vélin, du *Perceforest* dont l'identité du premier propriétaire ne fait pas l'unanimité de la critique: Gilles Roussineau l'attribuant à François Ier lui-même, le catalogue des imprimés de la bibliothèque du Château de Chantilly évoquant la présence des „armes de Chateaubriand".[96]

4 Conclusion

Par l'étude des livres publiés et de la manière dont ils sont publiés puis vendus, il est possible de dégager une politique éditoriale. Cependant, pour valider et étayer certaines de nos observations et pour pouvoir juger de la spécificité de la

---

94 Paris, BnF, Rés Y² 23.

95 Sur cet individu, Jean-Marc Chatelain, 'Les Livres dans les cabinets d'amateurs français du XVIIe siècle'. In: *La Licorne et le bézoard. Une histoire des cabinets de curiosités.* Éd. par Dominique Moncond'huy. Poitiers 2013, p. 348–357.

96 Chantilly, BC, XII H 19–24. Chantilly, BC, Page de présentation des *Livres imprimés rares du Cabinet du duc d'Aumale* (http://www.bibliotheque-conde.fr/expo/expo_ed_imprimes_rares.htm, consulté le 20 juillet 2017); *Chantilly. Le cabinet des livres. Imprimés.* Paris 1905, p. 305; *Perceforest. Quatrième partie.* Éd. par Gilles Roussineau. Paris, Genève 1987 (Textes littéraires français 343), p. XXXIV.

politique de Galliot, il serait nécessaire de disposer d'une approche quantitative et comparative plus large. Une telle approche comparative, tant en synchronie avec les libraires parisiens contemporains qu'en diachronie avec ceux qui ont précédé Galliot du Pré, permettrait de pouvoir juger de cette politique et d'évaluer ce qui relève de *topos* éditoriaux, de stratégies plus précises ainsi que de logiques de mise en page, par exemple adaptées au contenu ou au type de contenu.

Cette étude sur la politique éditoriale d'un libraire dont la publication d'œuvres médiévales reste somme toute marginale a permis de dégager plusieurs indices qui tendent à confirmer la conscience de l'émergence, à la fin des 1520, d'un nouveau paradigme dans la production de la littérature et de sa consommation. À ce sujet, il est indéniable que Galliot suit un mouvement de rénovation de la langue française et qu'il participe du programme culturel mis en place par François Ier; les prologues allographes des livres qu'il publie insistent tant sur le processus philologique de révision et de correction du livre (voulant rétablir certains textes à „leur naturel",[97] „à leur vraye intelligence",[98] „en leur entier"[99]) que sur le processus de modernisation et d'ornementation ou d'actualisation auquel il soumet les textes anciens.

Cependant, il ne faut pas oublier que Galliot reste un marchand qui cherche à vendre des produits qui se vendent: dans certains cas, en présentant voire en accentuant le caractère ancien et renommé de l'auteur; dans d'autres, en gommant l'historicité du texte et en le présentant comme une œuvre tout à fait contemporaine. Il faut donc nuancer la vision d'un Galliot sensible et soucieux de diffuser la littérature médiévale. Ce que nous voulions démontrer.

Bibliographie

Albert, Sophie, 'Recycler Meliadus: la réception de l'identité héroïque dans l'imprimé *Meliadus de Leonnoys* (1528)'. In: *Cahiers de recherches médiévales et humanistes* 24 (2012), p. 487–503 (aussi en ligne: URL: http://crm.revues.org/12961; DOI: 10.4000/crm.12961, consulté le 20 juillet 2017).

---

97 „Maistre Pierre Pathelin restitué à son naturel" (*Farce de Maistre Pierre Pathelin*, 1532, page de titre, Paris, BnF, Rés. Y[e] 1284).

98 „reveues, corrigees et restituees à leur vraye intelligence" (François Villon, *Oeuvres*, éd. Clément Marot, 1533, privilège, Paris, BnF, Rés. Y[e] 1297); voir aussi: „pour laquelle chose restituer en meilleur estat et plus expediente forme pour l'intelligence des lecteurs et auditeurs" (*Le Roman de la Rose*, 1526, prologue allographe *Preambule du livre*, Munich, BSB, 2° P.O. gall. 24 d, fol. ^{2} v°).

99 „reveues et remises en leur entier par Clement Marot" (François Villon, *Oeuvres*, éd. par Cl. Marot, 1533, titre).

Amstrong, Adrian, *Technique and technology. Script, Print, and Poetics in France 1470–1550*. Oxford 2000 (*Oxford Modern Languages and Literature Monographs*).

Balsamo, Jean, 'La collection des anciens poètes français de Galliot du Pré (1528–1533)'. In: *L'analisi linguistica e letteraria* 8 (2000), p. 179–194.

Balsamo, Jean, 'La première génération des traducteurs de l'italien en français (1500–1535)'. In: *Passeurs de textes II. Gens du livre et gens de lettres à la Renaissance*. Éd. par Chiara Lastraioli et al. Tours 2014, p. 15–31.

Bianciotto, Gabriel, 'Le roman d'*Isaïe le Triste*: les imprimés'. In: *Ensi firent li ancessor. Mélanges de philologie médiévale offerts à Marc-René Jung*. Éd. par Luciano Rossi, Christine Jacob-Hugon et Ursula Bähler. Alessandria 1996, p. 623–639.

Bossuat, Robert, 'Vasque de Lucène, traducteur de Quinte-Curce (1468)'. In: *Bibliothèque d'Humanisme et Renaissance* 8 (1946), p. 197–245.

Bouvier, Yann, 'Antoine Escalin des Aimars (1498?–1578) de la Garde-Adhémar au siège de Nice: le parcours d'un ambassadeur de François Ier'. In: *Recherches régionales. Alpes-Maritimes et contrées limitrophes* 48 (2007), p. 73–100.

Bratu, Cristian, 'Denis Sauvage: the Editing of Medieval Chronicles in Sixteenth-century France'. In: *Studies in Medieval and Renaissance History*, 3rd Series, 7 (2010), p. 255–278.

Brown, Cynthia J., *Poets, patrons, and Printers. Crisis of Authority in Late Medieval France*. London 1995.

Brun, Robert, '*La Mer des histoires* de Pierre Le Rouge offerte à Charles VIII'. In: *Humanisme actif. Mélanges d'art et de littérature offerts à Julien Cain*. Vol. 2 Paris 1968, p. 191–197

Cappello, Sergio, 'Les éditions de romans de Jean II Trepperel'. In: *Raconter en prose. XIVe-XVIe siècle*. Éd. par Paola Cifarelli, Maria Colombo Timelli, Matteo Milani et Anne Schoysman. Paris 2017, p. 121–145.

Cerquiglini-Toulet, Jacqueline, 'Clément Marot et la critique littéraire et textuelle: du bien renommé au mal imprimé Villon'. In: *Clément Marot "prince des poètes françois", 1496–1996. Actes du Colloque international de Cahors en Quercy, 21–25 mai 1996*. Éd. par Gérard Defaux et Michel Simonin. Paris 1997 (Colloques, congrès et conférences sur la Renaissance 8), p. 157–164.

Chantilly. Le cabinet des livres. Imprimés. Paris 1905.

Charon-Parent, Annie, *Les métiers du livre à Paris au XVIe siècle (1535–1560)*. Genève 1974 (EPHE. Sciences historiques et philologiques. Histoire et civilisation du livre 6).

Charon-Parent, Annie, 'Aspects de la politique éditoriale de Galliot Du Pré'. In: *Le Livre dans l'Europe de la Renaissance. Actes du XXVIIIe Colloque international d'études humanistes de Tours [juillet 1985]*. Éd. par Pierre Aquilon et Henri-Jean Martin. Paris 1988, p. 54–67.

Charon-Parent, Annie, 'Du Pré, Galliot'. In: *Dictionnaire encyclopédique du livre*. Éd. par Pascal Fouché, Daniel Péchoin, Philippe Schuwer et al. T. 1. Paris 2002, p. 836–837.

Charon, Annie, Claire Lesage et Ève Netchine, *Le livre entre le commerce et l'histoire des idées. Les catalogues de libraires (XVe – XIXe siècle)*. Paris 2001.

Chartier, Roger (éd.), *Les usages de l'imprimé, 15e-19e siècle*. Paris 1987.

Chartier, Roger, *La main de l'auteur et l'esprit de l'imprimeur: XVIe-XVIIIe siècle*. Paris 2015.

Chatelain, Jean-Marc, 'Les Livres dans les cabinets d'amateurs français du XVIIe siècle'. In: *La Licorne et le bézoard. Une histoire des cabinets de curiosités*. Éd. par Dominique Moncond'huy. Poitiers 2013, p. 348–357.

Chavy, Paul, 'Les Traductions Humanistes de Claude de Seyssel'. In: *L'humanisme français au début de la Renaissance. Colloque international de Tours*. Éd. par André Stegman. Paris 1973, p. 361–376.

Chavy, Paul, 'Les traductions humanistes au début de la Renaissance française: traductions médiévales, traductions modernes'. In: *Canadian Review of Comparative Literature* 1981, p. 284–306.

Chenaye-Desbois, François de la, *Dictionnaire de la noblesse contenant les généalogies, l'histoire [. . .]*. T. VI, 2e éd. Paris 1773.

Chiron, Pierre, 'L'édition des *Œuvres* de Villon annotée par Clément Marot, ou comment l'autorité vient au texte'. In: *Littératures classiques* 64 (2007), *La note d'autorité. Aperçus historiques (XVIe-XVIIIe s.)*, p. 33–51.

Cockshaw, Pierre et Christiane Van den Bergen-Pantens, *Les Chroniques de Hainaut ou les Ambitions d'un Prince Bourguignon*. Bruxelles 2000.

Colombo Timelli, Maria, 'La *Tresplaisante et recreative hystoire du trespreulx et vaillant chevallier Perceval le Galloys. . .* (1530), mise en prose tardive du "cycle" du Graal'. In: *Le Moyen Français* 64 (2009), p. 13–54.

Colombo Timelli, Maria, '*Perceval le Galloys* (1530), première "traduction" moderne du cycle du Graal'. In: *'Un paysage choisi'. Mélanges de linguistique française offerts à Leo Schena*. Éd. par Giovanna Bellati et Leo Schena. Turin, Paris 2007, p. 119–128.

Connat, Madeleine, 'Galliot Dupré et sa famille: documents inédits'. In: *Bibliothèque d'Humanisme et Renaissance* 4 (1944), p. 427–435.

Coq, Dominique, 'Les débuts de l'édition en langue vulgaire en France. Publics et politiques éditoriales'. In: *Gutenberg-Jahrbuch* (1982), p. 59–72.

Coq, Dominique, 'Les incunables: textes anciens, textes nouveaux'. In: *Histoire de l'édition française. Tome 1. Le livre conquérant. Du Moyen Âge au milieu du XVIIe siècle*. Éd. par Martin Henri-Jean, Chartier Roger et Vivet Jean-Pierre. Paris 1983, p. 203–227.

Coq, Dominique, 'Les politiques éditoriales des premiers imprimeurs parisiens et lyonnais (1470–1485)'. In: *Legenda aurea: sept siècles de diffusion*. Éd. par Brenda Dunn-Lardeau. Montréal 1986.

Cornilliat, François, '*Or ne mens'. Couleurs de l'éloge et du blâme chez les 'Grands Rhétoriqueurs'*. Paris 1994.

Crescenzo, Roberto, 'Louis Le Roy et le statut de traducteur des Anciens au XVIe siècle'. In: *Travaux de literature* 20 (2007), p. 215–227.

Croizy-Naquet, Catherine, *Écrire l'histoire romaine au début du XIIIe siècle. L'Histoire ancienne et les Faits des Romains*. Paris 1999.

Defaux, Gérard, *Le Poète en son jardin. Étude sur Clément Marot et 'L'Adolescence clémentine'*. Paris 1996.

Delalain, Paul, *Notice sur Galliot du Pré, libraire parisien de 1512 à 1560*. Paris 1890.

Delalain, Paul, *Notice complémentaire sur Galliot du Pré, libraire parisien de 1512 à 1560*. Paris 1891.

Delisle, Léopold, 'Anciennes traductions françaises du traité de Pétrarque sur les remèdes de l'une et l'autre fortune'. In: *Notices et extraits des manuscrits de la Bibliothèque nationale et autres bibliothèques* 34 (1891), p. 273–304.

Duché-Gavet, Véronique, 'Le statut du traducteur (1526–1554)'. In: *Travaux de littérature 20 (2007), Le statut littéraire de l'écrivain*. Éd. par Lise Sabourin, p. 202–214.

Dufournet, Jean, 'Denis Sauvage et Commynes. La première édition des *Mémoires'*. In: *Convergences médiévales. Épopée, lyrique, roman. Mélanges offerts à Madeleine Tyssens*. Éd. par Nadine Henrard, Paola Moreno et Martine Thiry-Stassin. Bruxelles 2001 (Bibliothèque du Moyen Âge 19), p. 161–171.

Dupré La Tour, Laurence, 'La traduction manuscrite du *Compendium Historial* d'Henri Romain'. In: *Revue d'histoire des textes* 5 (1977), p. 137–168.

Frappier, Jean, 'Sur le Perceval en prose de 1530'. In: *Fin du Moyen Âge et Renaissance. Mélanges de Philologie française offerts à Robert Guiette*. Anvers 1961, p. 233–247.

Frieden, Philippe, 'Le *Roman de la Rose*, de l'édition aux manuscrits'. In: *Perspectives médiévales* [en ligne] 34 (2012) (URL: http://peme.revues.org/290; DOI: 10.4000/peme.290, consulté le 20 juillet 2017).

Genette, Gérard, *Seuils*. Paris 1987 (Poétique).

Gilmont, Jean-François et Alexandre Vanautgaerden (éd.), *La page de titre à la Renaissance*. Turnhout 2008.

Guérout, J., *Le Palais de la Cité à Paris des origines à 1417. Essai topographique et archéologique*. Paris 1949 [extrait de *Paris et Ile-de-France. Mémoires* 1 (1949–1953)].

Guillerm, Luce, *Sujet de l'écriture et traduction autour de 1540*. U. de Lille III 1988 (thèse de doctorat inédite).

Harf-Lancner, Laurence et Emmanuel Baumgartner, *Seuils de l'œuvre dans le texte médiéval*. Paris 2002.

Hériché Pradeau, Sandrine, 'La traduction du *De remediis utriusque fortunae* de Pétrarque par Jean Daudin: la rhétorique et la contrariété'. In: *Traduire au XIVe siècle. Évrart de Conty et la vie intellectuelle à la cour de Charles V*. Éd. par Joëlle Ducos et Michèle Goyens. Paris 2015, p. 267–292.

Lazard, Madeleine, 'Clément Marot éditeur et lecteur de Villon'. In: *Cahiers de l'Association internationale des études françaises* 32 (1980), p. 7–20.

Lefèvre, Martine, 'La production imprimée: lectures et postérité du *Roman de la rose*'. In: *Le Roman de la rose. L'art d'aimer au Moyen Âge*. Éd. par Nathalie Coilly et Marie-Hélène Tesnière. Paris 2014, p. 157–161.

Lesage, Claire, Ève Netchine et Véronique Sarrazin, *Catalogues de libraires 1473–1810*. Paris 2006.

Lestringant, Frank, *Clément Marot, de 'L'Adolescence clémentine' à 'L'Enfer'*. Padova 1998.

Mann, Nicholas. 'La fortune de Pétrarque en France. Recherches sur le *De remediis*'. In: *Studi francesi* 37 (1969), p. 1–15.

Matoré, Georges, 'Le temps au XVIe siècle'. In: *L'Information grammaticale* 32 (1987), p. 3–8.

McFadden Smith, Margaret, *The Title Page. Its Early Development 1460–1510*. London 2000.

McKenzie, Donald F., *Bibliography and the Sociology of Texts*. Cambridge 1999.

La Mer des hystoires, traduction française du 'Rudimentum noviciorum'. Éd. par Nelly Sciardis. Paris 2004.

Modernités 5 (1994). *Ce que modernité veut dire*. Éd. par Yves Vadé.

Mombello, Gianni, 'Claude de Seyssel: un esprit modéré au service de l'expansion française'. In: *Culture et pouvoir au temps de l'Humanisme et de la Renaissance*. Éd. par Louis Terreaux. Genève 1978, p. 71–122.

Morisse, Gérard, 'Pour une approche de l'activité de Sébastien Gryphe, libraire-imprimeur lyonnais du XVIe siècle'. In: *Revue française d'histoire du livre* 126–127 (2005–2006), p. 13–68.

Mounier, Pascale, *Le roman humaniste. Un genre novateur français (1532–1564)*. Paris 2007.

Le Moyen Français 69 (2011), *Antoine Vérard*. Éd. par Paola Cifarelli, Maria Colombo Timelli et Anne Schoysman.

Nichols, Stephen G., 'Marot, Villon et le *Roman de la Rose*. A Study in the Language of Creation and Re-creation'. In: *Studies in Philology* 63 (1966), p. 141–142.

Ornato, Ezio, 'L'évaluation quantitative des stratégies éditoriales. Problèmes méthodologiques et techniques'. In: *Les stratégies éditoriales à l'époque de l'incunable: le cas des anciens Pays-Bas*. Éd. par Chiara Ruzzier, Xavier Hermand et Ezio Ornato. Turnhout 2012, p. 133–203.

Ouvry-Vial, Brigitte et Anne Réach-Ngô (éd.). *L'acte éditorial. Publier à la Renaissance et aujourd'hui*. Paris 2010 (Études et essais sur la Renaissance 89).

Perceforest. Quatrième partie. Éd. par Gilles Roussineau. Paris, Genève 1987 (Textes littéraires français 343).

Pettegree, Andrew et al. (éd.), *French Vernacular Books. Books Published in the French Language before 1601*. Leiden 2007.

Pittion, Jean-Paul, *Le livre à la Renaissance. Introduction à la bibliographie historique et matérielle*. Turnhout 2013 (Nugae humanisticae sub signo Erasmi 15).

Réach-Ngô, Anne, 'L'écriture éditoriale à la Renaissance. Pour une herméneutique de l'imprimé'. In: *Communication et Langages* 154 (2007), p. 41–57.

Réach-Ngô, Anne, 'La mise en recueil des narrations à la Renaissance ou l'art de la bibliothèque portative'. In: *L'Acte éditorial. Publier à la Renaissance*. Éd. par Brigitte Ouvry-Vial et Anne Réach-Ngô. Paris 2010 (Études et essais sur la Renaissance 89 / Pratiques éditoriales 1), p. 125–148.

Réach-Ngô, Anne, 'Instances et stratégies éditoriales à la Renaissance: de la fabrique du livre à la fabrication de l'auteur'. In: *La fabrication de l'auteur*. Éd. par Marie-Pier Luneau et Josée Vincent (dir.). Québec 2010, p. 333–362.

Réach-Ngô, Anne (éd.), *Créations d'atelier. L'éditeur et la fabrique de l'œuvre*. Paris 2014.

Réach-Ngô, Anne, 'Performance et paratextes éditoriaux à la Renaissance'. *Textes en performance*. Éd. par Ambroise Barras et Éric Eigenmann. Genève 2006, p. 183–197.

Réach-Ngô, Anne, *L'Écriture éditoriale à la Renaissance. Genèses et promotion du récit sentimental français (1530–1560)*. Genève 2013.

Le recueil des repues franches de maistre François Villon et de ses compagnons. Éd. par Jelle Koopmans et Paul Verhuyck. Genève 1995 (Textes littéraires français 455).

Regalado, Nancy, 'Gathering the Works: The "Œuvres de Villon" and the Intergeneric Passage of the Medieval French Lyric into Single-Author Collections'. In: *L'Esprit créateur* 33 (1993), p. 87–100.

Richer, Adrien, *Vies de Jacques Cassard et du capitaine Paulin*. Avignon 1817.

Rigolot, François, 'Clément Marot et l'émergence de la conscience littéraire à la Renaissance'. In: *La Génération Marot. Poètes français et néo-latins (1510–1550), Actes du Colloque international de Baltimore, 5–7 décembre 1996*. Éd. par Gérard Defaux. Paris 1997, p. 21–34.

Runnalls, Graham, 'La vie, la mort et les livres de l'imprimeur-libraire parisien Jean Janot d'après son inventaire après décès (17 février 1522 n. st.)'. In: *Revue belge de philologie et d'histoire* 78 (2000), p. 797–851.

Ruzzier, Chiara, Xavier Hermand et Ezio Ornato, *Les stratégies éditoriales à l'époque de l'incunable: le cas des anciens Pays-Bas*. Turnhout 2012.

Rychner, Jean, 'Observations sur les textes incunables du *Testament* de Villon. I. L'édition de Jean Dupré, Lyon, vers 1490'. In: *Mélanges offerts à Félix Lecoy. Études de langue et de littérature du Moyen Âge offertes à Félix Lecoy par ses collègues, ses élèves et ses amis*. Paris 1973, p. 529–539.

Rychner, Jean, 'Observations sur les textes incunables du *Testament* de Villon. II. L'édition de Germain Bineaut, Paris, 1490'. In: *Mélanges de linguistique et de philologie et littérature médiévales offerts à Monsieur Paul Imbs*. Éd. par Robert Martin et Georges Straka. Strasbourg 1973 (Travaux de linguistique et de littérature 11/1), p. 615–620.

Sansy, Danièle, 'Texte et image dans les incunables français'. In: *Médiévales* 22–23 (1992), p. 48–70.

Schuwer, Philippe, *Traité pratique d'édition*. Paris 1997.

Schuwer, Philippe, 'Politique éditoriale'. In: *Dictionnaire encyclopédique du livre*. Éd. par Pascal Fouché, Daniel Péchoin, Philippe Schuwer et al. T. 3. Paris 2011, p. 303–304.

Schwarz, Theodor, *Über den Verfasser und die Quellen des 'Rudimentum novitiorum'*. Rostock 1888.

Servet, Pierre, 'D'un Perceval l'autre. La mise en prose du *Conte du Graal* (1530)'. In: *L'œuvre de Chrétien de Troyes dans la littérature française – Réminiscences, résurgences et réécritures*. Éd. par Claude Lachet. Lyon 1997, p. 197–210.

Simonin, Michel, 'Peut-on parler de politique éditoriale au xvıᵉ siècle? Le cas de Vincent Sertenas, libraire du Palais'. In: *Le Livre dans l'Europe de la Renaissance. Actes du XXIIIᵉ colloque international d'Études humanistes de Tours*. Éd. par Pierre Aquilon et Henri-Jean Martin. Paris 1988, p. 264–281.

Spiegel, Gabrielle, *Romancing the Past. The Rise of Vernacular Prose Historiography in Thirteenth-Century France*. Berkeley 1993.

Taylor, Jane H.M., *Rewriting Arthurian Romance in Renaissance France. From Manuscript to Printed Book*. Woodbridge 2014.

Thiry, Claude, 'Marot, éditeur de Villon'. In: *Villon entre mythe et poésie. Actes du colloque organisé les 15, 16 et 17 décembre 2006 à la Bibliothèque historique de la Ville de Paris*. Éd. par Jean Dufournet et Marcel Faure. Paris 2011 (Colloques, congrès et conférences sur le Moyen Âge 9), p. 281–290.

Thorel, Mathilde, 'Pratiques de l'intitulation au XVIᵉ siècle'. In: *L'Acte éditorial. Publier à la Renaissance*. Éd. par Brigitte Ouvry-Vial et Anne Réach-Ngô. Paris 2010 (Études et essais sur la Renaissance 89 / Pratiques éditoriales 1), p. 165–183.

Tilley, Arthur, 'A Paris Bookseller – Galliot du Pré'. In: *Studies in the French Renaissance*. Cambridge 1922, p. 168–218.

Tran, Trung, 'Le texte illustré au xvıᵉ siècle, stratégie éditoriale ou création littéraire?'. In: *L'acte éditorial. Publier à la Renaissance et aujourd'hui*. Éd. Brigitte Ouvry-Vial et Anne Réach-Ngô. Paris 2010 (Études et essais sur la Renaissance 89), p. 59–88.

Van Hemelryck, Tania, 'Du *Perceforest* manuscrit à l'imprimé de Galliot du Pré (1528). Un long fleuve tranquille?'. In: *Le Roman français dans les premiers imprimés*. Éd. par Anne Schoysman. Paris 2016 (Rencontres 147 / Civilisation médiévale 17), p. 159–174.

Van Hemelryck, Tania, 'La ou les traductions françaises des *Annales historie illustrium principum Hanonie* de Jacques de Guise? L'éclairage de la tradition manuscrite'. In: *Le Moyen Français*, 51–52–53 (2003), *Traduction, dérimation, compilation. La phraséologie*. Éd. par Giuseppe Di Stefano et Rose M. Bidler, p. 613–625.

Van Hoorebeeck, Céline, *Livres et lectures des fonctionnaires des ducs de Bourgogne (ca 1420–1520)*. Turnhout 2014 (Texte, Codex et Contexte 16).

Veyrin-Forrer, Jeanne, 'Antoine Augereau, graveur de lettres, imprimeur et libraire parisien (1534)'. In: *La lettre et le texte. Trente années de recherches sur l'histoire du livre*. Éd. par Jeanne Veyrin-Forrer. Paris 1987, p. 3–50.

Vial, Jean, 'Formules publicitaires dans les premiers livres français'. In: *1500–1900. Gutenberg-Jahrbuch* 1958, p. 149–154.

Villon, François, *Testament / Lais / Poésies diverses*. Éd. par Jean Rychner et Albert Henry, Genève 1974–1977 (Textes littéraires français 207, 208, 239, 240).

Viollet-le-Duc, Eugène, *Dictionnaire raisonné de l'architecture française du XI*e *au XVI*e *siècle.* Paris [1860?].

Wahlen, Barbara, *L'écriture à rebours. Le Roman de Meliadus du XIII*e *au XVIII*e *siècle.* Genève 2010 (Publications romanes et françaises 252).

Weinberg, Bernard, 'Guillaume Michel dit de Tours. The Editor of the 1526 *Roman de la Rose*'. In: *Bibliothèque d'Humanisme et Renaissance* 11 (1949), p. 72–85.

Wijsman, Hanno, *Luxury Bound. Illustrated Manuscripts Production and Noble and Princely Book Ownership in the Burgundian Netherlands (1400–1550)*. Turnhout 2010 (Burgundica 16).

Winn, Mary B., *Anthoine Vérard, Parisian Publisher (1485–1512). Prologues, Poems and Presentations*. Genève 1997 (Travaux d'Humanisme et Renaissance 313).

Wright, Edith A., '*La Mer des Hystoires*, Paris 1488'. In: *Boston Public Library* 11 (1959), p. 59–74.

II Publication Strategies

Julia Frick

Visual Narrative: The *Aeneid* Woodcuts from Sebastian Brant's Edition of Virgil (Strasbourg 1502) in Thomas Murner's Translation of the *Aeneid* (Strasbourg 1515)

Abstracts: Thomas Murner's translation of Virgil's *Aeneid* into German (Strasbourg: Johann Grüninger 1515) is accompanied by a selection of 112 of the 143 *Aeneid* woodcuts from the complete edition of Virgil's works edited by Sebastian Brant. The latter had been published by Johann Grüninger in Strasbourg in 1502, thirteen years before Murner's translation. Research has demonstrated that Brant was involved in the production of the woodcuts as a "concepteur": the extremely detailed interpretation of the text by means of images implies a thorough knowledge of Virgil's text, while the resulting visual narrative, in addition to the textual understanding supplied by the Latin writing, creates a striking and absorbing display. It can be demonstrated that Thomas Murner knew Brant's edition and this raises the question of whether Murner was influenced by the familiar woodcuts in his translation of the *Aeneid*. He, just like Brant, attributed great value not only to the illustrative and mnemonic function of the image, but also to the close relationship between the text and the image. Indeed, the influence of the *Aeneid* illustrations on Murner's understanding of the Latin text can be observed in some places in his translation, demonstrating a dual translation process: the transposition of the Latin text into a pictorial form, which was then translated back into the German language.

Thomas Murner übersetzte als erster Vergils *Aeneis* in die deutsche Sprache (Straßburg: Johann Grüninger 1515). Seiner Übersetzung ist eine Auswahl von 112 der 143 *Aeneis*-Holzschnitte beigegeben, die der von Sebastian Brant betreuten Gesamtausgabe der Werke Vergils entstammen. Johann Grüninger hatte sie im Jahr 1502, 13 Jahre vor Murners Übersetzung, in Straßburg verlegt. Die Forschung hat herausgearbeitet, dass Brant bei der Herstellung der Holzschnitte als 'Concepteur' tätig war: Die äußerst detailreiche Umsetzung des Textes ins Bild setzt eine intensive Kenntnis des vergilischen Textes voraus und eröffnet als visuelles Narrativ neben dem sich aus der lateinischen Schriftlichkeit speisenden Textverständnis eine ostentative Aufnahme durch das visuelle Medium. Thomas Murner hat Brants Ausgabe nachweislich gekannt, was die Frage aufwirft, ob Murner sich bei seiner *Aeneis*-Übersetzung von den ihm bekannten Holzschnitten hat beeinflussen lassen, maß er doch selbst ebenso wie Brant nicht nur der illustrativen und memorativen Funktion des Bildes, sondern auch dem engen Bezug von Text und Bild großen Wert bei. Tatsächlich ist der Einfluss der *Aeneis*-Illustrationen auf das Verständnis des lateinischen Textes an einigen Stellen in Murners Übersetzung zu beobachten, was den Vorgang eines doppelten Übersetzens dokumentiert: das Überführen des lateinischen Textwortes in eine picturale Formel, die wiederum in die deutsche Sprache rückübersetzt wird.

Julia Frick, University of Zurich

Thomas Murner (1475–1537) was the first to translate Virgil's *Aeneid*, a key poetic text in the world of Western education, into German.[1] In line with the printing tradition of the *Aeneid*, the Supplement, written by the Italian Humanist Maffeo Vegio (1407–1458) in Pavia in 1428, is appended to Murner's translation of Virgil's twelve books. It has been considered an integral part of Virgil editions since its *editio princeps* (Venice: Adam von Ambergau, 1471)[2]; known as the 13th book, its content positions the Supplement at the end of the *Aeneid* and employs the prophecies given in the epic to drive the plot forward to a conclusion allegedly intended by Virgil.[3]

Furthermore, the first printed edition of 1515 adds a selection of 112 of the 143 *Aeneid* woodcuts to the German text, all derived from Sebastian Brant's (1457–1521) major complete edition of Virgil's work; they had already appeared in an identical fashion in Strasbourg in Johann Grüninger's work thirteen years prior to Murner's translation.[4] The reuse of the woodcuts, which, for economic reasons, was common and natural at the time, has remarkable historical and cultural significance in this particular instance.

---

1 [Thomas Murner,] *Vergilij maronis dryzehen Aeneadischen Bücher von Troianischer zerstörung / vnd vffgang des Römischen Reichs. durch doctor Murner vertütst.* Strasbourg: Johann Grüninger, 1515 (VD16 V 1426). An edition with an introductory analysis has been compiled by this author at the Albert-Ludwigs-University of Freiburg in the context of a DFG project (supervisor: Prof. Nikolaus Henkel). See Julia Frick, *Thomas Murners 'Aeneis'-Übersetzung. (Straßburg 1515). Lateinisch-deutsche Edition und Untersuchungen.* Diss. Freiburg i. Br. 2016 (the publication is planned for 2019). For general information on Murner, see Franz Josef Worstbrock, 'Murner, Thomas'. In: *Deutscher Humanismus 1480–1520. Verfasserlexikon.* Ed. Franz Josef Worstbrock. Vol. 2. Berlin, New York 2013, cols. 300–368.

2 It has been evidenced as far back as the middle of the sixteenth century and earlier in printed editions of Virgil. See *Das Aeneissupplement des Maffeo Vegio.* Ed. and transl. by Bernd Schneider. Weinhein 1985, p. 13f.; Cf. *Maffeo Vegio. Short Epics.* Ed. by Michael C. J. Putnam. Cambridge 2004 (The I Tatti Renaissance Library 15).

3 The three significant prophecies in the *Aeneid* also have a metatextual function as they hand the reader a key to understanding the poetry. In addition to Jupiter's prophecy in the first book (*Aen.* 1.257–296), the Augustan presence is identified as the aim of Roman history in the prediction of the sixth book (*Aen.* 6.791–795; 881–853) and in the description of the shield in the eighth book (*Aen.* 8.626–729). Cf. Ernst A. Schmidt, 'Vergils Aeneis als augusteische Dichtung'. In: *Von Göttern und Menschen erzählen. Formkonstanten und Funktionswandel vormoderner Epik.* Ed. by Jörg Rüpke. Stuttgart 2001 (Potsdamer altertumswissenschaftliche Beiträge 4), p. 89.

4 *Publij Virgilij Maronis opera cum quinque vulgatis commentariis expolitissimisque figuris atque imaginibus nuper per Sebastianum Brant superadditis exactissimeque reuisis atque elimatis.* Strasbourg: Johann Grüninger, 1502 (VD16 V 1332).

As Werner Suerbaum has correctly remarked in his commendable *Handbuch der illustrierten Vergil-Ausgaben,* instead of analysing the relationship between the illustrations and the German text, the more rewarding question is whether Murner was influenced by his knowledge of the woodcuts when writing his translation of the *Aeneid.*[5] This question is addressed in this essay.

1 Brant's Edition of Virgil in the Context of Grüninger's Publishing Programme

Johann Grüninger opened a printing business in Strasbourg in 1483.[6] His publications included both Latin and German texts in a variety of disciplines and genres.[7] He maintained active relationships with the leading personalities of Humanism in the Upper Rhine, including Sebastian Brant, Jakob Wimpfeling, Gregor Reisch, Heinrich Bebel, Jakob Locher and Martin Waldseemüller.[8] Some

---

5 Werner Suerbaum, *Handbuch der illustrierten Vergil-Ausgaben 1502–1840. Geschichte, Typologie, Zyklen und kommentierter Katalog der Holzschnitte und Kupferstiche zur Aeneis in Alten Drucken. Mit besonderer Berücksichtigung der Bestände der Bayerischen Staatsbibliothek München und ihrer Digitalisate von Bildern zu Werken des P. Vergilius Maro.* Hildesheim, New York 2008 (Bibliographien zur klassischen Philologie 3), p. 181.
6 For more on Grüninger, see Charles Schmidt, *Zur Geschichte der ältesten Bibliotheken und der ersten Buchdrucker zu Strassburg.* Strasbourg 1882. p. 112–118; Charles Schmidt, *Répertoire bibliographique strasbourgeois jusque vers 1530. I. Jean Grüninger 1483–1531.* Strasbourg 1894; Paul Kristeller, *Die Strassburger Bücher-Illustration im XV. und im Anfange des XVI. Jahrhunderts.* Leipzig 1888 (Beiträge zur Kunstgeschichte. N. F. VII); Hermann Römer, 'Hans Grüninger und die Buchdruckerfamilie Reinhard aus Markgröningen'. In: H.R., *Markgröningen im Rahmen der Landesgeschichte. I. Urgeschichte und Mittelalter.* Markgröningen 1933, p. 277–331; François Ritter, *Histoire de l'imprimerie alsacienne aux XV*[e] *et XVI*[e] *siècles.* Strasbourg, Paris 1955, p. 81–110; and the more recent publications by Ferdinand Geldner, *Die deutschen Inkunabeldrucker. 2 vols. 1. Das deutsche Sprachgebiet. 2. Die fremden Sprachgebiete.* Stuttgart 1968–1970, p. 71–75; Miriam U. Chrisman, *Bibliography of Strasbourg Imprints 1488–1599.* New Haven 1982; Christoph Reske, *Die Buchdrucker des 16. und 17. Jahrhunderts im deutschen Sprachgebiet. Auf der Grundlage des gleichnamigen Werkes von Josef Benzing.* Wiesbaden 2007 (Beiträge zum Buch- und Bibliothekswesen 51), p. 871f.
7 The GW attributes 209 printed editions to Grüninger and the VD16 a further 310. Reske (see note 6), p. 871 lists around 400 printed editions.
8 For more on literary life in Strasbourg, see Klaus Manger, *Literarisches Leben in Strassburg während der Prädikatur Johann Geilers von Kaysersberg (1478–1510).* Heidelberg 1983 (Heidelberger Forschungen 24); Miriam U. Chrisman, *Lay Culture, Learned Culture. Books and Social Change in Strasbourg 1480–1599.* New Haven 1982; Stephen Mossman, Nigel F. Palmer

Humanist scholars occasionally worked as proof-readers for Grüninger's printing business[9]: Johann Adelphus Muling,[10] Matthias Ringmann[11] and Gervasius
Sopher.[12] Latin editions of the Classics, which Grüninger had been publishing
since the end of the fifteenth century, made up a significant proportion of his
publications. These included editions of the works of Virgil, Terence, Horace,
Cicero, Plautus, Ovid and Ptolemy.[13] This focus gained a higher profile with five

---

and Felix Heinzer (eds), *Schreiben und Lesen in der Stadt. Literaturbetrieb im
spätmittelalterlichen Straßburg*. Berlin 2012 (Kulturtopographie des alemannischen Raums 4).

9 For more on the profession of *corrector* in the Early Modern Period, see Heinrich Grimm,
'Von dem Aufkommen eines eigenen Berufszweigs Korrektor und seinem Berufsbild im
Buchdruck des XVI. Jahrhunderts'. In: *Gutenberg-Jahrbuch* 39 (1964), p. 185–190; Jürgen Geiß,
'Herausgeber, Korrektor, Verlagslektor? Sebastian Brant und die Basler *Petrarca*-Ausgabe von
1496'. In: *Sebastian Brant. Forschungsbeiträge zu seinem Leben, zum 'Narrenschiff' und zum
übrigen Werk*. Ed. by Thomas Wilhelmi. Basel 2002, p. 83–102.

10 Muling was intermittently employed by Grüninger as an editor and proofreader from 1505
to *c.* 1513. See Franz Josef Worstbrock, 'Muling, Johann Adelphus'. In: *Deutscher Humanismus
1480–1520'. Verfasserlexikon*. Ed. by Franz Josef Worstbrock. Vol. 2. Berlin, New York 2013,
col. 27. Muling is also named in the colophon of Murner's teaching on logic, *Logica memorativa*
(VD16 J 661), as a *castigator*: *Nobis quoque plurimam gratiam referes* [i.e. *candide lector*]:
Necnon Ioanni Adelpho: viro secundum cor nostrum: huius operis castigatori. (fol. Nv^v) "You
(i.e. dear reader) will offer us profuse thanks, but offer them also to Johann Adelphus, a man
very dear to us and the corrector of this work."

11 Ringmann worked as a proof reader for Grüninger in 1505–1506. See Franz Josef
Worstbrock, 'Ringmann, Matthias'. In: *Deutscher Humanismus 1480–1520. Verfasserlexikon*.
Ed. by Franz Josef Worstbrock. Vol. 2. Berlin, New York 2013, col. 727.

12 Cf. Reske (see note 6), p. 871.

13 P. Vergilius Maro, *Bucolica. Mit einem Kommentar des Hermannus Torrentinus*. [Strasbourg:
Johann Grüninger]. GW M49908; P. Terentius Afer, *Comoediae. Mit einem Kommentar des Guido
Juvenalis, Jodocus Badius Ascensius und Johannes Egidius*. Strasbourg: Johann Grüninger 1.
XI.1496. GW M45481; further edition 1499: GW M45485; further edition 1503: VD16 T 361;
Q. Horatius Flaccus, *Opera*. Ed. by Jacobus Locher Philomusus. Strasbourg: Johann Grüninger 12.
III.1498. GW 13468; M. Tullius Cicero, *Somnium Scipionis*. [Strasbourg: Johann Grüninger after
1500]. GW 6. Sp.622a; P. Vergilius Maro, *Opera*. Ed. by Sebastian Brant. Strasbourg: Johann
Grüninger 1502. VD16 V 1332; P. Terentius Afer, *Comoediae sex*. Strasbourg: Johann Grüninger
1503. VD16 T 361; P. Vergilius Maro, *Opera [Manuale Vergilianum]. Mit einem Kommentar des
Jodocus Badius Ascensius*. Strasbourg: Johann Grüninger 1505. VD16 ZV 15224; T. Maccius
Plautus, *Comoediae*. Ed. by Johann Adelphus Muling. Strasbourg: Johann Grüninger 1508. VD16
P 3379; T. Maccius Plautus, *Comoediae quattuor (Amphitryo. Aulularia. Duo Captivi et Menechmi)*.
Strasbourg: Johann Grüninger 1511. VD16 P 3401; further editions: VD16 3434; 3444; 4312.
P. Terentius Afer, *Comoediae*. Ed. by Thomas Vogler. Strasbourg: Johann Grüninger 1511. VD16
T 370; *Ovidii Nasonis Fastorum libri*. [Strasbourg: Johann Grüninger *c.* 1521]. VD16 O 1612; *Claudii
Ptolemaei [...] opus Geographiȩ*. Ed. by Lorenz Fries. Strasbourg: Johann Grüninger 1522. VD16
P 5210; further edition: VD16 P 5211.

translations of classical texts into German, which were published at the same time as the Latin Classic editions were being printed: Terence, Livy, Caesar, Virgil's *Bucolics* and *Aeneid*.[14] The translations of these ancient texts were partly produced by the same Humanist writers Grüninger employed as scholarly proof-readers for the Latin texts (Muling, Ringmann). Three of the five translations (Terence, Virgil's *Bucolics* and *Aeneid*) were published shortly after the Latin editions issued by Grüninger.[15] Both the editions of the Classics and the translations display similarities in terms of the (folio) format and are characterised by the addition of woodcuts as paratextual elements. This choice testifies to the contemporary interest in ancient classical texts and translations, as well as in the presentation of textual content through the medium of images.[16]

---

14 For more on the reception of ancient Classics in Germany, see Franz Josef Worstbrock, *Deutsche Antikerezeption 1450–1550. Teil I: Verzeichnis der deutschen Übersetzungen antiker Autoren. Mit einer Bibliographie der Übersetzer*. Boppard am Rhein 1976 (Veröffentlichungen zur Humanismusforschung 1). The numbers in the following list of translations are those used by Worstbrock: P. Terentius Afer, *Comoediae*. German (anonymous). Strasbourg: Johann Grüninger 5. III.1499. GW M45583. Worstbrock, *Antikerezeption*, no. 408; Titus Livius, *Ab urbe condita*. German by Bernhard Schöfferlin/Ivo Wittich. Strasbourg: Johann Grüninger 1507. VD16 L 2103. Worstbrock, *Antikerezeption*, no. 246; C. Iulius Caesar, *Commentarii de bello Gallico. Commentarii de bello civili*. German by Matthias Ringmann Philesius. Strasbourg: Johann Grüninger 1507 VD16 C 54. Worstbrock, *Antikerezeption*, no. 43. Further edition: Strasbourg: Johann Grüninger 1508. VD16 C 55. Worstbrock, *Antikerezeption*, no. 44; P. Vergilius Maro, *Bucolica*. German by Johann Adelphus Muling. Strasbourg: Johann Grüninger [1508–1509]. VD16 V1529. Worstbrock, *Antikerezeption*, no. 426; P. Vergilius Maro, *Aeneis*. German by Thomas Murner. Strasbourg: Johann Grüninger 1515. VD16 V 1426. Worstbrock, *Antikerezeption*, no. 427.

15 Some of these Latin and German publications are being examined in the Bochum DFG project 'Klassiker im Kontext' (director: Prof. Bernd Bastert, Prof. Manfred Eikelmann). For more on this, see http://staff.germanistik.rub.de/klassiker-im-kontext/das-team/ [Accessed: 20/10/2018].

16 For the distribution of elaborate text-image units in the printing of the fifteenth and sixteenth centuries, see Joachim Knape, 'Mnemonik, Bildbuch und Emblematik im Zeitalter Sebastian Brants'. In: *Mnemosyne. Festschrift für Manfred Lurker zum 60. Geburtstag*. Ed. by Werner Bies, Hermann Jung and Manfred Lurker. Baden-Baden 1988 (Bibliographie zur Symbolik, Ikonographie und Mythologie, supplementary vol. 2), p. 133–178. The so-called 'picture books' are included in the research into predecessors of emblem books. See Seraina Plotke, 'Emblematik vor der Emblematik. Der frühe Buchdruck als Experimentierfeld der Text-Bild-Beziehungen'. In: *ZfdPh* 129 (2010), p. 127–142; Karl A. E. Enenkel, 'Illustrations as Commentary and Reader's Guidance. The Transformation of Cicero's *De officiis* into a German Emblem Book by Johann of Schwarzenberg, Heinrich Steiner, and Christian Egenolff (1517–1520; 1530/31; 1550)'. In: *Transformations of the Classics via Early Modern Commentaries*. Ed. by Karl A. E. Enenkel. Leiden, Boston 2014 (Intersections 29), p. 167–259. [For text-image relations, see also the articles by Potysch, p. 273–295 and Schaeps, p. 297–324, in the present volume.]

Grüninger ascribed great importance to providing his books with illustrations. He ran his own workshop for the production of the woodblocks, presumably from *c.* 1495 to *c.* 1506, in which famous artists of the time, such as Hans Baldung Grien, Hans Wechtelin, Hans Schäufelein and Urs Graf, worked to a high artistic standard.[17] Those of Grüninger's printed publications that were accompanied by numerous woodcuts included in particular the Latin Classics: the 1496 edition of Terence (GW M45481) contained 159 illustrations,[18] each composed of several partially sawn woodcuts, which were then joined together.[19] With a few expansions, the Terence woodcuts were also used in the German translation of Terence published in 1499 (GW M45583), as well as to illustrate two further Latin editions in 1499 (GW M45485) and 1503 (VD16 T 361). Some of them were combined with newly designed illustrations to adorn the complete edition of the works of Horace, finished on 12 March 1498, under the supervision of Jakob Locher (GW 13468).[20] In the period between 1500 and 1502, Grüninger had many woodcuts made[21] to illustrate three editions overseen by Sebastian Brant,[22] as well as other printed

17 For more on the artists employed by Grüninger, see Reske (see note 6), p. 871. See also Kristeller (see note 6), p. 18.

18 For the importance of Grüninger's edition of Terence "nicht nur für die Textkritik und die Geschichte der Buchkunst [...], sondern ebenso für die Theaterwissenschaft und die Kostümgeschichte", see Stephan Füssel, 'Die Bedeutung des Buchdrucks für die Verbreitung der Ideen des Renaissance-Humanismus'. In: *Die Buchdrucker im 15. und 16. Jahrhundert*. Ed. by Barbara Thiemann. Hamburg 1999, p. 134.

19 See Anneliese Schmitt, 'Tradition und Innovation von Literaturgattungen und Buchformen in der Frühdruckzeit'. In: *Die Buchkultur im 15. und 16. Jahrhundert*. 2nd half-volume. Ed. by Barbara Thiemann. Hamburg 1999, p. 103. Römer (see note 6), p. 291, refers to the edition of Terence's *Comedies* published by Johann Trechsel in Lyon in 1493 (GW M45397), which he considers to be a model for Grüninger's edition of Terence because of the similarity of the illustrations.

20 For more information, see Christoph Pieper, 'Horaz als Schulfibel und als elitärer Gründungstext des deutschen Humanismus. Die illustrierte Horazausgabe des Jakob Locher (1498)'. In: *Transformations of the Classics via Early Modern Commentaries*. Ed. by Karl. A. E. Enenkel. Leiden 2014, p. 61–90.

21 Dupeux, Lévy and Wirth list over 600 woodcuts that Grüninger had produced at this time. Cf. Cécile Dupeux, Jacqueline Lévy and Jean Wirth (eds), *La gravure d´illustration en Alsace au XVIᵉ siècle*. 3 vols: *1. Jean Gruninger: 1501–1506. 2. Georg Husner, Johann Prüss, Bartholomäus Kistler, Wilhelm Schaffner, Mathias Hupfuff, Johann Schott, Johann Wähinger, Martin Flach, Johann Knobloch. 3. Jean Grüninger: 1507–1512*. Strasbourg 1992–2009, here: vol. 1, p. 16.

22 The lawyer Sebastian Brant became syndic of the town of Strasbourg in 1501 and Chancellor of the Imperial City in 1503. See Joachim Knape, 'Brant (Titio), Sebastian'. In: *Deutscher Humanismus 1480–1520. Verfasserlexikon*. Ed. Franz Josef Worstbrock. Vol. 1. Berlin, New York 2008, cols. 247–283; Thomas Wilhelmi (ed.), *Sebastian Brant. Forschungsbeiträge zu seinem Leben, zum 'Narrenschiff' und zum übrigen Werk*. Basel 2002.

publications:[23] in 1501, the edition of *Consolatio Philosophiae* was published with 60 woodcuts (VD16 B 6404)[24]; the edition of *Der Heiligen Leben* (VD16 H 1471), in which the passions of the saints were illustrated through 240 woodcuts, was issued a year later,[25] in 1502; in that same year, the edition of Virgil's works (VD16 V 1332) appeared. Brant's edition of Virgil is considered by scholars to be the undisputed masterpiece of the art of book production in Strasbourg at the time: "chef-d'oeuvre d'illustration strasbourgeoise de l'époque".[26] This first completed cycle of images of Virgil's works includes 214 woodcuts, of which 137 accompany the text of the *Aeneid* and another six illustrate the Supplement, Maffeo Vegio's 13th book.[27] The remaining 71 woodcuts are distributed among Virgil's *Bucolics, Georgics* and the *Carmina minora*. With four exceptions,[28] Grüninger had them made specifically for this edition. In the colophon of the publication, he emphasised the huge and financial cost: „Impressum [...] operaque et impensa non mediocri magistri Iohannis Grieninger" (fol. 34[r] of the Appendix).[29]

Grüninger did not only use the woodcuts to illustrate Johann Adelpus Muling's translation of the *Bucolics*[30] and Thomas Murner's translation of the

---

23 These include the *Legenda sanctae Catharinae* in Latin and German (GW M31820; GW M31822), the *Destillierbuch* (GW 05595) and the *Pestbuch* (GW 05596) by Hieronymus Brunschwig, the chivalric romances *Hug Schapler* (GW 12589) and *Die Königstochter von Frankreich* (GW 06707), as well as a German *Hortus sanitatis* (GW M09739). See Dupeux, Lévy and Wirth (see note 21), vol. 1.

24 The images are, for the most part, composed of two to three woodblocks of varying artistic quality whose original use is yet to be determined. See Dupeux, Lévy and Wirth (see note 21), vol. 1, p. 19f. and the illustrations on p. 95–118.

25 Brant's contribution to the edition is admittedly unclear. Cf. Dupeux, Lévy and Wirth (see note 21), vol. 1, p. 20f. and the illustrations on p. 119–196. For more information, see Nikolaus Henkel, 'Das Bild als Wissenssumme. Die Holzschnitte in Sebastian Brants Vergil-Ausgabe, Straßburg 1502'. In: *Schreiben und Lesen in der Stadt. Literaturbetrieb im spätmittelalterlichen Straßburg*. Ed. by Stephen Mossman, Nigel F. Palmer and Felix Heinzer. Berlin 2012 (Kulturtopographie des alemannischen Raums 4), p. 389–419, here p. 392.

26 Dupeux, Lévy and Wirth (see note 21), vol. 1, p. 16.

27 They are briefly described in Suerbaum, *Handbuch* (note 5), p. 135–152.

28 Three woodcuts came from the 1501 print of Boethius's *Consolatio Philosophiae*, one from the Terence edition printed in 1496. See Bernd Schneider, '"Virgilius pictus" – Sebastian Brants illustrierte Vergilausgabe von 1502 und ihre Nachwirkung. Ein Beitrag zur Vergilrezeption im deutschen Humanismus'. In: *Wolfenbütteler Beiträge* 6 (1983), p. 204, note 9.

29 The description *magister* probably does not refer to an academic title, but to a 'master craftsman'; indeed, Grüninger wrote to Willibald Pirckheimer on 17/12/1529 that he "nit latin kann". Quoted in Reske (see note 6), p. 871.

30 P. Vergilius Maro, *Bucolica*. German by Johann Adelphus Muling. Strasbourg: Johann Grüninger, [1508–1509] (VD16 V1529); Franz Josef Worstbrock, 'Adelphus Mulings

Aeneid, but also other translations of the Classics: a woodcut appeared in Ringmann's 1507 printed translation of Caesar (VD16 C 54), although the link between the text and the image is somewhat looser.[31] Around 50 illustrations from the Virgil edition, along with the woodcuts from *Hug Schapler* (GW 12589) and *Die Königstochter von Frankreich* (GW 06707), were also used to illustrate the printed edition of the translation of Livy begun by Bernhard Schöfferlin and continued from 1507 by Ivo Wittich (VD16 L 2103)[32]; some woodcuts were used several times. For the Livy edition, Grüninger only had 39 of the 254 illustrations newly made.[33]

The woodblocks from the Virgil edition were re-used in a printed publication of Virgil in 1517 in Lyon, where Grüninger had sold them after extensive use.[34] He was presumably connected to this city through his relative Markus Reinhard, who owned the second printing press in Lyon with Nikolaus Philippi in 1477.[35] The woodblocks travelled to Venice later: in 1552, Virgil's *Opera* were published by Tommaso Giunta who appropriated some of Grüninger's original

---

Vergilübersetzung'. In: *ZfdA* 102 (1973), p. 204–206, proves that the date estimated in VD16 of [ca. 1520] is not tenable due to the form of the name Mülich and the fact that Muling only dealt with the translation of ancient authors around 1510.

31 A woodcut from the beginning of the third book of the *Aeneid*, depicting the preparation of the Trojans to leave Antandrus for the promised land (VD16 V 1332, fol. 183^v), appears at the beginning of the second book of *Bellum civile* (VD16 C 54) under the caption: *Des andern buochs Figur Wie der Legat C. Trebonius die stat Massiliam im namen des Keisers belegeret Ouch von einem Schiffsstryt* (fol. 88^r). In the Virgil woodcut, however, the name rotuli identify the people as Anchises and Aeneas and the city as Troy. For more on this, cf. Schneider (see note 28), p. 226. Cf. also Dupeux, Lévy and Wirth (see note 21), vol. 3, p. 9 and the illustrations p. 59–72.

32 The translation started by Schöfferlin may have been conceived in the environment of the Württemberg court for Count Eberhard in Bart, who had named Schöfferlin a life member of the Council in 1488. Ivo Wittich first published the translation, expanded by a third part (Livy's fourth decade), in 1505 through Johann Schöffer in Mainz (VD16 L 2105) and dedicated it to Maximilian I. See Franz Josef Worstbrock, 'Wittich, Ivo'. In: ^{2}*VL* 10 (1999), cols. 1290–1292. For more on Schöfferlin and his translation, see Carla Winter, *Humanistische Historiographie in der Volkssprache. Bernhard Schöfferlins 'Römische Historie'*. Stuttgart, Bad Cannstatt 1999 (Arbeiten und Editionen zur mittleren deutschen Literatur. N. F. 6); Walter Röll, 'Schöfferlin, Bernhard'. In: ^{2}*VL* 8 (1992), cols. 810–814.

33 See Dupeux, Lévy and Wirth (see note 21), vol. 3, p. 10 and the illustrations on p. 73–96.

34 P. Vergilius Maro: *Opera*. Lyon: Jacobus Saccon, 1517. For more on this edition, see Suerbaum, *Handbuch* (note 5), p. 182f.

35 Römer (see note 6), p. 280, speaks of a close kinship. The exact nature of the kinship has, however, not yet been confirmed (p. 282f.). Markus Reinhard returned to Strasbourg in 1482, presumably at first to join Grüninger's printing business. Contact between Grüninger and Lyon might have been established from this time.

illustrations for his work.[36] They were also often re-cut – not only for editions of Virgil[37] – and their motifs can be found in most illustrated editions of Virgil until partway through the seventeenth century.[38] The remarkable impact of Grüninger's edition of Virgil reveals the importance of his workshop in the realm of book production in the Upper Rhine around the year 1500. According to François Ritter, his illustrations were the highpoint of the art of bookmaking in Strasbourg: "Il n'en demeure pas moins qu'il est l'un des plus importants parmi les imprimeurs strasbourgeois."[39]

2 The Woodcuts from Brant's Edition of Virgil (Strasbourg 1502)

The model for the complete edition of the works of Virgil supervised by Brant was the Virgil edition published in Venice in 1491 by Philippus Pincius and edited by the Italian Humanist Antonio Mancinelli (GW M49944). In addition to Virgil's three principal works (*Bucolics, Georgics, Aeneid*), it included the so-called *Appendix Vergiliana*, a series of short poems that had become attached to Virgil's work over the course of its transmission.[40] Mancinelli's edition appended five commentaries to Virgil's works for the first time in printing history[41]: commentaries by the late classical grammarians Servius and Tiberius

---

36 See Schneider (see note 28), p. 231. For Giunta's edition of 1552, see Suerbaum, *Handbuch* (note 5), p. 248–250.

37 Thus, a mirror image recut of Fama from Brant's edition of Virgil (fol. 215ᵛ) is displayed as the title woodcut of the printed edition of a text by the same name (*Fama*), published by Hieronymus Rodler in Simmern in 1534 (VD16 F 592). Cf. Jacob Klingner, *Minnereden im Druck. Studien zur Gattungsgeschichte im Zeitalter des Medienwechsels*. Berlin 2010 (Philologische Studien und Quellen 226), p. 210, note. 44.

38 For more on the 'afterlife' of Grüninger's Virgil woodcuts, see Suerbaum, *Handbuch* (note 5), p. 54.

39 Ritter (see note 6), p. 109. [For Strasbourg, see also the article by Bertelsmeier-Kierst in the present volume, p. 37–40.]

40 Cf. Leighton D. Reynolds (ed.), *Texts and Transmission. A Survey of the Latin Classics.* Oxford 1983, p. 433–440. See also Henkel, 'Das Bild' (note 25), p. 382. For the individual poems, see the anthology *Die Appendix Vergiliana. Pseudepigraphen im literarischen Kontext.* Ed. by Niklas Holzberg. Tübingen 2005 (Classica Monacensia 30).

41 Cf. Martin Davies and John Goldfinch (eds), *Vergil. A Census of Printed Editions 1469–1500.* London 1992, p. 68.

Claudius Donatus, as well as by the Humanists Antonio Mancinelli, Domizio Calderini and Cristoforo Landino. They are printed in separate blocks marked with the names of the commentator.

Brant's edition of Virgil is introduced by a propempticon written by the editor (fol. Ai^v–Aii^r/KT 397) and is followed by Cristoforo Landino's proem to Virgil's works (fol. Aii^v–Aiiii^r) and Aelius Donatus's Life of Virgil (Aiii^r–Av^v).[42] A separate foliate Appendix is appended to Virgil's main work that contains both Maffeo Vegio's 13th book and the *Carmina minora*. Brant uses the five commentaries from Mancinelli's edition as closing paratexts, although he changes their presentation. He brings together the different details that relate to the same location or lemma: lower-case letters above relevant words in the main text refer to the commentaries appended to Virgil's text, which thus appear "nicht mehr wie in den Vorgängerausgaben als eigene kohärente Texte [...], sondern je 'parzelliert'".[43]

The woodcuts demonstrate this rich interpretation not only of the Virgilian text, but also of the commentaries added to it and reveal the expertise of an evident connoisseur of ancient literature and mythology. Research has demonstrated that Brant was closely involved in the production of the woodcuts as a 'concepteur'[44]: the craftsmen employed in Grüninger's woodcarving workshop worked on the basis of Brant's presumably sketchy preliminary drawings, labelled with details about each individual illustration, which assumes a lively exchange between the editor and the artists realising the work.[45] The narratorial sequence of images, the "Bild-'Erzählung'",[46] in addition to the textual understanding supplied by the Latin writing, creates an engrossing display through the visual medium.

---

42 For KT, see note 48.

43 Henkel, 'Das Bild' (note 25), p. 394.

44 Henkel, 'Das Bild' (note 25), p. 394. Brant supervised the printing of the edition of Virgil and was apparently able to prevent the *Carmina Priapea*, which he believed to be offensive, from being printed in the Appendix of the edition. Cf. Nikolaus Henkel, 'Die *Carmina Priapea* in Sebastian Brants Vergil-Ausgabe (1502). Strategien einer angeleiteten Kommunikation. Mit einem Anhang: Die Sammlung der Vergil-Epitaphien der Straßburger Ausgabe'. In: *Sebastian Brant und die Kommunikationskultur um 1500*. Ed. by Klaus Bergdolt. Wiesbaden 2010 (Wolfenbütteler Abhandlungen zur Renaissanceforschung 26), p. 379–410.

45 The fact that the printmakers and cutters presumably had no knowledge of Virgil's text or of Latin can be seen, for instance, in the erroneous name inscriptions on the woodcuts. Cf. Henkel, 'Das Bild' (note 25), p. 391, note 46.

46 Henkel, 'Das Bild' (note 25), p. 389.

In the introductory and closing poems of the edition, Brant explains the intended purpose of the *pictae tabellae* (KT 397, v. 1), as he called the woodcuts, of his Virgil[47]: they are intended for the unschooled (*indocti*, KT 397, vv. 9f.) and the simple folk (*rusticoli viri*, KT 389, v. 4), for whom the images would open a door to participation in the ancient cultural heritage.[48] As an example of this mode of reading, Brant points to a passage from the first Book of the *Aeneid* in which Aeneas and his companion Achates examine the reliefs in Juno's temple in Carthage, which shows scenes from the Trojan War (*Aen.* 1.441–493): "Dardanium Aenan doctum non legimus usquam: / picturam potuit perlegere ille tamen" (KT 397, vv. 11f.).[49] The possibility, thanks to the first complete image cycle of the works of Virgil, of making the ancient body of knowledge accessible to those who, due to a lack of Latin education, are reliant upon the visual display, refers back to the topos of the *pictura* as *litteratura laicorum*.[50] It has long been a consensus among researchers that Brant's statement is not to be taken literally,[51] yet the woodcuts demonstrate an exceptionally high density of scholarly knowledge that stems not only from the primary texts of the classical poet, but is also taken from the Late Antiquity and Humanist commentaries added to them. A thorough knowledge of them is necessary to truly 'read' the images and

---

47 For more on the impact of Brant's edition of Virgil, see Schneider (see note 28), p. 202–262.

48 The poems are printed in: Sebastian Brant, *Kleine Texte*. Ed. by Thomas Wilhelmi. 3 vols. Stuttgart, Bad Cannstatt 1998 (Arbeiten und Editionen zur mittleren deutschen Literatur N. F. 3): "Hic legere historias commentaque plurima doctus | nec minus indoctus perlegere illa potest" (KT 397, vv. 9f.). "The scholar can here read stories and numerous commentaries, yet the unlearned is no less able to read them [by observing]." The closing poem expresses it thus: "Virgilium exponant alii sermone diserto. | Et calamo pueris: tradere et ore iuuet. | Pictura agresti voluit Brant atque tabellis: | Edere eum indoctis: rusticolisque viris" (KT 389, vv. 1–4). "Others seek to explain Virgil with scholarly discourse and teach the boys through favourable speech and written word (with a stylus); Brant wanted to issue him with simple pictures and tables for unlearned and simple people."

49 "We do not read anywhere that the Trojan Aeneas was educated but he was able to read the picture."

50 For more on this argument, see Michael Curschmann, 'Pictura laicorum litteratura? Überlegungen zum Verhältnis von Bild und volkssprachlicher Schriftlichkeit im Hoch- und Spätmittelalter bis zum Codex Manesse'. In: *Pragmatische Schriftlichkeit im Mittelalter. Erscheinungsformen und Entwicklungsstufen*. Ed. by Hagen Keller, Klaus Grubmüller and Nikolaus Staubach. München 1992 (Münstersche Mittelalter-Schriften 65), p. 211–229.

51 In contrast, see Craig Kallendorf, *Virgil and the Myth of Venice. Books and Readers in the Italian Renaissance*. Oxford 1999, p. 162, who considers the recipients of the edition of Virgil to be "poorly educated, humble folk".

to understand the relationship between the elements they represent. These are mostly an illustration of a combination of scenes that summarise several plot sequences,[52] some of which refer to textual passages of over hundred lines.

As Brant states in a poem in the Appendix of the Virgil edition, the woodcuts have, on the one hand, a memorative function as a mental visualisation of what is read: "The image keeps the book in memory" ("memori seruat mente figura librum", fol. 35ᵛ).[53] On the other hand, the richness of detail and the great complexity of some of the illustrations offer literati the possibility of a scholar's game based on the recognition of the particular literary work depicted in the image; and, finally, the woodcuts also hold a learning process for the scholars: "jeder, auch der beste Kenner, ist nicht so weit fortgeschritten, dass er nicht noch mehr lernen könnte und sollte."[54] This learning process for the litterati takes place though the living and vivid transfer of the textual content into a visual medium, which guarantees a maximum presence for that which is represented.

The illustrated narrative of the woodcuts accompanying the Latin text in the Strasbourg 1502 Virgil edition offers a "Höchstmaß an minutiöser sinnstiftender Differenzierung"[55] and, as such, is comparable to the process of translation: both illustration and translation aim to communicate to the recipient a coherent image of the text that corresponds to contemporary vision and understanding.[56] Thus, the woodcuts transpose the ancient material to the era of c. 1500 north of the Alps[57]: half-timbered houses, bay

52 Cf. Suerbaum, *Handbuch* (note 5), p. 53.

53 For more on the combination of text and image in Brant's edition of Virgil, see Joachim Hamm, 'Zu Paratextualität und Intermedialität in Sebastian Brants *Vergilius pictus* (Straßburg 1502)'. In: *Intermedialität in der Frühen Neuzeit. Formen, Funktionen, Konzepte*. Ed. by Jörg Robert. Berlin, Boston 2017 (Frühe Neuzeit 209), p. 236–259.

54 Henkel, 'Das Bild' (note 25), p. 410.

55 Henkel, 'Das Bild' (note 25), p. 409f.

56 Eleanor W. Leach, 'Illustration as Interpretation in Brant's and Dryden's Editions of Vergil'. In: *The Early Illustrated Book. Essays in Honor of Lessing J. Rosenwald*. Ed. by Sandra Hindman. Washington 1982, p. 175–210, discusses the type of interpretative illustration of Virgil's *Bucolics* and *Aeneid* in Brant's and Dryden's editions of Virgil. She sees illustration and translation as two parallel paths "to convey the reader a coherent image couched within the understandable contemporary idiom" (p. 175).

57 A knowledgeable commentary of selected woodcuts is provided by Vergil, *Aeneis*. Ed. by Manfred Lemmer. Translated by Johannes Götte. Leipzig 1979, p. 365f.; Schneider (see note 28), p. 202–262, examines the Virgil edition with an analysis of individual woodcuts, taking into account their historical reception.

windows and battlements, even church towers with bells and crosses reflect the typical building designs of German towns in the late Middle Ages (Strasbourg 1502, fol. 121^r, 159^r, [222^r]); the clothes, the hair and beard styles belong to the period 1500 (fol. 145^v, 151^r); the heroes fight in the manner of knights (fol. 171^v, 406^v, 408^v); Turnus's infantry even displays the 'Bundschuh' on its banner (fol. 319^v).[58] Christian elements are encountered in the depiction of the jaws of hell (fol. 265^v, 268^v) and the death of Aeneas, whose soul escapes from his mouth in the shape of a small figure (fol. 5^v of the Appendix) – a common depiction in images of the death of Mary, for example.[59] Conversely, the pagan world of the gods is represented in "barbarischer Nacktheit",[60] to quote Lemmer, as not belonging to the Christian sphere (fol. 133^r, 212^v). The visual transfer of the textual content to the contemporary conceptual world and the translational practice in Murner's German version of the *Aeneid*, which aims to provide a cultural transposition of the ancient text,[61] demonstrate the appropriation of the ancient Classics in accordance with the respective contemporary local conditions.[62]

---

58 For more on the uprisings of peasants in the Upper Rhine in the period from 1493 to 1517, see Georges Bischoff, *La guerre des Paysans. L'Alsace et la révolution du Bundschuh, 1493–1525*. Strasbourg 2010.

59 See Josef Myslivec, 'Tod Mariens'. In: *LCI* 4 (1994), cols. 334–338.

60 Vergil, *Aeneis* (note 57), p. 365.

61 For more on Murner's translational practice, see Julia Frick, 'Renaissance eines antiken Klassikers. Thomas Murners Übersetzung von Vergils *Aeneis* (1515)'. In: *ZfdA* 146 (2017), p. 351–368 and the examination of Murner's translation currently in preparation (see note 1).

62 For more on this method in Brant's edition of Virgil, see also Werner Suerbaum, 'Titelbilder zu den Aeneis-Büchern vom Humanismus bis zum Neoklassizismus. Geschichte, Typen und Tendenzen der Aeneis-Illustration in gedruckten Vergil-Ausgaben und -Übersetzungen von 1502–1840'. In: *Philologia antiqua* 1 (2008), p. 103. Gerlinde Huber-Rebenich shows that the assimilation of ancient materials into the contemporary era was the common reception form in the sixteenth century, using the example of Ovid's *Metamorphoses* in her article 'Ovids Göttersagen in illustrierten Ausgaben des 15. und 16. Jahrhunderts'. In: *Wechselseitige Wahrnehmung der Religionen im Spätmittelalter und in der Frühen Neuzeit. II. Kulturelle Konkretionen (Literatur, Mythographie, Wissenschaft und Kunst).* Ed. by Ludger Grenzmann, Thomas Haye and Nikolaus Henkel et al. Berlin, Boston 2012 (Abhandlungen der Akademie der Wissenschaften zu Göttingen N.F., 4), p. 185–207. A "historisierende, das meint: antike Formen aufnehmende Darstellungsweise" would, according to Henkel, 'Das Bild' (note 25), p. 389, note 44, hardly be possible north of the Alps at this time.

3 The Influence of the Virgil Woodcuts on Thomas Murner's Translation of the *Aeneid* (1515)

A collation of eleven contemporary editions of the *Aeneid* using indexed samples led to the identification of the 1509 Strasbourg edition published by Johannes Schott (VD16 V 1409) as being the likely model for Murner[63]; it has been shown that the commentary to the Latin edition, which is restricted to basic knowledge, found its way into Murner's German verse.[64] Furthermore, the use of the 1502 Strasbourg Virgil edited by Sebastian Brant (VD16 V 1332) is noticeable: the edition of Murner's translation opted to recycle the former's arguments and especially its woodcuts. It has been proven that Murner knew Brant's edition. In his work *Honestorum poematum condigna laudatio* (1503), he explicitly highlights the benefit of the Virgil woodcuts in offering a visualisation of great impact:

> Uidistin Uirgilium in hac nostra imperiali vrbe Argentina formis diuersis impressum et imaginibus decorum vt fere vitali precepto Eolus ipse tempestates videatur sonoras excitare, Ilium destrui bello, vrbisque Rhome menia noua visionis iucunditate exurgere et cetera id generis.[65]

Murner is referring here to the extremely detailed interpretation of Virgil's text and the commentary through the visual medium of images that present the events with vivid detail to the eye of the beholder. His statement can be read as a contemporary judgement on the high quality and far-reaching effect of the Virgil woodcuts,[66] seeing the close correspondence of the reality created by

---

63 The following editions were collated: Strasbourg 1470 (GW M49727); Venice 1471 (GW M49738); Nuremberg 1492 (GW M49940); Venice 1492 (GW M49944); Venice 1494 (GW M49953); Paris 1500–1501 (GW M49979); Venice 1500 (GW M49969); Cologne 1501 (VD 16 ZV 19185); Strasbourg 1502 (VD 16 V 1332); Strasbourg 1505 (VD 16 ZV 15224); Strasbourg 1509 (VD 16 V 1409).

64 For more on Murner's model, see Frick, 'Renaissance' (note 61), p. 356–362.

65 Thomas Murner, *Honestorum poematum condigua* [read: *condigna*] *landatio* [read: *laudatio*]. Strasbourg 1503. VD16 M 7038, fol. b i[r]. "Have you seen the Virgil printed in our Imperial town of Strasbourg with different typefaces and decorated with images which makes it seem as if Aeolus himself is stirring thunderous storms with an almost living command, that Troy is being destroyed in a war, that the walls of the new Rome are being vividly and pleasantly raised and more of the like." Murner refers here to the following woodcuts from Brant's complete edition of Virgil's works (VD16 V 1332): Aeolus (fol. 124[v]); the destruction of Troy (fol. 172[v]; also fol. 166[v] or 168[v]); the 'new' Rome (Appendix fol. 3[r] and 3[v]).

66 According to Suerbaum, *Handbuch* (note 5), p. 54, the Virgil woodcuts dominated Virgil illustrations in "leichten Abwandlungen und Nachschnitten vor allem in Venedig sowie in Lyon und Paris" until the first quarter of the seventeenth century.

literature with everyday life as the measure of the value of visual art.[67] As Joachim Hamm correctly supposes,[68] this appreciation of Brant's edition may have prompted Murner to give his translation of the *Aeneid* to Grüninger in order to be printed, whereas the majority of his vernacular works written around the time of the composition of the German *Aeneid* were published in Strasbourg by Matthias Hupfuff.[69] The translation fitted Grüninger's publishing programme perfectly, since it assigned an important place to the ancient Classics. Murner himself, like Brant, ascribed great value not only to the illustrative and memorative function of woodcuts, but also to the close relationship between the text and the image[70]; he always ensured that his books were decorated with visual elements.[71]

---

67 Similarly presented is the praise with which Jakob Locher considers the woodcuts in the Preface to Grüninger's second Latin edition of Terence (GW M45485): *Viva omnia sunt* (fol. 1ᵛ).

68 Cf. Hamm (see note 53), p. 256.

69 Cf. Worstbrock, 'Murner, Thomas' (note 1), cols. 333–339. For more on Hupfuff and his printing business in Strasbourg, see Oliver Duntze, *Ein Verleger sucht sein Publikum. Die Straßburger Offizin des Matthias Hupfuff (1497/98–1520)*. München 2007 (Archiv für Geschichte des Buchwesens 4).

70 He emphasises this in his teaching materials for the study of law, such as the *Chartiludium Institute* (VD16 M 7028), in which he ascribes to pictures the function of an important memory aid: "Accipite igitur ex nobis [...] totius institute cognitionem apud alios multis verbis inculcatam. hic autem figuris et typis sic ordinatam vt illis breui valeatis et textus intelligentiam atque perfectam et exactissimam memoriam ac quasi specularem tueri." (fol. a iiᵛ). "Receive therefore from me [...] the knowledge of the whole *Institutiones*, which is inculcated by others with many words, but is here arranged with images and styles which will help you to understand the text within a short period of time and to be able to keep it fully and with great accuracy – visually as it were – in memory." The illustrations of Murner's works are documented by Moritz Sondheim, 'Die Illustrationen zu Thomas Murners Werken'. In: *Elsaß-Lothringisches Jahrbuch* 12 (1933), p. 5–82. For more on the relationship between text and image in Murner's writings, see Maria Wolters, *Beziehungen zwischen Holzschnitt und Text bei Sebastian Brant und Thomas Murner. Mit einem Exkurs über die Illustrationen des Wälschen Gastes*. Strasbourg 1917, p. 28–44.

71 He also repeatedly devoted himself to drawing: he is believed to have drawn most of the templates for the 36 illustrations for his *Badenfahrt* (VD16 M 7022) himself, a spiritual and allegorical interpretation of bathing as a cleansing of the sinner by Christ, the 'bath attendant'. Cf. Dupeux, Lévy and Wirth (see note 21), vol. 2, p. 19 and the illustrations on p. 223–231. For more on the illustrations of *Badenfahrt*, see also Birgit U. Münch, 'Periculosus catus. Subversive Kritik in Bildern und Texten Thomas Murners'. In: *Von der Freiheit der Bilder. Spott, Kritik und Subversion in der Kunst der Dürerzeit*. Ed. by Thomas Schauerte, Jürgen Müller and Bertram Kaschek. Petersberg 2013, p. 196–217. The illustrations in Murner's translation of Sabellicus's universal history are also believed to be Murner's own work. See Tilman Falk, 'Die Illustrationen zu Murners Sabellicus-Übersetzung'. In: *Thomas Murner. Elsässischer Theologe und Humanist, 1475–1537. Eine Ausstellung der Badischen Landesbibliothek Karlsruhe und der Bibliothèque nationale et universitaire de Strasbourg*. Karlsruhe 1987, p. 112–130, p. 114.

Table 1: Related Virgil Editions

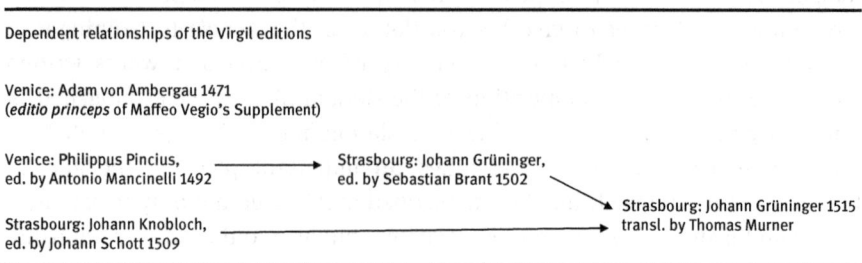

Dependent relationships of the Virgil editions

Venice: Adam von Ambergau 1471
(*editio princeps* of Maffeo Vegio's Supplement)

Venice: Philippus Pincius, ————————▶ Strasbourg: Johann Grüninger,
ed. by Antonio Mancinelli 1492   ed. by Sebastian Brant 1502

                                                                    ▶ Strasbourg: Johann Grüninger 1515
Strasbourg: Johann Knobloch, ———————————————————————▶ transl. by Thomas Murner
ed. by Johann Schott 1509

Brant's carefully calculated intermedial arrangement of the *Vergilius pictus*, which correlated and enabled the interaction of the woodcuts, the Virgilian text and the commentary,[72] loses its functionality in the *editio princeps* of Murner's translation: the extra information provided by the woodcuts points nowhere due to the absence of the commentaries. Yet, the influence of the illustrations on the understanding of the Latin text can be shown in some places of Murner's translation of the *Aeneid*, where details of the images that are not clearly based on the Latin text and its commentaries, nevertheless find their way into Murner's German verse.[73]

Book 1 (Fig. 1, fol. 12ᵛ-13ʳ): Eneas and Achates (both far right) examine the images of Juno's temple in Carthage that depict scenes from the Trojan War (*Aen.* 1.455f./M 1.897–899): a fighting Hector in the top left box, middle, Antomedon (read: Automedon), Vlisses and Dolon, Diomedes thrusting a sword into the side of Rhesvs (*Aen.* 1.471/M 1.925); right, Achilles killing Troilvs (*Aen.* 1.475f./M 1.932–934) from his chariot. In the bottom left box, Trojan women pray before the statue of Pallas (*Aen.* 1.479f./M 1.943–946); middle, Achilles and Priamvs (*Aen.* 1.487/M 1.959f.) with Mennon laid out (*Aen.* 1.489/M 1.963); right, Patesilea (read: Penthesilea) in battle (*Aen.* 1.491/M 1.965).

A Trojan woman wearing a veil and a long cloak is kneeling with folded hands before the statue of Pallas Athena; the two women behind her have raised their arms in a gesture of lament. The Latin text states that the Trojan women approached the goddess "suppliciter, tristes et tunsae pectora palmis"

---

72 Cf. Hamm (see note 53), p. 257.
73 The description of the woodcuts follows the entries in the edition. See Frick (see note 1), vol. 2. The line references are to the Latin text of the *Aeneid* as found in *P. Vergili Maronis Opera*. Ed. by R.A.B. Mynors. Oxford 1969 and Murner's German text in the above-mentioned edition respectively.

(*Aen.* 1.481). The kneeling posture with folded hands in the picture so vividly illustrates a gesture of supplication (*suppliciter*) that Murner picks up on it in his translation and applies it to all the Trojan women:

Darnach sach er ein gantze schar
   Troyanscher frauwen kummen dar,
Mit zersteuwtem har vnd weinen,
   rungent ir hend / die zart vnd reinen;
Für die göttin knüwten all
   vnd clagten des kriegs vngefall.
Die göttin wolt ir hören nit,
   wendt ir augen / veracht ir bit. (M 1.943–950)[74]

The fourth book offers a particularly marked example of the phenomenon of transposing details of the images to the German text. It can be traced to two woodcuts:

(Fig. 2, fol. 57ᵛ): DIDO and ANNA stand in the foreground next to the funeral pyre that has been erected and decorated with garlands (*Aen.* 4. 504–507/M 4.1070–1074), to their left, the priestess is standing at the altar with a sickle (*Aen.* 4.483/M 4.1022f.). In the background, to the left, a room can be seen with a bed with a cover adorned with a portrait of ENEAS (*Aen.* 4.508/M 4.1077–1079). He himself is sitting in a ship back right, admonished by Mercury to leave (*Aen.* 4.554–558/M 4.1188–1193).

(Fig. 3, fol. 60ʳ): In the middle image, DIDO is standing on the upper-most step of a stairway leading to the burning pyre on which the bed with Aeneas's portrait has been placed. She pierces her breast with the sword (*Aen.* 4.663f./M 4.1422), whilst IRIS flies in from the right to cut a lock from DIDO's hair (*Aen.* 704/M 1504). With loose hair and raised arms, a wailing ANNA (*Aen.* 4.667–674/M 4.1438–1444) and other followers approach from the left.

In the Latin text, there is a bed on the pyre, which is used as a repository for clothes, a sword and an *effigies* (*Aen.* 4.506f.). Although the commentary on this passage of the text does indeed clarify that this effigy is an image of

---

74 "Then he saw a large company of Trojan women coming with dishevelled hair and crying, wringing their pure and delicate hands; they all knelt before the goddess and lamented the horrors of the war. The goddess would not listen to them, turned her eyes away and left their plea unheeded."

Fig. 1: Bayerische Staatsbibliothek München, Res/2 A.lat.a. 349, fol. 12^v-13^r.

Fig. 1: (continued)

Von Eneas

Darnach sie auch grusam betracht
an manche warnung da gedacht
Da mit sie was gewarnet worden
zü kummen in celischen orden
So ducht sie alle zeit on syn
wie er sie ließ vnd fier da hyn

Das sie da funde nut allein
vnd het ir Dienerin kein
Auch sücht Tyrischen in ein land
Da menschen nit gewonet hand
Gleich wie Pentheus sah die schar
Der helschen göttin kummen dar.

Wie dido btruglich ir schwester zu iré tod rüsté ließ

Fig. 2: Bayerische Staatsbibliothek München, Res/2 A.lat.a. 349, fol. 57ᵛ.

Das.IIII.Buoch LX

zü welschem land in lenden an
Eneam den vntruwen man
Ist voɪ göttern also gschehen
so vɪich doch das er müß sehen
Hefftig mit krieg vmb triben werden
vertriben von des landes erden

Von seinem sun Julo kum
vnd ßilff müß berlen vmbundum
Die seinen sehen sol erschlagen
vnd keinen friden mög erjagen
Doch wart frid geben im da mit
das er das reich erßole nit

Auxiliū
implorat

Wie sich vßliebe Dido selbs ertödtet.

Fig. 3: Bayerische Staatsbibliothek München, Res/2 A.lat.a. 349, fol. 60ʳ.

Aeneas (*imago*), it does not specify its exact nature.[75] Murner's translation, by contrast, offers a very precise description of the *effigy*:

[...] super	[Dido] hat / auch dar gebracht
exuuias	Eneas cleidung vnd sein schwert,
ensemque	ein bildung, die sie mit gferdt
relictum	Hat wircken lassen vff das bett
Effigiemque toro	von Enea conterphet (M 4.1075–1079)[76]
locat haud ignara	
futuri.	
(*Aen.* 4.506f.)	

The translation adopts the knowledge presented in the woodcuts: two depictions show a bed adorned with a coverlet with a portrait of Aeneas. It is only some 150 lines later that the reader of the Latin edition learns the origin of Brant's idea of the *effigies Aeneae*: with regard to *Dardanij rogum capitis* (*Aen.* 4.640), Servius states: *in quo [rogo] eius* [i.e. *Aeneae*] *imago fuerat* (fol. 228ᵛ). In this, Murner's translation is based on the first mention of the funeral pyre, thus suggesting that he may have taken his cue from the visual medium.

Furthermore, the woodcut on fol. 57ᵛ (Fig. 2) shows Dido with loose hair, whereas, in the Latin text, this is the attribute of the priestess: "crines effusa sacerdos" (*Aen.* 4.508). In Murner's translation, it is Dido whose hair flows loose: "Jr [i.e. Dido's] gelbes har ab lassen hangen" (M 4.1082).

Book 5 (Fig. 4, fol. 67ᵛ): Duel between ENTELLVS and DARES. The two opponents are standing opposite each other on an enclosed battlefield, armed with *caestus* (blunt instruments resembling pipes) (*Aen.* 5.426f./M 5.854f.). Two crossed swords lie before them. To the left behind ENTELLVS stands ACESTES with his followers, to the right behind DARES are ENEAS, ASTANIVS (read: Ascanius) and ACHATES.

The practice of the ancient boxing matches, in which opponents would wind leather strips sometimes filled with iron or lead (*caestus*) around their hands, no longer existed by 1500. Rather, in the Middle Ages and the Early Modern period, the *caestus* was understood to be a kind of blunt instrument – a type of club that could be studded or filled with lead. This idea is documented

---

75 Servius refers only to Dido's wish to be united, even in death, with a visual presence of her beloved: "exprimit affectum amantis: quo etiam in morte amici imagini vult coniungi" (Strasbourg 1502, fol. 225ᵛ).

76 "Dido had also brought Aeneas's clothes and his sword there, as well as an effigy of Aeneas that she had had embroidered on the bed, at her own request."

Von Eneas

ich hab verdienet die erste kron
Vß macht/wiewol vß falschë glück
der fail schier anderst ward geschickt
Mit solchen worten zeugt er an
den wüst in seinem antlit stan
Darzů all sein beschißne glider
verwüstet waren hin vnd wider
Eneas lacht in fründtlich an

vnd gab dem selben für sein lan
Ein hübschen schilt vß sunderm gunst
gemacht mit Sidimaonis kunst
Genummen von einß pfosten stat
Neptuno er in dar gehencket hat
Den gab er bald dem iungen man
der mit in het das best gethan.

Et clypeum

Wie vmb kostliche gaben gekempffet ward.

post vbi
confecti

Ls es mit lauffen was gethon
vñ yeder het verdienten lon
Sprach Eneas ist kein gsel
der nun dem andern kempffen wel
Mit krafft vñ auch võ freiem můt

als man dan mit kolben tůt
Mit freien armen vngebunden
zwo gaben bot er da zů stunden
Er setzt in für zwyfaltig eer
wer da ein vberwinder wer

Fig. 4: Bayerische Staatsbibliothek München, Res/2 A.lat.a. 349, fol. 67ᵛ.

by the relevant dictionaries, although with reference to the earlier gloss: for the lemma *plicholp*, the Old High German dictionary describes a "mit Blei (Bleiknöpfen) besetzter kurzer dicker Stock",[77] the Middle High German dictionary also contains relevant entries (*blīkiule/blīkolbe*) with a reference to the Viennese Codex of the thirteenth century (Cod. Vindob. 901), which, in addition to Latin keywords, also offers a Latin-German lexicon with the lemma *blicolbe* for *cestus*.[78] In the Old High German and Old Saxon vocabulary glosses, the entry *plikolbin* is given the meaning "lead-studded club"[79]; Lorenz Diefenbach, analysing the glossaries of the Middle Ages and the Early Modern period, lists the German interpretaments *bliecule, stritkolb, eysener kolb* and *kempfkolben* for *cestus*.[80] In accordance with this contemporary idea, the *caestus* from the Latin text (*Aen.* 5.379 *et passim*) are represented in the image as pipe-like blunt instruments. Murner also renders them as *kolben* (M 5.763 *et passim*) in his translation.

Book 6 (Fig. 5, fol. 82ᵛ): CHARON hurries after having seen the golden bough in ENEAS' hand (*Aen.* 6.406/M 6.863f.) so that the latter and SYBILLA can cross the river in his boat (*Aen.* 408–10/M 869–871), passing by the three-headed Cerberus (*Aen.* 6.417/M 6.884f.) and a Hell mouth with flickering flames on the left side with its negative heraldic connotations. Wailing shapes sit on the bank in the foreground, waiting to cross.

In Virgil's *Aeneid*, it is Sibylla who shows ferryman Charon the golden bough that entitles them to descend into the Underworld; this action is poetically integrated into her speech: "[...] At ramum hunc" (aperit [i.e. Sibylla] ramum qui veste latebat) | "Agnoscas." (*Aen.* 6.405f). On the woodcut, however, Aeneas is the one represented with the golden bough in his hand, which he also produces from under his garment in Murner's text: "Den [i.e. guldnen zweig] er mit kleid verborgen hat, | Eneas bald herfürher that" (M 6.863f.).[81]

Book 10 (Fig. 6, fol. 140ᵛ): In the foreground, two pairs of knights are fighting each other with raised lances; in the middle, between them, a human body with a severed head is lying on the ground. The middle-ground shows a duel between PALLAS and LAVSVS (*Aen.* 10.433f./M 10.921f.): The latter strikes out

---

77 Cf. *Althochdeutsches Wörterbuch*. Vol. 1. Ed. by Elisabeth Karg-Gasterstädt and Theodor Frings. Berlin 1968, col. 1212.

78 Cf. *Mittelhochdeutsches Wörterbuch*. Vol. 1. Ed. by Kurt Gärtner, Klaus Grubmüller and Karl Stackmann. Stuttgart 2013, col. 4878.

79 Cf. Rudolf Schützeichel, *Althochdeutscher und Altsächsischer Glossenwortschatz*. Vol. 1. Tübingen 2004, p. 430.

80 Lorenz Diefenbach, *Glossarium Latino-Germanicum mediae et infimae aetatis*. Unmodified reprint of the Frankfurt am Main 1857 edition. Darmstadt 1968 (Supplementum Lexici Mediae et Infimae Latinitatis), p. 116.

81 "Aeneas soon produced [the golden bough] that he had hidden under his robe."

Von Eneas
Wie Charon die Sybillin vnd Eneam verfieret.

Ærgo
iter

Aenach vollentens ire ſtroß
vñ kamē zů dem fluſſe groß
So bald ẟ ſchiffmā ſie erſaħ
ſtil gond durch den walde ẟ;
Vnd zů dem waſſer zů ħin gan
fieng er zům erſten reden an

Vnd ſchalt ſie darzů ħartigklich
du ſeieſt wer du wölleſt glich
das du ħar gaſt gewapnet dich
Was kumſtu ħar das ſag mir an
gang nit fürt bleib ſtillen ſtan
Der geiſt allein iſt diſe ſtat

Quiſq;
es

Fig. 5: Bayerische Staatsbibliothek München, Res/2 A.lat.a. 349, fol. 82ᵛ.

Von Eneas
Wie Turnus Pallassen anrante vnd erstach.

interea
soror

Das sie da beid nit zamen kemen
sunder ein andern tod in nemen
Von eim stærckern grössern feind
von dem sie beid erschlagen seind
Da zwischen Juturna Turnum mant
das er Lauso thet ein beistandt

Er kam geloffen fliegent har
mittel durch die gantze schar
So bald er seine gsellen sahe
stond ab dem krieg er zü in lahe
Ich wil Pallanta greiffen an
selber/ist mir ein eben man

Solus
ego

Fig. 6: Bayerische Staatsbibliothek München, Res/2 A.lat.a. 349, fol. 140ᵛ.

with his sword whilst PALLAS thrusts his lance against LAVSVS's shield. TVRNVS is standing behind: he is following the admonition of his sister Juturna, who is floating in a cloud to his left, and hurrying to the aid of LAVSVS (*Aen.* 10.439/M 10.933f.); after having jumped from the chariot (right) (*Aen.* 10.453/M 10.954), he pierces PALLAS with a lance (*Aen.* 10.482–485/M 10.1019–1026).

Whereas, in the Latin text, Turnus comes running in his chariot to take up the fight against Pallas ("qui [i.e. Turnus] volucri curru medium | secat agmen", *Aen.* 10.440), for Murner, he is coming on foot, as in the illustration: "Er kam geloffen fliegent har | mittel durch die gantze schar" (10.935).[82] In addition to the visual representation, Murner's translation may be traced back to the reading "volucri cursu" (at a flying run) for "volucri curru" (in a flying, quick chariot). However, the variant *cursu* for *curru* has not been attested in any of the contemporary editions of Virgil examined.

The 'translation' of the textual wording and of knowledge derived from the text in its pictorial form allowed the *litterati* to play a scholarly game, testing their own specialist knowledge using the images and thereby provides a learning process that occurs through the living and vivid transposition of the textual content into a visual medium. Murner, as a *doctus*, participated in this learning process: pictorial elements[83] that have no clear source in Virgil's Latin text or the commentaries added to it have found their way into Murner's German text. The repeated integration of pictorial details into the translation demonstrates the memorative effect of the *pictae tabellae* (KT 397, v. 1) that place the textual content before the reader's eyes in a living visualisation, thus allowing a deepened understanding of the Virgilian text. The woodcuts permitted a tangible process of dual translation: the transposition of the Latin text into a pictorial formula, which was then back-translated into German. The mediation process of Virgil's *Aeneid* takes place through the complementary composition of text and image, which guarantees a living and vivid representation of the written content. The interaction of the *Aeneid* woodcuts with Murner's translation allowed recipients unfamiliar with the Latin language to participate in an ancient body of knowledge, transposed into a pictorial language as early as 1500 and supported by a cultural transfer realised through both a visual and a linguistic medium.

---

82 "At a flying run, he passed through the whole company."
83 Cf. Henkel, 'Das Bild' (note 25), p. 410.

Bibliography

Althochdeutsches Wörterbuch. Vol. 1. Ed. by Elisabeth Karg-Gasterstädt and Theodor Frings.
Berlin 1968.

Bischoff, Georges, *La guerre des Paysans. L'Alsace et la révolution du Bundschuh, 1493–1525.*
Strasbourg 2010.

Brant, Sebastian, *Kleine Texte.* Ed. by Thomas Wilhelmi. 3 vols. Stuttgart, Bad Cannstatt 1998
(Arbeiten und Editionen zur mittleren deutschen Literatur N. F. 3).

Chrisman, Miriam U., *Bibliography of Strasbourg Imprints 1488–1599.* New Haven 1982.

Chrisman, Miriam U., *Lay Culture, Learned Culture. Books and Social Change in Strasbourg
1480–1599.* New Heaven 1982.

Curschmann, Michael, '*Pictura laicorum litteratura*? Überlegungen zum Verhältnis von Bild
und volkssprachlicher Schriftlichkeit im Hoch- und Spätmittelalter bis zum Codex
Manesse'. In: *Pragmatische Schriftlichkeit im Mittelalter. Erscheinungsformen und
Entwicklungsstufen.* Ed. by Hagen Keller, Klaus Grubmüller and Nikolaus
Staubach. München 1992 (Münstersche Mittelalter-Schriften 65), p. 211–229.

Davies, Martin and John Goldfinch (eds), *Vergil. A Census of Printed Editions 1469–1500.*
London 1992.

Diefenbach, Lorenz, *Glossarium Latino-Germanicum mediae et infimae aetatis.* Unmodified
reprint of the Frankfurt am Main 1857 edition. Darmstadt 1968 (Supplementum Lexici
Mediae et Infimae Latinitatis).

Duntze, Oliver, *Ein Verleger sucht sein Publikum. Die Straßburger Offizin des Matthias Hupfuff
(1497/98–1520).* München 2007 (Archiv für Geschichte des Buchwesens 4).

Dupeux, Cécile, Jacqueline Lévy and Jean Wirth (eds), *La gravure d'illustration en Alsace au
XVIe siècle.* 3 vols: *1. Jean Gruninger: 1501–1506. 2. Georg Husner, Johann Prüss,
Bartholomäus Kistler, Wilhelm Schaffner, Mathias Hupfuff, Johann Schott, Johann
Wähinger, Martin Flach, Johann Knobloch. 3. Jean Grüninger: 1507–1512.* Strasbourg
1992–2009.

Enenkel, Karl A. E., 'Illustrations as Commentary and Reader's Guidance. The Transformation
of Cicero's *De officiis* into a German Emblem Book by Johann of Schwarzenberg, Heinrich
Steiner, and Christian Egenolff (1517–1520; 1530/31; 1550)'. In: *Transformations of the
Classics via Early Modern Commentaries.* Ed. by Karl A. E. Enenkel. Leiden, Boston 2014
(Intersections 29), p. 167–259.

Falk, Tilman, 'Die Illustrationen zu Murners Sabellicus-Übersetzung'. In: *Thomas Murner.
Elsässischer Theologe und Humanist, 1475–1537. Eine Ausstellung der Badischen
Landesbibliothek Karlsruhe und der Bibliothèque nationale et universitaire de
Strasbourg.* Karlsruhe 1987, p. 112–130.

Frick, Julia, *Thomas Murners 'Aeneis'-Übersetzung (Straßburg 1515). Lateinisch-deutsche
Edition und Untersuchungen* (forthcoming 2019).

Frick, Julia, 'Renaissance eines antiken Klassikers. Thomas Murners Übersetzung von Vergils
'Aeneis' (1515)'. In: *ZfdA* 146 (2017), p. 351–368.

Füssel, Stephan, 'Die Bedeutung des Buchdrucks für die Verbreitung der Ideen des
Renaissance-Humanismus'. In: *Die Buchdrucker im 15. und 16. Jahrhundert.* Ed. by
Barbara Thiemann. Hamburg 1999, p. 121–161.

Geiß, Jürgen, 'Herausgeber, Korrektor, Verlagslektor? Sebastian Brant und die Basler
Petrarca-Ausgabe von 1496'. In: *Sebastian Brant. Forschungsbeiträge zu seinem Leben,*

zum '*Narrenschiff*' *und zum übrigen Werk*. Ed. by Thomas Wilhelmi. Basel 2002, p. 83–102.

Geldner, Ferdinand, *Die deutschen Inkunabeldrucker. 2 vols.: 1. Das deutsche Sprachgebiet. 2. Die fremden Sprachgebiete*. Stuttgart 1968–1970.

Grimm, Heinrich, 'Von dem Aufkommen eines eigenen Berufszweigs Korrektor und seinem Berufsbild im Buchdruck des XVI. Jahrhunderts'. In: *Gutenberg-Jahrbuch* 39 (1964), p. 185–190.

Hamm, Joachim, 'Zu Paratextualität und Intermedialität in Sebastian Brants *Vergilius pictus* (Straßburg 1502)'. In: *Intermedialität in der Frühen Neuzeit. Formen, Funktionen, Konzepte*. Ed. by Jörg Robert. Berlin, Boston 2017 (Frühe Neuzeit 209), p. 236–259.

Henkel, Nikolaus, 'Die *Carmina Priapea* in Sebastian Brants Vergil-Ausgabe (1502). Strategien einer angeleiteten Kommunikation. Mit einem Anhang: Die Sammlung der Vergil-Epitaphien der Straßburger Ausgabe'. In: *Sebastian Brant und die Kommunikationskultur um 1500*. Ed. by Klaus Bergdolt. Wiesbaden 2010 (Wolfenbütteler Abhandlungen zur Renaissanceforschung 26), p. 379–410.

Henkel, Nikolaus, 'Das Bild als Wissenssumme. Die Holzschnitte in Sebastian Brants Vergil-Ausgabe, Straßburg 1502'. In: *Schreiben und Lesen in der Stadt. Literaturbetrieb im spätmittelalterlichen Straßburg*. Ed. by Stephen Mossman, Nigel F. Palmer and Felix Heinzer. Berlin 2012 (Kulturtopographie des alemannischen Raums 4), p. 389–419.

Holzberg, Niklas (ed.), *Die Appendix Vergiliana. Pseudepigraphen im literarischen Kontext*. Tübingen 2005 (Classica Monacensia 30).

Huber-Rebenich, Gerlinde, 'Ovids Göttersagen in illustrierten Ausgaben des 15. und 16. Jahrhunderts'. In: *Wechselseitige Wahrnehmung der Religionen im Spätmittelalter und in der Frühen* Neuzeit. *II. Kulturelle Konkretionen (Literatur, Mythographie, Wissenschaft und Kunst)*. Ed. by Ludger Grenzmann, Thomas Haye and Nikolaus Henkel et al. Berlin, Boston 2012 (Abhandlungen der Akademie der Wissenschaften zu Göttingen N. F., 4), p. 185–207.

Kallendorf, Craig, *Virgil and the Myth of Venice. Books and Readers in the Italian Renaissance*. Oxford 1999.

Klingner, Jacob, *Minnereden im Druck. Studien zur Gattungsgeschichte im Zeitalter des Medienwechsels*. Berlin 2010 (Philologische Studien und Quellen 226).

Knape, Joachim, 'Mnemonik, Bildbuch und Emblematik im Zeitalter Sebastian Brants'. In: *Mnemosyne. Festschrift für Manfred Lurker zum 60. Geburtstag*. Ed. by Werner Bies, Hermann Jung and Manfred Lurker. Baden-Baden 1988 (Bibliographie zur Symbolik, Ikonographie und Mythologie, supplementary vol. 2), p. 133–178.

Knape, Joachim, 'Brant (Titio), Sebastian'. In: *Deutscher Humanismus 1480–1520. Verfasserlexikon*. Ed. by Franz Josef Worstbrock, vol. 1. Berlin, New York 2008, cols. 247–283.

Kristeller, Paul, *Die Strassburger Bücher-Illustration im XV. und im Anfange des XVI. Jahrhunderts*. Leipzig 1888 (Beiträge zur Kunstgeschichte. N. F. VII).

Leach, Eleanor W., 'Illustration as Interpretation in Brant's and Dryden's Editions of Vergil'. In: *The Early Illustrated Book. Essays in Honor of Lessing J. Rosenwald*. Ed. by Sandra Hindman. Washington 1982, p. 175–210.

Manger, Klaus, *Literarisches Leben in Strassburg während der Prädikatur Johann Geilers* von Kaysersberg *(1478–1510)*. Heidelberg 1983 (Heidelberger Forschungen 24).

Mittelhochdeutsches Wörterbuch. Ed. by Kurt Gärtner, Klaus Grubmüller and Karl Stackmann. Vol. 1. Stuttgart 2013.

Mossman, Stephen, Nigel F. Palmer and Felix Heinzer (eds), *Schreiben und Lesen in der Stadt. Literaturbetrieb im spätmittelalterlichen Straßburg*. Berlin 2012 (Kulturtopographie des alemannischen Raums 4).

Münch, Birgit U., 'Periculosus catus. Subversive Kritik in Bildern und Texten Thomas Murners'. In: *Von der Freiheit der Bilder. Spott, Kritik und Subversion in der Kunst der Dürerzeit*. Ed. by Thomas Schauerte, Jürgen Müller and Bertram Kaschek. Petersberg 2013, p. 196–217.

Myslivec, Josef, 'Tod Mariens'. In: *LCI* 4 (1994), cols. 334–338.

Pieper, Christoph, 'Horaz als Schulfibel und als elitärer Gründungstext des deutschen Humanismus. Die illustrierte Horazausgabe des Jakob Locher (1498)'. In: *Transformations of the Classics via Early Modern Commentaries*. Ed. by Karl. A. E. Enenkel. Leiden 2014, p. 61–90.

Plotke, Seraina, 'Emblematik vor der Emblematik. Der frühe Buchdruck als Experimentierfeld der Text-Bild-Beziehungen'. In: *ZfdPh* 129 (2010), p. 127–142.

Putnam, Michael C. J. (ed.), *Maffeo Vegio. Short Epics*. Cambridge 2004 (The I Tatti Renaissance Library 15).

Reske, Christoph, *Die Buchdrucker des 16. und 17. Jahrhunderts im deutschen Sprachgebiet. Auf der Grundlage des gleichnamigen Werkes von Josef Benzing*. Wiesbaden 2007 (Beiträge zum Buch- und Bibliothekswesen 51).

Reynolds, Leighton D. (ed.), *Texts and Transmission. A Survey of the Latin Classics*. Oxford 1983.

Ritter, François, *Histoire de l'imprimerie alsacienne aux XVe et XVIe siècles*. Strasbourg, Paris 1955.

Röll, Walter, 'Schöfferlin, Bernhard'. In: ²*VL* 8 (1992), cols. 810–814.

Römer, Hermann, 'Hans Grüninger und die Buchdruckerfamilie Reinhard aus Markgröningen'. In: H.R., *Markgröningen im Rahmen der Landesgeschichte. I. Urgeschichte und Mittelalter*. Markgröningen 1933, p. 277–331.

Schmidt, Charles, *Zur Geschichte der ältesten Bibliotheken und der ersten Buchdrucker zu Strassburg*. Strasbourg 1882.

Schmidt, Charles, *Répertoire bibliographique strasbourgeois jusque vers 1530. I. Jean Grüninger 1483–1531*. Strasbourg 1894.

Schmidt, Ernst A., 'Vergils Aeneis als augusteische Dichtung'. In: *Von Göttern und Menschen erzählen. Formkonstanten und Funktionswandel vormoderner Epik*. Ed. by Jörg Rüpke. Stuttgart 2001 (Potsdamer altertumswissenschaftliche Beiträge 4), p. 65–92.

Schmitt, Anneliese, 'Tradition und Innovation von Literaturgattungen und Buchformen in der Frühdruckzeit'. In: *Die Buchkultur im 15. und 16. Jahrhundert*. 2nd half-volume. Ed. by Barbara Thiemann. Hamburg 1999, p. 9–120.

Schneider, Bernd, '"Virgilius pictus" – Sebastian Brants illustrierte Vergilausgabe von 1502 und ihre Nachwirkung. Ein Beitrag zur Vergilrezeption im deutschen Humanismus'. In: *Wolfenbütteler Beiträge* 6 (1983), p. 202–262.

Schneider, Bernd (ed. and transl.), *Das Aeneissupplement des Maffeo Vegio*. Weinhein 1985.

Schützeichel, Rudolf, *Althochdeutscher und Altsächsischer Glossenwortschatz. Bearbeitet unter Mitwirkung von zahlreichen Wissenschaftlern des Inlandes und des Auslandes. Herausgegeben im Auftrag der Akademie der Wissenschaften zu Göttingen*. 12 vols., Tübingen 2004.

Sondheim, Moritz, 'Die Illustrationen zu Thomas Murners Werken'. In: *Elsaß-Lothringisches Jahrbuch* 12 (1933), p. 5–82.

Suerbaum, Werner, *Handbuch der illustrierten Vergil-Ausgaben 1502–1840. Geschichte, Typologie, Zyklen und kommentierter Katalog der Holzschnitte und Kupferstiche zur Aeneis in Alten Drucken. Mit besonderer Berücksichtigung der Bestände der Bayerischen Staatsbibliothek München und ihrer Digitalisate von Bildern zu Werken des P. Vergilius Maro*. Hildesheim, New York 2008 (Bibliographien zur klassischen Philologie 3).

Suerbaum, Werner, 'Titelbilder zu den Aeneis-Büchern vom Humanismus bis zum Neoklassizismus. Geschichte, Typen und Tendenzen der Aeneis-Illustration in gedruckten Vergil-Ausgaben und -Übersetzungen von 1502–1840'. In: *Philologia antiqua* 1 (2008), p. 99–201.

P. Vergili Maronis Opera. Ed. by R.A.B. Mynors. Oxford 1969.

Vergil, *Aeneis*. Ed. by Manfred Lemmer. Translated by Johannes Götte. Leipzig 1979.

Wilhelmi, Thomas (ed.), *Sebastian Brant. Forschungsbeiträge zu seinem Leben, zum 'Narrenschiff' und zum übrigen Werk*. Basel 2002.

Wilhelmi, Thomas (ed.), Sebastian Brant. Kleine Texte. 3 vols. Stuttgart, Bad Cannstatt 1998 (Arbeiten und Editionen zur mittleren deutschen Literatur N. F. 3).

Winter, Carla, *Humanistische Historiographie in der Volkssprache. Bernhard Schöfferlins 'Römische Historie'*. Stuttgart, Bad Cannstatt 1999 (Arbeiten und Editionen zur mittleren deutschen Literatur. N. F. 6).

Wolters, Maria, *Beziehungen zwischen Holzschnitt und Text bei Sebastian Brant und Thomas Murner. Mit einem Exkurs über die Illustrationen des Wälschen Gastes*. Strasbourg 1917.

Worstbrock, Franz Josef, 'Adelphus Mulings Vergilübersetzung'. In: *ZfdA* 102 (1973), p. 203–210.

Worstbrock, Franz Josef, *Deutsche Antikerezeption 1450–1550. Teil I: Verzeichnis der deutschen Übersetzungen antiker Autoren. Mit einer Bibliographie der Übersetzer*. Boppard am Rhein 1976 (Veröffentlichungen zur Humanismusforschung 1).

Worstbrock, Franz Josef, 'Wittich, Ivo'. In: [2]*VL* 10 (1999), col. 1290–1292.

Worstbrock, Franz Josef, 'Muling, Johann Adelphus'. In: *Deutscher Humanismus 1480–1520. Verfasserlexikon*. Ed. by Franz Josef Worstbrock. Vol. 2. Berlin, New York 2013, col. 255–277.

Worstbrock, Franz Josef, 'Murner, Thomas'. In: *Deutscher Humanismus 1480–1520. Verfasserlexikon*. Ed. by Franz Josef Worstbrock. Vol. 2. Berlin, New York 2013, cols. 333–339.

Worstbrock, Franz Josef, 'Ringmann, Matthias'. In: *Deutscher Humanismus 1480–1520. Verfasserlexikon*. Ed. by Franz Josef Worstbrock. Vol. 2. Berlin, New York 2013, col. 725–740.

Nicolas Potysch
Dasselbe nochmal: Narratives Potenzial von Bildwiederholungen in frühneuzeitlichen Romanen

Abstracts: Illustrated novels are characterized by the material co-existence of written text and images. This combination of figuration and writing allowing intersemiotic interpretation reached new heights with the technical advances of the turn of the sixteenth century. The multiple use of the same image within one illustrated narrative is a little-studied phenomenon linked to this special type of text. Up to now, research has mainly concentrated on the historical conditions of production to explain these repetitions. One could, however, also ask what the narrative consequences of such multiple uses of identical illustrations are. In this contribution, an attempt is made to partially answer this question by means of a close reading of a small extract of Georg Wickram's *Ritter Galmy* (1539), a typical example of duplication within one novel.

Illustrierte Romane zeichnen sich durch die materiale Gleichzeitigkeit von Bild und Schrift, d. h. durch eine bisemiotische Konfiguration der Buchseite, aus, die aufgrund technischer Innovation erst an der Schwelle vom 15. zum 16. Jahrhundert eine Hochkonjunktur erfährt. Durch sie werden intersemiotische Interpretationsspielräume eröffnet, für die die Wechselbeziehung der unterschiedlichen Zeichensysteme konstitutiv ist. Die mehrfache Verwendung identischer Bilder innerhalb eines Romans stellt dabei ein kaum untersuchtes Phänomen dar, das primär als Ausdruck marktwirtschaftlichen Kalküls verstanden wird. Stattdessen stehen im Zentrum der folgenden Überlegungen die narrativen Konsequenzen solcher Bildwiederholungen, die anhand eines Close-Readings eines knappen Auszugs aus Georg Wickrams *Ritter Galmy* (1539) exemplarisch vorgeführt werden.

Auch wenn uns die Gleichzeitigkeit von Bild und Schrift in *einem* Artefakt heute in unterschiedlichen literarischen und nicht-literarischen Kontexten vertraut oder gar als Standardfall erscheint (man denke z. B. an Printwerbung oder generische Schrift-Bild-Formen wie den Comic),[1] so handelt es sich dabei am Übergang vom 15. zum 16. Jahrhundert doch um eine Konfiguration, die

---

[1] So proklamiert Susanne Blazejewski gar: „Die Kombination von Wort und Bild stellt heute *in allen Medien* den Normalfall dar." (Susanne Blazejewski, *Bild und Text – Photographie in autobiographischer Literatur: Marguerite Duras' 'L'amant' und Michael Ondaatjes 'Running in the Family'.* Würzburg 2002, S. 14; Hervorhebung NP).

Nicolas Potysch, Ruhr-Universität Bochum

aufgrund technischer Innovation für den literarischen Markt gerade erst attrak-
tiv geworden war. Diese Attraktivität war in erster Linie eine wirtschaftliche,
bei der die Rentabilität der verantwortlichen Offizin und die gesicherte finan-
zielle Situation der mit der Buchproduktion verbundenen Akteure (Autor, Set-
zer, Reißer, Schneider, Lektor, Drucker, etc.) im Zentrum stand. Darüber hinaus
stellt die Entwicklung effizienter Drucktechniken und -maschinen aber auch im
Sinne einer Schlüsseltechnologie die ‚Bedingung der Möglichkeit‘ für die Her-
ausbildung literarischer Genres dar,[2] deren genuines Merkmal die semiotische
Verschränkung von Schrift und Bild ist. Wenngleich diese Korrelation bereits
verschiedentlich ausführlich beschrieben wurde,[3] so existieren doch bis dato
kaum beachtete Phänomene, die sich ausgerechnet in dieser von Experimenten
und Unwägbarkeiten bestimmten Sondierungsphase moderner Buchproduktion herausgebildet haben und denen bis in die Gegenwart hinein *systematische* Relevanz zukommt. Eines dieser Phänomene wird im Folgenden mitsamt
dem damit verbundenen narrativen Potenzial näher differenziert und analy-
siert: die *Bildreplik*, d. h. die *intra*textuelle weil roman*interne* Mehrfachverwen-
dung einer identischen Bildtextur.[4]

Ich beginne meine Argumentation mit der Darlegung des exemplarischen, historischen Gegenstands und des Phänomens, wobei ich an geeigneter Stelle abbre-
chen werde.[5] Derart skizziere ich die Herausforderung, die Bildwiederholungen

---

2 Eine Technologie ist dann eine Schlüsseltechnologie, wenn durch sie zugleich die
technischen Möglichkeiten einer Gesellschaft geradezu sprunghaft ansteigen und eine gesell-
schaftliche Entwicklung beschleunigt oder überhaupt erst ermöglicht wird. Vgl. dazu Mae
Keary, 'Key Technologies – Chasing the Gap'. In: *Aslib Proceedings* 43/5 (1991), S. 161–172.
3 Vgl. dazu beispielsweise das formal und nicht inhaltlich gedachte Genre des ‚Bildbuchs‘,
das Knape als „feste[s] und verbreitete[s] Prinzip der Buchgestaltung im Bereich der Moralistik
und Satire" (S. 153) bezeichnet. Vgl. Joachim Knape, 'Mnemonik, Bildbuch und Emblematik im
Zeitalter Sebastian Brants (Brant, Schwarzenberg, Alciati)'. In: *Mnemosyne. Festschrift für Manfred Lurker zum 60. Geburtstag.* Hg. v. Werner Bies und Hermann Jung. Baden-Baden 1988,
S. 133–178.
4 Zum systematischen Anspruch, Bilder als Texte bzw. Texturen zu beschreiben, der sich
maßgeblich aus der Semiotik speist vgl. z. B. Hartmut Stöckl, *Die Sprache im Bild, das Bild in
der Sprache: Zur Verknüpfung von Sprache und Bild im massenmedialen Text. Konzepte, Theorien, Analysemethoden.* Berlin, New York 2004; Thomas M. Susanka, *Foto/grafie. Zur Rhetorik
von Medium und Bild. Mit einer Fallstudie zu James Nachtwey.* Berlin 2015; Ulla Fix und Hans
Wellmann, 'Sprachtexte – Bildtexte. Bemerkungen zum Symposion *Bild im Text – Text und
Bild* vom 6.–8. April 2000 in Leipzig'. In: *Bild im Text, Text im Bild.* Hg. v. Ulla Fix und Hans
Wellmann. Heidelberg 2000, S. XI–XVII.
5 Ausführlicher widme ich mich dieser Thematik anhand weiterer Beispiele – aus dem *Fortu-
natus* (1509), Georg Wickrams *Ritter Galmy* (1539), Georg Messerschmidts *Brissonetus* (1559),
Thüring von Ringoltingens *Melusine* (1587) in der Fassung des *Buchs der Liebe* und Karl Arnold

innerhalb des Lektüreprozesses für die Intersemiose – also die das einzelne Zeichensystem überschreitende Bedeutungszuweisung von Schrift *und* Bild – und die Konstruktion einer global sinnkonstanten, erzählten Welt darstellen.

1 Bildwiederholungen im *Ritter Galmy* I

Der 1539 in Straßburg bei Jacob Frölich veröffentlichte und vermutlich von Georg Wickram verfasste Roman *Ein schoene und liebliche History von dem edlen und theüren Ritter Galmien* berichtet vom Aufstieg des jungen Ritters Galmy am Hofe des bretonischen Herzogs.[6] Der Ritter, der bald in höfischer Minne zur Frau seines Lehnsherrn entbrennt, ist trotz seines ritterlichen Erfolges nach einer Intrige gezwungen, ins Exil in die Dienste des schottischen Königs zu fliehen. Lediglich um seine verehrte Herzogin zu schützen, kehrt er als Mönch verkleidet in die Bretagne zurück und gewinnt für sie einen Gerichtskampf, ein Gottesurteil, durch das ihre moralische Unversehrtheit bewiesen wird. Nachdem der bretonische Herzog bald darauf an einer Krankheit verstirbt, kann Galmy aus dem Exil zurückkehren, die Herzogin wenig später ehelichen und selber zum Herzog der Bretagne erhoben werden. Bei der Lektüre des Romans begegnen insgesamt 61 Bilder,[7] denen jedoch nur 37 Druckstöcke zugrunde liegen. Die Ursache für diese Diskrepanz erklärt sich dadurch,

---

Kortums *Jobsiade* (1824) – in *Wiederholt doppeldeutig in Bild und Schrift – Ambiguität im durchbilderten Roman*. Hannover 2018.

6 Als eines der Zentren der Reformation kommt Straßburg auch als deutsch-französischer Kontaktzone im 16. Jahrhundert maßgeblicher Einfluss auf den Buchmarkt und das Druckergewerbe der Zeit zu. Josef Benzig geht dabei so weit, superlativisch zu betonen: „L'importance de Strasbourg pour l'histoire de l'imprimerie n'est plus à démontrer" (Josef Benzig, *Bibliographie Strasbourgeoise*. Bd. 1. Baden-Baden 1981, S. 5). Unabhängig davon, ob diese Einschätzung uneingeschränkt zu teilen ist, konnte Straßburg daher wohl bereits in der Frühzeit des erstarkenden, ortsfesten, deutschen Buchmarkts auf eine handwerkliche Tradition sowie auf ein ausgeprägtes Selbstverständnis und -bewusstsein der dazugehörigen Berufsstände zurückblicken. Damit ein Buch wie der *Ritter Galmy* in diesem wirtschaftlichen Umfeld zum Bestseller werden konnte – Gotzkowsky verzeichnet alleine für das 16. Jh. 13 Ausgaben –, musste es sich entweder durch einen besonders günstigen Preis oder eine hohe Qualität gegenüber dem breiten Konkurrenzangebot auszeichnen. Vgl. Bodo Gotzkowsky, *'Volksbücher'. Prosaromane, Renaissancenovellen, Versdichtungen und Schwankbücher. Bibliographie der Deutschen Drucke. Teil I: Drucke des 15. und 16. Jahrhunderts*. Baden-Baden 1991, S. 443–448. [Vgl. für die Bedeutung von Straßburg als Druckzentrum auch den Beitrag von Bertelsmeier-Kierst in diesem Band (Seite 37).]

7 Den verbreiteten Ausdruck Illustration vermeide ich trotz seiner erhellenden Etymologie konsequent, da mir mit seiner Verwendung sowohl im deutsch- als auch englischsprachigen

dass innerhalb des Romans acht Bilder zweimal, fünf dreimal, zwei viermal und nur die übrigen 22 singulär dargeboten werden. Die Bildtexturen sind – von einer Ausnahme abgesehen – immer ungefähr am Kapitelanfang gesetzt, jedoch beziehen sie sich nicht zwingend auf die dort unmittelbar beschriebenen Ereignisse. So es die Seitenaufteilung erlaubte, wurde offenbar versucht, die Bilder unmittelbar unter oder innerhalb der Kapitelüberschrift einzufügen. Der sorgfältige Satz und die hohe Qualität des im Oktav-Format vorliegenden Romans fallen auf und lassen auf eine sorgfältige Produktion und nennenswerte Fertigungskosten schließen. Mit Ausnahme des quadratischen Titelbildes sind sämtliche Bilder als leichte Querrechtecke (Verhältnis 7:8) geboten, wobei jedes Bild erneut von einer kräftigen schwarzen Linie gerahmt wird. Während die Bildtextur auf der Titelseite ca. zwei Drittel des Satzspiegels einnimmt, kommt den anderen Bildern etwa drei Fünftel der bedruckten Seitenfläche zu.

Da offensichtlich weniger Holzschnitte angefertigt wurden, als Kapitel vorhanden sind, liegt möglicherweise zunächst der Gedanke nahe, die Wiederholungen dadurch zu erklären, dass Frölich bzw. Wickram dem Leser für jedes Kapitel ein *Leitbild* bieten wollte und so gezwungen war zu wiederholen. Aufgrund zweier Überlegungen ist diese Annahme jedoch wenig plausibel. Erstens verfügt nicht jedes Kapitel über genau ein Bild: Im 54. Kapitel, das mit fünfeinhalb Seiten keineswegs besonders umfangreich ist, finden sich anders als in den sonstigen Kapiteln zwei Bildtexturen, von denen außerdem *keine* mehrfach gebraucht wird. Zweitens wäre das Bildprogramm des Romans leicht für eine solche Situation anzupassen gewesen – die Offizine verfügten in der Regel über einen großen Bestand an Druckstöcken. Außerdem wird begründet gemutmaßt, dass Wickram nicht nur den Wortlaut des *Ritter Galmy*, sondern auch die dazugehörigen Bilder genauestens plante.[8] Wäre die obige These zutreffend, so hätte das Verhältnis von Bildtextur zu Kapitel auch über die Kapitelanzahl oder weitere Holzschnitte reguliert werden können.

Bei der Lektüre des Romans begegnet auf fol. 9ʳ ein Bild (s. Abb. 1), das eine intime Szenerie zeigt: Eine Frau, die ihrer prunkvollen Kleidung nach wohl von edlem Stande ist, steht am Bett eines offensichtlich erkrankten oder sterbenden

---

Raum eine implizite und explizite Aufwertung des Illustrierten, d. h. der Schrift und eine Abwertung des Illustrierenden, den Bildern, verbunden scheint.

8 Vgl. Peter Schmidt, 'Literat und "selbstgewachsener Moler". Jörg Wickram und der illustrierte Roman der Frühen Neuzeit'. In: *Künstler und Literat. Schrift- und Buchkultur in der europäischen Renaissance.* Hg. v. Bodo Guthmüller, Berndt Hamm und Andreas Tönnesmann. Wiesbaden 2006, S. 143–194.

Mannes und leistet diesem Beistand. Sie hat seine rechte Hand mit ihrer gefasst und sieht den Kranken unverwandt an. Am rechten Bildrand steht eine weitere Frau – ihrem Gewand nach wohl eine Zofe – die ebenfalls den Kranken betrachtet. Die Identifikation der dargestellten Figuren innerhalb der Romanepisode ist in diesem Fall unproblematisch bereits anhand der Kapitelüberschrift möglich: „Wie die *Hertzogin* mit jren *Junckfrawē* den *Ritter Galmien* heymsuochet / jn auff seinem betth ligen findet / Und wie der Ritter von der Hertzogin gedroest ward" (fol. 8ᵛ, Hervorhebungen NP]).

Die Herzogin betritt somit in standesgemäßer und anständiger Begleitung „jre[r] Junckfrawē" (fol. 8ᵛ) das Gemach des Ritters Galmy. Dort spricht sie mit dem leidenden, im Bett liegenden Ritter – der dann auch der Männergestalt im Bild zugeordnet werden kann – und vergewissert sich, dass die Botschaft von der Minnekrankheit des Ritters, die Galmys Freund Friderich ihr übermittelte, der Wahrheit entspricht. Das anfängliche Zögern des Ritters, sich seiner Herrin zu offenbaren, überwindet die Herzogin dadurch, dass sie „zuohandt die beyden junckfrawen / mit sampt deß Ritters knaben / in jr gemach schicken theht" (fol. 9ʳ), nicht ohne jedoch explizit zu betonen: „Dieweil ich doch verstanden hab / du [=Galmy] mich nicht anderst / dann in züchten und eeren liebhabest / und allein meines drostes begeren thuost" (fol. 10ᵛ).

Nach einem längeren Dialog, in dem Galmy der Herzogin seine Liebe gesteht, überreicht sie ihm – relativ unvermittelt – einen Ring als Liebesgabe. Mittels dieses „zeychen warer unn rechter liebe" (fol. 11ᵛ) schließt sie so einen Treuebund mit ihrem Ritter. Besondere Aufmerksamkeit legt die Schrift-Bild-Textur dabei auf das Motiv der ‚Hand'. Galmy berichtet seiner Geliebten, wie er sich vor kurzem auf einem Jagdausflug in sie verliebt hat: „[S]o bald aber ewer schoene weisse hand / inn die mein verschlossen ward / augenblicklich mich ein brinnender flamn umb mein herz entzünden thet / und von solchen tag an / die liebe sich in mir staetigs gemeret / und so krefftigklich zuogenumnen" (fol. 11ᵛ). Im Kontext dieser Aussage erhält die Tatsache, dass das Bild die Herzogin just in dem Moment zeigt, als sie dem Ritter erneut „ir schneeweisse hand bieten thet" (fol. 11ᵛ), zusätzliche Brisanz – entzündete diese Geste doch die Liebe des Ritters. Der Krankenbesuch der Herzogin ist schließlich von Erfolg gekrönt: Der Ritter gesundet durch die Fürsorge seiner Herrin. Die Medizin, die der Bildbetrachter in der dargestellten Glasphiole der Zofe vermuten mag, findet sich dabei schriftlich als „koestlich confeckt unn latwergen" (fol. 12ʳ) wieder. Wie genau der Leser sich allerdings eine Medizin für einen liebeskranken Ritter vorzustellen hat, wird nicht verraten, doch deutet es der körperliche Kontakt zwischen Ritter und Herzogin im zuvor erotisch aufgeladenen Händereichen und der pointierten Hervorhebung, dass die Herzogin sich „aller einig bey dem Ritter" (fol. 9ʳ)

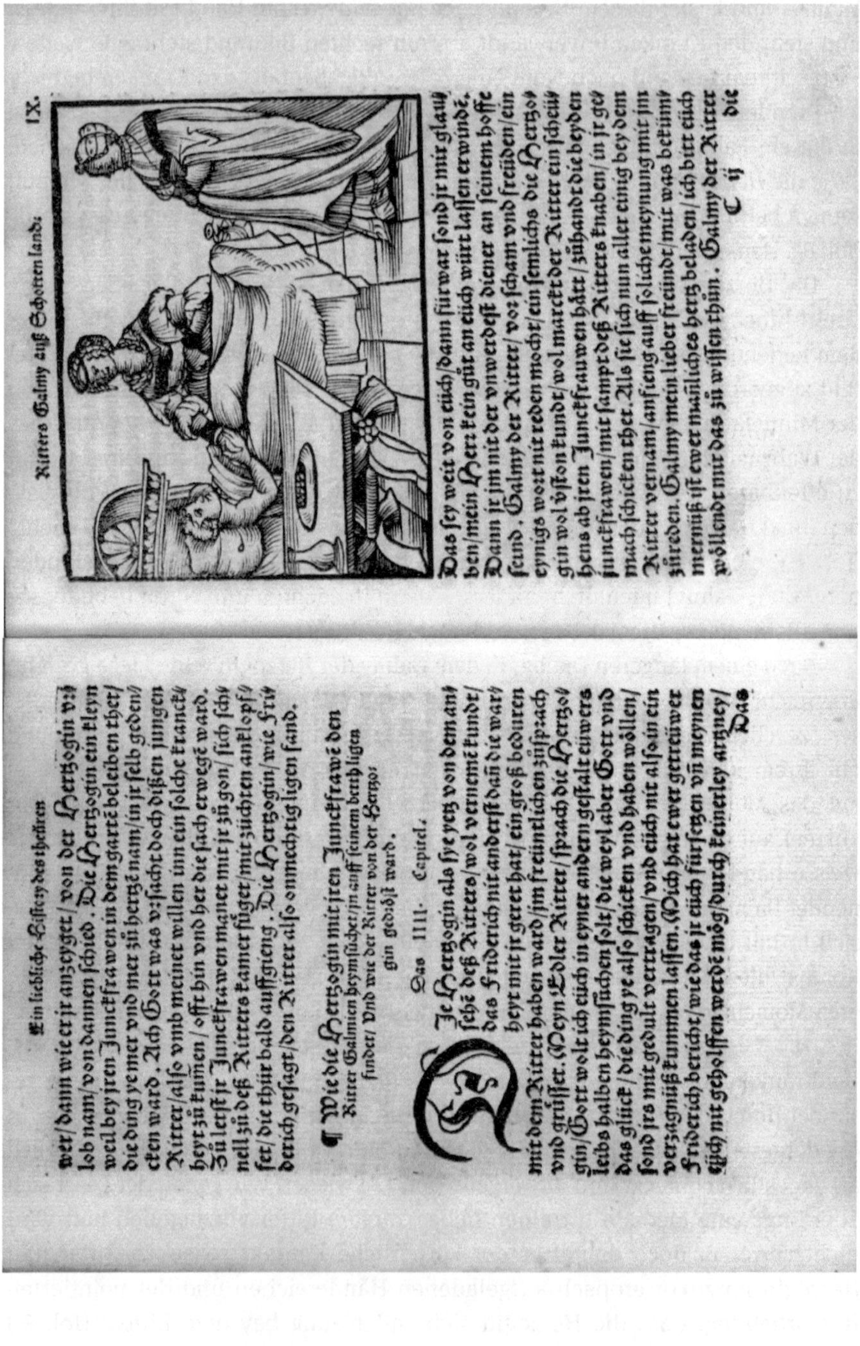

Abb. 1: *Ritter Galmy* (1539): fol. 8^{v}–9^{r}.

befand, an. Zudem endet die intime Zweisamkeit der beiden Liebenden mit der erneuten Betonung des erotischen Moments:

> Die zeit aber kam / das die Junckfrawen jrem befelch nach / schier kummen sollten / die Hertzogin guot bedunckt / ein abscheyd von dem Ritter zuo nemmen / also sprach. Mein aller liebster Galmy / uns wil nit lenger gezymmen / bey einander zuo bleiben / deßhalben ich ein freündlich urlob von dir beger / im ihr schneweisse hand bieten thet. (fol. 11ᵛ)

Im Fortlauf der Ereignisse steigt Galmy erst weiter am herzoglichen Hofe auf, indem er sich und seinem Lehnsherren Ruhm und Anerkennung auf einer Vielzahl von Turnieren erwirbt, bevor er dann aufgrund einer erpresserischen Intrige, in deren Zentrum seine Minne zur Herzogin steht, ins Exil nach Schottland flüchten muss. Nur für einen gerichtlichen Zweikampf kehrt er verkleidet zurück und verhindert so, dass eine weitere Verschwörung seine Herrin auf den Scheiterhaufen bringt.

Wenn dann auf fol. 134ʳ (s. Abb. 2) das Bild von fol. 9ʳ erneut begegnet, stellt dies den Leser bzw. die Leserin vor ein Dilemma: Die Bedeutung, die dem Bild eingangs des Romans im vierten Kapitel zugewiesen wurde – Herzogin und Galmy im Zwiegespräch im Gemach des Ritters – ist hier innerhalb der erzählten Welt unmöglich, da Galmy nach wie vor in Schottland weilt und aktuell von seinem Vertrauten Friderich besucht wird.

Stattdessen legen der folgende Passus und das erneut dargebotene Bild eine andere Krankenbett-Situation nahe:

> Nun begab sich in der zeit / die weil Friderich inn Schottenland was / das der Hertzog inn ein schwere kranckheyt fiel / Darvon ein neüwes leydt inn gantzem Britanien endtston thett. Als aber vil mit jm versuochet / unnd als umb sunst was. Der Hertzog zuo letst von diser welt verschied. (fol. 135ʳ)

Der Herzog ist plötzlich sehr schwer erkrankt, die Ärzte können ihm nicht mehr helfen und so stirbt er bzw. liegt in der Momentaufnahme des Bildes im Sterben. Ihm kommt daher in der Bildtextur wohl die Position zu, die zuvor der kranke, im Bett liegende Galmy eingenommen hat. Die Herzogin hält auch seine Hand und spendet ihm Trost. Eine Hofdame mit einer Phiole in der Hand nimmt die Position der „vil mit jm versouchenden" Ärzte ein.

Aber wer wird durch die Bildtextur nun im Bett liegend vor Augen geführt – Galmy oder der Herzog? Handelt es sich um eine Sterbe- oder eine Genesungsszene? Diese durch die Wiederholung induzierten Irritationen gilt es zu verarbeiten. Bevor ich hier nun mit meiner Auslegung des *Ritter Galmy* fortfahre,

trete ich daher einen Schritt von dieser Einzelinterpretation zurück und konzentriere mich auf das Wechselspiel von Wiederholung und Irritation.

In jüngerer Zeit ist ein erstarktes Interesse an der Durchbilderung der Werke Wickrams (primär) seitens der mediävistischen Forschung zu beobachten.[9] Die Fragestellungen folgen dabei zwar einem materialphilologisch sensibilisierten Bewusstsein für die Bedeutsamkeit der Korporalität und Materialität der spezifischen Gegenstände, sind jedoch in vielen Fällen noch immer stark auf die von der Schrift diktierte Linearität der Ereignisabfolge fokussiert, die seitens der Bildtexturen dann nur noch unterstrichen bzw. unterstützt wird – Subvention statt Kooperation. Derart entstehen Scheuklappen, die den Blick zwar für einzelne Merkmale der Textur schärfen, gleichzeitig aber andere aus dem Gesichtsfeld verdrängen. So verzeichnet die editionsphilologische Ausgabe der Werke Wickrams von Bolte und Scheel (1901) beispielsweise zwar die Tatsache der Durchbilderung,[10] reproduziert jedoch keine einzige der Bildtexturen und erwähnt auch die mehrfache Verwendung derselben nicht. Erstmals deskriptiv erfasst ist die multiple Bildwiederholung bei Bodo Gotzkowsky, wenngleich die numerischen Angaben fehlerhaft sind.[11] Peter Schmidt und Hubertus Fischer fordern schließlich, dass die poetologische Bedeutung und die narrative Funktion, die den Bildtexturen in Wickrams Werken zukommt, zu untersuchen seien.[12]

Eine exemplarische Arbeit, die eine programmatische Veränderung im Umgang mit Wickrams durchbilderten Romanen markiert, stellt Rafael Kuchs „Intermediales Erzählen im frühneuzeitlichen illustrierten Roman. Zu Struktur und Wirkung der Medienkombination bei Jörg Wickram" dar. Auch bei Kuch finden

---

9 Vgl. u. a. Dieter Kartschoke: 'Ritter Galmy uß Schottenland und Jörg Wickram aus Colmar'. In: *Daphnis* 31 (2002), S. 469–489; oder Raphael Kuch, *Intermediales Erzählen im frühneuzeitlichen illustrierten Roman*. Köln, Weimar, Wien 2014. Eine ausführliche Übersicht findet sich bei Catherine Drittenbass und André Schnyder (Hgg.), *Eulenspiegel trifft Melusine. Der frühneuhochdeutsche Prosaroman im Licht neuer Forschungen und Methoden*. Amsterdam, New York 2010.

10 Johannes Bolte und Willy Scheel (Hgg.), *Georg Wickrams Werke. Erster Band. Galmy – Gabriotto*. Bd. CCXXII. Tübingen 1901 (Bibliothek des literarischen Vereins in Stuttgart), S. XX–XI.

11 Vgl. Gotzkowsky (vgl. Anm. 6), S. 443; und Bodo Gotzkowsky, *Die Buchholzschnitte Hans Brosamers zu den Frankfurter 'Volksbuch'-Ausgaben und ihre Wiederverwendungen*. Baden-Baden 2002, S. 77.

12 Vgl. Schmidt (vgl. Anm. 8) und Hubertus Fischer: 'Wickrams Bilderwelt. Vorläufige Bemerkungen'. In: *Vergessene Texte – Verstellte Blicke. Neue Perspektiven der Wickram-Forschung*. Hg. v. Maria Elisabeth Müller und Michael Mecklenburg. Frankfurt am Main 2007, S. 199–214. [Zum Einfluss von Bildern auf die Interpretation eines Werkes siehe auch den Beitrag von Frick in diesem Band, S. 254–267.]

sich Ansätze dazu, die Narration nicht als *Schriftgeschichte* unterstützt durch bildliche Hinzugaben, sondern als Schrift-Bild-Geschichte zu verstehen. Dabei fällt jedoch auf, dass Kuch wenig auf systematische Aspekte, wie die theoretischen Grundlagen und die erforderliche Modellierung eines intersemiotischen Narrativs, eingeht. Anders als in den Vorarbeiten und Werkausgaben des (frühen) 20. Jahrhunderts zu Georg Wickram erfährt die 1539er Ausgabe des Ritter Galmy bei Kuch eine detaillierte Beschreibung, bei der auch das Durchbilderungsprogramm inklusive der Bildwiederholungen erfasst wird.[13] Insbesondere die folgende Hypothese erscheint vor den bisherigen Überlegungen anschlussfähig: „Dabei [= in der Rezeption der Bildwiederholung] schwingt die ursprüngliche Semantik der Bilddarstellung zwangsläufig folienartig mit und regt zur relationalen Verknüpfung mit der neuen Semantik an".[14] – Hier wird Ambiguität beschrieben, ohne dann allerdings aus diesem Nebeneinander der Semantiken einen interpretativen Mehrwert abzuleiten. Ohne die notwendigen semiotischen und textuellen Grundlagen wird die Wiederholung von der Schrifttextur aus gedacht und an diese angepasst. Friktionen, Kontraste oder Irritationserfahrungen finden dabei kaum Beachtung. Die Wiederholung, so scheint es, hat primär Konsequenzen für das Bild selbst – Kuch spricht sogar von einer „durch die wiederholte Verwendung des Druckstocks erzeugte[n] Ambiguität der Bilderzählung".[15]

Dass diese Ambiguität aber auch auf Ebene des Schrift-Bild-Textes Konsequenzen hat oder gerade erst auf ihr verortet ist, bleibt hier unberücksichtigt. Gerade für die Auseinandersetzung mit dem Ritter Galmy stellt Kuchs Arbeit daher einerseits einen eindrücklichen Vorläufer und andererseits jedoch eine deutliche Kontrastfolie dar, liegen bei ihm die Deutungs- und Erzählmacht letztlich dann doch beim Schrifttext:

> Gemäß den Beteuerungen des Erzählers und der Figuren handelt es sich dabei um eine keusche Liebe, die an sich nicht im Widerspruch zur Beziehung der Herzogin zu ihrem Gatten steht. Dennoch birgt sie die ständige Gefahr missverstanden zu werden und muss daher unbedingt geheim gehalten werden.[16]

Für diese Keuschheit der Liebe, die – wie ich im Folgenden zeigen werde – im Zentrum der von mir vorgestellten Romanepisode steht, finden sich ausreichend Belege innerhalb des Schrifttexts. Die Logik der Erzählung würde also nahelegen, dass die keusche Minne zwar als sexuelle Liebe missverstanden werden kann, letztlich aber moralisch integer bleibt. Dass dem nun möglicherweise gar nicht

---

13 Vgl. Kuch (Anm. 9), S. 46–96.
14 Kuch (Anm. 9), S. 234.
15 Kuch (Anm. 9), S. 115.
16 Kuch (Anm. 9), S. 47.

so ist – und das nicht nur, weil der Erzähler und die beteiligten Figuren ständig die moralische Integrität beteuern – werde ich im letzten Teil der Argumentation im Detail zeigen. Mittels der Bildwiederholung – und dem mit ihr einhergehenden unklaren Status des Bildes als Pro- oder Analepse – wird eine zusätzliche Stimme in das Erzählgeflecht des Romans eingewoben, die in der Schrifttextur so überhaupt nicht vorhanden ist. Um diese Lesart zu plausibilisieren und die narrative Funktion der Bild*wiederholung* hervorzuheben, trete ich nun den bereits angesprochenen Schritt vom konkreten Gegenstand zurück und frage nach den Mechanismen und Strukturen, die für den präsentierten Romanauszug auf einer systematischen Ebene relevant sind.

2 Ambiguität, Sinnkonstanz und epistemische Gewissheit

Auf einer systematischen Ebene bedeutet *Ambiguität zu erfahren*, nicht (länger) sicher sein zu können, *wofür etwas* oder *wie etwas in Relation zu etwas anderem* steht. Im ambigen Fall liegen folglich stets mindestens zwei konkurrierende, ähnlich plausible (Be-)Deutungsvarianten *von* bzw. *in Bezug auf* etwas vor. Dieses *etwas* kann dabei als Ausspruch, als Schrift, Bild, Geste oder Ton, kurz: in verschiedenen semiotischen Systemen begegnen. In dem Moment, wenn sich aufgrund weiterer Informationen Gewissheit einstellt, *wie* eine Struktur zu deuten ist, endet dieser Zustand – diese *kognitive Patt-Situation*[17] – vielleicht sogar unbemerkt. Das literarische Potenzial, das dieses Phänomen für Erzähltexte aus Schrift und Bild – und die damit verbundenen *Intersemiose* – darstellt, ist vielgestaltig und von unterschiedlicher Komplexität. Daher werde ich mich in den folgenden Überlegungen insbesondere auf die narrative Ebene beschränken, wobei ein materialphilologischer Zugang – also eine Konzentration auf die konkrete Gestalt des Untersuchungsgegenstands anstelle einer Rekonstruktion der Produktionsumstände oder -intentionen – das Fundament bilden wird.

　　Der Wunsch nach *eindeutiger Sinnzuweisung* und *epistemischer Gewissheit* markiert eine anthropologische Präferenz. Als sinngenerierende Subjekte sind Rezipienten bereit, im Umgang insbesondere mit *literarischen* Texten ko-produzierend tätig zu werden. Das Wissen darum, dass Schrift- und Bildtextur in dieser Form nicht kontingent sind, sondern in der Regel das Resultat von einer

---

17 Claudia Pinkas, *Der phantastische Film. Instabile Narration und die Narration der Instabilität*. Berlin, New York 2010, S. 39.

bis vielen Produktionsentscheidungen sowie der damit verbundenen bewussten Freigabe darstellen, fundiert diese Bereitschaft. Pointiert lässt sich somit festhalten: Dadurch, dass Rezipienten davon ausgehen, dass sich Bild und Schrift aufeinander beziehen bzw. in einer – wie auch immer gearteten – Relation zu einander stehen, ist ihr Verhalten auf die Identifikation möglicher Konnektoren bzw. Verweise von einem System auf das andere hin sensibilisiert. Sie nehmen eine semantische Kohärenz der Gesamttextur (auf globaler Ebene) an, die letztlich unabhängig davon ist, welche semiotischen Ressourcen ihr zugrunde liegen.[18] Es scheint somit weitaus schwieriger zu sein, Schrift und Bild in einem Buch derart zu kombinieren, dass sich zwischen den beiden Texturen – auch trotz der (Bedeutungs-)Anreicherung durch den Rezipienten – keine plausiblen Sinnbezüge herstellen lassen.

Mittels *salienter* Strukturen und der dadurch möglichen Markierung von (Einzel-)Elementen kann Einfluss auf den für die Interpretation fundamentalen Prozess der *Inferenz*bildung genommen werden.[19] Dadurch, dass bestimmte inhaltliche oder formale Elemente aus der sie umgebenden Ko-Textur herausstechen, wird ihr Stellenwert für den Rezeptionsprozess und die Bedeutungsgenese prominenter. Texturen lassen sich aus dieser Perspektive als komplexe Salienz*geflechte* beschreiben, für deren Faktur in der Forschung bereits mehrfach die Metapher der *Spur* als Beschreibungskategorie genutzt wurde.[20] Diese Metapher erscheint mir hilfreich, um sich den Prozess der Bedeutungszuweisung zu vergegenwärtigen: Ausgehend von einem initialen Verstehensmoment kombiniert der Rezipient die weiteren Informationen sukzessive unter Anbindung an das Vorangegangene. Dadurch werden die Bedeutungen der Komponenten zusammengesetzt und bilden so eine zusammenhängende Einheit, die durch ein *globales semantisches Feld*,[21] das Hans

---

18 Eine Konsequenz, die sich völlig stimmig zu den Prämissen und Schlussfolgerungen der IBE-Theorie (=*Inference to Best Explanation*) verhält. Vgl. dazu Peter Lipton, *Inference to the best explanation*. 2. Aufl. New York, London 2004.

19 Als *Salienz* verstehe ich gemäß Susan Fiske und Shelley Taylor „making a piece of information more noticeable, meaningful, or memorable to audiences. An increase in salience enhances the probability that receivers will perceive the information, discern meaning and thus process it, and store it in memory" (Robert M. Entman, 'Framing: Toward Clarification of A Fractured Paradigm'. In: *Journal of Communication* 43 (1993), S. 51–58, hier S. 53.) Vgl. auch Susan T. Fiske und Shelley E. Taylor, *Social Cognition*. New York 1991, S. 246.

20 Vgl. Maximilian Scherner, 'Textverstehen als "Spurenlesen"'. In: *Text und Grammatik*. Hg. v. Peter Canisius u.a. Bochum 1994, S. 317–340; Monika Schwarz, 'Kohärenz – Auf den materiellen Spuren eines mentalen Phänomens'. In: *Gesprochene Sprache – transdisziplinär. Festschrift für Gottfried Meinhold*. Hg. v. Margret Bräunlich u.a. Frankfurt am Main 2001, S. 151–160.

21 Juri Michailowitsch Lotman, *Die Struktur literarischer Texte*. München 1972, S. 360.

Hörmann *Sinnkonstanz*[22] genannt hat, gekennzeichnet ist – sodass zum Beispiel die Genese einer in sich stimmigen erzählten Welt erst möglich und
plausibel wird. Diese Spuren liegen in der konkreten Verwendungssituation
für den Rezipienten nicht gleichmäßig ausgeprägt vor. So erscheinen einige
(subjektiv) auffälliger und überdecken andere, die erst wieder an einer ganz
anderen Stelle der Textur salient wirken und bei einer *Relektüre* unter anderen
Gesichtspunkten deutlicher hervortreten könnten.

Bei der Rezeption von Romanen aus Schrift und Bild – *illustriert, bebildert,
bimodal, durchbildert*, etc. – handelt es sich um einen Spezialfall des Textverste-
hens: um „semiotisch integriertes Gesamtverstehen",[23] in dessen Umfang die bis-
her beschriebenen Prozesse kombiniert Anwendung finden. Textverstehen zielt
dabei als eine „Folge von perzeptiven und kognitiven Operationen [...] auf den
Sprache[=Schrift]-Bild-Abgleich und eine kontextsensible Sinnzuschreibung".[24]
Die Geschichte eines Romans, die Spezifizierung der Figuren(-konstellationen)
und die Funktion des Erzählers werden aus sämtlichen Komponenten des literar-
rischen Artefakts prozessiert.

Unter dieser Perspektive richte ich nun den Blick „auf die binnentextuellen
Verfahren der Erzeugung von Ambiguität als einem Doppelsystem einander
gegenseitig ausschließender Deutungsmöglichkeiten in einem Text".[25] Eine
Narration wird erst dann *ambig*, wenn der Rezipient

> jeweils nur die eine *oder* die andere Sichtweise der Ereignisse akzeptieren [kann], wobei
> der Text selbst keinerlei Hinweis auf die Präferenz der einen oder der anderen Lesart gibt.
> Ein ambiguer Text erzeugt [...] somit stets eine unmögliche Situation für den Leser,
> indem er ihn mit verschiedenen Deutungsangeboten konfrontiert, die einander gegensei-
> tig ausschließen [...].[26]

---

22 Hans Hörmann, *Meinen und Verstehen. Grundzüge einer psychologischen Semantik*. Frankfurt am Main 1976, S. 205, 208–212.
23 Werner Holly, 'Audiovisuelle Hermeneutik. Die Zeitgebundenheit des Bild-Verstehens am
Beispiel der Medienberichterstattung'. In: *Linguistische Hermeneutik. Theorie und Praxis des
Verstehens und Interpretierens*. Hg. v. Helmuth Feike und Angelika Linke. Tübingen 2007,
S. 387–422, hier S. 390.
24 Hartmut Stöckl, 'Sprache-Bild-Texte lesen. Bausteine zur Methodik einer Grundkompetenz'. In: *Bildlinguistik*. Hg. v. Hans-Joachim Diekmannshenke, Michael Klemm und Hartmut
Stöckl. Berlin 2011, S. 43–70, hier S. 55.
25 Pinkas (vgl. Anm. 17), S. 39. Im Gegensatz dazu vertritt Marina Münkler ein weites Ambi-
guitätsverständnis, das auch widersprüchliches Figurenverhalten einschließt – dies wäre
noch im Detail zu prüfen. Vgl. Marina Münkler, *Narrative Ambiguität: Die Faustbücher des 16.
bis 18. Jahrhunderts*. Göttingen 2011.
26 Pinkas (vgl. Anm. 17), S. 39–40 (Hervorhebung NP).

Die Herausforderung besteht somit nicht in der *Vermeidung* der Ambiguitätserfahrung, sondern in der *Integration* derselben in den eigentlichen Textsinn. Allgemeine Interpretationsoffenheit, die sich aus Merkmalen der Textur oder aber auch subjektiven Eigenschaften des Rezipienten speist, und der Spezialfall Ambiguität lassen sich demnach deutlich voneinander unterscheiden. Mit Blick auf analytische Präzision sollte Interpretationsoffenheit daher graduell im Rahmen eines Kontinuums verstanden werden. Ambiguität lässt sich demgegenüber durch die Analyse der intra- oder intertextuellen Verweissysteme einer Textur, mittels der zwei (oder mehr) äquivalent plausible Lesarten einer Textstelle und damit gegebenenfalls des gesamten Textes möglich werden, verorten.[27]

Das strukturbildende Moment der *Wiederholung*, für das Bildrepliken eine spezifische Form der Ausprägung darstellen, kann innerhalb narrativer Großformen eng mit der Etablierung bzw. Destabilisierung sinnkonstanter Entwürfe einer erzählten Welt verbunden sein. Ein Bild innerhalb eines Romans als die Wiederholung eines vorangehenden zu verstehen, d. h. die erfolgte Segment-Iteration zu erfassen, bedeutet, dass „die Wahrnehmung eines Elementes (A) ausdrücklich von dem Bewußtsein begleitet wird, es handele sich hier in der Tat um die Wiederholung eines Früheren (also um A^0 oder genauer $^0[A]$)".[28] Das *wiederholte* Bild wird ebenso wie das *sich wiederholende* Bild damit zu einer *intratextuellen Abbildung* des jeweils anderen. In diesem engen Sinne stellt der erneute Verweis auf ein Motiv oder die Anspielung auf spezifisches textinternes oder -externes Wissen zwar eine Wiederaufnahme dar, genügt aber nicht der engen Identitätsbeziehung, die für eine Wiederholung konstitutiv ist. Eine Wiederholung wird als solche nur durch das Vorangehen bzw. das Nachfolgen von etwas Identischem ersichtlich, A und A^0 sind nur in Relation zueinander *wiederholt* bzw. *wiederholend*.

---

27 Die Ambiguität eines Textes ist nicht immer eine im strengen Sinne narrative, wenngleich die Übergänge zwischen den unterschiedlichen Subklassen noch nicht ausreichend ausgeleuchtet wurden. Pinkas Studie zur Gestalt des phantastischen Films aus filmnarratologischer Sicht gründet ebenso wie Martínez' eher fiktionstheoretische Ausarbeitung *Doppelte Welten* auf Tzvetan Todorovs Ausführungen zum Phantastischen. Die Übergänge zwischen Narratologie im strengen Sinne und Fiktionstheorie erscheinen hier fließend – gleichwohl bleibt offen, wie sich die narrative Ambiguität einer Geschichte und die aus der Unklarheit, ob ein Text die Attribute fiktiv, faktual oder phantastisch verdient, resultierende Deutungsoffenheit zueinander verhalten. Vgl. Tzvetan Todorov, *Introduction à la littérature fantastique*. Paris 1970; Matias Martínez, *Doppelte Welten. Struktur und Sinn zweideutigen Erzählens*. Göttingen 1996; Pinkas (vgl. Anm. 17).
28 Eckhard Lobsien, *Wörtlichkeit und Wiederholung: Phänomenologie poetischer Sprache*. München 1995, S. 15–17.

Insbesondere für die Struktur der Erzählung und die Gestalt der erzählten Welt hat eine solche *Bezugnahme durch Iteration* Konsequenzen. Der bis zu diesem Zeitpunkt der Textgenese sinnkonstante Entwurf der erzählten Welt gerät ins Stocken. Narrative Gewissheit, die sich zuvor etablierte, wird instabil:

> Der Tendenz nach hebt jede Wiederholung die bis dato geleistete Synthesearbeit und die in ihr begründete und durch sie erworbene Sicherheit in der Lektüre wieder auf, und die lineare Sukzession, die Ausgedehntheit des Textes tritt wieder, wie zu Beginn einer jeden Lektüre, als Grundorientierung in Funktion. A und A^0 stehen nebeneinander; ihre Wiederholung entautomatisiert die subjektive Aneignung des Textes [...].[29]

Auf diese Weise kommt es zu einer Erhöhung der kognitiven Verarbeitungsleitung, die der Rezipient für die Genese eines Gesamttextes aufbringen muss. Der Herausforderung, die wiederholte Bildtextur im Rahmen des Schrift-Bild-Abgleichs in die Narration einzubinden, korrespondiert dabei zusätzlich die *Integration* der Wiederholung selbst. Die daraus gegebenenfalls resultierende Ambiguität dient hier als narratives Mittel, um neben einer allgemeinen Vagheit der Interpretationen *distinkte, erzählte Welten* einander gegenüber zu stellen. Diese können sich auf Ebene der Figuren, der Ereignisse, der Handlungen, des Modus, des Erzählers oder auch hinsichtlich der kausalen oder temporalen Ordnung derselben unterscheiden. Da Rezipienten in der Lage sind, unter Rückgriff auf unterschiedlichste epistemische Ressourcen (textinternes sowie textexternes Wissen) und unter Anwendung verschiedener kognitiver Kompetenzen, komplexe Bedeutungseinheiten zu konzeptualisieren, stellen semiotisch verschränkte Texturen somit ein erhebliches Potenzial bereit. Die Textgenese erfolgt auch hier sukzessive, aber nicht ohne Vorausdeutungen, Annahmen, Rückgriffe, Revisionen und Korrekturen – sie ist nicht an die gegenständliche Linearität der Textur gebunden. Epistemische Gewissheiten, die in der Lektüre über Identifikations-, Relations- und Schlussfolgerungsprozesse generiert werden, geraten so (*wiederholt*) instabil – so sehr, dass alles bis hin zur *mimetischen Unentscheidbarkeit* zu zerfallen droht.[30]

---

29 Lobsien (vgl. Anm. 28), S. 10–11.
30 Vgl. Matias Martínez und Michael Scheffel, *Einführung in die Erzähltheorie*. 10. überarbeitete und aktualisierte Auflage. Köln 2016, S. 109–110.

3 Bildwiederholungen im *Ritter Galmy* II

Das literarische Potenzial, das sich daraus ergibt, Bildwiederholungen in eine narrative Großform wie den Roman integrieren zu können, zeigt sich nun beispielsweise an der Konstruktion einer ambigen Narration. Hier markiert nicht etwa die Auflösung der gleichzeitigen Zweiwertigkeit, sondern die Synthese der irritierenden Simultaneität auf einer höheren Textebene den Fluchtpunkt. Statt zu fragen, welche Version die plausiblere ist, gilt es zu fragen, warum hier zwei oder mehrere Versionen in gegenseitiger Konkurrenz entworfen werden.

Dabei sind für die folgende Lesart mindestens die nachstehenden drei Prämissen zu nennen, deren Aussetzung zwar möglich ist, mir aber im Kontext literarischer Texturen wenig sinnvoll erscheint:

1. Soll nach narrativen Möglichkeiten gefragt werden, die sich aus der Bildwiederholung ergeben, so ist auszuschließen, dass die Doublette(n) entweder nicht wahrgenommen oder aber bewusst übergangen werden. Ersteres erscheint wahrnehmungspsychologisch mit Blick auf die Identitätsbeziehung der beiden Texturen zueinander unwahrscheinlich;[31] letzteres bleibt dem Rezipienten überlassen, impliziert aber eine Bewertung der Iteration als versehentlich, fehlerhaft oder bedeutungslos für die Geschichte.[32]

2. Wenngleich eine *Re-Semantisierung*, also die Umdeutung einer bereits mit einer ersten Lesart versehenen Textur, zweifelsohne möglich ist, so wird dadurch die erste Lesart nicht etwa überschrieben und getilgt. Vielmehr existieren beide bzw. im Fall multipler Verwendung alle Lesarten simultan und distinkt fort, insbesondere dann, wenn eine die beiden Lesarten

---

31 Verwandt wären hier Überlegungen zur *Funktionalen Gebundenheit*, d. h. zur Unfähigkeit, ein Artefakt einer anderen Funktion zuzuführen.

32 Davon unbenommen ist die Hypothese, dass Bildwiederholungen auch eine ökonomische Attraktivität zukommt. Die Möglichkeit der mehrfachen Verwendung desselben Druckstocks beinhaltet gleichzeitig die Option, Kosten, wie sie z. B. durch die Anfertigung eines weiteren Druckstocks entstehen würden, zu sparen; vgl. Manuel Braun, 'Illustration, Dekoration und das allmähliche Verschwinden der Bilder aus dem Roman (1471–1700)'. In: *Cognition and the Book. Typologies of Formal Organisation of Knowledge in the Printed Book of the Early Modern Period.* Hg. v. Karl A. E. Enenkel und Wolfgang Neuber. Leiden 2005, S. 369–407, hier S. 382. Eine solche Hypothese bedarf jedoch der detaillierten Aufarbeitung der jeweiligen historischen Produktionsumstände, will sie nicht Spekulation bleiben, und läuft zudem beständig Gefahr, einer Selbstinszenierung der am Produktionsprozess beteiligten Akteure im Sinne der *dissimulatio artis* zu unterliegen. In jedem Fall – und zwar unabhängig davon, ob die Bildwiederholung literarisch oder merkantil motiviert Einzug in den Roman fand – ist sie Bestandteil der Textur und kann nicht einfach übergangen oder mit Verweis auf ihre Kontingenz bzw. als für die Interpretation irrelevant marginalisiert werden.

rahmende Struktur existiert. Somit gilt diese Prämisse vornehmlich für den *intra*textuellen Wiederholungsfall und ist stark von weiteren Einflussgrößen (Distanz der wiederholten Elemente zueinander, Fortlauf der Lektüre, etc.) abhängig. Für die *inter*textuelle Wiederholung, wie sie z. B. zwischen Wickrams *Ritter Galmy* und weiteren Romanen, wie *Der Jungen Knaben Spiegel* (1554), zu beobachten ist,[33] wäre diese Vorannahme daher differenzierter zu formulieren.

3. Da bei der Konstruktion der erzählten Welt des *Ritter Galmy* sowohl Schrift als auch Bild – im gegenseitigen Abgleich – einbezogen werden, können Bilder nicht als Zierrat marginalisiert werden, obgleich ihnen natürlich auch eine schmückende Funktion zukommt. Auf narrativer Ebene stellt sich die Frage, wer innerhalb der Logik des Romans Verantwortung für die Bilder und die Wiederholung derselben zeichnet. Dies ist nicht mit der Frage danach zu verwechseln, welche historische Produktionsinstanz die Verschränkung von Bildern und Schrift in diesem Fall initiiert bzw. umgesetzt hat.

Bevor nun ausgehend von diesen Prämissen und den vorangehenden Überlegungen die Auslegung der Bildwiederholung *als* literarischem Mittel und die damit einhergehenden narratologischen Konsequenzen fokussiert werden, subsumiere ich knapp die eingangs der Argumentation formulierte Lektüresituation:

Das erste Mal begegnet das Bild (Abb. 3) im vierten Kapitel des Romans und kann dort gemeinsam mit den schriftlich geschilderten Ereignissen der erzählten Welt zu einer plausiblen Lesart 1 kombiniert werden. Bei der zweiten Konfrontation mit dem Bild im 58. Kapitel – und dem damit verbundenen Wiedererkennen – wird diese etablierte Lesart 1 erneut aufgerufen, jedoch unmittelbar verworfen, da sie sich im Kontext der erzählten Ereignisse als inadäquat für diese Romanpassage erweist. Im Rahmen des erneut erforderlichen Verstehensprozesses erfolgt eine Re-Semantisierung der Textur an deren Ende eine Lesart 2 steht, die sich hinsichtlich zentraler Merkmale (z. B. Figurenidentität im Bild) von Lesart 1 unterscheidet. Innerhalb des Romans hat sich das Bild als ambige Textur erwiesen; die Lesarten 1 und 2 existieren simultan, distinkt und exklusiv fort.

Aus dieser Koinzidenz ergibt sich die Frage nach dem Verhältnis von Lesart 1 und Lesart 2 zueinander. Da es nach der Wiederholung unmöglich ist, die eine Bedeutung ohne die andere zu verstehen, gilt es, die in Schrift und

---

33 Im Roman *Der Jungen Knaben Spiegel,* der 15 Jahre nach der *History von dem edlen und theüren Ritter Galmien* erschienen ist, begegnen vier Bildtexturen erneut – dann jedoch singulär –, die bereits im *Ritter Galmy* mehrfach verwendet wurden.

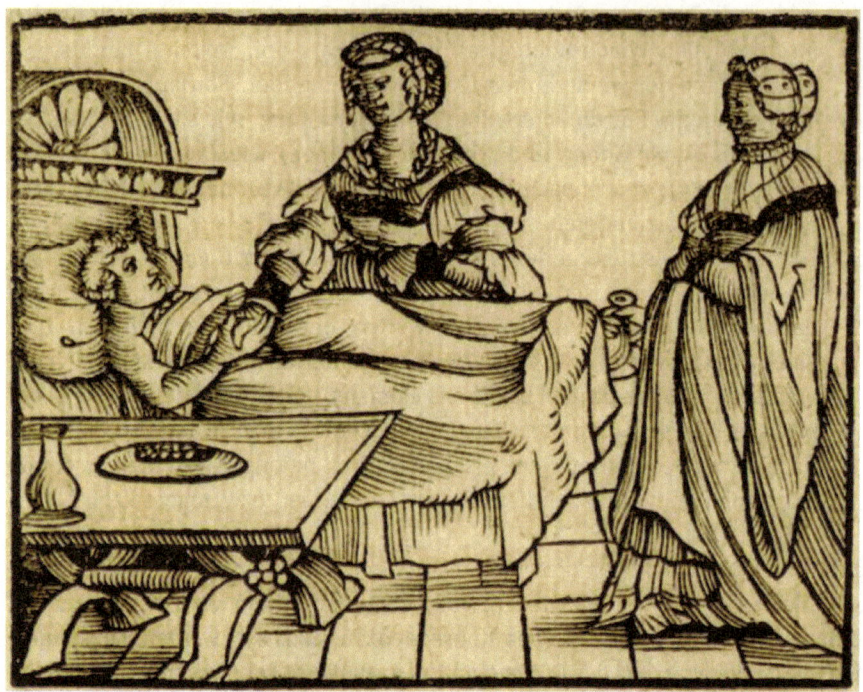

Abb. 3: *Ritter Galmy* (1539): fol. 9ʳ, 134ʳ.

Bild vorliegenden Ereignisse des vierten und 58. Kapitels vor der Folie der weiteren bzw. vorangehenden Romanhandlung mit- und gegeneinander zu interpretieren:

Auf einer übergeordneten Ebene fällt schließlich eine strukturelle Ähnlichkeit der betreffenden Romanepisoden auf – eine Frau besucht einen im Bett liegenden Mann. Beide Situationen sind aus dieser allgemeinen Perspektive vergleichbar. Mit Ausnahme der vertauschten Männerfigur im Bett ist das im Bild dargestellte Figurenensemble möglicherweise identisch (die jeweiligen Zofen werden nicht eigens benannt) – so scheint es: Auffällig ist, dass die Krankheit des Herzogs ebenso unversehens vermittelt wird wie zuvor die Genesung des Ritters. Dem bildlichen Austausch der Männer korrespondiert zudem eine Permutation der Männer auf Handlungsebene. So wie der Herzog nämlich Galmys Platz im Krankenbett einnimmt, nimmt Galmy im unmittelbaren Fortlauf der Ereignisse den Platz des Herzogs im Bett der Herzogin und an der Spitze der Hofgesellschaft ein. Dieser chiastische Tausch rahmt die wechselseitige Liebessituation, denn um eine solche handelt es sich explizit, spricht doch die Herzogin in direkter Rede davon, dass sie Galmy „von dem tag an liebhaben wil / in gleichem" (fol. 135^r), wie er sie begehrt.

Platonisch und damit moralisch unzweifelhaft ist dieses Liebesverständnis – wenngleich der Erzähler dies mehrfach beteuert – zwischen Herrin und Vasall keineswegs, bereut sie doch erneut in Figurenrede ausdrücklich, dass sie nicht „in eyner andern gestalt eüwers [= Galmys] *leibs* halben heimsuochen" (fol. 8^v) kann und fordert von ihrem zuküenftigen Geliebten, er solle es „mit gedult vertragen" (fol. 8^v). Diese Geduld macht sich dann auf fol. 134^r rasch bezahlt. Nachdem der Herzog, der dem Liebesglück im Wege stand, verstorben ist, überschlagen sich sogleich die Ereignisse: Bereits vier Seiten nach dem abrupten Tod des Herzogs schließt Galmy die Herzogin in seine Arme (s. Abb. 4). Dabei ist das Bild der Wiedervereinigung des Liebespaars sogar von dem Satz gerahmt: „So bald Galmy der Ritter von seinem gsellen vernan / das der Her- [Abb. 4]-tzog tod was / sich von stund an bereyten thet" (fol. 135^v–136^r). Schließlich gipfelt die plötzlich rasant voran getriebene Handlung in der Hochzeit der beiden Liebenden. Im Anschluss erhält Galmy zudem den Titel eines bretonischen Herzogs. Obwohl der Schrifttext Galmys Ernennung zum neuen Herrscher der Bretagne nicht explizit problematisiert, wird doch betont, „das noch keyn Jar vschinen war / das der Hertzog gestorben was" (fol. 138^r).

Reflektiert man die Ereignisse unter Berücksichtigung dieser Aussage und vor dem Hintergrund der Parallelstruktur, die die Ambiguität der Schrift-Bild-Textur eröffnet, so wird – insbesondere vor dem Hintergrund der Entsprechung von liebeskrankem Ritter und sterbendem Herzog – eine Problematisierung der Situation ersichtlich: Auch wenn die erzählte Welt zeitlich nicht exakt zu verorten ist, lassen die geschilderten gesellschaftlichen Strukturen eine zeitliche Einordnung im Zeitraum vom 12. bis 13. Jahrhundert zu.[34] Zu dieser Zeit setzte sich das gelehrte Römische Recht in der Bretagne zunehmend gegen das altgediente Gewohnheitsrecht mit seinen römischen, englischen und keltischen Einflüssen durch. Während das Englische Gewohnheitsrecht, das die Waliser und Inselkelten bei ihrem Exodus aus England besonders im 5. und 6. Jahrhundert mitbrachten, verlangt, dass Witwen „dem Tod des Ehemannes zwölf Monate lang unverheiratet blieben",[35] da sie sonst die „Morgengabe und allen anderen

---

[34] Von etwa 1341 an wird die gesamte Bretagne für mehrere Jahrzehnte bis 1379 vom Bretonischen Erbfolgekrieg erschüttert, von dessen destabilisierender Wirkung der Roman jedoch nicht berichtet. Außerdem ist die Blütezeit des Ritterstandes zu diesem Zeitpunkt bereits Vergangenheit. Die starken Landesherren und die deutlich ausgeprägte höfische Gesellschaft legen hochmittelalterliche Strukturen nah.

[35] Jens Roehrkasten, 'Witwe, Englisches Recht'. In: *LexMA*, Band IX. Stuttgart, Weimar 1999, S. 279.

Abb. 4: *Ritter Galmy* (1539): fol. 136ʳ.

durch den ersten Ehemann erhaltenen Besitz verlieren"[36] sollten, fordert das Römische Recht – dessen Einfluss in der Bretagne bis ins 13. Jahrhundert stark
bleibt – die vollständige und dauerhafte Infamie der Witwe, sollte diese neu heiraten (wollen). Konkret bedeutet dies den Verlust des gesellschaftlichen Rechtsschut-
zes und der Rechtsfähigkeit der Witwe.[37] Demgegenüber schließt das Römisch-

---

36 Roehrkasten (vgl. Anm. 35).
37 Vgl. Irene Fuchs, *Die Ehrenstrafen der Vergangenheit und Gegenwart.* Diss. Köln 1928;
Benno Löbmann, *Der kanonische Infamiebegriff in seiner geschichtlichen Entwicklung: unter besonderer Berücksichtigung der Infamielehre des Franz Suarez.* Leipzig 1956; Satu Lidman, *Zum
Spektakel und Abscheu: Schand- und Ehrenstrafen als Mittel öffentlicher Disziplinierung
in München um 1600.* Frankfurt am Main, Berlin, Bern 2008.

Kanonische Recht, dessen Etablierung „in Nordfrankreich [...] schon im 13. Jh."[38] seinen Anfang nahm und „bereits Ende des 15. Jahrhunderts als abgeschlossen angesehen"[39] werden kann, eine Wiederheirat grundsätzlich nicht mehr aus. Folglich lässt sich die erneute Heirat der Herzogin innerhalb des Trauerjahres nur mit den Vorgaben des Römisch-Kanonischen Rechts in Einklang bringen, da es innerhalb des Romans zu keiner unmittelbaren moralischen Ächtung der Herzogin kommt und sie auch nicht aller Titel und Besitztümer beraubt wird. Sie muss sich allerdings der „verwilligung aller Landtsherrn" (fol. 137^v) für die schnelle Hochzeit und den damit verbundenen Männertausch sicher sein.

Die Herzogin besteht hier offenbar einen moralischen Grenzgang, der zwar vom neu-etablierten Römisch-Kanonischen Recht gebilligt, aber deshalb gesellschaftlich noch lange nicht selbstverständlich wird. Somit ist die Ehe zwischen Galmy und der Herzogin nichts Widerrechtliches, taugt allerdings wohl kaum länger – trotz aller Beteuerungen des Erzählers, dass es sich bei der bretonischen Herzogin um ein Musterbild weiblicher Tugend handele – als sittsames Vorbild. Zwar ist während der gesamten Romanhandlung bis zum Tod des Herzogs präsent, dass die Herzogin sich von zwei Männern angezogen fühlt, doch zeigt die Bildreplik dies konzentriert an zwei zentralen Stellen auf – mit ihr erhält eine weitere Stimme Einzug in das Erzählgeflecht, die nicht identisch ist mit der des Erzählers.

Die Parallelkomposition der Ereignisse, die in der bildlichen Entsprechung und dem Austausch der Männerfigur an der Seite der Herzogin gipfelt, wird erst im Moment einer *scheinbaren Redundanz*, die durch die Replik in den Rezeptionsprozess eintritt, vor Augen geführt. Der strategische Einsatz der Möglichkeit, unterschiedliche Figuren der Geschichte den dargestellten Figuren im Bild zuzuordnen und die daraus resultierende Ambiguität der Bildelemente heben hier die Brisanz des Männertauschs, d. h. die Besetzung der Position an der Seite der Herzogin gleich durch zwei männliche Figuren der Handlung, auf eine Art und Weise hervor, die in einem Konkurrenz- bzw. Kooperationsverhältnis zur (ausschließlich schriftlich vermittelten,) wertenden Erzählerstimme steht.

Gleichzeitig – und das mag von systematischem Mehrwert sein – wird die *Spannung* zwischen Figuren- und Erzählerrede, die ohnehin im Roman angelegt ist, zusätzlich betont. Anstelle der anfangs stabilen Situation eines *heterodiegetischen* Erzählers (*nullfokalisiert*), der sich in Vorausdeutungen und Einblicke in das

---

38 Filippo Ranieri, 'Römisches Recht, Rezeption'. In: *LexMA*, Bd. VII. Stuttgart, Weimar 1999. S. 1015.
39 Ranieri (vgl. Anm. 38).

Innenleben der Figuren zu erkennen gibt, erscheint hier eine *homodiegetische*, wertende Erzählsituation wahrscheinlicher. Inwieweit auf systematischer Ebene eine Korrelation zwischen dem Modus der Erzählung (insbesondere Distanz) und dem Vorhandensein von Bildrepliken als Stilelement zwischen Vorausdeutung und Rückblende existiert, wäre nun Gegenstand einer anderen Abhandlung.

Bibliographie

Benzig, Josef, *Bibliographie strasbourgeoise*. Bd. 1. Baden-Baden 1981.

Blazejewski, Susanne, *Bild und Text – Photographie in autobiographischer Literatur: Marguerite Duras' 'L'amant' und Michael Ondaatjes 'Running in the Family'*. Würzburg 2002.

Bolte, Johannes und Willy Scheel (Hgg.), *Georg Wickrams Werke. Erster Band. Galmy – Gabriotto*. Tübingen 1901 (Bibliothek des literarischen Vereins in Stuttgart 222).

Braun, Manuel, 'Illustration, Dekoration und das allmähliche Verschwinden der Bilder aus dem Roman (1471–1700)'. In: *Cognition and the Book. Typologies of Formal Organisation of Knowledge in the Printed Book of the Early Modern Period*. Hg. v. Karl A. E. Enenkel und Wolfgang Neuber. Leiden 2005, S. 369–407.

Drittenbass, Catherine und André Schnyder (Hgg.), *Eulenspiegel trifft Melusine. Der frühneuhochdeutsche Prosaroman im Licht neuer Forschungen und Methoden*. Amsterdam, New York 2010.

Entman, Robert M., 'Framing: Toward Clarification of A Fractured Paradigm'. In: *Journal of Communication* 43 (1993), S. 51–58.

Fischer, Hubertus, 'Wickrams Bilderwelt. Vorläufige Bemerkungen'. In: *Vergessene Texte – Verstellte Blicke. Neue Perspektiven der Wickram-Forschung*. Hg. v. Maria Elisabeth Müller und Michael Mecklenburg. Frankfurt am Main 2007, S. 199–214.

Fiske, Susan T. und Shelley E. Taylor, *Social Cognition*. New York 1991.

Fix, Ulla und Hans Wellmann, 'Sprachtexte – Bildtexte. Bemerkungen zum Symposion Bild im Text – Text und Bild vom 6.–8. April 2000 in Leipzig'. In: *Bild im Text, Text im Bild*. Hg. v. Ulla Fix und Hans Wellmann. Heidelberg 2000, S. XI–XVII.

Fuchs, Irene, *Die Ehrenstrafen der Vergangenheit und Gegenwart*. [Diss.] Köln 1928.

Gotzkowsky, Bodo, *'Volksbücher'. Prosaromane, Renaissancenovellen, Versdichtungen und Schwankbücher. Bibliographie der Deutschen Drucke. Teil I: Drucke des 15. Und 16. Jahrhunderts*. Baden-Baden 1991.

Gotzkowsky, Bodo, *Die Buchholzschnitte Hans Brosamers zu den Frankfurter „Volksbuch"-Ausgaben und ihre Wiederverwendungen*. Baden-Baden 2002.

Holly, Werner, 'Audiovisuelle Hermeneutik. Die Zeitgebundenheit des Bild-Verstehens am Beispiel der Medienberichterstattung'. In: *Linguistische Hermeneutik. Theorie und Praxis des Verstehens und Interpretierens*. Hg. v. Helmuth Feike und Angelika Linke. Tübingen 2007, S. 387–422.

Hörmann, Hans, *Meinen und Verstehen. Grundzüge einer psychologischen Semantik*. Frankfurt am Main 1976.

Kartschoke, Dieter, 'Ritter Galmy uß Schottenland und Jörg Wickram aus Colmar'. In: *Daphnis* 31 (2002), S. 469–489.

Keary, Mae, 'Key Technologies – Chasing the Gap'. In: *Aslib Proceedings* 43/5 (1991), S. 161–172.

Knape, Joachim, 'Mnemonik, Bildbuch und Emblematik im Zeitalter Sebastian Brants (Brant, Schwarzenberg, Alciati)'. In: *Mnemosyne. Festschrift für Manfred Lurker zum 60. Geburtstag*. Hg. v. Werner Bies und Hermann Jung. Baden-Baden 1988, S. 133–178.

Kuch, Raphael, *Intermediales Erzählen im frühneuzeitlichen illustrierten Roman*. Köln, Weimar, Wien 2014.

Lidman, Satu, *Zum Spektakel und Abscheu: Schand- und Ehrenstrafen als Mittel öffentlicher Disziplinierung in München um 1600*. Frankfurt am Main, Berlin, Bern 2008.

Lipton, Peter, *Inference to the best explanation*. 2. Aufl. New York, London 2004.

Löbmann, Benno, *Der kanonische Infamiebegriff in seiner geschichtlichen Entwicklung: unter besonderer Berücksichtigung der Infamielehre des Franz Suarez*. Leipzig 1956.

Lobsien, Eckhard, *Wörtlichkeit und Wiederholung: Phänomenologie poetischer Sprache*. München 1995.

Lotman, Juri Michailowitsch, *Die Struktur literarischer Texte*. München 1972.

Martínez, Matias, *Doppelte Welten. Struktur und Sinn zweideutigen Erzählens*. Göttingen 1996.

Martínez, Matias und Michael Scheffel, *Einführung in die Erzähltheorie*. 10. überarbeitete und aktualisierte Auflage. Köln 2016.

Münkler, Marina, *Narrative Ambiguität: Die Faustbücher des 16. bis 18. Jahrhunderts*. Göttingen 2011.

Pinkas, Claudia, *Der phantastische Film. Instabile Narration und die Narration der Instabilität*. Berlin, New York 2010.

Potysch, Nicolas, *Wiederholt doppeldeutig in Bild und Schrift – Ambiguität im durchbilderten Roman*. Hannover 2018.

Ranieri, Filippo, 'Römisches Recht, Rezeption'. In: *LexMA*. Bd. VII. Stuttgart, Weimar 1999. S. 1015.

Roehrkasten, Jens, 'Witwe, Englisches Recht'. In: *LexMA*. Bd. IX. Stuttgart, Weimar 1999. S. 279.

Scherner, Maximilian, 'Textverstehen als "Spurenlesen"'. In: *Text und Grammatik*. Hg. v. Peter Canisius u.a. Bochum 1994. S. 317–340.

Schmidt, Peter, 'Literat und "selbstgewachsener Moler". Jörg Wickram und der illustrierte Roman der Frühen Neuzeit'. In: *Künstler und Literat. Schrift- und Buchkultur in der europäischen Renaissance*. Hg. v. Bodo Guthmüller, Berndt Hamm und Andreas Tönnesmann. Wiesbaden 2006, S. 143–194.

Schwarz, Monika, 'Kohärenz – Auf den materiellen Spuren eines mentalen Phänomens'. In: *Gesprochene Sprache – transdisziplinär. Festschrift für Gottfried Meinhold*. Hg. v. Margret Bräunlich u.a. Frankfurt am Main 2001, S. 151–160.

Stöckl, Hartmut, *Die Sprache im Bild, das Bild in der Sprache: Zur Verknüpfung von Sprache und Bild im massenmedialen Text. Konzepte, Theorien, Analysemethoden*. Berlin, New York 2004.

Stöckl, Hartmut, 'Sprache-Bild-Texte lesen. Bausteine zur Methodik einer Grundkompetenz'. In: *Bildlinguistik*. Hg. v. Hans-Joachim Diekmannshenke, Michael Klemm und Hartmut Stöckl. Berlin 2011, S. 43–70.

Susanka, Thomas M., *Foto/grafie. Zur Rhetorik von Medium und Bild. Mit einer Fallstudie zu James Nachtwey*. Berlin 2015.

Todorov, Tzvetan, *Introduction à la littérature fantastique*. Paris 1970.

Jef Schaeps

Old-Fashioned in Order to be Modern: *Seghelijn van Iherusalem* and its Woodcuts

Abstracts: *Seghelijn van Jherusalem* is a fourteenth-century verse narrative, extant in one manuscript and six printed editions. Since the 1983 publication of Ingrid van de Wijer's doctoral thesis on the text, interest has increased and *Seghelijn* has been the subject of several studies. These investigations always concern the text, whereas the woodcuts in the printed editions have received little attention. In this contribution these woodcuts and especially the title illustrations are the main focus of interest. The first edition appeared in Delft (1483–86, Jacob Jacobszoon van der Meer), while subsequent ones were published in Antwerp (1511, Hendrick Eckert van Homberch; before-1517, attributed to Claes de Grave; 1517, Claes de Grave; 1520, Hendrick Eckert van Homberch; *c.* 1530–40, Hendrick Peeterssen van Middelburch). All these editions have woodcuts on the title page but not one of these was designed for this specific work. All were fifteenth-century cuts re-used in a new setting. This article argues that this was a deliberate, rather than a convenient or careless, choice: re-editions of medieval narratives were furnished with older woodcuts as indicative of the genre. This is illustrated by the edition of 1517 in which an older woodcut is framed within a more modern, contemporary woodcut border. This shows that although the printer had access to modern designs, he opted to illustrate *Seghelijn* with an older (indeed old-fashioned) frontispiece.

Seghelijn van Jherusalem ist ein Versroman aus dem vierzehnten Jahrhundert, der in einer Handschrift und sechs Drucken überliefert wurde. Seit Ingrid van de Wijer 1893 ihre Dissertation dem Text widmete, hat das Interesse am *Seghelijn* zugenommen und ist der Text Gegenstand einiger Studien gewesen. Diese befassen sich ausschließlich mit dem Text, während die Holzschnitte, die in den Drucken vorkommen, bis heute wenig Aufmerksamkeit erregt haben. Thema des vorliegenden Beitrags sind die Holzschnitte, insbesondere die Titelillustrationen. Der erste Druck erschien in Delft (1483–86, Jacob Jacobszoon van der Meer), während spätere Ausgaben in Antwerpen publiziert wurden (1511, Hendrick Eckert van Homberch; vor 1517, Claes de Grave zugeschrieben; 1517 Claes de Grave; 1520, Hendrick Eckert van Homberch; ca. 1530–40, Hendrick Peeterssen van Middelburch). Alle Ausgaben enthalten Holzschnitte auf dem Titelblatt, aber keiner davon wurde speziell für eine *Seghelijn*-Ausgabe angefertigt. In allen Fällen handelt es sich um eine Wiederverwendung älterer Holzschnitten aus dem fünfzehnten Jahrhundert. In diesem Beitrag wird argumentiert, dass das nicht nur eine Frage der Unachtsamkeit oder der Bequemlichkeit war, sondern eine bewusste Entscheidung: Ausgaben mittelalterlicher narrativer Erzählungen wurden vorzugsweise mit älteren Holzschnitten versehen zur Charakterisierung der Gattung. Illustrativ in dieser Hinsicht ist die 1517-Ausgabe, bei der ein älterer Holzschnitt in einen modernen, zeitgenössischen Rahmen eingefasst wurde. Sie zeigt, dass der Herausgeber zwar über moderne Materialien verfügte, für den *Seghelijn* aber eine ältere (und somit altmodische) Abbildung wählte.

Jef Schaeps, Leiden University

Seghelijn van Iherusalem is a fourteenth-century chivalric verse romance, written by an otherwise unknown author named Loy Latewaert.[1] The text has been transmitted in a single manuscript and dates from around 1412–1415. Its six printed editions were published between circa 1485 and 1540.[2] "Not a work of genius" is one of the milder, if still pejorative, judgments that have been used to characterize *Seghelijn*, yet in the first century after the invention of printing the text enjoyed considerable popularity.[3] *Seghelijn* is one of the rare examples of Dutch chivalric verse romances that made it into print.[4] Moreover, the printed editions of *Seghelijn* make up the highest number of editions in the corpus of Dutch printed romances (a number only equalled by the famous Charlemagne romance *Karel ende Elegast*, which was also printed six times before 1540). The text of *Seghelijn*, its genesis and its transmission have received a measure of scholarly attention in recent decades. The illustrations in the printed editions, however, have been studied less extensively.[5] The aim of this article is to take a closer look at the woodcuts, especially those on the title-pages, to explore their origin and to see what their occurrence can tell us about the use and function of woodcuts in early printed editions of narrative literature in general.

1 Historiography and Summary of the Text

The first one to devote any attention to *Seghelijn van Iherusalem* was Henrik van Wyn, who described the text as "a concoction of foolish inventions".[6]

---

1 His name is mentioned in the last lines of the 1511 edition, published in Antwerp by Hendrick Eckert van Homberch: "Die dit dichte en[de] heft bescreuen | Was gheheeten loylate waert" (fol. 68). The name is now commonly spelled Loy Latewaert.
2 The manuscript is kept in the Staatsbibliothek in Berlin (Ms. Germ. fol. 922). The dating, mentioned in Ingrid van de Wijer, 'Segheliin van Iherusalem, tekstoverlevering van een Middelnederlands ridderdicht'. In: *Quaerendo* 14 (1984), p. 273–303 (p. 284), is based on the manuscript's watermarks. There will have been older manuscripts, now lost, that go back to the middle of the fourteenth century.
3 Van de Wijer, 'Segheliin van Iherusalem' (note 2), p. 273: "geen hoogvlieger." [On the popularity of *Seghelijn van Jherusalem* and *Karel ende Elegast* both in manuscript and in print, see the article by Besamusca and Willaert in this volume, p. 71–72, p. 82 and p. 83.]
4 See on the exceptional status of *Seghelijn* as a narrative printed in verse: Rob J. Resoort, 'Het raadsel van de rijmdrukken'. In: *Nederlandse Letterkunde* 3 (1998), p. 327–344.
5 So far, only Van de Wijer, 'Segheliin van Iherusalem' (note 2), has paid attention to the illustrations.
6 Henrik van Wyn, *Historische en letterkundige avondstonden*. Amsterdam 1800, p. 315, note b: "een saamenweefzel van dwaaze verdichtzelen."

W.J.A. Jonckbloet, in his authoritative *Geschiedenis der Nederlandsche letter-kunde* (History of Dutch literature), spoke of "wild romantic tales combined with vulgar fantasies and miracles."[7] Jacob Verdam, who published a transcription of the manuscript and compared this to the printed editions, ascribed the negative assessments to a rather careless transmission of the text from manuscript to printed version.[8] To Verdam we also owe the dating of the text to around 1330–1350. Of all the authors who wrote about narrative literature in the Early Modern period, only Emile Van Heurck devotes a passage to *Seghelijn*, while Luc. Debaene includes the book in his major work on Dutch prose romance, listing it in a seperate section of popular books that do not meet the generic definition of 'prose romance' and are therefore left without commentary.[9] Ingrid Van de Wijer published an extensive study of *Seghelijn* in 1983, focusing on the codicology and transmission of the text.[10] Some of her findings were published in an article, aimed at an international audience.[11] Finally, W.P. Gerritsen and A.G. van Melle included *Seghelijn* in their 1993 survey of medieval narrative literature, in an essay written by G.H.M. Claassens.[12] In recent years *Seghelijn* has been the subject of a reappraisal, resulting in a number of articles, centering around at the linguistic, literary and cultural aspects of the text.[13]

---

7 W.J.A. Jonckbloet, *Geschiedenis der Nederlandsche letterkunde*. Vol. 1. Groningen 1868, p. 332: "[…] wilde romantiek huwt zich daarin dan ook aan de wansmakelijkste legende-wonderen." And even though Jonckbloet somewhat toned down this judgment in the later editions of his *Geschiedenis* (2nd edition: 1873–1874, 3rd edition: 1881–1886, 4th edition (posthumous): 1882–1892), his negative verdict persisted.

8 Jacob Verdam (ed.), *Seghelijn van Jherusalem naar het Berlijnsche handschrift en den ouden druk*. Leiden 1878, p. IV and XII.

9 Emile Van Heurck, *Les livres populaires flamands*. Antwerpen 1931, p. 28; Luc. Debaene, *De Nederlandse volksboeken. Ontstaan en geschiedenis van de Nederlandse prozaromans, gedrukt tussen 1475 en 1540*. Antwerpen 1951, p. 267.

10 Ingrid van de Wijer, *Segheliin. Codicologische, bibliographische en tekstkritische studie en editie* (diss. Leuven). 2 vols. Leuven 1983.

11 Van de Wijer, 'Segheliin van Iherusalem' (note 2).

12 G.H.M. Claassens, 'Seghelijn van Jheruzalem'. In: *Van Aiol tot de Zwaanridder. Personages uit de middeleeuwse verhaalkunst en hun voortleven in literatuur, theater en beeldende kunst*. Ed. by W.P. Gerritsen and A.G. van Melle. Nijmegen 1993, p. 299–300.

13 See for example: G.H.M. Claassens, 'Die kerstenwet stercken. Kruisvaartideologie en kritiek in de Seghelijn van Jhersualem'. In: *TNTL* 107 (1991), p. 235–273; G.H.M. Claassens, 'Dat en is sonder reden niet. Over de zeven vragen van Seghelijn van Jhersualem'. In: *Spiegel der Letteren* 40 (1998), p. 25–54; An Faems, 'Nu hoert, ghi heren, ende verstaet ende neemt exempel aen desen man. De functie van het vertellerscommentaar in Seghelijn van Jhersualem'. In: *Millennium* 15 (2001), p. 114–139; G.H.M. Claassens, 'Membra disiecta: excessief geweld in de ridderroman Seghelijn van Jhersualem'. In: *Kabaal! Feest en strijd in de Nederlandse literatuur*. Ed. by Elke Brems, An Faems and Eveline Vanfraussen. Leuven 2004, p. 25–55. More

Seghelijn is an indigenous Middle Dutch text, consisting of a compilation of narrative elements known from many other texts. Born in Jerusalem to an Islamic family, son of King Pridus and Queen Braffeleur, it is foretold that Seghelijn will kill his father. His mother hides him from his father's persecution and Seghelijn is raised by a fisherman. While still a young man Seghelijn is engaged by his father as a courtier without being recognised. His luck doesn't last long, however, and soon he has to flee the court due to a conspiracy. This is the start of a rollercoaster of wondrous and exciting adventures: Seghelijn defeats giants and other adversaries, he sleeps with seven virgins on seven consecutive days and fathers seven sons. For this he is imprisoned for fifteen years and after his release he joins his seven sons, who were to become the Seven Wise Men of Rome, in an attempt to end the siege of their hometown Oliferne. Finally he marries Emperor Constantine's daughter Florette. This seems to initiate a more quiet phase in Seghelijn's life, but it does not last long. Empress Helen takes Seghelijn on a succesful journey to find the Holy Cross, but in the meantime his wife Florette is subjected to a heinous series of atrocities. After Constantine and Helen's deaths, Seghelijn becomes the new Emperor. Due to further conspiracies, Seghelijn accidentally kills his parents when they visit Rome on a pilgrimage, thus fulfilling the prophecy from his childhood. After having been suspected of adultery by Seghelijn, Florette dies of grief. Seghelijn withdraws into the wilderness for some years, only to be elected pope later on.[14]

The son who is separated from his parents and destined to kill them, the wandering through many regions and countries, the service of kings and emperors, the succession of some of the most unlikely adventures and the final apotheosis – these are elements borrowed from other well-known stories, which have been gathered here into a kaleidoscopic trip through medieval imagery.

2 Printed Editions and their Woodcuts

The first printed edition of *Seghelijn van Jerusalem* was published in Delft by Jacob Jacobszoon van der Meer between 1483 and 1486 (ISTC is00366400;

---

references can be found in the online *Bibliografie van de Nederlandse taal- en literatuurwetenschap* (BNTL, www.bntl.nl).

14 For a more comprehensive summary see Van de Wijer, 'Segheliin van Iherusalem' (note 2) and Claassens, 'Seghelijn van Jherusalem' (note 12).

GW 12790).[15] *Seghelijn* was not the first narrative text that van der Meer published. In May 1479, during his companionship with Mauricius Yemantszoon van Middelborch, he had produced an edition of the history of Alexander the Great (ISTC ia00401000; GW 892) and in January 1483 he had printed *Hystorie van die seven wise mannen van Romen* (ISTC is00450150; GW 12877). Both texts followed earlier editions by Gerard Leeu in Gouda. Like all books printed by Jacob van der Meer and Mauricius Yemantszoon – they had started their career in January 1477 with the famous Delft Bible – *Dat leven ende dat regiment des coninc Alexanders* did not have a separate title-page, nor were there any woodcuts included in the book. The *Hystorie van die seven wisen mannen van Romen* was also devoid of a title-page, but in this case the publisher used a series a woodcuts, starting with an image opposite the first page.[16] Other narrative texts followed. The prose version of *Reynaert de Vos* is dated 4 June 1485 (ISTC ir00136000; GW 12726) and is more or less contemporary with the undated *Seghelijn*. Later, in 1487–1488, van der Meer produced an edition of *Karel ende Elegast* (ISTC ic00204700; GW 12601) and a second edition of *Die historie van die seven wijse mannen van Roemen*, undated but produced between April 1487 and August 1491 (ISTC is00450300; GW 12879).

When van der Meer printed *Seghelijn*, he was unable to rely on any previous editions. As a novelty he inserted a title-page before the start of the text.[17] Around ten years after the introduction of printing in the Low Countries, title-pages were still a rarity. Books started either with the text, a preceding table, or a blank page. The title-page of *Seghelijn* has the title at the top of the page and two small woodcuts of a knight and a nobleman on horseback (Fig. 1). The title reads: *Die historie va[n] seghelijn van iherusalem*. The two woodcuts actually represent chess pieces, which van der Meer had already at his disposal in his workshop. They were cut, together with 14 other woodcuts, for Jacobus de Cessolis' book on chess, in a Dutch translation entitled *Scaecspel* that had been

---

15 Ina Kok, *Woodcuts in Incunabula Printed in the Low Countries*. 4 vols. Houten 2013 (hereafter cited as Kok) dates the book between 14 February 1483 and 25 March 1486. A unique copy is kept in the University Library in Ghent (Res. 1405).

16 The book contains 16 full-page woodcuts, including many repeats. See Kok (note 15), nr. 32.

17 This was already noted by Ursula Rautenberg, 'Die Entstehung und Entwicklung des Buchtitelblatts in der Inkunabelzeit in Deutschland, den Niederlanden und Venedig – Quantitative und qualitative Studien'. In: *Archiv für Geschichte des Buchwesens* 62 (2008), p. 1–105: "Die Ausgabe des Versromans *Seghelijn van Jerusalem* [...] zeigt möglicherweise eine der ersten illustrierten Titelseiten." (p. 69). Based on this fact Rautenberg is inclined to date *Seghelijn* to the end of the time period, set by Kok (see note 15), that is 1486. [For title-pages, see also the contribution by Syrovy in the present volume, p. 351–374.]

published on 14 February 1483 (ISTC ic00412000; GW 6537).[18] Nevertheless, the woodcuts are appropriate here. *Seghelijn* abounds in knights and noblemen and the way they are printed, opposing each other with raised lances, corresponds to the many combats Seghelijn would be involved in. Title pages with more than one woodcut are otherwise unknown during this period. When a book does have a title-page with an illustration, it is always just one and, in this period, these often represent devotional images or a *magister cum discipulis* scene. By printing the woodcuts close to the title, leaving a large part of the page blank, one of the later owners of the only known copy in Ghent was incited to add a few woodcuts of their own. A scene of the circumcision and two separate architectural side pieces have been pasted onto the title-page.[19] They stem from the printing shop of Gerard Leeu and date from shortly after the printing of *Seghelijn*.[20] It is likely that the same owner added three more biblical woodcuts to the reverse side of the title-page.[21] There are no other woodcuts included in the book, neither printed nor added by a later hand. The edition by van der Meer is the only one to have been published in the Northern Netherlands; all consecutive editions were published in Antwerp.

Some 25 years later a new edition of *Seghelijn* was printed and published by Hendrick Eckert van Homberch.[22] Like van der Meer, Eckert resided originally in Delft, but in 1500 he had relocated to Antwerp. He was in the possession of many woodcuts he had purchased from earlier printers such as Jacob Bellaert from Haarlem and Gerard Leeu who had been active in Gouda and Antwerp. Eckert's edition of *Seghelijn* is dated 16 March 1511 (Fig. 2). The title-page is of a type common in the second decade of the sixteenth century: the first words of the title (preceded by an ornament) are cut from a woodblock

---

18 The date of *Scaecspel* determined the *terminus post quem* for *Seghelijn*, see Kok (see note 15).

19 Van de Wijer, *tekstkritisch studie en editie* (note 10) apparently felt unsure about whether the woodcuts were printed or added manually through pasting. She writes: "werden waarschijnlijk later opgeplakt" [tr. probably pasted in at a later time] (p. 101). In her article in *Quaerendo* (note 2, p. 289) she just mentions the woodcuts, without saying anything about their status. Rautenberg (see note 17) was misled by a photograph or digital image: she describes the circumcision scene as part of the printed book (p. 69).

20 William Martin Conway, *The Woodcutters of the Netherlands in the Fifteenth Century*. Cambridge 1884. For the circumcision see Conway, 9.2.11 and Kok (see note 15), 74.11. For the sidepieces see Conway 10.7 (3) and 12.11.7; and Kok (see note 15), 85.96 and 85.108.

21 Conway (see note 20), 10.6.116, 10.6.129 and 12.3.10; and Kok (see note 15), 85.16, 85.48 and 85.66.

22 *een seer / schone historie van seghelijn van iherusalem* (NK 1322). There is a unique copy in the Koninklijke Bibliotheek in The Hague (KW 227 A 4).

Fig. 1: Title-page of *Seghelijn van Iherusalem*, Delft, Jacob Jacobszoon van der Meer, 1483–1486 (Ghent, University Library).

and printed in red. The remaining part of the title is set underneath in type and printed in black. Finally a narrative woodcut is printed below the text, in this case with an additional ornamental frieze. The title reads: *een seer schone historie van seghelijn van iherusalem* (a very beautiful history of Seghelijn of Jerusalem). The woodcut shows a combat scene in front of city walls. The page's design (woodcut title, remainder of the title in type and woodcut image) was common within title-pages from this period and, moreover, one that is not confined to narrative literature alone but can be found in other genres as well.[23] Although the woodcut may be appropriate to the story of the romance, in fact it dates from 1483–1485, when it was used by Jacob Bellaert in *Historie van den vromen ridder Jason* (ISTC i100111000; GW M17467) and reused in *Vergaderinge der historien van Troyen* (ISTC i100116000; GW M17453).[24] In these books the woodcut represents King Apollo fighting King Zetephius. Since scenes from Greek and Roman history were usually represented by medieval knights, the woodcut was apparently considered fit to illustrate *Seghelijn*. Bellaert's woodcut passed into the hands of Gerard Leeu and thence to Hendrick Eckert.

The third edition of *Seghelijn* is, unfortunately, not dated, nor does it have the name of a publisher. It is generally attributed to the Antwerp printer and publisher Claes de Grave (Fig. 3).[25] The title-woodcut (*Die historie va[n] seghe/ lijn van iherusalem*) is reused in the next edition from 1517, which has De Grave's name in the colophon, making it likely that he was also the publisher of the earlier edition. This third edition of the text of *Seghelijn* is usually re-ferred to as the pre-1517 edition. Besides the title, the page displays a large woodcut with narrative scenes and it takes the viewer some time to decipher the illustration which should actually be read from foreground to background. In the front, we find a walled city that is guarded by a giant, standing on the bridge leading to the city's gate. In the next scene the giant is having a sword fight with a knight. Subsequently, the giant is defeated by the knight and in the hindmost scene the giant has disappeared, while the knight is resting next to a river, holding a larger hand in his own gloved hand. Even further in the back-ground an approaching army on horseback is visible. This is an illustration of

---

23 Conway (see note 20), 11.6.13 and Kok (see note 15), 160.13. The woodcut is repeated on k2, being the sole woodcut in the book.

24 *Jason* is to be dated between 10 December 1483 and 5 May 1485, *Troyen* is dated 5 May 1485. [Cf. the contribution by Besamusca and Willaert in the present volume, p. 73.]

25 The unique copy, kept at Leiden University Libraries (1498 C 3), lacks the last pages with a supposed colophon. NK 1323.

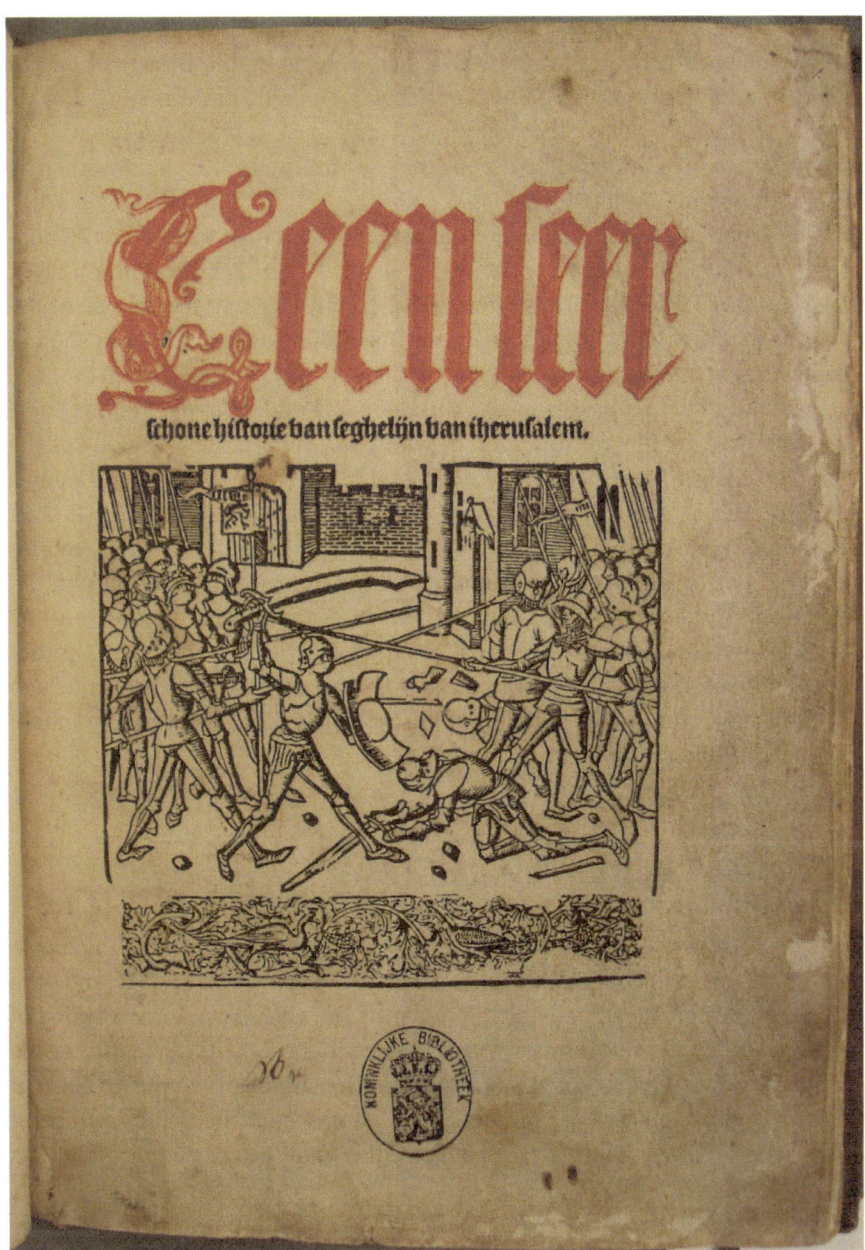

Fig. 2: Title-page of *Seghelijn van Iherusalem*, Antwerp, Hendrick Eckert van Homberch, 1511 (The Hague, KB).

a well-known Antwerp legend, the defeat of the giant Druon Antigoon, who ruled the city as a tyrant, by the young hero Silvius Brabo. Brabo cut off the giant's hand and threw it into the river Scheldt. Not only did this story provide the city of Antwerp with a legendary and heroic past, it also gave meaning to the city's name. To throw a hand, or as they say in Dutch, 'een hand werpen' is taken as the origin of Antwerpen.

The woodcut was initially produced for the *Cronike van Brabant*, published by Roelant van den Dorpe in Antwerp in February 1497 (ISTC ic00475000; GW 6667).[26] These Chronicles contain a large number of woodcuts, the majority much smaller than this page-filling scene. The print shop of Roelant van den Dorpe, which only published ten books, closed in 1501, one year after Roelant passed away. The woodcuts of the *Cronike* were at some point acquired by Jan van Doesborch, who used them in new editions of the same Chronicles, published in 1512, 1518 and 1530. The 1512 edition as well as the 1518 edition contain the Druon Antigoon – Brabo woodcut, in 1512 in a more pristine condition than in the pre-1517 *Seghelijn*. Pre-1517 thus implies post-1512. Both Van Doesborch editions of the Chronicles from the second decade also contain two woodcuts that have been re-used in the pre-1517 *Seghelijn*: two small battle scenes printed next to each other and another larger battle scene.[27] They also originate from Van den Dorpe's *Cronike*, where the two smaller ones were still joined. In 1512, however, they were separated, although printed as if joined.

3 The 1517 Edition by De Grave

Claes de Grave was a publisher active in Antwerp from the second to the fourth decade of the sixteenth century. He had started his firm in 1511 and, the following year, managed to obtain a privilege to be able to print (for a period of six years) all books not formerly printed in Brabant. Like the majority of his competitors, De Grave's firm was located near the Cam[m]erpoort, the centre of the book publisher's quarter, in a building named after the nearby cathedral *Onser liever vrouwen* (Our Lady), an address he would keep until the end of his

---

26 *Die alder excellentste cronyke van Brabant*. For the Brabo woodcut: Conway (see note 20), 37.1.25 and Kok (see note 15), 306.25.
27 Conway (see note 20), 37.1.27 and 30; and Kok (see note 15), 306.32 and 306.35.

Fig. 3: Title-page of *Seghelijn van Iherusalem*, Antwerp, Claes de Grave (attr.), before 1517 (Leiden, UB).

career. De Grave's firm produced on average three books a year, which makes it likely that he had revenues from other sources as well.[28] His production is rather diverse, including devotional works (some Lutheran), Bibles, government publications, prognostications and scientific books (botany, medicine, history, law). At the beginning of his career he cooperated with Thomas van der Noot from Brussels a number of times who, in those instances, probably acted as the printer. However, towards the end of his working life, in the 1530s, Willem Vorsterman was his partner. Although the majority of his books were printed in the vernacular, *Seghelijn* is his only verse romance.

De Grave's pre-1517 edition had a title-page with a single woodcut, apart from the book's title, which was cut from a woodblock as well. Different from Eckert van Homberch, whose two editions (1511 and its 1520 reprint, which is discussed below) looked almost identical, De Grave made a radical change for his 1517 edition (Fig. 4).[29] The title was printed from the same woodcut but had now become part of a page covered by a multitude of smaller woodcuts. The central woodcut shows a well-known biblical scene, the Fall of Jericho, originating from the workshop of Gerard Leeu.[30] It was part of a large series of biblical woodcuts that Leeu employed in a number of books, although the presumed Bible or other book for which they were intended has not survived.[31] Claes de Grave must have acquired the woodcut, and others from the same series, before January 1516, when he used some of them in his illustrated *Bibel int corte ghetranslateert*.[32] The three border pieces, at the top, bottom and left margins, were copied from a Basel border. Finally De Grave added seven small decorative pieces to fill out the remaining voids. The effect is visually intimidating, the result of an unrestrained *horror vacui* that leaves the spectator baffled. The stylistic incongruity resulting from the combination of all these different parts is perhaps the most conspicuous characteristic of this

---

28 The USTC lists 87 publications with Claes de Grave's name, published between 1511 and 1543. Most years he produced two to five titles but some years remained without any output at all, while the years 1520 and 1539 were exceptional thanks to a large number of government publications.

29 *Die historie va[n] seghe/lyn van iherusalem* (NK 1324). A unique copy is kept in the Koninklijke Bibliotheek in The Hague (KW 227 A 14).

30 Conway (see note 20), 10.6.68; not in Kok but belonging to her series 85.

31 Conway (see note 20), p. 56 suggests „[…] that the series would be found solely in a book for which it was specially intended, […]". The Old Testament scenes were used by Leeu in several Ludolphus de Saxonia editions, the New Testament ones only turned up with later printers in the sixteenth century and were apparently never employed by Leeu.

32 NK 366.

Fig. 4: Title-page of *Seghelijn van Iherusalem*, Antwerp, Claes de Grave, 1517 (The Hague, KB).

title-page. Chronologically they range from the 1480s (for the biblical scene) to 1517 (for the border pieces).

The border that De Grave had copied for this edition of *Seghelijn* had originally been cut for the 1515 edition of Erasmus' *Adagia*, published by Johann Froben. This was a famous edition. In 1513 Froben had illegally, in other words without the author's consent, published an edition of the *Adagia*, copied from the earlier version, printed in Venice by Aldus Manutius. Although Erasmus was not happy with this pirated edition, he did admire the skill displayed by Froben and decided to have the 1515 edition published by him.[33] It had a woodcut on the title-page displaying 'portraits' of Greek and Roman philosophers and writers, but on the second page, framing the preface to the reader, a four-part border was used (Fig. 5), the one that was copied two years later by Claes de Grave. The left part shows Eve, holding the snake, standing on a decorative column. The part on the right, somewhat wider, shows two columns, the front one similar to the one in the left piece, the one in the back of a more plain nature, with a putto standing on top. The upper part shows garlands of peapods with a cherub's head in the centre, while the bottom part has two winged angels, standing next to vessels and flanking an empty shield. The border was designed by the artist Urs Graf, who signed it twice: the bottom part has his usual monogram, VG, while the letters VRS are inscribed on the column in the left piece. The letters MVA on the same column should probably be read as EVA, who tops that column.[34] The border was one of two stylistically related four-part borders that Graf designed simultaneously and that were used the next year, in various combinations, in an even more famous book, the *Novum Instrumentum*, Erasmus' edition of the New Testament in Greek (1516). Parts of these two borders can also be found in later editions of the *Novum Instrumentum*, those of 1519 and 1522 (Fig. 6).

Urs Graf was, along with Hans Holbein, the most prominent artist in Switzerland and the author of a great number of woodcuts for publishers in Basel. His border for Erasmus' *Adagia* was inspired by a slightly older one by Albrecht Dürer that had been used in a number of books, edited by his close

---

33 Margaret Mann Phillips, *The Adages of Erasmus. A Study with Translations.* Cambridge 1964, p. 119–121. The evolution of Erasmus' cooperation with Johann Froben can be traced through Erasmus' letters, which lead from an angry humanist in 1513 to one involved in a whole range of publishing projects with Froben in 1515.
34 This is the suggestion of Hieronymus Frank, *Oberrheinische Buchillustrationen, 2. Basler Buchillustration, 1500–1545.* Basel 1984, p. 144–145, No. 175.

Fig. 5: Erasmus, *Adagia*, Basel, Johann Froben, 1515 (Munich, SB).

Fig. 6: Erasmus, *Novum Testamentum*, Basel, Johann Froben, 1522 (Munich, SB).

friend Willibald Pirckheimer. These editions of Greek and Roman authors were published in Nuremburg by Friedrich Peypus. The first book to include Dürer's border was a 1513 edition of Plutarchus' *De his qui tarde*, where it framed the first text page (Fig. 7).[35] In later books the border was used on the title-page. These included editions of (again) Plutarchus, Nilus and Lucianus Samosatensis.[36] Unlike Graf's design, which consisted of four separate parts, Dürer's border was a true border woodcut forming a single image, creating continuity in the design, with the text field conceived as an illusionistic tablet hanging in front of the columns, stairs, fabled creatures and angels. Although the execution of the woodcut is generally attributed to Dürer's workshop, the design must have been his: Pirckheimer was Dürer's closest friend in Nuremberg and it is unlikely that the artist delegated his friend's request for a woodcut border to his workshop without being involved in the design.

Graf's four-part woodcut border is not a slavish copy of Dürer's but the dependency is obvious. The two columns on the right are almost identical, although Graf replaced Dürer's satyr with a putto. The garlands at the top are very similar but whereas Dürer put some fabulous creature at the centre where the garlands meet, Graf chose a cherub's head. For the bottom part Dürer depicted four angels, two holding Peypus' coat of arms and two blowing a trumpet. They were more or less copied by Graf, not in the bottom part used in the 1515 *Adagia*, but in the second border used in the *Novum Instrumentum* of 1516. For the left part of the woodcut, Dürer created a complicated architectural setting with steps, a baluster, a heron on a column and dangling grapes. Graf replaced these with a single column of elaborate design, not unlike the one on the right side, with the figure of Eve on top.

By copying the woodcut border by Urs Graf, inspired by Albrecht Dürer and using it in his edition of *Seghelijn*, Claes de Grave introduced a specimen of Renaissance book design into the Low Countries. Designs of such modernity were still a rarity and although notions such as 'old-fashioned' or 'modern' or stylistic concepts such as 'gothic' and 'renaissance' may be anachronistic to use here, De Grave must have been aware that he was copying something not seen before in his homeland. The woodcutter must also have taken some pride

---

35 VD16 P 3634. This, and the books mentioned in the next note, can be accessed through the VD16 website.

36 Plutarchus, *De vitanda usura*, 1515 (VD16 P3783 and P3784), Lucianus Samosatensis, *De ratione conscribendae historiae*, 1515 (VD16 L3033 and L3034), Nilus, *Sententiae morales*, 1516 (VD16 N1759 and 1760) and Lucianus Samosatensis, *Piscator seu reviviscentes*, 1517 (VD L3033).

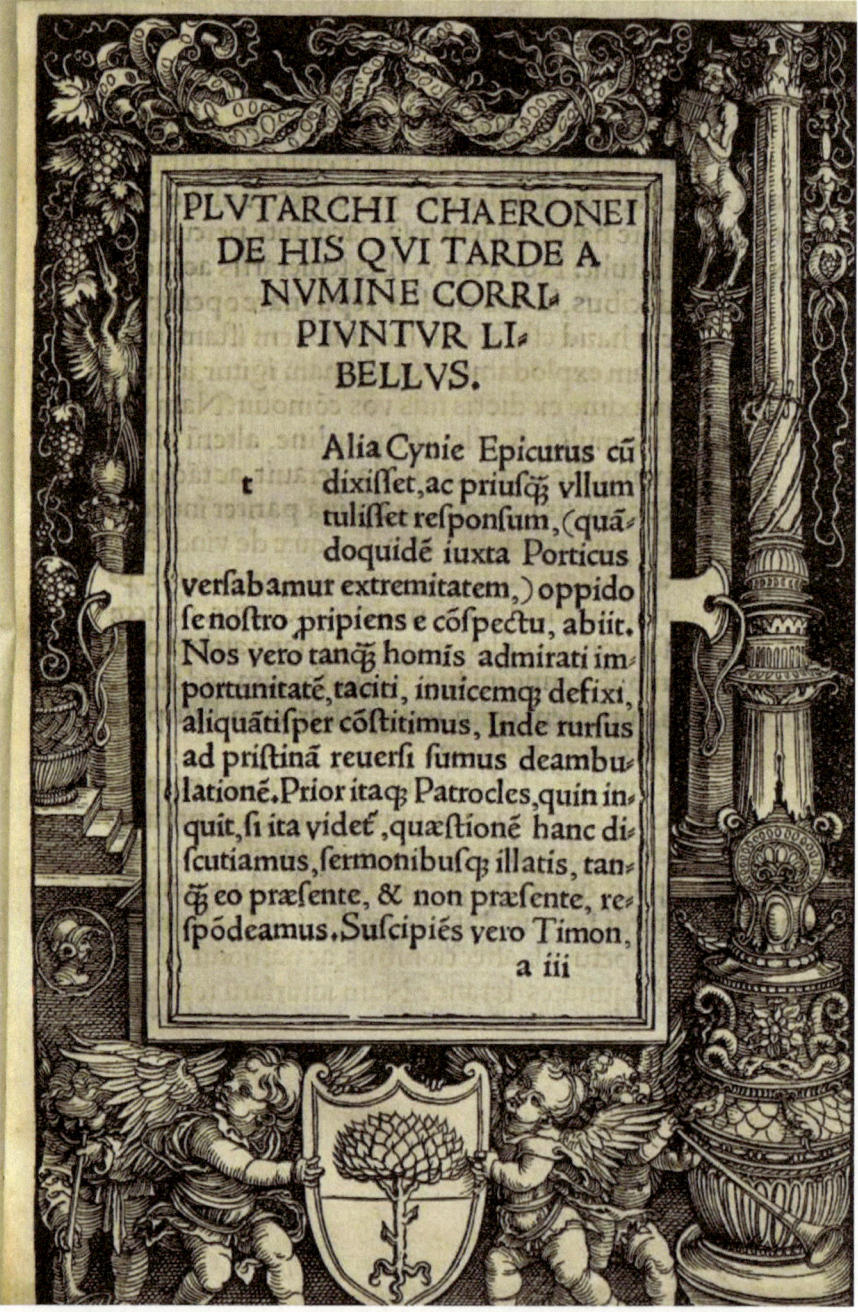

Fig. 7: Plutarchus (W. Pirckheimer ed.), *De his qui tarde*, Nuremberg, Friedrich Peypus, 1513 (Munich, SB).

Fig. 8: Detail of Fig. 4.

in his work. He signed the design with his monogram inscribed on the lower right side on a tablet (Fig. 8). Indecipherable as it is (J * S?), it is one of the old-est signatures to be found in book decoration in the Low Countries.[37] That De Grave did not fully embrace or even appreciate the innovative nature of the de-sign can be deduced from his only partial application (he left out the right part), the combination with a much older woodcut and the repeated use in books, none of which contains a contemporary text. After *Seghelijn*, parts of the border – never all four together – were used by De Grave in *Den grooten Cathoon* (1519 and 1535), *Somme ruyrael* (1520 and 1529) and Ludolphus de Saxonia's *Vita Christi* (1521, in Dutch).[38] In this last book, De Grave used the border not on the title-page, but to frame the Lentullus-portrait of Christ, ex-changing the left and right parts and thus ignoring Urs Graf's discerning char-acteristic of making the right side – corresponding to the outer margin of the page – wider. The combination of Urs Graf's design with much older woodcuts

---

37 I * B is another option. I haven't been able to find another example in early book decoration in the Low Countries. The monogram is not registered in G.K. Nagler, *Die Monogrammisten*. 5 vols. Munich 1858–1879.
38 NK 542, 543, 481, 482 and 1411.

such as we saw in *Seghelijn* was repeated in the other books. Thus, although Claes de Grave introduced a state-of-the-art woodcut border in the Low Countries, the way he applied it was outdated.

4 *Seghelijn* Editions after 1517

In 1520 Hendrick Eckert van Homberch republished his *Seghelijn* (Fig. 9).[39] This edition is almost identical to the one he had published in 1511, the two title-pages being virtually indistinguishable. There is a slight change in the spelling of the title: *schone historie van seghelijn van iherusalem* became *schoone hystorie van seghelijn van Iherusalem*. But the composition of the title-page remained the same, although the decorative border piece below the narrative woodcut was replaced by a different one. While the 1511 edition had no other woodcuts but the titular one, repeated twice in the text, the 1520 edition used a different woodcut for the book's interior, which was repeated four times.[40] And, like the titular woodcut used earlier in Bellaert's *Jason*, the one inside the book, showing a military tent camp, was used by Bellaert as well, but in a different book, the 1485 *Vergaderinge der historien van Troyen* (ISTC i100116000; GW M17453), where it represented the siege of Troy by the Greeks.[41]

The last edition of *Seghelijn* to be published in the Low Countries (or anywhere, for that matter) was again printed in Antwerp, by Hendrick Peetersen van Middelburch around 1540.[42] Like Claes de Grave before him, Peetersen used a woodcut from Roelant van den Dorpe's *Cronike van Brabant* on the title-page (Fig. 10).[43] It represents a battle scene that originally was meant to portray the Battle of Cordoba (1236) but could equally be applied to one of the many battles Seghelijn was involved in. The space underneath the battle woodcut was filled by Peetersen with stock images from his workshop. The lower border piece includes a coat-of-arms with the initials IL. These refer to Jacob van Liesveldt, making it probable that van Liesveldt was the publisher and Peetersen the printer. Peetersen (or van Liesveldt) could have borrowed the

---

39 NK 3364. The Österreichische Nationalbibliothek in Vienna holds the only known copy (66.E.39). [On Hendrick Eckert van Homberch see also the contribution by De Bruijn in this volume, p. 113–115.]

40 The woodcut can be found on fols. E1, F5, G1 and H2.

41 The woodcut: Conway (see note 20), 11.7.10; and Kok (see note 15), 162.10.

42 NK 3365. A unique copy is kept in the Bibliothèque nationale de France in Paris (Res-YI-27).

43 Conway (see note 20), 37.1.42; and Kok (see note 15), 306.42.

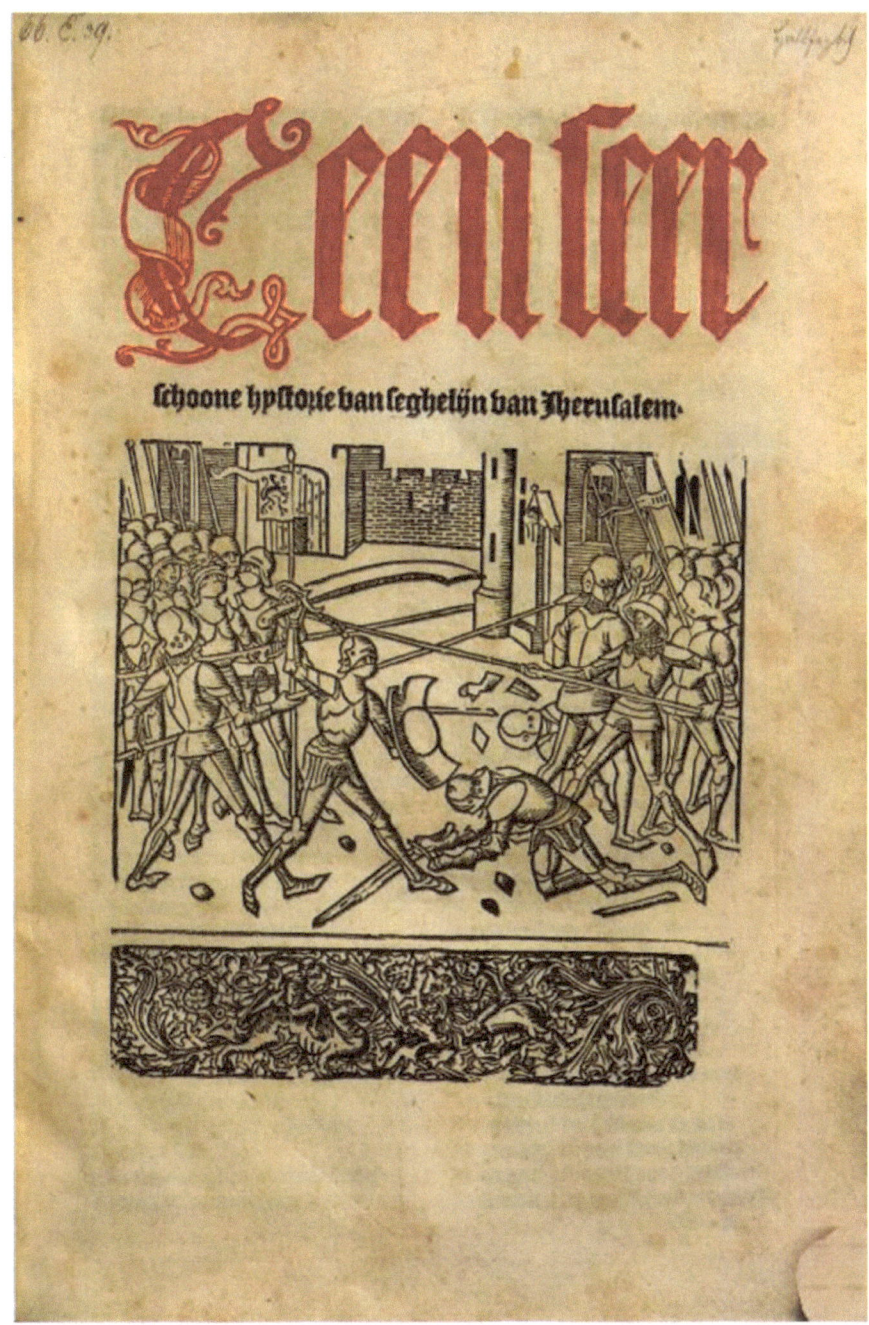

Fig. 9: Title-page of *Seghelijn van Iherusalem*, Antwerp, Hendrick Eckert van Homberch, 1520 (Vienna, ÖNB).

Fig. 10: Title-page to *Seghelijn van Iherusalem*, Antwerp, Hendrick Peetersen van Middelburch for Jacob van Liesveldt, 1540 or earlier (Paris, BN).

battle woodcut from Jan van Doesborch. Some copies of Van Doesborch's Chronicles, using van den Dorpe's woodcuts, were actually printed for Peetersen.[44] This could be an argument to date Peetersen's *Seghelijn* closer to 1530, when van Doesborch and Peetersen were collaborating.[45]

5 Use and Re-Use of Woodcuts in Narrative Prose

Without exception, all the woodcuts that have been used in the six editions of *Seghelijn* are examples of the re-use of existing woodcuts. Not one woodcut was produced with the purpose of illustrating the *Seghelijn* text itself. The 1483–1486 edition by Jacob Jacobszoon van der Meer was illustrated by slightly older woodcuts from Van der Meer's own stock (*Scaecspel*, 1482–1484). The 1511 and 1520 editions by Hendrick Eckert van Homberch employed the same woodcut on their title-pages, an image originating from Jacob Bellaert, to be dated between 1483 and 1485 (*Jason*). The pre-1517 edition by Claes de Grave used a woodcut from Roelant van den Dorpe's Chronicles (1497), while the 1517 edition from the same publisher once more had a woodcut from Gerard Leeu on the title-page, one of a series of biblical prints, dated on or before 1487. This woodcut was surrounded by border pieces that were newly cut, although probably not specifically for this *Seghelijn* edition. These border pieces were copied after a Basel border designed by Urs Graf. The book contains a few woodcuts from Van den Dorpe's Chronicles to illustrate the text. The 1520 edition by Hendrick Eckert used, apart from the already mentioned title-page cut, woodcuts from a different book published by Jacob Bellaert, dated 1485 (*Vergaderinge der historien van Troyen*). The final edition from around 1540 or somewhat earlier, was published by Jacob van Liesveldt and again uses a woodcut from van den Dorpe's Chronicles on the title-page, one not used before in a *Seghelijn* edition.

So all the title woodcuts, with the exception of the copies after Urs Graf in the 1517 edition, date from before 1500. They were cut for different texts that served different needs and were intended for different audiences. Jacob Bellaert's

---

44 Peter J.A. Franssen, *Tussen tekst en publiek. Jan van Doesborch, drukker-uitgever en literator te Antwerpen en Utrecht in de eerste helft van de zestiende eeuw*. Amsterdam 1990, p. 85, No. 62. Franssen mentions that a number of the copies of *Van Brabant die excellente cronike* (1530) were printed for either Michiel Hillen van Hoochstraten or Hendrick Peetersen.

45 There is perhaps one other edition of *Seghelijn*, the title identical to the Van Liesveldt / Peetersen edition, dated 1564. It is mentioned by the USTC and located in the Bodleian Library in Oxford. I haven't been able to consult this copy to see if it is indeed a different edition or a bibliographical error.

Jason, which was the source for the title woodcut of the 1511 and 1520 editions, can be considered a literary text of a similar kind to *Seghelijn*. But Roelant van den Dorpe's Chronicles, providing woodcuts for the editions of pre-1517, 1517 and around 1540, is not a romance but a chronicle, even though not all the histories presented by Van den Dorpe meet our standards of reliable history. Lastly, the image that Claes de Grave used for the 1517 edition was a biblical image. Its subject, the fall of a city (actually Jericho), was perhaps not completely at odds with some of the stories in *Seghelijn*, although the soldiers carrying the Ark of Covenant may have struck an odd note even to contemporary readers. One might expect that publishers would be willing to produce new woodcuts for a book such as *Seghelijn* whose popularity lasted throughout the first half of the sixteenth century. The opposite was the case. This reliance on older woodcuts was a characteristic *Seghelijn* shared with many narrative and historical texts in the sixteenth century.

To name just one example, the history of *Margariete van Limborch* has been the subject of a recent study by Rita Schlusemann.[46] This romance, published as *Een schoone historie va[n] margariete[n] va[n] limborch* in 1516 by Willem Vorsterman in Antwerp, contains a large number of woodcuts. With the exception of the title illustration and the coat of arms on the verso, the book has 40 woodcuts, including a few repeats. Although some of them seem to have been made especially for this text, the majority had a history of previous use in older books, including books from the fifteenth century. An important source again was Roelant van den Dorpe's Chronicles from 1497, the same source from which several *Seghelijn* illustrations were borrowed. The double scene that was used in the pre-1517 and the 1517 editions of *Seghelijn* can also be found in *Margariete*. Vorsterman probably borrowed or purchased the woodblocks from Jan van Doesborch who had used many blocks from van den Dorpe to illustrate his own updated version of the Chronicles, *Die alder excellenste cronyke*, published in 1512. Other sources for the woodcuts in *Margariete* were a bit more recent, like the *Vier Heemskinderen* (1508). Apart from re-used images, *Margariete* contains a few copies after older illustrations to *Godevaert van Boloen* (1486) and *Destructie van Jherusalem* (c. 1505). Schlusemann's thorough research has demonstrated that there was a lively trade in woodblocks among printers and publishers, a subject that is far from exhausted.[47]

---

46 Rita Schlusemann, *Schöne Historien. Niederländische Romane im deutschen Spätmittelalter und in der frühen Neuzeit*. Berlin 2016.
47 Schlusemann (see note 46), p. 69–89. To the publishers mentioned by Schlusemann as former owners of some of the woodblocks (Jan van Doesborch, Jan Seversz) can be added Claes

In general it can be said that woodcuts on the title-page of a book had a dual function. Firstly title-pages, including woodcuts, had an advertising function in a period when books were often sold without a cover. Whether purchased in a bookshop (often connected to a printer's workshop), on a market, or from a hawker, books were usually sold as a set of unbound quires. The title-page was thus an important feature of the book in transmitting information to the customer. In fact, the development of the title-page as such, and as the main source of information about the book, can be attributed to this practice of selling books without a prefabricated binding.[48] Woodcuts supported this function. They could enhance the book's appeal and draw the customer's attention through their design.

Secondly, woodcuts on title-pages contributed to the identification of genres. The early sixteenth century saw an enormous increase in book production. Not only did the number of printers and publishers rise, they produced more books than their predecessors.[49] The national and international book trade intensified and perhaps most of all, the position of authors changed. While the fifteenth century saw many existing texts from the manuscript age being printed and distributed, the sixteenth century produced an increasing number of new texts. These developments asked for a market strategy which did not yet exist for the printed book. With enlarged production, a greater variety of texts and a wider clientele, thanks to an improved literacy, publishers had to think of ways of reaching their public. Diversification was instrumental in this process. Specialisation became more common among publishers, especially towards the middle of the sixteenth century. Some publishers specialised in humanist texts, others in religious and devotional texts and others again in narrative literature. During the years between 1515 and 1540, the title-page plus woodcut developed in such a way that it became easy to recognise a humanist text, a devotional tract, a herbal or a narrative text at a glance. The discerning characteristic for this last category was that the woodcuts were often of a narrative nature, representing a scene from a story, and of a stylistically old-fashioned character. This was underlined through the use of older, fifteenth century images.

---

de Grave, owner of a wedding scene, used by him in *Dat regime[n]t vanden huwelijcken staet* (1512): Schlusemann p. 86 and 259, No. B 40.

48 See Margareth M. Smith, *The Title-Page, its Early Development 1460–1510*. New Castle, London 2000, passim but especially chapters one (p. 25–34) and six (p. 91–108); Rautenberg (see note 17), passim.

49 The USTC lists 2061 books printed in the Low Countries before 1501 (1473–1500), while a calculation for the period 1501 to 1530 results in 3624 books (retrieved December 2017).

The use of older woodcuts in sixteenth century books has been described by, amongst others, Carsten-Peter Warncke and Christine Boßmeyer as an instance of the typological character of fifteenth and sixteenth century woodcuts.[50] A woodcut of a battle could serve many goals. Its generic quality made it suitable to be used in different books, describing different battles. The same can be said of city-views or portraits.[51] Nevertheless this is not the complete story. For example, Boßmeyer refers to the repeated use of the same woodcut of a city view in the *Weltchronik* of Hartmann Schedel (1490) for the portrayal of many different cities while at the same time the *Weltchronik* contains large woodcuts which have been specifically designed to illustrate one city only.[52] Both tendencies thus existed side by side, the use of typological or generic images to cover a range of specific subjects as well as the use of increasingly 'naturalistic' images to portray the world. However, the stylistic characteristics of these images and their functionality have largely been ignored. Outmoded images were well suited to indicate the nature of the books they adorned. They visualised the ancient and traditional character of the texts that were often also emphasized in the textual elements on the title-pages. The practice of employing older, or older-looking, woodcuts was thus a conscious decision on the part of the publisher / printer, in order to characterise their texts.[53]

And this is exactly what the publishers of *Seghelijn* did. The generic character of the woodcuts they employed suited the text well, for a woodcut of the siege of a city could function in different contexts and be used for sieges from different times and places. Indeed this proved to be a distinguishing characteristic of much narrative literature in the sixteenth century. Apart from the already-mentioned *Margariete*, this can be demonstrated by other narrative texts as well, such as *Die distructie van Troyen* (Jan van Doesborch, 1508–1515), *Hystorie van Olyvier van Castillen* (Hendrick Eckert van Homberch, *c.* 1510) and *Die historie van Peeter van Prove[n]cen* (Willem Vorsterman, *c.* 1517). That this was not just a matter of the careless use of already available woodcuts, but

---

50 Carsten-Peter Warncke, *Sprechende Bilder – sichtbare Worte. Das Bildverständnis in der frühen Neuzeit*. Wiesbaden 1987, p. 64–80; Christine Boßmeyer, *Visuelle Geschichte in den Zeichnungen und Holzschnitten zum "Weißkunig" Kaiser Maximilans I*. 2 vols. Ostfildern 2015. Textband, p. 217–223.
51 Examples of this can be found in Warncke (see note 50) and Boßmeyer (see note 50).
52 Boßmeyer (see note 50), p. 217.
53 The development of the illustrated title-page in the sixteenth-century Low Countries and the function of the woodcut in the publisher's strategy is the subject of a study scheduled for publication in 2020. This will also contain a more extensive evaluation of the use of woodcuts in narrative texts. [For old-style title-pages, see also the article by Syrovy in the present volume, p. 351–374.]

a conscious choice by the publisher, is demonstrated by the 1517 edition of *Seghelijn* from the printer's shop of Claes de Grave. Here he combined, on the title-page, a fifteenth-century woodcut with border pieces copied after a book printed by the trendsetting firm of Johann Froben. There can be little doubt that De Grave was fully aware of the impact the stylistically innovative design of Urs Graf's woodcuts would make in the Low Countries. His decision to include a much older woodcut must have been the result of his intention to characterise the genre of narrative literature with an image customers would recognise as typical for much narrative literature.

Bibliography

Boßmeyer, Christine, *Visuelle Geschichte in den Zeichnungen und Holzschnitten zum "Weißkunig" Kaiser Maximilans I.* 2 vols. Ostfildern 2015.

Claassens, G.H.M., 'Die kerstenwet stercken. Kruisvaartideologie en kritiek in de *Seghelijn van Iherusalem'*. In: *TNTL* 107 (1991), p. 235–273.

Claassens, G.H.M., 'Seghelijn van Jheruzalem'. In: *Van Aiol tot de Zwaanridder. Personages uit de middeleeuwse verhaalkunst en hun voortleven in literatuur, theater en beeldende kunst.* Ed. by W.P. Gerritsen A.G. van Melle. Nijmegen 1993, p. 299–300.

Claassens, G.H.M., 'Dat en is sonder reden niet. Over de zeven vragen van Seghelijn van Jherusalem'. In: *Spiegel der Letteren* 40 (1998), p. 25–54.

Claassens, G.H.M., 'Membra disiecta: excessief geweld in de ridderroman Seghelijn van Jherusalem'. In: *Kabaal! Feest en strijd in de Nederlandse literatuur.* Ed. by Elke Brems, An Faems and Eveline Vanfraussen. Leuven 2004, p. 25–55.

Conway, William Martin, *The Woodcutters of the Netherlands in the Fifteenth Century.* Cambridge 1884.

Debaene, Luc., *De Nederlandse volksboeken. Ontstaan en geschiedenis van de Nederlandse prozaromans, gedrukt tussen 1475 en 1540.* Antwerpen 1951.

Faems, An, 'Nu hoert, ghi heren, ende verstaet ende neemt exempel aen desen man. De functie van het vertellerscommentaar in Seghelijn van Jhersualem'. In: *Millennium* 15 (2001), p. 114–139.

Frank, Hieronymus, *Oberrheinische Buchillustration, 2. Basler Buchillustration, 1500–1545.* Basel 1984.

Franssen, Peter J.A., *Tussen tekst en publiek. Jan van Doesborch, drukker-uitgever en literator te Antwerpen en Utrecht in de eerste helft van de zestiende eeuw.* Amsterdam 1990.

Heurck, Emile van, *Les livres populaires flamands.* Antwerpen 1931.

Jonckbloet, W.J.A., *Geschiedenis der Nederlandsche letterkunde.* Vol. 1. Groningen 1868.

Kok, Ina, *Woodcuts in Incunabula Printed in the Low Countries.* 4 vols. Houten 2013.

Mann Phillips, Margaret, *The Adages of Erasmus. A Study with Translations.* Cambridge 1964.

Nagler, G.K., *Die Monogrammisten.* 5 vols. Munich 1858–1879.

Rautenberg, Ursula, 'Die Entstehung und Entwicklung des Buchtitelblatts in der Inkunabelzeit in Deutschland, den Niederlanden und Venedig – Quantitative und qualitative Studien'. In: *Archiv für Geschichte des Buchwesens* 62 (2008), p. 1–105.

Resoort, Rob J., 'Het raadsel van de rijmdrukken'. In: *Nederlandse Letterkunde* 3 (1998), p. 327–344.

Schlusemann, Rita, *Schöne Historien. Niederländische Romane im deutschen Spätmittelalter und in der frühen Neuzeit*. Berlin 2016.

Smith, Margareth M., *The Title-Page, Its Early Development 1460–1510*. New Castle, London 2000.

Verdam, Jacob (ed.), *Seghelijn van Jherusalem naar het Berlijnsche handschrift en den ouden druk*. Leiden 1878.

Warncke, Carsten-Peter, *Sprechende Bilder – sichtbare Worte. Das Bildverständnis in der frühen Neuzeit*. Wiesbaden 1987.

Wijer, Ingrid van de, *Segheliin. Codicologische, bibliographische en tekstkritische studie en editie* (diss. Leuven). 2 vols. Leuven 1983.

Wijer, Ingrid van de, 'Segheliin van Iherusalem, tekstoverlevering van een Middelnederlands ridderdicht'. In: *Quaerendo* 14 (1984), p. 273–303.

Wyn, Henrik van, *Historische en letterkundige avondstonden*. Amsterdam 1800.

Anna Katharina Richter

Ritter, Romance, Rewriting. Überlegungen zur dänischen Erzählliteratur in der Frühdruckzeit am Beispiel der Historie von *Persenober oc Constantianobis* (1572)

Abstracts: *Persenober oc Constantianobis*, published in 1572 by Laurentz Benedicht in Copenhagen, is an early modern Danish translation and adaption of the Old French 'roman courtois' *Partonopeu de Blois* (twelfth century). This article outlines the way in which different forms of transformation and *rewriting,* or *Retextualisierung* (Joachim Bumke), have been realized in this edition. Another, now lost, edition from 1560, as well as a manuscript in Old Danish from ca. 1500, originally derived from the *Partalopa saga*, which is a thirteenth- or fourteenth-century Old Norse-Icelandic prose adaption of the French romance, can be considered as precursors in this complex process of translation, adaptation and rewriting. The 1572 edition, the oldest complete Danish version in print, reveals some characteristics of paratextual and rewriting which seem to be unique in the Danish transmission: an epilogue and the transformation of an important passage (the first meeting between Persenober/Partonopeu and the princess Constantianobis/Melior) that strengthens the importance of the moral choices of the noble protagonists. Thus, the narrative can offer both *nutz und kurtzweyl* (usefulness and entertainment) and models for identification to its (mostly aristocratic) readership in sixteenth-century Denmark.

Der 1572 beim Kopenhagener Buchdrucker Laurentz Benedicht erschienene dänische Druck der Historie von *Persenober oc Constantianobis* ist die früheste erhaltene gedruckte dänische Übersetzung und Bearbeitung des ursprünglich altfranzösischen 'roman courtois' von *Partonopeu de Blois* (12. Jahrhundert). Im Folgenden sollen unterschiedliche Darstellungsformen von Transformation, *rewriting* oder Retextualisierung (Joachim Bumke) in diesem dänischen Frühdruck erläutert werden. Seine Vorgängertexte – ein nicht erhaltener früherer Druck von 1560 sowie ein dänisches Manuskript von ca. 1500, das auf die altnorwegisch-isländische *Partalopa saga* zurückgeht, eine im 13. oder 14. Jahrhundert entstandene Prosaübersetzung und Adaption des altfranzösischen Versromans – werden ebenfalls in die Untersuchung miteinbezogen. Der dänische Druck von 1572 weist einige Besonderheiten hinsichtlich der Paratexte und Formen von *rewriting* auf, die als einzigartig in der dänischen Überlieferungsgeschichte der Erzählung anzusehen sind: eine Nachschrift und insbesondere textuelle Veränderungen in einer zentralen Passage (welche die erste Begegnung des Protagonistenpaares betrifft). Insbesondere durch letzteres Verfahren wird dem Text ein deutlich moralisierender Duktus verliehen, der ihn mit einem sowohl *nutz* als auch *kurtzweyl* vermittelnden Identifikationsangebot für seine (vorwiegend adlige) Leserschaft im vormodernen Dänemark ausstattet.

Anna Katharina Richter, Universität Zürich

1 Dänische *Partonopeu*-Fassungen

1572 erschien beim Kopenhagener Buchdrucker Laurentz Benedicht ein Büchlein im Oktavformat mit dem Titel:

> Persenober. En lystig oc skøn Historie paa Riim/ om Konning Persenober oc Drotning Constantianobis. Lystig at høre oc læse. Nu nylige offuerseet oc Corrigerit/ Rettere end hun vaar før. Prentet i Kiøbenhaffn/ aff Laurentz Benedicht. 1572.[1]

> (Persenober. Eine unterhaltsame und schöne Historie in Versen/ über König Persenober und Königin Constantianobis. Vergnüglich zu hören und zu lesen. Nun unlängst durchgesehen und korrigiert/ richtiger als sie zuvor war. Gedruckt in Kopenhagen/ von Laurentz Benedicht. 1572.)[2]

Es handelt sich hierbei um eine frühneuzeitliche dänische Bearbeitung des anonymen französischen Versromans *Partonopeu de Blois*, welcher nach bisherigem allgemeinem Forschungskonsens in den Jahren 1180–1185, möglicherweise jedoch, wie jüngere Arbeiten zeigen, schon einige Jahre früher (1170–80), verfasst wurde[3] und mit zahlreichen Übersetzungen und Bearbeitungen in vielen europäischen Sprachen zu einer der beliebtesten und sehr weit verbreiteten mittelalterlichen Erzählungen gehörte.[4] Der französische Erzählstoff ist vermutlich über eine norwegisch-isländische Prosabearbeitung nach Dänemark gekommen.[5] Diese heute nicht mehr bekannte Fassung war aller Voraussicht nach sowohl die Vorlage für die gedruckte Überlieferung der Erzählung als auch für die einzig bekannte Handschrift des Textes, die im Manuskript Codex Holmiensis K 47 (Königliche Bibliothek Stockholm) zusammen mit fünf anderen höfischen Versromanen in dänischer Sprache überliefert ist.[6] Dieses Manuskript,

---

1 Königliche Bibliothek Kopenhagen, Sign. LN 1325, 8°. Vgl. auch die digitalisierte Edition auf *Early European Books*: https://search.proquest.com/eeb/docview/2090302028 (letzter Zugriff am 27.5.2019).
2 Diese und alle folgenden Übersetzungen aus den skandinavischen Sprachen von mir, AKR (sofern nicht anders angegeben).
3 Zur Datierungsfrage des *Partonopeu*-Romans vgl. Sif Rikhardsdottir, *Medieval Translations and Cultural Discourse. The Movement of Texts in England, France and Scandinavia*. Cambridge 2012, S. 118; sowie Penny Eley, *Partonopeus de Blois. Romance in the Making*. Cambridge 2011, S. 11–15.
4 Vgl. Birgit Nyborg (Hg.), *Tre riddersagaer: Sagaen om Partalopi. Sagaen om Flores ok Blankiflor. Sagaen om Bevers*. Oslo 2005, S. 54; und Rikhardsdottir (vgl. Anm. 3), S. 113–151.
5 Auf die komplexe Transmissionsgeschichte wird hier unten näher eingegangen.
6 Siehe hierzu die digitalisierte Edition von Jonathan Adams und Marita Akhøj Nielsen des in den Jahren 2002–2006 durchgeführten Forschungsprojekts von *Det Danske Sprog- og Litteraturselskab* (Gesellschaft für dänische Sprache und Literatur, DSL, welche der Universität Kopenhagen und der Königlichen Bibliothek angeschlossen ist): https://tekstnet.dk/manuscript-descriptions/stockholm-k47 (Beschreibung der Handschrift Cod. Holm. K 47) sowie https://tekstnet.dk/persenober-og-konstantianobis/1 (Edition). Zur Handschrift Cod. Holm. K 47 bemerken die Herausgeber: „Den tidligst kendte tekst af den danske *Persenober og Konstantianobis* findes i stockholmhåndskriftet K 47 fra

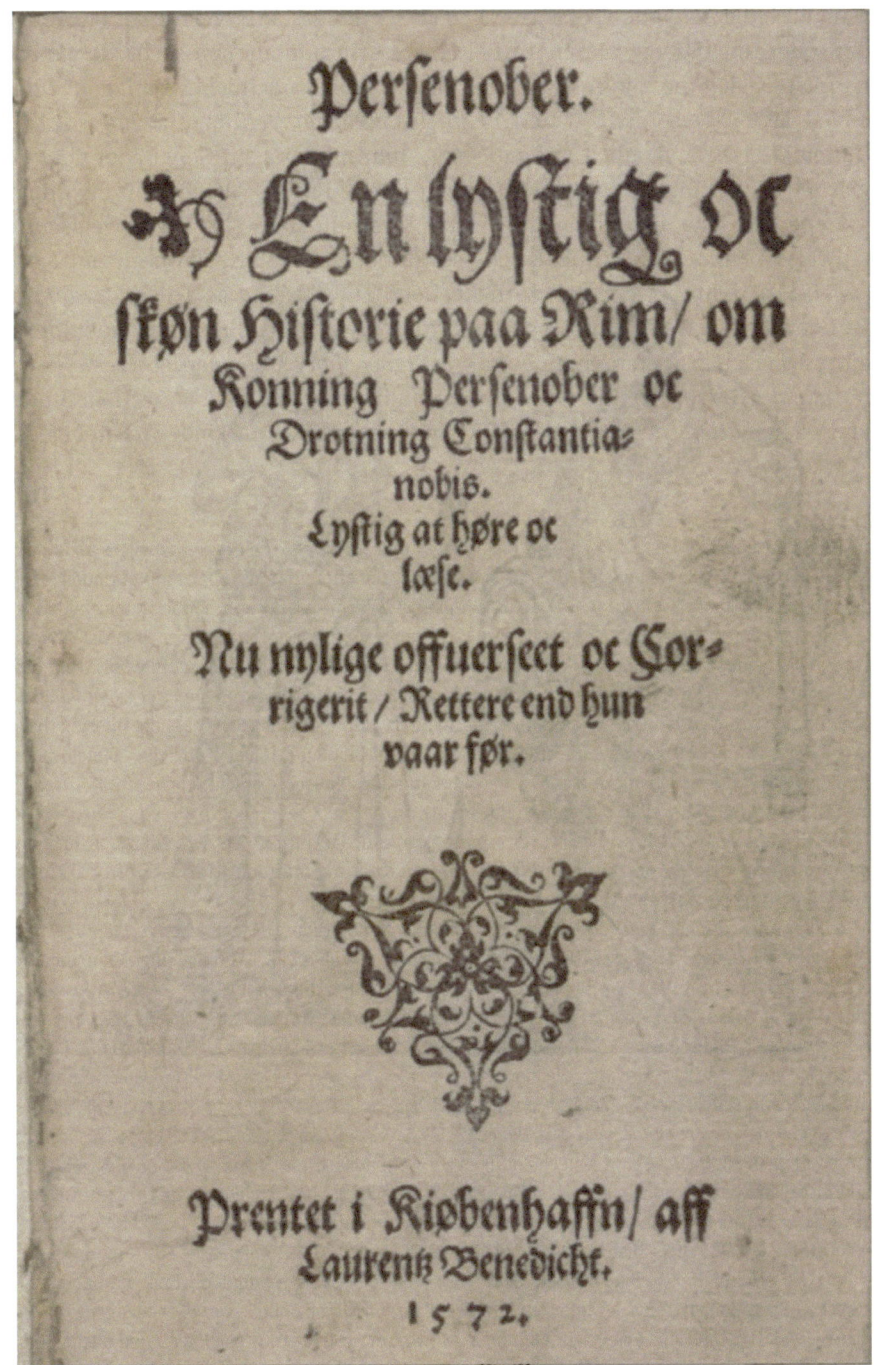

Abb. 1: *Persenober oc Constantianobis*, Kopenhagen 1572. Titelblatt (Bl. A1r) (© Königliche Bibliothek Kopenhagen/Early European Books).

vermutlich die Abschrift einer älteren Vorlage, ist auf das ausgehende 15. Jahrhundert oder um 1500 zu datieren.[7] Bei allen darin enthaltenen sechs Romanen handelt es sich um dänische Übersetzungen volkssprachlicher Vorlagen: Drei davon sind Übersetzungen und Bearbeitungen der berühmten *Eufemiavisor* (Eufemia-Lieder), nämlich Anfang des 14. Jahrhunderts auf Geheiß der norwegischen Königin Eufemia (Regierungszeit 1299–1313) ins Altschwedische übertragene höfische Erzählungen, welche ihrerseits teilweise altnorwegische, teilweise kontinentale (französische sowie deutsche) Vorlagen besitzen: *Ivan Løveridder* (Ivan Löwenritter, zurückgehend auf Chrétien de Troyes' *Yvain ou Le Chevalier au lion*), *Flores oc Blantzeflor* (Flores und Blanzeflor, nach dem altfranzösischen Versroman *Floire et Blancheflor*) und *Hertug Frederik af Normandi* (Herzog Fredrik aus der Normandie, eine Erzählung aus dem Stoffkreis der *matière de Bretagne*).[8] Die anderen drei Texte sind *Persenober oc*

---

ca. 1500. Sjuskefejl i teksten tyder afgjort på, at der er tale om en afskrift. Det underbygges af, at den ældste bevarede trykte udgave fra 1572 har læsemåder, som efter al sandsynlighed er oprindelige og går tilbage til et fælles forlæg for K 47 og trykkene. Blandt disse passager er den mest iøjnefaldende et helt vers, der mangler i K 47, men dårligt kan undværes, fordi det indeholder rimordet til vers 1247." (Die früheste bekannte Textfassung des dänischen *Persenober und Konstantianobis* stellt die Handschrift Stockholm K 47 von ca. 1500 dar. Flüchtigkeitsfehler im Text deuten auf jeden Fall darauf hin, dass es sich hierbei um eine Abschrift handelt. Dafür spricht auch, dass der älteste erhaltene Druck von 1572 Lesarten aufweist, die aller Wahrscheinlichkeit nach auf eine gemeinsame Vorlage für K 47 und die Drucke zurückgehen. Am auffälligsten ist dabei ein Vers, der in K 47 fehlt, aber unverzichtbar ist, weil er das ergänzende Reimwort zu Vers 1247 enthält.).

7 Die *Persenober*-Erzählung datiert der Text selbst auf das Jahr 1484. Vgl. die ausführliche Beschreibung des Manuskripts unter https://tekstnet.dk/manuscript-descriptions/stock holm-k 47-lang-beskrivelse (letzter Zugriff am 27.5.2019).

8 Zu den schwedischen *Eufemiavisor* vgl. die kommentierte Edition: *Eufemiavisorna*. Bde. I (*Flores och Blanzeflor. Hertig Fredrik av Normandie*) und II (*Ivan Lejonriddaren*). Textredigering, kommentarer och ordförklaringar av Henrik Williams. Inledning av Bo Ralph. Stockholm 2018 (Svenska klassiker utgivna av Svenska Akademien); Gösta Holms, 'Eufemiavisorna'. In: *Medieval Scandinavia: An Encyclopedia*. Hg. v. Philip Pulsiano. New York 1993, S. 171–173; Jürg Glauser (Hg.), *Skandinavische Literaturgeschichte*. 2. Aufl. Stuttgart, Weimar 2016, S. 30–31; Stefanie Würth, 'Eufemia. Deutsche Auftraggeberin schwedischer Literatur am norwegischen Hof'. In: *Arbeiten zur Skandinavistik. 13. Arbeitstagung der deutschsprachigen Skandinavistik 29.7.–3.8.1997 in Lysebu/Oslo*. Hg. v. Fritz Paul. Frankfurt a. M. 2000 (Texte und Untersuchungen zur Germanistik und Skandinavistik 45), S. 269–281; und insbesondere den Sammelband von Olle Ferm et al. (Hgg.), *The Eufemiavisor and Courtly Culture, Time, Texts and Cultural Transfer*, Papers from a Symposium in Stockholm 11–13 October 2012. Stockholm, Kunglig Vitterhets Historie och Antikvitets Akademien 2015 (Konferenser 88). – Zum Manuskript Cod. Holm. K 47 siehe insbesondere Jürg Glauser, 'Höfisch-ritterliche Epik in Dänemark zwischen Spätmittelalter und Frühneuzeit'. In: *Festschrift für Oskar Bandle zum 60. Geburtstag am 11. Januar 1986*. Hg. von Hans-Peter Naumann unter Mitwirkung von Magnus von Platen und Stefan Sonderegger. Basel, Frankfurt a. M. 1986 (Beiträge zur nordischen Philologie 15), S. 191–207.

Constantianobis sowie *Dværgekongen Laurin* (Zwergenkönig Laurin) und *Den kyske Dronning* (Die keusche Königin). Die Historie von *Persenober* steht in dieser Handschrift genau in der Mitte, an vierter Stelle, auf Bll. 169^v bis 196^r; sie leitet damit die zweite Hälfte der Ritterromane in diesem Manuskript ein, in denen die Liebe als zentrales Thema behandelt wird.[9]

Vor dem genannten Kopenhagener Druck von 1572 erschien bereits 1560 eine frühere Ausgabe, vermutlich ebenfalls in Kopenhagen, welche zwar nicht mehr erhalten ist, auf die der Benedicht-Druck von 1572 sowohl im Titel als auch am Ende seines eigentlichen Erzähltextes jedoch verweist.[10] Noch ein weiterer, allerdings unvollständiger dänischer Druck aus dem späten 16. Jahrhundert ist überliefert, der auf die Zeit 1572–1600 datiert wird, diesmal vermutlich aus einer Offizin in Norddeutschland.[11] Im Jahr 1700 scheint der letzte nachgewiesene Druck in Kopenhagen erschienen zu sein, wahrscheinlich gab es dazwischen noch die eine oder andere, nicht mehr erhaltene Ausgabe aus dem 17. Jahrhundert.[12] Der Druck von 1572 stellt somit die älteste vollständig erhaltene Druckfassung des Textes in Dänemark dar.

2 Höfische Literatur in der Frühdruckzeit in Dänemark

In welchem literarhistorischen Kontext steht nun die Produktion eines Textes wie die dänischen Adaptionen des *Partonopeu*-Romans in ihrer handschriftlichen Fassung und ihren gedruckten Versionen? Nach der Einführung des Buchdrucks in Dänemark und Schweden in den letzten Jahrzehnten des 15. Jahrhunderts[13] druckte vor allem der aus den Niederlanden eingewanderte,

---

9 Vgl. Glauser, 'Höfisch-ritterliche Epik' (Anm. 8), S. 192–193 und https://tekstnet.dk/persenober-og-konstantianobis/about#K47ogPK (letzter Zugriff am 27.5.2019).

10 Vgl. J.P. Jacobsen et al. (Hgg.), *Danske Folkebøger fra 16. og 17. Aarhundrede*. Bd. VI. København 1925, S. 149– 207 (Text) und S. 511–513 (Bibliographie), im Folgenden mit *DF* VI abgekürzt. Zur Ausgabe von 1560 s. hier, S. 512. Der Verweis auf den Vorgängerdruck findet sich in der Ausgabe von 1572 auf Bl. D8r.

11 Diese Ausgabe befindet sich in der Königlichen Bibliothek Kopenhagen, Sign. LN 1325a 8° und wird nicht in *Danske Folkebøger* erwähnt, vgl. *DF* VI, S. 511–513.

12 Die Ausgabe von 1700 befindet sich ebenfalls in der Königlichen Bibliothek Kopenhagen, Sign. Hielmst. 1865 8°. Vgl. auch die Angaben in *DF* VI, S. 512.

13 1482 wurde in Odense von Johan Snell das erste Buch überhaupt in Dänemark gedruckt (*Obsidionis Rhodiae urbis descriptio* des Guillaume Caoursin), bereits zuvor druckte er dort wohl ein Messbuch (*Breviarum Ottoniense*, undatiert). Vgl. hierzu Glauser, *Skandinavische Literaturgeschichte* (Anm. 8), S. 55 und generell zum (frühen) Buchdruck in Dänemark auch Henrik

ab 1489 in Kopenhagen tätige Gotfried von Ghemen (dän. Gotfred af Ghemen) als erster permanent etablierter dänischer Drucker neben Schriften für die 1479 gegründete Kopenhagener Universität auch volkssprachliche Texte.[14] Das erste auf Dänisch gedruckte Buch in seiner Offizin war *Den danske Rimkrønike* (Die dänische Reimchronik) 1495, bald darauf folgten frühe Romane und andere Erzähltexte, die zumeist nach kontinentalen Textvorlagen bearbeitet und ins Dänische übersetzt wurden: *Flores oc Blantzeflor* (1504 und 1509), *Jesu barndoms bog* (Das Buch von der Kindheit Jesu, 1508), *Karl Magnus krønike* (Chronik von Karl dem Großen, 1509 und nochmals 1534). Weitere, bei verschiedenen Druckern in Kopenhagen und auch in Norddeutschland erschienene Erstdrucke dänischer früher Romane sind *Griseldis* (1528), *Sigismunda* (1528), *Ion presth* (dänische Version der *Epistola presbiteri Johannis*, 1510), *Marcolfus* (1540), *En Ræffue Bog, som kaldes paa Tyske Reinicke Foss* (Ein Fuchsbuch, das auf Deutsch Reinicke Fuchs heißt, 1555) und im Jahre 1560 dann der eingangs erwähnte, heute verlorene dänische (Erst?)Druck von *Persenober oc Constantianobis*, um nur einige Beispiele zu nennen.[15] Die ‚große Welle' gedruckter Übersetzungen meist (hoch- oder nieder-)deutscher Vorlagen von didaktischen und erzählenden Historienbüchern und Frühromanen setzt in Dänemark ab den 1530er Jahren ein.[16] In der Regel im Oktavformat und ohne aufwendige Illustrationen gedruckt, waren sie von Beginn an für eine relativ kostengünstige Publikationsform vorgesehen, welche häufige Nachdrucke ermöglichte:

> Bereits im 16. Jahrhundert verwendet man für diese Texte in der Regel kleinere Druckformate (meist Oktav), was belegt, dass von Anfang an eine Aufteilung des Gattungsspektrums auf Formate und Ausstattung vorgenommen wird: Neben großformatigen Prachtwerken mit repräsentativem Charakter (Bibeln, Chroniken usw.) gibt es handlichere Bücher für weniger öffentliche Lesesituationen. Die zahlreichen Drucke dieser Historienbücher, die oft in rascher Folge wieder aufgelegt wurden, zeigen, wie die neue Medialitätsform gleich nach der Einführung des Buchdrucks für die Erfahrung imaginärer Welten eingesetzt wird.[17]

Horstbøll, *Menigmands medie. Det folkelige bogtryk i Danmark 1500–1840*. København 1999 (Danish Humanist Texts and Studies 19).

14 Dazu Glauser, *Skandinavische Literaturgeschichte* (Anm. 8), S. 56.

15 Siehe dazu Glauser, *Skandinavische Literaturgeschichte* (Anm. 8), S. 31 und S. 59–60.

16 Vgl. hierzu Glauser, *Skandinavische Literaturgeschichte* (Anm. 8), S. 59–60 und Anna Katharina Richter, *Transmissionsgeschichten. Untersuchungen zur dänischen und schwedischen Erzählprosa in der frühen Neuzeit*. Tübingen, Basel 2009 (Beiträge zur nordischen Philologie 41), S. 17–22.

17 Glauser, *Skandinavische Literaturgeschichte* (Anm. 8), S. 60. [Anderswo in Westeuropa scheint ein Folio- oder Quartformat für frühe Romane geläufiger gewesen zu sein. Siehe für die Benutzung des Quartformats in England den Beitrag von Boffey (Seite 138), für die Verwendung des Folioformats bei französischen Artusromanen den Beitrag von Montorsi (Seite 174)

Zahlreichen der oben genannten Texte ist gemeinsam, dass sie fremdsprachige, d. h. mittelalterliche kontinentaleuropäische (häufig deutsche oder französische) Übersetzungsvorlagen hatten. Viele dieser Erzählungen wurden um 1500 aus dem Hoch- oder Niederdeutschen übersetzt, doch nicht wenige weisen bereits eine ältere Transmission innerhalb Skandinaviens auf: Bereits im 13. und 14. Jahrhundert wurde nämlich in Norwegen und Island ein großes Textkorpus an altfranzösischen Erzählungen (Romane, *fabliaux* und *lais*) der *matière de Bretagne*, dazu die *lais* der Marie de France, Erzählungen aus der *matière d'aventure* wie auch aus der Gattung der französischen Heldensage (*chansons de geste* aus der *matière de France*) sowie Texte aus dem Anglonormannischen (etwa die *Tristan*-Erzählung) ins Altnorwegische übertragen. Bergen und Oslo stellten dabei Zentren dieser umfangreichen Vermittlertätigkeit dar, von denen aus die neuen Erzählformen und Genres wie Rittersagas (*riddarasögur, romances*), die eingangs erwähnten *Eufemiavisor* und auch die Balladen in die anderen nordischen Länder und Sprachen verbreitet wurden. In Schweden und in Dänemark wurden die höfischen Versromane dann im 14. und 15. Jahrhundert adaptiert, in Form von Bearbeitungen und Übersetzungen.[18] Wurden jedoch Texte wie etwa die *Karlamagnús saga* (Saga von Karl dem Großen), eine Kompilation von Texten aus dem Karls-Kreis mit französischen und lateinischen Vorlagen, bereits im 13. Jahrhundert ins Altnorwegische und im 14. Jahrhundert ins Altschwedische übertragen, folgte Dänemark erst relativ spät mit der Adaption der mittelalterlich-höfischen Erzähltradition, nämlich ab ca. 1450. Es gibt nur sehr wenige literarische Textzeugnisse aus dieser Zeit, eines der wichtigsten ist die bereits erwähnte Handschrift Cod. Holm. K 47.[19]

---

und für die Buchformate in Augsburg bzw. im deutschen Südwesten den Beitrag von Bertelsmeier-Kierst (Seite 37) in diesem Band.]

18 Hierzu ausführlich Glauser, *Skandinavische Literaturgeschichte* (Anm. 8), S. 31 und Jürg Glauser, 'Romance (Translated *riddarasögur*)'. In: *A Companion to Old Norse-Icelandic Literature and Culture*. Hg. v. Rory McTurk. Oxford 2005, S. 372–387; sowie Marianne E. Kalinke, 'Norse Romance (*Riddarasögur*)'. In: *Old Norse-Icelandic Literature. A Critical Guide*. Hg. v. Carol J. Clover und John Lindow. Toronto u.a. 2005, S. 316–363.

19 Zur (verspäteten) Rezeption in Dänemark siehe Glauser, 'Höfisch-ritterliche Epik' (wie Anm. 8), S. 192. Studiert man das Textkorpus, das die Dänische Sprach- und Literaturgesellschaft im Rahmen des erwähnten Digitalisierungsprojekts als „Texte aus Dänemarks Mittelalter 1100–1550" erarbeitet hat, wobei Handschriften wie Frühdrucke berücksichtigt wurden, ist die große Anzahl an Gesetzestexten auffallend, ebenso sind historische Texte wie Chroniken und religiöse Texte wie Legenden oder das sehr beliebte Buch von der Kindheit Jesu (*Jesu barndoms bog*, 1508) vertreten. Narrative Texte stellen insgesamt eher eine Untergruppe dar. Wie die dänische Literaturwissenschaftlerin Pil Dahlerup jedoch mit Verweis auf die Balladenrezeption und auf bildliche Darstellungen in Kirchen usw. vermutet, ist wohl anzunehmen, dass höfische Literatur auch schon früher bekannt war, wir jedoch keine Textzeugnisse aus dieser Zeit erhalten haben,

3 Die Transmission der *Persenober*-Historie und ihr europäischer Hintergrund

Auch die Transmission der *Persenober*-Historie in Skandinavien verlief zunächst über eine Adaption und Übersetzung einer französischen Vorlage in einen altnorwegischen Prosatext: Die spätmittelalterliche *Partalopa saga* zählt zu den *romances*, den übersetzten *riddarasögur* (Rittersagas). Ihre Vorlage dürfte eine (eventuell verlorene) französische Textversion sein, die genaue Entstehungszeit der Saga ist jedoch unklar, entweder im 13. Jahrhundert am norwegischen Königshof (im Zuge der vorhin erwähnten ‚Welle' mit Übersetzungen aus dem Altfranzösischen, ähnlich wie in der Transmission von *Flores oc Blantzeflor*, der ja dann später mit *Persenober* auch im selben dänischen Manuskript Cod. Holm. K 47 enthalten ist) – oder etwas später, vor dem 14. Jahrhundert direkt auf Island.[20]

Die europäische Handschriftenüberlieferung des *Partonopeu de Blois* lässt sich in zwei Textgruppen unterscheiden: Ebenso wie das mittelenglische Fragment von ca. 1450, die dänische Handschrift Cod. Holm. K 47, die spanische Prosaversion und eine katalanische Übersetzung davon gehört auch die altnorwegische *Partalopa saga* zur sogenannten Z-Gruppe (hier beginnt die Erzählung in Griechenland, der ursprünglichen Heimat der Protagonistin Melior).[21] Unterschieden davon

---

vgl. Pil Dahlerup, *Dansk litteratur. Middelalder*. Bd. II: *Verdslig litteratur*. København 1998, S. 265–267.

20 Die Saga ist in zwei Redaktionen, A und B, überliefert. Vgl. die maßgebliche Edition: *Partalopa saga*. Hg. v. Lise Præstgaard Andersen. Copenhagen 1983 (Editiones Arnamagnæanæ, Series B, Bd. 28). Marianne E. Kalinke verweist in dieser Diskussion auf die deutliche Bearbeitung des französischen Romans durch den Sagaautor (insbesondere das Motiv der *maiden-king* anstelle der Fee in der Figurendarstellung der Prinzessin Melior/Marmoria) und spricht sich für eine Entstehung der Saga in Island aus. Vgl. dazu Marianne E. Kalinke, 'Scribe, Redactor, Author: The Emergence and Evolution of Icelandic Romance'. In: *Viking and Medieval Scandinavia* 8 (2012), S. 171–198, hier insbesondere S. 186–189; vgl. dazu auch die Angaben bei Pulsiano (Anm. 8), S. 497 und Rikhardsdottir (vgl. Anm. 3), S. 21–22 und S. 116–120; sowie Marianne E. Kalinke, 'Clári saga, Hrólfs saga Gautrekssonar, and the Evolution of Icelandic Romance'. In: *Riddarasögur. The Translation of European Court Culture in Medieval Scandinavia*. Hg. v. Karl G. Johansson und Else Mundal. Oslo 2014, S. 273–292, hier S. 285.

21 Im französischen Text wird die weibliche Hauptfigur zunächst „une damoisele" oder „la dame" genannt, schließlich mit ihrem Namen, Melior. Als Textgrundlage für den französischen Roman dient die Ausgabe *Le Roman de Partonopeu de Blois. Édition, traduction et introduction de la rédaction A (Paris, Bibliothèque de l'Arsenal, 2986) et de la Continuation du récit d'après les manuscrits de Berne (Burgerbibliothek, 113) et de Tours (Bibliothèque municipale, 939), par Olivier Collet et Pierre-Marie Joris*. Paris 2005 (im Folgenden mit *Le Roman* abgekürzt). Zur Namensgebung vgl. *Le Roman*, V. 1129, V. 1243 und V. 1763). In der *Partalopa saga* heißt die Prinzessin Marmoria (vgl. *Partalopa saga* (vgl. Anm. 20), S. 1), im dänischen

werden die Texte der sogenannten Y-Gruppe (hier beginnt die Geschichte in Frankreich, der Heimat von Partonopeu), nämlich der französische Versroman und die davon ausgehenden, mehr oder weniger direkten Übersetzungen des Textes ins Englische, ins Hoch- und Niederdeutsche, ins Niederländische und ins Italienische.[22] In der Forschung wurde die Vermutung geäußert, dass der Druck aus Laurentz Benedichts Offizin von 1572, wohl auch der verlorene von 1560 sowie die in der Handschrift Cod. Holm. K 47 überlieferte Version des Textes möglicherweise letzten Endes auf eine gemeinsame, verlorene norwegisch-isländische Vorlage zurückgehen. In diesem Fall wäre das wohl eine Version der *Partalopa saga*, welche älter sein muss als die heute (wie häufig in der Überlieferung altnorwegischer und isländischer Texte des Mittelalters) allerdings nur noch in späteren Fassungen erhaltenen isländischen Handschriften dieser Saga, von denen die älteste das Manuskript AM 533 4to (Reykjavík, Stofnun Árna Magnússonar í íslenskum fræðum, ca. 1450–1500) ist. Es existierte jedoch bereits zuvor in der (verlorenen) *Ormsbók* aus dem 14. Jahrhundert ebenfalls eine Version der *Partalopa saga*.[23] Möglicherweise hat es Varianten der Saga gegeben, die dem dänischen *Persenober*-Versroman näherstehen als die heute erhaltenen Sagamanuskripte.[24] Vielleicht stellt die Version in Cod. Holm. K 47, die sich größtenteils an die Saga, teilweise wiederum enger an den französischen Text hält, aber auch eine eigene originale dänische Bearbeitung einer oralen Tradition dar, etwa wegen der zahlreichen eigenwilligen dänischen Eigennamen.[25] Aufgrund der unklaren Quellenlage ist jedoch bei all

---

Manuskript Cod. Holm. K 47 sowie in den dänischen Drucken aber Constantianobis, vermutlich als Ableitung vom Namen ihrer Heimatstadt Konstantinopel, im dänischen Text Constantia. Zu dieser Variante (sowie zu den anderen Namensänderungen, etwa Meliors Schwester Urrake, die in der dänischen Tradierung zu Fraga/Frago wird), siehe *DF* VI, S. LXI.

22 Zu den Textgruppen vgl. *Partalopa saga* (vgl. Anm. 20), S. XIII–XIV sowie Kalinke, 'Scribe, Redactor, Author' (Anm. 20), S. 186.

23 Vgl. *Partalopa saga* (vgl. Anm. 20), S. XLVIII–LVLXV; Nyborg (vgl. Anm. 4), S. 56–58; Rikhardsdottir, (vgl. Anm. 3), S. 119–120; sowie Kalinke, 'Clári saga' (Anm. 20), S. 285.

24 Vgl. hierzu *DF* VI, S. LIX–LX und Nyborg (vgl. Anm. 4), S. 57.

25 Dies vermutet Dahlerup (vgl. Anm. 19), S. 270. Bereits der dänische Herausgeber des Versromans im 19. Jahrhundert, Carl Joakim Brandt, äußert sich zur eigenwilligen Namensgebung in der dänischen Tradierung („Constantianobis" möglicherweise aufgrund eines Missverständnisses oder weil der dänische Bearbeiter um 1500 ihren Namen vergessen und sich einfach am Ortsnamen Konstantinopel, wo die Geschichte beginnt und wo ihr Vater regierender König ist, orientiert hätte). Vgl. Carl Joakim Brandt (Hg.), *Romantisk Digtning fra Middelalderen*. Bd. III. København 1877, S. 334. Klärungen zu der- resp. denjenigen genauen Textfassung(en), die der dänischen Tradierung (für Handschrift und Druck) zugrunde liegt resp. liegen, stehen noch aus, ebenso genauere Angaben zur Entstehung des Manuskripts Cod. Holm. K 47 selbst.

diesen Überlegungen zu Vorlagen und wechselseitigen Abhängigkeiten der nordischen *Persenober*-Texte große Vorsicht geboten und es bedürfte einer detaillierten Untersuchung.

Vor diesem komplexen transmissionshistorischen Hintergrund und angesichts der Tatsache, dass die Frühdruckzeit in Skandinavien noch lange durchaus „von der Gleichzeitigkeit, dem Neben- und Miteinander und der Mischung der Überlieferungsträger Handschrift/Buchdruck geprägt"[26] war, ist auch der 1572 in Laurentz Benedichts Offizin erschienene *Persenober*-Druck zu betrachten. Wie auch immer die genaue Überlieferung des Textes im Norden verlaufen ist: Zusammen mit der bereits 1504 und 1509 gedruckten Erzählung von *Flores oc Blantzeflor*[27] sowie der *Karl Magnus Krønike* (1509, 1534), beide bei Gotfred af Ghemen, stellt der *Persenober* jedenfalls einen der explizit höfischen Erzähltexte aus dem Mittelalter dar, die in der dänischen Frühdruckzeit des 16. Jahrhunderts auftreten und den Übergang von der Handschrift zum Druck erlebt haben. Auch wenn, wie erwähnt, die Details der Abhängigkeitsverhältnisse zwischen der den *Persenober*-Roman enthaltenden Handschrift (Cod. Holm. K 47) und den frühen *Persenober*-Drucken nicht ganz geklärt sind, so stellt das Manuskript in jedem Fall ein wichtiges Bindeglied zwischen der Handschriftenkultur und dem beginnenden Buchdruck in Dänemark dar. Ganz offensichtlich versprachen sich Drucker wie Gotfred af Ghemen und Laurentz Benedicht von den ursprünglich aus dem französischen Mittelalter stammenden Versromanen *Flores oc Blantzeflor* und *Persenober* einen entsprechenden Absatz bei ihrer Käuferschaft – neben anderen, ebenfalls mehrfach aufgelegten Frühromanen und Erzähltexten wie *Sigismunda*, *Griseldis* (beide Erstdruck 1528), *Marcolfus* (1540), *Uglspil* (Eulenspiegel, vor 1571), *Fortunatus* (1575), *Magelona* (1583) und anderen.[28]

---

26 Glauser, *Skandinavische Literaturge*schichte (Anm. 8), S. 56. [Vgl. für die Entwicklung von der Handschrift zum Druck in den anderen Sprachgebieten die Beiträge von Bertelsmeier-Kierst (Seite 36), Besamusca und Willaert (Seite 68) und Sánchez-Martí (Seite 144) in diesem Band.]

27 Die beiden *Flores*-Drucke aus dem Jahre 1504 sind nur fragmentarisch erhalten (beide enthalten denselben Textausschnitt, nämlich sechs Blätter, Bl. 3, 4 und 5, sowie jeweils Teile von Bl. 1, 6 und 7, beide mit demselben Holzschnitt auf Bl. 1ʳ) und befinden sich im Besitz der Uppsala Universitetsbibliotek (Sign. Danica vet. 26, 8° und Danica vet. 26a, 8°). Der erste vollständige Druck *Flores oc Blantzeflor* 1509 gehört zur Sammlung der Königlichen Bibliothek Kopenhagen, Sign. LN 67, 8ᵗᵒ (digitalisiert auf *Early European Books*).

28 Vgl. Glauser, *Skandinavische Literaturgeschichte* (Anm. 8), S. 59–60.

4 Transformationen: *Rewriting* als Modell für die Adaption und Bearbeitung von Erzähltexten in der dänischen Frühdruckzeit

Preist der Druck von 1572 gleich im Titel seinen potentiellen Leserinnen und Lesern die Erzählung als „lystig oc skøn Historie"[29] an, welche „nu nylige offuerseet oc Corrigerit"[30] sein soll, so rekurriert er hier auf eine für diese Textsorte gebräuchliche und auch im deutschen Sprachraum verbreitete Rhetorik und Textproduktionspraxis.[31] Die dänische *Persenober*-Erzählung ist ein gutes Beispiel dafür, wie ein Erzähltext im Prozess eines produktiven und kreativen *rewriting* mehrfach bearbeitet, adaptiert und nachgedruckt wurde, wobei der (meist anonyme) Übersetzer durchaus in den Text eingreifen, Kürzungen vornehmen und auch ganze Passagen abändern und ‚korrigieren' konnte – insbesondere vor dem Hintergrund, dass es sich um einen volkssprachlichen Erzähltext handelt.[32] Im Folgenden soll *rewriting* oder *Retextualisierung*, wie Joachim Bumke für die zahlreichen Bearbeitungs-, Übersetzungs- und Adaptionsprozesse mittelalterlicher Texte vorgeschlagen hat,[33] auch als eine Form von (durchaus positiver) ‚Manipulation' verstanden werden, wie es der belgische Übersetzungstheoretiker André Lefevere formuliert hat:

> Translation is, of course, a rewriting of an original text. All rewritings, whatever their intention, reflect a certain ideology and a poetics and as such manipulate literature to function in a given society in a given way. Rewriting is manipulation, undertaken in the service of power, and in its positive aspect can help in the evolution of a literature and a society. Rewritings can introduce new concepts, new genres, new devices and the history of translation is the history also of literary innovation, of the shaping power of one culture upon another.[34]

---

29 „unterhaltsame und schöne Historie" (*Persenober* 1572, Bl. A1ʳ).
30 „jetzt unlängst durchgesehen und korrigiert" (*Persenober* 1572, Bl. A1ʳ).
31 Vgl. Richter, *Transmissionsgeschichten* (Anm. 16), S. 17 und ausführlich in: Lauritz Nielsen, *Dansk bibliografi: med saerligt hensyn til dansk bogtrykkerkunsts historie*. 3 Bde. København 1919–1935.
32 Für die mittelalterliche Übersetzungspraxis vgl. etwa Rikhardsdottir (vgl. Anm. 3), S. 5 und zu volkssprachlicher Literatur ebda., S. 116: „The notion of textual fidelity was in fact foreign to a mindset that viewed vernacular texts and stories not as singular and fixed entities, but rather as collective material to draw on in the creative process."
33 Vgl. Joachim Bumke und Ursula Peters (Hgg.), *Retextualisierung in der mittelalterlichen Literatur*. Sonderheft *Zeitschrift für Deutsche Philologie* 124 (2005), hier insb. S. 1–5.
34 André Lefevere, *Translation, Rewriting and the Manipulation of Literary Fame*, London, New York 1992, S. vii.

Der dänische *Persenober*-Druck von 1572 mit seinen unterschiedlichen ‚Vorgänger-Texten' – nämlich dem mittelalterlichen französischen *Partonopeu*-Roman, der altnorwegischen *Partalopa saga*, dem Ms. Cod. Holm. K 47, dem Erstdruck von 1560 – stellt mithin ebenfalls ein *rewriting* dar. Erzählungen wie *Persenober oc Constantianobis* dokumentieren die komplexe Transmission und damit auch Transformation höfischer Texte mit einer langen kontinental-europäischen Tradition, sie machen die *mouvance* des Textes, seine Unfestigkeit und seinen Reichtum an *variance* im Laufe seiner Manuskript- und Drucktransmission deutlich.[35] In den unterschiedlichen Bearbeitungs- und Übersetzungsstufen zeigt sich nämlich eine Produktivität und Kreativität, die die Rezeption und auch die Kontinuität höfischer Literatur in Skandinavien veranschaulicht.

Im Folgenden sollen drei Beispiele für solche produktiven Äußerungsformen von *rewriting* am dänischen *Persenober*-Druck von 1572 gezeigt werden: erstens Auslassungen resp. Ellipsen, die eine Akzentverschiebung in der Erzählung evozieren, zweitens eine Nachschrift an den Leser sowie drittens eine Textstelle, deren Bearbeitung durch den dänischen Übersetzer eine moralisierende Steuerung der zeitgenössischen Rezeption und eine Besonderheit in der dänischen Tradierung darstellt. An diesen Beispielen soll verdeutlicht werden, auf welche Weise der Text im Umfeld der Frühdruckzeit in Dänemark für sein Publikum adaptiert wurde. Ich werde mich also primär auf diese Druckversion beziehen und je nachdem auch die Manuskriptfassung Codex Holm. K 47, die *Partalopa saga* und die französische Fassung vergleichsweise heranziehen.[36] Der komplexen gesamtskandinavischen *Partonopeu*-Transmission vermag dieser kurze Beitrag freilich nicht Rechnung zu tragen, doch soll immerhin ein erster Einblick in das dänische Material gewonnen werden.

---

35 Mit *mouvance* wird auf die Begriffsbildung bei Paul Zumthor in seinem *Essai de poétique médiévale* von 1972 rekurriert, vgl. Paul Zumthor, *Toward a Medieval Poetics*. Übers. v. Philip Bennett. Minneapolis 1992, vgl. insb. S. 40–76; *variance* nach Bernard Cerquiglini, *Éloge de la variante: historie critique de la philologie*. Paris 1989 und *Unfestigkeit* geprägt durch Joachim Bumke, zuerst in *Die vier Fassungen der 'Nibelungenklage'. Untersuchungen zur Überlieferungsgeschichte und Textkritik der höfischen Epik im 13. Jahrhundert*. Berlin, New York 1996, vgl. insb. S. 53–60.

36 Auch wenn die französische Fassung zur Y-Textgruppe gehören, ist es in der Forschung unumstritten, dass die altnorwegische Saga auf einer französischen Vorlage beruht. Vgl. *Partalopa saga* (vgl. Anm. 20), S. XIII.

5 *Rewriting* I: Abweichungen, Ellipsen

Allein über die zahlreichen Unterschiede zwischen den skandinavischen Textversionen (d.h. der *Partalopa saga* und den dänischen Textzeugnissen der frühen Neuzeit) und dem französischen *Partonopeu* ließe sich vor dem Hintergrund der Translation französischer *romances* nach Skandinavien im Mittelalter sehr viel sagen.[37] So sind etwa viele der ausführlichen Turnier- und Kampfschilderungen des französischen Textes in der Saga wie auch im Manuskript Cod. Holm. K 47 und im Benedicht-Druck 1572 ausgelassen worden, ebenso retardierende Erzählmomente, außerdem die Differenz zwischen Heidentum und Christentum, die langen Dialoge und die psychologisierende Darstellung der Figuren, insbesondere in der Liebesgeschichte zwischen Partonopeu (resp. Partalopi/ Persenober) und Melior (resp. Marmoria/ Constantianobis).[38]

In diesem überblicksartigen Beitrag, der nur einige exemplarische Textbeispiele auswählen und daran die Charakteristika der dänischen Transmissionsgeschichte dieses Romans zeigen kann, sollen solche *rewriting*-Prozesse, auch und gerade mit ihren Auslassungen oder Abweichungen als Repräsentationen textueller Dynamik, Unfestigkeit und *mouvance* verstanden werden.

Zunächst einmal fällt auf, dass etwa der gesamte Prolog und die beim Trojanischen Krieg beginnende Genealogie (*Pré-histoire*) des französischen Textes schon in der *Partalopa saga* und auch im dänischen *Persenober* 1572 ausgelassen sind. Dadurch entfällt die Rhetorik des Erzählers, wie er im französischen *Partonopeu* agiert, in diesem einleitenden Teil[39]; geblieben ist im dänischen Druck an dieser Stelle die nur sehr kurze einleitende Formel des anonymen Ich-Erzählers: „It Euentyr vil ieg sige fra/ I huo som der vil lyde paa/ Aff en mectig Konnig rig/ Mand finder icke nu mange slig." (Bl. A2ʳ).[40] Am Anfang der Erzählung in Laurentz Benedichts Druck steht (aufgrund der Zugehörigkeit zur Y-Textgruppe) denn auch nicht die Jagd in den Wäldern der Ardennen, sondern die Schilderung von Prinzessin Constantianobis' Kindheit und Jugend, von ihrer außerordentlichen Klugheit und Schönheit (Bl. A2ʳ), dann folgt der Tod von ihres Vaters (Bl.

---

37 Vgl. Rikhardsdottirs (vgl. Anm. 3) ausführliche Analyse auf S. 113–163. Sie vergleicht beispielsweise den altnorwegischen Sagatext mit den beiden mittelenglischen Versionen sowie mit der französischen Textfassung (ebda., S. 152–163).

38 Vgl. zu diesen Auslassungen (für die Sagafassung) Lise Præstgaard Andersens Kommentar in *Partalopa saga* (vgl. Anm. 20), S. XXIII–XXV.

39 Vgl. *Le Roman* (vgl. Anm. 21), S. 70–94 (VV. 1–498).

40 „Ein Abenteuer will ich erzählen, allen, die zuhören mögen, von einem mächtigen und reichen König; seinesgleichen findet man heutzutage nicht mehr viele." (Diese und folgende Zitate beziehen sich auf die erwähnte Ausgabe von Laurentz Benedicht, Kopenhagen 1572.)

A2^v–A3^r) und die Aufforderung des königlichen Rates an Constantianobis, einen Ehegatten zu wählen (Bl. A3^r). Constantianobis lässt hierauf zwölf Ritter zu sich rufen und sendet sie aus, um einen geeigneten Kandidaten zu suchen (Bl. A3^r–A3^v). Der zwölfte Ritter überreicht der Prinzessin bei seiner Rückkehr einen Brief mit der Beschreibung eines jungen Mannes, der ihr schließlich am meisten zusagt – es ist Persenober, der Neffe des französischen Königs (vgl. Bl. A4^r). Constantianobis gelangt mittels ihrer zauberischen Kräfte nach Frankreich und überzeugt sich selbst – unsichtbar für die anderen – am Hofe des französischen Königs von der Wahrheit der Beschreibung des Prinzen, er gefällt ihr und sie würde ihn wohl gern als Ehemann auswählen. In dieser ganzen ersten Passage stimmt die Druckfassung mit der Version in der Handschrift Cod. Holm. K 47 fast wortwörtlich überein.[41]

In der *Partalopa saga* ist der Anfang ganz ähnlich, doch wird der Akzent anders gesetzt: Hier dominiert das Motiv der *meykongr* (*maiden-king*) aus der isländischen Erzähltradition – Prinzessin Marmoria, der ihre Berater ebenfalls zur Heirat raten, damit das Reich einen Souverän bekommt, will ihre Autorität und Unabhängigkeit als Herrscherin nicht aufgeben, heiraten würde sie nur einen in Ritterlichkeit und Klugheit ihr würdigen Mann, den sie aber nicht unter den Prinzen ihres Landes finden kann.[42] Als sie mittels Zauberei nach Frankreich gelangt, weil sie von den Tugenden des französischen Königssohns gehört hat, und diesen, nämlich Partalopi, dann auch selbst zu sehen bekommt, gefällt er ihr durchaus. Jedoch will sie ihre Unabhängigkeit als Herrscherin nicht aufgeben und beschließt daher, Partalopi zwar für sich zu gewinnen, aber:

> ok kom henni þat jhvg at hon matti slikann mann eignazt þo at eigi vissi hennar radgiafar treystir hon ok svo vel sinvm klerkdomi at | hon matti hann lata fara hvert er hon villdi en þvi gerdi hon þetta at hon villdi ǫngvann mann lata vera sier rikara ef hon mætti rada ok sa hon þat sem var at sa mvndi keisari verda yfir allri Grecia er hennar feingi ok sa mvndi rikari verda en hon ok þotti henni þat mikil minkan at heita sidan keis<ar>ina þar er advr het hon meykongvr yfir P(artalopa) ok morgvm ǫdrvm hǫfdingivm. Sidan for hon aptvr til Mikla gardz ok gerdi sier þat ihvg at hon skylldi leyniliga med þessu mali fara ok fa hann þo allt at einv [...] ok let svo fyrir vinvm sinvm at hon villdi ǫngvm manni giptazt þeim er þar vissi hon deili.[43]

(Es kam ihr in den Sinn, einen solchen Mann zu bekommen, auch wenn ihre Berater nichts [davon] wussten. Und sie vertraute so sehr auf ihre Klugheit [gemeint sind ihre

---

41 Vgl. https://tekstnet.dk/persenober-og-konstantianobis/2.
42 Vgl. *Partalopa saga* (vgl. Anm. 20), S. 8–9 und S. 2–3 (Text) bzw. S. 130–131 (engl. Übersetzung); dazu auch Kalinke, 'Scribe, Redactor, Author' (Anm. 20), S. 187–189.
43 Vgl. *Partalopa saga* (vgl. Anm. 20), S. 7–9.

zauberischen Künste], dass sie ihn überallhin gehen lassen konnte, wohin sie nur wollte. Und dies tat sie, weil sie keinen Mann mächtiger als sie selbst sein lassen wollte, wenn es nach ihr ging. Und für sie war es so, dass derjenige, welcher sie heiratete, Kaiser über ganz Griechenland werden würde und dieser wäre dann mächtiger als sie. Dies schien für sie eine große Herabsetzung ihrer Stellung zu bedeuten, dass sie dann Kaiserin heißen würde und nicht wie zuvor *meykongr* über Partalopi und alle anderen Fürsten. Daraufhin reiste sie zurück nach Konstantinopel und beschloss, dass sie dies heimlich regeln und ihn [Partalopi] gleichwohl bekommen würde. Sie [...] gab vor ihren Freunden vor, niemanden der Männer zu heiraten, die ihr bekannt waren.)[44]

Sif Rikhardsdottir verweist an dieser Stelle auf die Bedeutung des *maiden-king*-Motivs in der isländischen Literatur und auf den markanten Unterschied zwischen dem Sagatext und den französischen und englischen Fassungen, wo die Hochzeit zwischen Melior und Partonopeu nur aufgrund der Jugend des Protagonisten aufgeschoben wird.[45] In der folgenden Episode wird daraufhin erzählt, wie Partalopi sich während eines Jagdausflugs verirrt und schließlich (implizit durch Marmorias Zauberkräfte) nach Konstantinopel und in ihr Schloss gelangt. Auch in den dänischen Textfassungen (Manuskript Cod. Holm. K 47 und Druck von 1572) folgen der Jagdausflug und die Reise Persenobers zum Feenschloss, welche als von Constantianobis' magischen Kräften gelenkt erscheinen.[46] Das Motiv der unabhängigen *maiden-king*-Herrscherin ist in den frühneuzeitlichen dänischen Versionen aber nicht mehr präsent und scheint somit ein Spezifikum der spätmittelalterlichen *Partalopa saga* in ihrem kulturell-literaturhistorischen Kontext zu sein.

---

44 Dt. Übersetzung von mir, AKR. Englische Übersetzung in der Ausgabe der *Partalopa saga*, vgl. *Partalopa saga* (vgl. Anm. 20), S. 133–134: „It entered her mind that she could get such a man, even though her counselors did not know [about it]. She also trusted so well in her learning that she could cause him to go where ever she wished. She did this, because she wanted to let no man be more powerful than herself, if she might have her way. She perceived that – as it was – that that one would become emperor of all Greece who married her, and that one would be more powerful than she. That seemed to her great abasement to be called afterwards empress where before she was called maiden-king over Partalopi and many other chieftains. After that she went back to Constantinople and took it into her head that she should secretly deal with this matter and get him nevertheless. She [...] pretended thus to her friends that she did not wish to marry any man of those she knew."

45 Vgl. Rikhardsdottir (vgl. Anm. 3), S. 121–123.

46 Im französischen Text geht die erste, sehr ausführlich geschilderte erotische Begegnung zwischen den beiden Protagonisten der Aussicht auf die Eheschließung voraus. Vgl. *Le Roman* (vgl. Anm. 21), VV. 1401–1564 und Eley (vgl. Anm. 3), S. 219, zur Jugend des Helden vgl. hier insb. S. 19–32.

6 *Rewriting* II: Zusätze im dänischen Druck von 1572

Wie dynamisch der Text in seinem Transmissionsprozess bleibt, zeigen zwei besondere Erweiterungen, die der Druck bei Laurentz Benedicht 1572 gegenüber der Handschrift Cod. Holm. K 47 besitzt, auf die bereits Brandt in seiner Ausgabe im 19. Jahrhundert kurz hingewiesen hat[47] und die im Folgenden präsentiert werden sollen.

6.1 Ein erweiterter Schluss

Zunächst einmal hängt der Druck aus Laurentz Benedichts Offizin 1572 einen erweiterten Schluss an das in der Handschrift erzählte eigentliche Ende der Historie an, welche dort mit der Hochzeit von Persenober und Constantianobis, deren Tod und der Datierung des Textes schließt. So heißt es im Manuskript Cod. Holm. K 47:

> giorde thieris brøllop i same stad/ the adhe och drwke och waræ glad/ sidhen bleff then edlæ mand/ konningh och herræ ower thet land/ the ende thieris liiff och finge roo/ och mon medh gud i hemerigh boo/ [196r] thenne bogh worte dikt i rym/ aar effter gusz fødsels tim/ thet wil jech seye obenbaræ/ twsind oc iiii hwndret aar/ firæ sindis tywe paa thet fierde amen   (*Persenober*, VV. 1580–1590, Bl. 195ᵛ–196ʳ)[48]

> (Sie hielten ihre Hochzeit in derselben Stadt, aßen und tranken und waren fröhlich. Danach wurde der edle Mann [Persenober] König und Herr über das Land. Sie beschlossen ihr Leben und fanden ihren Frieden; mögen sie nun mit Gott im himmlischen Reiche wohnen. Dieses Buch wurde in Verse gesetzt im Jahre – das will ich offenbaren – eintausendvierhundertvierundachtzig Jahre nach der Geburt des Herrn, Amen.)

Hier fügt der Druck nach der Krönung Persenobers noch zehn neue Zeilen ein (vgl. Bl. D7ʳ–D7ᵛ) und berichtet in diesem eingeschobenen Passus von der Aufteilung des Reiches unter den drei Söhnen des Herrscherpaares (welche in der Handschrift gar nicht vorkommen), des Weiteren von der Bekehrung des

---

47 Carl Joakim Brandt, *Romantisk Digtning fra Middelalderen*. Bd. II. København 1870, S. 378–382; und Brandt, *Romantisk Digtning* III (Anm. 25), S. 334–335.
48 Lemmatisierter Text zitiert nach der Online-Edition: https://tekstnet.dk/persenober-og-konstantianobis/10

heidnischen Königs, um dann ebenfalls in einem formelhaften Gebet des anonymen Ich-Erzählers, in das Zuhörer und Leser eingeschlossen sind, zu enden:

> Nu befaler ieg alle mand/ Gud Fader Søn og Hellig Aand/ Gud vnde oss alle den euige ro/
> At wi maa bliffue vdi en stadig tro/ Paa vor siste ende/ Naar wi skulle fare vdaff dette
> elende/ Nu er denne Bog til ende/ Gud oss sin Naade sende. Amen./ Ende paa denne His-
> torie.   (*Persenober* 1572, Bl. D7^r–D7^v)

> (Nun empfehle ich jedermann Gottvater, Sohn und dem Heiligem Geist. Möge Gott uns
> allen die ewige Ruhe schenken, auf dass wir in einem festen Glauben verbleiben an unse-
> rem Lebensende, wenn wir dieses irdische Elend verlassen. Nun ist dieses Buch zu Ende.
> Gott möge uns seine Gnade schenken, Amen. Ende dieser Historie.)

Das Motiv von der Aufteilung des Königreiches unter die Kinder findet sich übri-
gens auch am Ende des in derselben Handschrift Cod. Holm. K 47 enthaltenden
Versromans von *Flores oc Blantzeflor*. Dort gibt es eine interessante Varianz: In
der Manuskriptversion wird von der Aufteilung der Herrschaft unter die zwei
Söhne und der einzigen Tochter des Paares erzählt, mit welcher implizit Berthe,
die Mutter Karls des Großen aus der französischen *Charlemagne*-Texttradition ge-
meint ist, Flores und Blantzeflor somit als Groß- und Stammeltern Karls des Großen figurieren. In der altnorwegischen *Flóres saga ok Blankiflúr* (entstanden im
13. Jahrhundert, Textzeugnisse jedoch erst aus dem 14. Jahrhundert erhalten)
sowie im altschwedischen *Flores* (1312) und interessanterweise dann (erst wieder)
in der Drucküberlieferung der dänischen Historie von *Flores oc Blantzeflor* ab
1509 sind es dagegen drei Söhne, keine Tochter.[49] Es ist bemerkenswert, dass
das (genealogische) Erzählen von der Kontinuität der Herrschaft bei *Flores oc
Blantzeflor* in der Manuskriptversion stärker betont wird, im *Persenober* dagegen
(nur) in der späteren Druckfassung.

6.2 Die Nachschrift „Til Læseren"

Im Anschluss an dieses „Ende der Historie" folgt als zweite Neuerung des Drucks
gegenüber dem Manuskript noch die Nachschrift „Til Læseren" (Bl. D7^v–D8^r)
und eine Vignette des Druckers. Diese Nachschrift ist ein neues paratextuelles
Element, das erst mit den Druckfassungen in die Transmission der dänischen

---

49 Vgl. hierzu Anna Katharina Richter, 'La transmission de Floire et Blancheflor au Danemark
(XVe–XVIIe siecles)', mit weiterführenden Literaturangaben, in: *L'Expérience des frontières et
les littératures de l'Europe médiévale*. Hg. v. Sofia Lodén und Vanessa Obry. Paris 2019 (Colloques, Congrès et Confèrences – Le Moyen Âge, 26, 1 vol.) (in Vorbereitung).

Historie hinzugekommen ist.[50] Hier lassen sich vier Aspekte ausmachen, die buch- und überlieferungshistorisch interessant sind: erstens die Datierung der Erzählung, die fast wortgetreu aus der Vorlage übernommen wird: „Denne Historie vaar sat paa rim/ Aar efter Guds fødzels time/ Det vi lieg sige obenbar/ Tusind firehundrit aar/ Firesindstiue paa det fierde/ Det skal vide baade lege oc lærde." (Bl. D7ᵛ).[51] Damit wird indirekt auf die Handschrift Cod. Holm. K 47 (oder ggf. eine andere, evtl. nicht erhaltene zeitnahe Handschrift) verwiesen und wird nicht nur – wie schon oben vermerkt – im Textkorpus selbst, sondern auch in der Nachschrift das Jahr 1484 als Genese der dänischen Textfassung angegeben. Zweitens nennt die Nachschrift auch einen namentlichen Übersetzer, einen gewissen Hendrick Christensen aus dem norwegischen Bergen, der den Text aus dem Deutschen ins Dänische übersetzt haben soll: „Den som Bogen aff tyske oc til danske vende/ Er født i Bergen iblant de haarde Steen/ [...] Hendrick Christensen er hans naffn" (Bl. D7ᵛ–D8ʳ)[52] und es wird drittens auf die Existenz der früheren Ausgabe von 1560 verwiesen. Viertens wird schließlich auf den konkreten Bearbeitungsprozess der vorliegenden Ausgabe aufmerksam gemacht und zugleich auch die für die frühen Romane sehr übliche, rezeptionslenkende wie auch ökonomisch relevante (indem der Text einer bestimmten Textsorte zugordnet, das Leserinteresse und damit auch die Kauf-

---

50 Der spätere Druck von 1700 übernimmt die Nachschrift aus dem Druck von 1572, stellt sie der Erzählung aber nunmehr als Vorwort voran. Ob es bereits im (verlorenen) Druck von 1560 auch eine solche Nachschrift gab, lässt sich nicht rekonstruieren; der Druck vom Ende des 16. Jahrhunderts ist unvollständig (s.o., Anm. 7), Drucke des 17. Jahrhunderts sind ebenfalls nicht erhalten. Vgl. dazu auch Brandt, *Romantisk Digtning* II (Anm. 25), S. 381–382 und *DF* VI, S. 408–416.
51 „Dieses Buch wurde in Verse gesetzt im Jahre – das will ich kundtun – tausendvierhundertvierundachtzig nach der Geburt des Herrn. Dies sollen sowohl Laien als auch gelehrte Leute wissen."
52 „Der das Buch aus dem Deutschen ins Dänische übersetzt hat, ist geboren in Bergen zwischen den harten Steinen [wohl eine Anspielung auf die felsige Küstenlandschaft vor Bergen?], Hendrick Christensen ist sein Name." – Bereits Brandt zweifelte jedoch an der Identität des Übersetzers Hendrick Christensen, die Herausgeber von *Danske folkebøger* ziehen einen „bogfører" (Buchführer) Henrik aus Bergen († 1560) als möglichen Übersetzer und Bearbeiter in Erwägung, vgl. dazu *DF* VI, S. LXIII. Dass nun ein (hoch- oder nieder-)deutscher *Partonopeu* als Übersetzungsvorlage für den dänischen Druck angegeben wird, macht die Frage nach den Vorlagen angesichts der unterschiedlichen beiden Haupt-Textgruppen nicht einfacher. Da die dänische Fassung mit der norwegisch-isländischen große Gemeinsamkeiten aufweist und es sich hier zudem um eine Nachschrift handelt, erscheint dieser Verweis wenig überzeugend. Er bedarf jedenfalls zusätzlicher Klärung, die noch aussteht und an dieser Stelle leider nicht beantwortet werden kann.

lust geweckt wird) Zuschreibung von „nutz und kurtzweyl" ausgesprochen –
gewissermaßen ein ‚Label', das einen hohen Wiedererkennungseffekt für das
zeitgenössische Lesepublikum besaß[53]:

> Der mand screff M.D. hundrit Aar/ Effter Christi Fødzel alt obenbar/ Oc der til lige Try-
> sinds tiue/ Ieg vil de ticke liuffe/ Da bleff Bogen først tryct paa ny/ Vdi den Kongelige
> Stad Kiøbenhaffn/ mangen til lærdom/ nytte oc gaffn/ Nu nylig offuerseet oc forbedrit/
> Oc mange steder Corrigerit.   (*Persenober* 1572, Bl. D7^v–D8^r)
>
> (Da man schrieb 1500 Jahre nach Christi Geburt und dazu noch sechzig Jahre, ich will
> nicht lügen, da wurde das Buch erstmals gedruckt in der königlichen Stadt Kopenhagen.
> Vielen zur Belehrung, zum Nutzen und zur Unterhaltung. Nun unlängst durchgesehen
> und verbessert und vielerorts korrigiert.)

Mit dem formelhaften „mangen til lærdom/ nytte oc gaffn" korrespondiert
auch der eingangs präsentierte Titel der Erzählung, „[e]n lystig oc skøn Historie [. . .] Lystig at høre oc læse" (Bl. A1^r), welcher in dieser oder ähnlicher Formulierung für die frühneuzeitlichen dänischen und schwedischen Historien
sehr häufig auftritt und von den gängigen deutschen Historienbuch-Titeln wie
etwa „Eine schöne und vergnügliche Historie" oder ähnlichen Formulierun-
gen übernommen ist.[54]

7 *Rewriting* III: Besonderheiten der frühneuzeitlichen dänischen Tradierung in Handschrift und Druck am Beispiel der nächtlichen Begegnung zwischen Persenober und Constantianobis

Abschließend sei darauf hingewiesen, dass die dänische Überlieferung im Ver-
gleich zur *Partalopa saga* einige korrigierte Passagen enthält. Eine davon findet

---

53 Zum Aspekt von Didaxe und Unterhaltung oder „nutz und kurtzweyl" der Prosahistorien
vgl. die für den deutschen Sprachraum einschlägige Literatur, grundlegend Jan-Dirk Müller,
'Volksbuch/Prosaroman im 15./16. Jahrhundert. Perspektiven der Forschung'. In: *Internationales Archiv für Sozialgeschichte der Literatur* 1 (1985), Sonderheft (Forschungsreferate), S. 1–128,
hier S. 84.
54 Vgl. Richter, 'La transmission' (Anm. 49).

sich sowohl im Manuskript Codex Holm. K 47 als auch im Benedicht-Druck und stellt m.E. ein interessantes Beispiel für einen textuellen Eingriff im Sinne der Lefevere'schen *manipulation* dar. Möglicherweise ist sie sogar ein einzigartiges, spezifisches Charakteristikum der dänischen Transmission des *Partonopeu-*Romans. Es geht um die erste Begegnung zwischen Persenober und Constantia-nobis, welche nachts im Schloss der Prinzessin stattfindet, wo der Held von un-sichtbaren Dienern bedient und wie von Feenhand köstliche Speisen serviert und schließlich zu einem mit zahllosen Edelsteinen geschmückten königlichen Bett geleitet wird, wo er sich schlafen legt. Schon bald bemerkt er jedoch, dass er dort nicht allein ist. Im französischen Roman wird an dieser Stelle der darauf-folgende „dialogue avec l'inconnue" ausführlich beschrieben, ebenso die an-schließende erotische Begegnung zwischen Partonopeu und „la dame", erst danach gibt nämlich Melior ihre Identität preis und es folgt das Tabu-/ Sichtversprechen.[55]

In der *Partalopa saga* entspinnt sich hier nur ein relativ kurzes, aber inte-ressantes Gespräch zwischen Partalopi und der ihm noch unbekannten Frau; es heißt dann abschließend:

> Nv skempta þav sier þa nott eptir þvi sem þeim likadi ok sofnvdv sidan jfógrv fadmlage ok godv[56]

> (Nun vergnügten sie sich in dieser Nacht ganz so, wie es ihnen gefiel und danach schlie-fen sie in einer schönen und guten Umarmung ein.)[57]

Der Sagatext nimmt hierin zwar sehr kurz, aber doch deutlich (der Rest mag der Phantasie des Lesers/Zuhörers überlassen worden sein) den Topos der Liebes-nacht auf – wobei es in dem dieser Textstelle unmittelbar vorausgehenden Pas-sus bezüglich der Macht- und Autonomieverhältnisse zwischen den beiden Protagonisten markante Unterschiede zur Darstellung im französischen *Parto-nopeu*-Roman gibt, wie Rikhardsdottir bemerkt.[58] Doch nochmals ganz anders ist der Wortlaut in der spätmittelalterlich-frühneuzeitlichen dänischen Tradie-rung und zwar in fast wörtlicher Übereinstimmung zwischen der Handschrift Cod. Holm. K 47 und dem Druck von 1572. Die delikate Textstelle ist hier

---

55 Vgl. *Le Roman* (vgl. Anm. 21), VV. 1105–1570.
56 *Partalopa saga* (vgl. Anm. 20), S. 33, Kap. 4, Z. 133–135 (nach der Handschrift AM 533 4to).
57 Engl. Übersetzung von Foster W. Blaisdell nach der Handschrift AM 533 4to: „Now they en-tertained each other that night according to that which pleased them and fell asleep afterward in a lovely and good embrace." (*Partalopa saga* (vgl. Anm. 20), S. 148).
58 Vgl. Rikhardsdottir (vgl. Anm. 3), S. 125–126.

wesentlich gekürzt und die eigentliche Liebesnacht sogar gänzlich weggelassen, als ob der Text eine Zensur durchlaufen hätte: Persenober ist zunächst allein, dann betritt Constantianobis das Zimmer und setzt sich zu Persenober ans Bett, woraufhin sich dieser zur Wand dreht und Christus um Schutz bittet, droht ihm doch als Eindringling in ihr Schloss das Todesurteil. In der folgenden Rede, die die Prinzessin an Persenober richtet, eröffnet sie ihm jedoch die Aussicht auf die gemeinsame Ehe (nach einer halbjährigen Wartezeit), unter der Bedingung, dass er das Tabugebot einhalten müsse:

> Det siger ieg dig sandelig/ At ieg vil dig til herre haffue/ Oc aldrig andre i min dage/ [. . .]
> Huer nat skalt du ligge hoss mig/ Dog maa de ticke andit være/ End du skalt ligge hoss
> mig met ære/ Oc ingen whøffuiskhed mig at byde/ Om du vilt mit raad lyde/ Det siger ieg
> dig sandelig/ Ieg vil om natten tale met dig/ Huad oss kand baade være til glæde/ [. . .]
> Met megen glæde oc ære/ Oc da skal vort Bryllup være.   (*Persenober* 1572, Bl. A8ʳ–A8ᵛ)[59]

> (Dies sage ich dir wahrlich: dass ich dich und keinen anderen zu meinem Herrn haben
> will [. . .] Jede Nacht sollst du bei mir liegen, doch soll es nicht anders sein als mit Ehre
> und du darfst mir gegenüber kein maßloses Benehmen zeigen. Wenn du meinem Rat
> folgst – das sage ich dir wahrhaftig – dann will ich mich des Nachts mit dir unterhalten,
> was uns beide erfreuen kann. [. . .] Mit Freude und Ehre soll dann unsere Hochzeit
> stattfinden.)

Auffallend ist die deutliche Betonung des anständigen, ‚richtigen‘ Benehmens, der Vokabel „Ehre" und der dagegengesetzte Gebrauch des Ausdrucks „whøffuiskhed" als dessen offensichtliches Gegenteil: Hier weichen der dänische Versroman wie auch die Druckfassung 1572 deutlich von der altnorwegischen Saga ab und zeigen eine einschneidende Bearbeitung, die eine pikante Passage wie diese bewusst auslässt. Nur ex negativo, in der Negierung („whøffuiskhed") beziehungsweise bloß in vorsichtiger, andeutender Rede („dann will ich mich des Nachts mit dir unterhalten, was uns beide erfreuen kann") wird skizziert, was narrativ noch möglich wäre. (Von nächtlichem „unterhalten" war im Sagatext allerdings nicht die Rede.)

---

59 Vgl. die entsprechende Formulierung in der Handschrift Cod. Holm. K 47 (Bl. 174ᵛ, VV. 336–371): „tha swared hanum then jomfrv righ/ thet seyer jech eder sannelig/ ath jech wil thik til herræ hawæ/ och aldrigh andræ i mynæ dawæ/ [. . .] hwær nat skalt thu legge hooss mægh/ dog maa thet jckj anned wæræ/ æn thu skalt leggæ hooss mæg medh æræ/ och jngen vhøwske mæg ath bydhæ/ om thu wilt myt rad lydhæ/ thet seyer jech thik sannelig/ jech wil om natten snakæ medh thik/ [. . .] medh mygel glede och æræ/ och tha skal wort brøllop w0eræ." (auf eine Übersetzung wird hier wegen der fast wortgetreuen Übernahme der Passage im oben angeführten Benedicht-Druck verzichtet.)

Das Substantiv „whøffuiskhed" ist erstmals für das Jahr 1444 im Dänischen belegt und zwar im Kontext geistlicher Ermahnungen.[60] In Jon Tursens dänisch-lateinischem Wörterbuch aus dem Jahre 1561 steht es als Übersetzung für die lateinischen Begriffe *immodestia, intemperantia* sowie als „whøffuiskhed i seder og facter" (maßloses Benehmen in Sitten und Verhalten) sogar für die noch gröbere *incivilitas*[61] und gibt damit deutlich eine moralische Wertung menschlichen Benehmens. Hier wird nicht nur ein textueller Eingriff, eine Kürzung und Zensur vorgenommen – die Schilderung der Liebesnacht wird ja komplett ausgelassen –, sondern auch eine semantische Verschiebung und ein im Lefevere'schen Sinne „manipulierendes" *rewriting*, das die *Persenober*-Version in der Handschrift K 47 und den Druck von 1572 im Gegensatz zur Saga deutlich in Richtung moralisierenden Erzählens transportiert. Von dieser Textstelle auf eine erstmals für die Handschrift Cod. Holm. K 47 realisierte, in die Drucktradition übernommene Adaption des Textes im adlig-klösterlichen Milieu und auch auf eine weibliche Kopistin resp. Bearbeiterin der Handschrift insgesamt zu schließen, wie bereits die Herausgeber von *Danske folkebøger* vermuteten,[62] ist unter diesem Gesichtspunkt möglich,[63] aber es ist auch nicht auszuschließen, dass *Persenober* auch von einem männlichen Kleriker niedergeschrieben worden sein könnte.

Die Retextualisierung bzw. das *rewriting* an dieser nicht unrelevanten Textstelle gibt der dänischen *Persenober*-Tradierung (der spätmittelalterlichen

---

60 Vgl. das digitalisierte Wörterbuch des Altdänischen, *Gammeldansk ordbog* (https://gammel danskordbog.dk/), das dieses Wort verzeichnet, etwa in spätmittelalterlichen dänischen Klosterregeln sowie in geistlichen Schriften des bedeutenden dänischen Humanisten, Schriftstellers, Reformators und Bibelübersetzers Christiern Pedersen (vor 1480–1554) aus dem Jahre 1515: https://gammeldanskordbog.dk/ordbog?aselect=uh%C3%B8viskhet&query=uh%C3%B8ffuisk het (Zugriff am 3.6.2019).

61 Vgl. die von der DSL digitalisierte Edition dänischer Wörterbücher des 16. und frühen 17. Jahrhunderts: http://renaessancesprog.dk/renaissance/ordboger/Tursen1561/142?query_id= 33476 (Zugriff am 9.6.17).

62 Dies auch unter Berücksichtigung der erwähnten Schlussformel des *Flores* in derselben Handschrift, vgl. *DF* VI, S. LXII: „Skriveren (Bearbejderen?) er ifølge Slutordene i Floresrimet en Kvinde, vel sagtens en Adelsdame eller Klosterjomfru, og hermed stemmer godt den for den danske Bearbejdelse ejendommelige Fremhæven af Persenobers Afholdenhed overfor Konstantianobis, der sikkert er udsprunget af Anstændighetshensyn og snarest kan antages at skyldes en Kvinde." (Der Schreiber (Bearbeiter?) ist den Schlussworten im *Flores*-Roman zufolge eine Frau, genauer gesagt eine Adlige oder ein Klosterfräulein; und dazu passt auch die für die dänische Bearbeitung eigentümliche Betonung der Abstinenz Persenobers gegenüber Konstantianobis, welche mit Sicherheit auf Gründe der Anständigkeit zurückzuführen ist und am ehesten auf eine weibliche Schreiberin schließen lässt.)

63 Vgl. Glauser, 'Höfisch-ritterliche Epik' (Anm. 8), S. 195.

Handschrift wie dem Frühdruck) damit eine individuelle Prägung. Durch die Verwendung eines Begriffes wie „whøffuiskhed" werden Assoziationen zu anderen Textsorten – etwa geistlichen Ermahnungen – geweckt und dem dänischen Publikum ein bestimmter, vertrauter Wertekosmos vermittelt. Hier wird wohl weniger der Aspekt des höfischen Liebesromans in den Mittelpunkt gestellt, sondern eher – neben der „kurtzweyl" (im Dänischen „gaffn" in der Formulierung der Nachschrift im Druck von 1572), die die Liebes- und Abenteuergeschichte ihren Lesern und Zuhörern in jedem Fall bietet – auf jeden Fall *auch* großen Wert auf den (moralischen) Vorbildcharakter der adligen Protagonisten gelegt. Ähnlichkeiten hierzu lassen sich auch im Fall der Transmission von *Flores oc Blantzeflor* finden, auf die schon hingewiesen wurde. Hier endet die Historie sowohl bereits in der altnordischen *Flóres saga ok Blankiflúr*, im altschwedischen *Flores* (1312) wie auch im dänischen *Flores*-Versroman (Manuskript Codex Holm. K 47) und im ersten vollständig erhaltenen *Flores*-Druck von 1509 (ebenfalls bei Gotfred af Ghemen in Kopenhagen) mit dem Rückzug des Protagonistenpaares ins jeweilige (Männer- bzw. Frauen-)Kloster. Andererseits wird aber, im Gegensatz zum *Persenober*, der Liebe, auch der körperlichen Liebe, zwischen Flores und Blantzeflor in derselben Handschrift und im Frühdruck durchaus narrativer Raum gegeben. Auch im *Persenober* selbst scheint die ausgeführte Passage auf eine Form von ‚Zensur' zu deuten, jedoch wird an anderer Stelle wiederum durchaus auch vom nächtlichen Beisammensein von Persenober und Constantianobis erzählt, wenn auch etwas verhalten, aber immerhin, und zwar in der handschriftlichen wie auch in der gedruckten Überlieferung (1572).[64] Die Thematisierung von Liebe, Keuschheit, Sexualität und die (oftmals auch ambivalente) Rolle moralisierenden Erzählens in den Texten der skandinavischen Frühdruckzeit ist komplex und macht nicht zuletzt gerade deshalb die Historien derart interessant.[65]

---

64 Vgl. *Persenober* 1572, Bl. B2^v–B3^r, mit dem eingeschobenen kurzen Erzählerkommentar: „Om natten der de laa tilsammen/ De talit met huer anden oc giorde gammen/ [...] Om natten den Jomffru giorde hannem blide./ Ieg vil det lade nu saa være/ Hand haffde der megen ære/ En nat laa hand hoss hendis side/ [...]." (Nachts lagen sie beieinander, sie sprachen miteinander und hatten ihr Vergnügen [...] Des Nachts erfreute ihn die junge Frau – ich will es dabei belassen – er hatte dabei viel Ehre. Eines Nachts lag er an ihrer Seite [...]." – Und kurz darauf (Bl. B4^r): „Da vaare de baade i hiertet blid/ Hand kyste hendis rosens mund/ Deris kierlighed vaar tusindlund." (Da wurden beide von Herzen froh, er küsste ihren Rosenmund, ihre Liebe war tausendfach). Fast wörtlich übereinstimmend auch im Versroman in der Handschrift Cod. Holm. K 47, vgl. https://tekstnet.dk/persenober-og-konstantianobis/4, VV. 485–503 resp. https://tekstnet.dk/persenober-og-konstantianobis/5, VV. 554–556.
65 Diese Thematik bedürfte einer ausführlicheren Darstellung. Hier kann nur auf Texte wie *Appolonius af Tyrus* oder *Euriolus oc Lucretia* (Dänisch 1591 resp. 1571/1594) verwiesen werden, die Diskursfelder wie Inzest, Liebe und Ehe behandeln. Vgl. Richter, *Transmissionsgeschichten*

Zurück zum „nutz und kurtzweyl" der Texte: Es es ist sicherlich anzunehmen, dass die Leserschaft der frühen gedruckten Romane in Dänemark[66] neben dem Unterhaltungswert, den mittelalterliche Texte wie *Persenober oc Constantianobis* zweifellos boten, in der erzählten fiktionalen Welt also durchaus auch noch Mitte des 16. Jahrhunderts ein Angebot an Identifikationsmodellen gefunden haben – im Sinne eines didaktischen „nutz" („lærdom oc nytte" in der Nachschrift) der Erzählung demonstrieren die fiktionalen Helden exemplarisches Handeln und Verhalten.

Es zeigt sich schließlich auch, dass die Retextualisierung eine Brücke zwischen der spätmittelalterlichen Handschrift und dem Benedict-Druck schlägt und der Übergang zwischen Manuskript- und Druckproduktion für narrative Texte wie *Persenober* in Dänemark keine eigentliche Grenze darstellt, sondern gerade „[die] Gebundenheit der höfischen Epik in Dänemark zwischen den Epochen späteres Mittelalter und frühe Neuzeit" und ihre Bedeutung „als transitorische Literatur"[67] bemerkenswert ist. Erzähltexte blieben zugleich konstant (in ihrer kontinuierlichen Präsenz auf dem Buchmarkt) als auch dynamisch in ihren *rewriting*-Prozessen.

Bibliographie

Brandt, Carl Joakim (Hg.), *Romantisk Digtning fra Middelalderen*. Bd. II. København 1870.
Brandt, Carl Joakim (Hg.), *Romantisk Digtning fra Middelalderen*. Bd. III. København 1877.
Braun, Manuel, 'Historie und Historien'. In: *Die Literatur im Übergang vom Mittelalter zur Neuzeit*. Hg. v. Werner Röcke und Marina Münkler. München 2004 (Hansers

---

(Anm. 16), S. 282–304 und für die narrative Komplexität der Historien zwischen moralisierendem Erzählen und „vergnüglichem" Inhalt exemplarisch für den deutschen Kontext Manuel Braun, 'Historie und Historien'. In: *Die Literatur im Übergang vom Mittelalter zur Neuzeit*. Hg. v. Werner Röcke und Marina Münkler. München 2004 (Hansers Sozialgeschichte der deutschen Literatur vom 16. Jahrhundert bis zur Gegenwart 1), S. 317–361, hier S. 321: „Fast alle Geschichten beanspruchen exemplarische Geltung, indem sie Moral zu vermitteln und Orientierung für die Lebenspraxis zu leisten vorgeben. Die Erzählung löst diesen Anspruch aber häufig nicht ein, ja sie konterkariert ihn immer wieder, weil sich der Stoff gegen die ihm auferlegte Deutung sperrt, weil Erzählmuster Eigensinn entfalten oder weil literarisches Sprechen Überschüsse produziert."

66 Die komplexe Thematik des Rezipientenkreises in der Frühdruckzeit (vermutlich primär Angehörige des Adels und des aufkommenden städtischen Patriziats) kann hier nur angedeutet werden. Vgl. dazu etwa Glauser, 'Höfisch-ritterliche Epik' (Anm. 8), S. 204 und Richter, *Transmissionsgeschichten* (Anm. 16), S. 20–21 mit weiterführender Literatur (vgl. dort S. 21, Anm. 71).

67 Glauser, 'Höfisch-ritterliche Epik' (Anm. 8), S. 207.

Sozialgeschichte der deutschen Literatur vom 16. Jahrhundert bis zur Gegenwart 1), S. 317–361.

Bumke, Joachim, *Die vier Fassungen der 'Nibelungenklage'. Untersuchungen zur Überlieferungsgeschichte und Textkritik der höfischen Epik im 13. Jahrhundert*. Berlin, New York 1996.

Bumke, Joachim und Ursula Peters (Hgg.), *Retextualisierung in der mittelalterlichen Literatur*. Sonderheft *Zeitschrift für Deutsche Philologie* 124 (2005).

Cerquiglini, Bernard, *Éloge de la variante: historie critique de la philologie*. Paris 1989.

Dahlerup, Pil, *Dansk litteratur. Middelalder*. Bd. II: *Verdslig litteratur*. København 1998.

Eley, Penny, *Partonopeus de Blois. Romance in the Making*. Cambridge 2011.

Eufemiavisorna. Bde. I (*Flores och Blanzeflor. Hertig Fredrik av Normandie*) und II (*Ivan Lejonriddaren*). Textredigering, kommentarer och ordförklaringar av Henrik Williams. Inledning av Bo Ralph. Stockholm 2018 (Svenska klassiker utgivna av Svenska Akademien).

Ferm, Olle et al. (Hgg.), *The Eufemiavisor and Courtly Culture, Time, Texts and Cultural Transfer*, Papers from a Symposium in Stockholm 11–13 October 2012. Stockholm, Kungliga Vitterhets Historie och Antikvitets Akademien (KVHAA), 2015 (Konferenser 88).

Glauser, Jürg, 'Höfisch-ritterliche Epik in Dänemark zwischen Spätmittelalter und Frühneuzeit'. In: *Festschrift für Oskar Bandle zum 60. Geburtstag am 11. Januar 1986*. Hg. v. Hans-Peter Naumann unter Mitwirkung von Magnus von Platen und Stefan Sonderegger. Basel, Frankfurt a.M. 1986 (Beiträge zur nordischen Philologie 15), S. 191–207.

Glauser, Jürg, 'Romance (Translated *riddarasögur*)'. In: *A Companion to Old Norse-Icelandic Literature and Culture*. Hg. v. Rory Mc Turk. Oxford 2005, S. 372–387.

Glauser, Jürg (Hg.), *Skandinavische Literaturgeschichte*. 2. Aufl. Stuttgart, Weimar 2016.

Holm, Gösta, 'Eufemiavisorna'. In: *Medieval Scandinavia: An Encyclopedia*. Hg. v. Philip Pulsiano. New York 1993, S. 171–173.

Horstbøll, Henrik, *Menigmands medie. Det folkelige bogtryk i Danmark 1500–1840*. København 1999 (Danish Humanist Texts and Studies 19).

Jacobsen, J.P. et al. (Hgg.), *Danske Folkebøger fra 16. og 17. Aarhundrede*. Bd. VI. København 1925.

Kalinke, Marianne E., 'Norse Romance (*Riddarasögur*)'. In: Carol J. Clover und John Lindow (Hgg.), *Old Norse-Icelandic Literature. A Critical Guide*. Toronto u.a. 2005, S. 316–363.

Kalinke, Marianne E., 'Scribe, Redactor, Author: The Emergence and Evolution of Icelandic Romance'. In: *Viking and Medieval Scandinavia* 8 (2012), S. 171–198.

Kalinke, Marianne E., 'Clári saga, Hrólfs saga Gautrekssonar, and the Evolution of Icelandic Romance'. In: *Riddarasǫgur. The Translation of European Court Culture in Medieval Scandinavia*. Hg. v. Karl G. Johansson und Else Mundal. Oslo 2014, S. 273–292.

Lefevere, André, *Translation, Rewriting and the Manipulation of Literary Fame*. London, New York 1992.

Müller, Jan-Dirk, 'Volksbuch/Prosaroman im 15./16. Jahrhundert. Perspektiven der Forschung'. In: *Internationales Archiv für Sozialgeschichte der Literatur* 1 (1985), Sonderheft (Forschungsreferate), S. 1–128.

Nielsen, Lauritz, *Dansk bibliografi: med saerligt hensyn til dansk bogtrykkerkunsts historie*. 3 Bde. København 1919–1935.

Nyborg, Birgit (Hg.), *Tre riddersagaer: Sagaen om Partalopi. Sagaen om Flores og Blankiflor. Sagaen om Bevers*. Oslo 2005.

Partalopa saga. Hg. v. Lise Præstgaard Andersen. Copenhagen 1983 (Editiones Arnamagnæanæ, Series B, 28).

Pulsiano, Phillip (Hg.), *Medieval Scandinavia: An Encyclopedia*. New York 1993.

Richter, Anna Katharina, *Transmissionsgeschichten. Untersuchungen zur dänischen und schwedischen Erzählprosa in der frühen Neuzeit*. Tübingen, Basel 2009 (Beiträge zur nordischen Philologie 41).

Richter, Anna Katharina, 'La transmission de Floire et Blancheflor au Danemark (XVe–XVIIe siecles)'. In: *L'expérience des frontières et les littératures de l'Europe médiéval*. Hg. v. Sofia Lodén und Vanessa Obry. Paris 2019 (Colloques, Congrès et Confèrences - Le Moyen Âge, 26, 1 vol.) (in Vorbereitung).

Rikhardsdottir, Sif, *Medieval Translations and Cultural Discourse. The Movement of Texts in England, France and Scandinavia*. Cambridge 2012.

Le Roman de Partonopeu de Blois. Édition, traduction et introduction de la rédaction A (Paris, Bibliothèque de l'Arsenal, 2986) et de la Continuation du récit d'après les manuscrits de Berne (Burgerbibliothek, 113) et de Tours (Bibliothèque municipale, 939), par Olivier Collet et Pierre-Marie Joris. Paris 2005.

Würth, Stefanie, 'Eufemia. Deutsche Auftraggeberin schwedischer Literatur am norwegischen Hof'. In: *Arbeiten zur Skandinavistik. 13. Arbeitstagung der deutschsprachigen Skandinavistik 29. 7.–3.8.1997 in Lysebu/Oslo*. Hg. v. Fritz Paul. Frankfurt a.M. 2000 (Texte und Untersuchungen zur Germanistik und Skandinavistik 45), S. 269–281.

Zumthor, Paul, *Toward a Medieval Poetics*. Übers. von Philip Bennett. Minneapolis 1992.

Daniel Syrovy

What's in a Name? On the Titles of Early Modern Narratives, in Particular Those of the Spanish *libros de caballerías*

Abstracts: Book titles in Early Modern narratives are a neglected field of study that can help us understand the formation of narrative genres. Examining the corpus of Spanish chivalric romances, this article shows how specific paratextual strategies developed by printers in the sixteenth century for the *libros de caballerías* have led to a generally homogeneous view of the genre. A diachronic reconstruction, however, suggests that the way the romances were titled and designed needs to be contrasted with the books' actual contents and narrative techniques. In this way, different sub-categories might be distinguished in part by their respective titles. The last section discusses an important alternative title in the transmission of *Don Quixote*.

Die Titel frühneuzeitlicher Erzählliteratur sind ein vernachlässigter Forschungsbereich, helfen uns jedoch, die Entwicklung von Erzählgattungen nachzuvollziehen. Eine Untersuchung des Textkorpus der Kastilischen Ritterromane zeigt, dass für die *libros de caballerías* von Druckern des 16. Jh. spezifische Strategien paratextueller Rahmung entwickelt wurden, die stark zur Auffassung beitrugen, es handle sich um eine homogene Gattung. Eine diachrone Rekonstruktion suggeriert jedoch, dass die Titel und visuelle Gestaltung der Romane gesondert von den inhaltlichen und erzähltechnischen Eigenschaften betrachtet werden müssen. Auf diese Weise können nicht zuletzt mehrere Untergattungen unterschieden werden. Das letzte Kapitel behandelt einen wichtigen alternativen Titel in der Überlieferung des *Don Quijote*.

1 Introduction

In contrast to the rather superficial treatment of the Spanish *libros de caballerías* by former generations of Hispanists, who valued them mainly as unworthy precursors to *Don Quixote*, the last 25 to 30 years have seen a marked increase in dedicated studies of the genre and of particular texts. Nevertheless, various fundamental problems still remain unsolved. They stem in part from the long scholarly tradition of regarding the *libros de caballerías* as a homogeneous group of texts, a point of view that derives among other things from specific paratextual strategies developed by printers in the course of the sixteenth century.

Daniel Syrovy, University of Vienna

Confronted with a corpus of approximately 220 extant editions of 67 romances (plus 20 unique manuscripts),[1] both differences and similarities between various editions (and their editorial presentation) can be highlighted, depending on the line of reasoning. In order to properly situate the Spanish *libros de caballerías* in the context of Early Modern narrative, as part of the 'history of the novel' and not least as a specific genre, a differentiated view of the romances is necessary. Distinguishing between the narrative and thematic content of particular romances on the one hand and the editorial history of the genre as a whole on the other hand, is one of the more important steps in this direction. For both aspects, much research is still to be done. Problematically, the way differences between the romances were homogenized even in the sixteenth century (scholars have called this the editorial genre or "género editorial" of the romances), can often obscure our view. This article aims to show how the title pages and title conventions of the romances contribute to these difficulties.

2 The Problem of Titles

Titles, despite being one of the most salient features of a literary text, have rarely been studied systematically. Franco Moretti's chapter in *Distant Reading* is an instructive example of how to look at the problem, comparing the semantics of titles of seventhousand eighteenth- and nineteenth-century British novels.[2] What has been written on the subject confirms that the phrasing of titles and the formation of genres are not independent from each other, which is why the lack of studies must be considered especially problematic for the fifteenth and sixteenth centuries. Looking at narrative forms and genres during the period of early print, it is not hard to observe tendencies towards genre-

---

1 The relevant bibliographies are Daniel Eisenberg and María Carmen Marín Pina, *Bibliografía de los libros de caballerías castellanos*. Zaragoza 2000 (digital edition: http://www.cervantesvir tual.com/obra/bibliografia-de-los-libros-de-caballeria-castellanos/; accessed 25 May 2017) and the Appendix included in José Manuel Lucía Megías and Emilio José Sales Dasí, *Libros de caballerías castellanos (siglos XVI-XVII)*. Madrid 2008, p. 295–308. Since several of the catalogued editions are lost or doubtful and others deliberately excluded, it is not easy to state precise numbers. Much of the information in Alexander S. Wilkinson (ed.), *Iberian Books*. Leiden, Boston 2010 is not very reliable. On the question of the manuscript diffusion of the romances, see Manuel Sánchez Mariana, 'La novela en manuscrito en los Siglos de Oro'. In: *Imprenta, libros y lectura en la España del* Quijote. Ed. by José Manuel Lucía Megías. Madrid 2006, p. 119–138.
2 Franco Moretti, *Distant Reading*. London, New York 2013, p. 179–210. Some observations on the titles of Spanish narratives in the 17th century, mainly concerning genre descriptors, can be found in Anne Cayuela, *Le paratexte au siècle d'or. Prose romanesque, livres et lecteurs en*

specific titles. Titles in fact are often phrased in a way that copies a successful predecessor. For example, even though the 1482–1483 first edition of Boiardo's epic poem about Orlando is lost, its title is usually reconstructed as *Libro de l'inamoramento de Orlando*, modelled on the [*Primo*] *libro del in amoramento de Carlo Ma[g]no* (first printed in Venice, 1481; GW 12613).[3] Today, however, the poem is known mainly as *Orlando innamorato*, due to Ludovico Ariosto's *Orlando furioso* (1516), formally a continuation of Boiardo's poem, which was so successful that it influenced the title form of the earlier text until today (Ariosto's title itself was modelled on Seneca's *Hercules furens*).

Similarly, Jorge de Montemayor's pastoral romance starts out as the pseudo-Latinate *Los siete libros de la Diana* in the early editions (Milan 1560?, Barcelona 1561, Lisbon 1565, …[4]), following the structure of titles such as *Metamorphoseon libri XV* and *Aeneidos libri XII*. Later on, it changes to *La Diana*, definitively so after 1613. This change may have been influenced by the shortening already present in the *Segunda parte de la Diana* (Venice 1568; USTC 337847), but it also coincides with a trend observable in other examples of the genre, a narrative style that after all started with *Arcadia del Sannazaro* (Naples 1504; USTC 991320). Examples include the *Primera parte de la Galatea dividida en seys libros* by Cervantes (Alcalá 1585; USTC 348149) reprinted in Paris in 1611 as *Galatea dividida en seys libros* and perhaps culminates with d'Urfé's *L'Astrée* (Paris 1607), of which two different 1607 editions exist that reflect the same change.[5]

These examples may be anecdotal, but they point toward a major issue: There is little stability regarding the phrasing of titles in the early period of print. Titling as well as book design certainly play an important part in the formation and recognizability of genres, but the complex dynamics of stylistic influence as well as market considerations are far from being well understood. Moreover,

---

Espagne au XVIIe siècle. Genève 1996, p. 248–265. [For title-pages, see also the articles by Van Hemelryck and Delsaux, p. 189–237 and by Schaeps, p. 297–324 in the present volume.]

3 See Andrea Canova, 'Introduction'. In: Matteo Maria Boiardo, *Orlando innamorato. L'inamoramento de Orlando.* Ed. by Andrea Canova. Milano 2011, p. 5–65, here p. 10–12. For the early edition, see GW 04607.

4 USTC 337840, 340124, 337842, respectively.

5 Both editions are by Toussaint du Bray, Paris 1607. One states "L'ASTREE | DE MESSIRE HONORE DURFE […]" (Ex. BNF, RES P–Y2–261); the other, likely the earlier one that still lacks the author's name, "LES | DOUZE LIVRES | D'ASTREE […]" (Ex. BNF, Rothschild–V, 2.18). Judging by the critical on-line editions (http://astree.tufts.edu and http://www.astree.paris-sorbonne.fr/, accessed 25 May 2017), part of the foliation has changed as well. Yet the editions must have succeeded each other quickly. In both cases, the privilege is dated 18 August 1607 and is for "un livre intitulé *L'Astrée*".

modern conventions further obscure particular traditions, something that is not only a problem with the Spanish chivalric romances but extends even to classical texts: The titles of Latin editions of Valerius Maximus from the first half of the sixteenth century, for example, are as diverse as *Prisci exempla, Facta et dicta memorabilia* and *Facinora memorabilia*.[6] The advantages of short titles as generally used today are therefore counterbalanced by a great loss of detail. It may be a type of problem that has less to do with establishing an 'ideal text' than with reconstructing processes of reception, but the distinction is not quite as clear-cut. With respect to medieval manuscripts, Richard Sharpe argues that our knowledge of certain texts is limited precisely by the inability to correctly identify certain branches of their transmission, among other reasons, because the catalogues collecting the information traditionally tend towards "conservatism or convenience rather than [...] evidence".[7] One of Sharpe's examples is a list of 53 known manuscripts of Isidore's *Sententiae*. Only eight of them contain the familiar title-word, while almost forty are a variation of *De summo bono*. Others include *De diuersis uirtutibus, De lapsis* and combinations thereof (e.g. "de summo bono et diuersis uirtutibus").[8]

While this may be a challenge for bibliography, book history and literary history, it is of crucial importance for understanding not only book transmission, but also other kinds of historical context. The information allows us to reconstruct processes of influence or developments in editing, but since a title has a major influence on a reader's understanding of a text, it also indicates the practical use of books as well as the public's expectations. Unfortunately, tools such as the otherwise invaluable Universal Short Title Catalogue (USTC), as well as most modern editions (including critical ones) are of little help because they mainly use normalized titles in the first place. Therefore, it is essential to go back to the original editions (or, increasingly, to digitizations) to record faithfully what the title-pages state exactly and what they look like. Additionally, the relationship between titles as given on title-pages and, on the

---

6 The full titles are: *Valerii Maximi Priscorum exemplorum libri nouem: diligenti castigatione emendati: aptissimisque figuris exculti* (Venetia: Zanis 1508; USTC 861756); *Valerij Maximi Romani generis viri facta et dicta memorabilia Jterum recognita et accuratiore castigatione impressa q[uae] scriptor ille illustris Cesari Claudio Tyberio neroni dedicauit...* (Lipsia: Landsberg 1509; USTC 700294); *Valerij Maximi Ciuis Romani de factis ac dictis memorabilib[us] Exemplor [um] Libri nouem: tum [pro]pter stili maturitatem: tum vero propter vite instructionem vtilissimi.* (Lipsia: Lotter 1514; USTC 697004); *Valerii Max. Libri 9. in quibus, quod philosophi alijque scriptores praeceptionibus, hic uir prudens & sapiens facinorum memorabilium exemplis tradit.* (Basilea: Petri 1540; USTC 700274).

7 Richard Sharpe, *Titulus. Identifying Medieval Latin Texts.* Turnhout 2006, p. 27.

8 Sharpe (see note 7), p. 91–93.

other hand, in incipits, colophons, privileges, as well as in the form of references in other texts, might throw even more light on these issues.[9]

3 The Titles of Spanish Chivalric Romances

The way the *libros de caballerías* were perceived as a genre in the sixteenth century, and often still are today, may serve as an example for why these methodo-
logical approaches have practical consequences. A question that is especially
vexing in this respect is that of short titles. For practical reasons, all modern
scholars use them to designate the Spanish chivalric romances, including in
bibliographies and in the series of new editions, the *Libros de Rocinante*, published by the Centro de Estudios Cervantinos in Alcalá de Henares. Short titles
are, of course, a quick and handy reference, even though they deviate from the
evidence of the books themselves. Moreover, the habit is anything but recent.
Short titles have been in use from antiquity on (on the outside of scrolls[10]) and
contemporaries of the *libros de caballerías* unsurprisingly used them as well.
Elisabetta Sarmati collects 93 fifteenth- and sixteenth-century witnesses com-
menting on the genre and all of them use short forms (except 33 who do not
mention specific titles at all). These forms are indistinguishable from the heroes
of the books: *Amadís, Primaleón, Don Clarián.*[11] It may be significant that only
twelve of the commentators have a generally positive view of the phenomenon
of *libros de caballerías*, but the titles as such do not appear plainly dismissive.
By contrast, as many as sixteen writers employ adjectival or plural forms of the
names, a negative strategy that Sarmati herself identifies as a "topos of abun-
dance". There is talk of *Amadises* and *Palmerines* and poisonous "cavallerías
amadísicas y espla[n]diánicas".[12] In addition, this sort of criticism often

---

9 Cf. Ursula Rautenberg, 'Die Entstehung und Entwicklung des Buchtitelblatts in der
Inkunabelzeit'. In: *Archiv für Geschichte des Buchwesens* 62 (2008), p. 1–105 and especially her
remarks on title-pages and colophons, p. 16.
10 See Revilo P. Oliver, 'The First Medicean MS of Tacitus and the Titulature of Ancient
Books'. In: *Transactions and Proceedings of the American Philological Association* 82 (1951),
p. 232–261, p. 243.
11 Elisabetta Sarmati, *Le critiche ai libri di cavalleria nel cinquecento spagnolo (con uno
sguardo sul seicento). Un'analisi testuale.* Pisa 1996, p. 115–179.
12 Sarmati's analysis of "Il *tópos* dell'abbondanza", *Le critiche* (see note 11), p. 54–56. The ob-
servation about the number of positive texts is her own and can be found on p. 61. The last
quotation is from Alejo Venegas, introducing Alvar Gómez's *Theológica descripción de los mis-
terios sagrados* (originally Toledo 1541), in Sarmati's transcription, text no. 14, p. 131.

concerns all popular fiction and some of the lists include titles like *La Celestina* or *La Diana* (also at times in plural forms) that are not part of the corpus of chivalric texts. This suggests that certain expectations of homogeneity and even interchangeability among the romances may have been related to, or underscored by, titling habits.

This notion is confirmed by one of the most extensive commentaries on the genre, *Don Quixote*, specifically chapter six of the first part, in which the curate sorts out the *hidalgo*'s library. All but two of the titles mentioned are given in short form. Cervantes does emphasize differences in quality, however, and the two exceptions are also the most highly esteemed: "*Los cuatro de Amadís de Gaula*" (a reference to the original volume by Garci Rodríguez de Montalvo containing books one through four) and "*Historia del famoso caballero Tirante el Blanco*".[13] The latter, interestingly, does not correspond to the actual book's title: *Los cinco libros d[e]l efforçado & inuencible cauallero Tirante el blanco de roca salada: Cauallero dela Garrotera* [...]. Only the colophon, in fact, states "famoso & inuencible" (fol. 288r; Valladolid 1511; USTC 347631). The evidence, therefore, remains ambivalent. In addition, *Don Quixote* treats some of the romances in an anthropomorphized manner. In fact, modern editions generally miss a fine point of the famous chapter, when Cervantes's phrase "las *Sergas de Esplandián*, hijo legítimo de Amadís de Gaula" [sic] is not set *recte*, like it is in all the early editions.[14] Since the character Esplandián is the son of the knight Amadís, the statement is ambiguous: It can mean either that the character is the son of the other (parsing it as "las Sergas de [Esplandian, [[hijo legítimo...]]") or that one book is the 'son' of the other (but then, surely, *Amadís de Gaula* is understood as a title as well, i.e. should be set in italics). This is not to say that every metonymic use of titles has such implications,[15] but in *Don Quixote* the effect is clearly intentional. Overall, short titles for the romances are commonly used, then, and this even extends to some of the title-pages, as we will see.

---

13 In Miguel de Cervantes, *El Ingenioso Hidalgo Don Quijote de la Mancha*. Ed. by John Jay Allen. Madrid 2001, *Amadís* is called "el mejor de todos los libros que de este género se han compuesto" (p. 130) and *Tirante* is "un tesoro de contento y una mina de pasatiempos" (p. 134).

14 Madrid 1605 (2), Lisbon 1605 (2), Valencia 1605, Brussels 1607, Madrid 1608, Milan 1610, Brussels 1611, Brussels 1617.

15 Compare the case of *La vida de Lazarillo de Tormes* (the earliest editions are from 1554 in Antwerp, Burgos, Alcalá; USTC 440153, 351133, 343114), which becomes *La segunda parte de Lazarillo de Tormes* (Antwerp 1555; USTC 440363); modern editions, in fact, avoid this construction (paralleled by the *Segunda parte de la Diana*, quoted above) either by calling the book *Segunda parte del Lazarillo de Tormes* (e.g. ed. Alfredo Rodriguez López-Vázquez. Madrid 2014; my emphasis), or by supplying *de la vida de*.

4 The Conservative Design of the *libros de caballerías* and its Development

Before looking more closely at the usage of short titles (or what may be taken for such) on the actual title-pages of some sixteenth-century editions of the *libros de caballerías*, a few words need to be said about the development of the chivalric title-pages in general. As already indicated, scholars have been talking about an editorial genre ("género editorial") in this respect, meaning that there had been a kind of 'standard design' of the chivalric romances for a long period of time. Influenced by the huge success of some of the early volumes, above all *Amadís de Gaula*, which dates from the first years of the sixteenth century, the title-pages of the romances in fact were strikingly conservative: The long titles were set in gothic type and usually printed with red and black ink. Most title-pages featured a large woodcut that covered the top half of the page, generally depicting a scene with a knight on horseback, and were often surrounded by a decorative border.[16]

The image of the knight was obviously intended to illustrate a particular text, but the high expenses connected with producing new woodcuts often led to their repeated use for different romances. This in turn strengthened the visual coherence of individual cycles and the whole genre, because the books resembled one another even more closely. Yet, perhaps out of a perceived shortcoming, in many cases the printers apparently tried to emphasize the informative character of the woodcuts by attaching the names of the knights to the images. Technically, there are at least four ways to accomplish this goal: In the first case, the woodcut itself includes the knight's name, most commonly on a banner. This was sometimes done by way of a separate piece superimposed on the image of the knight.[17] Another method has the name printed with type inside the empty

---

16 Knights are, however, not the only subject of the woodcuts. There are also war scenes, sieges, heraldic motifs and sometimes religious or courtly scenes. This typology is taken in a simplified form from José Manuel Lucía Megías, 'Imprenta y lengua literaria en los Siglos de Oro: el caso de los libros de caballerías castellanos.' In: *Edad de Oro* 23 (2004), p. 199–229, here p. 208. A more extensive study of the design features of the whole corpus can be found in José Manuel Lucía Megías, *Imprenta y libros de caballerías*. Madrid 2000, p. 140–324. [For old-style title-pages, see also the article by Schaeps, p. 321–323, in the present volume.]

17 Beginning with the *Amadís* of 1508 (Zaragoza: Coci; USTC 342622) we find a handful of such cases, generally before 1550, for instance *Las Sergas de Esplandián* (Burgos: Juan de Junta 1526; USTC 348400) (see Fig. 1), or *Clarián de Landanís* (Sevilla: Jacobo & Juan Cromberger 1527; USTC 338312). *Belianís de Grecia* (Burgos: Martín Muñoz 1547; USTC 336254) looks as if the knight and his name were on the same woodcut.

space of the image, allowing for the woodcut's re-use while still creating the impression that the name belonged to the illustration.[18] In a third variation, an empty banner in the woodcut image is filled with type printing. This can be found on the title-page of a 1566 *Primaleón* (Lisboa: Manuel João; USTC 343200) and a much later book very closely modelled on it, *Choronica del mvy valiente* [...] *Amadis de Grecia* (Lisboa: Lopes 1596; USTC 342631; see Fig. 3).[19] The last option, to which we will return, is to print a knight's name in type above the woodcut, just outside the frame (see Fig. 5).

Sometimes, the reuse of woodcuts also clarifies processes of transmission. A very interesting example comes from the printing house of the Crombergers.[20] One particular woodcut is first preserved on the title-page of the *Historia del caballero Cifar* (Sevilla: Jacobo Cromberger, 1512; USTC 337405). Since the *Cifar* is not properly a *libro de caballerías*, it is surprising that a more or less faithful copy of the image is used by Antonio de Salamanca in Rome for the title-page of his *Amadís* of 1519 (USTC 802205; see Fig. 6), where it is also repeated three more times at the start of the individual books within the volume. By itself, the *Cifar* – a text from the 1300s that Cromberger edited in order to cash in on the new fashion of chivalric romances[21] and apparently no great success, as there are no reprints or further editions – seems unlikely to have influenced the design of an edition of *Amadís*. Yet, it is well known that in the course of three generations, the Crombergers constantly reused woodcuts.[22] The image in question, too, is still used 28 years after the *Cifar* on the title-page of an edition of *Primaleón* (Sevilla:

---

18 For instance, *Las Historias del muy noble* [...] *cauallero don Claria[n] de landanis* (Toledo: Juan de Villaquiran, 1518; USTC 344400), or *Los quatro libros del muy noble* [...] *Felix magno* (Sevilla: Trujillo 1549; USTC 342952; see Fig. 2). *El octavo libro de Amadis* (Sevilla: Jacobo & Juan Cromberger 1526; USTC 337574), includes six small woodcuts of crowned king/knight figures with their respective names.

19 In the case of *Silves de la Selva* (Sevilla: De Robertis 1546; USTC 342635) the name is typeset but split into three pieces of text ("Dō", "Silues dela sel", "ua."), aligned at 135° 0° and 225° angles to coincide with a woodcut banner (see Fig. 4).

20 In general, cf. Clive Griffin, *The Crombergers of Seville. The History of a Printing and Merchant Dynasty*. Oxford 1988.

21 For textual aspects and editorial strategies in the *Cifar* itself, see Juan Pablo Mauricio García Álvarez, 'Procedimientos textuales de impresor en el *Libro del caballero Zifar* (Cromberger, 1512): El caso de los epígrafes'. In: *Zifar y sus libros. 500 años*. Ed. by Karla Xiomara Luna Mariscal, Axayácatl Campos García Rojas and Aurelio González. México 2015, p. 265–308; and Juan Manuel Cacho Blecua, 'El género del 'Cifar' (Sevilla, Cromberger, 1512)'. In: *Thesaurus* LIV/1 (1999), p. 76–105.

22 Griffin (see note 20), p. 185 mentions that his microfiche-appendix "contains approximately 1,500 examples of woodcuts and decorative blocks used by the Cromberger press at Seville, but nevertheless does not represent all the blocks used in Cromberger editions."

Fig. 1: *Las Sergas de Esplandián* (Burgos 1526). Biblioteca de Catalunya Bon. 8-III-17: title-page.

Fig. 2: *Félix Magno* (Sevilla 1549). Biblioteca de Catalunya Bon. 9-III-8: detail.

Fig. 3: *Amadís de Grecia* (Lisbon 1596). Österreichische Nationalbibliothek 40.R.33/9: detail.

Juan Cromberger, 1540; not in USTC) and it serves again as an illustration on fol. 66v of Jácome Cromberger's 1545 *Cirongilio de Tracia* (USTC 342231). More interestingly, however, it was also used at the beginning of book four in Cromberger's

Fig. 4: *Silves de la Selva* (Sevilla 1546). Biblioteca de Catalunya Bon. 9-III-22: detail.

1526 *Amadís* (USTC 344299), replacing an omitted passage of text (fol. 201v: see Fig. 7[23]). The title-page of this edition features the much more famous woodcut of Amadís, accompanied by another knight and two squires, which the Crombergers used for a number of volumes and editions of the whole cycle (see Fig. 5).[24] But it is the reuse of the earlier image within the 1526 book that gives us a decisive hint why that particular woodcut may have been imitated in Rome in 1519. As indicated above, the *Cifar* was quickly printed to have a chivalric text available after the success of earlier romances. Is very likely, therefore, that the image on its title-page had already been used before, specifically for the lost 1511 *Amadís* of Sevilla,

---

23 Together with an additional small woodcut on fol. 202r, it takes the place of Garci Rodríguez de Montalvo's prólogo to book four of *Amadís*, as is pointed out by Rafael Ramos, 'Problemas de la edición zaragozana del *Amadís de Gaula* (1508)'. In: *Libros de caballerías (de "Amadís" al "Quijote"). Poética, lectura, representación e identidad*. Ed. by Eva Belén Carro Carbajal, Laura Puerto Moro and María Sánchez Pérez. Salamanca 2002, p. 319–342, here p. 336 no. 17.

24 Parts of this woodcut were inspired by the image on the title-page of the 1521 *Amadís* (Zaragoza: Coci; USTC 348441), an illustration from an earlier edition of Titus Livius (Zaragoza: Coci 1520; USTC 337649). See Juan Manuel Cacho Blecua, 'Iconografía amadisiana: las imágenes de Jorge Coci'. In: *eHumanista* 16 (2010), p. 1–27, here p. 18–19. The argument centers on the unnatural body position of the walking horse in 1526, which corresponds to that of a standing horse in the 1521 Zaragoza *Amadís*.

Fig. 5: *Amadís de Gaula* (Sevilla 1526) Biblioteca nacional de Portugal RES. 454 V: title-page.

Fig. 6: *Amadís de Gaula* (Rome 1519). Biblioteca de Catalunya Bon. 8-IV-11: title-page.

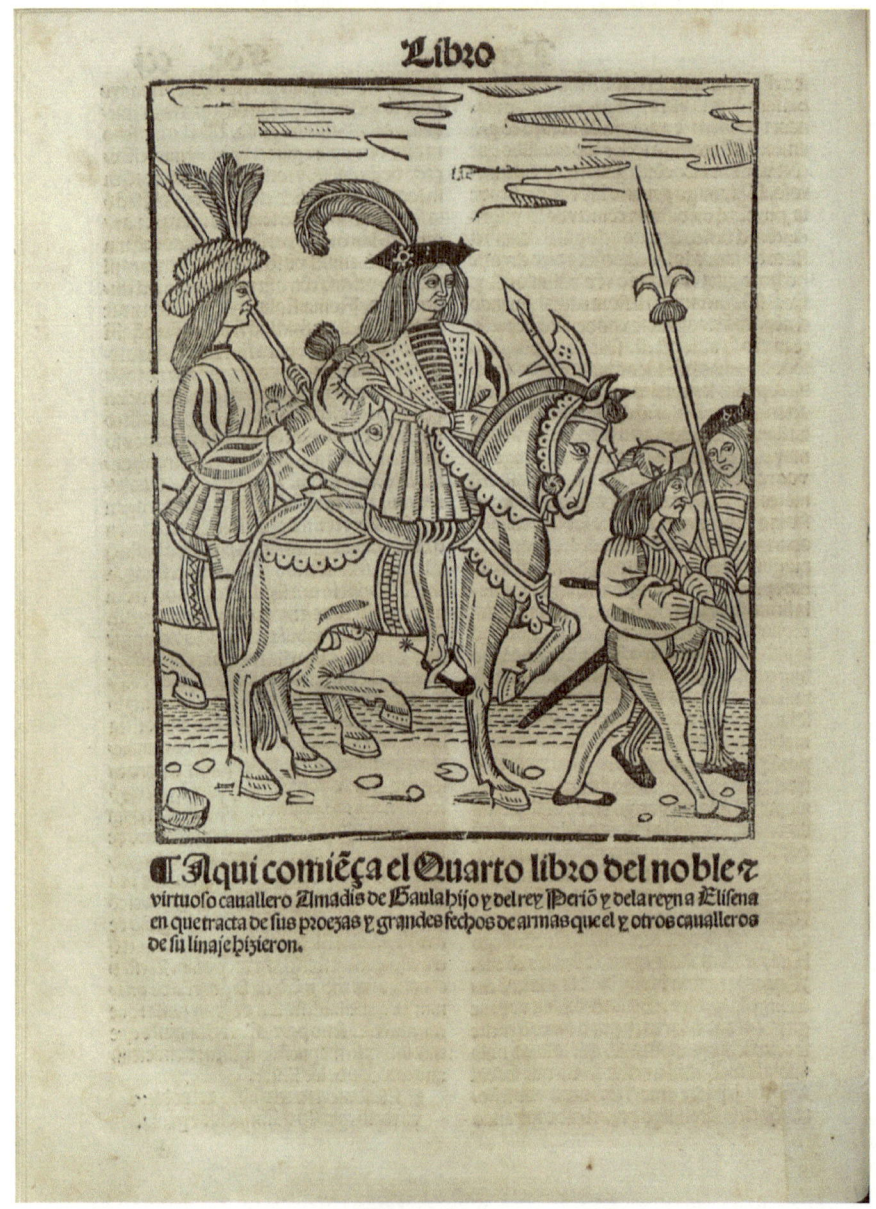

Fig. 7: *Amadís de Gaula* (Sevilla 1526) Biblioteca nacional de Portugal RES. 454 V: f. 201v.

which is supposed to have been Cromberger's. This would not only explain why the printer once again adapted the image for the 1526 *Amadís*, but why it featured in the 1512 *Cifar*, as well: It made the medieval text look exactly like the biggest success so far of the new chivalric genre. It also makes perfect sense for the Roman edition to closely follow the look of Cromberger's 1511 *Amadís*, a connection underlined by the fact that many of the illustrative woodcuts in the 1519 edition look almost exactly like the illustrations in Cromberger's 1526 *Amadís*, in turn presumably modelled on the same printing house's earlier edition.[25] Since the artistic quality of the Roman woodcuts, especially regarding facial expressions and other details, is considerably lower than that of Cromberger's 1526 edition, it is unlikely that they could have been the model for the latter. It is conceivable that both editions go back to an unknown, still earlier print, but it seems quite convincing that *Amadís* in 1511 looked very much like the 1519 imitation. Which is to say, very close to the 1526 edition, with the exception of the title-page and the prologue to book four.[26]

This clearly shows how certain design features of the romances were repeated over decades. By the early 1530s, the template had become part of the genre's tradition. This is especially striking when contrasted with the development of book design in general.[27] In Spain, books of all genres had by and large followed a similar pattern to that of the romances around 1490–1515 (woodcut, red-and-black ink, long titles). A decade later, the situation is more complicated. Even though Spain lagged behind Europe in this respect, mostly for economic reasons, as Lucía Megías argues, there was a general shift toward a more modern title-page in roman type, with the year and place of impression.[28]

---

25 Importantly, the first known edition of *Amadís* (Zaragoza: Coci 1508; USTC 342622) did not have any illustrative woodcuts in the text, cf. Cacho Blecua, 'Iconografia amadisiana' (note 24), p. 8.

26 Similar conclusions were reached in a paper by Maria Cristina Misiti, but in a more hypothetical manner, because the author was unable to directly compare the two books and examined only Cromberger's 1531 *Amadís* (USTC 338329) where many illustrative woodcuts are actually different from those used in 1526. See Maria Cristina Misiti, 'Alcune rare edizioni spagnole pubblicate a Roma da Antonio Martínez de Salamanca'. In: *El libro antiguo español. Actas del segundo Coloquio Internacional (Madrid).* Ed. by María Luisa López-Vidriero and Pedro M. Cátedra. Salamanca 1992, p. 307–323; Lucía Megías, *Imprenta y libros* (note 16), p. 147–149. The question is raised again by Folke Gernert, 'Antonio Martínez de Salamanca, impresor y Francisco Delicado, corrector. Libros españoles en la imprenta italiana a través de sus ilustraciones'. In: *Nápoles – Roma 1504. Cultura y literatura española y portuguesa en Italia en el quinto centenario de la muerte de Isabel la Católica.* Ed. by Javier Gómez-Montero. Salamanca 2005, p. 205–242.

27 For the chronological development of title-pages, see Rautenberg (see note 9), p. 16.

28 Lucía Megías *Imprenta y libros* (note 16), p. 436–437.

This affected the romances too, only more slowly. From this point on, their formal conservatism is most apparent by a comparison with the *libros de caballerías* printed outside of Spain. But while some features of the old-style design were long kept in place, presumably as a marker of genre, even they were adapted to a degree. From 1526 onwards, many editions feature a date on the title-page (and in many cases full information about printer and place, which was only legally required after 1558). The colophon was generally retained as well, but it served as much as a feature of the narration as for giving necessary details of the edition. Often printed before the tables of contents, in the case of a Leuven edition of *Amadís* from 1551 (USTC 440043) dividing the text into two quarto-volumes, there is only a 'colophon' at the end of volume two.

A more drastic change of the outward appearance of chivalric romances can, generally speaking, be observed only by the 1580s. At that time, the books still featured woodcuts of knights, but they tended to be placed like vignettes in the middle of the page.[29] Most significantly, there is now an overall change from gothic to roman type for the romances, a trend that had begun about twenty years earlier.[30]

---

29 For instance *Florisel de Niquea* (Zaragoza: Domingo de Portonaris Ursino 1584; USTC 338102), two editions of the *Sergas de Esplandian* (Zaragoza: de Portonaris 1587 (colophon: 1586); USTC 342628; and Alcalá de Henares: hered. Juan Gracián 1588; USTC 345710); or the *Chronica de* [...] *Lisvarte de Grecia* [...] *Y de Perion de Gaula* (Zaragoza: Puig, Escarilla 1587; USTC 337172). There is also a lone exception as early as 1551, the *Libro segvndo, De la quarta y gran parte de la Choronica del excelente Principe don Florisel de Niquea* (Salamanca: Andrea de Portonariis 1551; USTC 338314), for which, however, an alternative traditional title-page (albeit with roman lettering) exists, which is reproduced in José Manuel Lucía Megías (ed.), *Amadis de Gaula 1508, quinientos años de libros de caballerías*. Madrid 2008, p. 150.

30 The earliest cases known to me that keep the old title-page format of woodcut and long title but already use roman type for the whole book are two editions by Francisco del Canto in Medina del Campo: *Libro del inuencible cauallero Primaleon* (1563; USTC 338787) and *El noueno libro de Amadis de Gaula* [...] *Amadis de Grecia* (1564; USTC 348405). These are followed by *Olivante de Laura*, extant in one copy with a torn title-page (Barcelona: Bornat 1564; USTC 337972), *La coronica delos muy valie[n]tes caualleros don Florisel de Niquea y el fuerte Anaxartes* [...] (Lisbon: Borges 1566; USTC 342633) and *La primera parte de la qvarta* [...] *de* [...] *Don Florisel de Niquea* (Zaragoza: Floresta 1568; USTC 337518), as well as the problematic 1551 Salamanca *Florisel* (mentioned in note 29). The practice of combining the old-style title-page with roman script is still in use much later, cf. *Tercera y quarta parte del imbencible principe do[n] Belianis de Grecia* [...] (Burgos: Pedro de Santillana 1579; USTC 336253) and *Libro septimo de Amadis, enel qual se trata [n] los grandes hechos en armas de Lisuarte de Grecia* [...] (Lisbon: Alonso Lopez 1587; USTC 344302). Unsurprisingly, there are several other anomalies: the *Primera parte de la grande historia del* [...] *principe Felixmarte de Yrcania* (Valladolid: Francisco Fernandez de Cordoba 1556; USTC 340371) is set in gothic, but has roman type title-page, privileges and prologue (a second variant, the incomplete copy of the Biblioteca de Catalunya, Bon. 8–III–15, adds information on a fictitious

Some printers, especially outside of Spain, never conformed to the familiar design. One *Palmerin de Oliua* (Venetia: Gregorio de Gregorijs, 1526; USTC 344509) did have an elaborate woodcut frame and a knight on horseback, but mixed roman and gothic type. Overall, it looked nothing like a typical chivalric romance. Another edition of the same text (Veneçia: Juan Paduan & Venturin de Rufinelli, 1534; USTC 802676) is not set in columns and exists with two different title-pages, only one of which is ostensibly 'chivalric'.[31] Finally, *Los tres libros del muy efforçado cauallero Primaleon* (Venecia: Nicolini de Sabio, 1534; USTC 337939) had a gothic title-page but was set in roman type without columns and with woodcut illustrations throughout. Even in Spain, though, there was at least one exception: The *Espeio de principes y cavalleros* (Zaragoza: Nagera 1555; not in USTC) is presented more than anything as a humanist text. Printed in roman script, it has a modern title-page with a printer's vignette surrounded by a large border, in the style of a three-dimensional frame complete with columns, statues, satyrs and a lion's head ("una orla complicada y clasicista").[32] This probably reflects the conscious attempt to renew certain aspects of the genre, as programmatically stated by its author, Diego Ortúñez de Calahorra, in a preface[33]:

> leyendo algunas desocupadas horas en estos libros, se recrea el animo, y se leuanta el coraçon, adelgazase el ingenio, auiua se el juyzio, despiertase el sentido. [...] Bien que no es mi intento de loar agora todo el requaje de libros de cauallerias que estan escriptos,

---

translation and the year 1557 onto the title-page, but retains 1556 in the colophon. See USTC 348325). One edition of *Lepolemo* (Toledo: Ferrer 1552/1553; USTC 346549) curiously uses roman type for the colophon only. The problem of gothic and roman types is extensively treated by Lucía Megías, *Imprenta y libros* (note 16), p. 433–447.

31 It is likely, however, that the chivalric woodcut does reflect a revision of the title-page in the common style of the genre (short title above; woodcut; long title below). A guess at the chronology is possible because the 'chivalric' title-page a) slightly revises the long title, from "nueuame[n]te restampado: y corregido: con su tabla" to "[...] restampado y corregido [...]", b) aligns the two-color print much more carefully, and c) corrects a typographical error of the other variant, where the word "grandes" (in red ink) reads "zrandes", printed over by a black "g". While that error could theoretically be a result of the resetting, this seems unlikely.

32 See Daniel Eisenberg's *Introducción a 'Espejo de Príncipes y cavalleros [El Cavallero del Febo]' de Diego Ortúñez de Calahorra* (http://www.cervantesvirtual.com/nd/ark:/59851/bmcjq193; accessed 25 May 2017).

33 Frank Willaert rightly remarked to me that the use of the word *Espejo* (mirror, *Speculum*) also emphasizes the humanist and didactic aspects. There is, however, a precedent: *Espejo de caballerías*, first published in Toledo in 1525, is a Spanish prose version of Boiardo's *Orlando innamorato*. The didactic dimension of *libros de caballerías* is in itself a complex question. See also Lucía Megías, *Imprenta y lengua* (note 16), p. 204.

porque no es menos sino que hay algunos que no hay enellos alegoria ni moralidad alguna, de que el lector se pueda aprouechar [. . .]

(a few spare hours' reading of these books will relax the mind, lift the heart, ease the
spirit, revive judgement and awaken the senses [. . .] Even so I do not intend to praise the
whole drove of *libros de caballerías*, because there are certainly some that have no allegorical or moral dimension which the reader may profit from)

He adds, conveniently hiding behind the guise of a fictitious translation, that
"[el] Espejo de Principes y caualleros [. . .] sera agradable en su lectura, tiene
alguna moralidad que a bueltas delas historias no sera tan enojosa quanto
prouechosa para el que lo leyere".[34] The text became a huge success and by
1562, it was also sold with a more traditional-looking woodcut title-page.[35]

Despite this apparent homogeneity, it would ultimately be important to contrast both the conservative and innovative tendencies of the printers of *libros de
caballerías* with the actual content and style of the texts. We know of a number
of books throughout the sixteenth century that were 'advertised' as though they
were chivalric romances. This applies to the medieval *Historia del caballero Cifar*
which Cromberger reedited in Sevilla in 1512, as well as to the spiritual tale of
the *Libro intitulado Peregrinacion de la vida del ho[m]bre puesta en batalla de-
baxo.* . . (Medina del Campo: Guillermo de Millis, 1552; USTC 340706) which was
presented with the typical ingredients of a *libro de caballerías*: the gothic lettering, a knight's name ("Cauallero del Sol") over a woodcut of the knight on
a horse surrounded by rich borders, while the actual text is a religious alle-
gory.[36] The differences can be large, as in the case of a spiritual tale, but for the
understanding of the genre, even smaller narrative differences can be of importance. This includes different modes of narration, which are not always directly
reflected in the editorial presentation of the books.

---

34 "The Espejo de Principes y caualleros is pleasant to read and has a moral dimension that,
being part of the story, is not bothersome so much as profitable for the reader."
35 The title-page of the edition Zaragoza: Miguel de Guesa 1562 (USTC 346243) is reproduced
in Lucía Megías, *Imprenta y libros* (note 16), p. 178; the edition Alcalá de Henares: Iuan Iñiguez
de Lequerica 1580 (USTC 340401) has a similar design but is set in roman type. The printer of
the first edition, Nagera (Nájera) was active only from *c.* 1550–1555, for details on him and his
production, mostly books of lyric *Romances*, see Giovanni Caravaggi, 'Esteban Godines de
Nájera y Juan Coloma'. In: *Revista de poética medieval* 28 (2014), p. 177–187.
36 See Emma Herrán Alonso, 'Las narraciones caballerescas espirituales'. In: *Amadís de
Gaula 1508. Quinientos años de libros de caballerías*. Ed. by José Manuel Lucía Megías. Madrid
2008, p. 265–270.

5 Long and Short Titles and Their Relation to Entrelacement as a Narrative Technique

One of the ways in which the current exclusive use of short titles for the romances obscures our view of the genre's complexities, is by reducing necessary information contained in the original titles. Many of the Spanish romances (excluding, significantly, most of *Amadís*) are in fact narrated in a particular style which constantly switches between different narrative strands (the technique usually called *entrelacement*). Clearly, several narrative strands require a number of heroes on an equivalent scale, to allow the writers to interrupt the narration at critical (and suspenseful) moments as often as possible. This is an aspect the long titles of the romances do reflect, because very often two or more names are mentioned. Moreover, at least 18 romances out of the overall 60 are now referred to by completely different names. *Febo el Troyano* was actually called *Primera parte del Dechado y Remate de grandes Hazañas...*, a title that went on to name three heroes and heroines – Febo, Hispalián dela Vengança and Clariana – and referred to "many others" ("otros muchos"). Sometimes, the names of heroes explicitly referred to in the long titles are simply dropped today. The *Demanda del sancto Grial* also originally mentioned two knights, Lançarote and Galaz on the original title-page. And *Silves de la Selva*, apart from Silves, also mentioned the characters Esferamundi, Amadís de Astra, Fortunián and Astrapolo on its title-page.[37] Similarly, the *Segunda parte del Espejo de Principes y Caballeros* explicitly named the Emperador Trabacio, Alphebo, Risocler, Claridiano, Claridiana, Poliphebo de Tinacria, Archisilora and "otros". The case of sequels is especially interesting, since it has a direct relevance for the audience's expectations. What we know now simply as *Roselao de Grecia* was presented as the *Tercera parte de Espejo de cauallerias*. On the 1550 title-page, Roselao was in fact only mentioned *after* another hero, don Roserín. Distinguishing between different sub-categories, in part identifiable by their titles, is obviously of great importance for reception processes, apart from narratological analyses.

---

37 We find similar schemes in *Belianís de Grecia*, parts III-IV (Belianís, Belfloran de Grecia); *Cristalián de España* (Cristalián, Luzescanio); *Felixmarte de Hircania* (Felixmarte, Florasán de Misia); *Florisel de Niquea* (Florisel, Anaxartes); *Lisuarte de Grecia* (Lisuarte, Perión de Gaula); *Morgante* (Morgante, Roldán, Renaldos); *Oliveros de Castilla* (Oliveros, Artus de Algarve); *Palmerín de Inglaterra* (Palmerín, Floriano del Desierto, Florendos); *Philesbián de Candaria* (Philesbián, Felinís); *Primaleón* (Primaleón, Polendos); *Rogel de Grecia* (= *Florisel de Niquea, tercera parte*) (Rogel, Agesilao).

Yet, as we indicated earlier, the habit of referring to the romances by short titles dates back as far as the sixteenth century. In part, this has to do with convenience, omitting some of the blurb-like information contained in the long titles.[38] It may also have to do with the running titles that had to abbreviate titles for technical reasons. There is also another feature of the title-page that emphasizes this development. We find that by 1526 at the latest, what looks like short titles tend to be featured on most romances. Usually set in type just above the woodcut, a certain ambiguity remains, because the name of the hero might sometimes be intended to identify the knight in the image. The 1526 *Amadís* of Jacobo and Juan Cromberger (USTC 344299) states "Amadis de gaula" above the woodcut (as though it identified the knight) in the same size of type as "Los quatro libros de Amadis de gaula", which is somewhat redundantly printed below.[39] The evidence of the whole corpus suggests, however, that while this feature may have in part originated as a legend for the illustration, it soon became a signal for the buyer, a kind of short title distinct from the long one containing more information. Other examples from the same period have a similar scheme to that of *Amadís* yet cannot be interpreted as a legend for the illustration. The title-page of *Historia del inuencible cauallero do[n] Polindo hijo del rey Paciano rey de Numidia [...]* (Toledo: 1526; USTC 337928) says "Primer libro de don Polindo" topmost above the woodcut. *El ramo que delos quatro libros de amadis sale: llamado Las sergas de Espla[n]dian hijo de Amadis de gaula [...]* (Burgos: Juan de Junta, 1526; USTC 348400) has the phrase "Las sergas de Espla[n]dian" in the same place (see Fig. 1). Both are, in terms of appearance and function, short titles. Moreover, the latter's title-page contains the name "Esplandian" on a banner inside the woodcut as well. This short title also allowed the printers to emphasize the fact that some romances belong to a cycle, as with another edition of the *Sergas*. Above the woodcut of *Las sergas del muy efforçado & inuencible cauallero Espla[n]dian hijo de Amadis de gaula* (Sevilla: Juan Varela de Salamanca, 1526; USTC 348330), we find the phrase "Quinto libro de Amadis".[40] All in all, we can distinguish an interesting functional

---

38 Some systematic thoughts on how titles act as blurbs informing the reader about the contents of the books are offered by Lucía Megías, *Imprenta y libros* (note 16), p. 258–276, but he does not consider the problem of various protagonists as a structural one (p. 273–275).

39 I have counted at least six of those ambiguous cases from 1546 to 1587.

40 A mixed form appears on another title-page (without a woodcut, but with a decorative border around the long title): Florisando. | Sexto libro de Amadis. [border] El qual trata delos | grandes & hazaño= | sos fechos d[e]l muy | valie[n]te y efforca= | do cauall[er]o Flori | sando principe | de Ca[n]taria su | sobrino: fijo | d[e]l rey don | Floresta[n] de Cerdeña. (Sevilla: Juan Varela de Salamanca 1526; USTC 342630).

development of the title-page, where a kind of short title is printed above the woodcut, with the long title below, but which is still in keeping with the traditional visual idiom and design template of the chivalric romances of ten or fifteen years earlier.[41] Since both the long titles and this particular variant of short title tells us a lot about the way the books were presented to their readers, they need to be considered as crucial information about the individual volumes.

6 The Title of *Don Quixote*

The problem of original titles and their current misrepresentations even reappears when we turn to what is usually perceived as the end point of the chivalric tradition in Spain: *Don Quixote*. In many ways, Cervantes's novel departs from the design (as well as the content) of the earlier *libros de caballerías*.[42] It is of course not set in gothic type, which by 1605 would have been unlikely for any romance, and only one early edition (Lisbon: Rodríguez 1605) divides the text into columns, in general unnecessary for the quarto format. The title-page of the *princeps* neither includes a chivalric-themed woodcut (instead there is a printer's vignette)[43]; and while the proper name "Quixote" is divided in two ("Qvi- | xote") and thus supposedly de-emphasized, as was the case with many earlier romances,[44] some scholars have suggested that this facilitates a pun.[45]

---

41 Indeed, some earlier romances feature the phrase "Con priuilegio" in the same spot above the woodcut: *Arderique* (Valencia: Juan Viñao 1517; USTC 344387), *Clarián de Landanís* (Toledo: Juan de Villaquiran 1518; USTC 344400) and *Claribalte* (Valencia: Juan Viñao 1519; USTC 336204). I have only found a single later example for this, *Valerián de Ungria* (Valencia: Francisco Díaz Romano 1540; USTC 336843).

42 The title-pages of *Don Quixote* are easily accessible in Manuel Henrich (ed.), *Iconografía de las Ediciones del Quijote de Miguel de Cervantes Saavedra. Reproducción en facsímile de las portadas de 611 ediciones con notas bibliográficas*. Valladolid 2005 [Barcelona 1905]. It served as the basis for most of the information in this section.

43 There are, however, knights pictured on the title-pages of three early editions: Lisboa: Rodríguez 1605; Lisboa: Crasbeeck 1605; Valencia: Mey 1605.

44 Of 120 examined title-pages, just under 40% have the name of the hero or heroes divided over two lines or otherwise abbreviated, e.g. "dō tri | stan de leonis"; "Pri- | maleō"; "reynaldos de mō | taluan".

45 See Emilo Torné, 'Arquitectura tipográfica del libro en el Siglo de Oro'. In: *Imprenta, libros y lectura en la España del* Quijote. Ed. by José Manuel Lucía Megías. Madrid 2006, p. 243–273, here p. 268. Torné quotes a paper by Augustin Redondo suggesting that "xote" on its own was equivalent to idiot, "tonto"; Redondo's article is now entitled 'De la portada al prólogo en el Quijote de 1605. Un problema de recepción' and is included in Augustin Redondo, *En busca del* Quijote *desde otra orilla*. Alcalá de Henares 2011, p. 17–40, here p. 24.

No matter which position one takes in the debate on whether *Don Quixote* is a genuine chivalric romance, there can be no doubt that its title is important for the reception of the novel.[46] As one of the most famous books in history, one does not expect to find any oversights in its publishing history, yet no recent edition known to me informs the reader about a very common alternative title of the novel. While all the early editions invariably have *El ingenioso hidalgo* [or: *caballero*, from the title of the 1615 second volume] *don Quixote de la Mancha*, in the second half of the seventeenth century, starting with a Brussels edition (Bruselas: Juan Mommarte, 1662), we suddenly find the title changed to *Vida y hechos del ingenioso cavallero don Quixote de la Mancha*. Moreover, this particular phrasing soon travelled back to Spain: In fact, from 1671 onwards (Bruselas: Pedro de la Calle, 1671), all known editions[47] exclusively feature this phrasing until the edition of the *Real Academia Española* in 1780 restored the original title. Most nineteenth-century editions then followed this lead, with a few exceptions (Madrid 1782; 1808; 1840; Barcelona 1841; 1845–1846).[48] Not to take into account this alternative title is a glaring omission, especially because of the way the text's interpretation shifted from ridicule to sublimity toward the end of the eighteenth century.[49] Once again, the title could significantly guide the way a text is read: In Spanish literature, the phrase *Vidas y Hechos* (Life and Deeds) is mainly associated with the lives of kings and saints, even with Jesus Christ.[50] As the exclusive title over a long period of *Don Quixote*'s transmission, the phrase must have influenced the interpretation of

---

46 I follow Lucía Megás and Sales Dasí (see note 1) in counting *Don Quixote* among the genuine *libros de caballerías*. Cf. also Daniel Syrovy, *Tilting at Tradition. Problems of Genre in the Novels of Miguel de Cervantes and Charles Sorel*. New York, Amsterdam 2013.

47 Antwerp 1673; Madrid 1674; an edition without place or date, reprinted by Henrich (see note 39) as # 25*; Antwerp 1697 (twice); Barcelona 1704; Madrid 1706; Madrid 1714; Antwerp 1719; Madrid 1723; Madrid 1730; Madrid 1735; Lyon 1736; London 1738; Madrid 1741; The Hague 1744; Madrid 1750 (twice); Madrid 1751; Barcelona 1755?; Amsterdam/Leipzig 1755; Tarragona 1757; Barcelona 1762; Madrid 1764; Madrid 1765 (twice); Antwerp 1770; Madrid 1771; Madrid 1777 (twice).

48 Cayuela (see note 2), talking about the "fluctuations des titres" of Spanish 17th century narratives, does say that "le *Quichotte* voit son titre modifié pour une edition flamande de 1662" (p. 264), but the reference to only "one Flemish edition" is evidently misleading.

49 Cf. Anthony Close, *The Romantic Approach to 'Don Quixote'. A Critical History of the Romantic Tradition in 'Quixote' Criticism*. Cambridge 1978.

50 Compare *Historia de la vida y hechos del imperador Carlos V.* (Barcelona: s.n. 1560?; USTC 350861); Antonio de Fuenmayor's *Vida y hechos de Pio V pontifice Romano* (Madrid: Luis Sánchez 1595; USTC 336370); and most importantly the *Flos sanctorum y historia general de la vida y hechos de Jesu Christo* (Zaragoza: Domingo de Portonariis 1580; USTC 342411; and at least twelve more editions before 1600).

the story of the mad hidalgo as that of a suffering, saint-like figure. Even apart from these questions of interpretation, the problem is fundamental for the transmission and reception of the novel. The complete omission of any reference to its alternative title in the common editions of *Don Quixote* will leave scholars at a loss to explain, for example, why Ludwig Tieck's 1799–1801 translation into German was printed as *Leben und Thaten des scharfsinnigen Edlen Don Quixote von la Mancha* (Berlin: Unger, 1799–1801, 4 vols.). That a general awareness of different historical titles is lacking even for a novel as popular and well-studied as *Don Quixote*, should make it obvious how much research there is still to be done in this respect.

Bibliography

Cacho Blecua, Juan Manuel, 'El género del 'Cifar' (Sevilla, Cromberger, 1512)'. In: *Thesaurus* LIV/1 (1999), p. 76–105.

Cacho Blecua, Juan Manuel, 'Iconografía amadisiana: las imágenes de Jorge Coci'. In: *eHumanista* 16 (2010), p. 1–27.

Canova, Andrea, 'Introduction'. In: Matteo Maria Boiardo, *Orlando innamorato. L'inamoramento de Orlando*. Ed. by Andrea Canova. Milano 2011, p. 5–65.

Caravaggi, Giovanni, 'Esteban Godines de Nájera y Juan Coloma'. In: *Revista de poética medieval* 28 (2014), p. 177–187.

Cayuela, Anne, *Le paratexte au siècle d'or. Prose romanesque, livres et lecteurs en Espagne au XVIIe siècle*. Genève 1996.

Cervantes, Miguel de, *El Ingenioso Hidalgo Don Quijote de la Mancha*. Ed. by John Jay Allen. Madrid 2001.

Close, Anthony, *The Romantic Approach to 'Don Quixote'. A Critical History of the Romantic Tradition in 'Quixote' Criticism*. Cambridge 1978.

Eisenberg, Daniel and María Carmen Marín Pina, *Bibliografía de los libros de caballerías castellanos*. Zaragoza 2000 (digital edition: http://www.cervantesvirtual.com/obra/bib liografia-de-los-libros-de-caballeria-castellanos/).

Eisenberg, Daniel, *Introducción a 'Espejo de Príncipes y cavalleros [El Cavallero del Febo]' de Diego Ortúñez de Calahorra* (http://www.cervantesvirtual.com/nd/ark:/59851/bmcjq193; accessed 25 May 2017).

García Álvarez, Juan Pablo Mauricio, 'Procedimientos textuales de impresor en el *Libro del caballero Zifar* (Cromberger, 1512): El caso de los epígrafes'. In: *Zifar y sus libros. 500 años*. Ed. by Karla Xiomara Luna Mariscal, Axayácatl Campos García Rojas and Aurelio González. México 2015, p. 265–308.

Gernert, Folke, 'Antonio Martínez de Salamanca, impresor y Francisco Delicado, corrector. Libros españoles en la imprenta italiana a través de sus ilustraciones'. In: *Nápoles – Roma 1504. Cultura y literatura española y portuguesa en Italia en el quinto centenario de la muerte de Isabel la Católica*. Ed. by Javier Gómez-Montero. Salamanca 2005, p. 205–242.

Griffin, Clive, *The Crombergers of Seville. The History of a Printing and Merchant Dynasty.* Oxford 1988.

Henrich, Manuel (ed.), *Iconografía de las Ediciones del Quijote de Miguel de Cervantes Saavedra. Reproducción en facsímile de las portadas de 611 ediciones con notas bibliográficas.* Valladolid 2005 [Barcelona 1905].

Herrán Alonso, Emma, 'Las narraciones caballerescas espirituales'. In: *Amadís de Gaula 1508. Quinientos años de libros de caballerías.* Ed. by José Manuel Lucía Megías. Madrid 2008, p. 265–270.

López-Vázquez, Alfredo Rodriguez (ed.), *Segunda parte del Lazarillo de Tormes.* Madrid 2014.

Lucía Megías, José Manuel and Emilio José Sales Dasí, *Libros de caballerías castellanos (siglos XVI-XVII).* Madrid 2008.

Lucía Megías, José Manuel, *Imprenta y libros de caballerías.* Madrid 2000.

Lucía Megías, José Manuel, 'Imprenta y lengua literaria en los Siglos de Oro: el caso de los libros de caballerías castellanos.' In: *Edad de Oro* 23 (2004), p. 199–229.

Lucía Megías, José Manuel (ed.), *Amadis de Gaula 1508, quinientos años de libros de caballerías.* Madrid 2008.

Misiti, Maria Cristina, 'Alcune rare edizioni spagnole pubblicate a Roma da Antonio Martínez de Salamanca'. In: *El libro antiguo español. Actas del segundo Coloquio Internacional (Madrid).* Ed. by María Luisa López-Vidriero and Pedro M. Cátedra. Salamanca 1992, p.307–323.

Moretti, Franco, *Distant Reading.* London, New York 2013.

Oliver, Revilo P., 'The First Medicean MS of Tacitus and the Titulature of Ancient Books'. In: *Transactions and Proceedings of the American Philological Association* 82 (1951), p. 232–261.

Ramos, Rafael, 'Problemas de la edición zaragozana del *Amadís de Gaula* (1508)'. In: *Libros de caballerías (de "Amadís" al "Quijote"). Poética, lectura, representación e identidad.* Ed. by Eva Belén Carro Carbajal, Laura Puerto Moro and María Sánchez Pérez. Salamanca 2002, p. 319–342.

Rautenberg, Ursula, 'Die Entstehung und Entwicklung des Buchtitelblatts in der Inkunabelzeit'. In: *Archiv für Geschichte des Buchwesens* 62 (2008), p. 1–105.

Redondo, Augustin, 'De la portada al prólogo en el Quijote de 1605. Un problema de recepción'. In: A.R., *En busca del* Quijote *desde otra orilla.* Alcalá de Henares 2011, p. 17–40.

Sánchez Mariana, Manuel, 'La novela en manuscrito en los Siglos de Oro'. In: *Imprenta, libros y lectura en la España del* Quijote. Ed. by J. M. Lucía Megías. Madrid 2006, p. 119–138.

Sarmati, Elisabetta, *Le critiche ai libri di cavalleria nel cinquecento spagnolo (con uno sguardo sul seicento). Un'analisi testuale.* Pisa 1996.

Sharpe, Richard, *Titulus. Identifying Medieval Latin Texts.* Turnhout 2006.

Syrovy, Daniel, *Tilting at Tradition. Problems of Genre in the Novels of Miguel de Cervantes and Charles Sorel.* New York, Amsterdam 2013.

Torné, Emilo, 'Arquitectura tipográfica del libro en el Siglo de Oro'. In: *Imprenta, libros y lectura en la España del* Quijote. Ed. by José Manuel Lucía Megías. Madrid 2006, p. 243–273.

Wilkinson, Alexander S. (ed.), *Iberian Books.* Leiden, Boston 2010.

List of Contributors

Christa Bertelsmeier-Kierst is Professor of Medieval and Early Modern German literature in Marburg. In her research and teaching of the High and Late Medieval period and Humanism, she adopts a pan-European perspective, focusing especially on cultural- and media-historical phenomena (e.g. the shift from manuscript to print) in the Middle Ages and Renaissance.

Bart Besamusca is Professor of Middle Dutch Textual Culture from an International Perspective in the Utrecht Centre for Medieval Studies at Utrecht University. He has published widely on medieval narrative literature, manuscripts, and early printed editions. He is currently supervising the research project 'The Multilingual Dynamics of the Literary Culture of Medieval Flanders (ca 1200 – ca 1500)'.

Julia Boffey is Professor of Medieval Studies in the Department of English at Queen Mary University of London. Her interests include Middle English verse, especially lyrics and dream poetry, and the relationship between manuscript and print in the late fifteenth and early sixteenth centuries.

Elisabeth de Bruijn is a postdoctoral fellow of the Research Foundation Flanders (FWO), affiliated with the department of Dutch studies at the University of Antwerp. Her research interests include medieval literature in border regions (the Middle Low German and the Rhine-Meuse area) as well as the study of literature from a cross-cultural perspective (particularly early printed romances in Western Europe).

Olivier Delsaux is Lecturer at the University of Louvain and at the University of Saint-Louis in Brussels and Secretary of the *Groupe de recherche sur le moyen français* (Research Group on Middle French). Like Tania Van Hemelryck, he specializes in the study of fourteenth- and fifteenth-century French language and literature from the perspective of their production and reception contexts, as books in particular (manuscripts and early printed editions).

Julia Frick is scientific assistant at the German Institute (Department of Medieval Literature) of the University of Zurich. Her main areas of research are Early Modern translations of Virgil's works, especially the German Humanism of the sixteenth century. She recently completed an edition of Thomas Murner's translation of the *Aeneid* (Strasbourg 1515).

Tania Van Hemelryck is Senior Research Associate at the FRS-FNRS, Professor at the University of Louvain and *Director of the Groupe de recherche sur le moyen français* (Reseach group on Middle French). Like Olivier Delsaux, she specializes in the study of fourteenth- and fifteenth-century French language and literature from the perspective of their production and reception contexts, as books in particular (manuscripts and early printed editions).

Francesco Montorsi received his PhD in French medieval literature from the University of the Sorbonne and the University of Gottingen and he is Maître de Conférences at the University of Lyon II. His research focusses on the reception of chivalric romances and the cultural exchanges between France and Italy at the end of the Middle Ages and during the Renaissance. He is currently writing a book on the representations of the ancient past in French medieval literature (twelfth to thirteenth centuries).

Nicolas Potysch works at the Department of German Studies at the Ruhr-University Bochum, Germany. He completed his PhD at the University of Tübingen with a monograph entitled *Wiederholt doppeldeutig in Bild und Schrift* (Hannover 2018). His main areas of research are illustrated novels, ambiguity and word play, narratives of radicalisation, August von Kotzebue, and emblematics.

Anna Katharina Richter, educated at the Universities of Kiel (Germany) and Uppsala (Sweden), is Senior Lecturer at the Scandinavian Department of the University of Zurich. Her main area of research is Early Modern Literature in Scandinavia, especially narratives/romances in the early printing period in Denmark and Sweden. She is also interested in Translation Studies and literature from the Faroe Islands.

Jordi Sánchez-Martí is Senior Lecturer in English Literature at the University of Alicante, where he teaches medieval and early modern literature. He has published articles on Middle English romances and recently completed a critical edition of Anthony Munday's translation of *Palmerin d'Oliva*, forthcoming from the Arizona Center for Medieval and Renaissance Studies.

Jef Schaeps has been curator of Prints & Drawings at Leiden University Libraries since 2005. Although his speciality is the sixteenth century, he also has an interest in contemporary drawing and printmaking. In 2020 he plans to finish his doctorate on illustrated title-pages in the Low Countries, 1473–1585. In 2016 he co-authored *For Study and Delight*, a survey of the Leiden collections of prints and drawings, from 1500 until the present day.

Daniel Syrovy works at the Department of Comparative Literature of the University of Vienna. His main areas of research are Early Modern narrative, especially in the Romance languages, and the study of Habsburg Censorship in the Italian provinces in the eighteenth and nineteenth centuries.

Frank Willaert is professor emeritus of Middle Dutch literature at the University of Antwerp and presently vice-president of the Royal Academy of Dutch Language and Literature. He has published mainly on medieval mysticism and on lyrical poetry. He is currently preparing an extensive book on the history of Middle Dutch love poetry in its European context between the end of the twelfth and the beginning of the fifteenth centuries.

Index of Manuscripts

Index of Titles

Index of Names